AUTOMOBILE REPAIR GUIDE

by Boyce Dwiggins

A Revision of AUTOMOBILE GUIDE
by Frederick E. Bricker

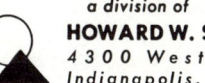

THEODORE AUDEL & CO.
a division of
HOWARD W. SAMS & CO., INC.
4300 West 62nd Street
Indianapolis, Indiana 46268

FOURTH EDITION

FIRST PRINTING—1978

Copyright © 1978 by Howard W. Sams & Co., Inc., Indianapolis, Indiana 46268. Printed in the United States of America.

All rights reserved. Reproduction or use, without express permission, of editorial or pictorial content, in any manner, is prohibited. No patent liability is assumed with respect to the use of the information contained herein. While every precaution has been taken in the preparation of this book, the publisher assumes no responsibility for errors or omissions. Neither is any liability assumed for damages resulting from the use of the information contained herein.

International Standard Book Number: 0-672-23291-X
Library of Congress Catalog Card Number: 78-50206

Foreword

The modern automobile is a complex combination of systems, each designed for maximum efficiency and for compatible relationship with all the others. Each system must be maintained in first-class operating condition, or it may affect the operation of the other related systems.

This book was prepared to guide the mechanic, operator, and owner in understanding the way in which an automobile works and to provide information on the repair that every car needs from time to time.

Various subjects such as front-wheel drive, speed control devices, and automobile air conditioning have been added in the revision of this book. Steam, electric, and turbine powered cars are also included in a look at possible future modes of transportation. It is believed that if the average person understands the operating principle of a device, he will be able to repair it more rapidly and with greater accuracy. This idea is followed in the text. Stress is placed on the explanations of how and why certain units operate as they do. Typical examples of repair procedures are explained; where applicable, trouble symptoms, their probable cause, and their possible remedies are listed. These lists should be of great help in diagnosing and correcting troubles that occur in any make or model of automobile.

Full use of illustrations is made to supplement the text and to make the explanations as clear as possible. Cutaway and exploded views show the actual construction features of various units, while other illustrations show the actual repair being made.

Special thanks are due every major automobile manufacturer for their cooperation in supplying information about their particular cars. Without their help, this book could not have been compiled.

Contents

CHAPTER 1

INTRODUCTION 9
 The car of the past—the car of today—the car of tomorrow—summary.

Chapter 2

STORAGE BATTERIES 22
 Battery fundamentals—battery capacity rating—battery design—battery maintenance—battery charging methods—battery testing—battery troubles and remedies.

CHAPTER 3

DISTRIBUTORS 45
 General construction, conventional distributor—spark advance—vacuum advance mechanism—general construction, electronic distributors—distributor testers—*Sun 500* distributor tester—*Delco-Remy* center-bearing plate—distributor troubles and remedies.

CHAPTER 4

SPARK PLUGS 80
 Spark plug construction—spark plug troubles—service procedures—spark plug possible troubles and remedies.

CHAPTER 5

FUEL PUMP AND FUEL SYSTEMS 95
 Operating principles—testing—servicing—fuel tanks and lines—fuel evaporation control system—principles of turbocharging—turbocharger troubleshooting—fuel injection—electronic fuel injection—fuel pump troubles and remedies—electronic fuel injection system troubles and remedies.

CHAPTER 6
CARBURETORS AND AIR CLEANERS 130
    Basic operating principles—carburetor types—carburetor adjustments—air cleaners—carburetor troubles and remedies.

CHAPTER 7
PISTONS, RINGS, AND ENGINE BLOCK 178
    Piston construction—piston replacement—inspection—piston rings—pistons and rings possible troubles and remedies.

CHAPTER 8
CRANKSHAFTS AND CONNECTING RODS 195
    Crankshafts—connecting rods—crankshaft and connecting rod possible troubles and remedies.

CHAPTER 9
CAMSHAFTS, LIFTERS, AND ROCKER ARMS 209
    Construction features—overhead camshafts—servicing—hydraulic valve lifters—hydraulic lifter troubles—mechanical valve lifters—cams, lifters, and rocker arm troubles and remedies.

CHAPTER 10
VALVES 235
    Valve assemblies—valve seats—valve guides—valve springs—valve troubles and remedies.

CHAPTER 11
ENGINE LUBRICATING, EMISSION CONTROL,
AND EXHAUST SYSTEMS 249
    Engine lubrication—pressure lubricating systems—engine oils—oil pumps—oil pressure indicators—crankcase ventilation—exhaust system controls—air injection reactor system—air injection pump—the exhaust sytem—lubricating system troubles and remedies.

CHAPTER 12
COOLING SYSTEMS 279
    Coolants—water jackets—radiators—water pumps—fans—thermostats—radiator caps—overflow tanks—coolant recovery system—draining the system—cooling system troubles and remedies.

CHAPTER 13

ENGINE TUNE-UP 296
    Tune-up troubles and possible remedies.

CHAPTER 14

TROUBLESHOOTING 303

CHAPTER 15

IGNITION TESTING 315
    Basic operating principles—trouble isolation—primary circuit tests—secondary circuit tests—transistor ignition systems—ignition timing—engine testers—ignition testing with a typical engine tester—basic scope patterns—the analog oscilloscope—highway safety-diagnostic testing.

CHAPTER 16

STARTERS AND ALTERNATORS 368
    Starters—starter brushes—starter drives—remote control starter switches—generators—alternators—alternator regullators—internal solid-state regulator—starter, generator, and alternator troubles and remedies.

CHAPTER 17

LIGHTING SYSTEMS 410
    Headlights—other lights—turn signals—headlight switch and circuit breaker—aiming the headlights—conventional turn signal troubles and remedies—sequential turn signal troubles and remedies—lighting troubles and remedies.

CHAPTER 18

INSTRUMENT PANEL 429
    Speedometer—fuel level—temperature indicator—charging indicator—oil pressure—instrument voltage regulator—speedometer troubles and remedies—fuel gauge troubles and remedies—temperature indicator troubles and remedies—charging indicator troubles and remedies—oil pressure indicator troubles and remedies.

CHAPTER 19

TIRE SERVICING 445
    Tire maintenance—tire types—tire repair—wheel balancing—tire troubles and remedies.

CHAPTER 20
STANDARD AND POWER BRAKES, DRUM AND DISC TYPES 469
Drum type—disc type—maintenance and adjustments—master cylinder—power brakes—power brake testing procedure—cleaning, inspection, and overhaul—brake light warning system—brake system troubles and remedies—standard brakes—power brakes.

CHAPTER 21
FRONT SUSPENSION, CHASSIS, SPRINGS, AND SHOCKS 513
Standard suspension—service procedures—air suspension—frame—springs—checking rear suspension—shock absorbers—suspension system troubles and remedies—standard system—air suspension system—spring and shock troubles and remedies.

CHAPTER 22
STEERING SYSTEM 544
Control linkage—steering gear—steering gear service and adjustment—power steering—power steering pumps—steering system troubles and remedies—Manual steering—power steering.

CHAPTER 23
FRONT WHEEL ALIGNMENT 581
Alignment factors—alignment procedures—adjustments—summary—wheel alignment troubles and remedies.

CHAPTER 24
CLUTCHES, MANUAL TRANSMISSION, AND OVERDRIVES 617
Clutches—3-speed transmission—4-speed transmissions—5-speed transmissions—overdrives—clutch system troubles and remedies—manual transmission troubles and remedies—overdrive unit troubles and remedies.

CHAPTER 25
AUTOMATIC TRANSMISSIONS 647
Torque converter—oil pump—planetary gears and controls—reverse clutch—governor—valve body—gearshift controls—transmission oil cooler—service—starting and towing precautions—automatic transmission troubles and remedies.

CHAPTER 26
DRIVESHAFTS, UNIVERSAL JOINTS, AND REAR AXLE ASSEMBLIES 666
Drive lines—drive shafts—universal joints—u-joint mounting—drive shaft angularity—service—rear axle assembly—differential—conventional differential—locking (anti-slip) differential—rear axle—rear axle service—differentials—rear axle noise diagnosis—wheel balancing precautions—drive shaft and universal joint troubles and remedies—rear axle troubles and remedies.

CHAPTER 27
FRONT-WHEEL DRIVE 702
Transmission-front suspension—drive axle—towing—rear suspension—transmission troubleshooting.

CHAPTER 28
ACCESSORIES 710
Speed control devices—controlled cycle wiper and washer system—fluid level indicator—sun roof—theft deterrent system—cruise control troubleshooting—wiper troubleshooting—washer troubleshooting.

CHAPTER 29
AUTOMOBILE AIR CONDITIONING 725
Basic principles of air conditioning—air conditioning system operation—component description—service and maintenance—installation procedures—trouble chart—air conditioning troubles and remedies.

CHAPTER 30
TABLES AND CHARTS 772
Conversion tables

INDEX 788

CHAPTER 1

Introduction

In the United States we like to measure our "go power" in ages. First was the Stone Age, but now we seem to be all wrapped up in several ages at one time — the Machine Age, Electronic Age, Atomic Age, Jet Age, and the Space Age — all in one hot package.

In 1969 man first walked on the moon. Astronaut Neil Armstrong strolled on the surface of the moon, 238,000 miles from Earth, for a longer period of time than Orville Wright, a bicycle mechanic, stayed in the air during the first powered flight at Kitty Hawk, North Carolina in 1903.

In 1976, the two-hundredth anniversary of our great nation was marked by an unmanned spacecraft making a soft landing on Mars. Mars, the nearest planet to Earth, is from over 34 million to just under 63 million miles away. At this distance it takes a radio signal, traveling at the speed of light (186,000 miles per second), from 3 to over 5.6 seconds to reach Earth.

What does the Space Age have to do with you, the auto mechanic? Plenty! Just a few short years ago — short, related to time and man's accomplishments — about the time Wright made his historic flight, someone said, — "You don't think that the general public will stand for the expense of paving streets and roads for the few who will own horseless carriages, do you?" Today it is possible to travel on paved highways and superhighways all over the United States, not to mention our adjoining countries, Canada and Mexico.

What then lies in the future? It is almost anybody's guess. Can you imagine entering a limited-access highway, then inserting a program-

Automobile Guide

med card into your "auto-computer" and doing nothing else until you reach your destination, though you may enter at Miami and your destination be New York, San Francisco, or any other major city in the United States? You may not even have to stop for fuel; a fuel cell may be all that is required. Oh yes, and your average speed may be in excess of one hundred miles per hour.

We have lots to do before that can happen however. But in order to do anything, we must have some basic training in our chosen profession. Training for a trade is as old as civilization itself. Though we have no way of being sure, it must be as old as the Stone Age itself. About four thousand years ago Babylonian law included provisions that insisted that artisians teach their craft to the younger generation.

Among many of Benjamin Franklin's inventions was a measuring device used to determine the distance between rural mail delivery stops for postal workers. This crude device (Fig. 1.) was the forerunner of the modern odometer. This device looks rather insignificant alongside a computer that can measure, in feet, the distance a spacecraft is from Earth, almost sixty-three million miles away, but it was a start.

Courtesy The Franklin Institute

Fig. 1. The first odometer.

Introduction

A former president of *General Motors Corporation* was once a bicycle mechanic. He took courses at night in a technical school. From bicycles he progressed to automobiles, and from automobiles to better automobiles. Mr. Walter P. Chrysler, founder of *Chrysler Motors Corporation*, started as an apprentice helper in a railway machine shop. They both added their ideas to what they had learned.

Modern technology is moving so rapidly that even while you're reading this book, man is working on a "better idea." Now he is working on cars that may be propelled by steam, electricity, or turbines. He works in secrecy and he will not disclose any of his ideas until he is satisfied with his work. Briefly, we will discuss some of the ideas now made public for the car of the future. Some ideas will fail where others will succeed, but man increases his knowledge even in failing.

The purpose of this book is to give you a basic understanding of today's car. From it you may learn, then add your ideas to what you have learned, for a better future in the automobile field.

THE CAR OF THE PAST

The development of the car would not have been possible without the development of the wheel. The earliest known form of a wheel, made of stone, dates back to the Bronze Age (about 3200 BC) according to a crude representation from Erech, an ancient Sumerian city, in a part of what is now Iraq.

Next came the three-wheeled cart, then the four-wheeled wagon. The four-wheeled wagon had limited use until certain problems were solved — problems that today seem very simple. Early carts and wagons could not be steered, but could only be turned by dragging or lifting the front end around corners. It took about a hundred years or so to develop the swiveling front axle.

In about the year 2000 BC the cart was transformed into a lighter military chariot and spoked wheels, made of wood, were adopted. To withstand the wear of rough roads, a "tire" of leather, copper, or wood studs was used.

Credit for the beginning of the "power plant" probably should go to Hero of Alexandria. Around 300 AD, in building the first known steam turbine, Hero was the first to convert steam pressure into mechanical energy. It was, however, another fourteen hundred years before Nicholas J. Cugnot developed the first known self-propelled vehicle, a steam-driven three-wheeled carriage. Only two models were built; one in 1769 and another in 1770. The 1770 model has been preserved and is on display in the Conservatorie des Arts et Metiers in Paris, France.

Also, in 1769, James Watt patented a new type of steam engine and originated a way of determining its power output. Known as the horsepower, this unit of power is still in use today.

In 1805 Oliver Evans ran his invention, the Orukter Amphibolos, through the streets of Philadelphia. In 1860 Etienne Lenoir patented, in France, the first gasoline-powered internal combustion engine. It was crude and noisy but worked, and was somewhat of a commercial success. In 1862 Alphonse Beau de Rochas filed for a patent, again in France, explaining the principle of a four-cycle gasoline engine. Though his description was reasonably accurate by today's standards, there is no record that he ever actually built a working engine.

George Brayton designed a two-cycle gasoline engine in 1872 and exhibited it at the Philadelphia Centennial Exposition in 1876. In 1878 Nikolaus A. Otto introduced an operational four-cycle engine called the "Otto Cycle." The model used to obtain a patent is on display at the Smithsonian Institution in Washington, D.C.

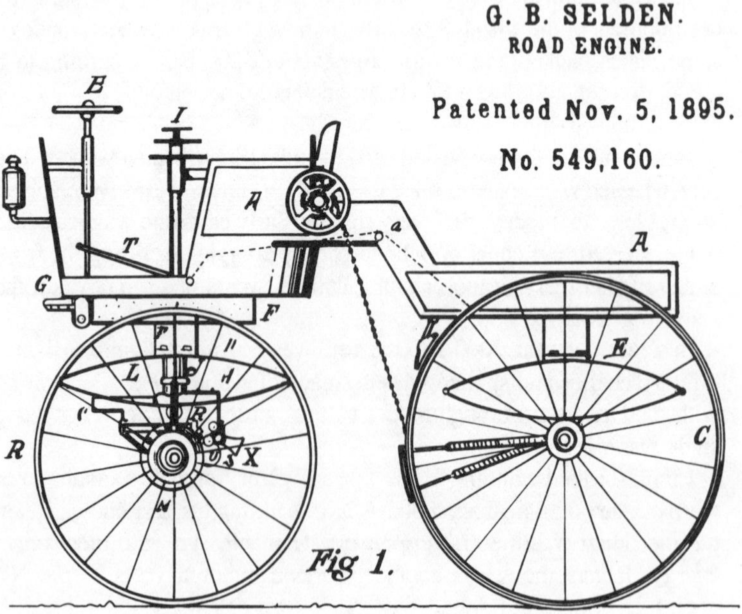

Fig. 2. Drawing for first automotive patent in the United States.

INTRODUCTION

The first United States patent for a two-cycle "road engine" (Fig.2) was issued to George B. Selden in 1879, a patent that was later to be challenged by a group of automobile builders led by Henry J. Ford.

In 1885 Gottlieb Daimler of Germany and Fernand Forest of France, working independently, perfected an engine design utilizing a carburetor. Daimler built the best engine and Forest built the best carburetor. Karl Benz improved Daimler's engine and Forest's carburetor, installed them in a tricycle, and added an electrical ignition system.

In 1888 John B. Dunlop reinvented the pneumatic tire, requiring sixty pounds of air pressure for inflation. The tire, originally invented in 1840, was developed for use on bicycles at that time.

Two brothers, Charles and Frank Duryea, drove their one-cylinder gasoline-powered carriage down the streets of Springfield, Massachusetts in September of 1893. In 1894, on July 4, Elwood Haynes made his first "run" in a similar carriage in Kokomo, Indiana.

In 1895 Frank Duryea won the Chicago Times race in a two-cylinder Duryea-built car. He completed the fifty-five mile course in eleven hours, averaging five miles per hour.

In 1896 Henry J. Ford made his first "run" down Bagley Avenue in Detroit in his "quadricycle." In that year a Duryea "Motor Wagon" was featured in the Barnum and Bailey Circus parade as a "freak."

The first companies for commercial motor vehicle production were formed in 1897. They were the *Pope Manufacturing Company* of Hartford, Connecticut and the *Winton Motor Carriage Company* of Cleveland, Ohio. Though Pope produced both electric and gasoline powered cars, twelve times as many electric cars were sold than gas in the first two years. The founder, Colonel Albert A. Pope, claimed; "You can't get people to sit over an explosion."

Development and technology began moving at a rapid pace after the turn of the century. Some of the important "firsts" are as follows:

1902: The American Automobile Association (AAA) was formed.
1903: George Selden formed an association to control the manufacture of automobiles in the United States, attempting to protect his patent of 1895.
Henry J. Ford founded the *Ford Motor Company* with a total capital of $28,000, supplied by a Detroit coal dealer, Alexander Malcumson.
1905: The Society of Automobile Engineers was founded, later to be known as the Society of Automotive Engineers (SAE).

Automobile Guide

1911: Selden's patent of 1895 was opposed by a group of independents led by Henry J. Ford. The U.S. Court of Appeals held Selden's patent valid, but only for cars equipped with two-cycle engines.
1912: The electric starter was developed by the *Dayton Engineering Laboratory Company*, now known as *Delco*.
1922: The balloon tire was introduced requiring only thirty pounds of air pressure.
1940: The first turnpike opened between Harrisburg and Pittsburgh, Pa.
1948: The one hundred millionth car was produced.
1950: The tubeless and puncture-proof tire was introduced.
1956: The Interstate Highway Act was passed.
1963: The first gas turbine cars were put on the road by *Chrysler*. The two hundred millionth car was produced this year.

It took some fifty-five years to produce the first one hundred million cars, but only fifteen years to produce the second hundred million. This event should now bring us to the car of today.

THE CAR OF TODAY

Today's car may be considered a truly remarkable piece of engineering. There are over fifteen thousand individual parts in the average car, each fitting with precision.

The car of today has features only dreamed of a few years ago. Features such as power steering, power disc brakes, electric door locks and trunk release, tilt steering wheel, speed control, electric window defogger (built into the glass), and air conditioning — to name a few. Additionally, today's car includes safety and pollution control features, such as lap and shoulder harness, fail-safe ignition, antilock brakes, engine clean-air equipment, and catalyst exhaust systems.

To get an idea of the potential for the automotive technician working on today's car, multiply the number of things that may go "wrong" with the car by 80,000,000. There are about that many cars on America's roads each day — eighty million.

How many things can go "wrong" with a car? The answer to that question could only be a guess, but if you were to pull one hundred cars off the road at random, you would find that only a few of them would

INTRODUCTION

have no mechanical problems. You would find something wrong with most of them. Some of them would have several problems.

Of the hundred cars, you would find: 350 steering system defects, 127 suspension system defects, and 38 brake system defects. That adds up to over 500 defects relating to steering and stopping the car alone, an average of five defects per car.

Table 1. Number of Worn Parts in 100 Cars Checked

Part	Count	Part	Count
Center control steering set	2	Radiator hose	1
Lower control arm bushing	2	Radius arm set	2
Upper control arm bushing	6	Rear grease seals	2
Front springs	10	Left axle shaft	1
Lower control arm set	38	Shocks and brackets	4
Upper control arm set	43	Upper control arm and bushings	8
Lower control rubber bumper	2	Idler arm pin and bushings	4
Shocks	72	Wheel cylinder cups	22
Weights	479	Brake lining	2
Tie rod ends	41	Dimmer switch	1
Upper control arm	23	Left front bearing	2
Pivot shaft bushings	78	Stabilizer link	1
Pivot shaft set	1	Center tie bolt	1
Grease fittings	3	Spring shackles	1
Rear main leaf	1	Inner upper shaft	5
Shims	17	Radius arm bushings	2
Master cylinder kit	2	Steering knuckle supports	2
Lower arm set	56	Tie rod and sleeve	1
Brake fluid	9	Spring leaves	3
Steering worm and tube	1	Headlight lens	1
Steering sector shaft	1	Headlight gasket	1
Kingpin and bushings	32	Pitman arm bushings	5
Drag links	4	Brake rod pins	3
Steering Pitman arm	5	Steering jacket bushings	2

Fantastic, yes, but we could go on and on. There are also electrical (battery, starter, alternator, ignition) and mechanical (engine, transmission, and drive train) defects. Actually, there is an *average* of over ten defects or potential defects in *each* car on the road today.

THE CAR OF TOMORROW

The car of tomorrow will probably be as different as the car of today is compared to the car of the past. It is pretty much a guess what the car of tomorrow will look like or, for that matter, when tomorrow will be.

AUTOMOBILE GUIDE

Look at the design and technological improvements of the car over the past twenty years or so. Try to imagine what the car will be like when you are in the prime of your career, twenty years or so from now.

Steam Power

Several companies are now working on a steam-powered engine. Steam-powered cars have long been a dream of many developers. Around the turn of the century the Stanley brothers introduced the *Stanley Steamer*. The *White Steamer* was introduced soon after, followed by the *Doble*. The last of the steamers, the *Doble*, was ready to run in 45 seconds from a cold start. It could travel 1000 to 2000 miles on 25 gallons of water, get 15 miles per gallon on kerosene, and used (on the average) one pint of oil every 500 miles. Only 24 *Dobles* were built when the company closed in 1930 with over $27 million in orders for the car. The *Dobles*, like *Stanley* and *White*, were years before their time. They were unable to solve many of their technical problems.

Perhaps one of the most interesting men in the field of steam power today is Mr. William P. Lear, Sr. With electronics as his background, Mr. Lear was president of *Quincy Radio Laboratory* at the age of 20, and at 22 was president of *Lear Radio Laboratory*. In 1954, at the age of 52, he was awarded the Horatio Alger Award, for his many achievements in the electronics field.

Mr. Lear founded (and funded with $10,000,000.00) *Lear Motors Corporation* dedicated to the future and to the air we breathe. Early in 1969, a *Lear Power System* had been developed. A steam engine power plant, it consisted of a vapor generator, motor, condenser, control system and auxiliaries (Fig. 3). A highly efficient delta-configuration motor contained 12 pistons in 6 cylinders and was only 18" long.

The *Lear* engines, Fig. 4, were to be installed in California Highway Patrol cars for testing. These engines would develop 300 horsepower and be capable of producing speeds of 130 miles per hour. The cars would have no transmission. Drive to all 4-wheels would be accomplished through a planetary differential and limited slip differential axles which split powerplant torque 60% to the rear wheels and 40% to the front wheels.

To start, just turn the key, and in thirty-seconds (even at − 30° F.) there would be full power available. Since speed of the engine is proportional to the speed of the car, fuel would be saved. The engine would not be running when the car was stopped. Since there is no transmission, reverse would be accomplished by reversing the engine.

INTRODUCTION

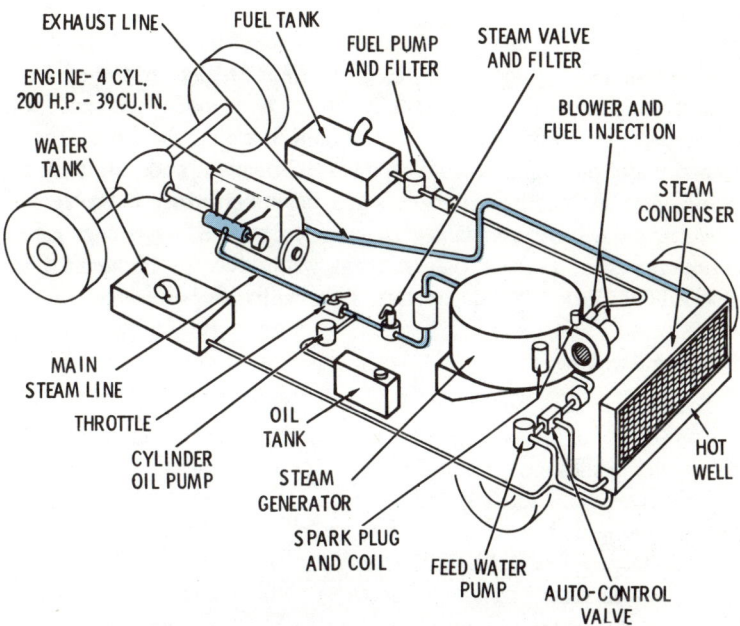

Fig. 3. Typical basic steam car design.

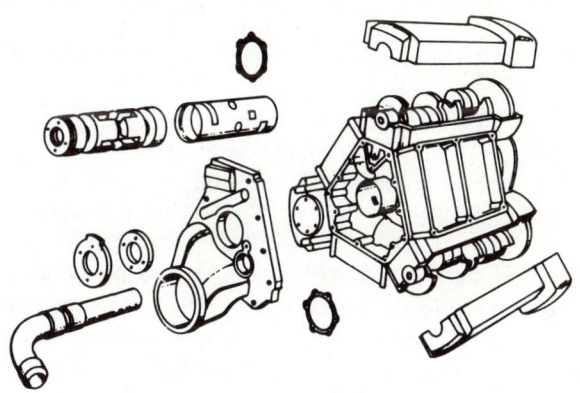

Fig. 4. LEAR DELTA engine.

Pushing a button on the dash would cause the engine to run backward instantly. To propel the air conditioner, charging system, power steering pump, and other accessories, a small auxiliary package (a steam turbine) would be installed, adding very little weight. In fact, the steam

Automobile Guide

engine and turbine would weigh only about two-thirds of what most gasoline engines weighed.

Unfortunately, by the end of 1969 the *Lear Steamer* had died. Mr. Lear had spent over $5,000,000.00 of his own money but had not developed a steam powered car that would run around the block. There were 5 major problems; low horsepower, lubrication, bulk, usability of liquid, and an inability to solve some basic performance problems.

Meanwhile, other companies are working on the steam engine for automotive use. Perhaps one of them will solve the problems that stopped Mr. Lear. Or, maybe, Mr. Lear will try again.

Electric Power

The electric car, though not new, has failed in the past. The main reason for its failure was the lack of a suitable power source. Several battery companies are now working on high energy storage batteries for experimental work relating to the electric car. One large company is experimenting with a fuel cell as a source of power for the electric car. During the past few years only 18 electric cars were produced in the United States according to the Electrical Vehicle Council.

One of the problems now facing developers is speed versus range. The *Yardney* manufactured by the *Yardney Electric Corporation* has a range of about 80 miles between battery charges but its top speed is only 25 miles per hour. The *Electrovair II (General Motors Corporation)* has a range of 40 miles between battery charges and has a top speed of about 80 miles per hour.

General Electric Corporation is working on an *ElectroCar*. Though there is still a lot of mystery on the *General Electric* experiments, it is believed they started working on the *ElectroCar* in early 1964. The GE experimental car employs a "hybrid" fuel cell quick-recharge metal-air battery.

A fuel cell is a continuous-feed electrochemical device in which the chemical energy of the reaction of a conventional fuel (hydrogen) and air (oxygen) is converted directly into useful electricity. It can operate continuously as long as fuel and air are available. The *ElectroCar* (it is believed) will have cruising speeds of 60 miles per hour and a range exceeding 200 miles. An electromobile service station will take a few minutes to "fill-up" and (since fuel cells produce water) drain some of the excess water from the storage tank.

General Electric board chairman, Mr. Gerald Phillippe, cautions however that the GE car is strictly a research vehicle. Such a car would

INTRODUCTION

be too expensive for the average driver. The *GE* family of fuel cells would cost $5,000.00 to $10,000.00 even in mass production. Others claim that the cost of fuel cell material is almost "dollar for dollar" the same as the cost of materials for the conventional gasoline engine, and that the selling cost could be about the same.

We talked earlier about the Space Age and man's walk on the Moon. *General Electric* played a large role in the space program. The Gemini space missions successfully utilized compact, efficient, powerful fuel cells made by *GE*. *General Electric* and *Monsanto Chemical Company* are teamed up working on a fuel cell-powered electric vehicle (M-37 tank) for the United States Army.

Automakers are predicting that in the next 5 to 10 years the electric car will be adopted on a limited basis. A driver should be able to pull into an electromobile service station with a low battery and pull out again in 5 minutes or so, with a fully charged battery on a rental or exchange basis. It is expected that oil companies will provide an exchange or rental service for the electric car driver of tomorrow.

Another type of electric car may also carry a small generator, powered by a steam or gas engine, that can operate continuously to keep the car batteries charged while the car is running, or it may run continuously day and night to keep the batteries up to full charge. Fig. 5 shows a cutaway of what such a car may look like as well as a simple wiring diagram of its components.

In a recent governmental agency study it has been determined, by today's technology, that the cost of an electric car would be about 20 percent higher than the cost of the current internal combustion engine car. Additionally, the cost of operation would be from 15 percent to 45 percent higher due partly to the high cost of generating the electrical power needed to recharge its batteries.

The high initial cost, cost of operation, and short range (now estimated to be about 50 miles in city driving) all have an adverse effect in the further development of the electric car.

Estimated annual sales, it is believed, would not exceed 2.5 million dollars — a drop in the bucket compared to current car sales.

Turbine Power

The first gas turbine engine was successfully demonstrated in a car in England in 1950 by *Rover*. Since that time the major automobile companies of the United States; *Chrysler*, *Ford*, and *General Motors* have been experimenting with gas turbine-powered cars.

AUTOMOBILE GUIDE

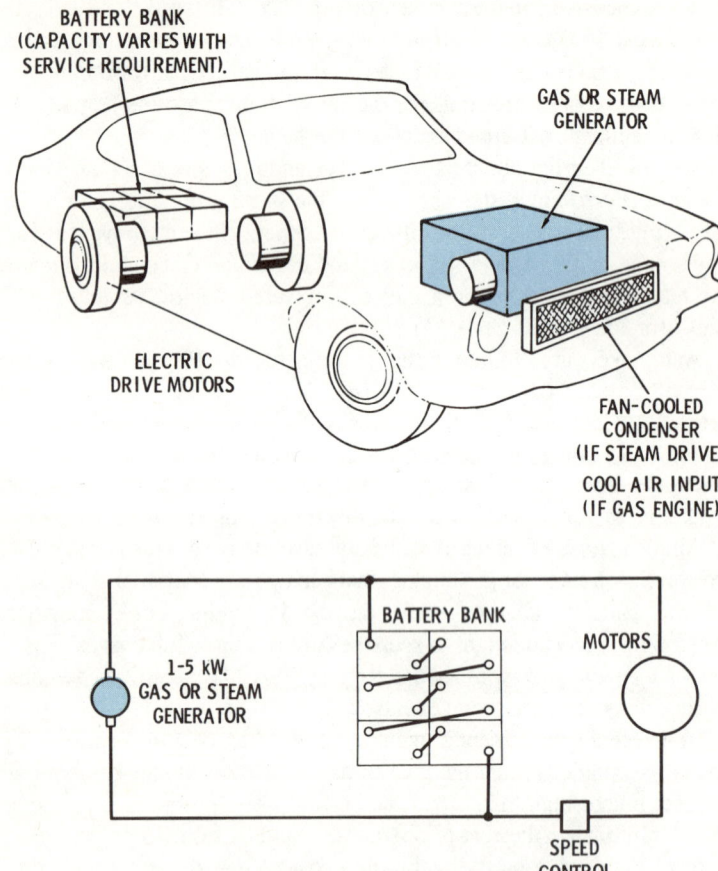

Fig. 5. Hybrid electric car and wiring diagram.

Although there are disadvantages, there are a number of advantages that make the turbine-powered car desirable. No transmission is required (as with the electric and steam-powered cars), it is a simple engine, it is small in size, light in weight, burns a wide variety of fuels, operates in almost any climate, and has low maintenance requirements.

The basic gas turbine engine consists of three main parts or sections. Shown in Fig. 6, they are: the air compressor, combustion chamber, and turbine. Briefly, here is how it works:

Air, at atmospheric pressure, is pulled into the air compressor where (applying a law of physics) its volume is decreased as its pressure is increased. Since compression of air causes a heat rise (another law of physics) the highly compressed air, at high temperature, is forced into the combustion chamber. In the combustion chamber a fuel nozzle (fuel injector) sprays in fuel, under high pressure, to mix with the moving hot air.

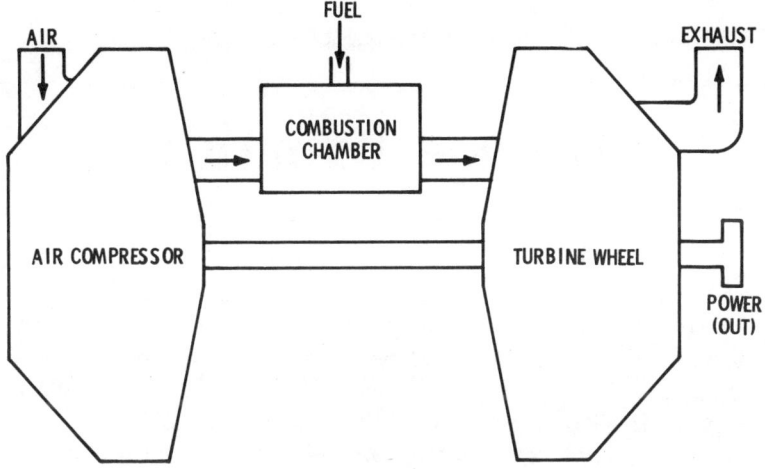

Fig. 6 Simple gas turbine engine.

The air/fuel mixture is ignited with a resistance-type spark plug. The air/fuel mixture in a turbine engine burns continuously, so once ignited the ignition may be turned off. The exhaust (products of combustion) leave the combustion chamber through a duct and fixed guides to enter the turbine unit. In the turbine unit these gases will deliver most of its energy to the turbine wheel.

In spite of the advantages, the turbine engine development has been very slow. The advancement of piston engine design and application has been ever improving, making it difficult for the turbine engine to be practical. The major disadvantages of the turbine engine for car application include high initial cost, delay in acceleration, and high fuel consumption. Experiments and tests continue in an effort to overcome the disadvantages, but for the immediate future the turbine engine car is still on the drawing boards.

CHAPTER 2

Storage Batteries

There are many types of storage batteries. Rather than discuss the various types, we will be concerned with the lead-acid battery commonly used in cars, trucks, and boats. The lead-acid storage battery may be thought of as a reservoir for the storage of electricity. It stores electrical energy in chemical form, and makes it available when needed — such as for starting the car engine.

The battery is perhaps one of the most often neglected parts of the car. If twenty cars were checked at random, one would need a new battery, five would need one (or both) battery cables replaced, and four should be recharged. Additionally, five of the remaining ten batteries will need replacement within the next twelve months.

Beginning in about 1950 the car manufacturers adopted a 12-volt battery ignition system. Prior to that time the 6-volt battery ignition system was widely used throughout the industry.

Today, the 12-volt battery ignition system is standard in *all* cars. Compare the 6-volt battery (Fig. 1) with the 12-volt battery (Fig. 2). Note that one is easily distinguished from the other by the number of filler caps. The 6-volt battery has 3 caps (or cells) while the 12-volt has 6 caps or cells.

The 12-volt ignition system was adopted for two main reasons. First, to provide adequate electrical power to supply the increasing number of electrical accessories used, and, secondly, to make available higher voltages to the ignition system for the newer high-speed, high-compression engines.

STORAGE BATTERIES

Courtesy Hayden Lynn Writing Service

Fig. 1. Illustrating a 6-volt automobile battery.

The advantage of doubling the voltage may be seen if it is realized that, in any direct-current electrical system, the power obtained is directly proportional to the product of current and voltage. Thus, with a 12-volt system, the same amount of electrical power can be delivered with half the amperage, because power is measured in watts, which are simply amperes multiplied by volts. When a generator is required to deliver, say 600 watts, this amount of power can be delivered in many ways, for example, 100 amperes at 6 volts or 50 amperes at 12 volts; since in each case the power obtained will be the same, or 600 watts.

Because it is the current flow in amperes that determines the conductor size needed, it follows that smaller and more economical wires

AUTOMOBILE GUIDE

Courtesy Hayden Lynn Writing Service

Fig. 2. Illustrating a 12-volt automobile battery.

can be used to deliver the same amount of power in a twelve-volt system that the much larger sizes would deliver in a six-volt system.

It should be noted that with the introduction of the 12-volt electrical system, numerous changes had to be made in the electrical accessories. Thus, for example, the battery, starter, generator, the various electric motors, light bulbs, etc., all had to be redesigned to operate at this higher voltage. The electrical circuits — that is, connections to the individual electrical units — will, however, be similar in both voltage systems.

BATTERY FUNDAMENTALS

An electrical battery consists of two or more individual units or *cells* producing electricity by certain chemical reactions. Electrical cells can be classified into one of two groups, namely: *primary* cells and *secondary* cells.

There are a number of different kinds of primary cells, one of the most familiar being the dry cell, such as used in a flashlight. All primary cells become exhausted in converting chemical energy into electrical energy, and they cannot be recharged by an electrical current as can a secondary cell.

Secondary cells, sometimes called *accumulators*, also convert chemical energy into electrical energy. The passing of an electrical current through the cells restores the chemical energy (or *charges* the cells) so that they are ready to supply electric current again when required. There are two types of secondary cells in general use today; these are the *lead-sulfuric acid* type and the *Edison* or *alkaline* type.

The lead-acid cell is made of plates of lead and lead oxide immersed in an electrolyte of sulfuric acid and water. Due to its economical and electrical advantages, the lead-acid storage battery is in general use for many purposes, the most common of which is for starting, and lighting the modern automobile.

In automobile installations, several cells are used in groups. The number of cells depends on the voltage requirements and the size depends on the service (amperage) required. A typical cell is shown in Fig. 3. The usual assembly method is to connect these cells in series — that is, the positive terminal of one cell is connected to the negative terminal of the next cell, and so on, to the end of the row.

With the cells in series, the voltage of the battery is the sum of the voltages of the individual cells. Thus, for example, a typical 12-volt storage battery has 6 cells with 11 plates per cell, a capacity of 70 ampere-hours at a 20-hour rate, and a rating of 840 watts.

BATTERY CAPACITY RATING

The battery industry has arrived at several accepted standards of battery performance which have been incorporated in the standards of the Association of American Battery Manufacturers (AABM), the Battery Council International (BCI), formerly part of the Society of Automotive Engineers (SAE), and the U.S. Government. The battery standards are as follows:

Cold Cranking Power — This rating gives the units of cranking power a given battery can deliver at 0° F. It is a new rating which replaces the old method of relating voltage and time as a method of

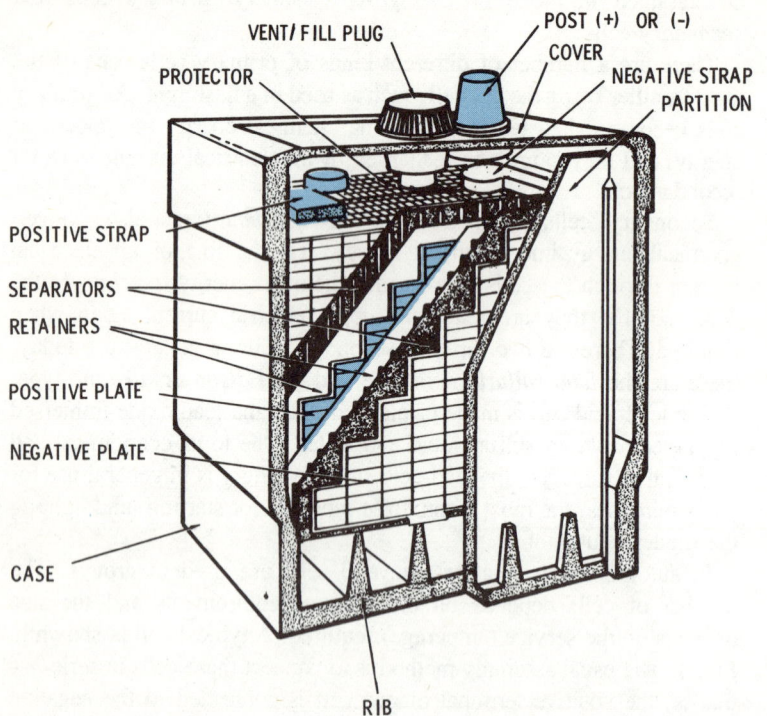

Fig. 3. Cutaway of one cell of a lead-acid storage battery.

measuring cranking ability. It is much more accurate because it allows the cranking capacity to be related to such significant variables as engine displacement, compression ratio, temperature, cranking time, condition of engine and electrical system, and lowest practical voltage for cranking and ignition. This test relates a discharge rating (in amperes) that a fully charged battery will maintain for 30 seconds without the terminal voltage falling below 7.2 volts for a 12-volt battery or 3.6 volts for a 6-volt battery.

Reserve Capacity — This is a measure of the minutes of 25-ampere output at 80° F and replaces the old 20-hour rating. It indicates how long (at 80° F) a fully charged battery will supply power for ignition, lights, and accessories in case of a charging failure or with the engine not running. The test continues until the voltage in the battery drops to 10.5 volts for a 12-volt battery or 5.25 volts for a 6-volt battery (the lowest practical voltages that meet the requirements).

STORAGE BATTERIES

BATTERY DESIGN

New battery designs have been introduced in recent years by some battery manufacturers in an effort to produce a better and more efficient battery. The different types of batteries require different methods of testing and servicing, therefore you should be familiar with them.

The early soft-cover type battery was shown in Fig. 2. Fig. 4 shows the hard-cover type battery with filler caps and top terminal posts. Fig. 5 shows the hard-cover type with top filler caps and recessed terminals on the side. Procedures for testing the hard cover batteries will be given later in this chapter.

Courtesy Hayden Lynn Writing Service

Fig. 4. Typical 12-volt hard-cover battery with top post.

Automobile Guide

Courtesy Hayden Lynn Writing Service

Fig. 5. A typical 12-volt hard-cover battery with side terminal connections.

A completely sealed and maintenance-free battery was introduced in 1971. It is maintenance free so far as internal service is concerned, but may, on occasion, require charging if found in a discharged condition. It has no vent or filler caps. Recessed terminals are located on the side. Shown in Fig. 6, it requires a different method of testing then does the other type battery. Unlike the other battery types, the sealed-type is claimed to have the following advantages:

1. Completely maintenance free. No water (or other additive) addition for the life of the battery.
2. Up to 35% more power, compared to earlier type batteries of the same size.
3. Higher performance level throughout its normal life.

STORAGE BATTERIES

4. Greatly reduced susceptibility to self-discharge, compared to earlier type batteries.

BATTERY MAINTENANCE

Most car storage batteries (except the sealed-type) are of the so-called "dry-type;" that is, the electrolyte is provided in a separate container and is added to the battery at the time of installation. This feature makes the maintenance of batteries in storage much simpler. In addition, the battery will be charged and ready for service as soon as it is filled. It is recommended, however, that a "fresh" battery be slowly charged after being filled with electrolyte whenever possible. Battery charging methods are given later in this chapter. If there is no time for charging however, the battery may be put directly into service.

Courtesy General Motors Corp.
Fig. 6. A sealed battery with side terminal connections.

29

Care of Dry-Charge Batteries

A "dry-charge" battery contains fully charged positive and negative plates, but no electrolyte. The plates are separated by high-quality microporous rubber separators.

A dry-charged battery should be stored in a dry place away from excessive heat, and should be kept in its original carton until ready to be put into service. This type of battery will retain its "charged" condition indefinitely if protected from moisture. Three years (36 months) of storage without maintenance usually produces no appreciable deterioration, provided the battery is stored properly.

After electrolyte has been added to a dry-charged battery it becomes a "wet" battery, and should be maintained in the same way as any other wet battery. It may be put into service without an additional charge if it has been stored properly. If one or more cells discharge gas violently after addition of electrolyte, and the specific gravity in any cell drops more than 25 points within 10 minutes, the battery should be charged before being put into service.

Preparing Dry-Charged Batteries for Service

To prepare dry-charged batteries for service, use only approved battery-grade acid electrolyte (1.265 sp. gr. at 80° F.). Care should be exercised in its use to prevent bodily injury or damage to clothing or other material resulting from physical contact with the electrolyte. Electrolyte should be added to dry-charged batteries in a location where water is readily available for flushing in case the electrolyte comes in contact with the body. Prompt flushing with water will prevent serious acid burns.

It is strongly recommended that a person filling batteries with electrolyte wear glasses (preferably safety glasses) to prevent possible damage to the eyes should any spattering of the electrolyte occur. Proceed as follows:

1. Remove the dry-charged (no electrolyte) battery from its original carton.
2. Remove the vent plugs and discard any seals found in the vent openings.
3. Using a glass or acid-proof plastic funnel, fill each battery cell with electrolyte. *Do not use a metal funnel.* Some "bulk" packaged electrolyte comes equipped with a dispensing hose, nozzle, and shut-off device. This should be used whenever

Storage Batteries

possible. The cell is properly filled when the electrolyte level rises to the split ring at the bottom of the vent well. Do not overfill. In most cases, some electrolyte will remain in the electrolyte container after the battery has been completely filled.

4. After filling the cells, wait five to ten minutes, and if necessary, add additional electrolyte to bring the level back up to the proper point.

Preparing Sealed-Type Battery for Service

Remove the battery from its original carton and check for obvious damage, such as a cracked or broken case that could permit loss of electrolyte. If no damage is noted:

1. Charge at maximum setting of charger for the length of time required to obtain 50 ampere-hours of charge. (Example: 50 amps for 1 hour, or 25 amps for 2 hours).
2. Connect a 300-amp load across the terminals for 15 seconds. This is to remove the surface charge.
3. Battery is now ready to be put into service.

Care of Wet Batteries

Batteries stored in new cars, as well as wet batteries in stock, must be given regular attention to prevent sulfation of their plates that may result from inactivity and self-discharge. All automotive-type wet batteries will slowly discharge while standing idle, whether stored in vehicles or in stock, and will self-discharge much faster when warm than when cold.

To minimize the extent of self-discharge, always store batteries fully charged and in the coolest possible place. At frequent intervals, check the level of the electrolyte and add water as required; also checking the specific gravity with a hydrometer. A boosting charge at a moderate rate, without excessive overcharge, must be given batteries in storage whenever the specific gravity falls to 1.250, corrected for temperature. Batteries used for display purposes or standing in cars in storage must be treated in the same manner as batteries in stock.

Level of Electrolyte

Water is the only component of the electrolyte which is lost as the result of charging and discharging, and it must be replaced before the electrolyte level falls to the tops of the separators.

If the water is not replaced, and the plates and separators become exposed, the acid may reach a dangerously high concentration that will char and disintegrate the separators and may permanently sulfate and impair the performance of the plates.

Plates cannot take full part in the chemical action unless they are completely covered by the electrolyte. Separators are no longer porous in the area that has dried out as a result of exposure; therefore, the corresponding area of the adjoining plates is rendered inactive and subject to continuous sulfation.

Battery Function

The battery in an automobile has three major functions:

1. It provides a source of energy for cranking the engine.
2. It acts as a stabilizer to the voltage in the electrical system.
3. It can, for a limited time, furnish energy when the demands of the electrical units in operation exceed the output of the generator.

In order for the battery to continue to function, it is necessary that the amount of current withdrawn from the battery be balanced by the current input from the generator so that the battery is maintained in a properly charged condition. If the output exceeds the input, the battery will become discharged and will be unable to supply sufficient energy.

The state of charge of the battery as well as the temperature of the electrolyte, has an important bearing on its capacity for supplying energy. Battery efficiency is greatly reduced when the temperature of the electrolyte decreases because a low temperature has a decided reducing effect on the electrochemial action. Under high discharge (such as cranking), the battery voltage drops to a lower value in cold temperatures than in warm temperatures.

In extremely cold climates, it is important to keep batteries in a nearly full-charged condition to avoid the possibility of freezing, which will damage any battery.

Care of Battery When Not in Use

Batteries in cars that are being stored over thirty days require care to prevent plate sulfation or other deterioration due to chemical action.

Before being placed in storage, the battery should be tested to assure that it is filled to the proper level and that it is fully charged. Batteries

STORAGE BATTERIES

should be checked every thirty days and given a boost charge of 25 percent of the ampere rating of the battery at a rate of five amperes.

Additionally, it is wise to disconnect the ground cable of the battery during the storage period.

BATTERY CHARGING METHODS

Because only direct current may be used for charging storage batteries, various types of current converters are used where only alternating current is available. The most commonly used equipment for converting alternating into direct current is the rectifier-transformer combination.

When direct current is available, it is a simple matter to arrange the charging equipment, since all that is necessary is to provide a suitable rheostat to control the charging current and an ammeter to accurately determine the rate of charge. See Fig. 7.

When alternating current only is available, it is necessary to use a rectifier with individual line rheostats and accurate meters. With either ac or dc apparatus, the batteries are charged in series and the charging rates are adjusted to the constant-current rate desired.

Selection of the correct charging equipment depends upon the type, make, and rating of the batteries to be charged, and the type of electrical power available. These factors, together with the number of batteries to

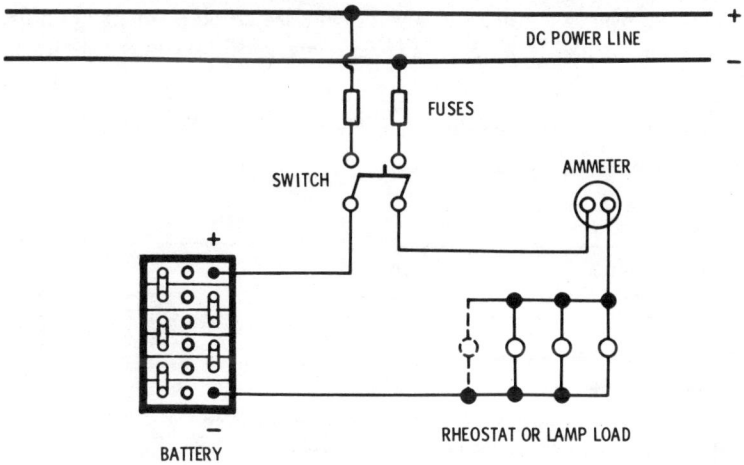

Fig. 7. Wiring diagram for constant-current battery charging when direct current is available.

33

AUTOMOBILE GUIDE

be charged simultaneously, will determine the size and type of battery equipment that will be required.

There are two separate methods of charging batteries. These differ basically in the rate of charge. In the "slow-charge" method, the battery is supplied with a relatively small amount of current for a relatively long period of time. In the "quick-charge" method, the battery is supplied with a high current for a short period of time.

The Slow-Charge Method

The slow-charge method, if properly applied, may safely be used under all possible conditions of the battery, provided the electrolyte is at the proper level in all cells. The battery may be fully charged by this method, unless it is not capable of taking a full charge.

The slow battery chargers commonly used in service stations are suitable for charging both 6- and 12-volt batteries on the same circuit. Each 12 volt unit must be considered as equal to two 6-volt batteries, and the charging rate must be adjusted so as not to exceed the amount determined by the smallest 12-volt battery on the line. Safe slow-charging rates are determined by allowing one ampere per positive plate per cell. Thus, the proper slow-charging rate for a battery with 11-plate cells is six amperes.

When putting batteries on the line, connect the positive charger lead to the positive battery terminal, and the negative charger lead to the negative battery terminal. If several batteries are to be charged on the same circuit, the batteries should be connected in series, as shown in Fig. 8.

As the batteries approach full charge, each cell will begin to gas or

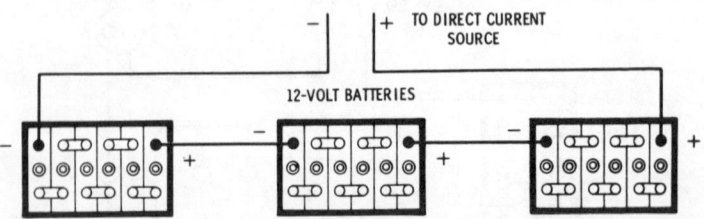

Fig. 8. Wiring diagram of a series hook-up for constant-current battery charging. When charging on a series (constant-current) line, connect the batteries in series and charge at a rate which is safe for the smallest battery. Continued charging at a high rate will result in high temperatures, which should be avoided.

Storage Batteries

bubble freely. The battery temperatures should not exceed 125° F during charge. If this temperature is reached, the battery should be cooled by reducing the charge rate or removal from the circuit. The battery is fully charged when three successive hourly hydrometer readings show no increase in specific gravity.

The Quick-Charge Method

It should be understood that a battery cannot be brought up to a fully charged condition by the "quick-charge" method. The battery can be substantially recharged or "boosted," but in order to bring the battery to a fully charged condition, the charging cycle must be finished by charging at a low or normal rate.

Used with care, a quick-charger will not damage a battery which is in good condition. A "quick-charge" must not be used, however, if any of the following conditions exist in the battery:

1. If the specific gravity readings are not uniform, the low reading cell may have an internal defect. Quick charging may cause considerable heat to develop, possibly enough to ruin the battery.
2. If the electrolyte is discolored with a brownish sediment, quick charging may produce an internal short and ruin the battery.
3. A sulfated battery will overheat during quick charging. Such a battery requires charging at half the normal "slow-charge" rate for from 60 to 100 hours to reconvert the crystalline lead sulfate into active material.
4. A battery which has been badly overcharged may quickly fail if placed on quick charge.
5. The cell voltages and the color of the electrolyte should be checked a few minutes after the battery has been put on quick charge. If the voltage readings are not uniform within 0.2 volt, or if the electrolyte has become discolored with brownish sediment, the quick charging should be stopped immediately. Charging may be continued by the "slow-charge" method.

A typical fast charger is illustrated in Fig. 9.

Charging the Sealed-Type Battery

The sealed-type battery should be charged at the maximum rate of the charger for the length of time required to obtain 50 ampere-hours of charge. If the charger does not have an ammeter, place one in series

35

Fig. 9. The ALLEN model 16-90 battery charger. This fast-charge unit is rated at 50 amperes at 12 volts or 100 amperes at 6 volts.

Courtesy Allen Electric & Equipment Co.

with the charger to determine the charging rate. If the charging rate is 10 amperes, the time required will be 5 hours (10 × 5 = 50). If the rate is 20 amperes, the time required will be 2.5 hours, etc., up to the maximum rate of the charger.

Charging rates as high as 75 amperes are recommended. At 75 amperes the charging time would be 2/3 hour (40 minutes). After charging, connect a 300 ampere load across the terminals for 15 seconds to remove the surface charge before putting the battery into service.

Precautions in Battery Charging

A battery charger must be connected in *parallel* with a battery. The positive terminal of the charger must be connected to the positive terminal of the battery. The two negative terminals must also be connected together. With any type or brand of battery charger, the positive terminal is a cable and clamp usually with red insulation. The negative cable usually has black or green insulation.

If a charger is connected in reverse polarity, the battery can be ruined very quickly, and may even explode due to the extreme heat developed in the electrolyte. If the battery is still in the automobile and connected to the electrical system, a reverse-connected charger can ruin a transistor-type regulator or damage the diodes in the alternator.

Most modern battery chargers are equipped with a protective device that lights a signal lamp when the charger is connected in reverse polarity. This device also prevents the flow of current until the polarity is correct.

BATTERY TESTING

There are several different ways of testing storage batteries to determine their state of charge, or to locate irregularities and identify worn-out batteries.

Specific Gravity Test

It is advisable to occasionally check the condition of the battery electrolyte with a hydrometer in order to determine whether the automotive charging system is maintaining the battery in a proper state of charge. This is particularly important during cold weather when the battery must deliver more power.

The hydrometer measures the percentage of sulfuric acid in the battery electrolyte in terms of specific gravity. As a battery drops from a charged to a discharged condition, the acid leaves the solution and enters the plates, causing a decrease in specific gravity of the electrolyte. By measuring the specific gravity of the electrolyte with a hydrometer, an indication of the approximate state of charge of the battery is obtained.

A hydrometer can be used only if there is sufficient electrolye above the battery plates to fill the hydrometer tube. *Do not take hydrometer readings immediately after refilling a battery with distilled water.* The specific gravity test cannot be made on the sealed-type battery.

To make a hydrometer test, remove the battery filler caps. Draw the electrolyte in and force it out of the hydrometer tube several times to bring the temperatures of the hydrometer float to that of the electrolyte. Then draw in just enough electrolyte to lift the float. Make sure the float is not binding on the side of the hydrometer tube. Read the specific gravity on the float scale.

The specific gravity of the electrolyte varies not only with the percentage of acid in the liquid, but also with a change in temperature. As temperature increases, the electrolyte expands so that the specific

Automobile Guide

gravity is reduced. As temperature drops, the electrolyte contracts so that the specific gravity increases. Unless these variations in specific gravity are taken into account, the reading obtained by the hydrometer may not give a true indication of the state of charge of the battery.

Correction can be made for temperature by adding .004 (usually referred to as 4 "points of gravity") to the hydrometer reading for every 10° F that the electrolyte is above 80°F, or subtracting .004 for every 10°F that the electrolyte is below 80°F. See Fig. 10.

If the electrolyte temperature is not too far from the 80°F standard or if only an approximate idea of the specific gravity reading is required, it will not be necessary to make the temperature correction. It should be noted that some hydrometers have built in thermometers and temperature-scale correction, which will simplify the operation of obtaining a true specific gravity reading.

A fully charged battery has a specific gravity reading of 1.280 to 1.300. A battery that has a specific gravity reading of 1.250 or less, with all cells reading evenly within 30 points (.030) of each other, requires recharging. A battery that has a specific gravity reading which varies more than 30 points between any two cells should be replaced and tested for cause of failure.

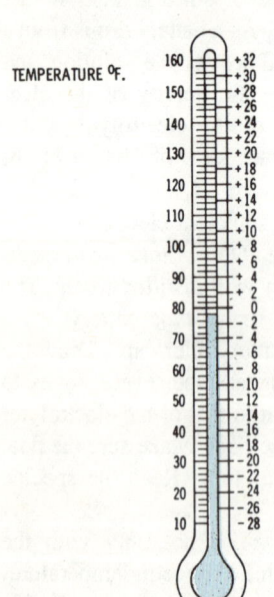

Fig. 10. Hydrometer reading correction chart.

STORAGE BATTERIES

High-Rate Discharge Test

Satisfactory capacity tests can only be made when the battery has a specific gravity reading of 1.215 or more at 80°F. If the specific gravity reading is below 1.215, the high discharge test should not be made.

To make the high rate discharge test (Fig. 11) connect a carbon pile rheostat in series with an ammeter and the battery as indicated schematically in Fig. 12. Be sure that the carbon pile control knob is rotated to the full resistance position *before* connecting.

The voltmeter clips must contact the battery posts only, and not the high rate discharge tester clips. Unless this is done, the actual battery-terminal voltage will not be indicated. Rotate the rheostat until the ammeter reads three times the ampere-hour rating of the battery (210 amps for a 70 ampere-hour battery). *NOTE: The sealed-type battery requires a 230-ampere load. With the battery under discharge for 15 seconds, read the terminal voltage.*

If the terminal voltage reads 9 volts (9.6 volts for the sealed-type) or more, the discharge capacity is satisfactory. If the reading is less than 9 volts (9.6 volts for the sealed-type), the battery must be completely recharged and tested again. For a 6-volt battery, the reading should be at

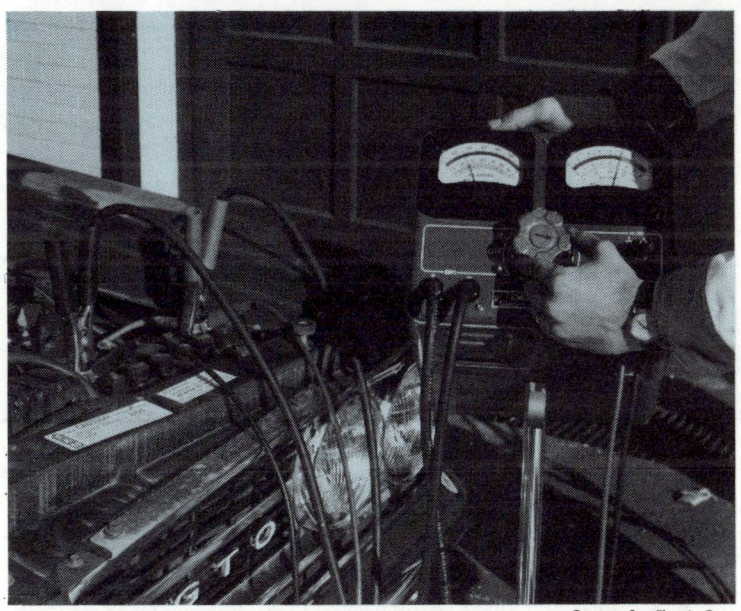

Courtesy Sun Electric Corp.

Fig. 11. Battery undergoing high-rate discharge test.

Automobile Guide

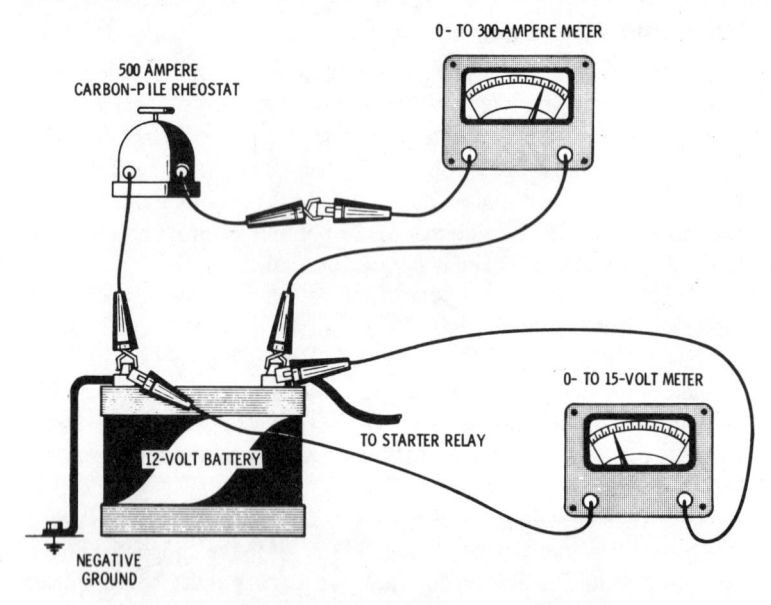

Fig. 12. Connections for a battery-capacity test.

least 4.5 volts. It is important that the rheostat be returned to the starting position following the test to avoid excessive battery drain.

Many different discharge testers are available. Figs. 13 and 14 illustrate two of these. The adjustable carbon pile is included in the instrument, and only four cables need be connected.

Undercharges Battery Conditions

Some of the more common causes of repeated undercharged battery conditions, other than those due to a defective battery, include:

1. Regulator improperly adjusted, low alternator output due to defective alternator or loose alternator belt(s).
2. Improper installation of "add-on" accessories or excessive use of accessories with engine not running.
3. Leaving headlamps or parking lights turned on, or leaving the doors open with the car unattended for extended periods.
4. Defective switch in underhood or trunk lamp circuit. If left burning long enough this small lamp will discharge a battery.
5. Self-discharge due to a dirty battery case or undercharging due to corroded or loose battery cables.

STORAGE BATTERIES

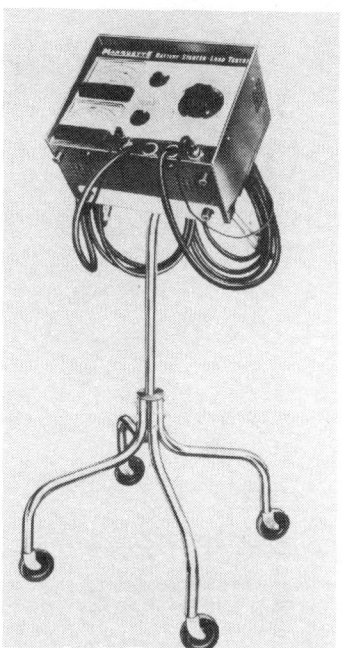

Fig. 13. The MARQUETTE battery-starter load tester.

Courtesy Marquette Manufacturing Co.

BATTERY TROUBLES AND REMEDIES

Symptoms and Possible Causes   *Possible Remedies*

Insufficient Charging Current to Battery

(a) Incorrect voltage regulator setting.
(b) Regulator contacts burned or oxidized.
(c) Glazed or burned generator commutator.
(d) Sulfated battery.

(e) Corroded battery terminals.

(a) Set regulator.
(b) Clean and adjust or replace regulator.
(c) Clean commutator and replace brushes.
(d) Charge battery at half the normal "slow charge" rate for 60-100 hours. Replace battery if necessary.
(e) Clean battery terminals and cables.

41

Automobile Guide

Fig. 14. The SUN model BST-10 battery-starter tester.

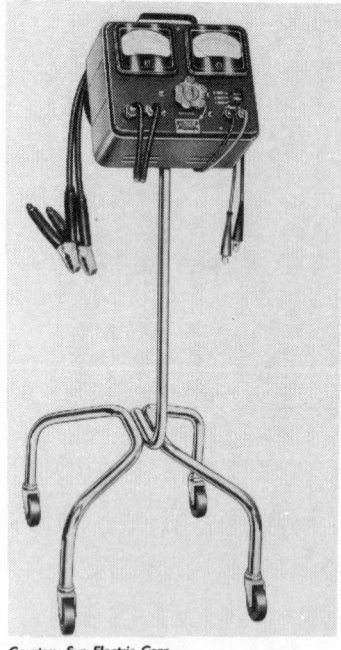

Courtesy Sun Electric Corp.

Symptoms and Possible Causes

(f) Loose connections in lighting, ignition, or regulator circuit.

(g) Slipping drive belt.

(h) Shorted or open alternator diodes.

(i) Grounded stator windings in alternator.

(j) Defective regulator fuse.

Possible Remedies

(f) Tighten connections. Note particularly regulator ground connection.

(g) Tighten drive belt.

(h) Replace defective diodes.

(i) Repair alternator. Replace stator.

(j) Replace fuse or replace regulator.

Excessive Lighting and/or Accessory Load

(a) Ground or short in lighting or accessory circuit.

(a) Repair circuit.

STORAGE BATTERIES

Symptoms and Possible Causes

(b) Unnecessary use of lights or accessories while parking.

(c) Stop light switch stuck closed.

(d) Battery under capacity.

(e) Defective accessory (radio, heater, cigarette lighter, etc.).

(f) Trunk or hood light switch stuck closed.

Possible Remedies

(b) Do not use lights or accessories when engine not running.

(c) Replace switch.

(d) Replace with larger capacity battery.

(e) Repair as necessary.

(f) Replace switch.

Internal Discharge of Battery

(a) Liquid level not maintained to proper level.

(b) Plate separators defective.

(c) Plates sulfated.

(d) Battery dirty.

(e) Case cracked (loss of liquid).

(a) Add water regularly.

(b) Replace battery.

(c) Charge the battery at half the normal "slow charge" rate for 60-100 hours. Replace battery if necessary.

(d) Clean battery.

(e) Replace battery.

Abnormal Starting Load on Battery

(a) Short trips (frequent use of starter).

(b) Defective starter.

(c) Difficulty in starting requiring excessive use of starter.

(d) Tight engine.

(a) If short trips are necessary, charge battery regularly.

(b) Repair starter.

(c) Correct starting problem as necessary.

(d) Repair engine as necessary.

Symptoms and Possible Causes

(e) Improper grade of oil in engine.
(f) Corroded battery terminals.
(g) Defective ground in starting circuit.

Possible Remedies

(e) Replace with proper engine oil.
(f) Clean battery terminals and cables.
(g) Clean and/or correct ground connections.

CHAPTER 3

Distributors

As its name implies, the distributor "distributes" the ignition spark to the spark plugs at the proper times and in the proper sequence to ensure maximum torque from the engine. The job of the distributor is also to "trigger" the exact instant that the spark is to occur. Its job is very exacting — it must trigger and distribute voltages that average 30,000 volts and must do so at very exact time intervals. Slight irregularities in the operation of the distributor caused by either mechanical or electrical misadjustments can result in very poor engine performance.

There are two types of distributor; conventional and electronic. The general construction details of both types are basically the same with the exception that the electronic distributor *does not have mechanical breaker points.*

GENERAL CONSTRUCTION, CONVENTIONAL DISTRIBUTOR

The breaker points in the distributor, shown in Fig. 1, open and close the circuit to the primary winding of the ignition coil. At the instant the points close, current begins to flow in the primary circuit and a magnetic field builds up around the primary coil. When the points open, the current flow stops and the magnetic field collapses rapidly. This sudden collapse builds up a very high voltage in the secondary winding of the coil. This high voltage is connected by a wire to the center terminal on the distributor cap. This terminal, in turn, is connected through a rotating contact to the rotor inside the distributor. The rotor turns with the distributor shaft and distributes, in the proper order, the high voltage

AUTOMOBILE GUIDE

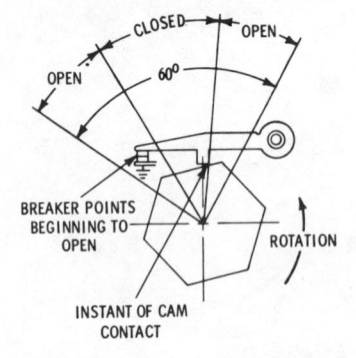

A. Points at the instant of opening.

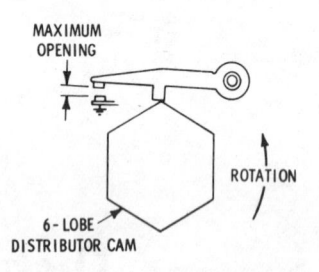

B. Points at maximum separation.

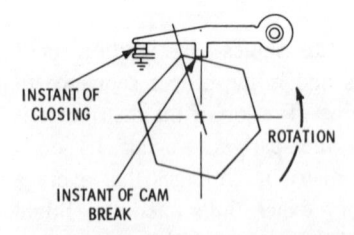

C. Points at the instant of closing.

Fig. 1. The cycle of breaker-point action in a six-cylinder engine. An eight-cylinder engine would have an eight-sided cam; a four-cylinder engine a four-sided cam. A change in dwell angle will change the opening time of the points, and this will be reflected in the ignition timing.

to the spark plugs. Fig. 2 shows a typical distributor for a 6-cylinder engine, while Fig. 3 shows the top view of the breaker plate used in another popular 6-cylinder distributor.

The parts that normally wear and require service are:

1. The breaker points.
2. The rubbing block.
3. The condenser.
4. The cam.
5. The shaft bearings.

Breaker Points

The breaker points are not subject to mechanical wear because they meet squarely and do not rub together. They are subject, however, to electrical wear. The sparking action at the points, as they open and close

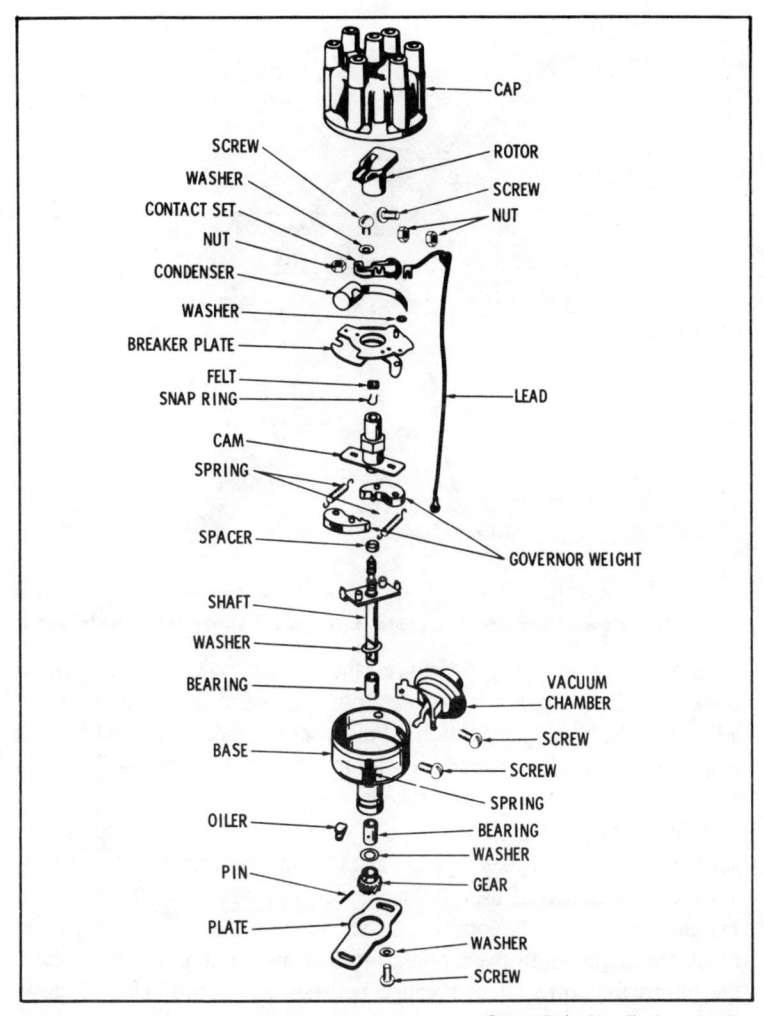

DISTRIBUTORS

Fig. 2. A typical distributor for a six-cylinder engine.

Courtesy Dodge Div., Chrysler Motors Corp.

the primary circuit, erodes the metal and sometimes causes metal to be transferred from one point to the other. Points that have been in service can be smoothed with an ignition file and left in service. It is not necessary to remove all traces of pits as this removes too much metal. Simply brighten the surface of the pitted point, and remove the small raised portion from the surface of the opposite point.

AUTOMOBILE GUIDE

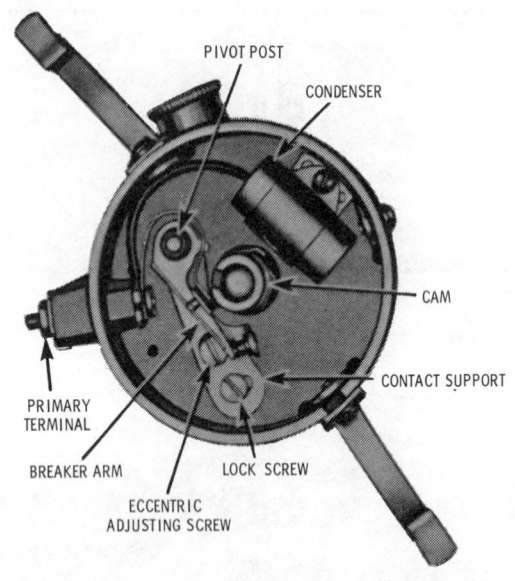

Courtesy Chevrolet Div., General Motors Corp.
Fig. 3. Top view of the breaker plate in a typical six-cylinder distributor.

Gap Setting — The gap between the breaker points at their widest separation (rubbing block on high point of cam, Fig. 1B) must be adjusted exactly to specifications. Points set too close will tend to burn and pit rapidly, while points set with too much separation will tend to cause ignition failure at high speeds.

A feeler gauge, dial indicator, or a dwell-angle meter can be used to set the point gap. A feeler gauge should only be used on new points, since the roughness of used points prevents an accurate setting. To set the gap on new points, loosen the lock screw(s) on the contact points, crank the engine until the rubbing block is on a high point of the cam, and insert the correct feeler gauge between the points. Use a screwdriver or appropriate tool to move the movable point back and forth until only a slight drag is felt when the feeler gauge is moved between the points.

A dial indicator can be used to set new or used points, as illustrated in Fig. 4. Clamp the dial indicator to the lip of the distributor and position the lever arm against the back of the movable point with the rubbing block on a cam flat. Set the dial indicator to zero and then crank the engine until the rubbing block is on a high point of the cam. The dial

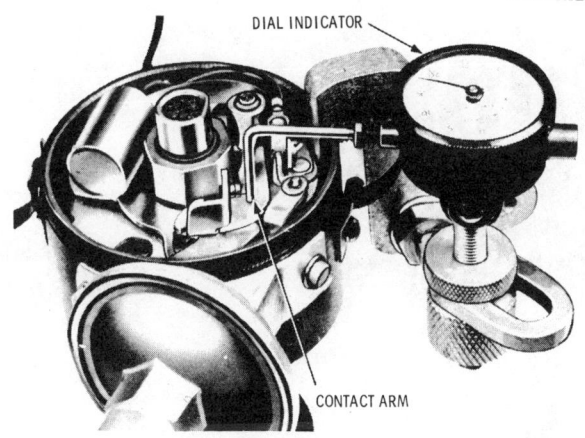

DISTRIBUTORS

Fig. 4. A dial indicator used to set point gap.
Courtesy Dodge Div., Chrysler Motors Corp.

indicator reading is the point gap. Adjust the breaker points until the reading agrees with the specifications.

A dwell meter is an electronic instrument that measures the point gap in terms of the cam rotation angle through which the points remain closed (Fig. 5). Some of the modern distributors have provisions for adjusting the point gap from outside the distributor housing (Fig. 6) without removing the distributor cap. On this type, a small window can be opened in the side of the distributor and a wrench inserted to adjust the gap while the engine is running. On older distributors, and on those new types without the window, the distributor cap must be removed and the engine cranked with the ignition off.

One lead of the dwell meter should be connected to ground and the other lead to the point terminal on the coil. The meter should be

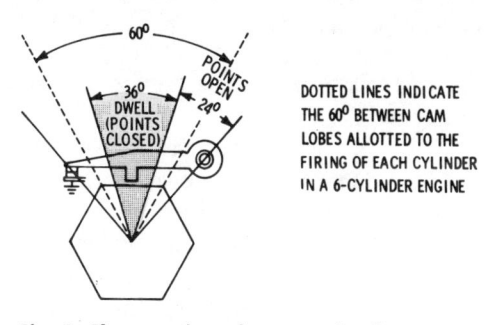

DOTTED LINES INDICATE THE 60° BETWEEN CAM LOBES ALLOTTED TO THE FIRING OF EACH CYLINDER IN A 6-CYLINDER ENGINE

Fig. 5. The meaning of contact dwell.

AUTOMOBILE GUIDE

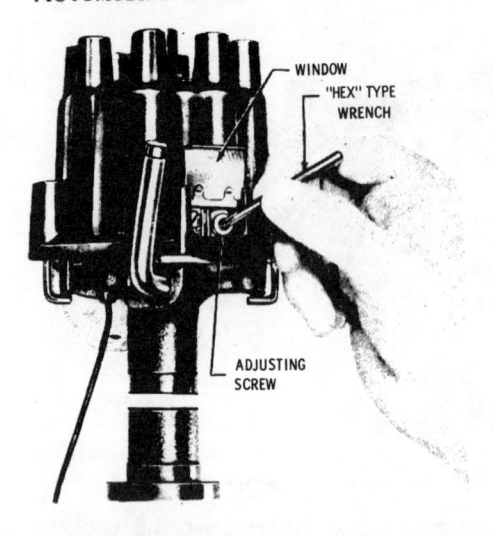

Fig. 6. Setting dwell angle on a modern distributor.

calibrated according to the manufacturer's instructions. Crank the engine, or start it, and adjust the point gap until the meter reading agrees with specifications.

Contact Pressure — The contact pressure, or the pressure with which the points are held together when they are closed, should be within the listed specifications. Weak tension will cause point chatter (bouncing) at high speeds, while excessive tension will cause extreme wear of the points, cam, and rubbing block.

Contact pressure is checked by placing the hooked end of a spring-tension scale over the movable breaker arm next to the point, as in Fig. 7. Pull the gauge at a right angle to the movable arm until the breaker points just begin to open. Read the scale. If the tension is not within specifications, adjust the spring tension as follows:

1. Disconnect the coil and the condenser leads at the breaker assembly terminal.
2. Loosen the lock nut holding the end of the spring. Move the spring toward the breaker arm pivot to decrease tension, or in the opposite direction to increase tension.
3. Tighten the lock nut and recheck the spring tension. Repeat the adjustment until the spring tension is correct.
4. Reconnect the coil and condenser leads at the breaker terminal. Tighten the holding nut securely.

DISTRIBUTORS

Fig. 7. Checking breaker arm spring tension.
Courtesy Sun Electric Corp.

Point Alignment — The rubbing block should be aligned so that it strikes the cam squarely. If this is not done, wear will be excessive. The points should be aligned so that they strike squarely over their entire surface (Fig. 8). This is particularly important with the vented type of points. Any misalignment of this type of points will cause premature wear, overheating, and pitting.

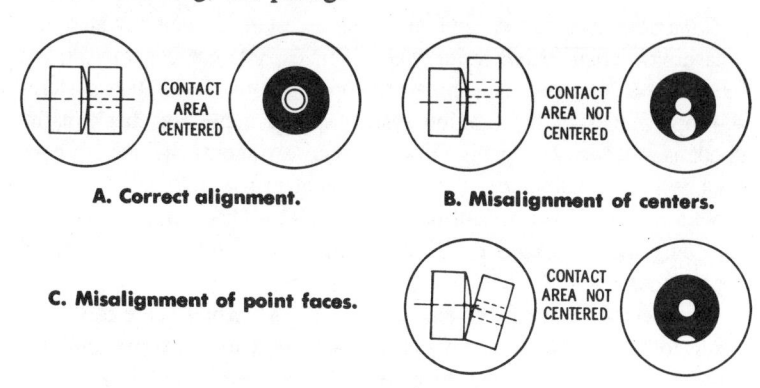

A. Correct alignment.

B. Misalignment of centers.

C. Misalignment of point faces.

Fig. 8. Alignment of breaker points.

51

Align the points by bending the stationary breaker-point bracket only. *Do not bend the movable arm.* After aligning the points, adjust the gap or the dwell angle.

The Rubbing Block

The rubbing block must follow the cam faces perfectly and must not wear excessively. The cam surface must be lubricated sparingly with cam lubricant. *Do not use engine oil to lubricate the cam.* On older types of points, the cam lubricant is very important, but the newer points generally have rubbing blocks made of nylon. This material has a very low coefficient of friction and does not wear quickly.

Excessive contact spring tension has a great effect on the life of the rubbing block. Adjust the spring tension to within specifications for minimum wear on the rubbing block.

When the rubbing block wears down, the points are not opened as widely and the dwell angle increases. When new points are installed, set the gap slightly on the high side (or the dwell angle on the low side) to compensate for the anticipated wear of the rubbing block.

The Condenser

There are three factors that affect condenser performance, and each must be considered when making tests. These are:

1. Capacitance.
2. Low insulation resistance.
3. High series resistance.

Capacitance — Every condenser has a certain capacity, which is a measure of its *electrical capacitance.* This capacitance can vary during the life of a condenser and impair the operation of the ignition system. A proper check of the ignition system should include a check of the condenser capacity. Most ignition service instruments include a means for checking capacitance. If the instrument in use does not have this function, or if an instrument is not available, a check can be made by replacing the suspected condenser with a new unit of the specified capacitance.

The specified condenser value is critical. The wrong value can cause metal to be transferred from one contact point to the other until the points are almost shorted together. Fig. 9 shows the results of a condenser of the wrong value.

DISTRIBUTORS

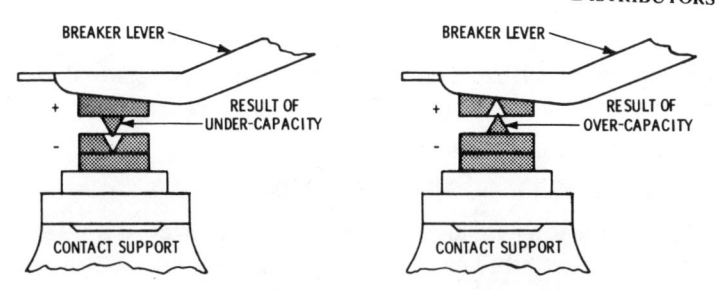

Fig. 9. Pitting of breaker contacts due to wrong condenser capacitance.

Low Insulation Resistance — The normal resistance of a good condenser should be several million ohms or more. The measured resistance of a faulty condenser could range from this value down to zero ohms. A low value of resistance in the condenser can upset the ignition system by acting as a shunt across the breaker points. The rapid increase and decrease of the magnetic field of the coil is slowed, and the output voltage from the coil will be much lower than normal. Most test instruments will measure insulation resistance.

High Series Resistance — High series resistance is usually a result of poor electrical connections within the condenser. The passage of current into and out of the condenser is reduced and again the output voltage from the coil is reduced. Most test instruments will measure series resistance.

The Cam

The distributor cam is pinned to the distributor shaft and must rotate with it. The wear of the rubbing block on the cam tends to round off the high points and reduce the gap setting. This naturally takes a long time, since the cam is made of a very hard, tough metal. If the proper dwell angle and gap setting cannot be obtained at the same time, the cam is worn and should be replaced.

The Shaft Bearings

The distributor shaft has a sleeve-type bearing at the top and bottom. Wear in these bearings will produce side play of the shaft and introduce irregularities in ignition timing. Side play can be checked with a dial indicator clamped to the distributor body with the lever arm contacting a circular portion of the shaft. Move the shaft to and from the indicator in various positions of its rotation. If the side play exceeds specifications, the bearings and/or the shaft must be replaced.

AUTOMOBILE GUIDE

Various specialized tools for removing and replacing distributor bearings are available. For best results, use tools approved by the manufacturer for replacing and burnishing the bearings.

SPARK ADVANCE

In order for an engine to develop maximum efficiency, it is necessary that peak pressures be developed in the cylinders near the start of the power stroke. It takes time for the fuel mixture in the cylinder to burn once ignition has been started by the spark plugs. Therefore, it is necessary for the spark to start the mixture burning *before* the piston reaches TDC at the end of the compression stroke and at the start of the power stroke. This is called *spark advance* and the advance which gives maximum engine power is called *optimum spark advance*.

The time it takes for a specific amount of mixture to burn does not vary greatly. The faster the piston moves, the earlier in the compression stroke the spark must occur in order to develop the maximum pressures at the top of the stroke. This results in a spark advance that varies directly with engine speed (Fig. 10), and is usually accomplished by a centrifugal advance mechanism, shown in Fig. 11. There is another action going on at the same time that must also be considered. As the

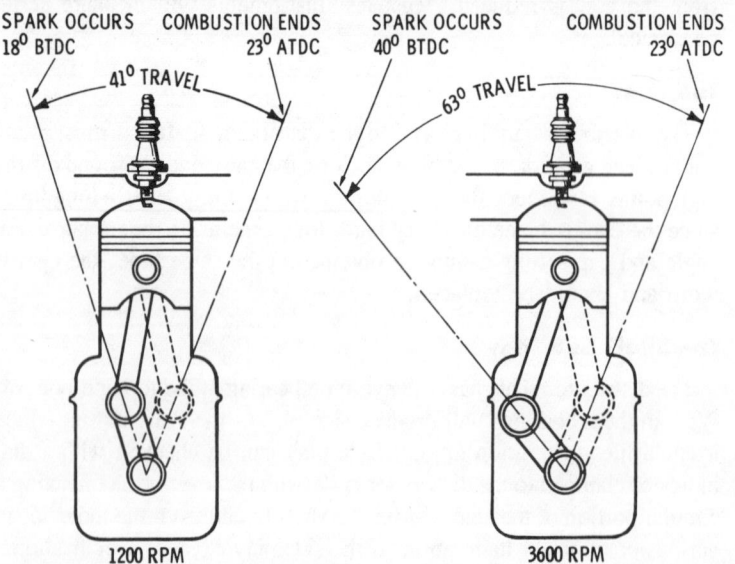

Fig. 10. Illustrating the spark advance which will vary due to engine r/min.

DISTRIBUTORS

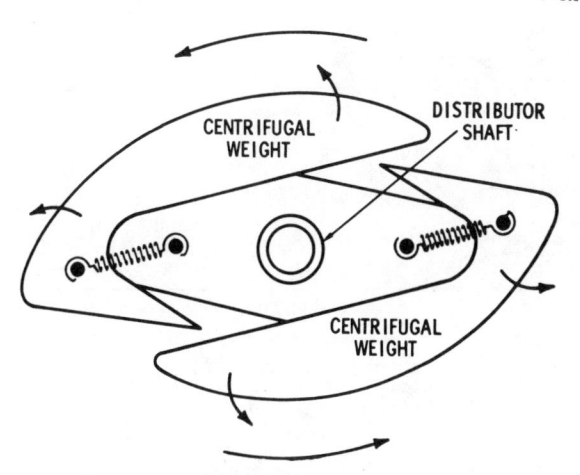

Fig. 11. Centrifugal weights which govern the spark advance.

throttle of an engine is opened, more fuel mixture is drawn into the cylinders. It takes a longer time to burn a larger charge of fuel, so another advance must be introduced which depends on how much fuel is going into the engine to ensure that maximum pressures are developed at the end of the compression stroke. This advance that must be added to the centrifugal advance is commonly called *vacuum advance*.

VACUUM ADVANCE MECHANISM

As mentioned earlier, as the mixture flowing into the cylinder is increased, the spark advance must also increase. A simple way of measuring the amount of fuel flowing into the engine is through the use of an auxiliary venturi in the carburetor. This venturi will develop a vacuum that depends upon how much fuel is flowing into the cylinder. As can be seen in the diagram (Fig. 12), this vacuum is applied to one side of the diaphragm in the vacuum chamber. Atmospheric pressure acting on the other side of this diaphragm is opposed by the spring and, as a result, causes movement of the operating rod to the left.

With increasing vacuum, the rod will move in proportion to the amount of vacuum applied to the chamber. This rod is usually connected to the distributor plate so that, as vacuum is introduced into the chamber, the plate is rotated opposite to the distributor shaft rotation, causing an ignition advance which depends upon the amount of charge being drawn into the cylinders. Under very high engine loading (that is,

Automobile Guide

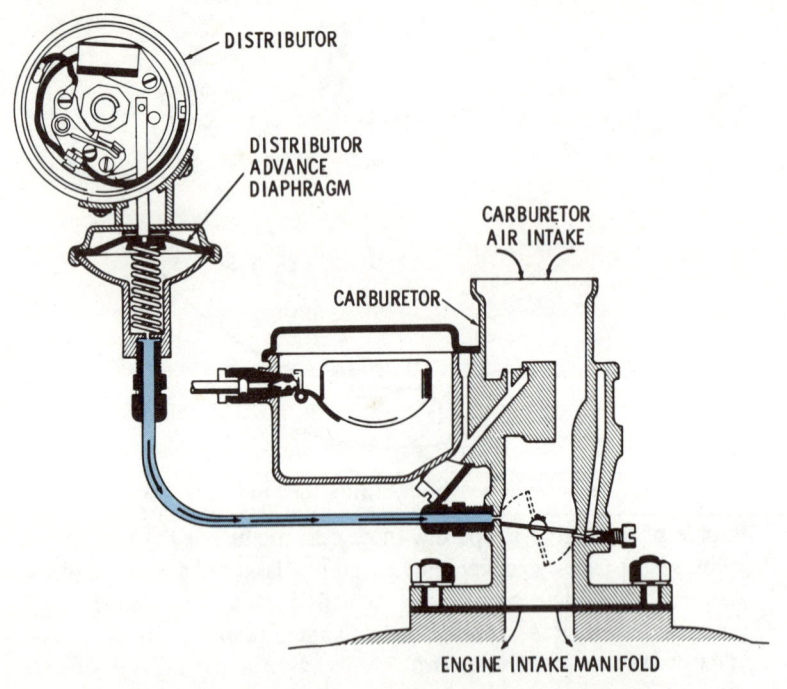

Fig. 12. Illustrating the vacuum advance mechanism.

when the throttle is floored), the spark must be retarded somewhat to prevent detonation or "ping." By connecting this diaphragm vacuum line through properly designed passages to the engine intake manifold, this effect is accomplished. When a wide-open throttle is approached, the engine manifold loses its vacuum and overrides the normal effect, resulting in a loss of vacuum advance under high engine loading. The centrifugal advance and vacuum advance work together in an automotive engine to produce the total advance necessary for the maximum efficiency of the engine.

In recent years, several changes have been made in the vacuum advance systems, primarily to assist in exhaust emission control. Briefly, we will discuss the *Delco* and *Autolite* systems.

One *Delco* system (Transmission Controlled Spark — TCS) allows vacuum to reach the vacuum advance at the distributor only when the transmission (automatic or standard) is in high gear with engine temperatures between 85°F and 220°F. Fig. 13 shows the TCS control solenoid closed, as would be the case when the engine temperature is

DISTRIBUTORS

above 85°F and below 220°F with the transmission in any gear except "high."

Fig. 14 shows the TCS solenoid open, as would be the case if the engine temperature were below 85° F, over 220° F, or the transmission were in "high" gear. Below 85°F the solenoid will open allowing distributor spark advance which will cause the engine to run faster for a rapid "warm-up." At 85°F the solenoid will close and remain closed during normal engine operating temperatures. If, however, the engine temperature reaches, or exceeds, 220°F the solenoid will again open, allowing spark advance to cause the engine to run faster, thereby cooling the engine. Whenever engine temperature drops below 220°F the solenoid will again close.

Another *Delco* system uses the Thermostatic Vacuum Switch (TVS), which also provides no vacuum advance at idle as long as the engine temperature is below 230°F. Note in Fig. 15 that manifold vacuum is

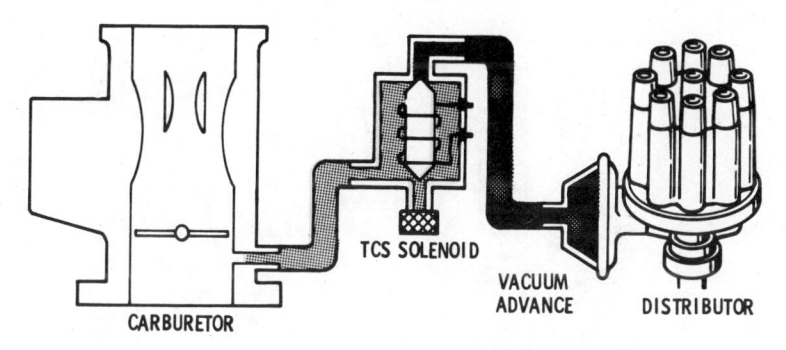

Fig. 13. TCS solenoid energized.

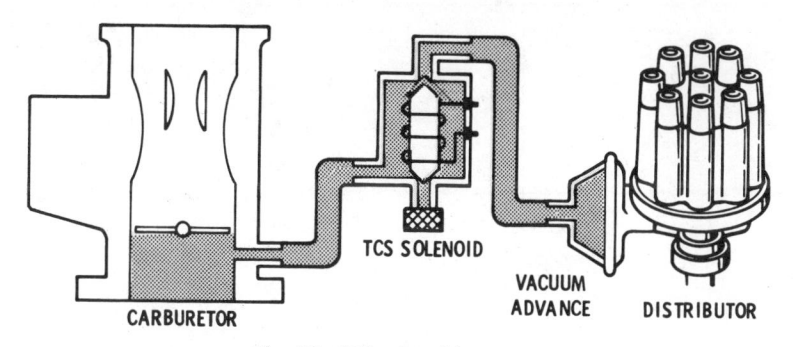

Fig. 14. TCS solenoid open.

57

Automobile Guide

"blocked" from the distributor by the thermostatic switch. Since the throttle plate is not open, no vacuum is available from the carburetor. Fig. 16 shows the throttle plate open (creating a carburetor vacuum), as would be the case in any "off-idle" condition. In this manner a vacuum would be applied to the distributor for normal operation.

Fig. 17 shows that the thermostatic vacuum switch has changed position, allowing full vacuum advance at idle, as would be the case if the engine temperature reaches 230°F or more. The function of the TVS is to allow full spark (vacuum) advance at idle when the engine temperature rises to 230°F or more, which would allow the engine to cool, so that normal operating temperatures can be maintained. The "no vacuum advance at idle" feature greatly reduces exhaust emission levels, during normal operating temperatures.

A Vacuum Control Valve (VCV) is used in the vacuum advance supply line of some *Autolite* equipped engines to provide advanced timing under certain prolonged idling conditions. The VCV, installed in

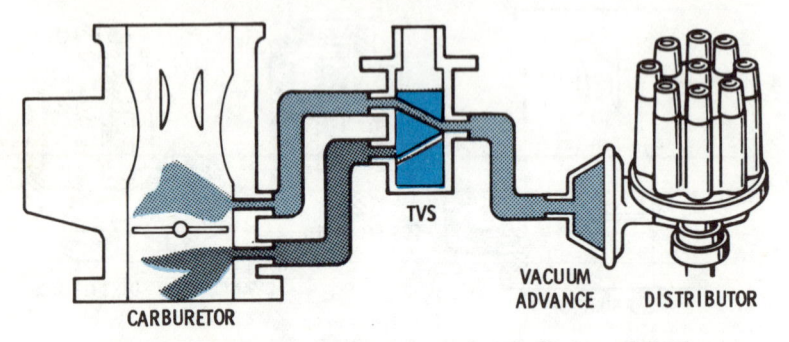

Fig. 15. TVS system with no vacuum at idle (below 230° F.).

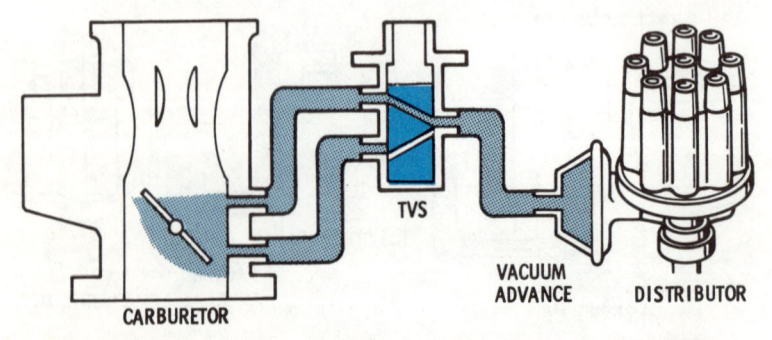

Fig. 16. TVS with vacuum advance off idle (at any temperature).

DISTRIBUTORS

the coolant outlet fitting, will sense engine coolant temperature. Normally, the valve connects normal source vacuum at the carburetor, to the distributor. However, should the engine temperature rise above normal, the valve will close the carburetor vacuum source and connect the distributor to an alternate vacuum source. Advanced ignition timing will cause an increase in engine speed which will continue until engine temperature returns to normal.

On other *Autolite*-equipped engines, a vacuum control valve is used in the vacuum system to provide additional control of timing. This device is used with the dual-diaphragm vacuum advance-retard unit, as shown in Fig. 18. During normal driving, the advance diaphragm is connected to a vacuum source on the carburetor. However, during deceleration periods, when intake manifold vacuum rises above a specific value, the deceleration valve closes off the carburetor vacuum to provide direct intake manifold vacuum to the distributor-advance diaphragm. This will cause maximum advance which will prevent "afterburning" (popping) in the exhaust system. When the engine slows down and is operating at idle, the valve shuts off manifold vacuum and opens the carburetor vacuum to the distributor.

GENERAL CONSTRUCTION, ELECTRONIC DISTRIBUTORS

The electronic distributor is about the same in construction as the conventional distributor (see Fig. 19). The main exception is, of course, the electronic distributor does not have conventional breaker points and a cam. It may or may not have a condenser depending on the type of distributor. Also, the electronic distributor may or may not have the coil built into the distributor cap.

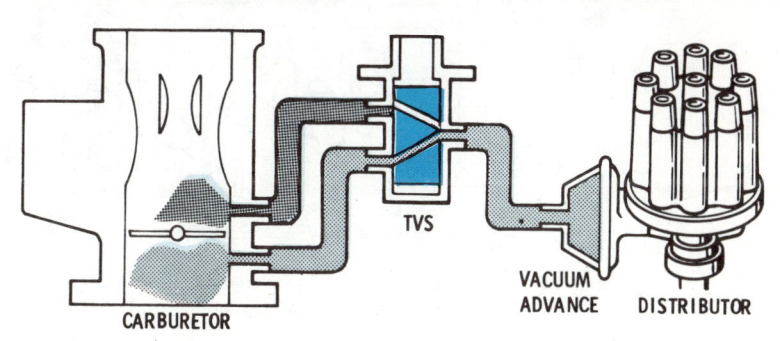

Fig. 17. Full vacuum advance at idle (above 230° F.).

AUTOMOBILE GUIDE

The breaker points and cam are replaced by a *sensor* and *trigger wheel*. The sensor is a small coil of wire and the trigger wheel is constructed of a nonmagnetic (nonferrous) material with "teeth" tipped with a magnetic (ferrous) metal.

The sensor coil is supplied an electrical current "signal" from an *electronic control device*. This signal is interrupted (triggered) when the ferrous metal of the trigger wheel passes through its magnetic lines of flux.

This electrical signal and its interruption is related to the "make" and "break" of conventional points which "charges" and "discharges" the coil at the proper interval to supply the required secondary voltage to the spark plugs.

Since there is no rubbing block, the cam angle will not normally change during the "life" of the sensor. Though the air gap setting is critical, once set there is no mechanical interference to change the setting. A defective sensor is replaced as a unit.

DISTRIBUTOR TESTERS

From a diagnostic point of view, the distributor is the heart of the automobile engine and, therefore, must be the subject of careful inspection in any case of poor engine performance.

There are several fundamental tests which must be made on a distributor to determine if it is performing its functions properly. They are:

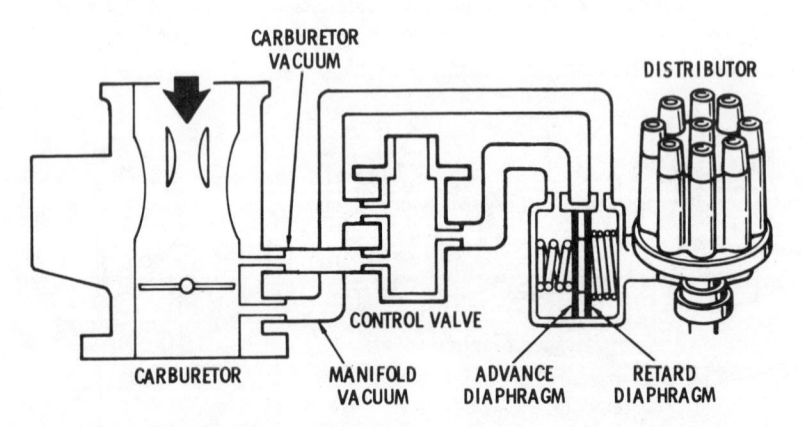

Fig. 18. Dual diaphragm system with vacuum advance control valve.

Distributors

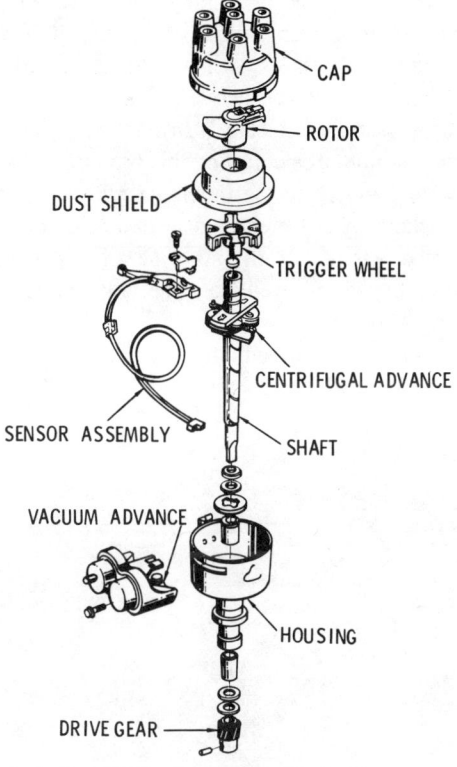

Fig. 19. Typical six-cylinder breakerless inductive discharge (BID) distribututor (exploded view).

1. Condenser tests.
2. Electrical resistance test.
3. Breaker point spring-tension test.
4. Cam lobe accuracy.
5. Breaker point alignment.
6. Breaker point dwell.
7. Breaker point dwell variation.
8. Centrifugal-advance calibration test.
9. Vacuum chamber diaphragm test.
10. Vacuum-controlled breaker plate test.
11. Vacuum spark-advance test.
12. Breaker plate spring-tension test.

61

AUTOMOBILE GUIDE

Distributor testers capable of making these tests are available from several manufacturers under various trade names. Fig. 20 shows a typical unit. Nearly all of these testers use the stroboscopic principle for one or more of the tests listed above.

A stroboscope is *an electronic instrument by which it is visually possible to stop motion*. Testers using this principle make it possible to see exactly what happens to the moving parts of a distributor and to determine the efficiency of the entire distributor assembly exactly as it is operating on the engine. With this type of tester, of course, the distributor assembly is removed from the automobile and placed in a special holder on the tester.

A variable-speed motor drive in the tester rotates the distributor shaft along with a dial upon which appears segments of light or arrow flashes.

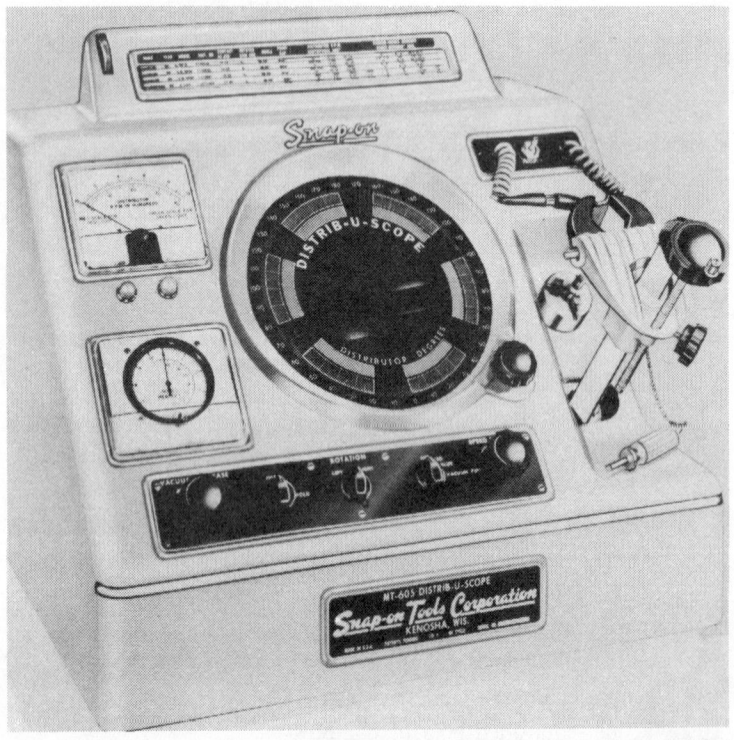

Courtesy Snap-on Tools Corp.

Fig. 20. DISTRIB-U-SCOPE is typical of the many distributor testers available.

DISTRIBUTORS

(See Fig. 21.) With the proper electrical connections made to the distributor, the light from a neon or similar lamp is controlled by the opening and closing of the point contacts in the distributor. Thus, for a distributor from a 6-cylinder car, the lamp will cause six arrow flashes or segments of light to appear during the time the distributor shaft (and the tester dial) makes one revolution. Each time the lamp flashes, it

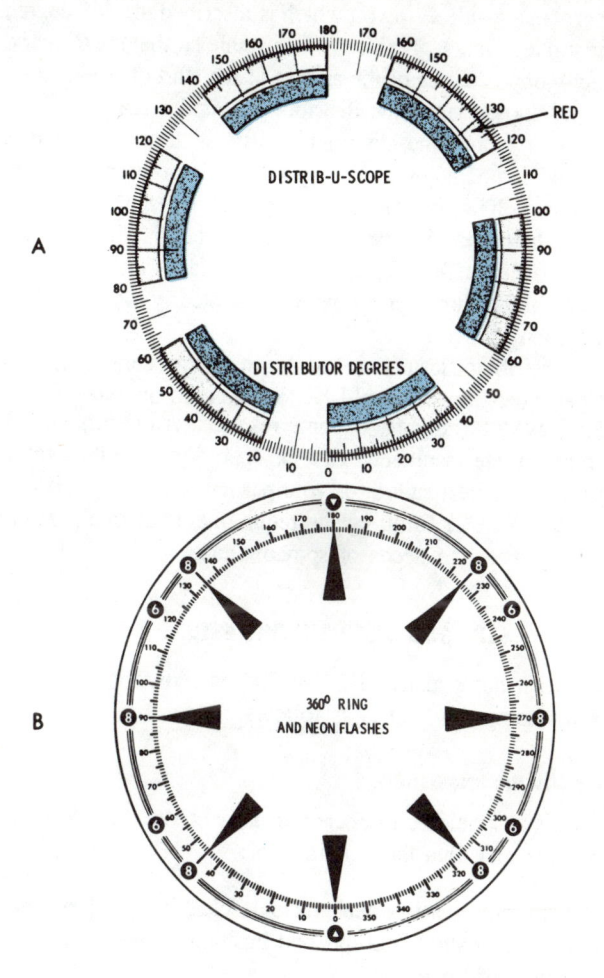

Fig. 21. Typical strobe patterns seen on distributor testers. Uneven synchronization, cam wear, play in the distributor shaft, and point bounce patterns; (A) SNAP-ON DISTRIB-U-SCOPE six-cylinder pattern; (B) ALLEN-TRONIC eight-cylinder pattern.

63

Automobile Guide

lights up the segment or arrow for an instant. Each time the flash occurs, however, the segment or arrow will be in a different position around the rim of the dial due to the rotation. This will cause the dial to appear to have six segments or arrows equally spaced around its circumference. A distributor for a 4-cylinder car would cause four segments or arrows to appear, and an 8-cylinder car, eight segments or arrows.

The dial rotates inside a ring on which is inscribed the 360 degrees of a complete circle. This degree ring is adjustable so that the 0° mark can be set directly opposite one of the arrows or the start of one of the light segments that appear when the distributor is under test.

The speed at which the distributor shaft is turned is read on a tachometer and can be adjusted by a speed-regulator knob from 0 r/min to a maximum of 3000 to 4000 r/min or more, depending on the make and model of the tester. Always keep in mind that the distributor-shaft r/min is only one-half the engine r/min. This fact must be taken into account unless the tachometer on the tester is clearly marked as engine r/min, as it many times is.

Nearly all distributor testers are similar in general construction to the units just described, but it should be remembered that specific makes and models may differ slightly in some respects. All testers have been designed for accurate results and ease of operation. The final selection of the type of tester best suited for your particular needs is left to your own judgment. A tester fulfilling the requirements of one person will not necessarily meet the needs of someone else.

SUN 500 DISTRIBUTOR TESTER

A typical distributor tester, the *Sun 500*, is shown in Fig. 22. The procedure for using this unit is as follows.

Distributor Visual Inspection

The distributor should be inspected visually before it is placed in the tester. Examine and note the condition of:

1. The distributor shaft. Check for side clearance and end play.
2. The distributor shaft bearings and bushings. Check for wear and smoothness of operation.
3. The flexible couplings. Check for wear.
4. Breaker plate bearings or bushings. Check for wear, smoothness of operation, and lubrication.

DISTRIBUTORS

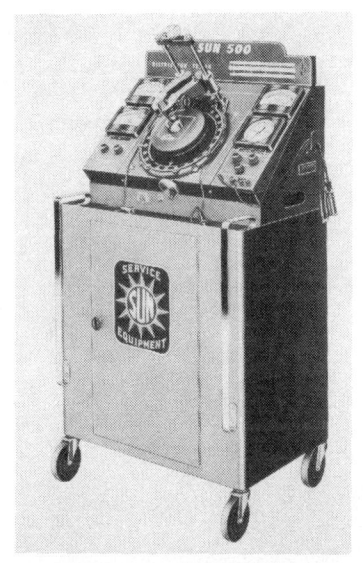

Fig. 22. SUN model 500 distributor tester.

Courtesy Sun Electric Corp.

5. Cam wick. Check for proper lubrication.
6. Breaker cam. Check for smoothness and lubrication.
7. Insulators, pigtails, and flexible internal leads. Check for breaks, loose connections, etc.
8. Contact points. Check alignment, pitting, and burning.
9. Rubbing block. Check for wear and lubrication.
10. Vacuum-advance linkage. Check for alignment, wear, and binding.

Distributor Mounting Procedure

Follow this procedure to mount the distributor on the tester.

1. Using the elevation crank, raise the clamp arms high enough to permit the shaft of the distributor being mounted to clear the drive chuck.
2. Position the distributor in the clamp with the vacuum chamber pointing to the right. Tighten the clamp arms securely on the machined surface of the distributor body. If the vacuum advance rotates the entire distributor, first install the proper collet on the distributor.
3. Using the elevation crank, lower the distributor until the gear, or about 3/4" of the tip of the distributor shaft enters the drive chuck,

or until the shaft engages the drive adapter if one is being used. Do not bottom the shaft in the chuck.
4. Tighten the chuck. (For *Delco-Remy* external adjustment-type distributors, approximately center the drive gear between its upper and lower limits of end-play travel before tightening the chuck.) Do not try to raise or lower the distributor after the drive chuck has been tightened.

Condenser Tests

To insure good ignition system performance, condensers should be tested for *series resistance* (which affects coil output); *capacitance* (which controls point arcing and pitting); and *leakage* (which determines whether the condenser insulation can withstand the stress of the ignition system). Condensers that fail one or more of these tests should be discarded.

Procedure — Follow these steps to test a condenser with the *Sun 500* Distributor Tester.

1. Flip the MOTOR SWITCH to give the proper direction of distributor rotation. Set the speed to zero r/min.
2. With the condenser test selector switch in the SERIES RESISTANCE position, connect the condenser test leads together.
3. Turn the condenser calibrate control clockwise from the OFF position.
4. Allow approximately 30 seconds for the tester to warm up and then adjust the calibrate control until the meter reads on SET LINE.
5. Rotate the distributor shaft until the cam holds the breaker points open.
6. Separate the test leads and connect one to the distributor primary terminal and the other to the distributor body. See Fig. 23.
7. With the test selector switch in the SERIES RESISTANCE position, the meter should read within the black bar at the right end of the scale. Failure to read in this area indicates a faulty condenser.
8. Set the test selector switch in the CAPACITY position and note the meter reading in microfarads. Compare with the manufacturer's specifications.
9. Set the test selector switch in the LEAKAGE position. The meter should read within the black bar at the left end of the scale. Failure to read within this area indicates a faulty condenser.

DISTRIBUTORS

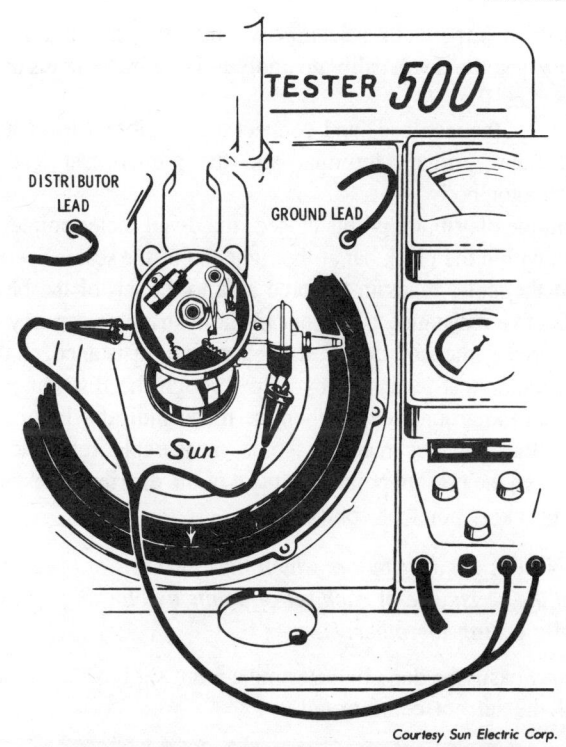

Fig. 23. One of the condenser test leads from the distributor tester is connected to the distributor housing and the other test lead is connected to the distributor primary terminal to test the condenser.

10. Set the test selector switch in the SERIES RESISTANCE position and turn the CONDENSER CALIBRATOR knob to the OFF position before disconnecting the test leads.

Distributor Resistance Test

This test indicates the electrical resistance of the distributor primary circuit from the primary terminal through the breaker points to the distributor body. Excessive resistance in any portion of the distributor primary circuit will prevent the coil from performing at full efficiency. Follow this procedure to make this test.

1. With the MOTOR SWITCH positioned for the correct direction of distributor rotation and the speed set to zero r/min, clip the distributor and ground leads of the tester together.

AUTOMOBILE GUIDE

2. Set the TACH-DWELL selector switch to the CALIBRATE position and adjust the dwell calibrate knob until the meter reads on the set line. See Fig. 24.
3. Separate the test leads and connect the distributor test lead to the distributor primary terminal and the ground test lead to the distributor body.
4. With the distributor points closed, the dwell meter pointer should read within the black bar at the right end of the scale. See Fig. 25.

If the meter reads in the blue area to the left of the black bar, excessive resistance is present in the distributor primary circuit. To locate the source of the excessive resistance, move the distributor test lead step by step through the distributor circuit toward the ground lead. When the meter indicates less resistance than the previous reading, some measurable resistance exists between the present point of contact of the distributor test lead and its previous point of contact.

NOTE: On distributors which have two sets of breaker points, test the resistance of each set of points by blocking one set open while testing the other.

This may easily be done by inserting a point-set box flap between the points of the set not being tested.

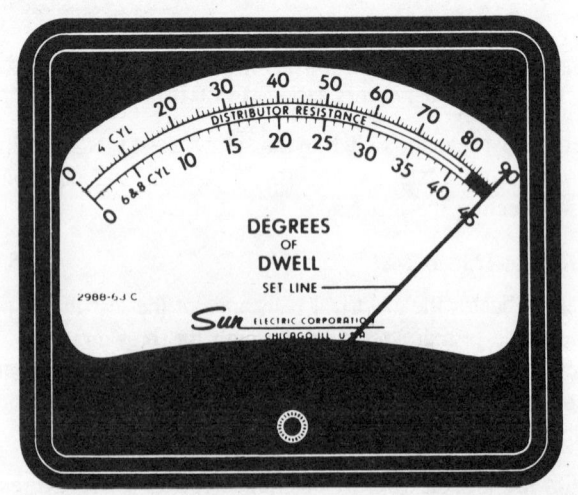

Courtesy Sun Electric Corp.

Fig. 24. To calibrate the dwell meter to make a resistance test, the dwell regulator is adjusted until the needle is in the position shown.

68

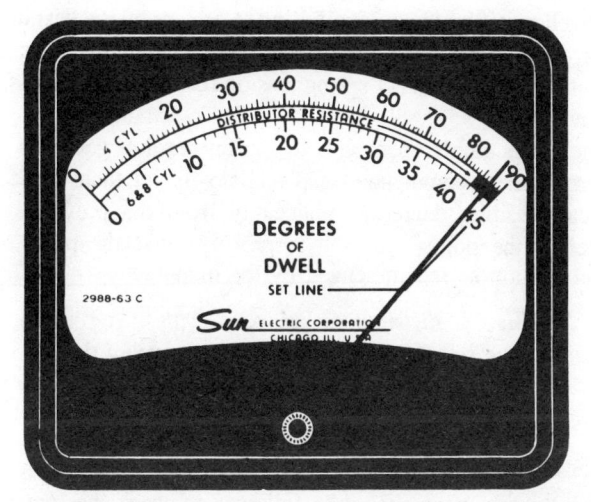

DISTRIBUTORS

Fig. 25. The dwell meter pointer in the direction shown indicates a satisfactory resistance condition in the primary circuit of the distributor.

Breaker-Point Spring-Tension Test

Proper tension of the breaker-point spring is important to obtain normal breaker-assembly life and to maintain full ignition system efficiency throughout the speed range of the engine. Excessive spring tension can cause rapid rubbing-block, cam, and contact wear. Insufficient spring tension may allow the points to bounce at high speeds, resulting in arcing and burning of the points and causing engine misfiring.

Follow this procedure to test the breaker-point spring tension:

1. Position the lazy hand of the spring-tension gauge on either side of the pointer, depending on whether the gauge will be pushed or pulled to open the points.
2. With the dwell meter calibrated, and the distributor test leads connected to the distributor as for the distributor-resistance test, place the end of the spring-tension gauge near the contact on the movable arm. See Fig. 26.
3. Slowly pull the spring-tension tester at right angles to the movable arm and gradually increase the pull.
4. Note the reading on the spring-tension scale at the instant the contacts separate. Contact separation will be indicated on the

AUTOMOBILE GUIDE

dwell meter by the pointer falling to zero or by the flashing of the arrow on the drive unit. Refer to the manufacturer's test specifications for the correct spring tension for the particular distributor under test.

5. Hold the points open with the spring-tension gauge to the approximate recommended gap and slowly let them close. If the scale reading decreases noticeably from the previous reading before the points close, it is probable that the pivot requires lubrication as recommended by the manufacturer.

NOTE: On distributors equipped with two sets of breaker points, one set must be held open while testing the other set. A piece of fiber can be placed between the contact points to hold them open.

Cam-Lobe Accuracy Test

The following steps should be followed to check the cam lobes for wear.

1. With the distributor test leads connected to the distributor as before, turn the TACH-DWELL switch to the position which corresponds to the type of distributor being tested (4, 6, or 8 cylinder.)

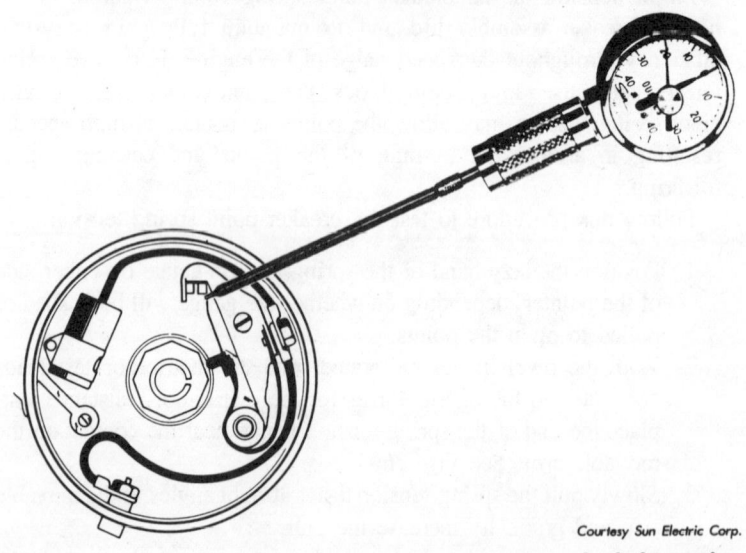

Courtesy Sun Electric Corp.

Fig. 26. Correct method of using a spring tension gauge to check the tension of the breaker point spring.

Distributors

2. Adjust the distributor speed to 1000 r/min.
3. Rotate the degree ring of the tester until the zero on the ring is aligned with one of the arrow flashes.
4. Observe the relative position of all the arrow flashes. All arrow flashes should be evenly spaced around the degree ring within 1°. The arrow flashes should be spaced at:

>90° for 4-lobe cams
>60° for 6-lobe cams
>45° for 8-lobe cams

Variations of more than 1° from the specified spacing indicates a worn cam or bent distributor shaft.

Breaker-Point Alignment Test

The following steps are necessary to check the breaker points for correct alignment.

1. With the distributor tester set as for the Cam-Lobe Accuracy Test, observe the slight arc appearing between the breaker points. If the points are properly aligned, the arcing will appear in the center of the contacts when viewed from above and from the side.
2. Reduce the tester speed to 200 r/min for the next test to follow.

Breaker-Point Dwell Test

Observe the dwell meter and, if necessary, adjust the point spacing until the dwell meter indicates the specific degrees of dwell.

On distributors equipped with dual points, it will be necessary to adjust the dwell on each set individually. To isolate each set for adjustment, the other set can be blocked open by inserting a piece of fiber between the contacts.

Additional information on point dwell and point adjustment is given later in this chapter.

Breaker-Point Dwell-Variation Test

1. While watching the dwell meter, vary the distributor speed from 200 to 1750 r/min. A dwell variation in excess of 2° indicates a worn distributor shaft or bushings.
2. Reduce the speed of the tester to 200 r/min for the next test.

AUTOMOBILE GUIDE

Centrifugal Advance Calibration Test

This test is made to determine if the ignition timing conforms to the manufacturer's specified advance curve throughout the operating speed range of the engine. A defective centrifugal advance unit will cause the engine to be out of time at certain speeds. This always results in a loss of engine performance and, in addition, may cause spark knock and/or overheating.

Perform the following steps:

1. Set the zero of the degree ring in line with the arrow flash that is nearest you.
2. Increase the distributor speed, pausing at each speed specified in the distributor manufacturer's manual to note if the amount of advance indicated by the arrow flash is within $\pm 1°$ (if no range is given) to the specified figure.
3. Momentarily exceed the highest speed specified as a check speed. Then, while returning the distributor speed back to zero, recheck at each test speed to see that the amount of advance at that speed is the same as it was in Step 2, and as specified. Any difference in readings requires correction be made for best engine performance.

If the advance in both steps 2 and 3 is excessive, the governor-weight springs are weak, or the wrong springs have been installed.

If the advance is insufficient in Step 2 and excessive in Step 3, the governor weights are sticking and should be freed.

If the advance is insufficient both on accelerations and deceleration, the governor spring tension is excessive.

Refer to the distributor tester's manual for the proper service procedure if the distributor fails any of the tests.

Vacuum-Chamber Diaphragm Test

Use the following procedure to test the vacuum-chamber diaphragm.

1. Insert the proper adapter in the vacuum-advance unit and tighten with a wrench to insure a good seal.
2. Attach the vacuum hose to the vacuum-advance unit and seal the hose with a metal clamp.
3. Adjust the VACUUM REGULATOR until the gauge reads 15 inches of mercury.
4. Release the vacuum hose clamp and observe the gauge. The gauge reading will momentarily fall to a lower value.

If the gauge reading returns to 15 inches within a few seconds, the vacuum chamber is airtight.

If the gauge reading fails to return to 15 inches, the vacuum chamber can be assumed to be leaky and must be replaced.

Vacuum-Controlled Breaker-Plate Test

The breaker-plate travel must be smooth and even or the plate will twist, changing the relationship between the cam and rubbing block and causing the dwell angle to change. Any change in dwell angle affects not only the quality of the ignition spark but also affects the timing.

Proceed as follows to check the breaker-plate action.

1. Adjust the speed control to 1000 r/min.
2. Adjust the vacuum to 0 with the vacuum-regulator knob, then increase it to 20 inches while watching the dwell-meter pointer for variations.
3. If the dwell reading varies more than ± 2° as the vacuum changes from 0 to 20 inches, it indicates worn breaker plate bushings and bearings, or intermittent distributor resistance. Check the condition of the distributor wiring, which may be broken within the insulation due to flexing.
4. Adjust the vacuum regulator to zero vacuum.

NOTE: This specification applies only to distributors with centrally located breaker-plate bearings.

On *Autolite* distributors, Models IAT, IBP, and IBR which have side-pivoted breaker plates, the dwell will normally vary by more than ± 2° when the vacuum unit is operated. No definite specifications are given by the manufacturer for the dwell variations of these distributors since the amount of variation varies with the individual distributor depending on the amount of maximum vacuum advance.

Vacuum Spark-Advance Test

The vacuum spark-advance adjusts the spark timing according to the load on the engine to provide peak fuel economy at moderate loads and full power without detonation at heavier loads. While making the test, look in particular for improper calibrations, sticky or erratic breaker-plate action, tilting of the breaker plate, or interference of the condenser with the breaker-plate action.

AUTOMOBILE GUIDE

Proceed as follows:

1. With no vacuum applied to the unit, set the zero of the degree ring in line with one of the arrow flashes. (Distributor speed is 1000 r/min.)
2. Adjust the vacuum regulator to apply the correct amount of vacuum for each specified check point in turn, and note the amount of advance obtained. Compare this amount with the manufacturer's specifications.
3. Momentarily exceed the highest vacuum value specified then reduce it and again note the advance obtained at each specified check point. See Figs. 27 and 28.

Courtesy Sun Electric Corp.

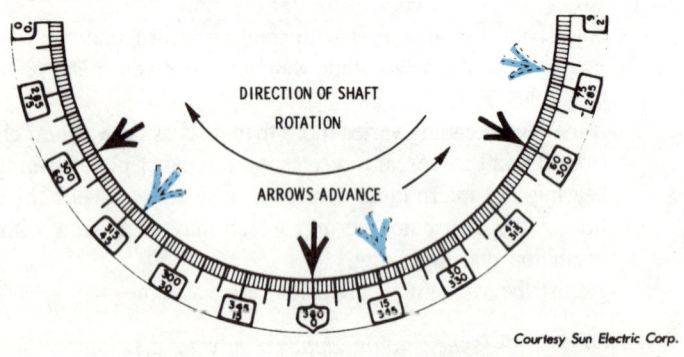

Fig. 27. Arrows will move in a counterclockwise direction when checking the centrifugal- and vacuum-advance mechanism on a distributor whose shaft rotates in a clockwise direction.

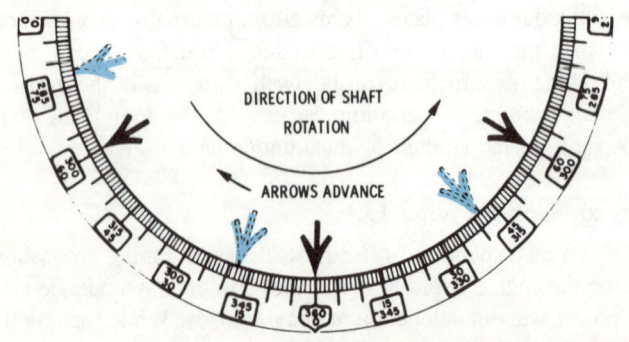

Fig. 28. Arrows will move in a clockwise direction when checking the centrifugal-and-vacuum-advance mechanism on a distributor whose shaft rotates in a counterclockwise direction.

DISTRIBUTORS

If the advance is excessive during both Steps 2 and 3, a week vacuum advance spring is indicated.

If advance is insufficient in Step 2 and excessive in Step 3, or is erractic in both Step 2 and 3, the distributor breaker plate is sticking or binding.

Refer to the distributor manufacturer's manual for the proper service procedure.

DELCO-REMY CENTER-BEARING BREAKER PLATE

Breaker-Plate Spring-Tension Test

This test is made to determine if the breaker plate is free to rotate correctly under the influence of the vacuum spark control unit. Excessive plate tension may cause sluggish action of the advance mechanism, resulting in erratic timing under changing loads.

To make this test, proceed as follows:

1. Remove the vacuum spark control unit from the distributor. Replace the small screw finger-tight in the plate to provide an attaching point for the spring-tension scale.
2. With the breaker plate pushed to the full retard position (full travel in the direction of cam rotation), hook the spring-tension scale on the screw, as shown in Fig. 29. Now pull the scale, noting the amount of pull necessary to start movement of the breaker plate.

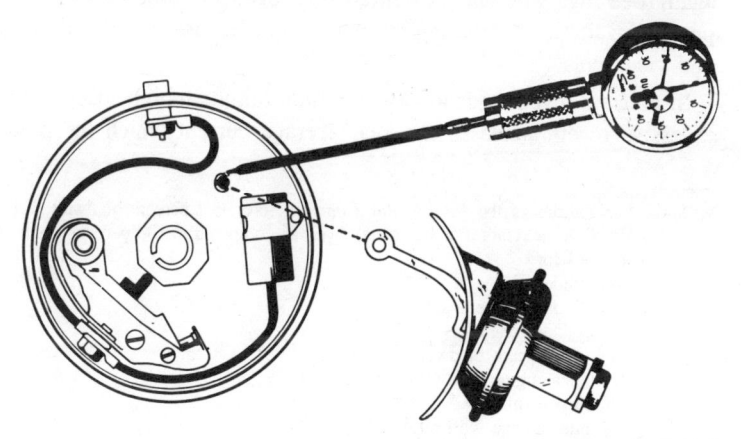

Courtesy Sun Electric Corp.

Fig. 29. Correct method of checking the spring tension of the breaker plate in a DELCO-REMY distributor.

75

AUTOMOBILE GUIDE

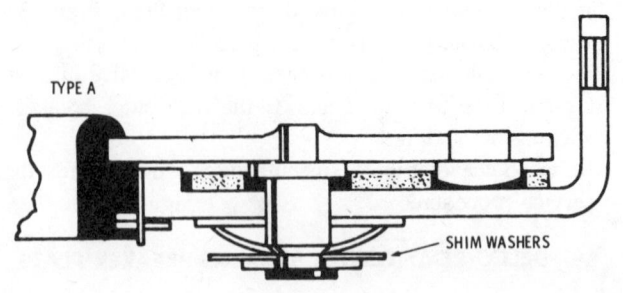

Courtesy Sun Electric Corp.
Fig. 30. Tension of a type-A breaker plate can be adjusted by adding or removing shim washers to the tension spring.

The amount of pull, as registered on the spring-tension scale, should not exceed 20 ounces for the type-A plate (Fig. 30), or exceed 15 ounces for the type-B plate (Fig. 31). The tension on a type-A breaker plate may be adjusted by adding or removing shim washers from the tension spring on the underside of the plate. The tension on a type-B breaker plate may be adjusted by stretching or replacing the helical plate-tension spring.

Distributor Point Dwell

Dwell or dwell angle is the number of degrees* through which the distributor shaft rotates from the time the points close until they open again (See Fig. 32). Thus, dwell angle is inversely proportional to the point gap; that is, increasing the point gap decreases the dwell angle, and vice versa.

Insufficient dwell tends to cause ignition failure at high speed, while excessive dwell increases the total average current which the points

---

*Some publications of the *Ford Motor Company* refer to "percent of dwell." The percent of dwell is the relation of the actual dwell as compared to 100 percent dwell. A 100 percent dwell for:
    a 4-cylinder engine is 90°
    a 6-cylinder engine is 60°
    an 8-cylinder engine is 45°
Examples of "percent of dwell" are:
    4-cylinder engine with 60 percent dwell
      is 60 percent of 90° or 54° dwell
    6-cylinder engine with 60 percent dwell
      is 60 percent of 60° or 36° dwell
    8-cylinder engine with 60 percent dwell
      is 60 percent of 45° or 27° dwell

DISTRIBUTORS

must handle, especially at low speeds. Excessive dwell usually leads to a very short point life.

After a distributor is initially timed to any given engine, any change in the dwell will result in a change of timing. This will require retiming the distributor, since the point rubbing block will make contact with the cam at a different place.

When dwell specifications are given with a high and a low limit, set the point dwell to the lower limit when new points are installed, to allow for rubbing block wear.

Contact-Point Gap and Dwell (Cam-Angle Relationship)

If a distributor cannot be adjusted so that the gap and dwell are within specifications at the same time, inspect for the following possibilities:

Courtesy Sun Electric Corp.

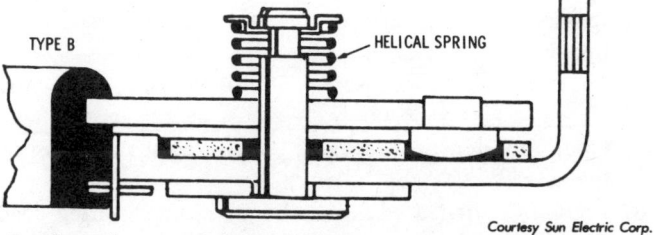

Fig. 31. Tension of a type-B breaker plate can be adjusted either by stretching or by replacing the helical tension spring.

DOTTED LINES INDICATE THE 60° BETWEEN CAM LOBES ALLOTTED TO THE FIRING OF EACH CYLINDER IN A 6-CYLINDER ENGINE

Courtesy Sun Electric Corp.

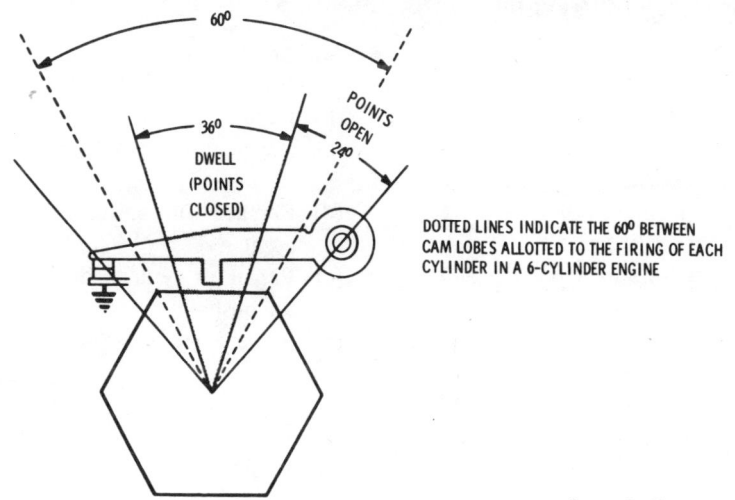

Fig. 32. An illustration of dwell angle.

77

1. Improper spring tension or sticky pivot.
2. Wrong point set installed.
3. Bent shaft, causing point gap to vary on each cam lobe.
4. Worn cam lobes or defective cam. (Compare point gap at each cam lobe if in doubt.)
5. Points floating, or not following the cam at high speeds.
6. Excessive resistance causing false dwell reading. In practically every case the remedy will be self-evident.

DISTRIBUTOR TROUBLES AND REMEDIES

Symptoms and Possible Causes *Possible Remedies*

Burned or Oxidized Points

(a) Ignition resistor shorted or bypassed.
(b) Improper value condenser.
(c) Open condenser (defective).
(d) Loose or corroded wiring connections.

(a) Replace resistor or connect into circuit.
(b) Replace with correct value condenser.
(c) Replace condenser.
(d) Correct wiring conditions.

Points Not Closing and/or Opening

(a) Point gap out of adjustment.
(b) Defective rubbing block.
(c) One or more lobes worn on cam.
(d) Incorrect point set.
(e) Intermittent point opening and/or closing.
(f) Defective breaker plate.

(a) Adjust point gap.
(b) Replace points.
(c) Replace distributor cam.
(d) Replace with correct points.
(e) Repair or replace distributor bushings.
(f) Replace breaker plate.

Crossfiring and/or Misfiring

(a) Defective distributor cap.
(b) Defective rotor.
(c) Defective plug wires.
(d) Distributor assembly dirty.

(a) Replace cap.
(b) Replace rotor.
(c) Replace plug wires.
(d) Clean distributor.

DISTRIBUTORS

Symptoms and Possible Causes *Possible Remedies*

Engine Will Not Start

(a) Defective sensor.
(b) Improper air gap.
(c) Defective control unit.

(a) Replace sensor.
(b) Correct air gap.
(c) Replace control unit.

Engine Surges

(a) Defective sensor leads.

(a) Repair leads or replace sensor.

Engine Misses

(a) Defective control unit.

(a) Replace control unit.

CHAPTER 4

Spark Plugs

The air/fuel charge in the cylinder of an automobile engine is ignited by a spark generated between the electrodes of the spark plug. Efficient engine performance demands that the spark must be adequate at all engine speeds and under all conditions to produce complete and proper ignition of the air/fuel mixture. Proper spark plug performance is one of the most important factors in maintaining good gas mileage and engine efficiency.

SPARK PLUG CONSTRUCTION

The spark plug has two important functions — to introduce a spark into the combustion chamber, and to seal the plug hole so that proper pressures are maintained in the cylinder.

The four main parts of a spark plug (Fig.1) are: the insulator, the shell, the internal seals, and the electrodes. The insulator prevents the high ignition voltage (up to 30,000 volts) from flowing in any direction except across the electrodes within the combustion chamber. Any cracks (either visible or invisible) in this insulator can cause misfiring because the crack becomes a path of low electrical resistance and shorts the high-voltage current to the shell.

The shell holds the plug together and acts to connect the ground electrode to the engine through the threads. The internal seals are made by a high-temperature, high-pressure cement. This special cement acts to seal the center electrode to the insulator and the insulator to the shell.

The electrodes operate at continuous high temperatures and are surrounded by corrosive gases. Special alloys are used in the electrodes

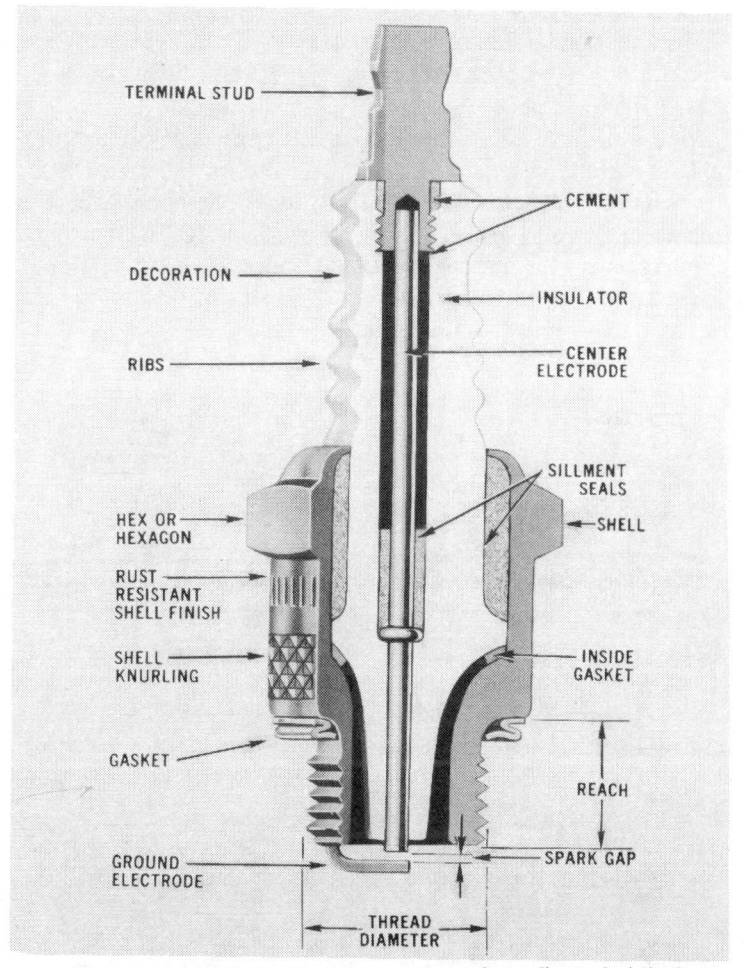

SPARK PLUGS

Fig. 1. Construction features of a modern spark plug.

Courtesy Champion Spark Plug Company

to resist corrosion from the burning combustion gases, and the destructive effects of the spark.

Some plugs have a taper seat while others use a soft copper washer (gasket) to seal the spark plug in the engine. The gasket is designed to be crimped or flattened when the plug is installed and tightened

81

Automobile Guide

properly. Fig. 2 shows several conditions of the gasket when the plug is properly and improperly tightened.

Spark plugs wear out, develop troubles, or can be of the wrong heat range for the engine because of a particular driver's driving habits. It is also possible to find the wrong type plug in an engine.

Most manufacturers recommend replacing spark plugs after 10,000 miles of average operation. Of course, operating conditions can modify this standard. An engine used exclusively for city driving, which means stop-and-go travel, frequent motor starts, and frequent cold-motor operation, may wear out the plugs at 5000 miles. The plugs in an engine used on the highway may last up to 25,000 miles or more before requiring replacement. An occasional cleaning and regapping *will* be required however.

A. A new gasket before installation.

B. When properly installed.

C. Insufficiently tightened when installed.

D. Excessively tightened when installed.

Courtesy AC Spark Plug Div., General Motors Corp.

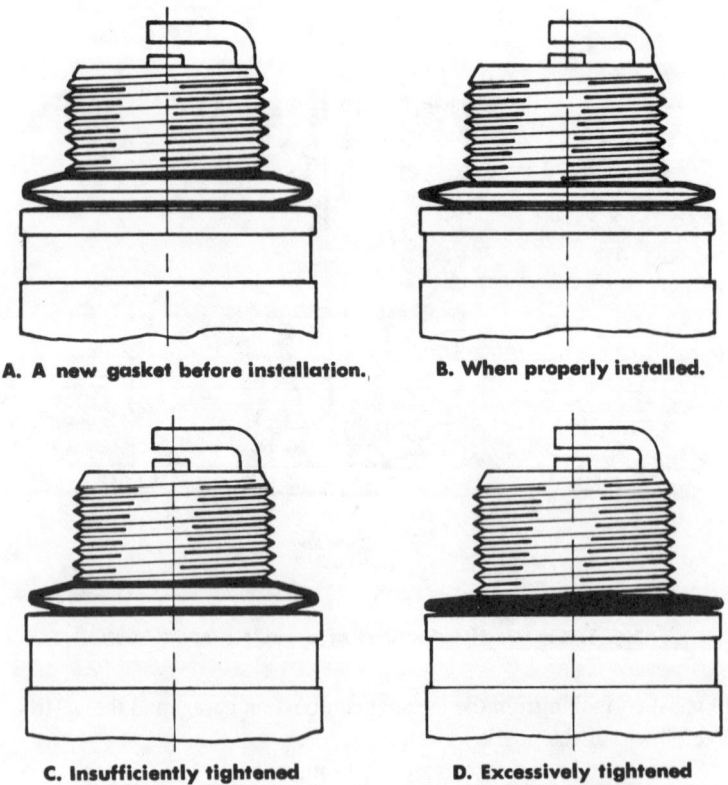

Fig. 2. The spark-plug gasket.

Spark Plugs

SPARK PLUG TROUBLES

Most spark plug wear is caused by the corrosive gases resulting from fuel combustion. These gases attack the electrodes and "eat" them away. The high-voltage spark *also* corrodes the electrodes and eats the metal away. Both of these factors cause the electrode gap to increase, and the spark has a greater distance to jump.

A much higher voltage is required to cause the spark to jump the wider gap. The ignition system often fails to provide this higher voltage, especially at high speeds, and the spark plug misfires. Cleaning and regapping of the electrodes will usually cure this condition if there is enough material remaining in the electrodes. The spark plug shown in Fig. 3 illustrates the condition of electrodes worn away enough that the plug cannot be regapped. Such a plug should be replaced. Worn out plugs cause loss of power, decrease in top speed, decreased gas mileage, hard starting, and general sluggish performance. Compare the worn plug in Fig. 3 with the good plug in Fig. 4

Spark plugs also get dirty. This condition is known as "fouling," of which there are several types.

Courtesy AC Spark Plug Div., General Motors Corp.
Fig. 3. Electrodes worn too thin for proper regapping.

83

Automobile Guide

Courtesy Champion Spark Plug Company
Fig. 4. A normal spark plug after use.

Oil Fouling

Wet, oily, black deposits (Fig. 5) on the firing end of the plug usually indicate that lubricating oil is leaking into the cylinder. This may occur because of worn piston rings, excessive valve stem-to-guide clearance, sticking valves, defective positive crankcase ventilation (PCV) valve, or a faulty fuel pump (if equipped with a double-action pump). Normally, plugs in this condition can be cleaned, regapped, and reinstalled.

If the black deposit is hard and glazed, it indicates that a low heat-range plug is being used in an oil-burning engine. Either a plug one heat range hotter can be used or the engine should be overhauled.

Gas (or Carbon) Fouling

Excessive fuel in the combustion chamber can cause dry, fluffy, black deposits (Fig. 6) to form on the spark plugs. This excess of fuel can result from prolonged idling, a faulty automatic choke, or a fuel mixture that is too rich. Use of a cold plug can also cause this type of deposit to form. Cleaning and regapping of the plug will restore engine performance, but the condition may recur. An engine tune-up or hotter-type plug will be necessary to eliminate the trouble.

SPARK PLUGS

Fig. 5. A cutaway view of an oil-fouled spark plug.

Fig. 6. A cutaway view of a gas-fouled spark plug.

AUTOMOBILE GUIDE

Lead Fouling

Deposits due to the burning of fuel scavengers (such as tetraethyl lead) cause red, brown, yellow, or white colors on the spark plug electrodes. While these deposits may look bad (Fig. 7), most of them are not harmful and have little effect on plug performance. If the combustion chamber temperatures become too high, however, these deposits may melt and form a shiny, glazed coating which will act as an electrical conductor and short out the plug. If the plug is not too heavily coated, these deposits can be removed by abrasive cleaning, and the plug can be used again.

SERVICE PROCEDURES

Ideally, spark plugs should be cleaned and regapped every 5000 miles. Inspection of the plugs while they are removed can frequently warn of engine troubles developing or of needed adjustments.

Courtesy Champion Spark Plug Company

Fig. 7. Scavenger deposits.

Spark Plugs

Removing Spark Plugs

1. Remove the plug wires carefully. Grasp the rubber insulator boot (not the plug wire) and pull it away from the plug slowly — do not jerk it.
2. Use the correct size deep-socket to fit the plug. The wrong size socket can break the shell or insulator and ruin the plug.
3. Loosen the plugs one turn, then use an air hose to blow the dirt away from the plug wells.
4. Remove the plugs and gasket (if a gasket-type plug is used). Inspect each plug as it is removed or keep them in order so that you can identify the cylinder each came from. Trouble in one particular cylinder can be found this way.

Cleaning Spark Plugs

Clean the top insulator and terminal of each plug. A rag moistened with a cleaning solvent will remove oil and grime. If the electrodes and threads of the plug are oily, clean the plug by brushing it in solvent. Dry the plug thoroughly with compressed air.

There are several approved plug-cleaning machines available. A typical unit is pictured in Fig. 8.

The operation of a typical unit is as follows:

1. Select the correct size of adapter, place the plug in the adapter, and the adapter in position on the cleaner.
2. Hold the plug and adapter down with one hand.
3. Press the cleaner hood all the way down for 3 to 5 seconds. This action starts the cleaning blast and also covers the top of the plug to protect the operator. Rotate both the plug and adapter during the cleaning blast.
4. Release the cleaner hood part way to stop the cleaning blast and to allow the compressed-air blast to blow the cleaning compound out of the plug.
5. Remove the plug and examine it for cleanliness. Steps 2 through 4 may have to be repeated to make sure that the entire surface of the insulator is clean.

Excessive cleaning can wear away the insulator. Use the cleaning blast cautiously. Fig. 9 shows a spark plug in which the insulator has been partially worn away by excessive blast cleaning.

Automobile Guide

Courtesy Champion Spark Plug Company

Fig. 8. A typical spark-plug cleaner.

After the plug has been cleaned, make sure that all the cleaning compound has been removed, especially from the threads. Clean the threads with a wire brush. Discard any plugs with stripped or otherwise damaged threads.

Regapping Spark Plugs

The cleaning operation does not always remove all the oxide or scale from the electrodes. Clean the firing surfaces of the two electrodes with a spark-plug or distributor-point file. Widen the gap, if necessary, to insert the file.

The plug should be regapped to the specifications of the car manufacturer (.035" for most domestic cars). Always use a round wire-type of gauge. The flat feeler gauge does not measure the gap correctly, as shown in Fig. 10.

The side electrode should be adjusted to set the gap. Use the adjusting notch which is part of most spark-plug gapping tools. Never try to adjust the center electrode, because this will break the insulator.

SPARK PLUGS

Fig. 9. Insulator tip worn down from excessive blast cleaning.
Courtesy AC Spark Plug Div., General Motors Corp.

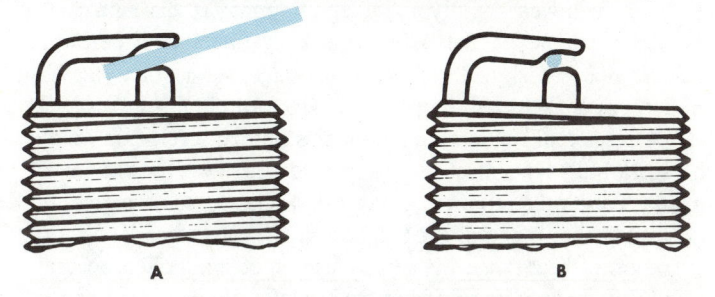

Fig. 10. Use of the gap gauge. A. A plain flat feeler gauge cannot accurately measure the true gap width. B. A round-wire gauge should always be used.
Courtesy AC Spark Plug Div., General Motors Corp.

If new plugs are being installed, check the gap setting and adjust to specifications.

Installing Spark Plugs

Always use a new gasket on either new or used plugs, except on those plugs which do not use gaskets. An old gasket will not seal properly and will allow gases to blow by.

89

AUTOMOBILE GUIDE

Make sure that the threads and gasket seats on the engine are clean. Screw the plug in by hand until it is finger tight on the gasket. Then tighten it with a wrench ½ to ¾ of a turn. If a torque wrench is being used, follow the recommended maximum torque shown in Table 1.

Table 1. Maximum Torque Values (in ft. lbs.)

Plug Thread	Cast Iron Heads	Aluminum Heads
10 mm	13-15	9-11
14 mm	26-30	18-22
14 mm*	15-20	15-20
18 mm	32-38	28-34
18 mm*	15-20	15-20
⅞"-18 mm	35-43	31-39

* Tapered seat spark plugs

Selection of Plugs

To give good performance in a particular engine, spark plugs must operate within a definite temperature range. If the plug temperature is too low; oil, carbon, and scavenger deposits will remain on the insulator and cause fouling and missing. If the plug temperature is too high, the electrodes will wear rapidly and preignition may result. Either of these conditions can prevent the engine from operating at peak performance.

An engine is designed for normal (average) service, and the original spark plugs are selected to operate satisfactorily in this type of service. Of course, not all engines are used in this normal service, in which case the spark-plug type must be changed to suit the eventual use of the engine. To suit the requirements of the various types of engine service, spark plugs are manufactured in various "heat ranges."

The term "heat range" is a classification of spark plugs according to their ability to transfer heat from the insulator tip to the cooling medium of the engine. The rate of heat transfer is altered by changing the distance the heat must travel to reach the cooling system. A "cold" plug has a short insulator tip and a thin, short shell, and transfers heat rapidly. A "hot" plug has a much longer insulator tip and a heavy shell so that heat is transferred much more slowly. Fig. 11 illustrates these two types of plugs. Fig. 12 shows a typical range of plugs from cold (on left) to hot (on right).

When other than normal operating conditions cause continual carbon or oil fouling, the spark plugs in use are too cold and a type one or two graduations higher (hotter) should be substituted. When preignition or

Spark Plugs

Courtesy Champion Spark Plug Company

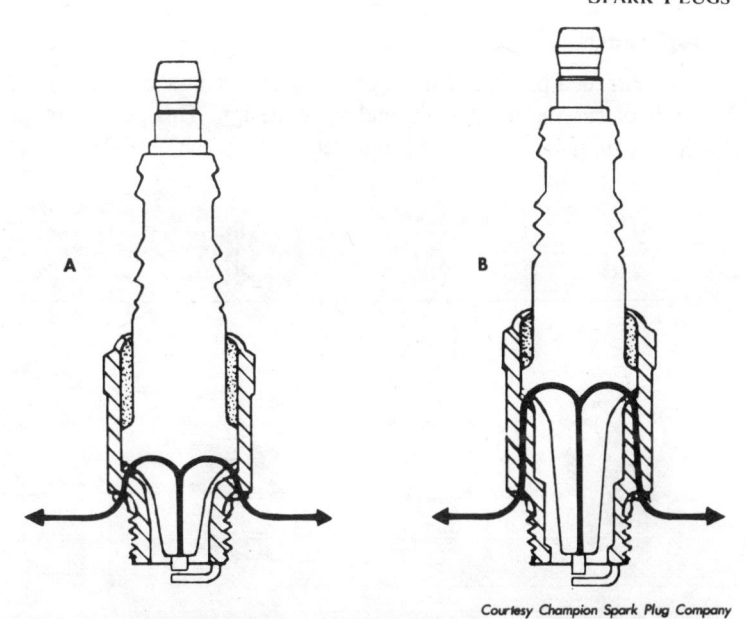

Fig. 11. Two spark plugs of different heat ranges. A. A cold-type with a short heat path. B. A hot-type with a long heat path.

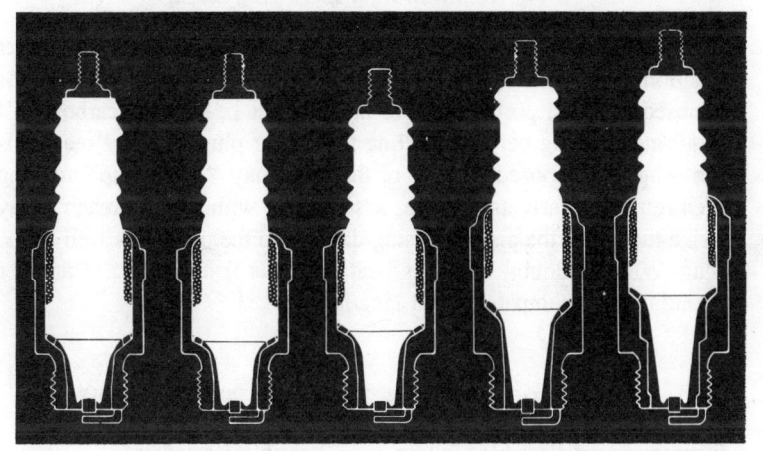

Courtesy Champion Spark Plug Company

Fig. 12. Insulator lengths vary from the cold plug at the left to the hot plug on the right.

rapid electrode wear is found, a type one or two graduations lower (cooler) should be used.

91

Plug Reach

The threaded portion of the spark plug that screws into the cylinder head is of varying lengths, depending on design. This part of the plug will vary from ⅜" to ¾", and is referred to as "reach," as shown in Fig. 13.

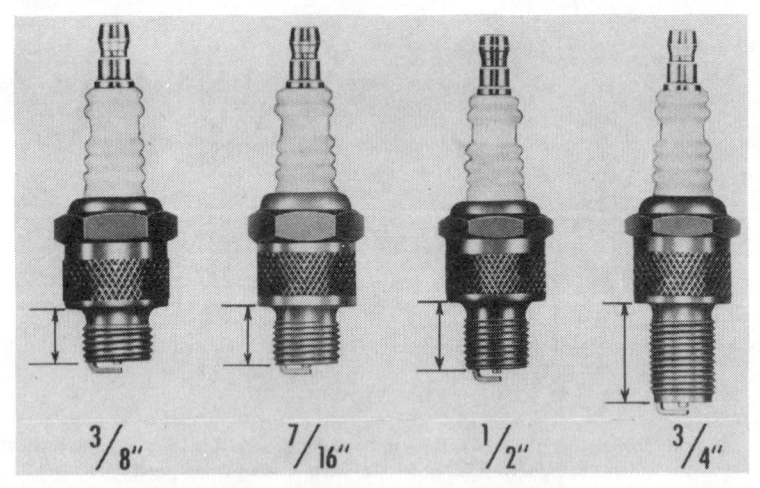

Fig. 13. Illustrating spark plug reach.

If the "reach" is too short, the electrodes will not be in proper position, and misfiring may occur under certain conditions. Also, the exposed threaded portion next to the cylinder head will "carbon up" requiring cleaning before installing the proper plugs. If the "reach" is too long, the exposed threads of the plug may "carbon up" making their removal nearly impossible. Also, a plug with a long "reach" may strike the top of the piston causing damage to the piston, as well as the plug. When in doubt, changing heat ranges or using a plug of another manufacturer, compare thread lengths.

SPARK PLUG POSSIBLE TROUBLES AND REMEDIES

Symptoms and Possible Causes   *Possible Remedies*

Oil Fouled — Oil Leaking Into Cylinder

(a) Worn or broken piston rings.

(a) Replace piston rings.

Spark Plugs

Symptoms and Possible Causes

(b) Excessive valve stem-to-guide clearance.
(c) Sticking valves.
(d) Broken valve spring.
(e) Oil deposit hard and glazed indicates low heat range plug used in oil-burning engine.

Gas Fouled

(a) Prolonged idling.

(b) Defective automatic choke.
(c) Fuel mixture too rich.
(d) Improper heat-range plug used.

Not Firing and/or Incorrect Firing

(a) Gap too wide.
(b) Dirty plug or closed gap.
(c) Defective plug wire.

(d) Defective plug.
(e) Plug wires crossed.

(f) Defective or dirty distributor cap.
(g) Incorrect plug (short plug used when long-reach plug should be used, for example).
(h) Plug wire disconnected.

Lead Fouled

(a) Improper heat-range plug.

Possible Remedies

(b) Repair, as necessary.

(c) Perform valve job.
(d) Replace valve spring.
(e) Use hotter range spark plug.

(a) Shut engine down when car will idle longer than two minutes.
(b) Repair or adjust choke.
(c) Adjust carburetor.
(d) Use hotter heat-range plug.

(a) Regap plug.
(b) Clean and regap plug.
(c) Replace plug wire (replace the set).
(d) Replace plug.
(e) Correct wires to proper firing order.
(f) Clean or replace cap.

(g) Replace with correct plug(s).

(h) Connect plug wire.

(a) Use colder heat range plug.

Symptoms and Possible Causes

(b) Fuel mixture too lean causing excessive combustion chamber temperatures.

Possible Remedies

(b) Adjust carburetor.

Electrode Flattened

(a) Excessive plug reach, allowing piston to strike bottom electrode.

(a) Use plug with correct reach.

CHAPTER 5

Fuel Pumps and Fuel Systems

The fuel pump in an automobile is used to move the gasoline from the tank to the carburetor in sufficient quantity to supply the requirements of the engine under all operating conditions. These conditions vary over wide limits, from idle to full speed and during periods of sustained full acceleration.

There are two types of fuel pumps in use on today's cars; mechanical (engine driven) and electromechanical or electric (electrically driven) pumps.

OPERATING PRINCIPLES

A diaphragm-type fuel pump, similar to the one in Fig. 1, is almost universally used. Most fuel pumps are actuated mechanically, although electric models are available for use on some cars. The operating principles of all mechanical fuel pumps are practically the same, regardless of their construction features or method of attachment to the engine. A filter unit is shown attached to the fuel pump in Fig. 1. Some pumps have a sediment bowl and filter that snaps on the bottom of the unit. Other pumps may have a sediment bowl and/or filter element on the inlet side.

The fuel pump is operated by the rotation of an eccentric on the camshaft. A flexible diaphragm in the pump is actuated by a combination of rocker-arm action and calibrated spring tension. On the intake stroke (Fig. 2A), the camshaft eccentric moves the rocker arm (by means of a push rod or by direct contact), causing the diaphragm to

AUTOMOBILE GUIDE

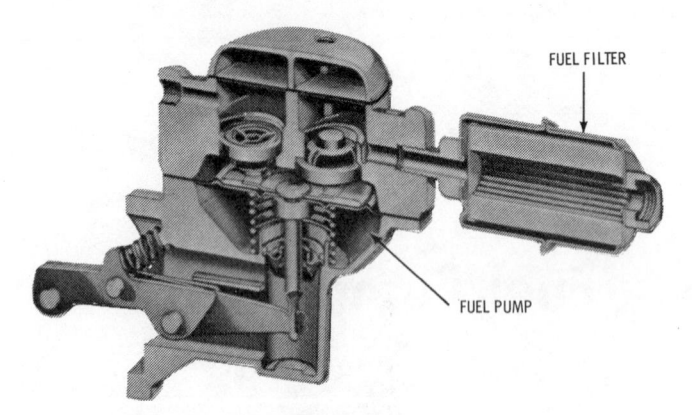

Fig. 1. A typical diaphragm-type fuel pump.

compress the diaphragm spring. This action draws gasoline from the fuel tank, through the intake valve of the pump, and into the fuel chamber. On the output cycle (Fig. 2B), the camshaft continues its rotation, and the force on the rocker arm is removed. The rocker arm rests on the low portion of the cam lobe, allowing the diaphragm spring to try and return the diaphragm to its normal position.

This action causes the intake valve to close, with the result that the gasoline in the fuel chamber is forced through the outlet valve by the pressure of the diaphragm and spring, and through the fuel line to the carburetor. The pulsator diaphragm and body dampens the fuel pump pulsations that otherwise would be felt by the inlet needle valve in the carburetor.

Gasoline is delivered to the carburetor only when the inlet valve of the carburetor is open. This valve is opened and closed by the level of gasoline in the float chamber of the carburetor. When the chamber is full, the valve is closed; when gasoline is used by the engine and the fuel level in the float chamber drops, the valve opens. With the carburetor inlet valve closed, the diaphragm spring in the fuel pump is not strong enough to force the diaphragm back to its normal position. Since the link on the rocker arm is designed to move the diaphragm only in the direction against the diaphragm spring, it exerts no force to move the diaphragm back to its normal position. Thus, with the diaphragm spring held in its fully compressed position by the fuel pressure acting on the diaphragm, the rocker-arm action continues, but no additional gasoline is drawn into the pump. The diaphragm remains in this stationary condition until there is again a demand for more gasoline to

Fuel Pumps and Fuel Systems

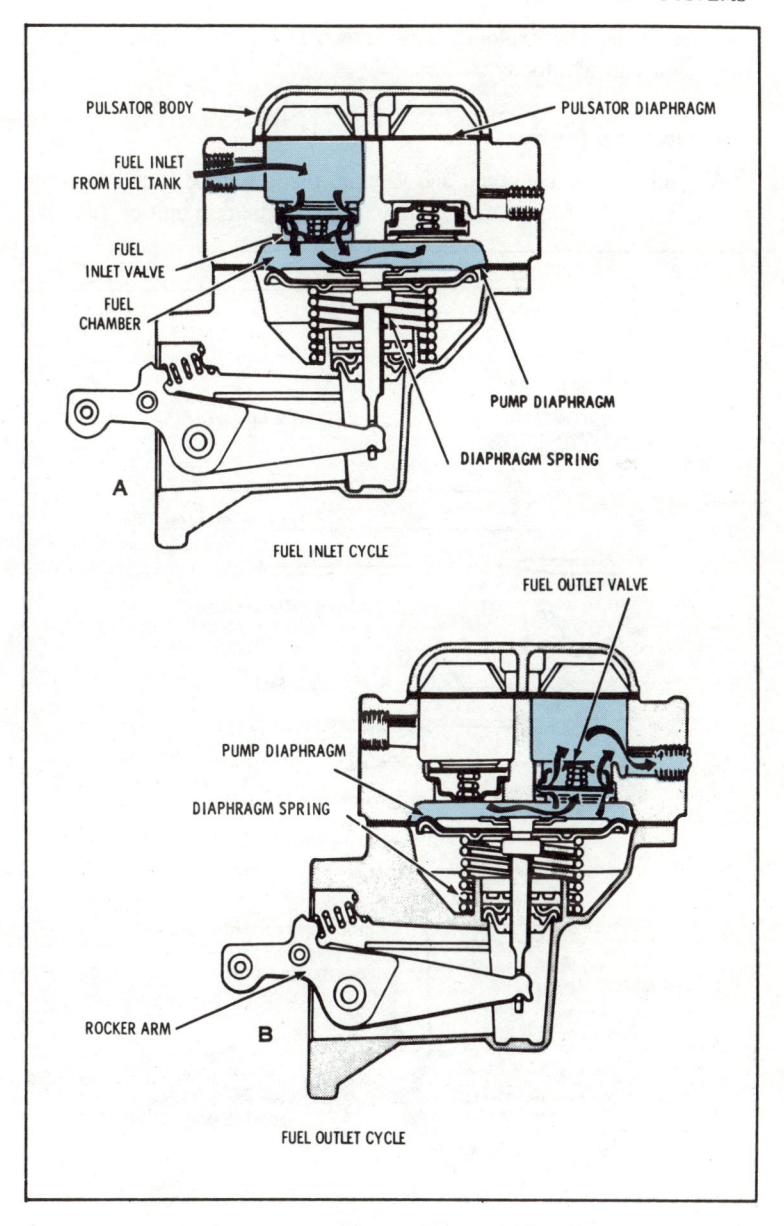

Fig. 2. Operation of a typical fuel pump; (A) Fuel intake cycle; (B) Fuel output cycle.

97

AUTOMOBILE GUIDE

the carburetor. The exploded view shown in Fig. 3 is typical of most fuel pumps in use today.

Combination Pumps

A combination fuel pump and vacuum pump will be found on some automobiles. A cross-sectional view of a combination unit of this kind

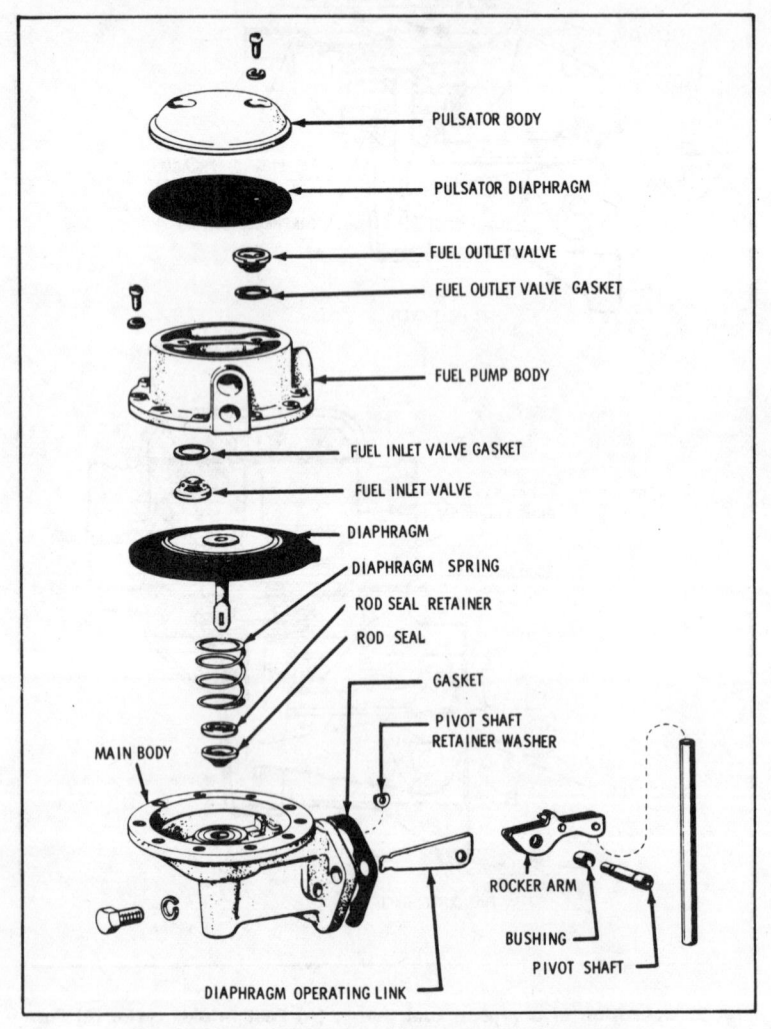

Fig. 3. An exploded view of a typical fuel pump.

FUEL PUMPS AND FUEL SYSTEMS

is shown in Fig. 4. The vacuum portion has nothing to do with the fuel system, but has merely been added to the fuel pump because of convenience. Its purpose is to furnish a nearly constant vacuum to the windshield wipers and various vacuum-actuated valves so their operation will not vary as the load on the engine changes.

The operation of the vacuum pump is very similar to the fuel pump except that more valves are used in the vacuum unit. A separate link to the rocker arm is used to actuate the vacuum pump.

The Electric Fuel Pump

The electric fuel pump may be of either the solenoid or turbine type. Some electric fuel pumps are found inside the fuel tank and are an integral part of the tank unit. This may include the sending switch for the fuel gauge.

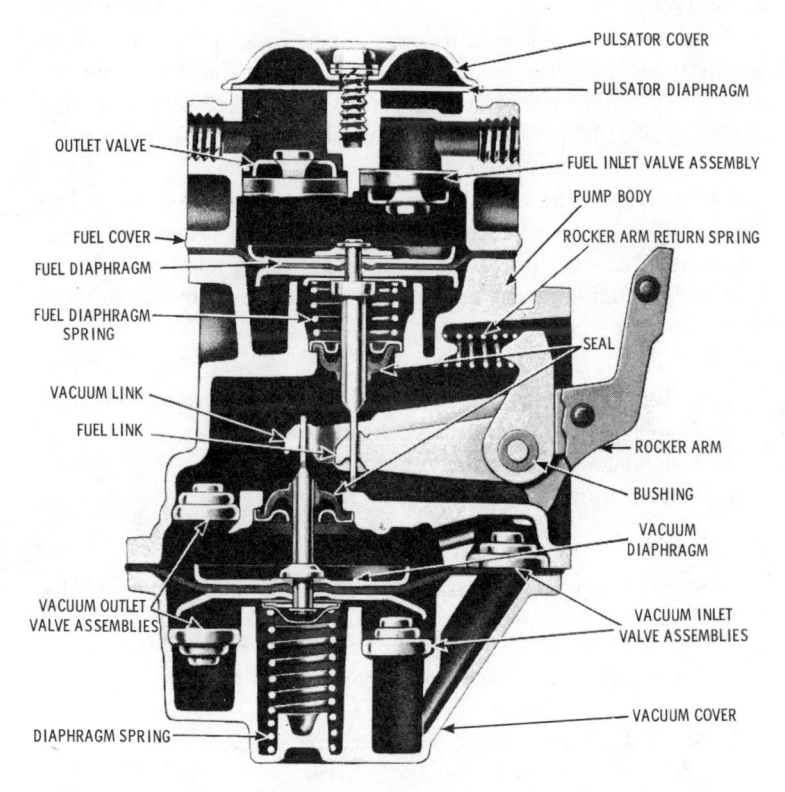

Fig. 4. Cross-sectional view of a combination fuel and vacuum pump.

Automobile Guide

The electric fuel pump is energized when the ignition switch is in the START position. After the engine has started and the ignition switch is in the ON position, the fuel pump is energized through the oil pressure switch. If for any reason the oil pressure should drop below 2-3 pounds per square inch, the electrical contact is broken to the fuel pump. This interruption of current stops the action of the fuel pump.

This system serves as a safety device to prevent engine damage that may occur if it is operated at low oil pressure. Of course, if the fuel pump is not operating no fuel is supplied to the engine and it will stop.

TESTING

Three tests — fuel-pump pressure, fuel volume, and fuel-pump vacuum — are necessary to determine if the fuel pump and fuel lines are in satisfactory condition.

If both the fuel-pump pressure and volume (rate of flow) are within specifications, then the pump and fuel lines are satisfactory. However, if the pump volume is within specifications, but the pressure is too high or too low, the fuel-pump vacuum test must be made to isolate the cause of trouble.

If both the pressure and vacuum are correct, but the volume is less than specified, inspect the fuel line for obstruction, crimps, or leaks. Replace the fuel filter (if the car is so equipped) and retest the volume.

High fuel-pump pressure and volume can be caused by one or more of the following:

1. Gasoline between the layers of the diaphragm, causing it to bulge.
2. Diaphragm too tight across its surface.
3. Diaphragm too strong (too rigid).
4. Rocker-arm link to diaphragm "frozen".
5. Diaphragm spring too strong.

Low fuel-pump pressure can be caused by one or more of the following:

1. Worn rocker arm, push rod, or rocker-arm pivot pin.
2. Punctured diaphragm.
3. Weak diaphragm spring.
4. Clogged valves in fuel pump.
5. Leaking or restricted fuel line.

FUEL PUMPS AND FUEL SYSTEMS

Fuel-Pump Pressure Test

A test of the fuel-pump pressure should be made with the pump on the engine, and using the following procedure:

1. Disconnect the fuel line at the carburetor and attach a fuel-pump pressure gauge between the line and the carburetor inlet, as in Fig. 5.
2. Start the engine and run at 500 r/min unless some other speed is specified.
3. Compare the pressure reading with the specifications (usually 3 to 5 psi). If the pressure is low, check for and correct any restrictions in the lines or filter, or any loose fittings that would allow air to enter the system. After correcting any defects, retest the pressure. If it is still low, repair or replace the fuel pump. If the pump pressure exceeds the specifications, the fuel pump should be repaired or replaced.

Fuel-Pump Volume Test

A test of the fuel-pump volume should be made with the pump on the engine, and only after it has been determined that the pressure is normal. Use the following procedure:

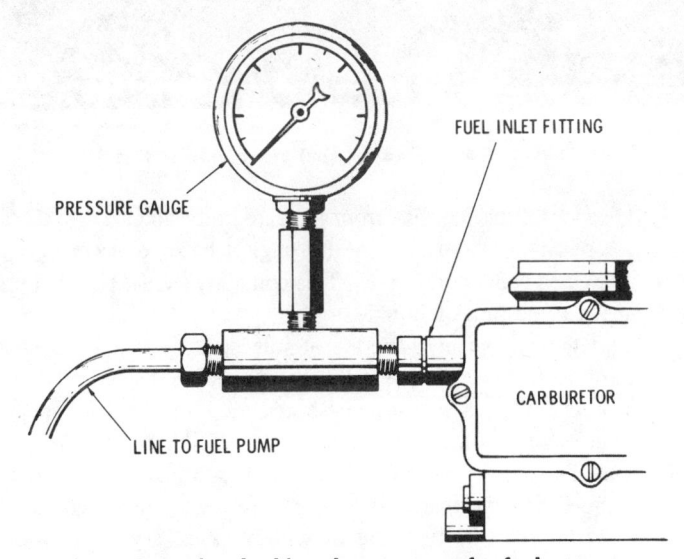

Fig. 5. Setup for checking the pressure of a fuel pump.

AUTOMOBILE GUIDE

Courtesy Sun Electric Corp.

Fig. 6. Performing the fuel-pump volume test.

1. Disconnect the fuel line from the carburetor and arrange to catch the discharge from this line (through a hose, if necessary) in a graduated container (Fig. 6). This container should be able to hold at least one pint of liquid.
2. Start the engine and operate at idle speed (the engine should continue to run a sufficient length of time on the gasoline in the float chamber). Note the time required to pump a specified quantity of gasoline into the container. Compare with the specifications (usually one pint in 15 to 20 seconds). If the quantity pumped is less than the amount specified, and there are no restrictions in the fuel line, it will be necessary to remove the pump for repair or replacement.

Fuel Pumps and Fuel Systems

Fuel-Pump Vacuum Test

A vacuum test of the fuel pump is made while it is installed on the engine, and using the following procedure:

1. Install a vacuum gauge between the inlet to the fuel pump and the fuel line to the gas tank.
2. Start the engine and run at idle speed.
3. Compare the gauge reading with the specifications (usually not less than 6 inches of mercury).
4. Stop the engine, The gauge should continue to indicate a vacuum for at least 10 seconds.

A reading less than the specified vacuum indicates a defective fuel pump which should be repaired or replaced. If vacuum is lost in less the 10 seconds after the engine is stopped, a defective pump or an air leak in the fuel line or fittings is indicated. The trouble must be isolated and corrected.

Fuel-Line Hose Leak Test

The fuel-line hose should be inspected occasionally for chafing, cracks, brittleness, rotting, and kinks or collapse.

The line can be tested for air leaks and restrictions by using the vacuum pump of a distributor tester.

1. Remove the flexible hose to be checked from the vehicle.
2. Hold your thumb over the end of the vacuum hose from the distributor tester and adjust the regulator until the vacuum gauge reads 10 inches of mercury.
3. Connect one end of the fuel-line hose to the vacuum hose of the tester. Hold your thumb over the free end of the fuel line hose. If the vacuum gauge reads less than 10 inches of mercury, the fuel-line hose leaks air. Observe the hose for signs of collapsing while making the test. The hose should also be inspected for internal deterioration while it is removed for this test. Any signs of leaks or damage should be cause for replacing the hose with a new one.

Vacuum-Pump Test

The following test is to be made only on the vacuum portion of combination pumps.

AUTOMOBILE GUIDE

1. Fully open the windshield-wiper valve and observe the wiper-blade speed as the engine is alternately idled and accelerated. The blade speed should be fairly constant regardless of engine speed or throttle opening. A dry windshield will slow the wiper speed. Take this into account, or spray the windshield with water during the test.
2. Inspect the hose connections at the pump, wiper motor, and control button, making sure the connections are airtight. Replace the hose if cracked or deteriorated.
3. If the wipers do not operate properly after correcting any leakage, detach both hoses at the vacuum pump and join them with a piece of tubing. Slowly increase the engine speed from idle to 1000 r/min; the wipers should run at full speed, operating on the engine vacuum only. If they do not, either the wiper motor or connecting tubing is defective. The vacuum pump is defective if the wipers operate properly on engine vacuum but not on pump vacuum.
4. A further test of the vacuum pump can be made by attaching a vacuum gauge to the inlet port (the port that normally is connected to the wiper motor) with the outlet hose disconnected. *(CAUTION: Always make sure the outlet port is open before making this test.)*
5. With the engine operating at 750 r/min, the gauge should show from 10 to 12 inches of vacuum. Less than 10 inches indicates a defective vacuum pump.

Electric Pump Testing

If the fuel pump is not operating because of lack of electrical power or because of a defective pump, the following simple test may determine the cause of malfunction:

1. Check for a proper ground at the pump. Make sure that the ground wire is securely fastened.
2. Check for proper voltage at the pump. If the engine is not running, this test must be made with the ignition switch in the START position.
3. If proper voltage is present with the ignition switch in the START position, but no voltage is present when the engine is running, trace the circuit back to the oil pressure switch.
4. If no voltage is present from the oil pressure switch, determine if the fault is a defective switch or low oil pressure.

Fuel Pumps and Fuel Systems

5. If voltage is not present in either of the above tests, repair or replace the defective wiring or switch, as necessary. If voltage is present in both of the above tests, replace the fuel pump.

SERVICING

Some fuel pumps, particularly the double-acting pump, may be dismantled for repairs. Most pumps, however, are sealed and must be replaced as a unit if found to be defective. The electric fuel pump *must* be replaced if found to be defective.

Repair kits are available to rebuild defective fuel pumps, and complete instructions are included for their use. Factory-rebuilt pumps are also available for most cars. An allowance is usually given for the old unit, if it is in repairable condition, when the rebuilt pump is purchased.

To repair a defective pump, the instructions given in the service manual should be followed. The procedure varies somewhat for each make and type of fuel pump, making it impractical to include a detailed description here. However, a few basic rules that apply to the repair of most fuel pumps are as follows:

1. Disconnect all lines from the pump unit.
2. Loosen the retaining bolts (usually 2) but do not remove them.
3. Jog the engine until the camshaft eccentric is in a position where the least amount of pressure is exerted on the rocker arm of the fuel pump.
4. Remove the retaining bolts and lift the pump and gasket free. If a pushrod is used to actuate the pump, it may have to be unhooked or removed before the pump can be lifted free. Discard the gasket, as a new one should be used when the pump is replaced.
5. Plug all openings in the pump assembly and thoroughly wash the exterior with solvent to remove all dirt and grease.
6. Scratch a mark on the cover or covers and the pump body to make sure of proper alignment when the unit is reassembled.
7. Disassemble the pump according to instructions, taking care not to damage any parts that may have to be used in the repaired unit.
8. Clean the various parts of the pump with a suitable solvent and blow out all passages in the body, housing, and cover with compressed air.
9. Inspect the pump body, valve housing, and cover for cracks, burrs, or damage. Examine all screw holes for stripped or crossed threads. Replace any defective unit.

AUTOMOBILE GUIDE

10. Inspect the valves for proper action and seating. If any part of the valve assembly is defective, replace the entire unit.
11. Inspect the diaphragm for pin holes, punctures, cracks, etc., and for torn or elongated screw holes around its circumference. Replace if any defect is found.
12. The diaphragm spring and rocker-arm spring should be replaced as they are very apt to be weak, corroded, or distorted.
13. Inspect the rocker arm, link, and rocker-arm pivot for signs of wear or distortion. Replace if necessary.
14. Reassemble the unit, taking care that the diaphragm is centered correctly. Never use shellac or gasket compound on the diaphragm.
15. Install the fuel pump on the engine, using a new gasket, and connect the fuel lines.

FUEL TANKS AND LINES

Fuel tanks and fuel lines generally do not require much service but, as a matter of practice, should be checked visually each time the car is on a service lift. Checking should include a careful inspection for cracks, dents, or rust.

Fuel Tanks

Most fuel tanks are of welded steel construction. They are, as a rule, located between the frame rails behind the rear axle of passenger cars. In station wagons they may be located behind the rear quarter wheelhouse, usually on the left side. Fig. 7 illustrates a typical passenger car fuel tank.

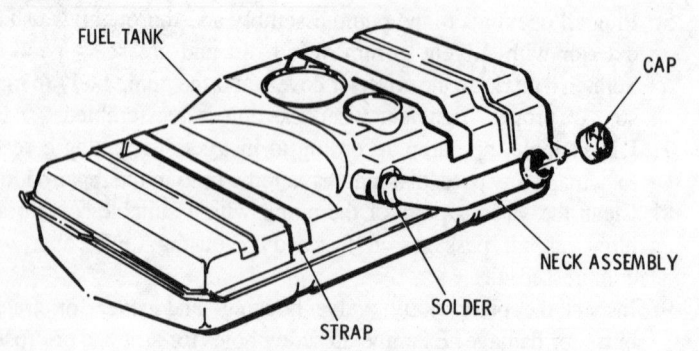

Fig. 7. Typical automotive fuel tank.

Fuel Pumps and Fuel Systems

Fuel tanks are generally secured with two sturdy metal straps held in place by bolts and nuts. Some are equipped with drain plugs so the fuel may be drained if necessary. If the tank is not equipped with a drain plug, the fuel must be siphoned for servicing.

The fuel meter assembly is a part of the fuel tank and may, in many cases, be serviced without removing the tank from the car or without draining the tank. The meter assembly, Fig. 8, contains the fuel delivery, vent, and return lines. It also contains the fuel gauge sending unit. The fuel inlet tube and filter is also a part of the assembly.

WARNING: Before servicing the fuel tank or any of its components, always: Remove battery negative (−) cable from the battery, wear safety glasses, place "No Smoking" signs around shop and have a CO_2 fire extinguisher handy. Place gasoline removed from the tank in an explosion-proof container.

If the fuel tank is to be repaired due to a leak *DO NOT USE AN OPEN FLAME*. Better still, send the tank to a professional for repairs. He is better equipped to handle the situation. Remember, gas fumes are highly flammable. An empty tank (filled with fumes) may explode.

Fuel Lines

The fuel lines extend from the fuel tank to the fuel pump. They are generally routed along the frame and are secured to the frame or

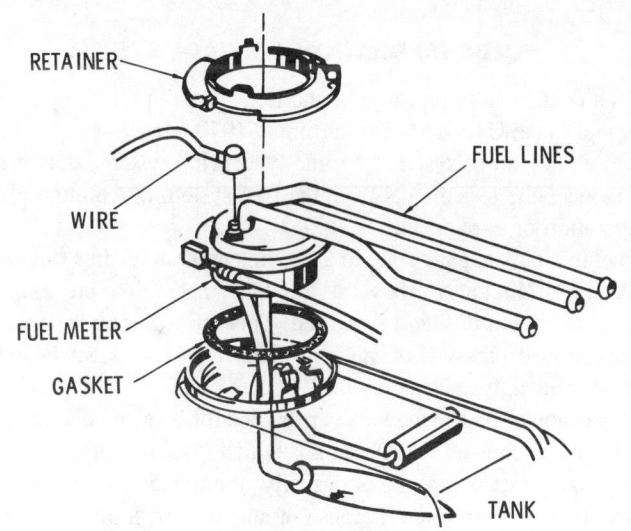

Fig. 8. Typical fuel tank meter assembly.

AUTOMOBILE GUIDE

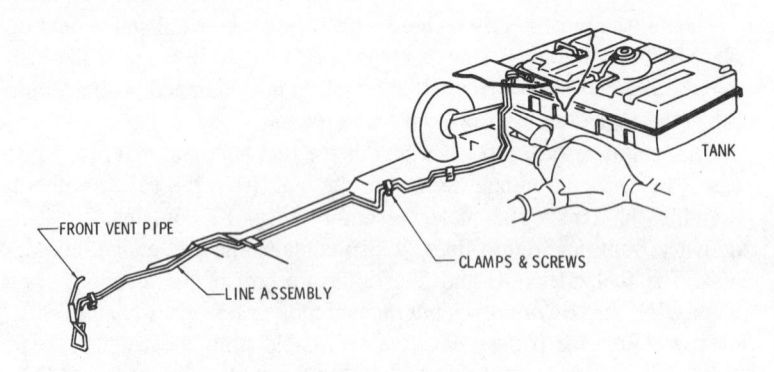

Fig. 9. Routing of fuel lines from fuel tank to fuel pump.

underbody with clamp and screw assemblies. Flexible rubber hoses are usually found at the fuel tank pickup and fuel pump.

Fuel lines are made of steel. Always replace hoses and lines of a fuel system with the same type and material as removed. Gasoline will cause rapid decomposition and early failure of certain types of synthetic materials. Under no circumstances should copper or aluminum tubing be used for fuel lines. Always use seamless steel tubing with double-flared fitting ends. Double flares may be made by using a commercially available double-flaring tool set.

FUEL EVAPORATION CONTROL SYSTEM

As an extra safety precaution, and to help minimize air pollution, all cars sold in the United States, starting in 1970, are equipped with a fuel evaporation control system of some type. This system, shown in Fig. 10, reduces the loss of fuel from the fuel system to the atmosphere by evaporation or expansion.

Fuel in a tank expands due to a rise in temperature. In a full tank this could result in an overflow at the filler neck. To prevent this, a "pressure-vacuum" filler cap is used. This cap will release only under a predetermined pressure or vacuum. This cap should not be replaced with any other type, such as the "vented" cap.

Expansion of fuel in the tank is provided for by a smaller tank, called a "thermal expansion volume tank," which is located inside the regular tank. The "expansion" tank, usually about 1.5 gallons, fills much slower than the main tank because of an "overfill limiter," so it stays essentially empty to allow for thermal expansion of the liquid fuel.

Fuel Pumps and Fuel Systems

Since the fuel tank is usually flat on top, four vent tubes are provided at each upper corner of the tank to allow for vapor (and some liquid) expansion whenever the car is parked at any incline. These four tubes run into a vapor-liquid separator. The purpose of the separator is just as its name implies, to separate the vapor from the liquid.

Since liquid is heavier than vapor, the liquid stays on the bottom of the separator and returns to the fuel tank through the liquid return line whenever the car is in the proper position (incline) for it to do so. The lighter vapor escapes through the vapor line into the crankcase air cleaner and into the crankcase. The liquid return line is the lowest point in the separator, while the vent to the crankcase is at the highest point in the separator. The crankcase vent also has a small orifice to minimize any liquid fuel transfer to the crankcase that might occur during maneuvering (fuel splashing) or incline parking.

Since fuel vapors are about three times heavier than any air that may be in the crankcase, the vapor will settle to the bottom. Along with any

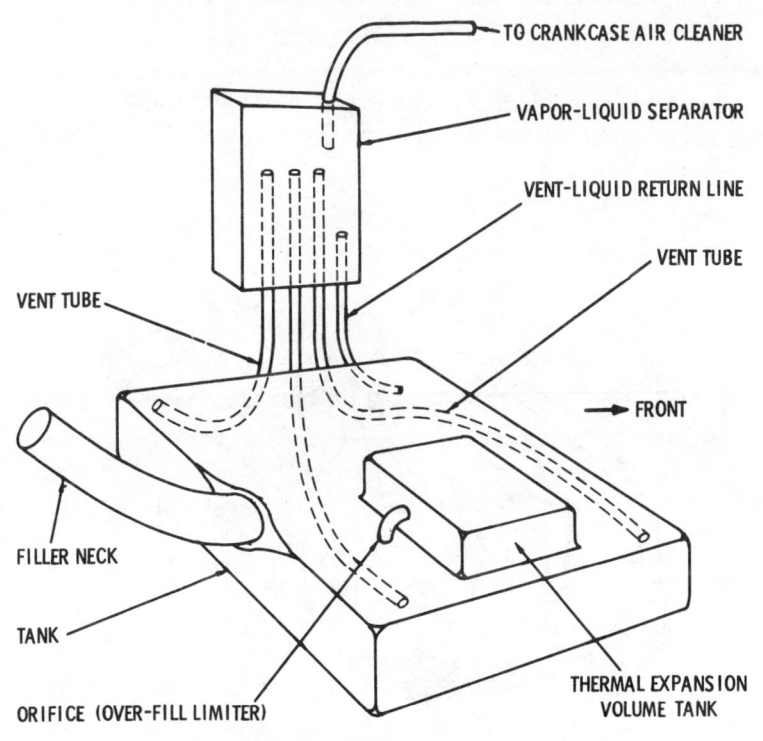

Fig. 10. Typical fuel evaporation control system.

normal crankcase vapor, the fuel vapor will be drawn (through the crankcase ventilation system) into the base of the carburetor to be burned by the engine during normal combustion.

The system should not require any normal servicing; however, a malfunctioning system may be indicated by fuel or vapor leaking from the filler cap. This would indicate a bad cap, defective seal between cap and filler neck, or one of the lines clogged.

PRINCIPLES OF TURBOCHARGING

In 1977, the *Buick Motor Division* of the *General Motors Corporation* introduced the first car factory-equipped with a turbocharged engine. The 231 c.i.d. Turbo V-6 engine is reported to have the performance of a V-8, while retaining the gas mileage of a V-6. Turbocharged engines, like naturally aspirated ones, may be equipped with either two- or four-barrel carburetors.

Description

A *turbocharger* (contraction of turbine-driven supercharger) is simply an exhaust-driven mechanical device (Fig. 11) to compress a larger

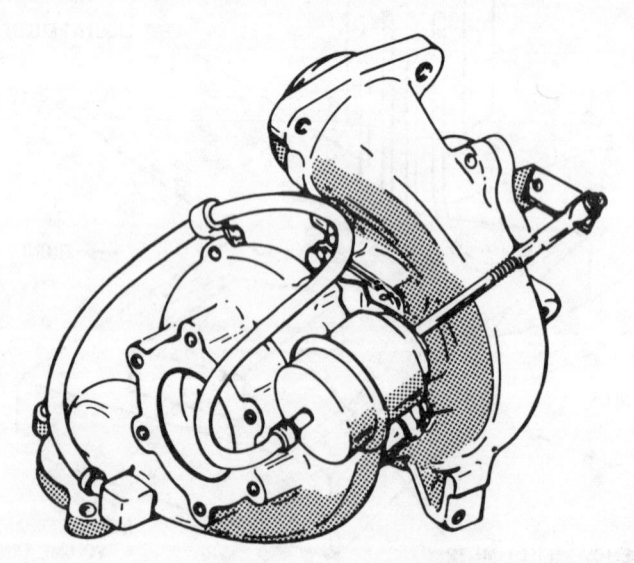

Courtesy Buick Motor Div., General Motors Corp.
Fig. 11. V-6 turbocharger.

Fuel Pumps and Fuel Systems

amount of air into the combustion chambers than the engine can draw on its own. This results in a denser air/fuel mixture and thus greater power developed during the combustion cycle.

The turbocharger consists of a single shaft with canted blades at either end, each enclosed and isolated from the other, having separate inlet and outlet ports. An oil-pressurized center shaft bearing greatly reduces the shaft's rotational friction, allowing it to spin at speeds in excess of 140,000 r/min, during full power operation.

Theory of Operation

Fig. 12 depicts simply, how a turbocharger is incorporated into the engine. The *turbine* blades are spun by escaping engine exhaust gases to a speed of about 30,000 r/min at a slow engine speed of 1500 r/min. Since the turbine and compressor blades share opposite ends of the same shaft, the *compressor* section also rotates at 30,000 r/min. Air is supplied to the engine by the intake stroke of the pistons, as in naturally aspirated engines. The turbocharger is not supplying any additional power at this point, and is acting only as an air/fuel mixture atomizer.

If the throttle is heavily depressed, such as when accelerating onto the freeway, more air and fuel are drawn into the combustion chambers and exhaust gas temperature and pressure greatly increases, causing the turbine to spin much faster—about 140,000 r/min. This, in turn, also causes the compressor section to pull large amounts of air through the carburetor—much more than the engine could pull on its own. This causes a pressurized condition, called "boost," to exist in the intake manifold and combustion chambers.

This is where the dramatic increase in available engine power becomes evident. The amount of "boost" present is now about 8 psia, literally packing the combustion chambers with additional air and fuel. This results in about a 50 percent increase in engine horsepower as compared to a naturally aspirated V-6.

Turbocharger Boost Control

If an automotive turbocharger were to operate unrestricted, the boost pressure would continue to climb as engine speed increased until a great strain was placed on pistons, rods, crankshaft, and head gaskets. To eliminate this problem, a special relief valve, called a *waste gate*, is employed. This valve senses the boost pressure in the intake manifold, and releases some exhaust gases to the outside air, before it reaches the

AUTOMOBILE GUIDE

turbocharger, when an excessive boost situation is developing. This relief valve is also known as a bypass valve, and as a "pop-off" valve.

Electronic Spark Control

A distributor-activated electronic spark control minimizes detonation in the combustion chambers (due to the leaning effect of low-octane

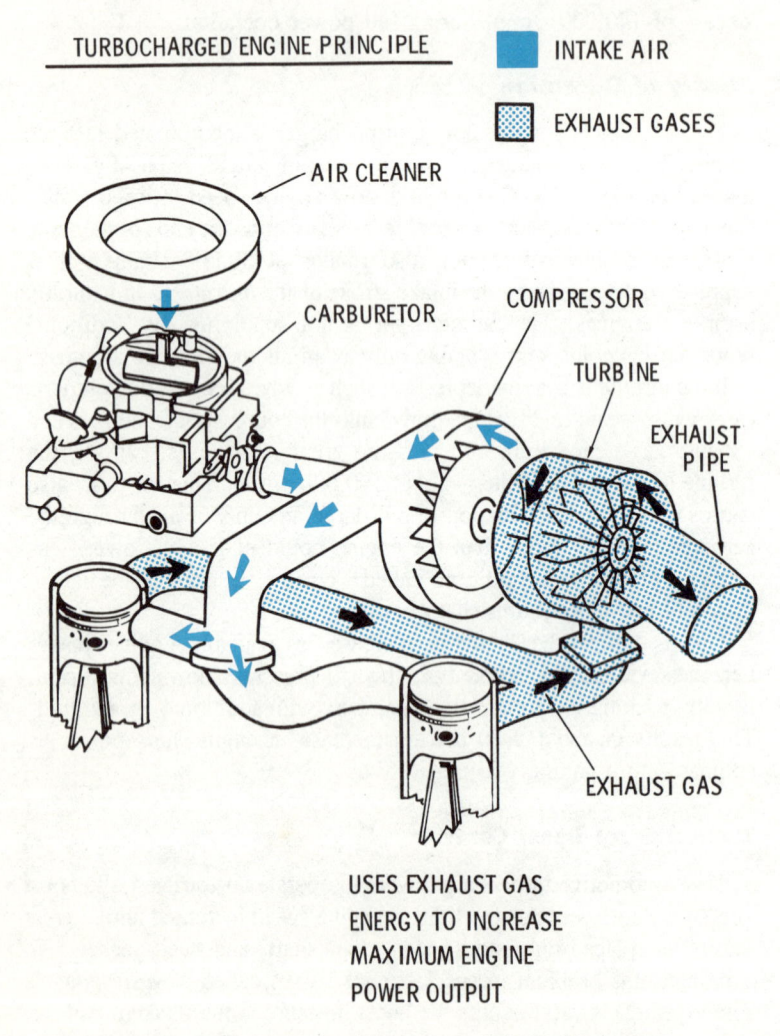

Fig. 12. Operating principles of a turbocharged engine.

Fuel Pumps and Fuel Systems

gas, magnified by the turbocharger) by retarding ignition timing up to 20°, in certain circumstances. This prevents the too-rapid burning of the dense air/fuel mixture provided by the turbocharger. Correct vacuum control, under these conditions, is provided by a vacuum bleed valve (two-barrel application) or a power enrichment control valve (four-barrel application).

Waste Gate Troubleshooting

Before testing a turbocharged engine, first be sure that there are no problems which may normally occur in a naturally aspirated engine. For example; burned points, fouled plugs, carburetor out of adjustment, etc.

The following simple tests are to determine fundamental turbocharger waste gate malfunctions:

1. Cut the tube from the compressor housing to the waste gate actuator assembly. Insert a tee and install a hand-operated vacuum/pressure pump with gauge.
2. Pump system up to 8 psia (16-in. Hg) and note actuator assembly operating rod. The rod should begin to open the waste gate.
3. If the rod moves, proceed with step 4. If the rod does not move, replace the actuator assembly and calibrate it to 8 psia.
4. Add a sufficient length of hose to the tee (step 1) to place the vacuum/pressure pump and gauge in the passenger compartment of the car.
5. Perform a 0-50 mph wide-open throttle test. Maintain top speed (50 mph) for three seconds, noting the pressure reading on the gauge.
6. The pressure should be 7-8 psia for two-barrel carburetors, and 8-9 psia for four-barrel carburetors.
7. If pressure is not as specified above, replace the actuator assembly and calibrate it to 8 psia.

Fig. 13 shows an exploded view of the *Buick* turbocharger, while Fig. 14 depicts a typical *Buick* turbocharger-to-engine mounting arrangement.

TURBOCHARGER TROUBLESHOOTING

Troubles encountered with *Buick* turbocharged engines are usually in one of two basic areas:

1. Engine detonation or poor performance.
2. Engine cranks but does not start.

Automobile Guide

The following tests should enable you to pinpoint the problem, which is usually electrical rather than mechanical. The manufacturer's service manual should be consulted for all repair procedures.

Engine Detonation or Poor Performance (Refer to Fig. 15)

1. Check all vacuum hoses and electrical wires for proper termination. If correct, proceed to step 2; if not, correct problem.
2. With ignition switch ON, check for voltage between lt. blue wire and black wire across *Electronic Spark Control* (ESC) relay. If voltage is present, proceed to step 3. If not, replace ESC relay.
3. Check engine timing, per manufacturer's specifications. Reconnect distributor vacuum advance after completion. If timing is correct, proceed to step 4. If not, correct timing.
4. At normal engine operating temperature:
   a. Connect a tachometer and a timing light meter to engine as per manufacturer's instructions.
   b. Turn air conditioner (if present) OFF.
   c. Set throttle fast idle cam on high step of cam.
   d. Engine r/min must be above 1800 r/min for test.
   e. Using a steel rod (such as a socket extension) tap the intake manifold near the detonation sensor with rapid light to medium taps. Do not tap sensor.
   f. Observe tachometer and timing light indication. Timing should retard 18° to 22°, and, r/min should drop 300 to 400 r/min while tapping on intake manifold. Values should return to normal within 20 seconds after tapping stops. If indicated response occurs, proceed to step 5. If not, proceed to step 6.
5. Follow this procedure if test in 4f was positive.
   a. Disconnect the four-wire connector from ESC at distributor.
   b. Using a jumper wire, connect socket no. 2 to pin no. 4 on the distributor side of the wiring harness connector.
   c. Check *High Energy Ignition* (HEI) distributor as recommended by manufacturer.
   d. After distributor testing and repair, remove jumper and reconnect ESC controller to distributor.
6. Follow this procedure if test in 4f was negative.
   a. Check connection from ESC to detonation sensor. If defective, replace. If not, proceed to step 6b.

Fuel Pumps and Fuel Systems

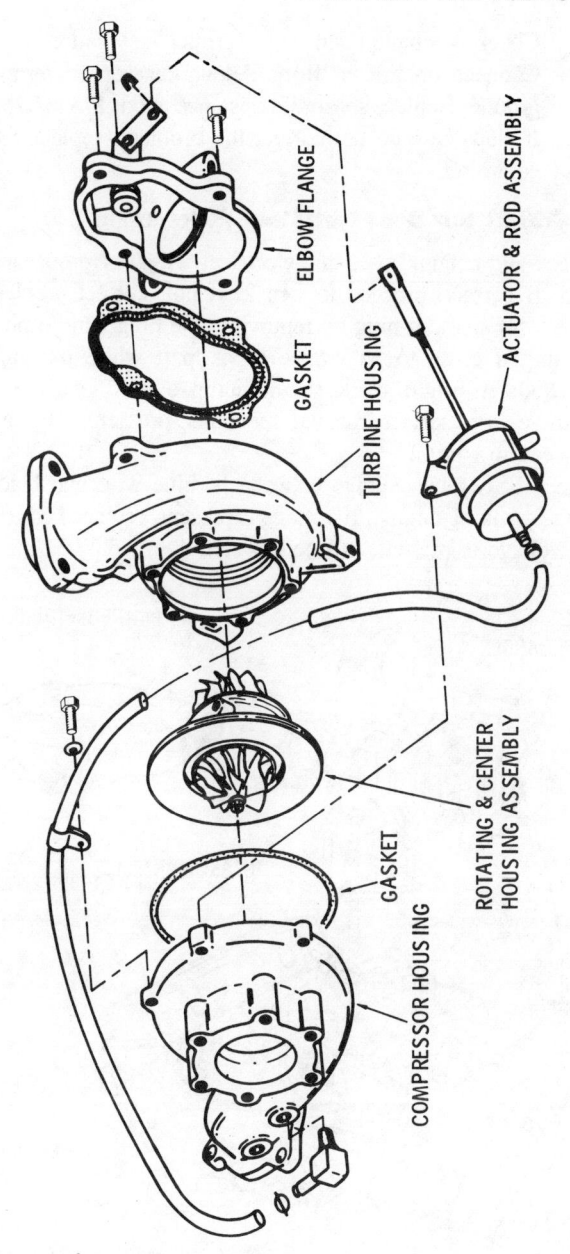

Courtesy Bear Mfgr. Co.
Fig. 13. Exploded view of the V-6 turbocharger.

115

AUTOMOBILE GUIDE

    b.   Check detonation sensor for proper installation.
    c.   Connect ohmmeter from detonation sensor terminal to ground. Replace sensor if resistance is not 175 to 375 ohms.
    d.   If steps 6a-c do not correct the problem, replace the ESC controller.

Engine Cranks But Does Not Start (Refer to Fig. 15)

1. Check all vacuum hoses and electrical wires for proper termination. If correct, proceed to step 2. If not, correct problem.
2. Check for spark at plug by removing one plug wire at plug, and holding it close to an engine block part while the engine is cranked. A bright spark should jump a 3/16" gap. If test is positive, see service manual for other problems. If negative, proceed to step 3.
3. Check ESC relay voltage between lt. blue wire and black wire while cranking engine. If voltage is present, replace ESC relay. If no voltage is present, proceed to step 4.

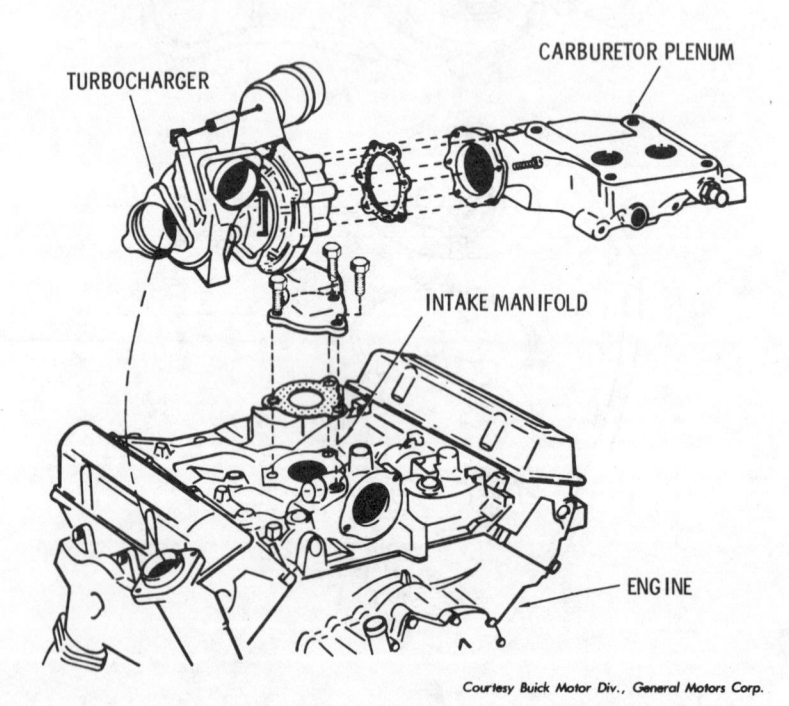

Courtesy Buick Motor Div., General Motors Corp.

Fig. 14. Turbocharger-to-engine mounting details.

Fuel Pumps and Fuel Systems

4. If voltage is under 7.0 volts, check for open circuit between "BAT" terminal on distributor and the ignition switch. If voltage is 7.0 volts or higher, proceed to step 5.
5. Follow this procedure if test 4 showed 7.0 volts or higher:

    a. Disconnect four-wire connector from ESC controller at distributor.

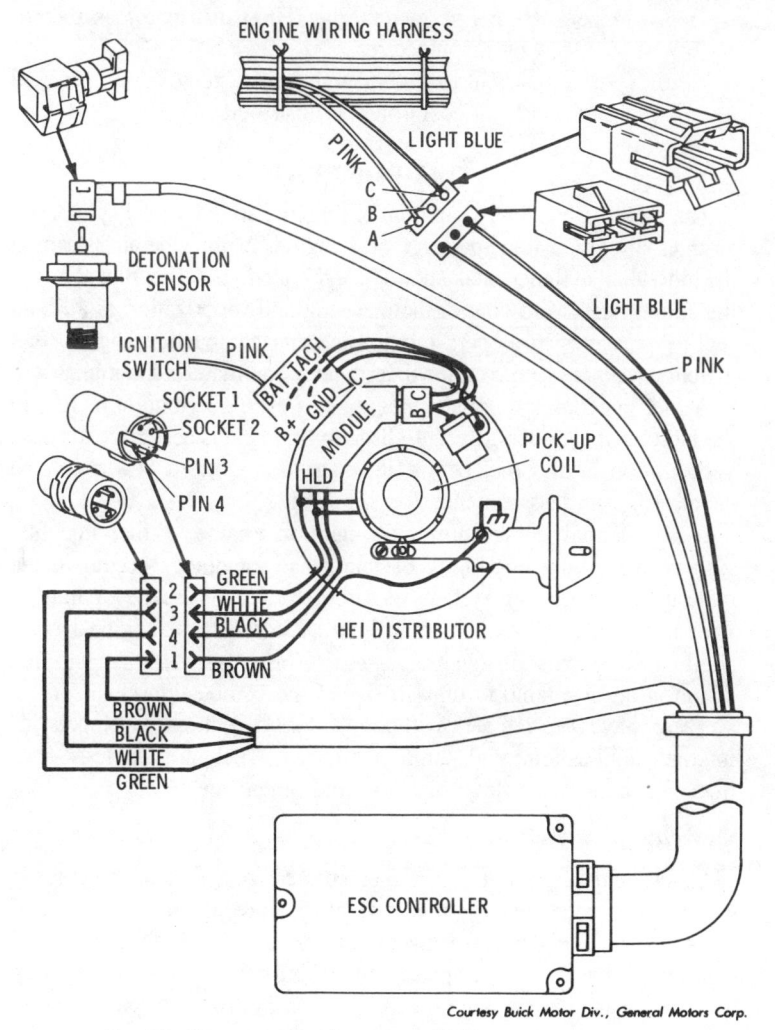

Courtesy Buick Motor Div., General Motors Corp.

Fig. 15. Electronic Spark Control (ESC) system diagram.

Automobile Guide

    b.   Using a jumper wire, connect socket no. 2 to pin no. 4 on the distributor side of the wiring harness connector.

    c.   Crank engine and re-check plug for a spark. If spark is present, replace ESC controller. If no spark is present, proceed to step 6.

6. Follow this procedure if test 5c was negative.
   a. Problem is not ESC controller. Leave jumper in the circuit.
   b. Check *High Energy Ignition* (HEI) distributor as recommended by manufacturer.
   c. After distributor testing and repair, remove jumper and reconnect ESC controller to distributor.

FUEL INJECTION

The forcing of a metered amount of fuel into an individual cylinder of an internal combustion spark-ignition engine, or into the air stream at the individual cylinder intake ports is *fuel injection*. A function of a fuel injection system is to control the metering and vaporization of a liquid fuel by pressure. In a spark-ignition internal combustion engine, fuel injection replaces a conventional carburetor and manifold combination.

A fuel injection system supplies a more even distribution of fuel to the individual cylinders. Because little (or no) heat is necessary to cause vaporization of the fuel before its distribution, more power can be developed with less tendency for knocking.

In an internal combustion spark-ignition engine, a fuel injection system avoids any possibility of icing that sometimes occurs in the metering or controlling systems of carburetors due to fuel evaporation. Fuel injection is necessary in an internal combustion engine having continuous combustion (such as a gas turbine) because the pumping action is not available to draw fuel into the combustion chamber.

There have been three methods of fuel injection developed for internal combustion spark-ignition engines. They are; metered port injection, continuous flow injection, and direct injection.

Methods of Injection

Metered Port Injection — The fuel required for a combustion cycle is metered into each intake valve port just before or during the intake stroke (before, or while the intake valve is open). This can either be controlled by a variable-displacement pump device, or by controlling the duration of the opening of a spray valve in a constant-pressure fuel supply system.

Fuel Pumps and Fuel Systems

Continuous Fuel Injection — A continuous flow fuel injection system supplies fuel directly to the intake ports. The quantity of fuel delivered is controlled by varying the pressure of the fuel supply system.

Direct Fuel Injection — Direct injection supplies fuel to individual cylinders, either by individual metering pumps (as in a diesel engine), or by a single metering pump with a distributor which directs each discharge stroke to an individual cylinder in a particular sequence.

Fig. 11 shows a typical direct fuel injection system. We will follow the flow of fuel from the fuel tank to the injector, through the overflow line back to the transfer pump.

System Components

Transfer Pump — The injector pump must be supplied with fuel under pressure because it has little or no suction ability. In order to supply fuel, under pressure, a transfer pump is used to transfer fuel from the supply tank to the injector pump. Note that the fuel must pass through a "secondary" filter before reaching the transfer pump and a "primary" filter before reaching the injector pump(s).

The transfer pump is a positive-displacement pump which will deliver fuel, through the filters, at a constant pressure of about 15 lbs. per sq. in. to the injector pump.

Injector Pump — The injector pump, sometimes referred to as a metering pump, serves two main purposes. First, it measures the fuel

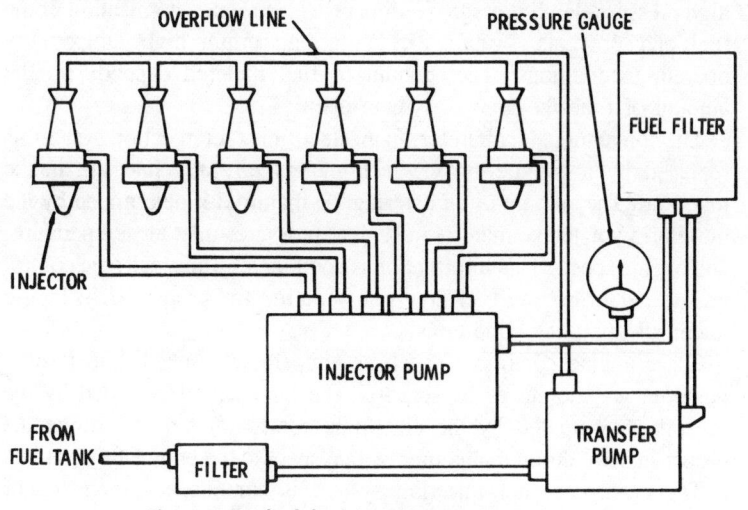

Fig. 16. Typical fuel injection system.

Automobile Guide

for each injection and combustion chamber, and secondly it puts a very high pressure (2400 to 3000 psi) on the fuel to the injectors.

Injector — The injector (also called "spray valve," "injector valve," and "injector nozzle") is a pressure-operated metering device to allow just the correct amount of fuel to enter the combustion chamber. Depending on engine design, the pressure of the spray will be from 1000 to 4000 psi.

Overflow Line — A certain amount of fuel seeps past the metering orifice of the injector nozzle to lubricate the closely fitted parts of the injector. This fuel seepage accumulates in the overflow line and drains back to the "inlet" side of the transfer pump.

ELECTRONIC FUEL INJECTION

The electronic fuel injection system (Fig. 12) monitors all engine operating conditions and electronically meters the fuel, controlling the air/fuel ratio necessary to meet those conditions. The electronic fuel injection system is basically one using an electrically operated fuel metering valve. When actuated, a small quantity of fuel is metered into the engine through individual injectors, one for each cylinder. The injectors' opening is timed so the fuel will be metered into the engine at the beginning of the cylinder intake stroke.

Fuel is supplied to the injector through a common fuel rail, under high pressure. High pressure feeding provides proper atomization of the fuel and prevents "vapor lock" during certain high temperature operating conditions. The amount of fuel metered depends on the amount of time the injector is held open.

The conventional carburetor, in an electronic fuel injection system, is replaced by a throttle body which meters *air only* into the intake manifold. The amount of air entering the manifold is determined by the monitoring of intake manifold absolute pressure, inlet air temperature, and engine speed. This information is computed by an electronic control unit to determine the fuel flow rate required for proper air/fuel ratio under all operating conditions.

Other engine conditions, such as temperature, speed, and throttle position, are monitored by sensors. The information provided by the sensors is computed by the electronic control unit to determine the proper injector duration and time with respect to the engine firing order.

The electronic fuel injection system is composed of four major sub-systems. They include the electronic control unit, the fuel delivery

Fuel Pumps and Fuel Systems

system, the air induction system, and the sensors. The proper function of each of these sub-systems are dependent, one on the other, for proper electronic fuel injection system operation.

Electronic Control Unit

The electronic control unit is a small pre-programmed analog computer. When the ignition switch is in the "ON" or "START" position the electronic control unit, powered by the car battery, receives signals from the sensors. This, in turn, activates the fuel pumps, fast idle valve, injection valves, and exhaust gas recirculating (EGR)* solenoid.

The optimum air/fuel ratios for various operating conditions are pre-programmed into the electronic control unit. Based on electrical signals received from the sensors, the computer issues signals to the injectors. This signal translates into a specific time duration for the injectors to be opened, depending on a variety of engine conditions.

Fuel Delivery System

The fuel delivery sub-system consists of seven major components in addition to the fuel supply and return lines. Those components; fuel tank, two fuel pumps, fuel filter, fuel rail, injector valves, and fuel pressure regulator, are responsible for the delivery of fuel to the cylinders and provide a means of returning excess fuel to the tank.

Fuel Tank — The fuel tank is somewhat different from that of a conventional tank in that it incorporates a reservoir below the sending unit and an in-tank (boost) fuel pump. The reservoir is provided to insure a constant supply of fuel to the in-tank pump under low fuel or severe maneuvering conditions. Excess fuel is returned to the tank through the reservoir, providing an additional means of insuring a constant fuel supply. The in-tank fuel pump is below the reservoir to insure a full prime under adverse conditions, as outlined.

Fuel Pumps — The in-tank (boost) pump and external (main) pump are electrical and are wired, in parallel, to the electronic control unit. The in-tank pump is an integral part of the fuel tank gauge unit. Its purpose is to supply fuel to the external chassis-mounted main pump and to prevent vapor lock on the suction side of the main pump.

The main pump is of a constant-displacement roller-vane type, incorporating a check valve to prevent back flow and to maintain fuel pressure when the pump is not operating. This pump includes an

---
*The EGR system is not a part of the electronic fuel injection system. It is, however, activated with the electronic fuel injection system.

Automobile Guide

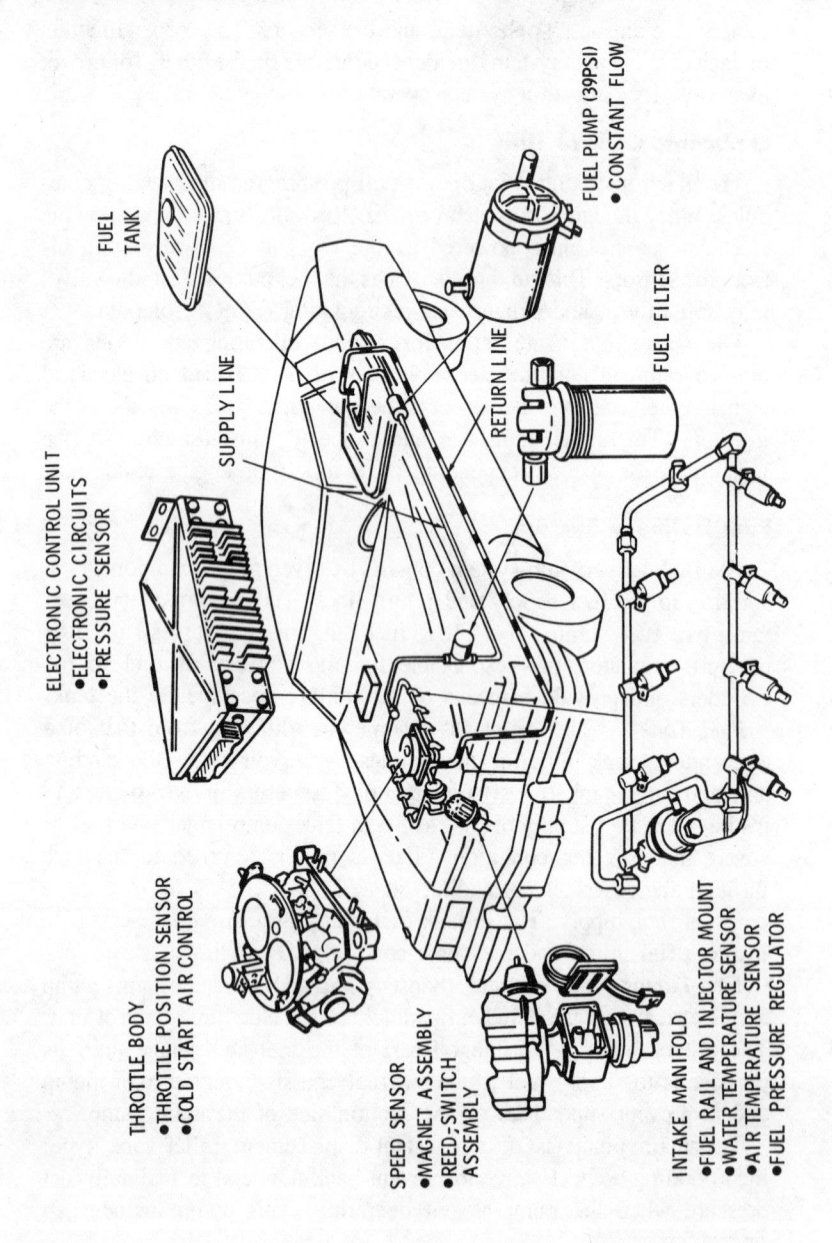

Fig. 17. Typical electronic fuel injection system.

Fuel Pumps and Fuel Systems

internal pressure relief valve which opens at 55 to 95 psi as a protection against excessive pressures.

Fuel Filter — The fuel filter consists of a disposable paper element housed in a metal casing. The fuel filter element is replaced by removing a can-type cover much like a miniature version of some types of standard oil filter cover. It is recommended that the filter element be replaced after the first 7500 miles, at 22,500 miles, and every 22,500 miles thereafter.

Fuel Rail — The fuel rail provides fuel flow passage for the pressure regulator and each of the injectors. The assembly generally consists of four pieces; right, left, front, and back rails. When servicing a fuel rail, always use a back-up wrench to prevent damage to the fittings.

Injector Valves — The solenoid-operated injector valves meter fuel to each cylinder based on a pulsed electrical signal from the electronic control unit. The signal strength (voltage) and duration (time) is determined by the electronic control unit based on information it receives from other sub-system sensors.

On signal, the valve opens for the proper time interval and gap to deliver the exact amount of fuel required for a particular operating condition. The injector valves are carefully calibrated and are a precision unit. As such, care must be taken when handling so the metering tips are not damaged.

Fuel Pressure Regulator — The fuel pressure regulator contains a fuel chamber and an air chamber. The two chambers are separated by a spring-loaded diaphragm. The air chamber, regulated by intake manifold vacuum, is connected to the throttle body by means of a hose. The changing intake manifold vacuum, under varying conditions, with the assist of the regulator spring, controls the diaphragm action. This action opens, or closes, an orifice in the fuel chamber to maintain a constant 39 psi pressure differential across the injectors. Excess fuel is returned to the fuel tank reservoir through the fuel return line.

Air Induction System

The air induction sub-system consists of three or four components, depending on the electronic fuel injection system. In addition to the throttle body assembly, intake manifold, and fast-idle valve assembly, some systems have an air solenoid valve.

Air for combustion enters the intake manifold through the throttle body. Primary air flow is controlled by the throttle valves very similar to a conventional carburetor system.

Throttle Body — The throttle body provides for variable air flow to the intake manifold. It is mechanically linked to the accelerator pedal much in the same manner as in a conventional carburetor system. Unlike the conventional carburetor however, the throttle body does not meter fuel.

An adjustment screw on the throttle body provides for a means to adjust the warm idle speed. Turning the adjustment screw clockwise (cw) decreases engine speed; counterclockwise (ccw) increases engine speed.

Intake Manifold — The intake manifold, with the exception of the omission of an exhaust heat passage, is basically the same as used on conventional gasoline engines. The electronic fuel injection manifold distributes only air to the cylinder intake ports however. Unlike the conventional intake manifold, additional ports are provided for the air temperature sensor and the injection valve assemblies.

Fast Idle Valve — The fast-idle valve is a thermally sensitive element electrically connected to the fuel pump circuit through the electronic control unit. The fast-idle valve provides a means of fast engine idle under varying ambient and engine temperature conditions, as required by the electronic control unit.

Some valves use an electric heater element for thermal conductivity while others sense coolant temperature. Either type serves basically the same purpose, similar to the automatic choke on conventional systems.

Air Solenoid Valve — The air solenoid valve is used on those systems having a coolant temperature sensing fast idle valve only. It is used to supplement the air supply from the fast idle valve to the throttle body during the engine warm-up period.

Sensors

Each sensor is electrically connected to the electronic control unit. Operating independently of each other, each sensor transmits an electrical signal relating to a specific operating condition. These signals are analyzed by the electronic control unit computer and converted into appropriate system commands.

Basically, there are five sensors; manifold absolute pressure sensor, throttle position switch sensor, two temperature sensors, and a speed sensor.

Manifold Vacuum Sensor — Changes in intake manifold vacuum, as a result of variable engine loads (speed, barometric pressure, and altitude), are monitored by the manifold vacuum sensor. This vacuum is

Fuel Pumps and Fuel Systems

translated into an electrical signal and transmitted to the electronic control unit computer.

Throttle Position Switch Sensor — The throttle position switch sensor detects throttle shaft movement and position. This information, translated into an electrical signal, is transmitted to the electronic control unit computer.

Temperature Sensors — There are usually two temperature sensors; one for air and one for coolant. The air sensor perceives intake manifold air temperature and the coolant sensor detects engine coolant temperature. An electrical signal is transmitted from both sensors to the electronic control unit computer.

It may be noted that, in most cases, both sensors are identical and may be interchanged. An ohmmeter is used to test the temperature sensors. In testing, resistance should be no greater than 1600Ω nor no less than 700Ω.

Speed Sensor — The speed sensor is an integral part of the high-energy ignition (HEI) distributor assembly. It consists of two components; a reed switch assembly, attached to the distributor shaft housing; and a rotor/magnet assembly, attached to (and rotating with) the distributor shaft.

The turning rotor/magnet, timed with the valve train, triggers the reed switch to provide a synchronization signal to the electronic control unit. This provides engine speed data for proper fuel scheduling to the right injector group at the proper intake valve timing interval.

FUEL PUMP TROUBLES AND REMEDIES

Symptoms and Possible Causes   *Possible Remedies*

Fuel Pump Leaks Gasoline

(a) Loose housing screws.   (a) Tighten screws.
(b) Ruptured or torn   (b) Install new diaphragm.
    diaphragm.
(c) Loose fittings.   (c) Tighten fittings.
(d) Threads stripped on   (d) Install new fittings.
    fittings.
(e) Damaged hose near   (e) Replace hose.
    fitting.
(f) Crack in pump   (f) Replace fuel pump.
    housing.

125

Symptoms and Possible Causes *Possible Remedies*

Fuel Pump Leaks Oil

(a) Hole in diaphragm.
(b) Leak at mounting flange.

(c) Damaged oil seal.

(a) Install new diaphragm.
(b) Install new gasket and tighten mounting bolts to required torque.
(c) Replace oil seal.

Insufficient Fuel Delivery

(a) Loose fuel-line fittings.
(b) Damaged diaphragm.
(c) Cracked or broken fuel line.
(d) Weak or broken diaphragm spring.
(e) Vent in tank restricted.

(a) Tighten fittings.
(b) Install new diaphragm.
(c) Replace line.
(d) Replace spring.
(e) Clean restriction or replace tank cup or vent.

Fuel Pump Noise

(a) Pump loose at mounting.
(b) Worn rocker arm or push rod.
(c) Broken or weak rocker arm

(a) Tighten mounting bolts.
(b) Replace worn unit.
(c) Install new spring.

Electric Pump Inoperative

While engine cranking only

(operative when engine is running)

(a) Defective ignition switch.
(b) Defective wiring; switch to pump.

(a) Replace ignition switch.
(b) Repair or replace wiring.

While engine running only

(operative when engine cranking)

(a) Low oil pressure.

(b) Defective oil pressure switch.

(a) Correct low oil pressure condition.
(b) Replace oil pressure switch.

FUEL PUMPS AND FUEL SYSTEMS

Symptoms and Possible Causes　*Possible Remedies*

(c) Defective wiring; switch to pump.
(c) Repair or replace wiring.

While engine cranking or running

(a) Defective fuse or circuit breaker.
(b) Defective wiring or harness.
(c) Loose or broken pump ground wire.
(d) Defective fuel pump.

(a) Replace fuse or circuit breaker.
(b) Repair or replace harness.
(c) Repair or replace as necessary.
(d) Replace fuel pump.

ELECTRONIC FUEL INJECTION SYSTEM TROUBLES AND REMEDIES

Symptoms and Possible Causes　*Possible Remedies*

Engine Cranks But Will Not Start

(a) Blown fuse.
(b) Broken or disconnected wire(s).
(c) Loose or defective connection (or ground).
(d) Defective throttle position switch.
(e) Defective speed sensor.
(f) Restricted fuel flow (line or filter).

(a) Replace fuse.
(b) Repair or replace as necessary.
(c) Repair as necessary.
(d) Replace switch.
(e) Replace sensor.
(f) Locate restriction and correct as necessary.

Engine Hard Starting

(a) Defective engine coolant sensor.
(b) Defective throttle position switch.
(c) Defective fuel pump.
(d) Defective fuel pressure regulator.

(a) Replace sensor.
(b) Replace switch.
(c) Replace fuel pump.
(d) Replace regulator.

AUTOMOBILE GUIDE

Symptoms and Possible Causes *Possible Remedies*

Engine Hesitates On Acceleration

(a) Disconnected or leaking manifold pressure sensor hose.

(a) Repair or replace hose as necessary.

(b) Restriction in manifold pressure sensor hose.

(b) Locate restriction. Repair or replace hose.

(c) Throttle position switch out of adjustment.

(c) Adjust switch to specifications.

(d) Defective throttle position switch.

(d) Replace switch.

(e) Malfunction (intermittent) of speed sensor.

(e) Determine problem and correct as necessary.

(f) Connection of jumper harness loose or defective.

(f) Repair connection as necessary.

(g) Loose connection at EGR solenoid.

(g) Repair connection.

(h) Defective EGR solenoid (cold engine only).

(h) Replace solenoid.

Rough Idle

(a) Disconnected or leaking manifold pressure hose.

(a) Repair or replace hose.

(b) Restriction in manifold pressure hose.

(b) Locate and correct as necessary.

(c) Loose connection at air temperature sensor.

(c) Repair connection.

(d) Loose connection at coolant sensor (cold engine).

(d) Repair connection.

(e) Loose connections at injector valve(s).

(e) Repair or correct as necessary.

(f) Defective engine coolant sensor.

(f) Replace sensor.

Poor Gas Mileage

(a) Defective coolant sensor.

(a) Replace sensor.

(b) Defective air temperature sensor.

(b) Replace sensor.

(c) Leaking or disconnected vacuum hose.

(c) Repair or replace hose as necessary.

Fuel Pumps and Fuel Systems

Symptoms and Possible Causes

(d) Leaking or disconnected manifold pressure sensor hose.

Possible Remedies

(d) Repair or replace hose as necessary.

Extended Fast Idle

(a) Loose electrical connection at fast idle valve
(b) Defective heating element in fast idle valve.
(c) Throttle position switch out of adjustment.
(d) Leak in vacuum system.

(a) Repair connection.

(b) Replace valve.

(c) Adjust to specifications.

(d) Locate and repair leak.

Poor or No High Speed Performance

(a) Throttle position switch out of adjustment (wide open position only).
(b) Defective or malfunctioning throttle position switch.
(c) Defective fuel pump.
(d) Restricted fuel filter.
(e) Restriction in fuel line.
(f) Defective wiring.

(a) Adjust to specifications.

(b) Replace switch.

(c) Replace fuel pump.
(d) Replace filter element.
(e) Locate and repair.
(f) Locate and correct.

Engine Starts, then Stalls

(a) Open electrical circuit.
(b) Loose electrical connection.
(c) Loose or defective connection at coolant sensor (cold or warm engine only).

(a) Locate and correct.
(b) Locate and repair.
(c) Repair as necessary.

CHAPTER 6

Carburetors and Air Cleaners

Automobile engines will not run on raw, liquid gasoline. Instead, the gasoline must be broken up into tiny drops, then vaporized to produce a highly combustible air/fuel mixture. This mixture is then introduced into the cylinders under controlled temperature, pressure, and time.

The device which mixes the gasoline and air is the carburetor. Not only does it mix the fuel and air, but it also automatically varies the proportion. It provides a richer mixture (a greater proportion of gasoline) for starting, idling, and acceleration, and a leaner mixture (a smaller proportion of gasoline) for part-throttle operation. In addition, the carburetor also regulates the engine speed and power by controlling the amount of the air/fuel mixture reaching the cylinders. In order to accomplish all these tasks, a carburetor has a variety of fixed and adjustable passages, jets, ports, and pumps arranged in systems or circuits.

BASIC OPERATING PRINCIPLES

Although a carburetor is relatively complicated, its basic operation depends simply on differences in pressure. An understanding of how these pressure differences are put to work in a carburetor will help in making adjustments and diagnosing carburetor troubles.

A piston moving down on the intake stroke draws air from the cylinder and from the intake manifold. This action creates a vacuum

CARBURETORS AND AIR CLEANERS

that draws atmospheric air through the only opening into the cylinder at that time — through the carburetor. This flow of air through the carburetor causes fuel to be drawn from the carburetor, through the manifold, through the intake valve, and into the cylinder.

The Venturi Principle

When air is passed rapidly through a tube having a small hole in the side, air will be drawn through the hole and into the air stream flowing through the tube, as shown in Fig. 1. If a hose is connected to this hole, and the opposite end of the hose is suspended in a liquid, the liquid will be pulled through the hose and will enter the air stream. This is shown in Fig. 2. The amount of liquid passing into the air stream in the tube will depend on how fast the air is moving past the hole in the side of the tube. The greater the velocity of the air, the greater will be the amount of liquid passing into the air stream.

If a "Y" is placed in the hose at a point below the level of the liquid, in a manner such as that shown in Fig. 3, both liquid and air will be pulled through the hose and into the air stream. The introduction of the air into the liquid helps to break up the liquid into smaller particles, making vaporization more complete.

For greater efficiency, a portion of the tube can be made with a smaller diameter. The air passing through the tube will speed up in the vicinity of the smaller diameter, and will also create an area of lower

Fig. 1. Air is drawn through a hole in the side of a tube through which a stream of air is passing.

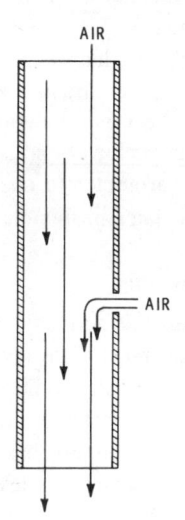

AUTOMOBILE GUIDE

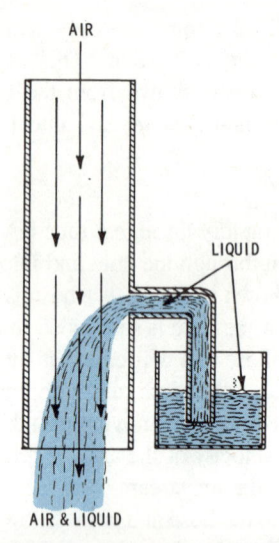

Fig. 2. Liquid from a container can be introduced into the air stream in the tube shown in Fig. 1, if a hose is connected from the liquid to the hole in the side of the tube.

pressure at the point where the air is passing on into the normal diameter of the tube. This restriction to the flow of air in the tube is known as a *venturi*. The action this restriction has on drawing fuel and air into the air stream is known as the *venturi effect*. Fig. 4 illustrates the principle of a venturi.

With the engine running at idle speed there is not enough air passing through the venturi to draw fuel into the air stream. In addition, the venturi effect is momentarily lost with sudden changes of engine operation, such as rapid acceleration. Other systems are therefore built into the carburetor to overcome these defects. These systems will be discussed later in this chapter.

Float System

The gasoline delivered by the fuel pump to the carburetor is contained in the fuel bowl. The level of the gasoline in the bowl must be kept constant under all conditions of engine operation. The float system in all carburetors operates on the same basic principle. As shown in Fig. 5, the typical carburetor has a float-operated needle valve and seat at the fuel inlet to control the level of the gasoline in the fuel bowl. When the fuel drops below a preset level, the float lowers and opens the needle

Carburetors and Air Cleaners

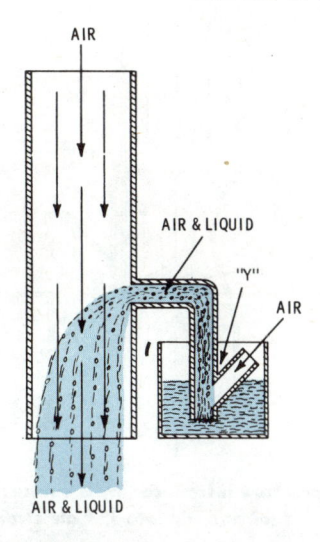

Fig. 3. If a "Y" is added to the hose below the level of the liquid with the open end of the "Y" exposed to the air, both air and liquid will be drawn into the air stream inside the tube.

valve, allowing gasoline to enter the bowl. When the fuel reaches the preset level, the rising float forces the inlet needle valve against the seat, shutting off the flow of gasoline from the fuel pump. In this manner the gasoline is kept at a constant level in the fuel bowl.

The fuel bowl is vented into the carburetor air horn to provide the proper air pressure to allow the gasoline to enter the passages in the throttle body of the carburetor during engine operation.

Throttle Valve

The throttle valve (Fig. 6) is a round disc, mounted on a shaft and located in the lower part of the throttle body. The throttle valve is pivoted by means of a mechanical linkage from the accelerator either to close off the air/fuel stream through the throttle body or to allow a variable amount of air/fuel to pass through. This action regulates the flow of the air/fuel mixture to the engine, thus controlling the engine speed.

Idle System

The idle system supplies the air/fuel mixture to keep the engine running when the throttle valve is completely closed. At idle there is

Automobile Guide

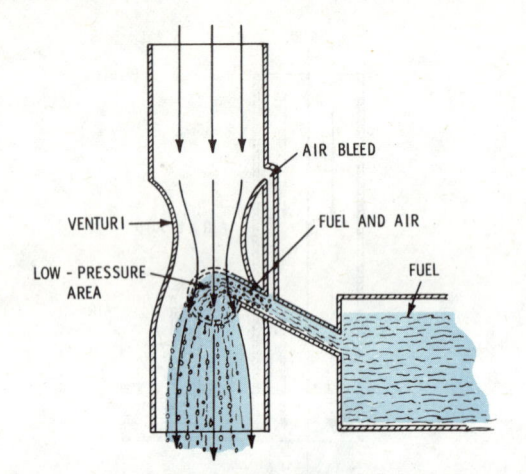

Fig. 4. The lower pressure introduced by a venturi in a tube helps to draw fuel and air into the air stream.

very little air flowing through the venturi because the throttle valve is closed, blocking most of the air flow. Thus, there is no venturi effect to draw fuel from the main fuel nozzle. To allow the engine to operate

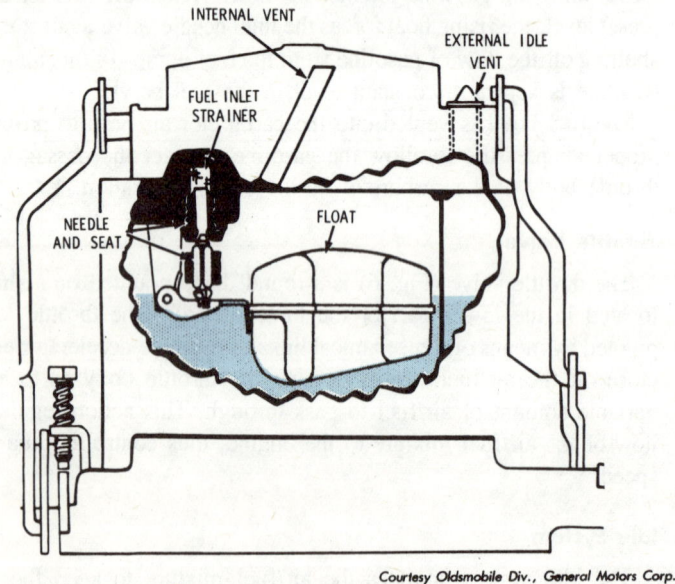

Courtesy Oldsmobile Div., General Motors Corp.

Fig. 5. A typical float system.

CARBURETORS AND AIR CLEANERS

THROTTLE VALVE OPEN   THROTTLE VALVE CLOSED

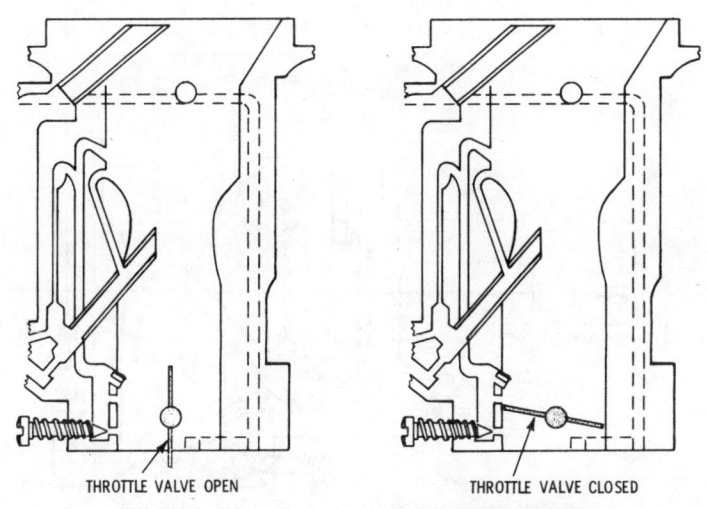

Fig. 6. The throttle valve controls engine speed.

under this condition, an idle port is placed just below the throttle valve, as shown in Fig. 7. Since the intake vacuum is high at idling speeds, the pressure differential between the air in the fuel bowl and the vacuum below the throttle valve forces fuel through the idle port into the air stream.

Gasoline flows from the fuel bowl through the idle tube on its way to the idle port. Air bleed holes opening into the idle tube introduce a metered amount of air into the gasoline in the idle system, and also act as vents to prevent siphoning of gasoline from the fuel bowl above idle, at high speeds, or when the engine is stopped. An adjustable needle valve controls the richness of the idle fuel mixture by regulating the amount of gasoline that passes through the idle port into the intake manifold.

Low-Speed System

When the throttle valve is opened slightly for low-speed operation, there is still insufficient air flow through the venturi to draw fuel from the main fuel nozzle. Since more fuel is needed than can be provided by the idle port alone, another port (Fig. 8) is located so that its opening is just above the throttle valve when it is closed, and in the low-pressure area when the throttle valve is in the low-speed position. Fuel is drawn from both ports in low-speed operation to provide the proper air/fuel ratio.

AUTOMOBILE GUIDE

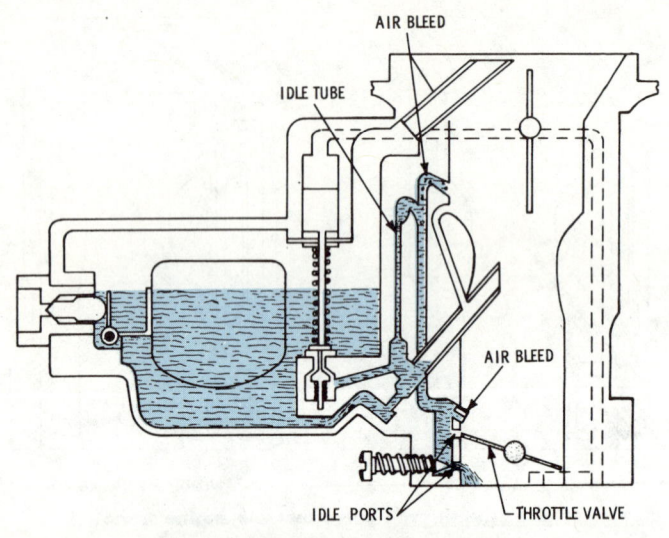

Fig. 7. The carburetor idle system.

High-Speed System

As the throttle valve is opened further, the air flow through the carburetor increases until, at some point, the venturi effect becomes

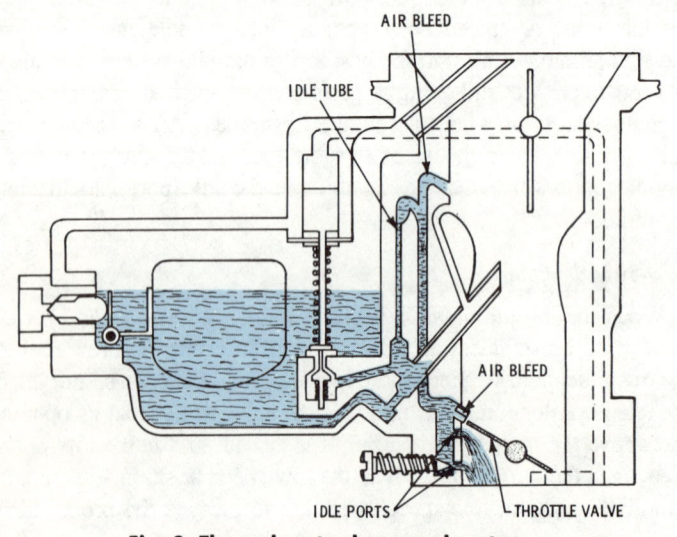

Fig. 8. The carburetor low-speed system.

CARBURETORS AND AIR CLEANERS

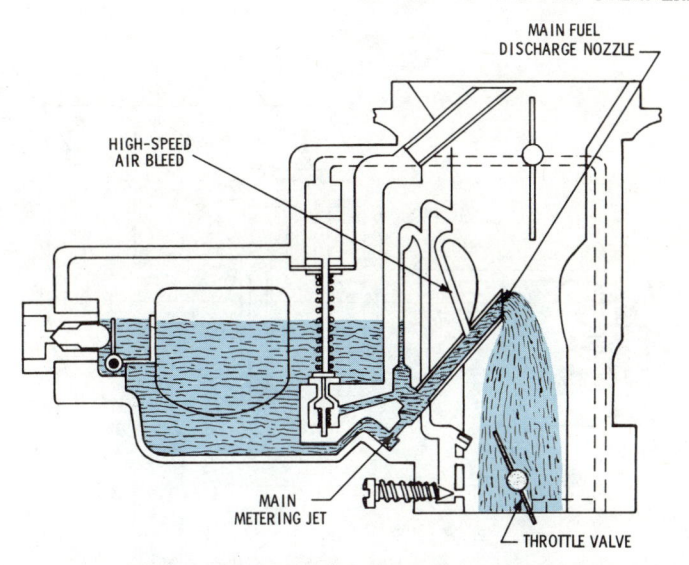

Fig. 9. The carburetor high-speed system.

great enough to draw gasoline from the main fuel nozzle. This action is shown in Fig. 9. Fuel from the low-speed system starts tapering off as the amount of fuel drawn from the main fuel nozzle increases, until finally the flow from the low-speed system stops completely.

The flow of gasoline during high-speed operation is from the fuel bowl, through the main passageway, through the main nozzle, and out into the air stream in the carburetor throat. An air bleed hole opening into the main passageway provides air to maintain the proper air/fuel ratio. An antisiphon bleed hole is also provided to prevent the gasoline from siphoning out of the fuel bowl when the engine is stopped.

Power System

During periods of increased load on the engine, or full-throttle operation, the ratio of the fuel to the air must be increased to provide a richer mixture. The additional fuel required is supplied by a power fuel system, such as the one in Fig. 10.

The power fuel system is controlled by intake manifold vacuum on most cars, but may be operated mechanically by accelerator action in a few instances. Manifold vacuum gives an accurate indication of the power demands placed on the engine, the vacuum being greatest under no-load conditions and decreasing as the load on the engine increases.

Automobile Guide

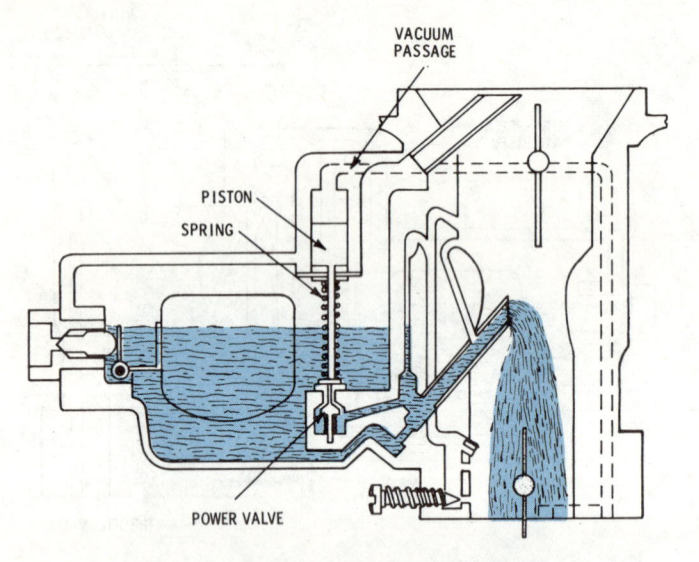

Fig. 10. The carburetor power system.

Manifold vacuum is transmitted from an opening in the throat at the base of the carburetor, through a passage in the body, to a power-valve chamber, where it acts on a piston or diaphragm. The engine vacuum at idle speeds or normal load conditions is great enough to hold the power valve closed against the tension of a calibrated spring. When the manifold vacuum drops due to an increased load on the engine, the spring opens the valve and allows additional gasoline to flow to the main fuel jet, enriching the mixture. In some carburetors, a metering rod may be lifted instead of a valve being opened. This is shown in the inset of Fig. 10.

Power circuits that are mechanically operated perform the same functions by moving a tapered metering rod in and out of a fixed-size jet. As the rod is moved out of the jet, the opening becomes progressively larger, allowing an increase in the flow of gasoline to the main fuel nozzle.

Accelerator-Pump System

Upon acceleration, the air flow through the carburetor increases almost immediately. There is, however, a brief interval before the fuel (which is heavier than air) can gain speed and maintain the desired balance of fuel and air. Unless this condition is corrected, the air/fuel

Carburetors and Air Cleaners

ratio will become leaner at a time when a richer mixture is actually required for more power. An accelerator pump is therefore provided to momentarily supply additional fuel until the flow from the main fuel nozzle increases.

The accelerator pump (Fig. 11) is operated by mechanical linkage connected to the throttle. When the throttle is suddenly opened, the spring-loaded plunger forces the required amount of gasoline past the discharge check valve and into the air stream of the carburetor. The spring loading provides for a continuation of fuel flow for a short period after the throttle is opened. Closing the throttle withdraws the pump plunger (Fig. 12), pulling gasoline into the pump cylinder through the inlet valve. This position of the pump plunger keeps the pump cylinder full of gasoline, ready for immediate use. A diaphragm-type pump is used on some carburetors instead of a plunger-type, but the principle of operation is the same.

Choke System

When a cold engine is being started, most of the gasoline discharged by the carburetor is unable to vaporize before it reaches the engine until the intake manifold heats up sufficiently. This means that a much larger quantity of fuel must be supplied to compensate for this lack of

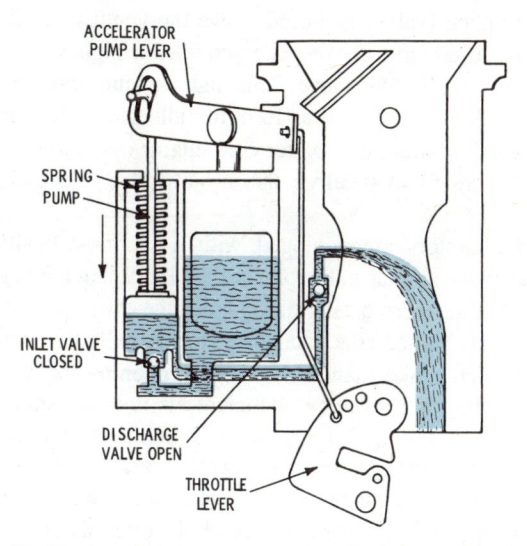

Fig. 11. The accelerator pump system during acceleration.

AUTOMOBILE GUIDE

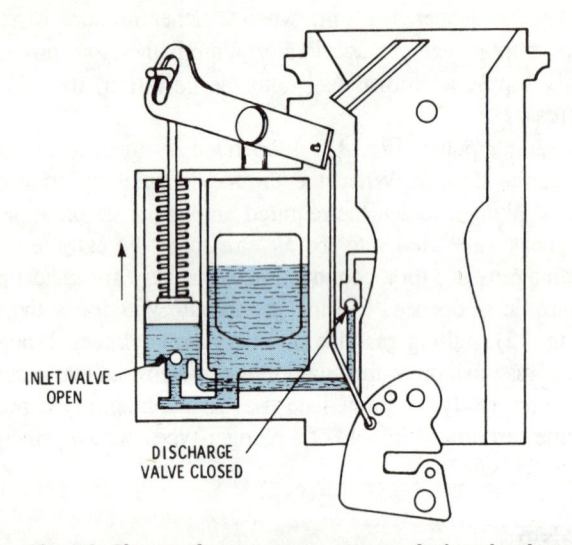

Fig. 12. The accelerator pump system during deceleration.

vaporization when starting and running a cold engine. In addition, the speed of the air through the carburetor is slow during starting which lowers the venturi effect, and little or no fuel is drawn from the main nozzle.

A choke plate (valve) is placed above the venturi, as shown in Fig. 13. When closed, this choke plate provides a high vacuum above as well as below the throttle valve. This high vacuum draws gasoline from the main fuel nozzle as well as from the idle ports, thus providing the extremely rich mixture needed for cold-engine operation. Choke valves may be operated manually, thermostatically, electrically, or by vacuum.

Most carburetors are equipped with a thermostatically-controlled automatic choke similar to the one in Fig. 14. When the engine is cold, the tension of the thermostatic spring holds the choke plate closed. After the engine has started, the vacuum piston is pulled downward by the vacuum in the intake manifold, partially opening the choke plate to prevent flooding and to allow sufficient air flow for smooth running. Exhaust-manifold gases heat the air in a tube leading into the thermostatic-spring housing. As the spring heats, it gradually loses its tension, allowing the vacuum piston to open the choke plate. When the engine reaches its operating temperature, the choke plate should be completely open. The choke plate in most carburetors is offset on its shaft so that

CARBURETORS AND AIR CLEANERS

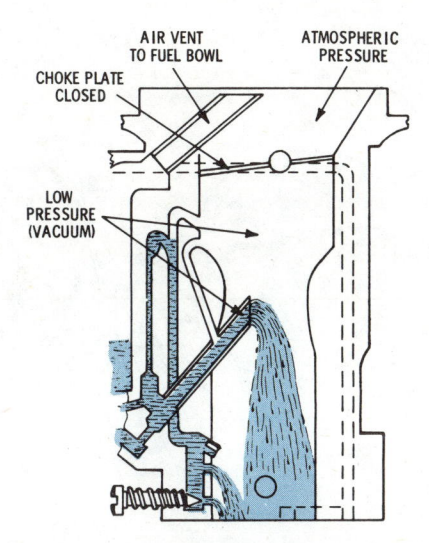

Fig. 13. The vacuum below the closed choke plate causes gasoline to flow from the main fuel nozzle and the idle ports.

the flow of air through the carburetor after the engine starts helps to hold the choke plate partially open against the thermostatic-spring tension.

Throttle-Return Check (Dashpot)

A dashpot is used on the carburetor of cars equipped with an automatic transmission. The purpose of this unit is to prevent the engine from stalling or hesitating when the throttle is closed suddenly. A dashpot (Fig. 15) operates in a manner similar to an automatic door check and this insures that the throttle will close gradually when the accelerator is released suddenly. The construction of dashpots differs depending on the manufacturer, and may be magnetically, hydraulically, or vacuum operated. Most units are sealed and are replaced rather than repaired if they become inoperative.

Throttle Linkage

Engine speed is controlled by the accelerator pedal moving a series of rods, levers, springs, etc., called the throttle linkage. This linkage is different in each particular make and model of car, and will even differ among the same make and model depending on the type of engine, carburetor, and transmission used. Besides opening and closing the

AUTOMOBILE GUIDE

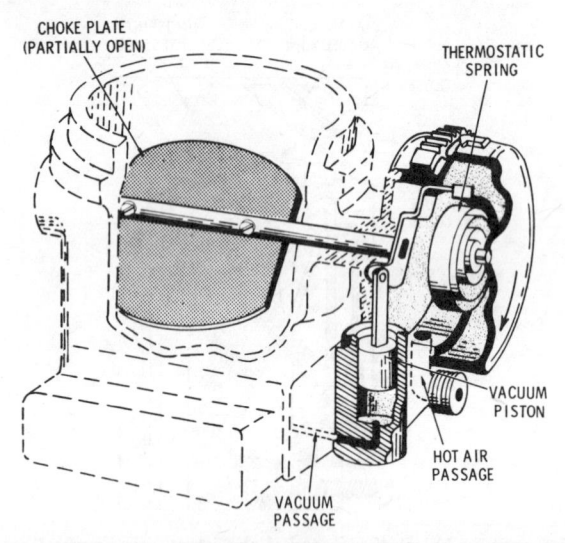

Fig. 14. A thermostatic spring and a vacuum piston automatically control the choking action on this carburetor.

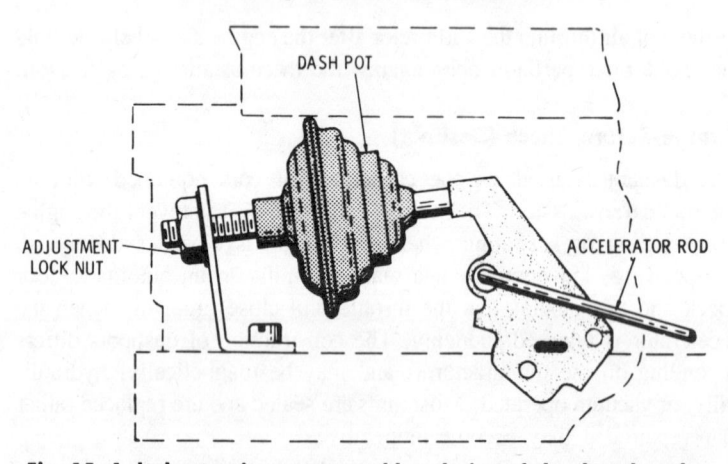

Fig. 15. A dashpot unit prevents sudden closing of the throttle valve.

throttle valve, the throttle linkage also activates the accelerator pump and the overdrive kickdown, and controls the automatic transmission shift speeds on cars so equipped.

Adjustments are provided on the throttle linkage to compensate for manufacturing tolerances and normal wear. Improper adjustment can change the idle speed, top speed, dashpot action, and the speeds at

CARBURETORS AND AIR CLEANERS

which the automatic transmission shifts, even if all other carburetor adjustments are correct.

CARBURETOR TYPES

Carburetors for domestic cars produced in the past ten years have been manufactured by *Carter, Holley, Ford, Rochester,* and *Stromberg*. The same basic carburetor may be used for several years on a particular make of car, with only minor changes being made from time to time. In other instances, there may be radical changes made each year with the model number of the carburetor remaining the same.

A carburetor may contain one, two, or four barrels. Also, the carburetor installation on a particular car may include a combination of two or three carburetors, each being a single, dual, or four-barrel unit.

An example of a single-barrel carburetor is shown in Fig. 16. This carburetor is used on certain 6-cylinder *Tempests* with a 215 cubic inch engine. The single-barrel carburetor shown in Fig. 17 is used on certain 223 cubic inch 6-cylinder *Ford* engines.

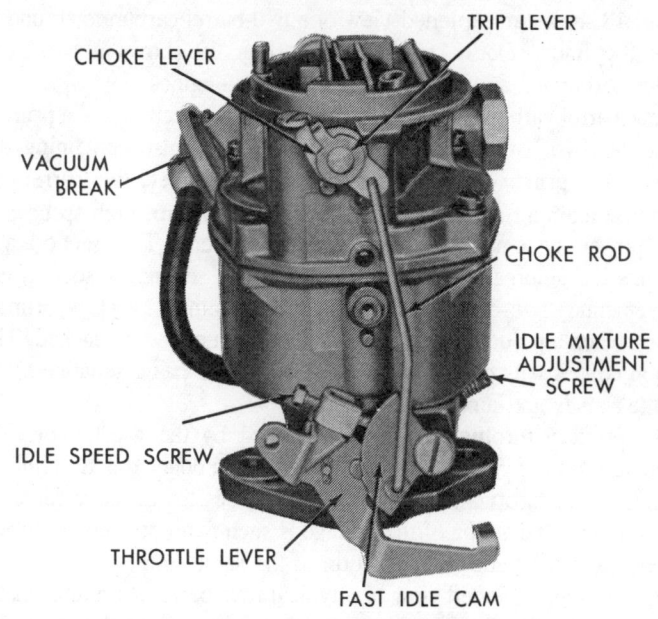

Courtesy Pontiac Motor Div., General Motors Corp.

Fig. 16. A ROCHESTER model BV single-barrel carburetor.

AUTOMOBILE GUIDE

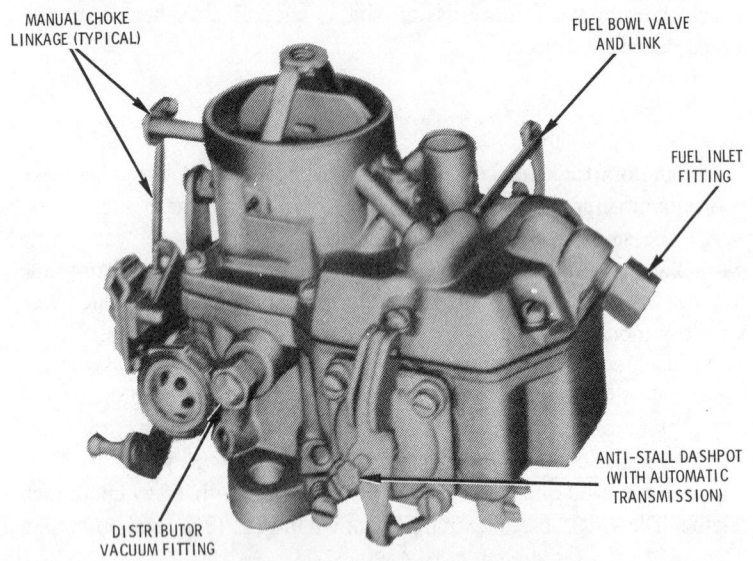

Fig. 17. A FORD single-barrel carburetor.

Fig. 18 shows an exploded view of a two-barrel carburetor found on some 8-cylinder *Dodge* engines while Fig. 19 shows a two-barrel *Holley* carburetor as used on some *Mercury* engines.

Four-barrel carburetors actually consist of two sections — a primary section of two barrels, and a secondary section, also containing two barrels. The primary section is essentially a complete two-barrel carburetor containing an idle system, low-speed system, high-speed system, power system, and an accelerating system. This section also contains the automatic-choke mechanism. The secondary section is a supplementary two-barrel carburetor which cuts in to assist the primary section when a predetermined car speed or engine load is reached. This section contains its own high-speed system, and has a separate set of throttle valves and auxiliary valves.

The primary throttle valves are operated by the accelerator. The secondary throttle valves are operated through a delayed-action linkage to the primary throttle-valve shaft which causes the primary valves to start to open. The action of the linkage is such that both sets of throttle valves reach the wide-open position at the same time.

Fig. 20 is an exploded view of a typical four-barrel carburetor that is used on a *Lincoln*. Combinations of carburetors are sometimes used to gain increased performance. An example of this is the dual four-barrel

CARBURETORS AND AIR CLEANERS

carburetor installation shown in Fig. 21. Each carburetor has a primary section (consisting of the two-barrelled forward half) and a secondary section (consisting of the two-barrelled rear half).

Fuel for idling is supplied by the primary section of both carburetors, but the fuel for all other operating conditions except hard acceleration or extreme high speeds is supplied by the primary section of the rear carburetor only. Only the rear carburetor is equipped with an automatic choke.

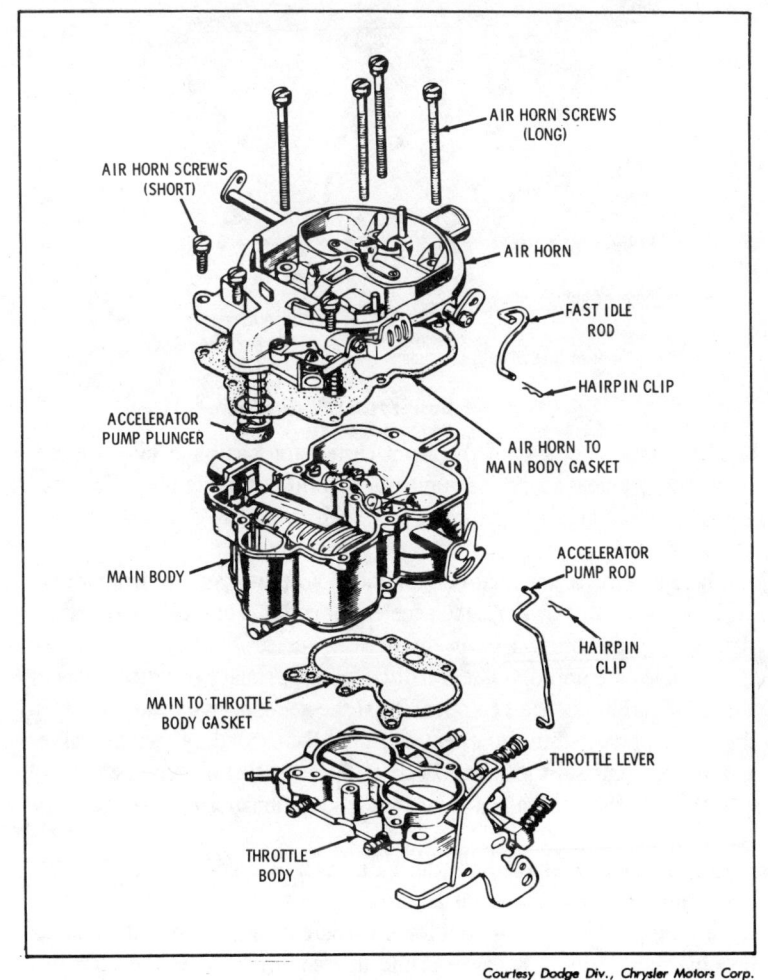

Courtesy Dodge Div., Chrysler Motors Corp.

Fig. 18. Exploded view of series WWC3 STROMBERG two-barrel carburetor.

Automobile Guide

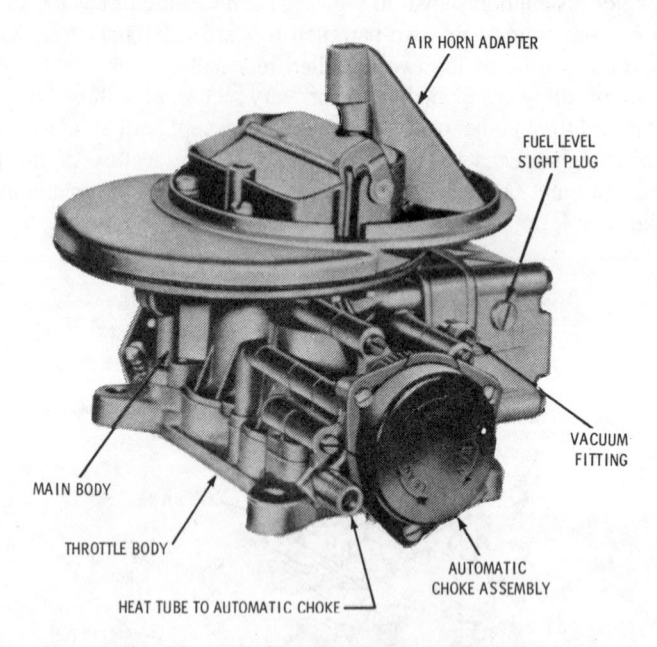

Fig. 19. A two-barrel HOLLEY carburetor.

The primary section of the front carburetor has fixed idle orifices, while the primary of the rear unit has both idle-mixture and idle-speed adjustments. Actually, the design is such that only one air-adjusting screw is used.

The operation of the dual-combination carburetor system from idle to wide open is as follows: As the accelerator pedal is gradually depressed, the primary throttle valves in the rear carburetor start to open. When these valves are approximately half open, the primary throttle valves of the front carburetor start to open. Next the secondary throttle valves in the rear carburetor start to open, and last, the secondary throttle valves in the front unit start to open. Each of the four sections open at such a rate that all throttle valves reach the wide-open position at the same time.

Combinations of three and four carburetors are sometimes used, but these are usually custom installations. The throttle linkage becomes rather complex with each additional carburetor added and adjustments become more critical because of the interaction between the carburetors. To achieve proper operation, trial and error is sometimes required.

CARBURETORS AND AIR CLEANERS

CARBURETOR ADJUSTMENTS

Adjusting a carburetor as part of a routine engine tune-up is comparatively simple. It is often more of a problem to locate the correct rod or screw than it is to adjust it. If the carburetor does not respond properly to routine adjustment a more "in depth" diagnosis is indicated. An electronic engine diagnostic center, such as the one shown in Fig. 22 is often used.

If the problem is determined to be the carburetor, it is usually necessary to disassemble it for cleaning and repairs. This phase of carburetor service, once outside the capabilities of the average car owner because of special tools and equipment required, is now possible. All necessary gauges and specific information for assembly is included with most carburetor repair kits.

Because of the large number of different models and types of carburetors — as well as the fact that information is included with the kit, the disassembly and internal repairs of carburetors will not be discussed in detail.

Inlet Fuel Filters

Most carburetors are equipped with some type of inlet fuel filter. This filter is essential to trap any rust or dirt particles that may have slipped past the fuel tank or fuel pump filters. Some filters are of the cartridge type and are secured to the fuel line just before the carburetor by clamps. To replace this type of filter, remove the inlet and outlet clamps (discard), slide out and discard the old filter. Install the new filter and clamps. Tighten both clamps securely, but do not overtighten.

Other filters are of the internal type, located just behind the inlet line fitting of the carburetor. To service this type of filter, proceed as follows:

1. Disconnect the fuel line at the carburetor with the correct size wrenches.
2. Remove the filter (or screen) and any gaskets or springs.
3. Wash the filter element or screen in solvent and dry with an air hose.
4. Replace the filter, gaskets, and springs in the correct order and direction. Some filters or screens are directional (Fig. 23) and should be installed with the larger, or open end toward the fuel inlet.
5. Always replace a paper-type filter with a new one.

Automobile Guide

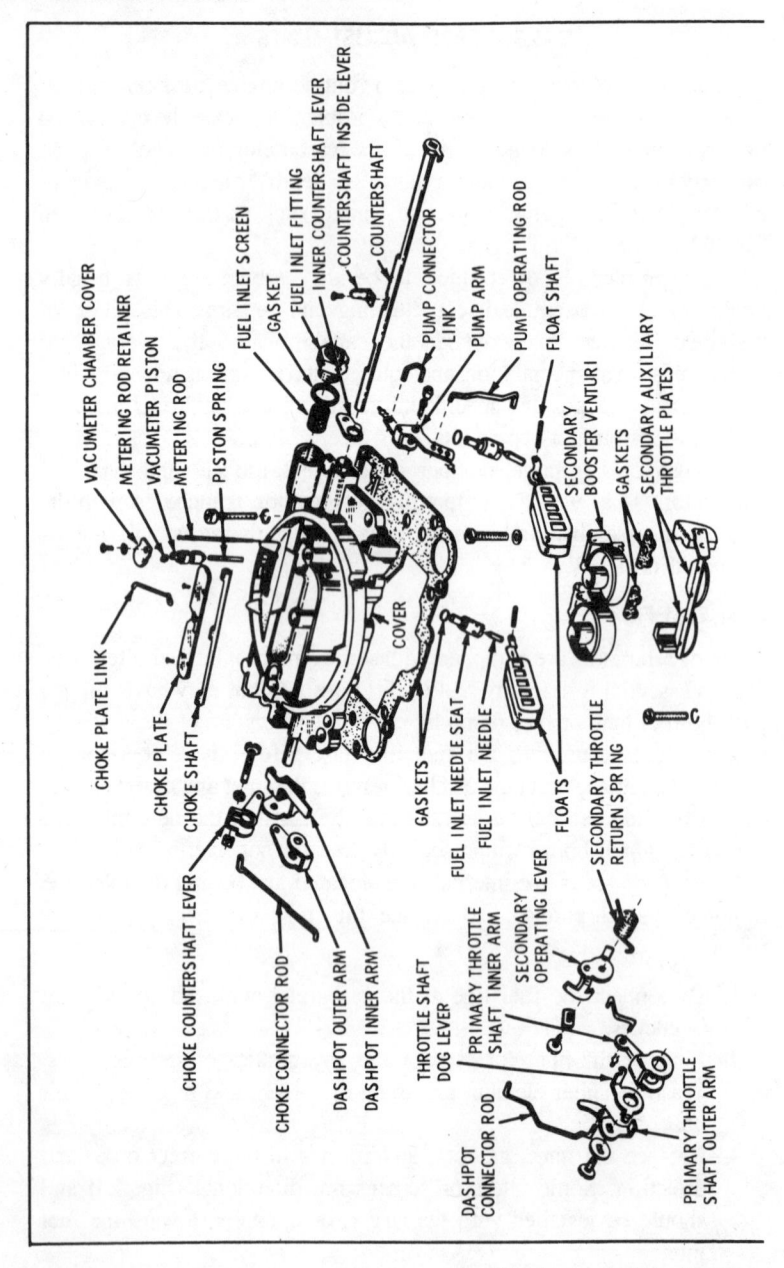

Fig. 20. An exploded view of a

Carburetors and Air Cleaners

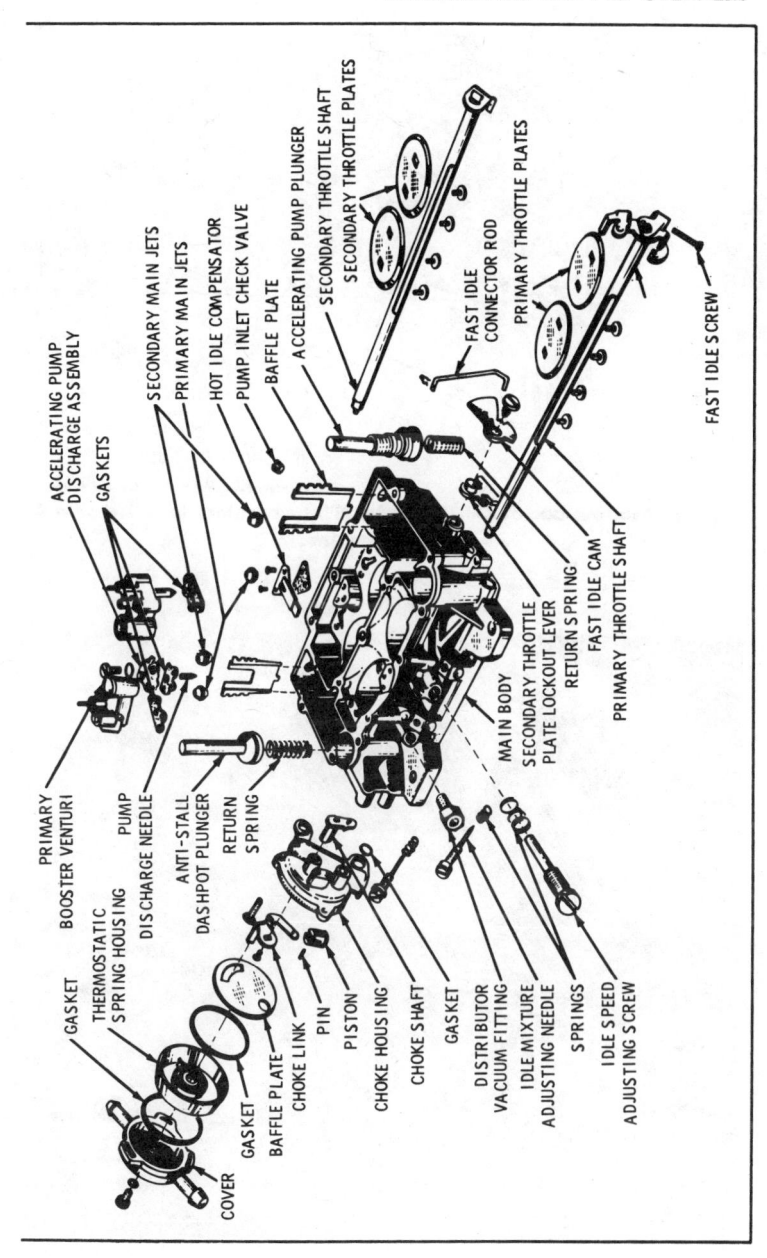

typical four-barrel carburetor.

149

AUTOMOBILE GUIDE

OMIT WHEN SYNCHROMESH
TRANSMISSION IS USED.

Courtesy Buick Motor Div., General Motors Corp.

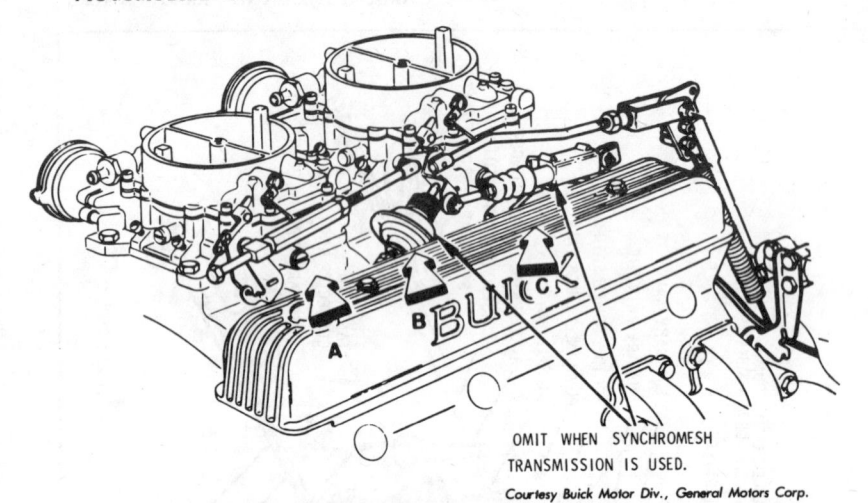

Fig. 21. Two four-barrel CARTER model AFB carburetors installed on a 425 BUICK engine.

Courtesy Sun Electric Corp.

Fig. 22. Using an electronic engine tester to test carburetor performance.

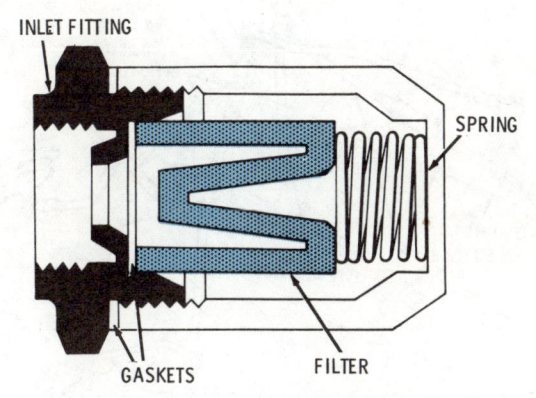

CARBURETORS AND AIR CLEANERS

Fig. 23. Cross-sectional view of the components in the fuel inlet of a ROCHESTER model BV carburetor.

Courtesy Pontiac Motor Div., General Motors Corp.

The rods, levers, springs, etc. which make up the throttle linkage should be inspected for looseness and binding. Check for proper adjustment of the linkage by completely depressing the accelerator pedal and noting whether the throttle plates are completely open, and whether they close completely when the pedal is released.

NOTE: On cars equipped with an automatic transmission, care must be taken not to disturb the linkage to the transmission. Note the point at which the transmission linkage is connected to the accelerator linkage. Adjustment of the accelerator linkage can usually be made between this point and the accelerator pedal without disturbing the linkage to the transmission. Follow the adjustment procedure recommended by the manufacturer.

An example of the throttle linkage on a car equipped with an automatic transmission is shown in Fig. 24.

Manual Choke

There are very few cars on the road today that are equipped with manual chokes. On those so equipped you will find a cable extending from the carburetor to the instrument panel, and adjustments of this type may be made as follows:

1. Pull the choke control knob fully out and check to see whether the choke plate in the carburetor is fully closed. If not, loosen the set

AUTOMOBILE GUIDE

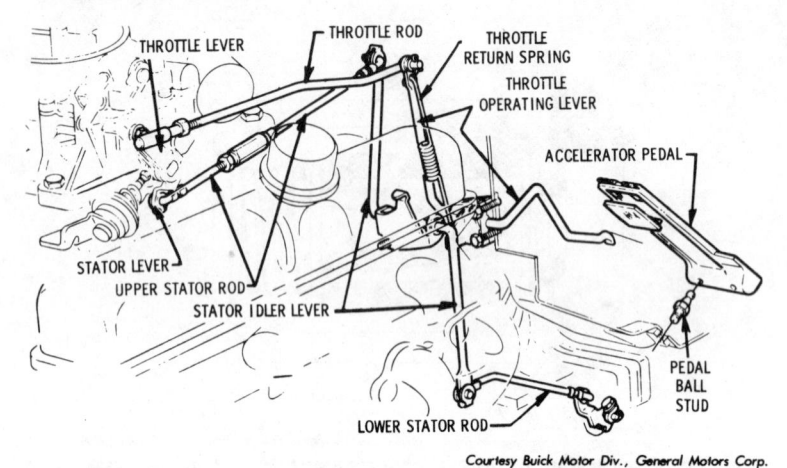

Fig. 24. The linkage to the throttle and automatic transmission in a BUICK is typical of the linkage on many automobiles.

Courtesy Buick Motor Div., General Motors Corp.

    screw holding the choke cable wire to the choke linkage on the carburetor, and close the choke plate by hand. Tighten the set screw and proceed to the next step.
2. Push the choke and control knob in completely. The choke plate in the carburetor should be in the full-open position.
3. Check for free operation by moving the control knob in and out. If it binds or hangs up at any point, check the entire length of the cable for sharp bends, kinks, or mechanical damage. Reroute the cable to remove any sharp bends, or replace it if kinks or cable damage is present.

Choke Rod (Automatic Choke)

    On cars equipped with an automatic choke, a choke rod connects the choke-plate lever to a fast-idle cam. This choke rod is sometimes called the fast-idle rod, and is shown on the carburetor in Fig. 25. The linkage shown is the direct type, although an indirect linkage may be found on some carburetors. To locate the choke rod, move the choke plate by hand and observe the movement of the various rods. Adjustment is sometimes required in order to cause the choke plate to open and close properly. This adjustment is usually made by bending the choke rod the necessary amount at the point specified by the manufacturer to lengthen or shorten it. The manufacturer's instructions should be carefully followed when making this adjustment.

Carburetors and Air Cleaners

An intermediate choke rod that is connected between the choke-plate lever and the automatic-choke mechanism is used in some carburetors. When the carburetor is so equipped, as in Fig. 26, this intermediate rod must be adjusted whenever the fast-idle (main) choke rod has been adjusted. Follow the manufacturer's instructions for making this adjustment. The procedure varies depending on the make and model of carburetor, but the general method is as follows:

1. Loosen the cover screws on the automatic-choke housing.
2. Hold the choke valve closed by lifting up on the intermediate choke lever.
3. Line up the specified mark on the automatic-choke cover with the index mark on the housing.
4. Tighten the cover screws on the housing.

Accelerator-Pump Linkage

A pump rod connects the throttle lever to the accelerator-pump lever (or arm). The construction of this linkage varies widely with the make and model of carburetor, but a typical example is illustrated in Fig. 27.

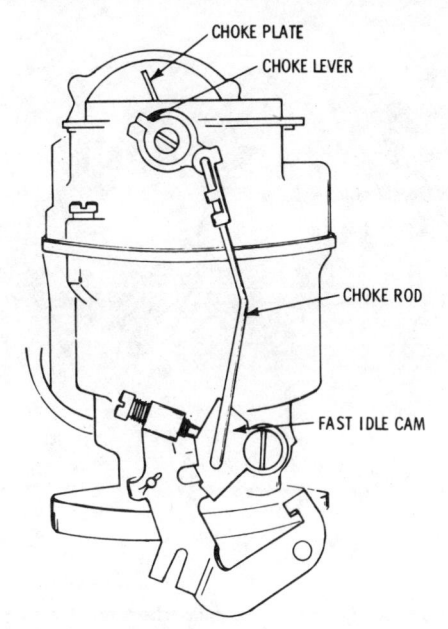

Fig. 25. An example of a direct choke linkage.

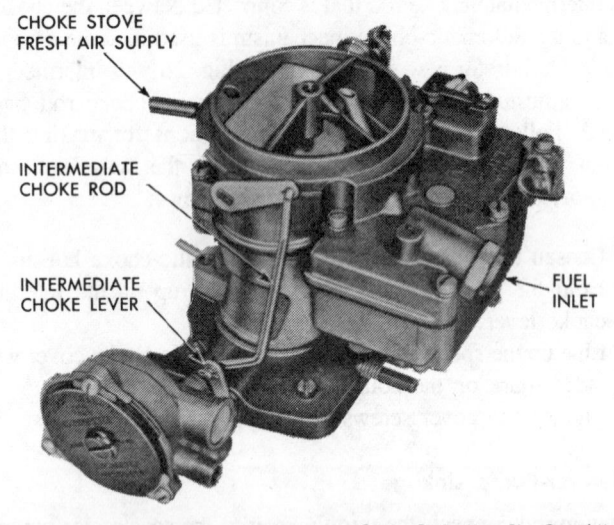

AUTOMOBILE GUIDE

Fig. 26. An example of a carburetor with an intermediate choke rod. This carburetor is a ROCHESTER model 2GC with two barrels.

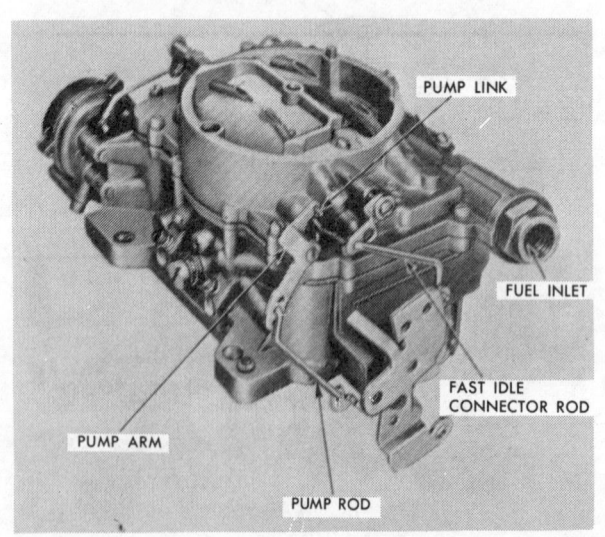

Fig. 27. A CARTER model AFB four-barrel carburetor showing the accelerator pump linkage.

The operation of the accelerator pump can be checked by looking in the air horn and rapidly moving the throttle lever. A noticeable stream of gasoline should spurt into the carburetor throat each time the throttle lever is moved. If no gasoline is noticed, the carburetor must be disassembled to check and repair the accelerator pump.

Movement of the throttle lever also allows a check to be made of the linkage to the pump. Some sort of adjustment is provided to lengthen or shorten the pump stroke for different temperature conditions. This adjustment feature is usually in the form of holes in either the throttle lever or pump arm (these holes are in the pump arm in Fig. 27). The pump stroke is changed by moving the accelerator-pump rod from one to another of the holes as specified for the season of the year. The adjustment of the pump stroke is made on some carburetors by bending the linkage rod.

Power-Valve Linkage

The linkage for the power valve does not have an external adjustment. Checking and adjustment requires disassembly of the carburetor and the use of special gauges and tools. The procedures and specifications recommended by the manufacturer must be strictly followed.

Idle Vent Valve Linkage

An idle vent valve (also called bowl vent and anti-percolator valve) will be found on many late-model carburetors. The purpose of this valve is to vent the vapors from the fuel bowl to the atmosphere when the throttle is closed. An example of the adjustment being made on this valve is pictured in Fig. 28. Some carburetors require partial disassembly to adjust this valve.

Secondary-Throttle Linkage

Four-barrel carburetors are essentially two dual carburetors divided into primary and secondary sides. The primary portion includes all circuits from idle to full power while the secondary side contains a lesser number of circuits and usually does not come into operation until some point between one-half and full-throttle position.

The secondary side of the carburetor is connected by a linkage to the primary side. On some carburetors, this linkage is made by a rod (Fig. 29) which must be bent in making adjustments. On certain other carburetors, the secondary system is not actuated by an external

AUTOMOBILE GUIDE

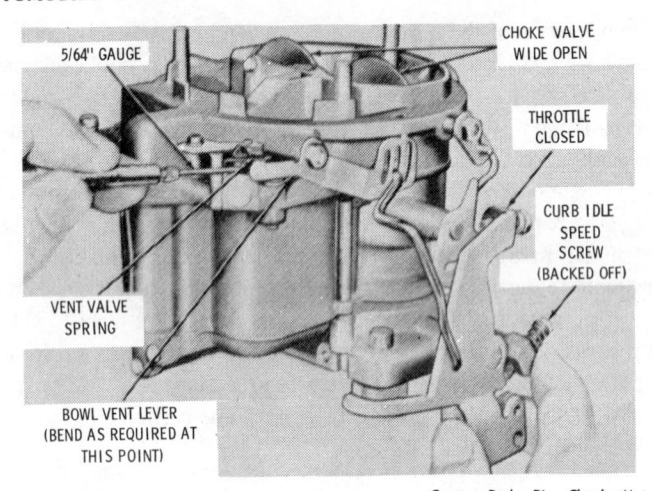

Fig. 28. Adjustment of the idle vent valve on a STROMBERG model WWC3 carburetor.

linkage, but by a vacuum-operated diaphragm connected to the secondary system. There are other types of secondary-throttle linkage, but the two just mentioned are the most common.

Choke and Fast-Idle Cam Linkage

To find and trace this linkage on a carburetor that is unfamiliar, the sequence of operation will be helpful. The thermostatic spring in the

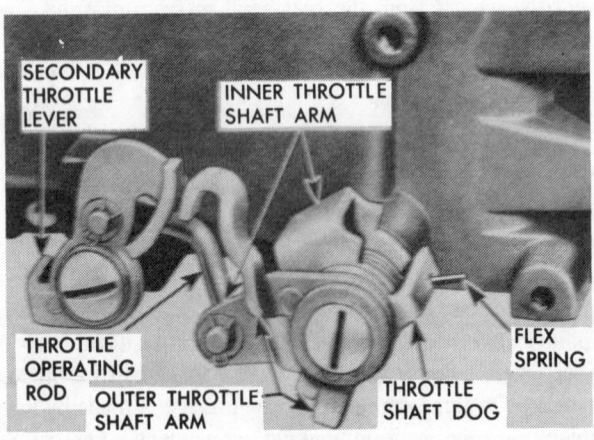

Fig. 29. Secondary throttle linkage on a CARTER model AFB carburetor.

CARBURETORS AND AIR CLEANERS

automatic choke closes the choke valve when the engine is cold. Since the choke rod is connected to the fast-idle cam, the closing choke lifts the cam until the fast-idle screw on the throttle lever contacts the highest point on the cam, providing a faster engine-idle speed. As the engine warms up, the choke opens, dropping the fast-idle cam which causes the idle screw to contact a lower step on the cam. Thus, the idle speed of the engine is reduced.

Anytime the engine temperature is below approximately 70°, the choke will be closed. The choke cannot completely close, however, as long as the fast-idle screw remains on the low step of the fast-idle cam. Therefore, when checking choke action, open the throttle slightly, which allows the fast-idle cam to rotate, closing the choke valve completely.

There are many variations in the choke linkage on different carburetors. The linkage can be traced on unfamiliar units in the following manner: Open the throttle slightly and move the choke plate with your fingers; look for movement of some type of arm at one end of the choke-plate shaft or countershaft; follow the moving parts to the choke linkage which operates the fast-idle cam. The cam is linked with the primary-throttle lever which can be identified by the idle adjusting screw and the connection running to the accelerator pedal. When these parts have been located, the operation of the choke and fast-idle cam linkage can be checked as follows:

1. Open the throttle slightly and check the action of the choke linkage. It should move without sticking or binding and without any looseness or free play.
2. With the engine warm, lift and release the choke rod. It should drop the idle cam of its own accord because of the weight of the choke-rod lever and/or any counterweights provided.

Choke Unloader

If the engine becomes flooded for any reason, the choke valve can be partially opened by depressing the accelerator pedal to the full extent of its travel. This causes an arm or projection (unloader) on the throttle lever to contact and rotate the fast-idle cam which forces the choke valve open. Check the operation of the unloader by opening the throttle fully. The choke plate should open partially under this condition. If adjustment is necessary, it is usually made by bending the unloader tang (Fig. 30) on the throttle lever. Follow the manufacturer's recommendations for proper adjustment.

AUTOMOBILE GUIDE

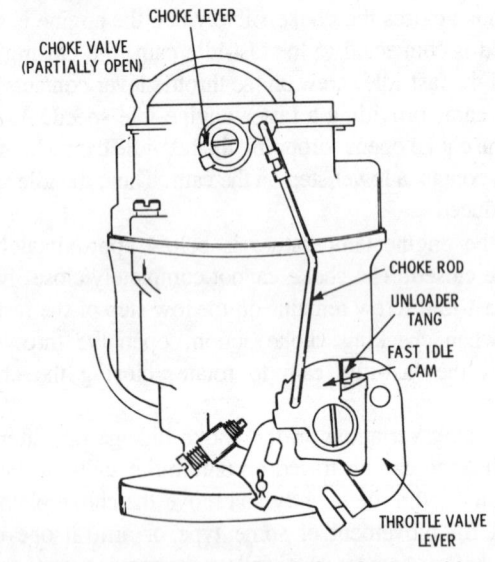

Fig. 30. The unloader partially opens the choke plate at wide-open throttle.

Automatic Choke

The automatic-choke mechanism on most cars is similar to the one shown in Fig. 31. This type of automatic choke is equipped with a thermostatic spring and a vacuum piston. The thermostatic spring coils up when cold and unwinds when warm. Thus, when the engine is cold, the spring holds the choke piston inward and the choke plate in a closed position (through mechanical linkage) prior to engine start.

When the engine starts, manifold vacuum acting on the piston in the choke housing moves the piston outward against the tension of the thermostatic spring, partially opening the choke plate to prevent stalling. As the engine warms up, manifold vacuum draws warm air from a heat chamber in the exhaust manifold. This warm air enters the choke housing and heats the thermostatic spring, causing it to unwind. Thus, the tension of the spring gradually decreases as the temperature of the air from the heat chamber increases, causing the choke plate to gradually open to the wide-open position when the engine reaches operating temperature.

If this type of choke requires adjustment, the alignment of the scribe marks on the choke cover with the index mark should be checked. Realign to specifications by loosening the three cover-retaining screws and rotating the cover the necessary amount (Fig. 32). If the choke is

CARBURETORS AND AIR CLEANERS

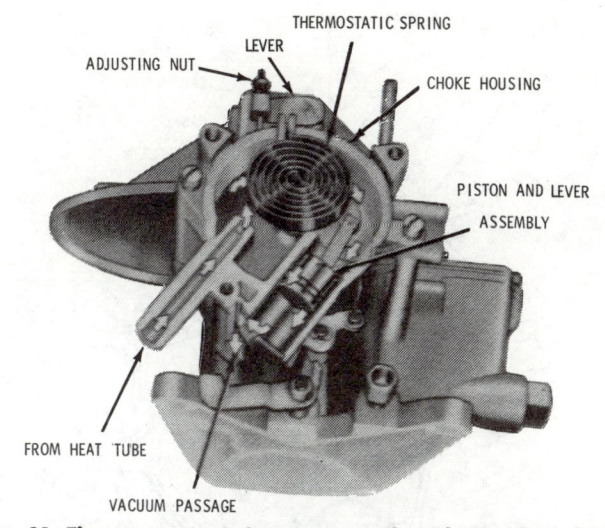

Fig. 31. The automatic choke system used on the two-barrel FORD carburetor.

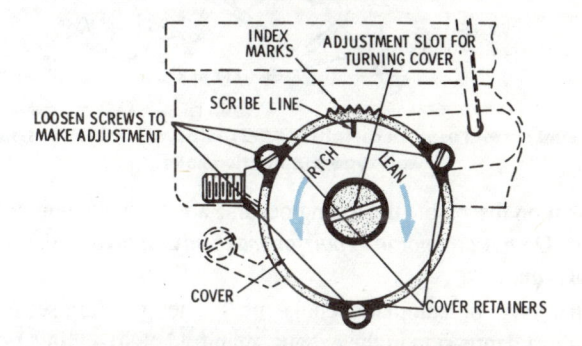

Fig. 32. Automatic choke adjustment.

sticking or sluggish, it may be necessary to remove the cover and free-up the mechanism. Special solvents are available with which to free the choke shaft and piston. If this does not correct the situation, the unit must be removed for repair or replacement.

The automatic choke used on most *Chrysler*-made cars is a well-type mounted in a cavity at the exhaust crossover passage of the intake manifold (Fig. 33). Other than cleaning, the choke requires no service. It is important, however, that the choke unit works freely in the well and at the choke shaft. Move the choke rod up and down to check for free

AUTOMOBILE GUIDE

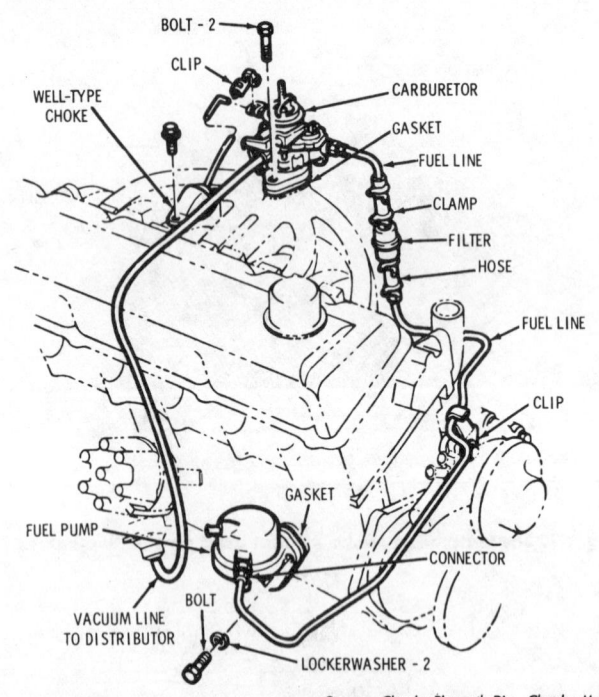

Courtesy Chrysler Plymouth Div., Chrysler Motors Corp.

Fig. 33. Fuel system used on certain PLYMOUTHS and VALIANTS showing the well-type automatic choke.

movement on the pivot. If binding occurs, a new choke unit should be installed. *Do not attempt to repair or make any change in the setting of the choke unit.*

Another type of automatic choke uses a temperature-sensing coil mounted in a depression in the exhaust manifold of six-cylinder engines (Fig. 34), and directly over the exhaust crossover passage in the intake manifold on V8 engines (Fig. 35). These automatic chokes are adjusted by bending the choke rod at the offset bend according to the instructions of the manufacturer. Lengthening the rod provides a richer mixture, while shortening the rod provides a leaner mixture.

Idle-Speed and Mixture Adjustments

The curb (hot) idle speed and mixture adjustments are relatively simple to make once the correct screw or screws have been located. The curb idle-speed screw is usually located either on the throttle lever, a

Carburetors and Air Cleaners

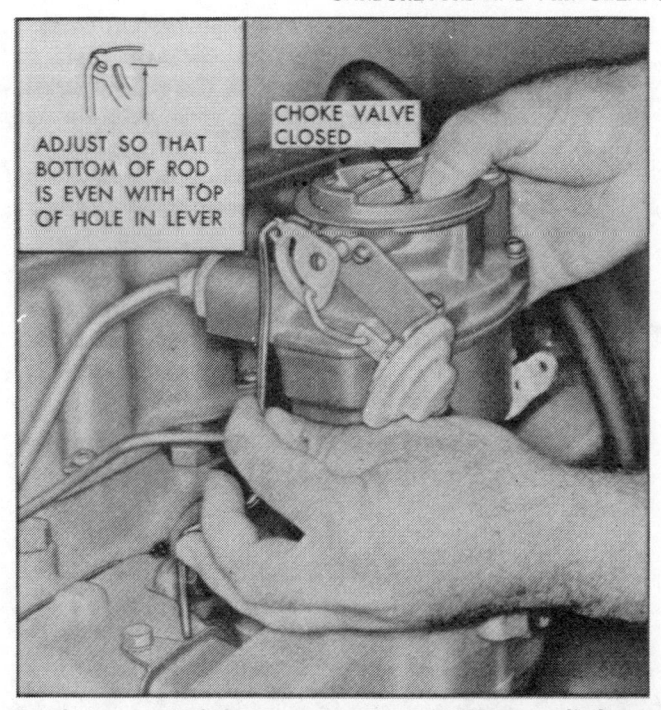

Fig. 34. The automatic choke arrangement on a CHEVELLE 6-cylinder engine.

cam, or in the carburetor body. This screw can be located by moving the throttle linkage and tracing the movement to the screw which stops the movement when the throttle is returned to the closed position (choke valve must be wide open). Do not confuse this screw with a separate fast-idle screw used on some carburetors (Fig. 36). The curb idle speed is always set with the engine at operating temperature (choke valve wide open).

The fast idle-speed screw is located by tracing the choke-rod linkage to the fast-idle cam. The fast-idle screw is the stop screw which contacts the highest step or point on the fast-idle cam when the throttle and choke are in the closed position. Some carburetors have only a single idle-speed screw (Fig. 37). With this type, the fast idle will be correct when the correct curb-idle adjustment has been made with the idle screw contacting the lowest step or point on the fast-idle cam.

Screws for adjusting the idle fuel mixture are provided in the carburetor throttle body, usually near the lower edge. Only one idle fuel-mixture screw is used on single-barrel carburetors (Fig. 38), while

Automobile Guide

Fig. 35. The automatic choke arrangement on a Chevelle 8-cylinder engine.

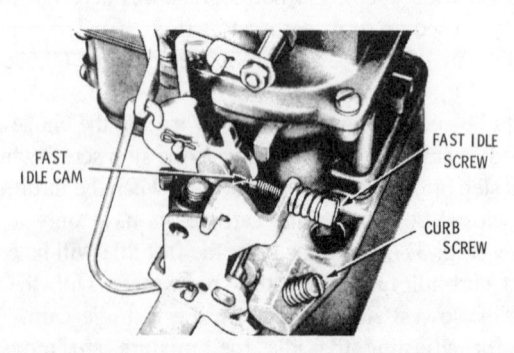

Courtesy Dodge Div., Chrysler Motors Corp.

Fig. 36. Some carburetors have a separate fast-idle adjustment in addition to the curb-idle adjustment.

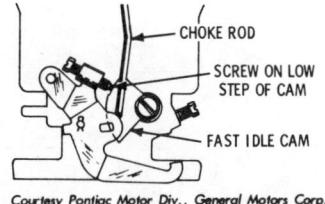

CARBURETORS AND AIR CLEANERS

Fig. 37. A single idle-speed screw is used on some carburetors. When the curb-idle speed is adjusted correctly, the fast-idle speed will automatically be correct.

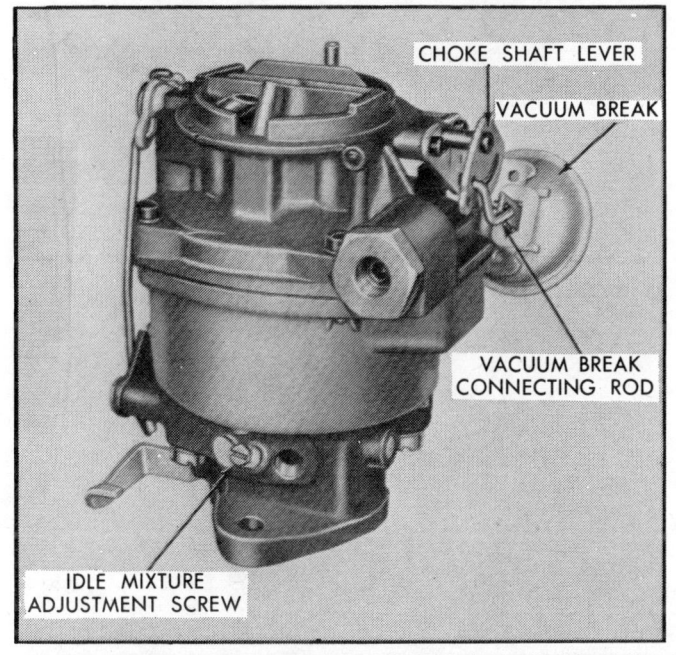

Courtesy Pontiac Motor Div., General Motors Corp.

Courtesy Pontiac Motor Div., General Motors Corp.

Fig. 38. A single-barrel carburetor has only one idle fuel-mixture adjusting screw.

Fig. 39 shows two idle-mixture screws on a four-barrel unit. The two mixture screws on some *Holley* carburetors are recessed in the carburetor body, as shown in Fig. 40, one on the left side and one on the right.

The actual adjustment of the curb idle speed, the fast idle speed, and the idle fuel mixture should not be made until all other systems that might affect engine performance have been checked and corrected. These include compression, fuel pump operation, manifold heat-control valve, throttle linkage, and ignition timing. After these have all been

Automobile Guide

Fig. 39. A four-barrel carburetor has two idle fuel-mixture adjustment screws.

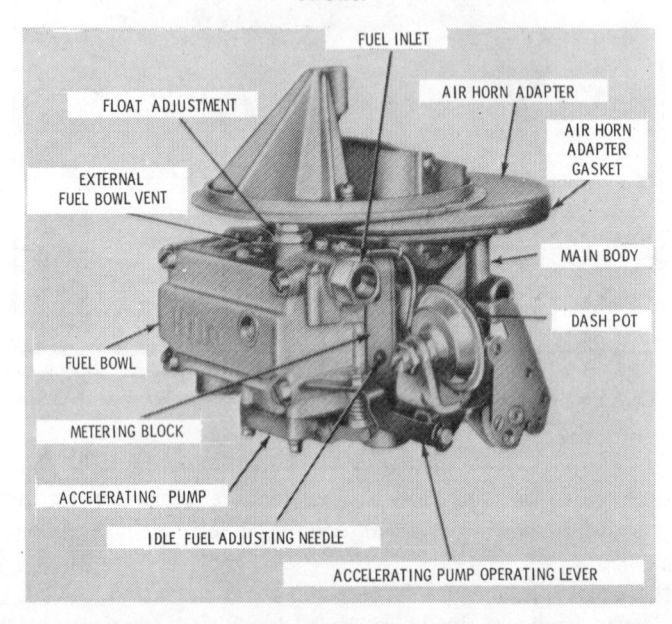

Fig. 40. The idle-mixture screws on two- and four-barrel HOLLEY carburetors are located differently than on other makes. Shown is the location on a two-barrel unit. The screws on a four-barrel HOLLEY carburetor are in a similar position.

164

checked and corrected, use the following procedure to set the curb-idle speed and idle fuel mixture:

1. Slowly turn the idle fuel-mixture screw clockwise until it gently seats. *Do not use a screwdriver — use fingers only.* Then turn the screw out (counterclockwise) the recommended number of turns. Backing the screw out from 1 to 1½ turns, unless otherwise specified, will usually give an average starting point for the adjustment.
2. Start the engine and set the hand brake. Allow the engine to run until it reaches its normal operating temperature. Follow the car manufacturer's recommendations as to the position of the shift lever, whether lights should be on or off, whether certain vacuum lines to accessories should be disconnected and taped, etc.
3. Turn the curb idle-speed screw slowly in or out until the engine is running at the idle speed specified by the manufacturer.
4. Turn the idle fuel-mixture screw slowly clockwise (toward a lean mixture) until the engine just starts to lag or run unevenly.
5. Now turn the screw slowly counterclockwise (toward a richer mixture) until the engine begins to run evenly.
6. Finally, set the idle fuel-mixture screw to a position midway between the lean and rich positions. If this is not the smoothest running idle position, compromise toward the rich (counterclockwise) position. When the carburetor has two idle-mixture screws, perform Steps 4, 5, and 6 for each screw.
7. If the idle speed of the engine has changed due to these adjustments, reset the idle-speed screw to obtain the specified speed.

Some carburetors have no fast-idle adjustment. When the curb idle speed is correct, the fast idle speed will automatically be correct. For those carburetors, however, that do have a fast-idle adjustment, use the following procedure:

1. Open the throttle enough to permit moving the fast-idle cam until the fast-idle screw contacts the high step on the cam.
2. Turn the fast-idle screw to obtain the specified fast-idle speed.

Multiple-Carburetor Adjustments

Some cars are equipped with multiple carburetors, such as three two-barrel carburetors, or two four-barrel units (see Fig. 21). The basic checks and adjustments described for single carburetors are applicable here, with the following variation.

On a three two-barrel installation, the center carburetor is a standard two-barrel unit and is adjusted in the normal manner. The front and rear carburetors are controlled from the center unit by a combination of vacuum and mechanical linkage. Since the front and rear units do not contain choke, idle, or part-throttle systems, no idle speed or idle fuel-mixture adjustments are necessary.

Check the vacuum connections for tightness, and the mechanical connections for free and smooth operation. Remove the air cleaners and, with engine running, open the throttle all the way. The throttle plates on all three carburetors should be fully opened under this condition. If they are not, adjustment of the vacuum valves or the front-to-rear carburetor throttle rod should be made as recommended by the manufacturer.

Each carburetor of a dual four-barrel installation is basically the same as the carburetor of a single four-barrel installation. Both contain idle-speed and mixture screws which must be adjusted until the best engine performance is obtained at the correct idle speed.

Linkage adjustments vary because some dual four-barrel installations are designed so both carburetors operate together from idle to full throttle. In other installations, the second carburetor starts to open when the first carburetor is at about half throttle. Thus, the manufacturer's instructions should be referred to when making linkage adjustments.

Dashpot Adjustments

The location of the dashpot varies on cars so equipped. Some are mounted on the body of the carburetor (Fig. 41), some are mounted either on the firewall in the engine compartment or at some point on the engine, as in Fig. 42, and in a few instances the dashpot is a built-in component inside the carburetor. The adjustment of all but the built-in units is similar. With the built-in dashpot, adjustment is made by bending the external lever that connects with the throttle linkage.

The adjustment of all but the built-in type dashpots is similar to the following procedure:

1. Complete the idle-speed and mixture adjustments and have the engine at operating temperature.
2. Hold the dashpot plunger in as far as possible with a screwdriver and measure the clearance between the plunger and the contact connected to the throttle mechanism (Fig. 43).

CARBURETORS AND AIR CLEANERS

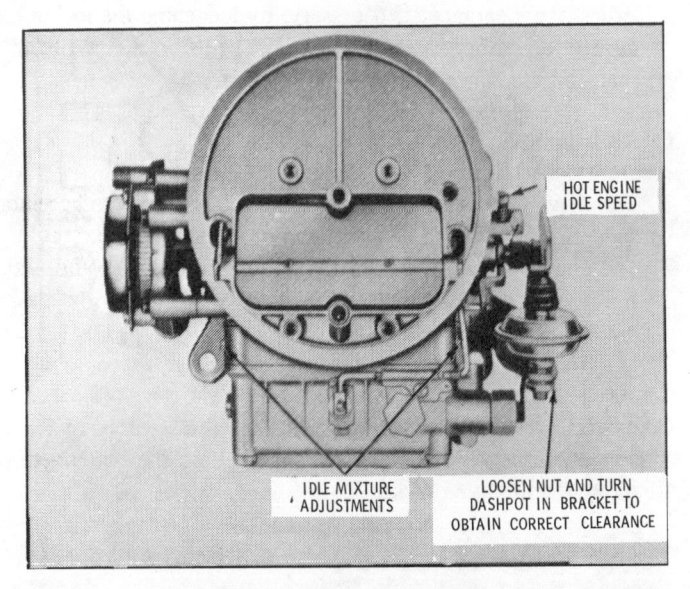

Fig. 41. Some dashpots are located on the body of the carburetor.

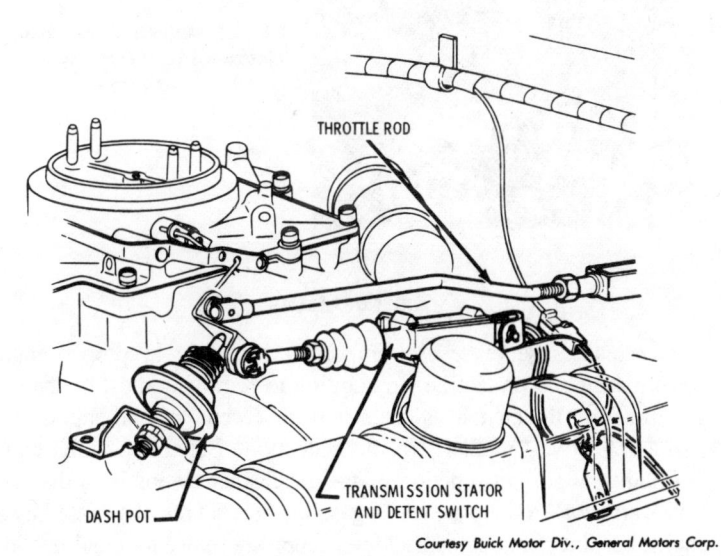

Courtesy Buick Motor Div., General Motors Corp.

Fig. 42. The dashpot on some BUICK automobiles is mounted on the engine instead of the carburetor.

AUTOMOBILE GUIDE

3. Adjust the clearance, if necessary, by loosening the locknut and turning the dashpot assembly in or out of its bracket to obtain the specified clearance. Tighten the locknut.

Check for correct adjustment as follows:

1. Test drive the car. Make a fast start, then release the accelerator suddenly, braking to a quick stop at the same time.
2. The engine should not hold at a high r/min, nor should it stall.
3. If the engine stalls, reduce the clearance between the dashpot plunger and throttle linkage.
4. If the engine rolls or surges, increase the clearance.

Complete carburetor servicing requires the disassembly of the unit and the use of special tools and gauges. Follow the manufacturer's instructions for this type of service.

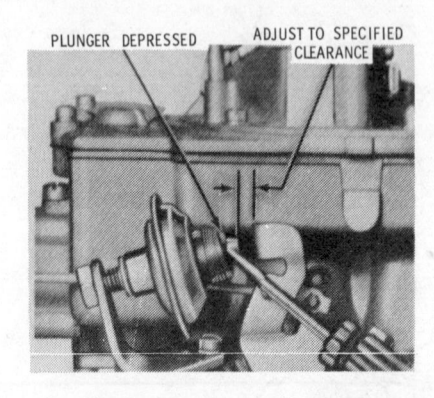

Fig. 43. Adjusting the dashpot clearance on a FORD two-barrel carburetor.

AIR CLEANERS

Air cleaners serve several important functions in proper engine performance and protection. In addition to removing most of the dust and dirt from the air that is taken into the carburetor and engine, it is also an effective "muffler" for the reduction of engine air-inlet noise.

Another important function of the air cleaner assembly is that of a "flash arrestor" to help prevent a gasoline fire that may be caused by an engine backfire. An engine backfire occurs when, due to a malfunction, the ignition "fires" the gasoline mixture back through the carburetor inlet.

Carburetors and Air Cleaners

Most air cleaner assemblies are equipped with an automatic air inlet temperature control device. This device is designed to improve carburetor operation and engine warm-up by keeping the air entering the carburetor at a temperature of 100°F or higher.

Filters

There are three types of air filters found in the air cleaner assembly. They are; paper, polyurethane over expanded metal, and polyurethane over paper. Regardless of the type, it is recommended that the filter be serviced every 12,000 to 24,000 miles. It should be serviced at more frequent intervals if the car is used primarily in dusty areas.

To service the paper filter, it is simply replaced. The polyurethane over expanded metal is serviced by washing it in clean mineral spirits or kerosene after first removing it from its expanded metal frame. After washing, it is squeezed dry. Never shake, swing, or wring dry. This practice may tear or damage the element. Dip in light engine oil and squeeze out the excess. Reinstall over expanded metal frame and replace in air cleaner.

The polyurethane over paper filter is serviced in the same manner as the polyurethane over expanded metal. When servicing this type filter, (Fig. 44) the paper element is replaced.

Thermostatic Control

The thermostatic control usually consists of a temperature sensor, vacuum motor, control damper, vacuum control hoses, heat stove, and the stove to the damper pipe, as shown in Fig. 45. The vacuum motor, controlled by the sensor, operates the air control damper. This action regulates the flow of hot air and/or underhood air to the carburetor inlet. Specific testing procedures are outlined in manufacturers service manuals. "Typical" testing procedures of the thermostatic air control are as follows:

1. Make a visual check of all connections, heat pipe, and hoses. Check for kinked or damaged hoses. Repair or replace any found to be defective.
2. Remove air cleaner cover and install temperature gauge (requires a special tool) as close as possible to the sensor. Re-install cover, less wing nut. Observe damper door through snorkel; passage should be open. If not, check for binds in linkage.

AUTOMOBILE GUIDE

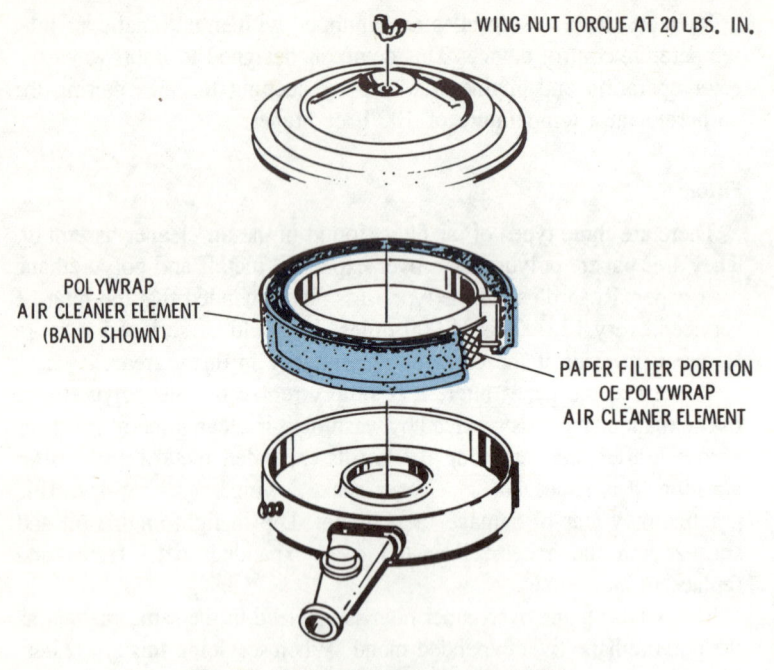

Fig. 44. Polyurethane-over-paper filter.

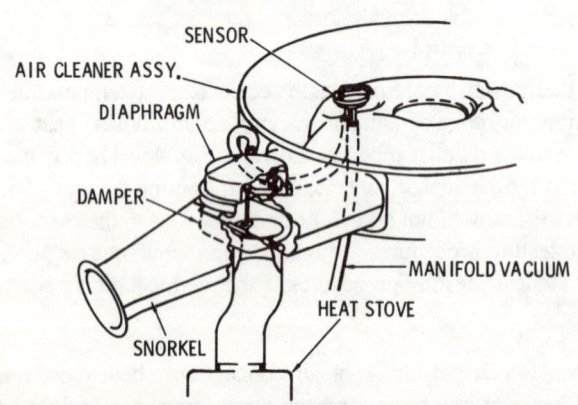

Fig. 45. Air filter thermostatic control assembly (typical).

NOTE: *Temperature must be below 85°F for this test.*

3. Start engine and allow to run at idle speed. If temperature is below 85°F, the snorkel passage should be closed. As soon as the

Carburetors and Air Cleaners

damper door begins to open, remove air cleaner cover and note temperature reading. It should be between 85°F and 115°F.

NOTE: If damper did not close completely when engine was started or did not open properly at the correct temperature, proceed with the vacuum motor test, step 4.

4. Turn off engine and disconnect vacuum hose at sensor unit. Apply minimum of 9.0" Hg vacuum. Damper door should completely close. With vacuum applied, clamp or bend hose to trap vacuum. Door should remain closed. If it does not, there is a vacuum leak in the hose or diaphragm assembly. Repair or replace as necessary.

NOTE: 9.0" Hg of vacuum can be pulled by mouth for this test.

CAUTION: Do not tighten the air cleaner wing nut tighter than 20 inch-pounds. Overtightening can distort the carburetor housing causing binding of the choke valve (butterfly).

CARBURETOR TROUBLES AND REMEDIES

Symptoms and Possible Causes   *Possible Remedies*

Flooding or Leaking Carburetor

(a) Cracked carburetor body.
(b) Defective main-body and/or fuel-bowl gasket.
(c) High fuel level or float setting.
(d) Fuel inlet needle not seating properly.
(e) Rupture of accelerator pump diaphragm.
(f) Excessive fuel pump pressure.
(g) Defective power valve gasket.

(a) Replace cracked unit.
(b) Replace defective gasket(s).
(c) Adjust float level.
(d) Inspect for dirt or wear. Remove dirt or replace worn parts.
(e) Replace diaphragm.
(f) Repair or replace fuel pump.
(g) Replace gasket.

AUTOMOBILE GUIDE

Symptoms and Possible Causes

(h) Ruptured power valve diaphragm.
(i) Leaking or defective carburetor float.

Possible Remedies

(h) Replace diaphragm.
(i) Repair or replace float.

Hard Starting

(a) Improper starting procedure causing engine flooding.
(b) Improper fuel level in carburetor.
(c) Improper idle adjustments.
(d) Fuel-inlet valve sticking or improperly seating.
(e) Incorrect fuel pump pressure.
(f) Improper or defective carburetor gasket and spacer combinations.
(g) Automatic choke set incorrectly.
(h) Choke plate or linkage binding.
(i) Broken or binding manual choke linkage.
(j) Restrictions or air leaks in the vacuum or hot-air passages to the automatic choke.
(k) Dirty carburetor air-cleaner element.
(l) Incorrect fast-idle adjustment.
(m) Incorrect accelerator-pump stroke.

(a) Use correct starting procedure.
(b) Adjust float level.
(c) Adjust low- and high-speed idle.
(d) Free-up or replace needle.
(e) Repair or replace fuel pump.
(f) Replace with correct combination.
(g) Adjust automatic choke.
(h) Free-up and adjust plate or linkage.
(i) Repair or replace linkage.
(j) Remove restrictions and repair air leaks.
(k) Service or replace air-cleaner element.
(l) Adjust fast idle.
(m) Adjust accelerator pump.

172

Carburetors and Air Cleaners

Symptoms and Possible Causes *Possible Remedies*

Stalling (Engine Cold)

(a) Incorrect idle fuel mixture.
(b) Engine idle speed too slow.
(c) Dirt, water, or ice in fuel filter.
(d) Positive crankcase-ventilation system defective.
(e) Fuel lines restricted or leaking air.
(f) Fuel tank vent restricted.
(g) Intake manifold or carburetor gaskets leaking.
(h) Carburetor icing.
(i) Incorrect throttle linkage adjustment.
(j) Clogged air bleeds or idle passages.
(k) Defective fuel pump.
(l) Defective or misadjusted automatic choke.

(a) Adjust idle fuel mixture.
(b) Adjust fast idle.
(c) Clean or replace filter element.
(d) Repair or replace defective parts.
(e) Remove restrictions, tighten fittings, or replace defective part.
(f) Remove restriction or replace gas cap.
(g) Tighten bolts or replace defective gasket.
(h) Use anti-icing fluid.
(i) Adjust throttle linkage.
(j) Disassemble carburetor and clean thoroughly.
(k) Repair or replace.
(l) Repair or adjust automatic choke.

Stalling (Engine Hot)

(a) Improperly adjusted or defective dashpot.
(b) Idle speed too slow.
(c) Incorrect idle fuel mixture.
(d) Worn or bent tip on idle fuel-mixture screw.
(e) Defective fuel pump.
(f) Coolant thermostat defective.
(g) Dirt, water, or ice in fuel filter.

(a) Adjust, repair, or replace.
(b) Adjust fast-idle speed.
(c) Adjust idle fuel mixture.
(d) Replace screw.
(e) Repair or replace.
(f) Replace thermostat.
(g) Clean or replace fuel-filter element.

Symptoms and Possible Causes

(h) Fuel tank vent clogged.

(i) Fuel lines clogged or leaking air.

(j) Carburetor icing.

(k) Throttle shaft too loose in body of carburetor.
(l) Incorrect or defective throttle linkage.
(m) Clogged air bleeds or idle passages.
(n) Leaking intake manifold or carburetor gasket.

Possible Remedies

(h) Remove restriction or replace gas cap.

(i) Remove restriction and tighten fittings or replace defective parts.

(j) Use anti-icer fluid (methanol) in fuel.

(k) Repair or replace parts as needed.

(l) Adjust or repair throttle linkage.

(m) Disassemble carburetor and clean thoroughly.

(n) Tighten bolts or replace gaskets.

Rough Idle

(a) Idle speed too slow.
(b) Incorrect idle fuel mixture.
(c) Damaged or worn idle-mixture screws.
(d) Dirt in idle fuel passages or air passages.
(e) Air leaks in fuel intake or intake manifold.
(f) Defective coolant thermostat.
(g) Incorrect fuel level in carburetor.
(h) Throttle plates or shafts bent, binding, or misaligned.
(i) Worn or damaged main metering jet.
(j) Fuel pump defective.

(a) Adjust idle speed.
(b) Adjust idle fuel mixture.
(c) Replace screws.

(d) Disassemble and clean carburetor thoroughly.
(e) Find and eliminate air leaks.
(f) Replace thermostat.

(g) Adjust float level.

(h) Repair, free, or replace damaged parts.

(i) Replace jet.

(j) Repair or replace fuel pump.

CARBURETORS AND AIR CLEANERS

Symptoms and Possible Causes

Poor Acceleration

Possible Remedies

(a) Incorrectly installed or adjusted accelerator-pump linkage.
(b) Defective check valves in accelerator pump.
(c) Dirt, water, or ice in fuel filter.
(d) Leaking accelerator-pump diaphragm.
(e) Defective fuel pump.
(f) Automatic choke malfunctioning.
(g) Clogged vent in gas cap.

(h) Clogged fuel line.
(i) Air leak in fuel line.

(j) Low fuel level in carburetor.
(k) Defective accelerator pump.

(a) Install properly or adjust.

(b) Repair or replace valves.

(c) Clean or replace fuel filter element.
(d) Replace diaphragm.

(e) Repair or replace pump.
(f) Repair or adjust as needed.
(g) Remove restriction or replace cap.
(h) Remove restriction.
(i) Tighten fittings or replace defective part.
(j) Adjust float level.

(k) Repair, adjust, or replace pump.

Choke Plate Jammed

(a) Engine backfires.
(b) Starting fuel mixture too lean.
(c) Accelerator not fully depressed before starting, causing engine to backfire.

(a) Set engine timing.
(b) Adjust carburetor for richer mixture.
(c) Use correct starting procedure.

Severe Transmission Engagement After Cold Start

(a) Fast-idle speed too high.

(a) Adjust fast-idle speed.

175

Automobile Guide

Symptoms and Possible Causes

(b) Throttle operating on highest point of the fast-idle cam.
(c) Binding or sticking throttle linkage, throttle valves or shafts, or accelerator pedal.

Possible Remedies

(b) Check automatic-choke adjustment.
(c) Repair or replace defective parts as needed.

Surging (Cruising Speed or Higher)

(a) Clogged main jets.
(b) Undersize main jets.
(c) Low fuel level in carburetor.
(d) Low fuel-pump pressure or volume.
(e) Clogged air bleeds.
(f) Clogged fuel filter.
(g) Vacuum passage to distriutor, clogged.

(a) Disassemble and clean carburetor. Replace jets if needed.
(b) Replace with proper size jets.
(c) Adjust float level.
(d) Repair or replace fuel pump.
(e) Disassemble and clean carburetor.
(f) Clean or replace fuel filter element.
(g) Remove restriction.

Reduced Top Speed

(a) Incorrect fuel level in carburetor.
(b) Incorrect fuel pump pressure or volume.
(c) Improper size or clogged main jet.
(d) Automatic choke not operating properly.
(e) Improper throttle linkage adjustment.

(a) Adjust float level.
(b) Repair or replace fuel pump.
(c) Clean or replace main jet.
(d) Repair, adjust, or replace automatic choke.
(e) Adjust throttle linkage.

CARBURETORS AND AIR CLEANERS

Symptoms and Possible Causes

(f) Clogged vacuum passage to venturi.
(g) Secondary throttle system defective.

Possible Remedies

(f) Clean or repair.
(g) Inspect secondary system for binding, sticking, bent shafts, wedged throttle plates, etc. Repair or replace as needed.

CHAPTER 7

Pistons, Rings, and Engine Block

The pistons and rings in an automobile are designed to withstand severe punishment. They must be able to operate effectively over a very wide range of temperatures and pressures. The area at the top of the piston must be sealed from the crankcase to prevent combustion blow-by and loss of compression, and also to prevent oil on the cylinder walls from entering the combustion chamber. All this must be done at temperature extremes ranging from below zero (when the engine is started in winter cold) to several hundred degrees plus after the engine has reached operating temperature. Pressure extremes range from the vacuum existing on the fuel-intake stroke to the several hundred pounds per sq. in. pressure exerted as the fuel-charge fires.

The engine block is that part of the engine on which all of the other parts are mounted or attached. It contains, among other components; the main bearings, pistons and connecting rods, crankshaft, timing gears and chain, and oil pump. Also, mounted to the engine block, are the intake and exhaust manifolds, cylinder head(s), water pump, oil pan, and transmission housing. The engine block is mounted to the car frame with rubber hardware, called "engine or motor mounts."

PISTON CONSTRUCTION

The majority of pistons in late-model cars are made of an aluminum alloy, and usually plated with tin to decrease friction and wear. Some cast iron pistons may still be found in older-model cars.

The aluminum alloy pistons are generally cam-ground, as shown in Fig. 1. This means that the piston, when cold, is not perfectly round;

PISTONS, RINGS AND ENGINE BLOCK

instead, it is slightly elliptical. As the temperature of this piston rises, the expansion along the diameter which passes through the piston-pin axis is greater than the expansion along the diameter across the thrust axis. Thus, the piston becomes circular at its operating temperature.

Aluminum alloy pistons should never be ground or honed in any way. If a piston is found to be oversize, the cylinder must be rebored or honed to obtain the proper fit.

Cast iron pistons found in some older-model cars can be machined slightly in most cases. Care must be taken if this operation is performed, however, to make sure the piston is not weakened, especially in the skirt area.

Pistons are designed for a particular make and model of car and cannot be used in other cars. This is true, even if the piston diameter and wrist-pin size is the same. For example, some pistons have full skirts, such as the one shown in Fig. 2, while others have partial skirts (Fig. 3). In addition, some pistons have flat tops (Fig.4), while others have recessed tops, such as the one shown in Fig. 5, or dome tops, such as the one shown in Fig. 6. Both the recessed top and dome top pistons are designed to increase the compression ratio of the engine.

PISTON REPLACEMENT

When an engine is to be overhauled or to be inspected for possible ring and/or piston replacement, the following procedure for removing the pistons is suggested:

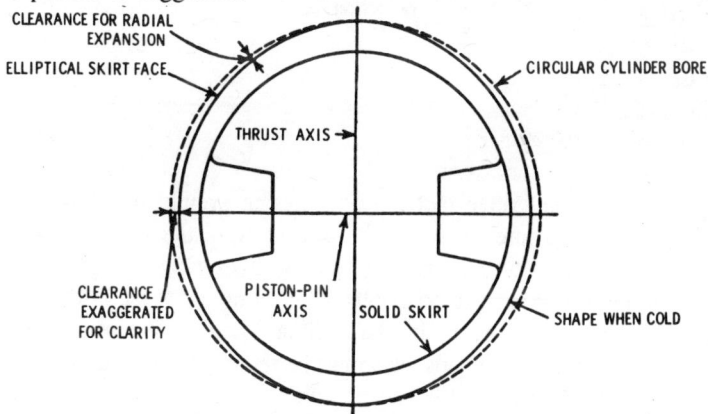

Fig. 1. Bottom view of a cam-ground piston showing its elliptical shape exaggerated for clarity.

AUTOMOBILE GUIDE

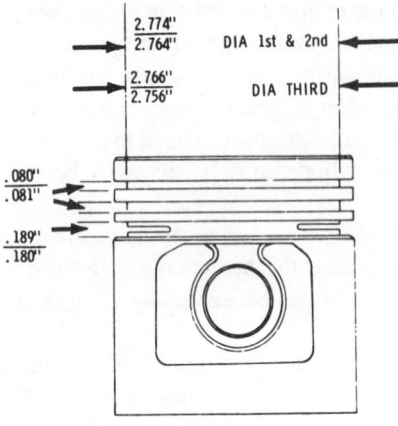

Fig. 2. A full-skirted piston.

Courtesy American Motors Corp.

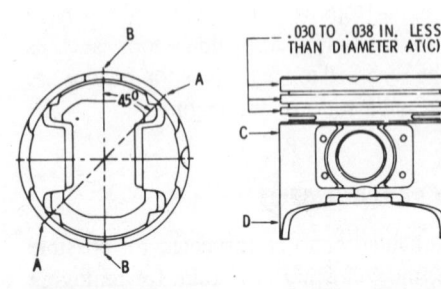

Fig. 3. A piston with a partial skirt.

THE ELLIPTICAL SHAPE OF THE PISTON SKIRT SHOULD BE .010 TO .012 IN. LESS AT DIAMETER (A) THAN ACROSS THE THRUST FACES AT DIAMETER (B). MEASUREMENT IS MADE 1/8 IN. BELOW LOWER RING GROOVE

DIAMETERS AT (C) AND (D) CAN BE EQUAL OR DIAMETER AT (D) CAN BE .0015 IN. GREATER THAN (C)

Courtesy Dodge Div., Chrysler Motors Corp.

1. Remove any ridge that may be present around the top of the cylinders before removing the pistons from the cylinder block. Keep the piston tops covered during this operation.
2. Rotate the crankshaft so that the connecting rod to the piston to be removed is centered in the cylinder bore. (The pistons and connecting rods in most cars must be removed from the top of the cylinder block.)
3. Identify the connecting-rod number and the direction of assembly of the cap (shown in Fig. 7), then remove the connecting-rod cap.

Pistons, Rings and Engine Block

4. Push the piston and rod assembly out of the cylinder bore. Take extra care to prevent the connecting-rod bolts from contacting and damaging the connecting-rod journal on the crankshaft.
5. Install the connecting-rod bearing cap on the rod.

INSPECTION

All deposits should be removed from the surface of the pistons. Any gum or varnish should be cleaned from the piston skirt, wrist pin, and rings with a suitable solvent. *Do not use a wire brush or a caustic cleaning solution.* Clean the ring grooves on the pistons with a ring-groove tool, such as the one shown in Fig. 8. Make sure the oil-ring slots (or holes) are clean.

Inspect the pistons for cracks at the ring lands, skirts, and pin bosses, and for scuffed, rough, or scored skirts. If any of these conditions exist, the affected piston or pistons should be replaced. Other conditions that call for piston replacement are excessive wear, a high stop on the lower inner portion of the ring grooves, spongy or eroded areas near the top of the piston, and wavy ring lands.

Wrist Pins

Replace any wrist pins that show signs of cracks or etching and/or wear. Check the wrist pin fit as recommended by the manufacturer. This

Fig. 4. A flat-top piston.

Courtesy Dodge Div., Chrysler Motors Corp.

AUTOMOBILE GUIDE

VALVE CLEARANCE RELIEF

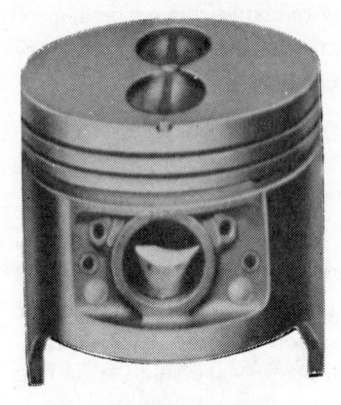

Fig. 5. A piston with recessed top to give clearance to the valves.

STANDARD PISTON

is usually given as a light thumb-press fit with both the piston and wrist pin at a normal temperature of approximately 70°F. If the fit of the wrist pin is not correct, new units should be installed. Most manufacturers supply oversize pins to be used if the old pins are loose. This means the wrist-pin hole in the piston must be reamed or honed to the correct size to accept the oversize pin. Some manufacturers do not recommend reaming or honing, or the use of oversize pins. Instead, they recommend replacement of both the piston and wrist pin.

The correct method of reaming a piston for an oversize wrist pin is to place the reamer in a vise and revolve the piston around the reamer. Set the reamer to the size of the existing pin bore, then expand the reamer

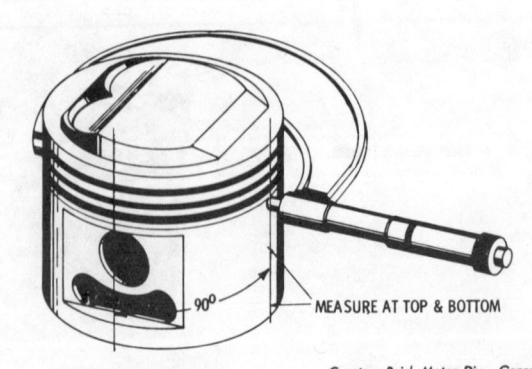

Courtesy Buick Motor Div., General Motors Corp.
Fig. 6. A piston with a domed top to increase the compression ratio.

182

Pistons, Rings and Engine Block

Fig. 7. Identifying connecting-rod number and direction of assembly.

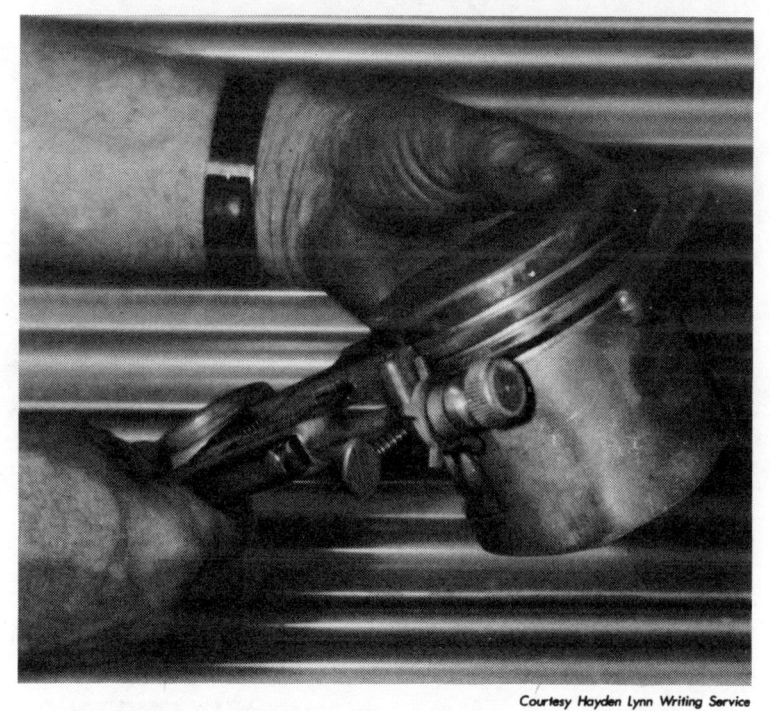

Courtesy Hayden Lynn Writing Service
Fig. 8. Using a ring-groove tool to clean piston ring grooves.

AUTOMOBILE GUIDE

slightly and make a trial ream. *Take a light cut.* Use a pilot sleeve of the nearest correct size in order to maintain alignment of the bores.

Check the hole size, using the new wrist pin to be installed. If the bore is too small, expand the reamer slightly and make another light cut. Continue this procedure until the proper fit is obtained. Check the fit of the wrist pin in the connecting rod and, if necessary ream or hone the rod until the pin fits according to specifications.

Engine Block

After removing the oil pan, cylinder head(s), water pump, and other related equipment, remove the old gasket material from the machined surfaces of the engine block. This task is accomplished with the use of a sturdy putty knife or gasket scraper. Take care, however, not to scratch or mar the machined mating surfaces. The block should then be thoroughly cleaned with solvent. Several types of degreasers are available for this purpose.

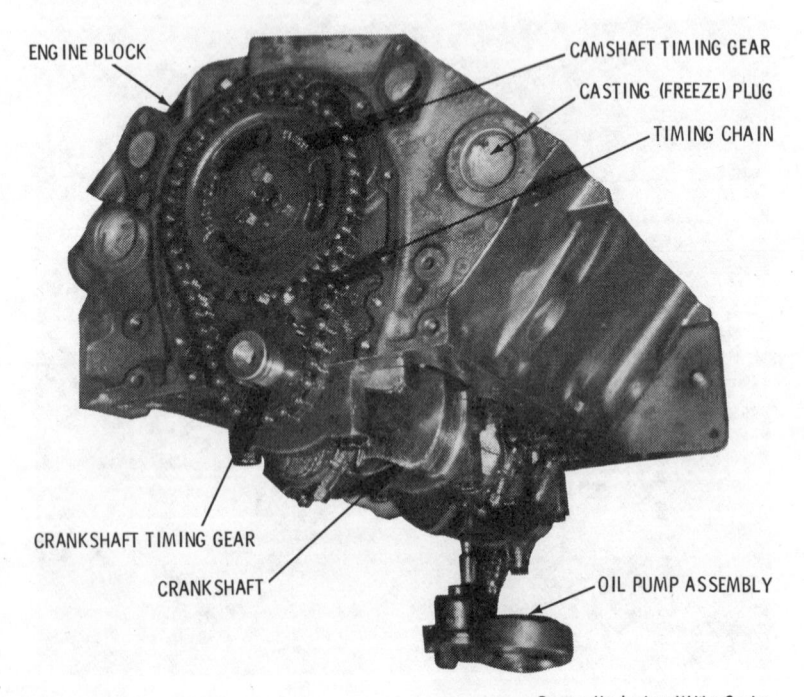

Courtesy Hayden Lynn Writing Service.
Fig. 9. Typical engine block.

Pistons, Rings and Engine Block

Remove any pipe plugs that seal oil passages, and blow out the passages, bolt holes, etc., with compressed air. Make sure that the threads in all bolt holes are clean and all passages are unobstructed. Dirt in the threads may cause binding and result in an incorrect torque reading during reassembly. Use a tap to "true" any damaged threads and to remove deposits. Obstructions in passages may cause restricted oil flow resulting in premature failure of engine parts due to lack of lubrication.

Carefully inspect all casting plugs (commonly called *freeze plugs*) for signs of corrosion or leakage (Fig. 9). If in doubt, replace all plugs. It is much easier to replace them with the engine block out of the car.

Inspect the block for cracks after it has been thoroughly cleaned. Small cracks that are not readily visibly may be detected by coating the suspected area with a mixture of 25% kerosene and 75% light engine oil. Wipe the area dry and immediately apply a coating of zinc oxide dissolved in wood alcohol. If cracks are present, the coating will become discolored at the defective area, indicating that the block should be replaced.

Check all machined gasket surfaces for burrs, nicks, scratches, and scores. Remove any minor imperfections with an oilstone. Check the flatness of the cylinder-block gasket surface. Regrind this surface if the flatness is not within the limits set up by the manufacturer. Do not remove more metal than recommended, because to do so will upset the

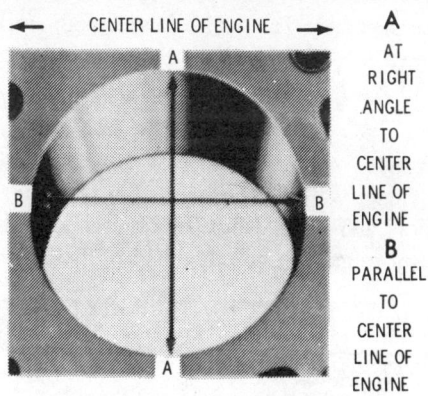

A AT RIGHT ANGLE TO CENTER LINE OF ENGINE

B PARALLEL TO CENTER LINE OF ENGINE

1. OUT-OF-ROUND = DIFFERENCE BETWEEN **A** AND **B**
2. TAPER = DIFFERENCE BETWEEN THE **A** MEASUREMENT AT TOP OF CYLINDER BORE AND THE **A** MEASUREMENT AT BOTTOM OF CYLINDER BORE

Fig. 10. Checking the out-of-round and taper conditions of a cylinder.

compression ratio and may result in damage to the engine after a short period of operation.

Inspect the cylinder walls for roughness, scoring, glazing, or other signs of wear. Check the cylinder bore for out-of-round and taper, making the measurements as shown in Fig. 10. Measure the diameter of each cylinder bore at the top, bottom, and middle, one set of readings with the gauge placed at right angles to the center line of the engine and another set of readings with the gauge parallel to the center line.

Reboring

Rebore and hone any cylinders that are deeply scored or that exceed the out-of-round and/or taper limits specified by the manufacturer. Before reboring any cylinder, all main-bearing caps must be in place and torqued to specifications so that the crankshaft bearing bores will not be distorted by the reboring operation.

Rebore and hone only the cylinder or cylinders that require it. *All pistons are the same weight (for a given car) whether they are standard or oversize; therefore, one or more different size pistons can be used without upsetting engine balance.* Rebore the cylinder with the most wear first to determine the maximum oversize necessary. If the cylinder cannot be refinished to fit the maximum oversize piston available, the block will have to be replaced.

Rebore the cylinder to within approximately 0.0015 inch of the required oversize diameter. This will allow enough stock for the final honing step to give the proper surface finish and pattern. Use clean, sharp 220- to 280-grit hones for the final operation.

Honing

Honing the cylinder walls is necessary after reboring, or to remove minor imperfections and glaze. This operation cannot be used to correct an excessive out-of-round or taper condition of the cylinder, however.

Fig. 11. A cross-hatch pattern on a correctly-honed cylinder wall.

PISTONS, RINGS AND ENGINE BLOCK

Usually, a few strokes of the hone will produce a satisfactory finish on the cylinder walls and within the required limits.

Before honing, stuff clean rags under the cylinders and over the crankshaft to keep the abrasive material from entering the crankshaft area. Honing should be done by moving the rotating hone up and down in the cylinder fast enough to produce a crosshatch pattern on the walls similar to the pattern in Fig. 11. Place the hone in the cylinder and expand the stones until the assembly can just be turned by hand. Connect a ½" electric drill to the hone and drive at drill speed while moving the hone up and down the entire length of the cylinder until the hone begins to run free. During this operation a liberal amount of kerosene, or other suitable cutting fluid, should be used to keep the

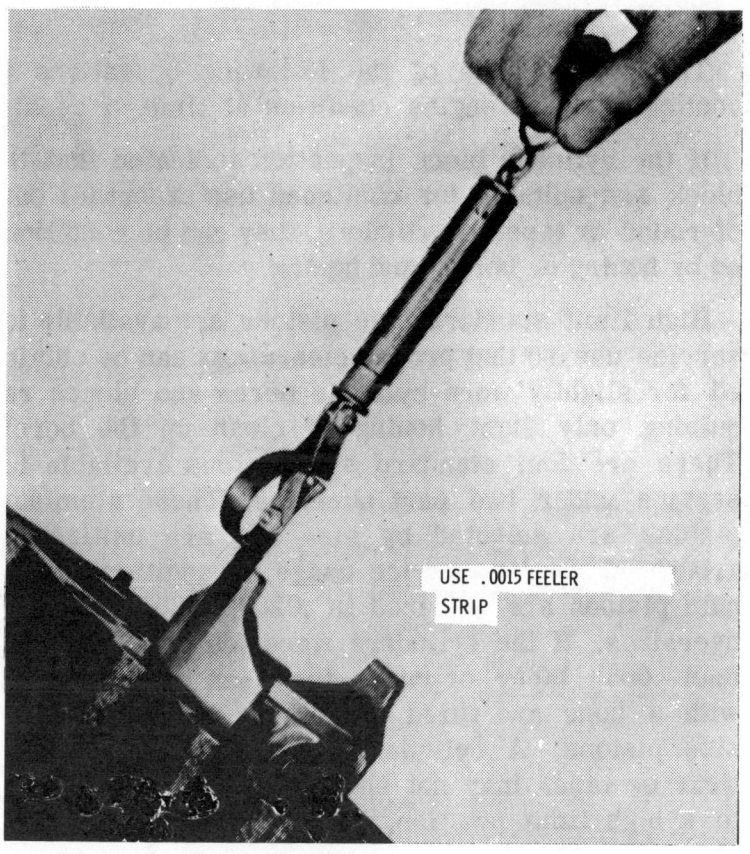

Fig. 12. Checking the fit of a piston.

stones clean. Move the hone up and down slowly with the first-cut rough stones, but more rapidly with the finish-cut fine stones. The final bore finish should show very fine and uniform scratches in a cross-hatch pattern having approximately a 45° to 60° included angle.

Expand the stones against the cylinder walls and repeat the honing operation until the desired bore diameter is obtained. The cylinder should be cleaned occasionally during the honing operation and the piston selected for that cylinder checked for the correct fit. *Allow the cylinder to cool and be sure it is clean and dry before the piston fit is checked.*

Mark each piston, after the correct fit has been obtained, to correspond with the cylinder to which it has been fitted. *Handle the pistons with care and do not attempt to force them into the cylinder.* Using force may permanently distort some types of pistons, making them unfit for use.

After the honing is completed, all abrasives must be removed from the engine parts. Hot water and soap is recommended to clean the cylinder walls. Scrub well with a stiff bristle brush, rinse with hot water, and dry thoroughly. The cylinder bores can be considered clean when they can be wiped with a white cloth without any dirt or particles appearing on the cloth. If any of the abrasive material is allowed to remain on the cylinder walls, it will rapidly wear the new rings and cylinder bores in addition to the bearings that are lubricated with the contaminated oil. The cylinder walls should be swabbed several times with light engine oil and a clean cloth and then wiped with a clean dry cloth. *The cylinders should not be cleaned with gasoline or kerosene.* Remove all abrasive material from other parts of the engine block.

Piston Fitting

The fit of each piston can be checked in the following manner:

1. Invert the piston (skirt end up) and insert in the top of the cylinder with a ½"-wide feeler strip of the recommended gauge between the piston and the cylinder wall. The gauge should be positioned on the side of the piston 90° from the wrist-pin holes, and connected to a spring scale.

   CAUTION: Handle the pistons with care and do not attempt to force them into the cylinder. Unless the cylinder has been bored or honed to the correct size, the pistons may be distorted and permanently damaged by careless handling.

PISTONS, RINGS AND ENGINE BLOCK

2. Insert the feeler strip and inverted piston into the cylinder so that the center of the wrist-pin hole is flush with the top of the cylinder block. See Fig. 12. Keep the feeler strip straight up and down and keep the wrist-pin hole parallel with the crankshaft axis.
3. Pull the feeler strip straight up and out from between the piston and cylinder wall, noting the amount of pull registered on the spring scale necessary to remove the ribbon.

NOTE: *The thickness of the strip and the recommended pull necessary to remove it depends on the car manufacturer's specifications. The strip is usually 0.0015" thick and the pull required varies from around 7 to 18 lbs. Check the specifications for the correct figure.*

4. If the scale reading is greater then the maximum pull specified, try another piston or lightly hone the cylinder to obtain the proper fit.
5. If the scale reading is less than the minimum pull specified, try another piston, or if standard size, try a standard high-limit piston if available. If the proper fit cannot be obtained, the cylinder must be rebored to the next oversize piston size.
6. Mark each piston, after fitting, to correspond with the cylinder to which it has been fitted.

PISTON RINGS

If new piston rings are installed without reboring the cylinders, the glaze on the cylinder walls should be removed. This is accomplished by using very fine stones and honing the walls very lightly. Be sure to remove all abrasives from the cylinder after this operation.

Select rings comparable in size to the piston being used. For example, use standard-size rings with standard-size pistons; use 0.010" oversize rings with 0.010" oversize pistons, etc. The rings must be checked for the correct clearance in the piston grooves and for the correct gap. The cylinders and piston grooves must be clean, dry, and free of carbon and burrs.

Nearly all cars, especially late models, use a three-ring piston. The two top rings are compression rings and the bottom ring is an oil control ring. This oil ring is usually an assembly of three or four separate parts — a top and bottom rail, a spacer, and often an expander. A set of typical piston rings is shown in Fig. 13.

Automobile Guide

The clearance of the rings in the piston grooves may be checked as shown in Fig. 14. The gauge should be inserted between the ring and its lower land, because any wear that has taken place will form a step at the inner portion of the lower land. If a relatively high step has been worn in the land, the piston should be discarded; installing new rings will be unsatisfactory because of excessive ring clearance. Rings are not available in oversize widths to compensate for ring-groove wear. The

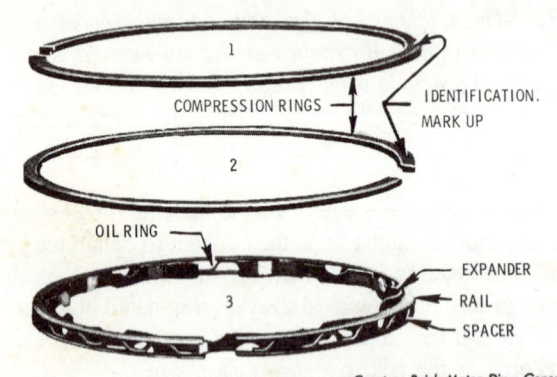

Courtesy Buick Motor Div., General Motors Corp.

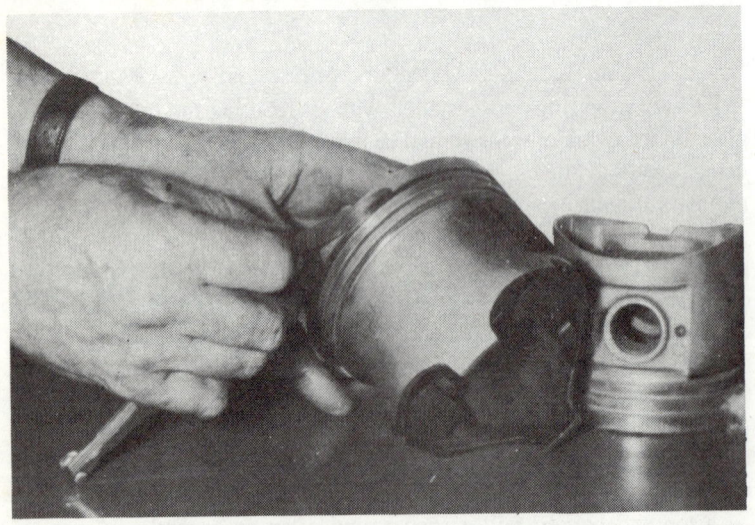

Fig. 13. A set of typical piston rings.

Courtesy Hayden Lynn Writing Service

Fig. 14. Checking piston-ring clearance.

PISTONS, RINGS AND ENGINE BLOCK

Courtesy Hayden Lynn Writing Service
Fig. 15. Checking piston-ring gap.

specified thickness of feeler gauge (usually 0.0015 to 0.003 inch for compression rings and 0.001 to 0.009 inch for oil rings) should slide freely around the entire ring circumference without binding.

The ring gap can be checked as shown in Fig. 15. Place the ring in the cylinder and, using the head of an inverted piston, press the ring down into the cylinder approximately 2 inches. Using the inverted piston insures that the ring will be square with the cylinder. Measure the gap between the ends of the ring with a feeler gauge. The gap should be from 0.010 to 0.015 inch on most cars. (Check the specifications for the correct gap.) If the gap is too wide, try another ring set. If the gap is too narrow, carefully file the ends of the ring until the correct gap is obtained.

AUTOMOBILE GUIDE

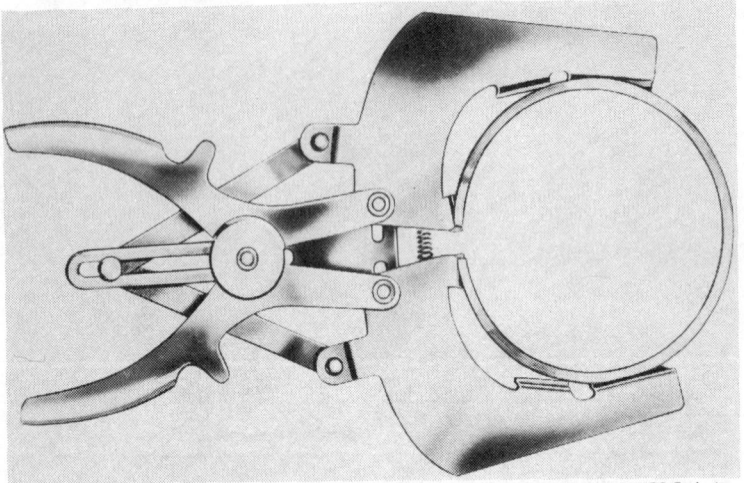

Courtesy AMMCO Tools, Inc.

Fig. 16. A typical piston ring expander.

It is important that each ring be fitted to its individual piston and cylinder. Clearly mark each ring set so that it will be installed in the proper cylinder. The oil ring should be installed first, following the specific instructions given on the package. The middle compression ring is installed on the piston next, followed by the top compression ring. A piston-ring expander (Fig. 16) should be used to install each ring with the identification mark on the ring oriented toward the top of the piston.

Before installing the pistons in the cylinders, position the gaps in the two compression rings so they are staggered and so that neither gap is in line with the gap in the oil ring. In addition, the gaps in the oil ring rails should be positioned so that they are not in line with each other or with the gap in the spacer. Stagger these rings so at least 1' separates the gaps.

To install the piston and ring assembly in the cylinder, a ring-compression tool, such as the one in Fig. 17, should be used. Lightly coat the pistons, rings, and cylinder walls with light engine oil. Install each piston in its respective cylinder with the identifying mark on the top of the piston toward the front of the engine. Push the engine through the ring compressor and into the cylinder by means of a wooden hammer handle placed in the center of the piston face. *Do not pound the piston into place. Use a steady push.*

Pistons, Rings and Engine Block

Fig. 17. Using a piston ring compressor.

Courtesy Hayden Lynn Writing Service

Be sure to install the pistons in the same cylinders for which they were fitted. Carefully guide the connecting-rod bearing into place on the crankshaft journal to avoid damage to the journal. Install the connecting-rod bearing caps and tighten to the specified torque.

IMPORTANT: *After installation of new pistons and rings, care should be taken in starting and running the engine for the first hour. Avoid high speeds until the parts have had a reasonable amount of break-in time so that scuffing or scoring will not occur.*

PISTONS AND RINGS
POSSIBLE TROUBLES AND REMEDIES

Symptoms and Possible Causes   *Possible Remedies*

Engine Noises

(a) Piston slap (excessive clearance between pistons and cylinders).

(a) Replace rings and/or knurl pistons

193

Symptoms and Possible Causes   *Possible Remedies*

(b) Broken piston.
(c) Piston rubs against cylinder head gasket.
(d) Tapered or out-of-round bores.
(e) Piston ring strikes "ridge" at top of cylinder bore.
(f) Carbon deposit on top of piston.
(g) Excessive side clearance of ring in piston groove.
(h) Worn or broken piston lands.
(i) Loose piston pin.

(b) Replace piston.
(c) Correct as necessary.

(d) Rebore block and replace rings.
(e) Ream ridge and replace rings.
(f) Clean piston.

(g) Use correct rings.

(h) Repair or replace piston.

(i) Tighten and/or replace lock screw or snap ring.

CHAPTER 8

Crankshafts and Connecting Rods

The crankshaft and connecting rods transform the reciprocating motion of the pistons into a rotary motion that is necessary to drive the car. These parts are subject to extreme stresses and strains, which means they must be constructed of special materials and with great precision if they are to perform satisfactorily.

CRANKSHAFTS

The crankshaft is cast or forged from a special steel alloy, after which its bearing surfaces are machined. A final grinding operation finishes the crankshaft to the close tolerances necessary in the modern automobile. The unit is then carefully balanced to prevent vibration at high engine speeds.

Replacement of the crankshaft or any of its bearings calls for the same precision as the original installation if satisfactory operation is to be expected.

Main Bearings

The crankshaft rotates in main bearings located at both ends and at certain intermediate points. The main bearings are supported by webs in the lower part of the engine block. The number of main bearings may vary between different makes and models of cars. Usually, however, 6-cylinder in-line engines (Fig. 1) will have four main bearings while 8-cylinder V-type engines (Fig. 2) will have five.

Automobile Guide

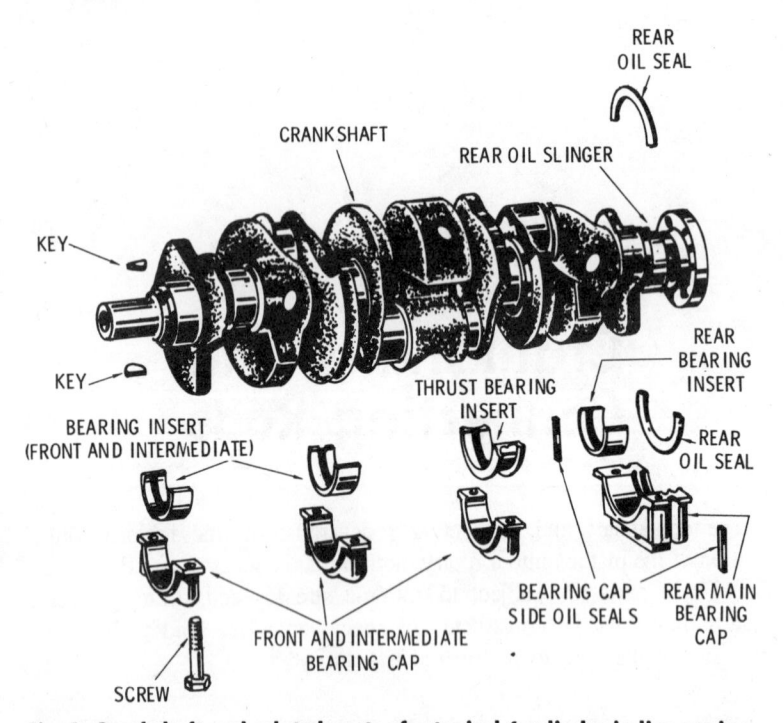

Fig. 1. Crankshaft and related parts of a typical 6-cylinder in-line engine.

Notice in Figs. 1 and 2 that one of the main-bearing inserts has a lip and is marked thrust bearing. The purpose of this bearing is to take the end thrust of the crankshaft. This thrust bearing is usually the 3rd main bearing back from the front of the engine.

All modern engines in domestic automobiles use bearing inserts in the main-bearing assemblies. Most manufacturers use a steel shell insert lined with babbit, although some late-model cars use other material, such as aluminum. One half of the shell fits into the bearing cap and the other half into a fixed recess in the lower part of the cylinder block. This type of shell insert has the advantage of being easily replaced (often without removing the crankshaft on certain cars) and does not require scraping and fitting. Its main disadvantage is that it cannot be line-bored or reamed to compensate for a warped crankshaft or block.

Notice that one-half of each bearing insert set is channeled to allow oil under pressure to enter from holes drilled in the crankshaft. In this way, the bearing is constantly supplied with oil to keep it lubricated.

CRANKSHAFTS AND CONNECTING RODS

Bearing Failure

Failure of the main-bearing inserts may be due to any one of a number of causes. The appearance of the defective insert will often provide the clue to the cause of failure. Fig. 3 shows the appearance of inserts that have failed due to the most common causes. Fig. 3A shows the results of abrasive material or dirt in the oil. Fig. 3B shows what may happen if the engine oil level becomes too low or if oil passages become clogged. Fig. 3C shows an insert that was seated improperly, possibly because it was distorted before installation or because dirt was present between it and the bearing seat. A tapered or out-of-round journal might cause the overlay material to be wiped out from the entire insert surface, as in Fig. 3D. An improperly ground journal might result in the type of failure shown in Fig. 3E. Fig. 3F shows what may happen

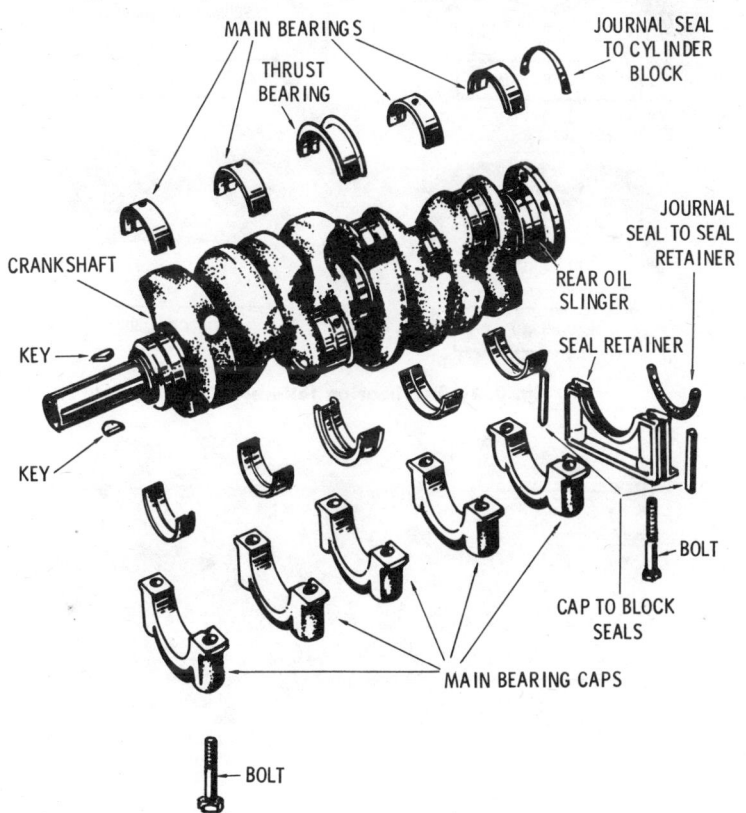

Fig. 2. Crankshaft and related parts of a typical 8-cylinder engine.

AUTOMOBILE GUIDE

A — SCRATCHED BY DIRT (SCRATCHES; DIRT IMBEDDED INTO BEARING MATERIAL)

B — LACK OF OIL (OVERLAY WIPED OUT)

C — IMPROPER SEATING (BRIGHT (POLISHED) SECTIONS)

D — TAPERED JOURNAL (OVERLAY GONE FROM ENTIRE SURFACE)

E — RADIUS RIDE (RADIUS RIDE)

F — FATIGUE FAILURE (CRATERS OR POCKETS)

Fig. 3. Typical bearing failures.

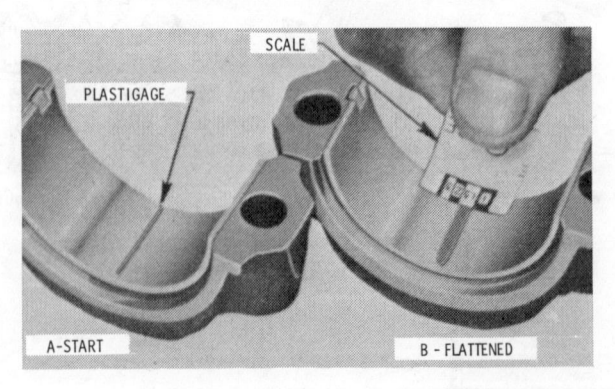

A - START (PLASTIGAGE) ; B - FLATTENED (SCALE)

Courtesy Buick Motor Div., General Motors Corp.

Fig. 4. Checking bearing clearance with PLASTIGAGE.

198

Crankshafts and Connecting Rods

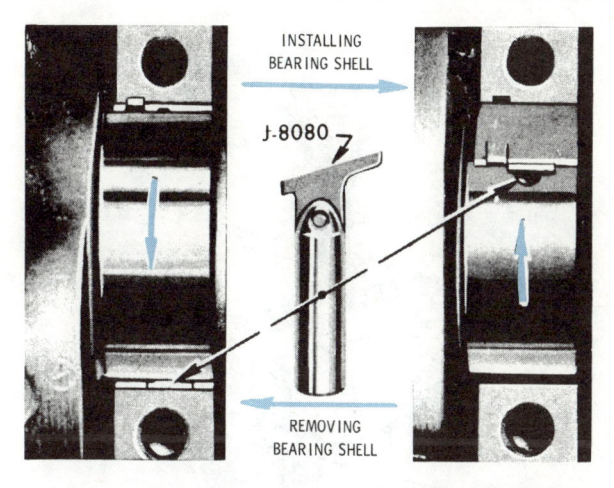

Fig. 5. A main-bearing insert removal and installer tool used on certain models of BUICK cars.

Courtesy Buick Motor Div., General Motors Corp.

Fig. 6. Typical rear-bearing oil seals.

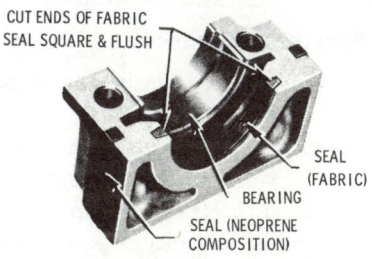

Courtesy Buick Motor Div., General Motors Corp.

when the bearing material becomes fatigued. This may be caused by defective material, sustained high-speed driving, continual engine overload, etc.

Any of the above conditions requires replacement of the defective inserts and correction of the fault that caused the failure. Sound judgment and proper inspections are necessary when evaluating bearing failure. Clean and inspect each bearing insert carefully. Remove any gum or varnish from the insert with a suitable solvent; do not remove by scraping. Clean and inspect the respective main-bearing journals on the crankshaft for cracks, scratches, grooves, or score marks. Dress any minor imperfections with a fine oil stone. If the journal is damaged, has a taper, or is out-of-round, it will have to be ground to size for the next undersize bearing.

AUTOMOBILE GUIDE

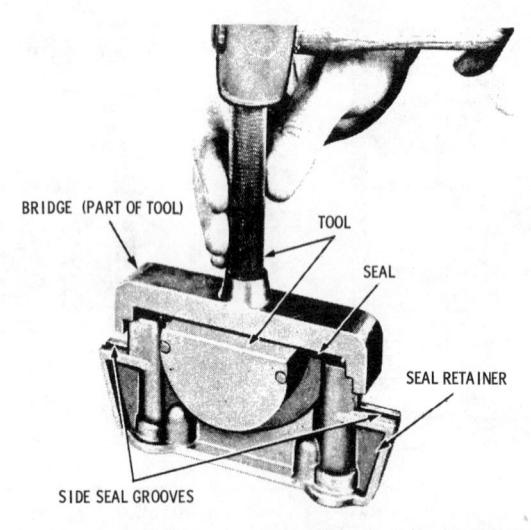

Courtesy Chrysler/Plymouth Div., Chrysler Motors Corp.
Fig. 7. Installing an oil seal in a PLYMOUTH engine rear-bearing cap.

Bearing Clearance

The clearance of main (and connecting-rod) bearings can be accurately checked by using *Plastigage*. This material consists of a wax-like plastic which compresses evenly between the bearing and journal surfaces without damaging either surface. *Plastigage* is manufactured by *Perfect Circle Corporation* and is available from most parts supplier's and car manufacturer's warehouse. *Plastigage* is manufactured in a variety of ranges, with type PG-1 (green) being the proper type for measuring the clearance of most main bearings.

To measure the clearance of a bearing, remove the cap and clean all oil from the bearing and journal surfaces (*Plastigage* is soluble in oil). Make sure all other main bearings are tightened to their specified torque. (If the engine is in the car, support the crankshaft with a jack to prevent its weight from giving an improper clearance reading). Place a piece of *Plastigage* lengthwise along the bottom center of the bearing cap, as shown in Fig. 4. Install the bearing cap and tighten to the specified torque. **DO NOT TURN THE CRANKSHAFT WITH THE PLASTIGAGE IN THE BEARING.**

Remove the bearing cap; the *Plastigage* will be found adhering to the bearing shell or the crankshaft journal. Do not remove it. Measure the flattened *Plastigage* with the scale printed on the *Plastigage* envelope.

CRANKSHAFTS AND CONNECTING RODS

The number within the graduation which most closely corresponds to the width of the flattened *Plastigage* indicates the bearing clearance in ten-thousandths of an inch. The measurement in Fig. 4 indicates a clearance of 0.0015″. If the bearing is not within the specified clearance, it should be replaced.

Measure the *Plastigage* at its widest point for the minimum clearance and at its narrowest point for the maximum clearance. If the *Plastigage* tapers toward the middle or ends, a difference in clearance exists, indicating a tapered condition, a low spot, or other irregularity of the bearing or journal. If the difference in clearance is 0.001″ or more, consideration to grinding the journal and installing undersize bearing inserts should be given. If no taper or out-of round condition exists, and the clearance is not over 0.003″ to 0.004″, or under 0.001″, the bearing

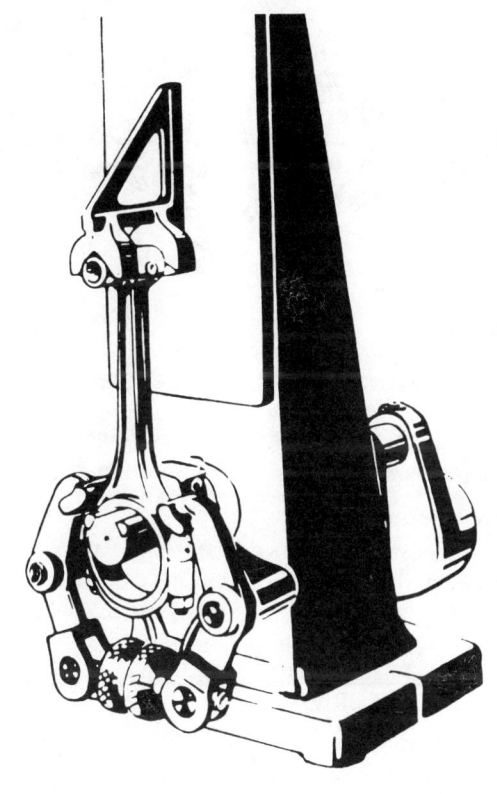

Courtesy AMMCO Tools, Inc.
Fig. 8. Checking connecting-rod for any possible bends.

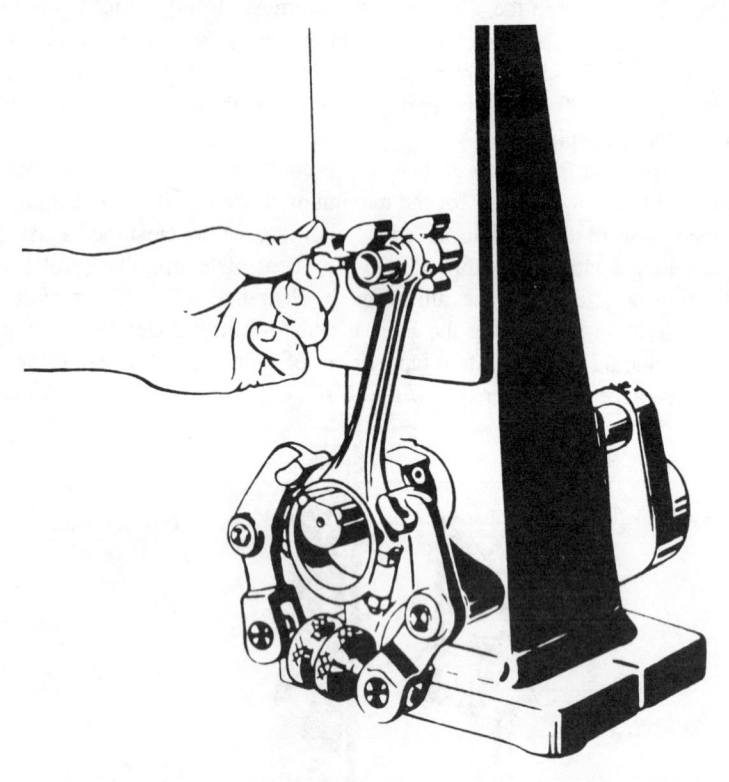

AUTOMOBILE GUIDE

Courtesy AMMCO Tools, Inc.
Fig. 9. Checking connecting-rod for possible twist.

fit is usually considered to be satisfactory, Consult the manufacturer's specifications for the recommended clearance limits.

Bearing Replacement

The main bearings on most cars can be replaced without removing the crankshaft. Special insert removal and installation tools are available to remove and install the upper inserts. Such a tool is shown in Fig. 5. The upper inserts are removed by placing the tool in the crankshaft journal oil hole and rotating the crankshaft in the proper direction. This causes the tang on the tool to engage the bearing insert and rotate it out of its seat. Care must be taken when removing inserts on the front and rear bearings to prevent the oil seal from also rotating out of position. Replace one bearing insert at a time, leaving the other bearings securely fastened.

CRANKSHAFTS AND CONNECTING RODS

When the inserts are installed, the ends extend slightly beyond the parting surfaces. This is normal in order that the inserts will be clamped tightly in place to insure positive seating and to prevent their turning. *The ends of the inserts must never be filed to bring them flush with the parting surfaces.*

Before installing the new bearing inserts, make sure the crankshaft journal and the bearing seats in the crankcase and cap are clean. Coat the inside surface of the upper bearing insert with engine oil and place it against the crankshaft journal so that any tang that is present will engage the notch in the crankcase when the insert is rotated into place. Rotate

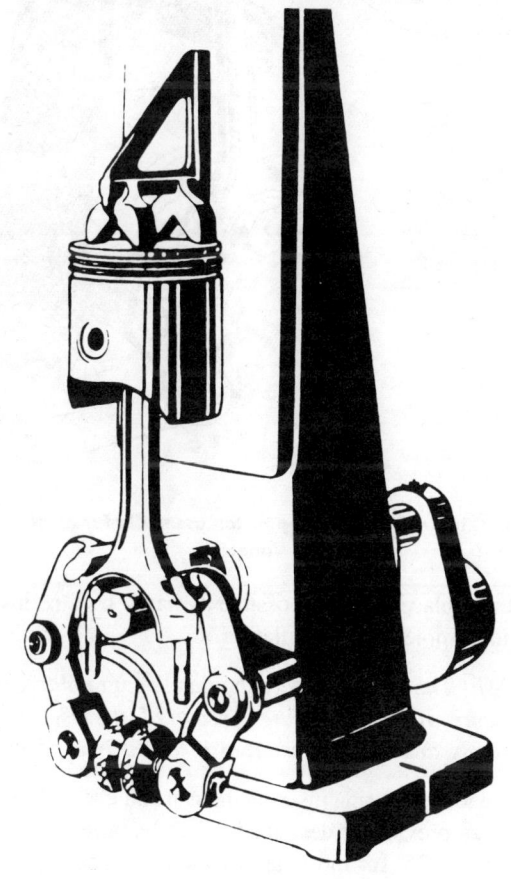

Courtesy AMMCO Tools, Inc.
Fig. 10. Checking connecting-rod and flat-top piston assembly for alignment.

203

Automobile Guide

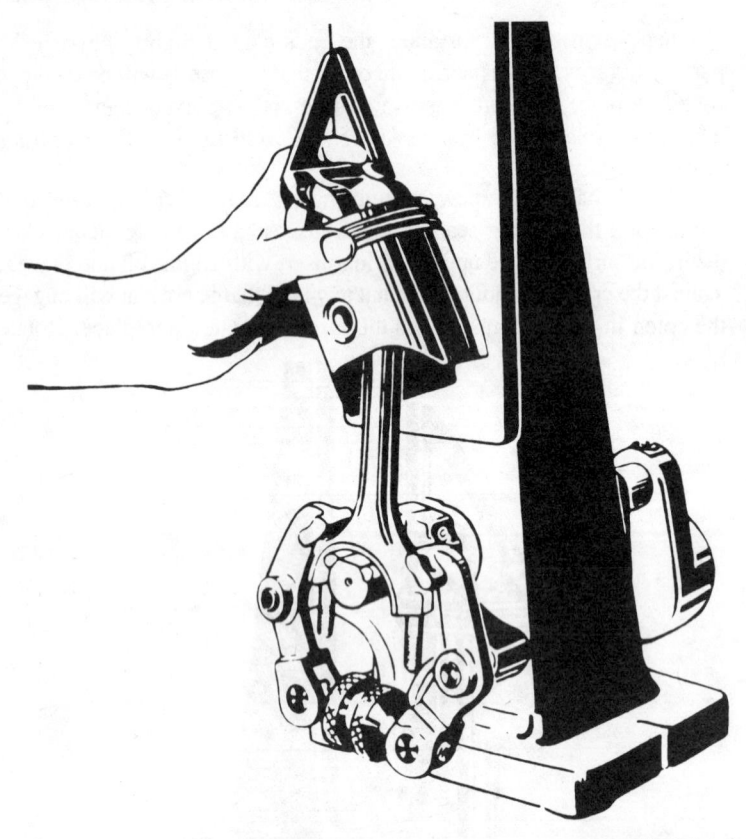

Courtesy AMMCO Tools, Inc.

Fig. 11. Checking rod and flat-top piston assembly for alignment at various angles.

the insert into place as far as possible by hand. Use the installation tool (Fig. 5) to complete the installation.

> NOTE: *The bearing insert should slide into place with very little pressure. If heavy pressure is required, the insert was not started squarely and will be distorted if forced into position.*

Place the lower bearing insert in the cap and check the clearance with *Plastigage* as previously described. The clearance should be between 0.005" and 0.0025" for most cars. If the clearance is greater than this, try the next undersize inserts, and check again with *Plastigage*. When the proper size insert has been determined, clean out all *Plastigage*, oil

Crankshafts and Connecting Rods

the insert, and reinstall the bearing cap. Tighten the cap bolts to the specified torque. *Under no circumstances should the ends of the bearing caps be filed to adjust for wear in old inserts or to obtain the proper clearance of new inserts. Neither do most car makers recommend shims to obtain proper clearance.*

If a thrust bearing has been disturbed or replaced, it is necessary to align the thrust surfaces of the inserts before the cap bolts are tightened. This is done on most cars by moving the crankshaft fore and aft the limit of its travel several times with the cap bolts finger tight. The end play of the crankshaft should be checked with a feeler gauge between the thrust bearing and its mating surface on the crankshaft. If outside the specified limits (usually from 0.002" to 0.010"), a new thrust bearing should be installed.

Oil Seals

Seals are pressed into grooves in the crankcase and rear bearing cap to seal against leakage of oil around the crankshaft. These seals can be

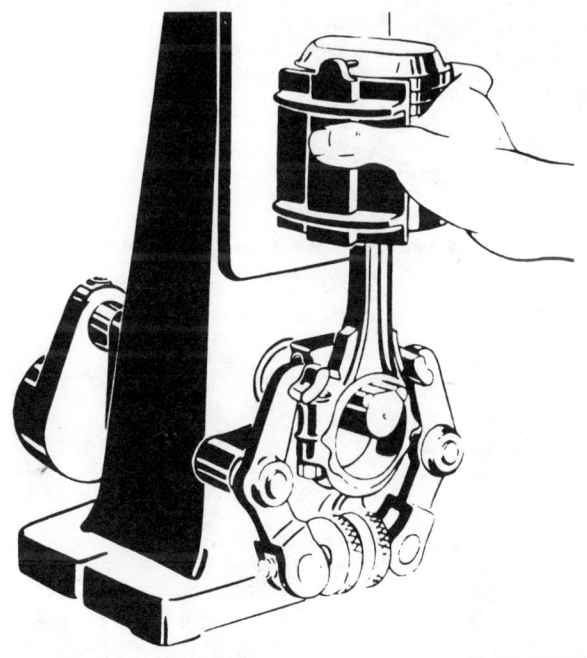

Courtesy AMMCO Tools, Inc.

Fig. 12. Checking connecting-rod and crown-top piston assembly for alignment.

AUTOMOBILE GUIDE

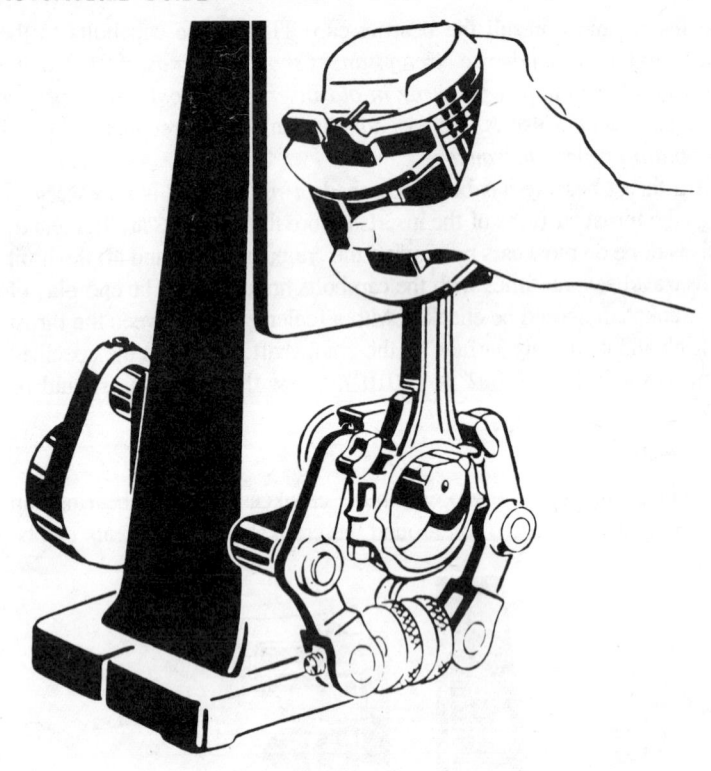

Courtesy AMMCO Tools, Inc.
Fig. 13. Checking rod and crown-top piston assembly for alignment at various angles.

Courtesy Hayden Lynn Wwiting Service
Fig. 14. Checking connecting-rod side clearance.

CRANKSHAFTS AND CONNECTING RODS

replaced in some cars without removing the crankshaft but not in others. Fig. 6 shows typical rear bearing oil seals. These are used on some model *Buicks* and consist of a braided fabric inner seal and neoprene composition side seal. Other makes and models may use other materials and different shape seals, but all are similar.

The seals are pressed into their grooves with a smooth object, such as a hammer handle or with an oil-seal installing tool (Fig. 7). The seal is placed in position and that portion trimmed off that protrudes above the cap.

Neoprene composition seals swell in the presence of oil and heat. Thus, they are undersize when first installed and may even leak for a short time until they have had time to swell and seal the opening.

CAUTION: The engine must be operated at a slow speed for a short time after braided-type seals have been installed.

CONNECTING RODS

The same general procedure is used in replacing rod bearings as for main bearings. The same type of bearing failure can occur and the same general procedure for checking bearing clearance is used.

A bent or twisted rod may cause bearing damage and eventual failure. In addition, piston and ring wear will almost surely take place, resulting in excessive oil consumption. Therefore, if such a condition is indicated or suspected, the rod should be checked. The instructions that accompany the tool should be carefully followed. Figs. 8 through 13 show connecting rods being checked using the *Ammco* model 3300 *ConRod* aligner. The following steps are taken for checking the connecting rod when using this tester:

Place the rod and pin assembly over the arbor and secure it by tightening the holding jaws with the knurled knob. The cap does not have to be on the rod for testing. Be sure that the rod is held firmly.

Rod and Pin Assembly — Check for bend (Fig. 8) by holding the checking block on the wrist pin so that the ground edge of the checking block is against the face plate. Check for twist (Fig. 9) by holding the checking block against the pin with ground edge against the face plate and at right angles to the rod.

Rod and Flat-Top Piston Assembly — Clean the carbon deposits from top of piston. Check for bend (Fig. 10) by holding the checking block on top of the piston. Be sure that the piston and rod are upright on the arbor. Check for twist (Fig. 11) by holding the checking block on the piston with piston "cocked" on the rod as far as possible.

Rod and Crown-Top Piston Assembly—Check for bend (Fig. 12) by holding "V" block firmly against the piston with ground edge of "V" block against the face plate. Check for twist, Fig. 13, by holding the "V" block as above, but "cock" piston as far as possible on the rod.

To replace or inspect a connecting-rod bearing, turn the crankshaft until the bearing is at the bottom of its travel. The cap bolts are easily reached in this position. Follow the procedure described for main bearings to inspect, replace, and measure clearances. Remove only one cap at a time and replace it before continuing to the next one. *Never interchange caps or connecting rods.*

After new bearing inserts have been installed, it should be possible to move the rod freely endways on the crankshaft journal, as allowed by the side clearance. If the rod cannot be moved, either the bearing is too much undersize or the rod is bent or twisted.

Side clearance of the connecting rods should be checked with a feeler gauge, as shown in Fig. 14. The clearance in V8 engines, where two connecting rods share the same journal, is measured between the two rods. On 6-cylinder engines, the clearance is measured between the connecting rod and shoulder on the crankshaft. The allowable clearance varies between different makes and models but is usually somewhere between 0.005″ to 0.030″.

CRANKSHAFT AND CONNECTING ROD POSSIBLE TROUBLES AND REMEDIES

Symptoms and Possible Causes　　*Possible Remedies*

Engine Noises

(a) Loose main bearing.
(b) Loose flywheel.
(c) Loose rod bearing.

(d) Loose piston pin.

(a) Repair as necessary.
(b) Correct as necessary.
(c) Inspect and correct as necessary; may be caused by oil that is too thin.
(d) Tighten and/or replace lock screw or snap ring. Repair as necessary.

CHAPTER 9

Camshafts, Lifters, and Rocker Arms

The purpose of the camshaft in an engine is to open and close each intake and exhaust valve at the correct time to provide for efficient engine operation. With the addition of extra lobes and/or gears, the camshaft may be used to operate the fuel pump, distributor, and oil pump.

The camshaft is rotated at one-half crankshaft (engine) speed, either by means of a pair of meshing gears, two sprocket gears and a chain, or two sprocket gears and a belt. In either event, the ratio of the crankshaft (drive) gear to the camshaft (driven) gear is 2:1. That is, there are half as many teeth or sprockets on the drive gear as there are on the driven gear.

The camshaft has a cam lobe for each valve; one intake and one exhaust. Thus, a four-cylinder engine has an eight-lobe cam, a six-cylinder engine has a twelve-lobe cam, and an eight-cylinder engine has a sixteen-lobe cam. There is an additional cam lobe if the fuel pump is driven off the camshaft.

In Fig. 1, as the camshaft rotates, the cam lobe moves up under the lifter. This action raises the lifter which in turn raises the push rod. The push rod in turn pivots the rocker arm causing a downward force on the valve stem, opening the valve. As the cam rotates further the valve spring closes the valve.

The camshaft and cam lobes must be machined and ground to very close tolerances. To give you an idea of how exacting the tolerances are, imagine that if the engine were running at 3000 r/min the camshaft

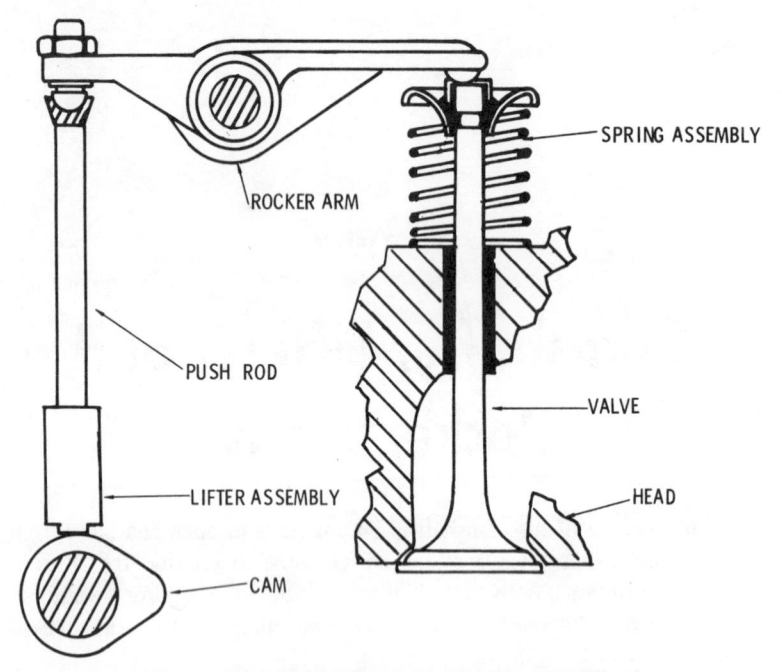

Fig. 1. Typical valve assembly (intake or exhaust).

would be turning at 1500 r/min. This means that each exhaust and each intake valve must open and close 1500 times each minute — and at just the right time. That means that 25 times each second each valve must be opened and closed. It is easy to see that the slightest error in cam lobe dimensions, arrangement, or grinding would greatly affect engine operation.

CONSTRUCTION FEATURES

The general construction features of all camshafts are similar, regardless of whether they are designed for 4-cylinder, 6-cylinder in-line engines or for V8 engines. The number and location of the cams and any gears they might have may be different, but the general appearance and material will be very similar.

Fig. 2 shows a camshaft used in a typical 6-cylinder engine, while Fig. 3 shows one for a V8. The principle difference between the two units is the number of bearing surfaces (4 for the 6-cylinder and 5 for the V8) and the number of cam lobes (12 for the 6-cylinder and 16 for the

Camshafts, Lifters, and Rocker Arms

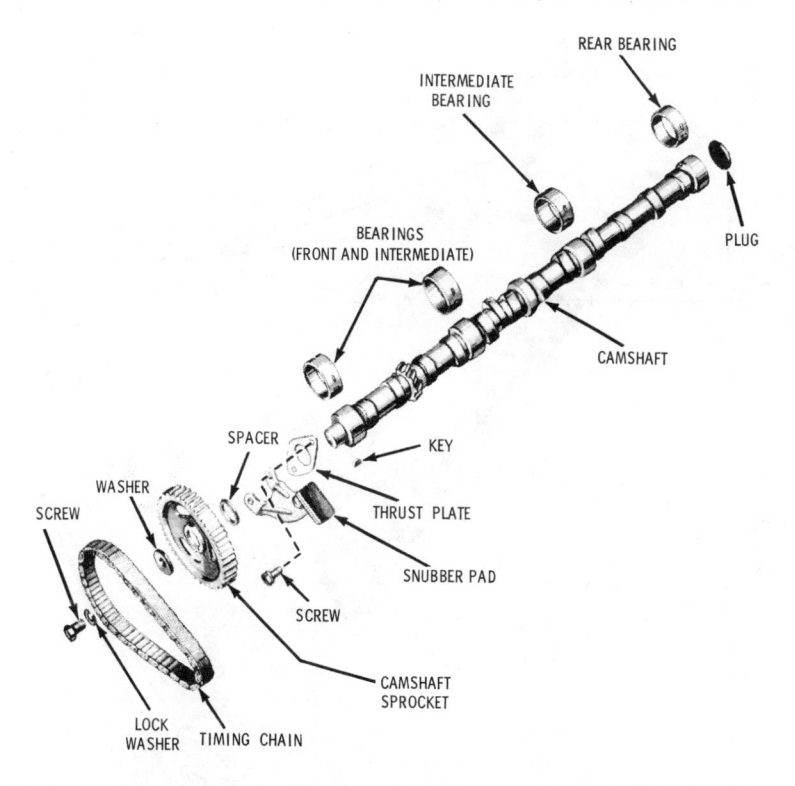

Fig. 2. A camshaft and related parts used on a typical 6-cylinder FORD.

V8). Even though camshafts may appear to be the same, they are seldom interchangeable from model to model and often not even from year to year in the same model. The reason for this is the many variables such as bearing journal diameters, cam lift and duration, length of shaft, accessories, etc.

The journals and cam lobes are precision ground and specially treated to produce a tough, wear-resistant surface. The shape and size of the cam lobes are critical and any appreciable wear that changes either of these factors will result in poor engine performance. Typical normal and abnormal wear patterns of cam lobes are shown in Fig. 4. Excessive wear of the lobe will cause late opening of the valve and a decrease in the amount of total lift. The latter condition can normally be compensated for by adjustment, but a late-opening valve cannot be corrected except by replacement of the camshaft.

211

AUTOMOBILE GUIDE

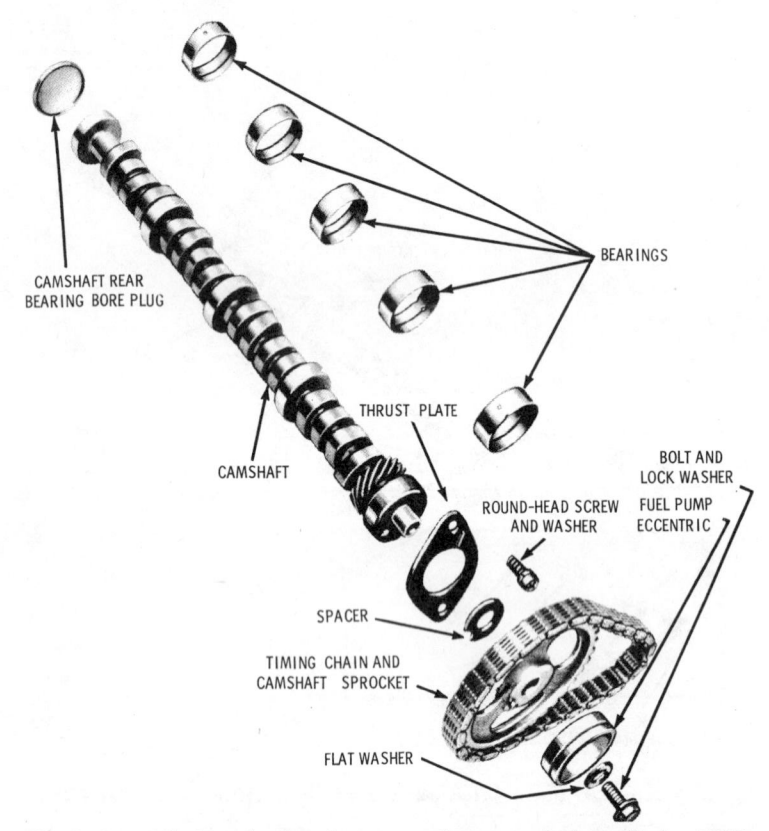

Fig. 3. A camshaft and related parts used on a typical 8-cylinder FORD.

OVERHEAD CAMSHAFTS

Some engines have a camshaft that is located above the valve train. Referred to as the "overhead cam" engine, the camshaft usually has seven bearing surfaces for a six-cylinder engine. Fig. 5 shows the location of the camshaft in relation to the valve train.

A passage is drilled the entire length of the camshaft with an oil hole drilled in the base circle of each cam lobe to supply lubrication (oil) to the cam pad surfaces of the rocker arm and the valve tip end. The cam pad surfaces are extra wide, operating against a cam lobe that is almost twice as wide as the standard lobe. This produces a very wide contact area and a very low contact pressure, for greatly increased reliability and durability.

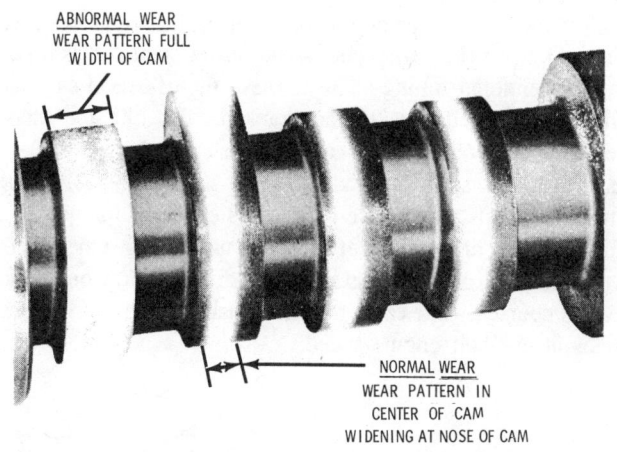

CAMSHAFTS, LIFTERS, AND ROCKER ARMS

Fig. 4. Examples of normal and abnormal cam-lobe wear.

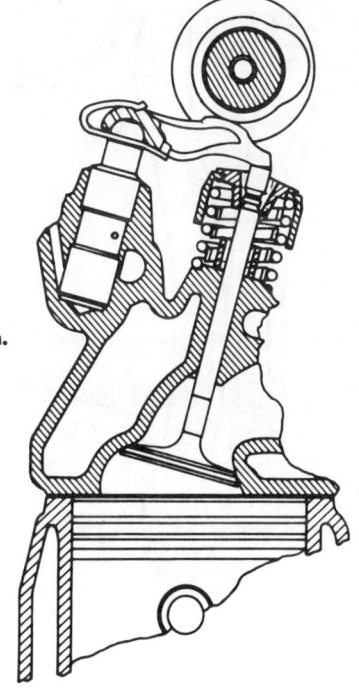

ABNORMAL WEAR
WEAR PATTERN FULL WIDTH OF CAM

NORMAL WEAR
WEAR PATTERN IN CENTER OF CAM WIDENING AT NOSE OF CAM

Courtesy Oldsmobile Div., General Motors

Fig. 5. Overhead camshaft valve train.

Automobile Guide

The overhead cam-type engine uses a fiberglass-reinforced rubber or nylon timing belt (Fig. 6). This special oil-resistant belt is used instead of the conventional timing chain to drive the overhead camshaft. The timing belt, located outside the crankcase is, like the chain type, protected by a metal cover. It connects the crankshaft (drive) sprocket, camshaft (driven) sprocket, and accessory sprocket(s). All sprockets in the timing system are surface-hardened steel for durability.

The accessory drive sprocket usually is used to drive the oil pump and distributor. Both oil pump and distributor operate at one-half engine speed. Of course — like conventional camshafts, the overhead camshaft operates at one-half engine speed.

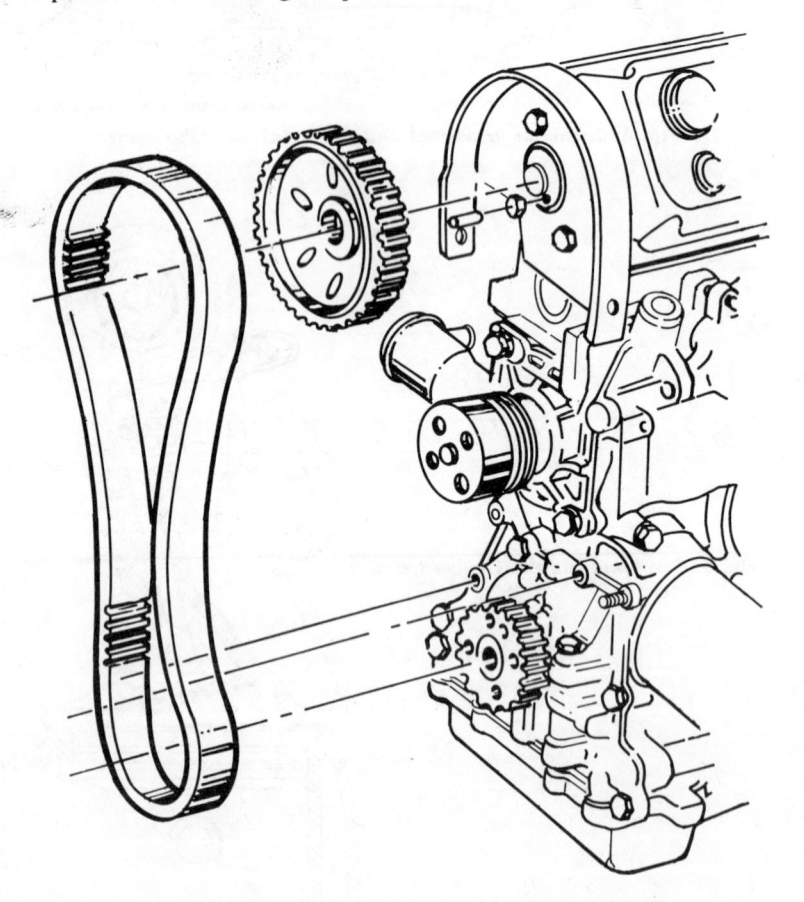

Fig. 6. Overhead cam timing gears and belt (typical).

Camshafts, Lifters, and Rocker Arms
SERVICING

The most usual type of service performed on the camshaft is replacement of bearing inserts. Cam lobes may become so worn that replacement of the shaft is necessary, and, occasionally, excessive and rapid bearing wear will be caused by a camshaft that is bent, requiring that it be straightened or replaced.

Bearing Replacement

Most camshaft bearings are of the steel-backed, babbit-lined, insert variety. Replacement of these units requires the removal of the camshaft. The removal procedure differs somewhat depending on the make and model of engine, but certain steps must be taken regardless of make or model.

The camshaft on most cars can be removed with the engine in the car provided the grille, radiator, fan, etc., are removed. On some cars, however, the engine must be removed before it is possible to remove the camshaft.

The camshaft is usually supported by 4 steel-backed, babbit-lined bearings in 6-cylinder engines, and 5 bearings in V8 engines. These bearings are pressed into the block and may or may not be line-reamed, depending on the make and model. The bearings on most camshafts are step-bored, being larger at the front bearing than at the back. This feature permits easier removal and replacement of the camshaft. A few cars, however, use the same size bearings throughout. Drilled galleries in the engine block supply oil under pressure to lubricate the camshaft bearings. It is therefore important that the oil hole in each bearing insert is lined up with the drilled hole in the block.

Camshaft Removal — The following steps should be followed to remove the camshaft (with engine out of the car):

1. Remove the cover from the timing chain and sprockets.
2. Remove the timing chain and sprockets, using the proper tools and procedure as recommended by the car manufacturer.
3. Remove the valve cover or covers.
4. Remove the valve push rods in sequence and place them in order in a rack so that they can be installed in their original positions.
5. Remove the hydraulic valve lifters or valve tappets through the push-rod openings, using a magnet or special tool if required.

Automobile Guide

Place the tappets or lifters in a rack in the correct order so they can be installed in their original positions.
6. Remove the distributor and shaft from the engine, following the procedure of the manufacturer.
7. Remove the oil pump and shaft, if driven directly from the camshaft.
8. Remove the fuel pump and push rod if driven by an eccentric on the camshaft.
9. Remove the camshaft thrust plate and spacer, if so equipped.
10. Carefully remove the camshaft by pulling it toward the front of the engine. *Use caution to avoid damaging the camshaft bearings, especially on those cars in which the bearing diameters are all the same.*

Inspection — Inspect the camshaft for scored or worn bearings. Bearing wear can be checked with inside and outside micrometers. Most manufacturers specify a maximum limit of from 0.004" to 0.006 " before bearing replacement is necessary. If only one exceeds the limit, all bearings should be replaced.

The camshaft journals should be checked for an out-of-round condition. If the journals are more than 0.001" out-of-round, either the camshaft should be replaced or the journals reground to a smaller diameter. Undersize bearings are available for some cars but not for others.

The camshaft should also be checked for alignment, especially if excessive bearing wear is evident. This is best done by the use of V-blocks and a dial indicator, as shown in Fig. 7. If the camshaft is more than 0.002" out of true, as read on the dial indicator as the camshaft is rotated, the camshaft should be straightened or replaced. *Use care in attempting to straighten the camshaft as it can be broken easily.*

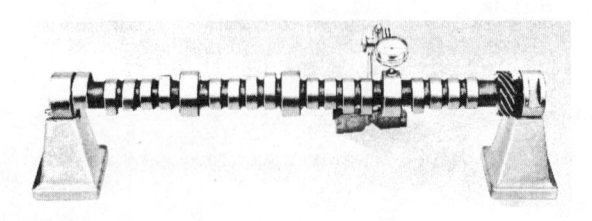

Fig. 7. Checking camshaft alignment.

Camshafts, Lifters, and Rocker Arms

Bearing Removal — If it is found necessary to replace the bearings, the following procedure is suggested for use on most cars:

1. Remove the crankshaft, if necessary.
2. Drive out the bore or expansion plug, in line with the camshaft and located at the rear of the engine block.
3. Remove the camshaft bearings using the special tool available for the particular engine being serviced.
4. Position the new bearings at the bearing bores such that the oil holes will align when the bearings are pressed into place.
5. Use the special tool (Fig. 8) to press the bearings into place. Follow the correct sequence as specified by the manufacture. Also make sure the correct size bearing (for taper-bored camshafts) is pressed into the correct bore.
6. Line-bore and ream the new bearings in engines requiring this operation.
7. Clean the rear expansion-plug recess thoroughly. Coat a new plug with oil-resistant sealer and install the plug with the flange facing out.

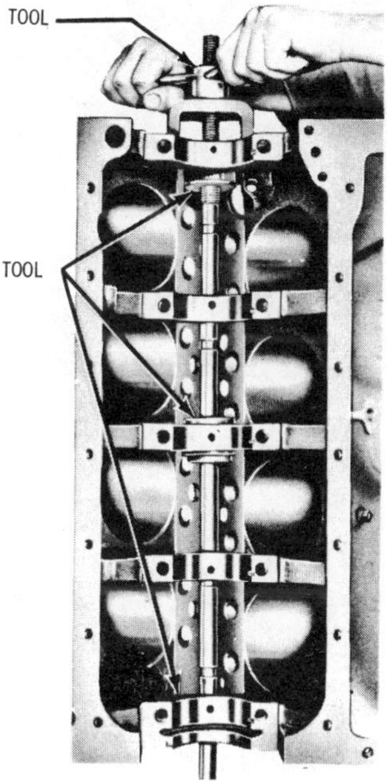

Fig. 8. Installing camshaft bearings in a FORD V8 engine, using special tools.

AUTOMOBILE GUIDE

8. Coat the camshaft with engine oil and install, using caution not to damage the bearing surfaces.
9. Install crankshaft (if removed) and other parts (flywheel, clutch housing, etc.) that may have been removed.
10. Position the sprockets and timing chain (or timing gears) on the camshaft and crankshaft (Fig. 9). Make sure the timing marks are positioned correctly, as specified by the manufacturer. Fig. 10 shows the correct alignment for most cars using a timing chain. An exception to this is shown in Fig. 11 for some 6-cylinder *Fords*. Here, the number of chain pins between timing marks determines the correct position of the sprockets. Fig. 12 shows the correct alignment of timing marks when timing gears are used instead of sprockets and a timing chain.

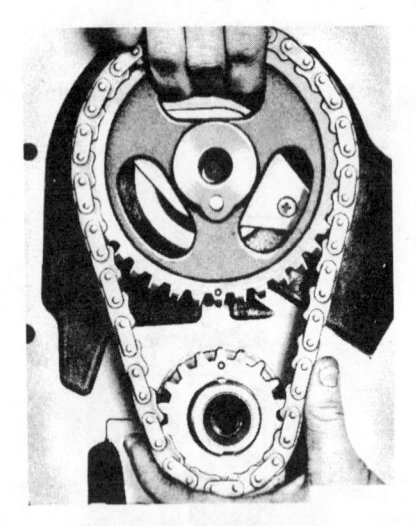

Fig. 9. Installing timing chain and sprockets.

11. Position the No. 1 piston on TDC after the compression stroke. Position the distributor and shaft in the block with the rotor at the No. 1 firing position and the breaker points open. Secure the distributor in place.
12. Install the oil pump and shaft. Follow the manufacturer's procedure for priming the pump. This varies, but requires either filling the pump with engine oil or packing it with a special lubricant before final assembly.
13. Install fuel pump and push rod.

CAMSHAFTS, LIFTERS, AND ROCKER ARMS

14. Install valve tappets (or hydraulic lifters) and valve push rods in their correct former positions. Perform any valve adjustment necessary.

15. Replace the rocker arm covers, using a new gasket.

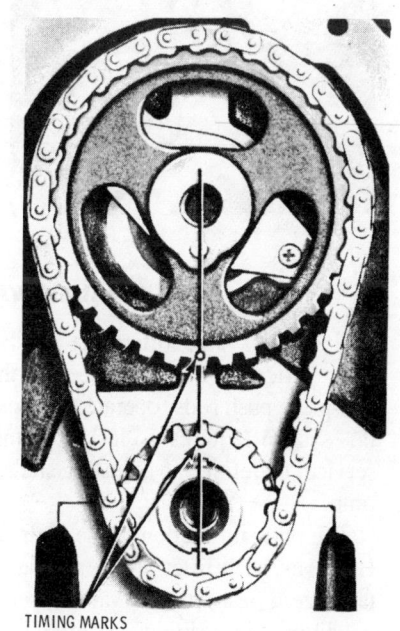

Fig. 10. Correct alignment of timing marks.

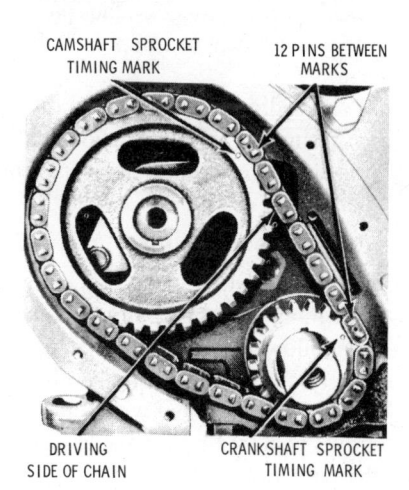

Fig. 11. Timing mark alignment on some 6-cylinder FORDS.

AUTOMOBILE GUIDE

Fig. 12. Example of timing mark alignment on timing gears.

TIMING MARKS

HYDRAULIC VALVE LIFTERS

Hydraulic valve lifters are used in most overhead-valve engines. These lifters ride on the lobes of the camshaft and, along with solid one-piece push rods, operate the rocker arms and valves. On most cars, this system requires no lash adjustment at the time of assembly or in service; therefore, no adjusting studs or screws are provided in the valve train.

The normal function of the hydraulic lifter is that of a cam follower. However, each lifter also serves as an automatic adjuster which maintains zero lash in the valve operating linkage under all operating conditions. In addition, the hydraulic lifter provides a cushion of oil to absorb operating shocks, thus promoting quiet valve operation. Periodic valve adjustment to compensate for wear of parts is completely eliminated.

The hydraulic lifters for the different makes and models of cars may vary slightly in construction features (Fig. 13), but the operating principles are virtually the same for all.

Operating Principles

The hydraulic lifter action on the camshaft is shown in Fig. 14. As shown, all parts of the lifter are housed in the main body, which is the cam follower. During manufacture, the body and plunger are machined to very close limits, with the plunger selectively fitted to each body to insure free movement with a minimum of clearance. The push-rod seat moves with the plunger and has a hemispherical seat to accept the end of the push rod.

CAMSHAFTS, LIFTERS, AND ROCKER ARMS

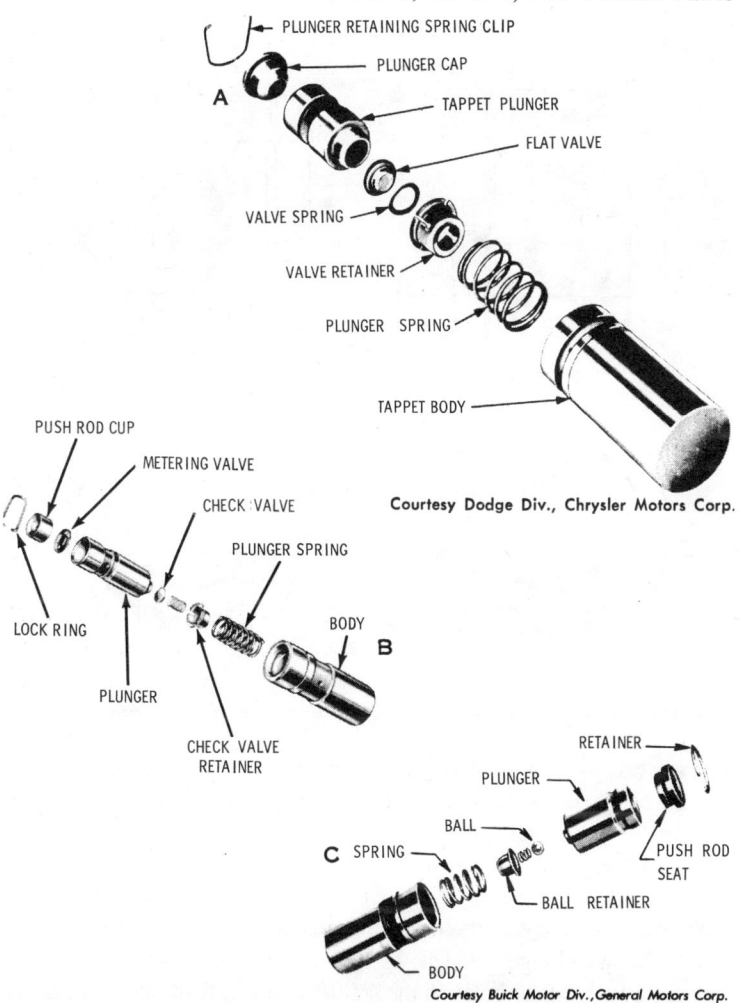

Fig. 13. Typical hydraulic valve lifters; (A) DODGE; (B) FORD; (C) BUICK.

The plunger is forced toward the upper end of the lifter body by a coil spring which also holds a check ball (or valve) retainer against the lower end of the plunger. A spring-wire retainer holds all the parts in the body when the push rod is removed from the seat.

When the valve lifter is installed in the engine, the push rod holds the plunger well below the spring-wire retainer ring at all times. In addition, the push rod also causes the entire assembly to press against

221

Automobile Guide

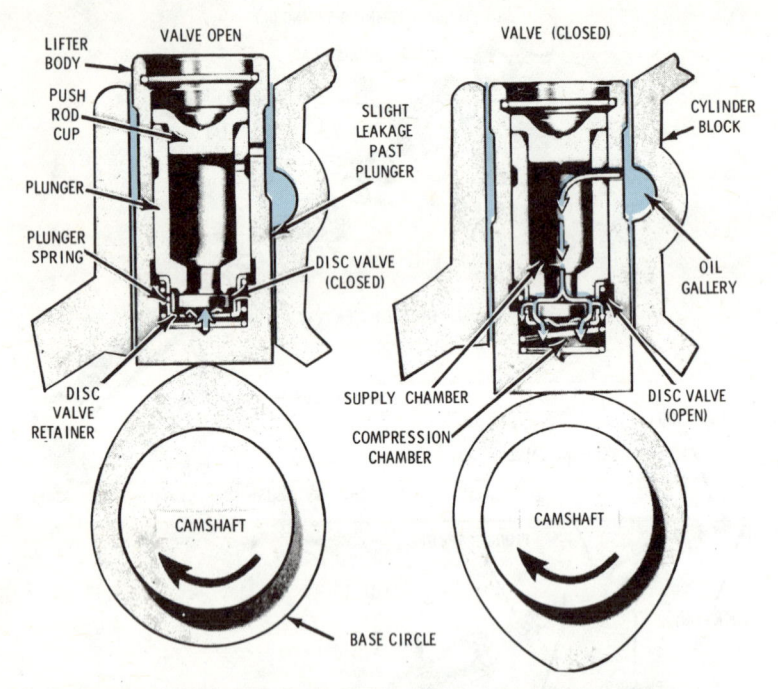

Fig. 14. Action of a hydraulic lifter as the camshaft rotates.

the camshaft with a load of several pounds (usually from 5 to 10 pounds). This pressure is sufficient to take up all lash clearances between the parts of the valve linkage without affecting the positive seating of the valve.

Oil is fed under pressure to all lifters through galleries in the crankcase. The oil enters the lifters through grooves and oil holes in the lifter body and plunger, and flows down into the chamber below the plunger through a feed hole. In the first few moments of operation after the engine starts, all air is forced out and the plunger and lower chamber is completely filled with oil.

At the start of each cycle of valve operation, the lifter body rests on the base circle of the camshaft. In this position, the plunger spring holds all lash clearance out of the valve linkage, and the check ball (or valve) rests on its retainer. Thus, conditions are such that the plunger feed hole is open to permit passage of oil into the lower chamber.

As the camshaft rotates, the cam lobe starts raising the valve lifter body, and the oil in the lower chamber starts flowing up through the

222

Camshafts, Lifters, and Rocker Arms

feed hole into the plunger. This action causes the ball or valve to seat against the plunger, preventing an appreciable loss of oil from the lower chamber. The lifting force against the body is thus transmitted through the entrapped oil to the check ball or valve and plunger so that the push-rod seat moves upward as a unit to operate the linkage to open the engine valve.

As the camshaft rotates further to close the engine valve, the valve spring forces the linkage and lifter to follow the cam lobe down. When the engine valve seats, the linkage and the lifter plunger stop moving, but the plunger spring now causes the lifter body to follow the cam down. Oil pressure holding the check ball or valve closed ceases when the plunger stops, allowing the ball or valve to drop down against its retainer. This action opens the feed hole in the plunger and permits the passage of oil once again into the lower chamber.

During the opening and closing action of the engine valve, a slight amount of oil escapes from the lower chamber through the clearance between the plunger and the body of the lifter. This oil returns to the crankcase. The slight loss of oil (called *leakdown*) is beneficial because it provides a gradual change of oil in the lifter. The opening of the plunger feed hole at the end of each cycle not only permits replacement of the oil lost from the lower chamber because of leakdown, but also permits control of the amount of oil in the lower chamber. The amount of oil compensates for expansion and contraction of valve linkage parts as the temperature of the engine changes.

When the temperature of the engine (and the oil) increases, the valve linkage parts expand, and the plunger in the lifter must move to a slightly lower position in the body to insure full closing of the engine valve. When the temperature of the engine decreases, the valve linkage parts contract, and the plunger must move to a slightly higher position to maintain zero lash in the valve linkage train.

HYDRAULIC LIFTER TROUBLES

Before disassembling any part of the engine to correct hydraulic lifter noise, check the oil pressure and oil level. The pressure should be within the specified limits (usually from 40 to 60 pounds at 1000 to 2000 r/min). The oil level should never be above the "full" mark on the dipstick, or below the "add oil" mark. Either of these two conditions can be the cause of noisy lifters, and severe damage to the engine if allowed to continue.

AUTOMOBILE GUIDE

An oil level above the "full" mark may result in the connecting rods dipping into the oil while the engine is running, causing the oil to foam. This foam will enter the lifters causing them to lose length, thus resulting in noisy operation.

Too low an oil level may allow the oil pump to take in air which, when fed to the lifters, again cause them to lose length, resulting in noisy operation. Any air leaks on the intake side of the oil pump will cause the same noisy lifter operation. Lifter noise due to air in the oil may be intermittent or constant, but will usually affect more than one lifter. When the fault has been corrected, the engine should be operated at fast idle for sufficient time to allow all the air in the lifters to bleed out.

The following is a list of noises that may be encountered, their probable cause, and the suggested remedy:

Rapping Noise Only When Engine Is Started — Any lifter that is on a camshaft lobe when the engine is stopped is under pressure of the valve spring. This will cause leakdown or escape of the oil in the lower chamber of the lifter. Thus, when the engine is started, a few seconds may be required to fill the lifter, especially in cold weather when the oil is sluggish. Noise from this source that occurs only occasionally is considered to be normal and requires no correction. If this noise occurs each time the engine starts, check for: (1) Oil too heavy for prevailing temperatures; (2) Excessive varnish in lifter. The remedy here is to: (1) Change to the recommended viscosity of oil for the prevailing temperatures; (2) Remove and clean varnish from valve lifter.

Intermittent Rapping Noise — A lifter noise that comes and goes every few seconds indicates leakage at the check ball or valve seat due to foreign particles, varnish, or defective valve or seat. Recondition the noisy lifters, checking carefully for the presence of grit or metal particles. If such foreign particles are present, a complete change of oil and filter is necessary, along with a thorough flushing of the system to remove the offending material.

Noisy Lifter Operation at Low or Idle Speeds — If one or more lifters are noisy at idle or at speeds up to 25 mph, but quiet at higher speeds, excessive leakdown or faulty check valve or seat is indicated. Faulty lifters may be detected by pushing down with equal pressure on each rocker arm while the engine is idling. Recondition the noisy lifters.

Noisy Lifter Operation at All Speeds — Check for high or low oil level in the crankcase. With the engine idling, strike each rocker arm on the push-rod side several sharp blows with a rawhide mallet. If the noise disappears, it indicates that foreign material was keeping the check valve from seating. Stop the engine and place the suspected lifters on the camshaft base circle (engine valve closed). If any lash clearance exists in any valve linkage, it indicates a stuck lifter plunger, a worn lower end on the lifter body, or a worn camshaft lobe. Recondition or replace the defective lifter or replace the camshaft as necessary, to correct the excessive clearance.

Noisy Lifter Operation at Normal Engine Temperature Only — If a lifter (or lifters) is noisy only when the engine is at normal operating temperature, excessively fast leakdown or a scored lifter plunger is indicated. Recondition the defective lifter.

Locating a Noisy Valve Lifter

A noisy hydraulic lifter can usually be located by operating the engine at idle speed and placing a finger on the face of each valve spring retainer in turn. If a lifter is not operating properly, a shock will be felt each time the valve seats.

NOTE: *Worn valve guides or cocked springs are sometimes mistaken for noisy lifters. If these parts are at fault, the noise may be dampened by applying a side thrust to the valve spring. If this does not appreciably reduce the noise, it can be assumed the lifter is at fault.*

Another method of identifying a noisy lifter is by the use of a piece of hose. With the engine idling, place one end of the hose near the end of the valve stem and the other end to your ear. Listen for a metallic click. Repeat this procedure on each intake and exhaust valve until the noisy lifter or lifters have been located.

Valve Lifter Service

The most common causes of hydraulic lifter troubles are dirt, gum, varnish, carbon deposits, and air bubbles. Less common troubles are caused by worn parts. If any of these causes exist (except for the presence of air bubbles), it will be necessary to remove the lifter for cleaning, repair, or replacement.

Dirt, gum, and varnish can prevent the check valve (or ball) from seating, causing a loss of hydraulic pressure. The plunger will force the oil back through the unseated valve into the plunger chamber during the time the push rod is being lifted. Dirt, gum, or varnish can also cause the plunger to stick or become sluggish, resulting in noisy operation. In the same manner, the body of the lifter may also stick in the bore. This will result in the engine valve remaining open at all times.

When it is necessary to remove one or more lifters, certain precautions should be observed. The following general procedure should be used:

1. Clean all dirt from cylinder heads, rocker-arm and valve-lifter covers, and any adjacent area. *It is of the utmost importance to avoid getting dirt into the hydraulic valve lifters.*
2. Remove the rocker arm and valve lifter covers as necessary to gain access to the valve lifters.
3. Remove the valve lifters that require service, following the procedure for the particular make and model of car being repaired.
4. Place the lifters in a wooden block having numbered holes or use another suitable method of identifying them according to their original position in the engine.
5. If less than a full set of lifters is being removed, immediately disassemble and inspect one or two lifters for the presence of dirt, gum, or varnish. If any dirt, gum, or varnish is found, all lifters should be removed for cleaning and inspection; otherwise it is necessary to service only those lifters that are not operating properly.
6. Examine the cam contact surface at the lower end of each lifter body. If this surface is excessively worn, galled or otherwise damaged, discard the lifter assembly and replace with a new unit.

Fig. 15 shows the appearance of the wear patterns on typical lifters. A lifter that has been rotating will have an overall wear pattern as shown in Fig. 15A, while a lifter that has not been rotating will have a pattern similar to the one in Fig. 15B. Either of these two conditions may be considered normal and such bodies may continue to be used. If any lifter shows the condition illustrated in Fig. 15C or D, it should be discarded and the mating camshaft examined for excessive wear or damage.

Disassembly and Cleaning — Observe the utmost cleanliness when disassembling and assembling a hydraulic valve lifter. *Never perform this operation on a dirty workbench.*

The internal parts of each hydraulic lifter are matched sets. Do not interchange with parts of other lifters. It is advisable to work on only

CAMSHAFTS, LIFTERS, AND ROCKER ARMS

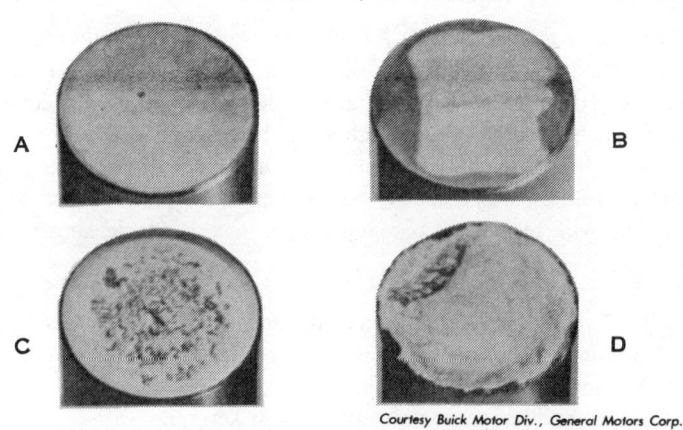

Courtesy Buick Motor Div., General Motors Corp.

Fig. 15. Lifter body wear patterns; (A) Rotating—normal; (B) Not rotating—normal; (C) Galled. Should be replaced; (D) Soft, worn. Should be replaced.

one lifter at a time to avoid mixing the parts. Keep the lifter assemblies in the proper sequence so that they can be installed in their original bores.

Use the following procedure to disassemble and clean:

1. Remove the plunger retainer ring with pliers or the special tool designed for this purpose. It may be necessary to depress the plunger to release the retainer ring. This can be done with a push rod.
2. Remove the push rod cup, metering valve (if so equipped), and plunger and spring assembly.
3. Invert the plunger and spring assembly and remove the check valve retainer. Next remove the check valve (ball or disc type) and spring.
4. Clean all parts in a suitable solvent that will remove all varnish and carbon.
5. Thoroughly wipe off all parts with a clean lint-free cloth, using a hard wiping action to remove any deposits. Rinse in clean kerosene.
6. Inspect the parts and discard the entire lifter assembly if any part shows signs of pitting, scoring, or galling. Replace the entire assembly if the plunger is not free in the body. The plunger should drop to the bottom of the body by its own weight.
7. Reassemble the lifter if all parts appear to be in good condition.

AUTOMOBILE GUIDE

Checking Leakdown Rate — Any reassembled hydraulic lifter or any unit suspected of being defective should be checked for correct leakdown rate. This is a test of how rapidly or slowly the oil from the lower chamber leaks past the plunger, allowing the plunger to settle toward the bottom of the lifter body. A certain amount of leakage is desirable in order that fresh oil will gradually be supplied to the lifter. Too rapid a leakdown, will result in noisy operation. Check for leakdown as follows:

1. Remove the push rod cup and completely submerge the lifter in an upright position in clean kerosene, or other liquid that might be recommended by the car manufacturer.
2. Allow the lifter to completely fill with kerosene.
3. Remove the lifter and replace the push rod cup.
4. Hold the lifter upright and force the plunger down with either a push rod or with special pliers (Fig. 16). If the plunger collapses almost instantly as pressure is applied, disassemble the lifter, clean and test again.
5. If the lifter still does not operate satisfactorily, replace with a new unit.

An alternate (and more accurate) test of the leakdown rate can be made by using one of the testers available commercially (Fig. 17). Proceed as follows:

1. Place the hydraulic lifter in the tester with the plunger facing upward. Pour hydraulic testing fluid into the test cup to a level that will cover the lifter assembly. Fluid for the tester can be purchased from the tester manufacturer. *Do not use kerosene as it will not provide an accurate test.*
2. Lower the ram on the tester until it rests in the push rod seat of the lifter. Adjust the length of the ram (if adjustable) until the pointer is in line with the starting mark as the ram contacts the push rod cup.
3. Pump the tester up and down through the full travel of the lifter plunger to force all air out of the lifter unit. Continue the pumping until considerable resistance is built up in the lifter.
4. Raise the weight arm of the tester to allow the lifter to completely fill with fluid, and then allow the ram and weight to force the lifter plunger downward. Measure the exact time it takes for the pointer

CAMSHAFTS, LIFTERS, AND ROCKER ARMS

to travel from the "Start Timing" mark to the "Stop Timing" mark.

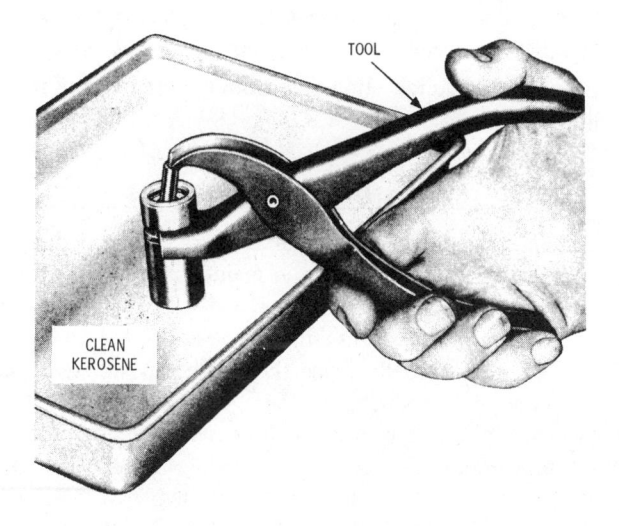

Courtesy Chrysler Plymouth Div., Chrysler Motors Corp.
Fig. 16. Testing a hydraulic lifter for proper leakdown.

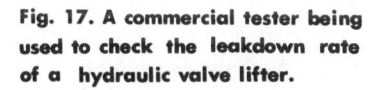

Fig. 17. A commercial tester being used to check the leakdown rate of a hydraulic valve lifter.

5. Compare the time with the specifications of the car manufacturer. Usually, a time of at least 10 seconds but less than 100 seconds indicates a satisfactory leakdown rate.

6. If the leakdown rate is not within specifications, disassemble the lifter and clean and inspect it. Reassemble and test the lifter again. If it still does not meet specifications, replace it with a new lifter. *Always test a new lifter before installing it in the engine.*
7. Bleed all hydraulic testing fluid from the lifter before installing it in the engine.

MECHANICAL VALVE LIFTERS

Cars equipped with mechanical valve lifters require periodic adjustment of the valve train mechanism to maintain the correct clearances. This adjustment is usually made on overhead-valve engines by means of an adjusting screw on the rocker arm (Fig. 18). The valve adjustment on an L-head engine is usually made directly below the valve stem by means of an adjustable stud (Fig. 19).

The valve adjustment is usually made with the engine at normal operating temperature. A feeler gauge of the specified thickness is inserted between the rocker arm and valve stem (overhead-valve engines) or between the adjusting stud and valve stem (L-head engines). The adjusting screw is turned in the proper direction until the correct clearance is obtained. This will be the point where the feeler gauge has a snug sliding fit during the time the valve is closed. When the correct clearance is obtained, the adjusting screw is locked in place by means of the locking nut provided.

NOTE: It is very important that the correct valve clearance be maintained. If the clearance is too small, the valve will open early and close late, causing rough engine idle and eventual warping and burning of the valve. If the clearance is too great, the valve will open late and close early, causing valve bounce and possible damage to the camshaft.

A more accurate valve clearance setting can be made by using a step-type ("go" and "no-go") feeler gauge, as shown in Fig. 20, instead of the common type. For example, if the desired valve clearance is 0.017 inch, a step-type gauge of 0.016 inch ("go") and 0.018 inch ("no-go") would be used. The "go" step should enter but the "no-go" step should not when the clearance is 0.017 inch.

Certain models of *Ford* cars have a zero-lash rocker arm that is used with mechanical lifters. This type of rocker arm, shown in Fig. 21, provides zero valve lash and minimizes valve train noise and wear.

Camshafts, Lifters, and Rocker Arms

Fig. 18. Valve clearance adjustment on an over-head valve engine that is equipped with mechanical lifters.

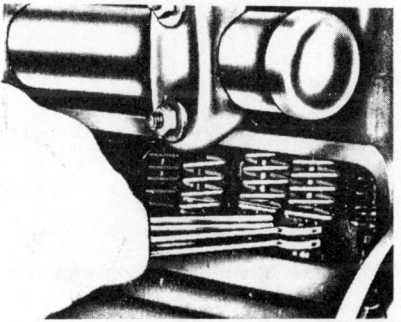

Courtesy American Motors Corp.

Fig. 19. Adjusting the valve clearance on an L-head engine equipped with mechanical lifters.

Courtesy American Motors Corp.

Fig. 20. Using a step-type feeler gauge to adjust valve clearance.

STEP-TYPE FEELER GAUGE

Adjustment of the valves differs somewhat when this type of rocker arm is used. The procedure is as follows, with the engine not operating:

1. Rotate the crankshaft until the piston associated with the valve to be adjusted is at the end of the compression stroke (both valves closed).

231

AUTOMOBILE GUIDE

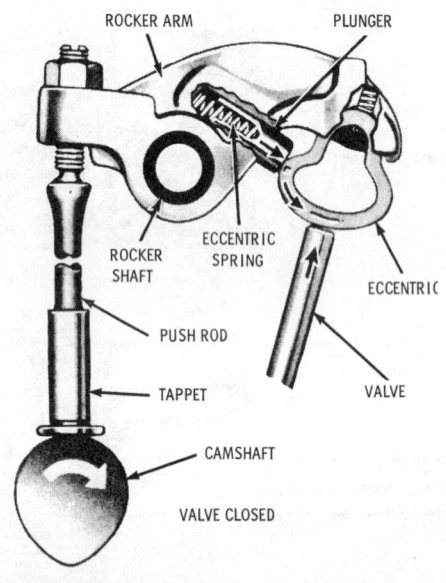

Fig. 21. Silent-lash rocker arm used on some models of FORD cars.

2. Push the rocker-arm eccentric toward the rocker arm until the eccentric spring (and plunger) is pushed completely into its bore

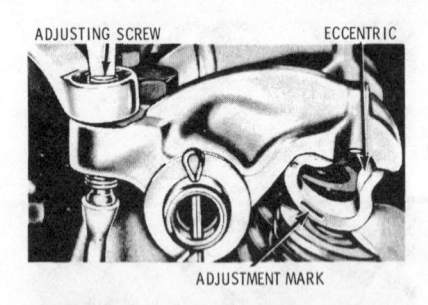

Fig. 22. Depressing the rocker-arm eccentric.

Fig. 23. Correct position of the eccentric.

232

CAMSHAFTS, LIFTERS, AND ROCKER ARMS

(Fig. 22). Turn the adjusting screw clockwise until the eccentric and plunger are held in that position.
3. Slowly turn the adjusting screw counterclockwise until the adjustment mark on the eccentric is exactly centered over the valve stem (Fig. 23). Tighten the lock nut to prevent the adjustment from changing.
4. Repeat the above procedure on all rocker arms, making sure the associated piston is at TDC at the end of the compression stroke.
5. Start the engine and operate it at normal idle speed. Observe the position of the adjustment mark on each eccentric. Make minor adjustments, as necessary, with the engine idling.

CAMS, LIFTERS, AND ROCKER ARM TROUBLES AND REMEDIES

Symptoms and Possible Causes   *Possible Remedies*

Engine Noises

(a) Hydraulic lifter(s) noisy.

(a) Change oil if dirty.
Repair or replace lifter(s).

(b) Plunger too tight in lifter body.

(b) Repair or replace lifter.

(c) Weak or broken plunger spring.

(c) Repair or replace.

(d) Plunger worn.

(d) Replace.

(e) Lock ring missing or improperly installed (if equipped).

(e) Repair or replace lock ring.

(f) Ball valve leaks.

(f) Repair or replace.

(g) Timing gear(s) loose.

(g) Replace or tighten gear(s).

(h) Timing gears misaligned.

(h) Correct as necessary.

(i) Improperly adjusted timing gear lash.

(i) Correct as necessary.

(j) Loose timing chain.

(j) Adjust or replace timing chain.

(k) Sprocket teeth worn, sprockets loose on shaft(s).

(k) Repair or replace as necessary.

(l) Sprockets misaligned.

(l) Align as necessary.

(m) Excessive camshaft bearing clearance.

(m) Correct as necessary.

Automobile Guide

Symptoms and Possible Causes

(n) Worn or damaged rocker arm(s) or rocker arm shaft.

Possible Remedies

(n) Repair or replace as necessary.

CHAPTER 10

Valves

Each cylinder in an engine has 2 valves — an intake valve which permits the air/fuel mixture to enter the cylinder, and an exhaust valve which permits the burned gases to escape. Thus, a 4-cylinder engine will have 8 valves (4 intake and 4 exhaust), a 6-cylinder engine will have 12 valves, and an 8-cylinder engine will have 16 valves.

Valves used in the modern engine are called "poppet" valves. The poppet valve is grouped into three general classifications, according to the shape of their heads: the "plain" valve, "mushroom" valve and "tulip" valve, as shown in Fig. 1.

Valves are usually made in one piece from special alloy steels. Intake valves are usually made of a chromium-nickel alloy. The exhaust valves, because of the extremely high temperatures they must withstand, are usually made of a silicon alloy.

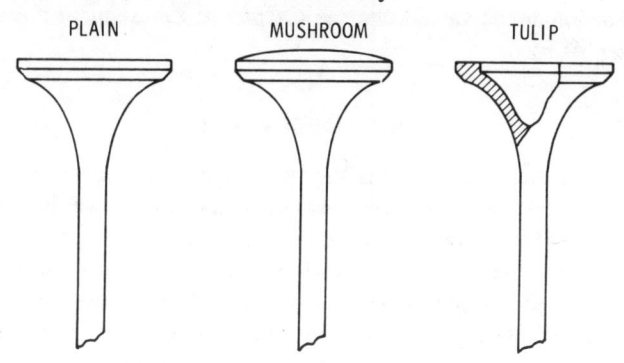

Fig. 1. Common types of poppet valves.

AUTOMOBILE GUIDE

On some engines, especially the air-cooled types, the exhaust valve may contain sodium in a sealed cavity extending from the head through the stem. The sodium helps to carry away heat from the head, through the stem, where it is conducted to the valve guide to aid in cooling. Normally, however, valve heads and seats are cooled by the transfer of heat to the adjacent metal and then to the water circulating through the engine water jacket, then to the radiator.

When the valves are closed, they must effectively seal the cylinder to prevent the escape of gas. This seal is made possible by the very accurate fit between the valve face and the valve seat. Valve grinding or refacing is necessary from time to time to renew the seal between the valve and its seat. Valve inserts of special high-temperature steel are used in some engines to aid in maintaining a good seal over prolonged periods of time.

The valves are kept in alignment with the valve seats by guides through which the valve stem extends. The valve guides and stems are precision fit to allow the valve stem to move freely up and down without any side play or passage of appreciable lubricant from one end of the guide to the other. The guides may be integral parts of the cylinder block or head, or they may be removable sleeves that can be replaced when worn.

The valves are opened by lobes on the camshaft rotating and applying pressure to the valve stem through the valve-train linkage. A typical linkage is shown in Fig. 2, where rotation of the camshaft against the tappet and push rod moves the rocker arm against spring tension of the valve stem opening the valve. The valves are closed by the pressure of the valve springs that act to move the valve against its seat when the camshaft lobes rotate out from under the valve tappet or lifter. For more information on the valve-train, see *Chapter 9: Camshafts, Lifters, and Rocker Arms.*

VALVE ASSEMBLIES

A typical valve assembly is shown in Fig. 3. An exploded view of both an intake and exhaust valve assembly is shown in Fig. 4. Generally, but not always, the exhaust-valve head will be of a smaller diameter than the intake-valve head. So that intake and exhaust valves are not mixed, the intake valve will generally have the word "IN" stamped on the head, and the exhaust valve will have "EX" stamped on the head.

VALVES

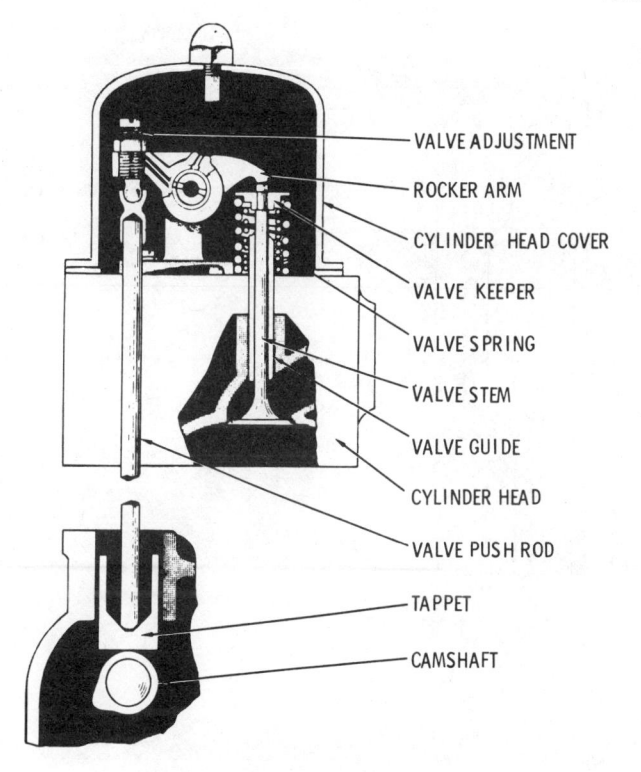

Fig. 2. Typical valve train linkage.

VALVE SEATS

Valve seats are present in an automobile engine to provide a perfect seal with the valves when the valves are closed. Any wear or distortion of either the valve face or the valve seat will destroy this perfect seal and make repair or replacement of these parts necessary, as damage to the engine is unavoidable.

The valve seats in most engines are an integral part of the engine block or cylinder head, having been machined into either of these units. When this type of seat becomes damaged or excessively worn, it becomes necessary to regrind it to effect a repair. Repeated regrinding will eventually result in the removal of too much metal, in which case the engine block or cylinder head will have to be discarded. This rarely happens, however, if care is taken in the grinding process, and if the valve train clearances are maintained.

AUTOMOBILE GUIDE

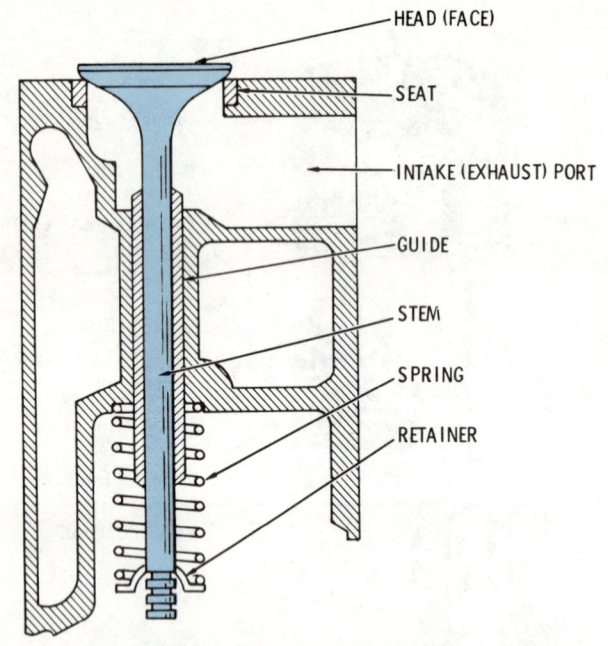

Fig. 3. Typical valve assembly.

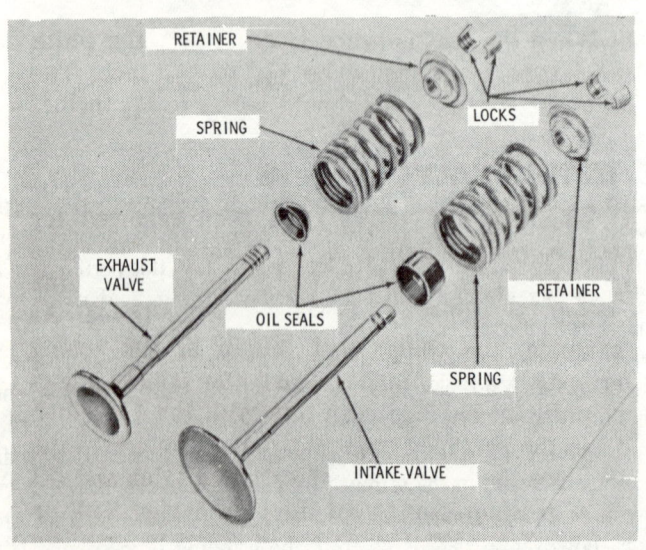

Fig. 4. Exploded view of an intake and exhaust valve assembly.

VALVES

Many engines have valve seat inserts, which means that those seats that cannot be reground to specifications can be removed and new units installed. In many cases it will be found that only the exhaust valve in each cylinder will have a valve seat insert — the intake valve will not.

The angle at which the valve seat is ground, as well as the width of the refinished face, is very important and must be maintained to specifications. Refacing the seat will always result in a greater seat width. This width can be brought back to specifications by removing metal either from the bottom of the seat with a grinding wheel having a greater angle than the wheel used to grind the face, or from the top of the seat with a wheel having less of an angle than the wheel used to grind the face. Fig. 5 shows the recommended angles for performing this operation on the valve seats in a certain model *Ford. Remember, these angles may be different for other makes and models.* Fig. 6 shows a scale being used to measure the seat width.

Not only must the angle and width of the valve seat be maintained, but also the runout must be held to close tolerances. A special gauge (Fig. 7) is used to check runout. If the reading exceeds the allowable limit (usually from 0.001 to 0.002 inch, depending on make and model of engine), the face must be reground.

The valve faces and seats in most engines are ground at the same angle. When this is the case, the final grinding operation can be accomplished by means of valve-grinding compound. It is becoming

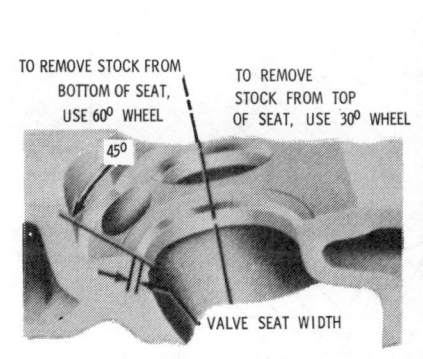

Fig. 5. Valve-seat refacing.

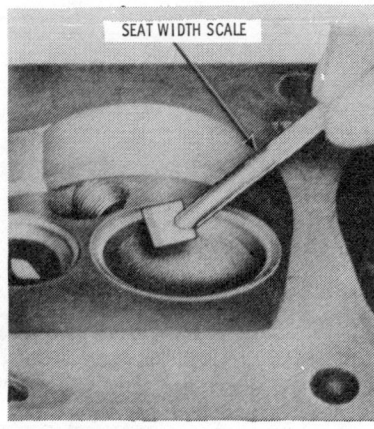

Fig. 6. Measuring the width of a valve seat.

239

Automobile Guide

more prevalent, however, to reface the valve at a slightly different angle than the valve seat to provide what is known as an *interference fit*. An example of this is shown in Fig. 8. In this particular engine, both the intake and exhaust valves have an interference fit with their seats. Some other cars may have this type of fit only on the exhaust valve. It is obvious that with the different angles between the valve face and seat, grinding compound cannot be used to finish the surfaces. Instead, refacing equipment must be utilized.

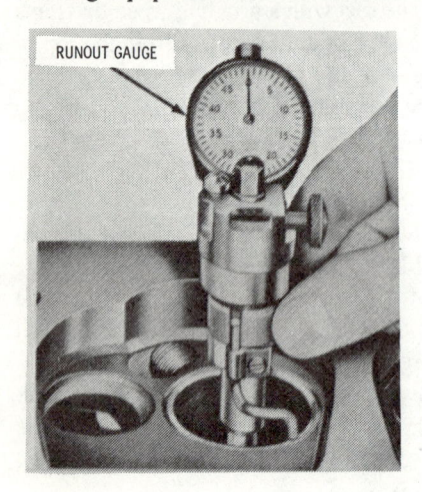

Fig. 7. Checking runout (concentricity) of a valve seat.

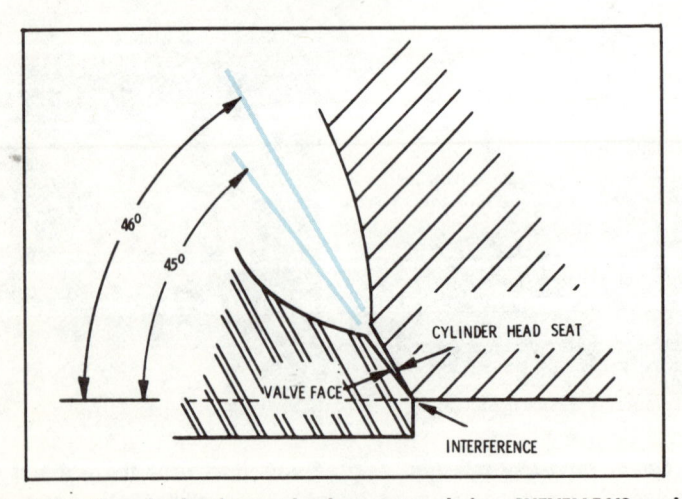

Fig. 8. Relation of valve-face and valve-seat angle in a CHEVELLE V8 engine.

VALVES

When refacing the valve seats, it is important to use the correct size valve-guide pilot for the refacing stones. This will insure a true and complete surface. After the refacing operation, measure the runout of the seat with the proper gauge (see Fig. 7). The total runout should not exceed the allowable limit which is usually 0.002 inch.

The overall contact of the valve face with the seat can be checked by lightly coating the valve seat with Prussian blue. Set the valve in place and rotate while applying a light downward pressure. If the blue is transferred to the center or upper half of the valve face (nearest the top of the head), the fit is satisfactory. If the blue is transferred to the extreme top edge, lower the valve seat with a stone of the proper angle (usually 30°). If the blue is transferred to the bottom edge of the valve face, raise the seat by using a stone of the recommended angle (usually 60°). When the seat is properly positioned, its width must be within the recommended specifications (usually from 3/64 to 3/32 inch).

VALVE GUIDES

Valve guides allow the valves to move up and down and provide accurate positioning of the valve face on the valve seat. The guides may be an integral part of the engine block or head, or may be in the form of inserts.

For those engines in which the guides are an integral part, valves with oversize stems are available when the guides (or valve stems) become excessively worn. For those engines with valve guide inserts, wear can be corrected by replacement of the guides and/or valves.

When wear of either the valve stem or the guide is suspected, both should be checked. The valve stem diameter can be measured with a micrometer. If the wear exceeds the specifications (usually 0.002 inch), the valve should be replaced.

The valve guide can be checked for wear by means of a gauge such as shown in Fig.9. With this method, the sleeve (Fig. 9A) places the valve at the correct position to obtain the proper measurement with the dial indicator. The gauge is fastened to the cylinder head and at right angles to the valve stem being measured. Move the valve to and from the indicator. The total reading should not exceed specifications (usually 0.010 to 0.015 inch).

If the valve-guide wear is excessive, the guide should be reamed for a valve with an oversize stem. Select the correct size reamer, (Fig. 10),

AUTOMOBILE GUIDE

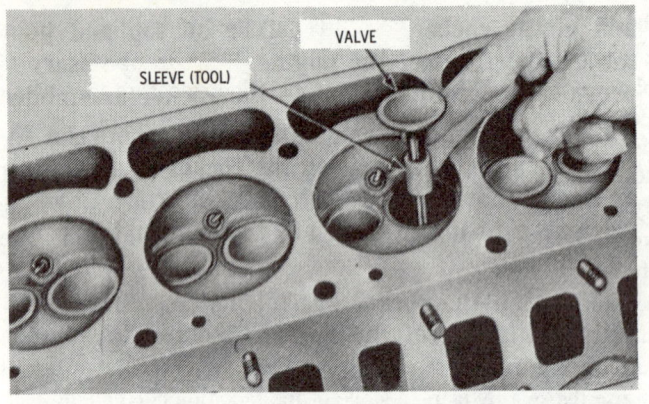

A. Special sleeve necessary for measuring valve guide wear.

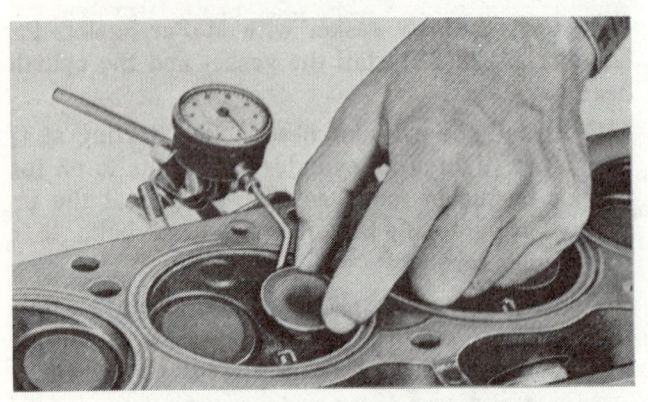

B. Dial indicator used to check valve guide wear.

Courtesy Chrysler Plymouth Div., Chrysler Motors Corp.

Fig. 9. Checking valve guide wear.

and slowly turn it by hand in the valve-guide bore. Clean the guide thoroughly before installing the new valve.

Never attempt to ream a valve guide from a standard size directly to the maximum oversize. Instead, ream in steps using sucessively larger reamers. In this manner the guide will be reamed true in relation to the valve seat.

Valve-guide insert replacement (in cars so equipped) is necessary when the old insert is worn beyond specifications. The insert can be removed and a new one installed by means of special tools and an arbor press, or by special tools and a hammer (for *Buicks*, shown in Fig. 11).

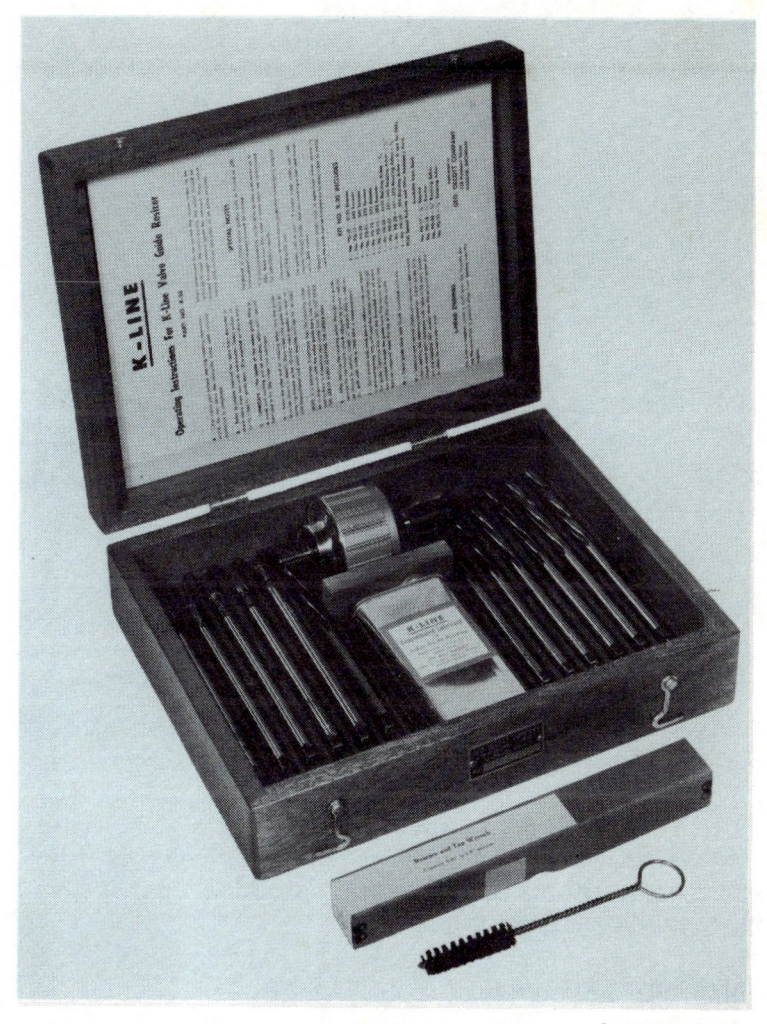

Fig. 10. Valve guide re-sizer set.
Courtesy K Line Tool Co.

After a new guide has been installed, it must be hand reamed to the correct size.

VALVE SPRINGS

Whenever the valves have been removed for inspections, reconditioning, or replacement, the valve springs should be tested. This is often

AUTOMOBILE GUIDE

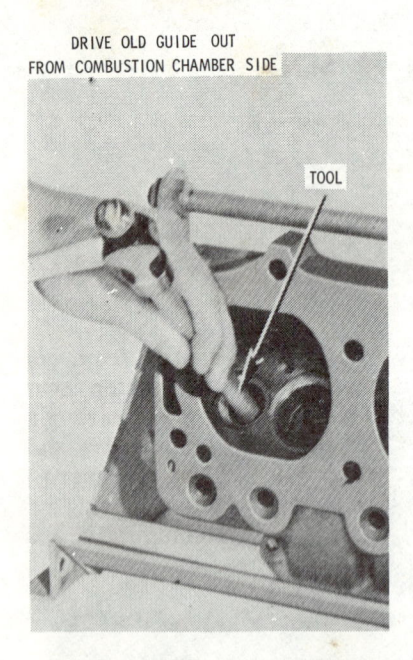

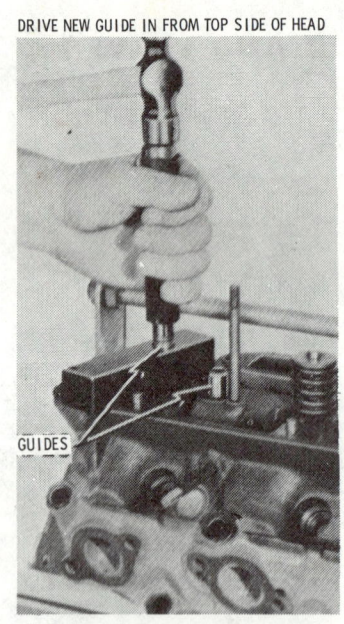

DRIVE OLD GUIDE OUT FROM COMBUSTION CHAMBER SIDE

DRIVE NEW GUIDE IN FROM TOP SIDE OF HEAD

Courtesy Buick Motor Div., General Motors Div.

Fig. 11. Removing and installing a valve guide in a BUICK engine.

overlooked, but the valve springs play a very important part in proper engine operation. A weak valve spring may cause unsatisfactory seating of the valve, resulting in rough engine idling and possible damage to the valve. A distorted spring or one with too much tension may cause excessive wear of the camshaft lobes. Therefore, testing the valve springs for correct pressure and squareness should be a part of every valve reconditioning operation.

Valve Spring Pressure

Each valve has only one spring on most cars. There are a few exceptions to this, however, one being certain *Buick* models that have two — one inside the other. The spring pressure is different for each car, ranging from as low as 70 pounds to as high as 280 pounds. The usual pressure, however, is from 100 to 150 pounds. Special tools are available for checking the valve spring pressure, one type being shown in Fig. 12.

To measure the pressure, the spring is compressed to a specified length, and the force necessary to hold it at this length is the valve

VALVES

spring pressure. A reading that varies more than 10 pounds from the specifications indicates the spring should be replaced.

Squareness

The valve spring should also be tested for distortion by using the method shown in Fig. 13. An ordinary machinist's or carpenter's square is placed on a flat surface with the valve spring positioned as shown. The length is measured as the spring is rotated. If the measurements vary by more than 1/16 inch, install a new spring. The overall length of the spring can also be measured with this setup and should agree with the specifications.

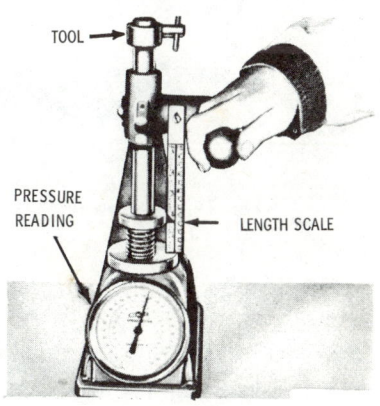

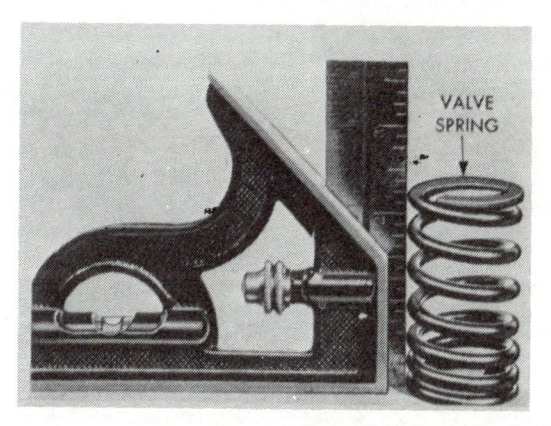

Fig. 12. Check valve-spring pressure.

Courtesy Chrysler Plymouth Div., Chrysler Motors Corp.

Fig. 13. Checking valve-spring squareness.

245

AUTOMOBILE GUIDE

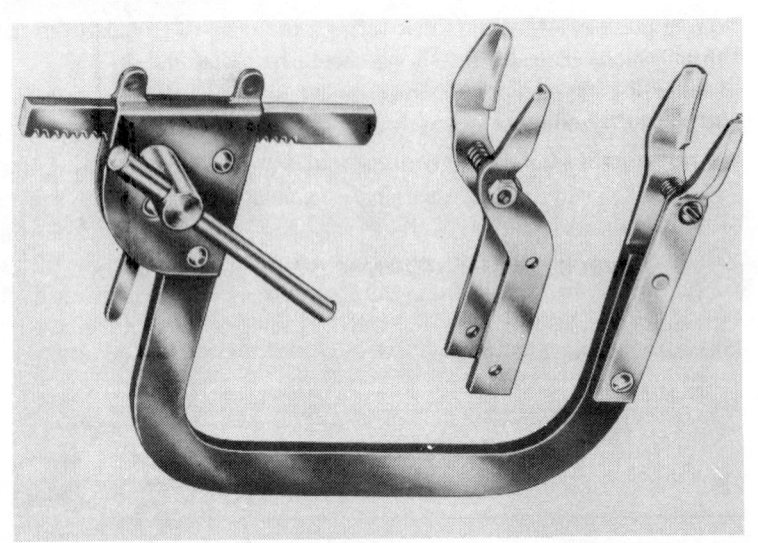

Courtesy AMMCO Tools Corp.
Fig. 14. Valve spring tool for valve-in-head engines.

Installation

Installation (or removal) of the valve spring requires the use of a compressor tool. These are available in different designs, many of them being made specifically for a particular make and model of engine. A typical tool for this purpose is illustrated in Fig. 14. This type of tool is used when the cylinder head is removed from the engine.

The valve springs can be installed in or removed from most engines with the cylinder head in place. To do this, the spark plug is removed from the cylinder that requires valve spring service and a threaded compressed-air adapter is inserted.

NOTE: *This adapter can be made from the body of a spark plug from which the porcelain has been removed and into which an air-hose adapter has been threaded.*

Connect an air hose to the adapter and maintain at least 90 lbs. of air pressure in the cylinder while the valve spring is being removed. The air pressure will hold the valve against its seat so the valve lock and upper retainer can be removed. A different type of spring compressor tool than the one shown in Fig. 14 will have to be used with this method. A plier-type tool (Fig. 15) is usually the handiest to use in this case.

VALVES

Fig. 15. Plier-type valve spring tool.

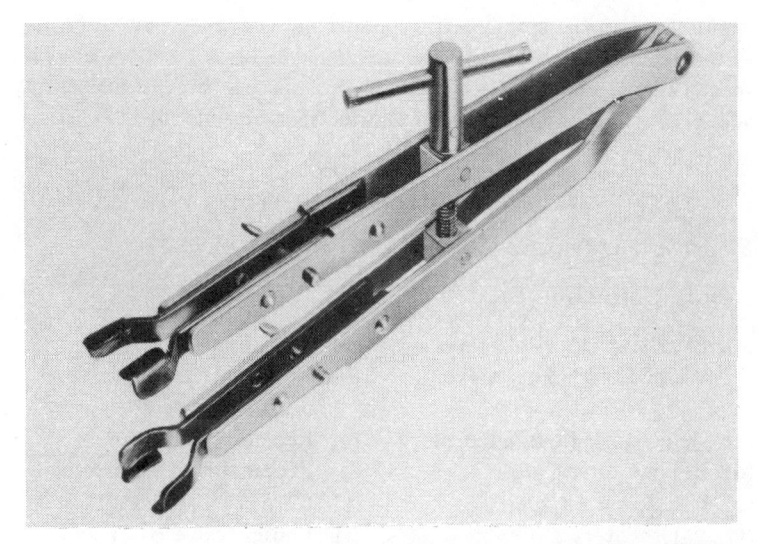

Courtesy AMMCO Tools Corp.

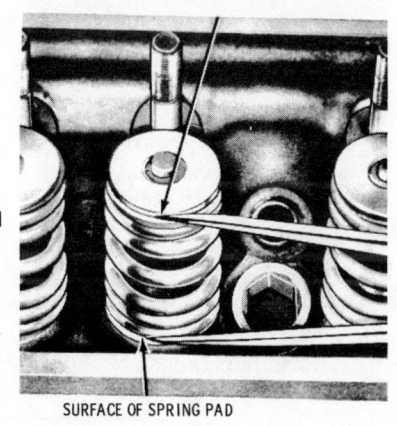

Fig. 16. Measuring the installed height of a valve spring.

SURFACE OF SPRING PAD

New oil seals should always be installed on the valve stems when the valve springs have been removed. In addition, replace any damaged spring shields (if used), or retainers.

Valve Spring Installed Height

The installed height of the valve spring should be checked especially if the valves or seats have been reground. This measurement is made from the top of the spring seat (or shim, if used) to the bottom of the spring retainer (Fig. 16). If the installed height is greater than the specifications, add the necessary number of spacers between the spring and its seat to bring the assembly to the recommended height.

VALVE TROUBLES AND REMEDIES

Symptoms and Possible Causes   *Possible Remedies*

Engine Noises

(a) Excessive tappet clearance.   (a) Adjust valves.
(b) Warped or sticking valve.   (b) Replace or repair valve as necessary.
(c) Defective hydraulic tappet.   (c) Replace tappet.
(d) Binding rocker arm.   (d) Repair rocker arm.
(e) Insufficient oil supply.   (e) Correct as necessary.
(f) Valve covers too tight.   (f) Loosen valve cover and tighten properly. (valve cover too tight will amplify normal valve noises).
(g) Valve face not concentric with valve stem (or valve seat face).   (g) Correct as necessary.
(h) Worn or damaged parts anywhere in valve system.   (h) Repair as necessary.
(i) Broken or weak valve spring(s).   (i) Replace spring(s).
(j) Excessive tappet/valve clearance.   (j) Adjust as necessary.
(k) Cocked valve spring(s).   (k) Correct as necessary.
(l) Cam surface rough.   (l) Regrind or replace cam.

CHAPTER 11

Engine Lubricating, Emission Control, and Exhaust Systems

One of the most important systems in an automobile is the one that lubricates the engine. Failure of this system will result in serious damage to the engine in a very short time. In the early days of automobiles, the engine was lubricated entirely by the *splash system*. This was satisfactory for the comparatively loose fitting parts then in use, provided the oil level was not allowed to get too low. As the power of engines was increased and greater precision used in fitting parts, the splash system was found to be inadequate. Thus, a combination of *splash and pressure* was used to distribute the oil to the various engine parts. Finally, the *full-pressure system* of lubrication was adopted and is used almost universally in the modern automobile engine.

ENGINE LUBRICATION

The lubricant (oil) in an engine actually performs four major functions (Fig. 1). It prevents metal-to-metal contact (lubricates) between moving parts; it assists in carrying heat away (cools) from the engine; it cleans (cleanses) the engine parts; and, it provides a seal between the piston rings and cylinder walls to prevent blow-by of combustion gases.

The primary function of engine lubrication is to reduce the friction between moving parts. Friction not only uses power that would otherwise be available to drive the automobile, but is also destructive and

Automobile Guide

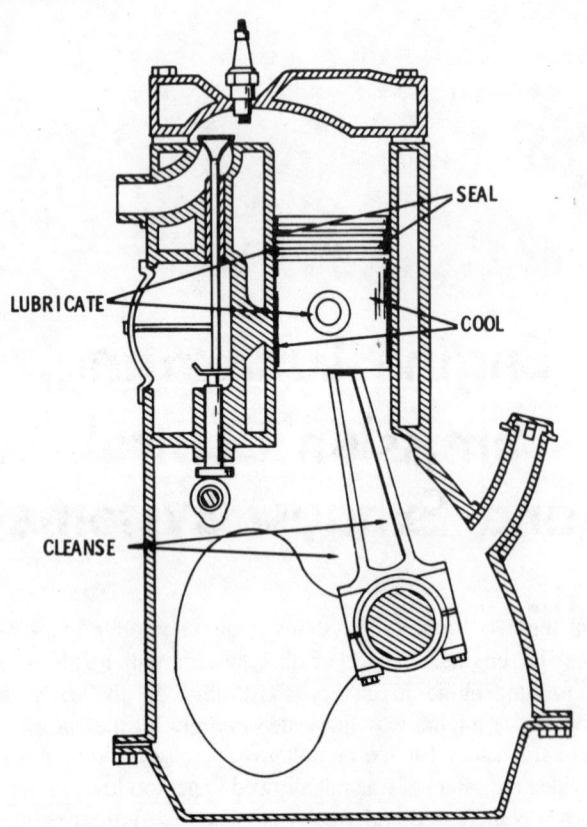

Fig. 1. Four major functions of motor oil.

creates heat that can destroy the moving parts. Moving parts that are deprived of oil will either melt, fuse, or seize after a very short period of operation. It is lubrication (oil) under pressure that makes possible the use of relatively simple and thin bearings and bushings in a modern engine.

The bearings at the crankshaft, connecting rods, wrist pins, camshaft, etc., are important points that must be constantly lubricated. In addition, other parts must be provided with an adequate supply of oil. For example, the valve stems must operate under stress and a wide range of temperature, and so require lubrication. Valve tappets and cams, gears, timing chains, and accessory drives also require a constant oil bath. In fact, any moving part must be bathed in oil while the engine is operating or else it will fail.

Engine Lubricating, Emission Control, and Exhaust Systems

The engine oil is heated through contact with the pistons and cylinder walls, after which it returns to the oil pan. Air flowing around the outside surface of the oil pan serves to cool the oil.

PRESSURE LUBRICATING SYSTEMS

All domestic cars manufactured today use a pressure-type engine lubricating system (Fig. 2). Oil from an oil-pan pump is delivered under pressure to various parts of the engine. Oil passages in the engine block deliver a constant flow of oil to the main bearings and connecting rod bearings. In order to direct the oil to the connecting-rod bearings, oil passages are drilled in the crankshaft. The oil enters these passages from openings in the main bearings and main journals. In some engines, these openings are merely holes that index (line up) once for every revolution of the crankshaft. This is sufficient to fill the oil passages in the crankshaft and furnish oil to the connecting-rod bearings. In other

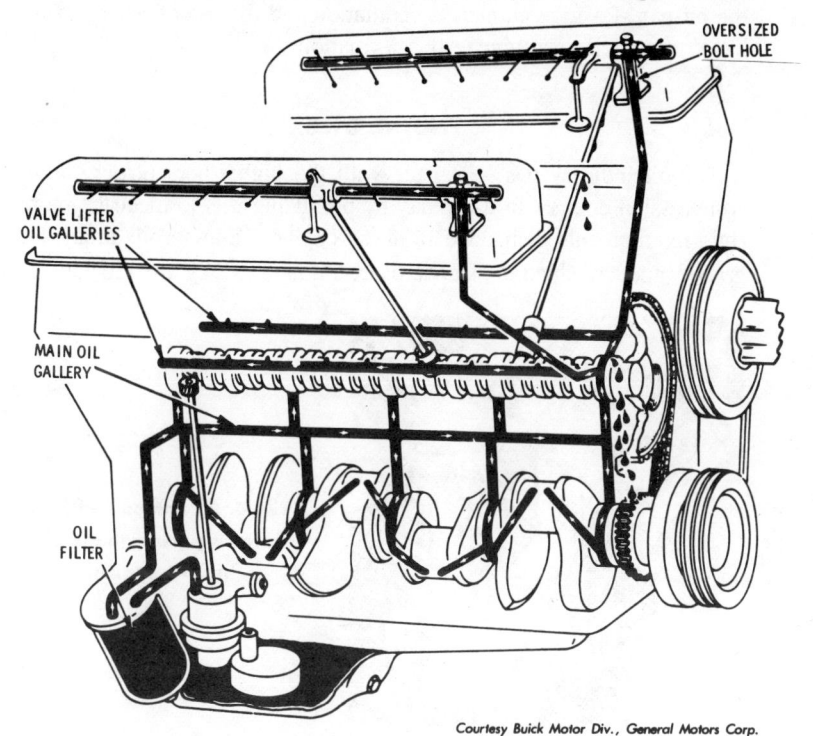

Courtesy Buick Motor Div., General Motors Corp.

Fig. 2. A typical pressure lubricating system.

Automobile Guide

engines, annular grooves are machined in the bearings through which oil can constantly pass into the passage through the crankshaft.

The cylinder walls are lubricated in most engines by means of a small groove or a drilled hole in the connecting-rod bearing that indexes with a matching hole in the connecting-rod journal once for every revolution of the crankshaft. This method is used most often in V8 engines where oil from the squirt hole in one connecting-rod bearing lubricates the opposite cylinder wall. For example, the No. 1 connecting rod lubricates the No. 5 cylinder, etc. As the crankshaft turns, the hole in the connecting-rod bearing aligns with the hole in the journal, causing a direct squirt of oil onto the cylinder wall (Fig. 3).

Piston pins are usually lubricated by the splash of oil created by the crankshaft. Moving parts not lubricated either by splash or by oil under pressure will be lubricated by dripping oil on its way back to the oil pan.

The formation of sludge will often clog the drain passages provided in the engine block to return the oil from the rocker-arm lubrication to the oil pan. Positive crankcase ventilation and the use of detergent oil has done much to minimize this formation.

ENGINE OILS

The oil industry has kept pace with the higher-horsepower, high-compression engines in use today by producing oils to meet the more rigid requirements demanded by these engines. Engine oils today are graded and classified to standards recommended by the Society of

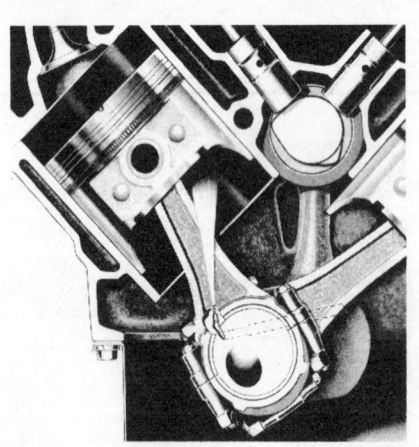

Fig. 3. A common method of lubricating the cylinder walls in a V8 engine.

ENGINE LUBRICATING, EMISSION CONTROL, AND EXHAUST SYSTEMS

Automotive Engineers (SAE) and the American Petroleum Institute (API).

It was, until about 1965, necessary to change engine oil every 1000 miles. This change interval has been greatly extended by the improved design of the modern engine, engine oils, and oil filters. Change intervals of 4000 to 6000 miles or more are common, provided the proper type of oil designated for the heavy-duty requirements of engines are used. The change interval, too, depends on the make and model of the car as well as the general driving conditions. Always follow the car manufacturer's recommendations for the correct change intervals as well as grade and type of oil.

Viscosity

The viscosity of an oil refers to its resistance to flow. When oil is hot, it will flow more readily than when it is cold. In cold weather, therefore, oil should be thin (low viscosity) to permit easy flow and, consequently, easier engine starting. In hot weather, oil should be heavier (high viscosity) to retard the rate of flow.

Oils are graded according to their viscosity by a series of SAE numbers. The higher the SAE number, the more viscous, or heavy, the oil (Fig. 4). This viscosity number has no connection with the lubricating qualities of the oil.

The oil most frequently used in automobile engines has SAE numbers of 10W, 20, and 30. For extreme cold conditions, SAE 5W is available, but when this weight is used, sustained high speeds (above 65 mph) should be avoided because of possible increased oil consumption.

Multi-viscosity oil is also available and becoming more and more popular. This type of oil is produced in many grades (5W-20, 10W-30, 10W-40, 20W-20, and 20W-50) which provides the starting ease of low-viscosity oil and the protection of high-viscosity for sustained driving. These multi-viscosity oils are generally acceptable by most car manufacturers.

Viscosity ratings tell us important facts about the characteristics of oil. For instance, a 10W-40 rated oil has the properties of a 10 viscosity oil (thin) at 0 F and the properties of a 40 viscosity oil (thicker) at 210 F.

The viscosity (SAE number) of the oil should be selected for the lowest anticipated temperature at which engine starting will be required, and not for the temperature at the time of oil change. The following temperatures and recommended viscosities are generally acceptable.

253

AUTOMOBILE GUIDE

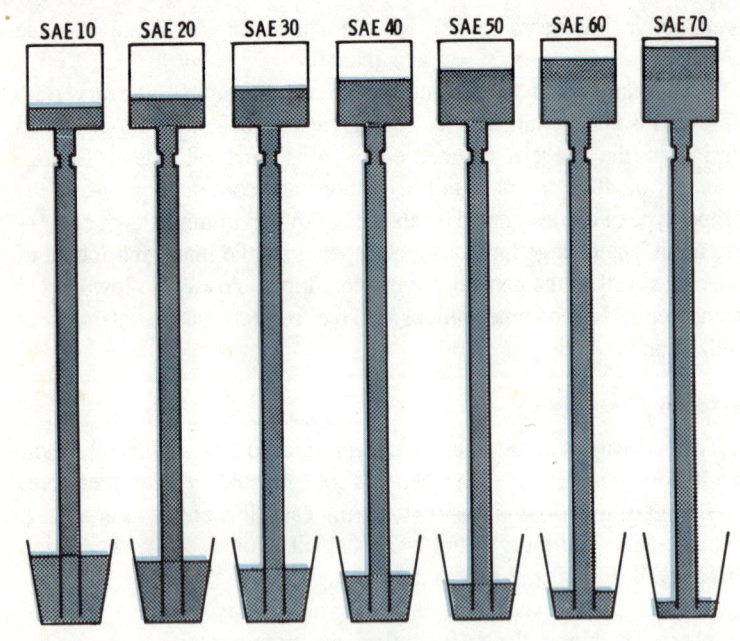

Fig. 4. Oil flow rate.

Chart 1: Oil Grades vs. Outside Temperature

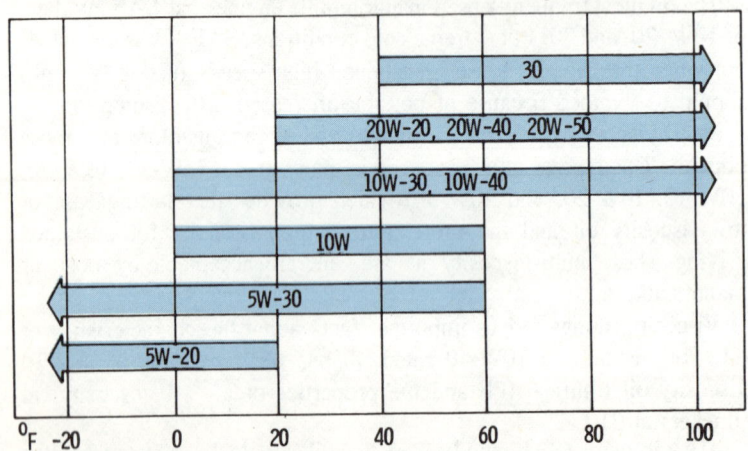

These viscosities are suggested for use in cars in good condition. A higher viscosity, such as SAE 30, may be required in high-mileage cars to decrease oil consumption.

254

ENGINE LUBRICATING, EMISSION CONTROL, AND EXHAUST SYSTEMS

Classification

There are several types of oil manufactured for use in automobile engines. For maximum engine protection and performance under all driving conditions, it is recommended that only an oil marked "API Service Classification — SE" be used. The letters "SE" should appear on the oil container singly or in combination with other designations. This oil is a heavy-duty detergent-type formulated to withstand severe service conditions in modern automobile engines.

Oils designated as types "SA" through "SD" are not recommended for use in automobile engines and should not be used except in emergencies when "SE" oil is not available.

"SA" is a light mineral oil, whereas "SD" is a petroleum product regarded as adequate for automotive service until about 1974, when it was replaced by "SE" grade oil.

Changing Oil

Oil does not wear out, but it does become contaminated and diluted. For this reason, the oil should be changed at the recommended intervals as determined by the car manufacturer for specific driving conditions.

Probably the most serious cause of engine oil deterioration is that of dilution. Dilution is caused by fuel vapor (and, in some cases, raw gasoline) leaking past the piston rings and mixing with the oil. Another cause of dilution is the condensation of moisture on the cylinder walls and crankcase. Leakage of fuel vapors into the oil pan occurs mostly during engine warm up when the fuel is not completely vaporized and burned. Water vapor enters the crankcase through normal engine ventilation and through the blow-by of exhaust gases. When the engine is not completely warmed up, these water vapors condense and combine with condensed fuel vapors and exhaust gases to form acid compounds in the crankcase. The acid thus formed can cause serious etching or pitting, resulting in rapid wear of wrist pins, bearings, and other moving parts of the engine.

Another result of water condensation is the emulsification that takes place when this water combines with the oil and any dirt or foreign matter present. In this way, sludge is formed that may clog oil lines and lubricating passages.

Raw gasoline drawn into the cylinders by excessive choke action or unvaporized fuel remains in a liquid state and drains past the piston rings into the oil pan. Here it is mixed with the oil. This mixture decreases the viscosity of the oil and causes it to lose some of its lubricating qualities. Presence of gasoline will not lower the oil level but will maintain or even raise it.

Many devices incorporated in the modern automobile engine help to minimize engine-oil dilution. The coolant thermostat, heat-control valve in the exhaust manifold, automatic choke, and crankcase ventilation are among the items that help control dilution.

Probably the greatest contributor to dilution is stop-and-go driving. Longer continuous driving allows the engine to reach operating temperature and evaporate any water or raw gasoline that may have mixed with the engine oil. For this reason, the oil should be changed at shorter intervals when the driving is principally stop-and-go or slow, short-time drives.

It is advisable to drain the crankcase only after the engine has become thoroughly warmed up to its normal operating temperature. Otherwise, the benefit of changing the oil is largely lost, as some of the suspended foreign material will cling to the sides of the oil pan and will contaminate the new oil.

Additives

Motor oils used in the modern cars of today, to meet exacting demands, use several additives to help increase the effectiveness of the oil to protect vital engine parts. High-speed high-temperature driving necessitates certain additives to help prevent engine damage.

Viscosity index improvers and a pour-point depressant is used to keep the oil at a low temperature thereby helping keep the viscosity index stable, since the higher temperatures of today's engines would tend to thin the oil.

Compounds are also used to help increase the anti-wear properties of the oil. Detergents are used to help keep sludge and varnish-forming materials suspended in the oil so they may be easily removed from the engine whenever the oil is drained (changed). Corrosion inhibitors (acid neutralizers) are used to counteract the action of any corrosion that might result if some acids are formed. Oxidation inhibitors are used to help slow down the process of oxidation at high temperatures, and foam inhibitors are used to help prevent bubbles from being formed in the crankcase by the churning action of the crankshaft (also to help those bubbles formed to break up quickly).

Additives are available for oil and fuel that are claimed by the manufacturer to improve general engine performance. Use of these

ENGINE LUBRICATING, EMISSION CONTROL, AND EXHAUST SYSTEMS

additional additives should, however, be up to the discretion of the car owner. Some claim that they help while others feel that the oil refiners have included all necessary additives.

Filters

An oil filter is standard equipment on most late-model automobiles. This unit filters the oil, removing most of the impurities that have been picked up by the oil as it circulates through the engine. There are two general types of filters on automobile engines at present — the full-flow and the partial-flow type.

An internal view of a full-flow filter is shown in Fig. 5. In this type, all of the circulating oil passes through the filter element before entering the main oil gallery. If the filter element should become so clogged that the oil cannot pass through it readily, a spring-loaded by-pass valve will open to allow oil to circulate freely. Under this condition, of course, no filtering action will take place. Regular replacement of the filter will prevent this from ever occurring.

In the partial-flow filter, only a portion of the total circulating oil passes through the filter element. The remainder is by-passed around the element.

In some cars, only the filter element and gasket needs replacement at the prescribed intervals. In other cars, the entire filter is discarded and a new unit installed. Follow the car manufacturer's instructions for changing the filter.

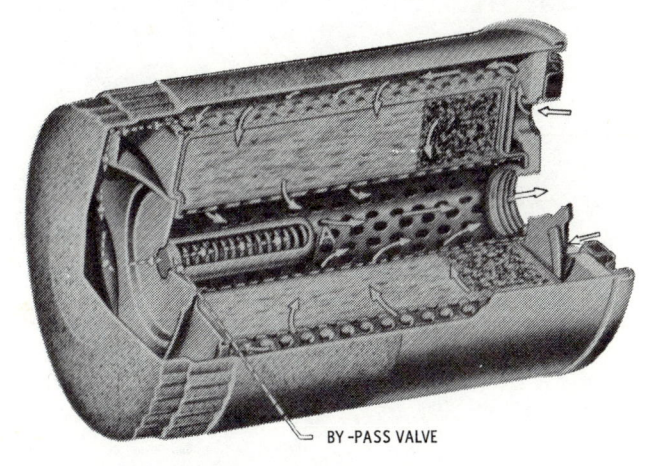

Fig. 5. Internal construction features of a full-flow type of oil filter.

AUTOMOBILE GUIDE

Most filter assemblies also contain an antidrain valve. This valve closes when the engine stops and holds the oil in the passages instead of allowing it to drain back to the oil pan. Thus, when the engine is started, oil is immediately available and engine lubrication starts at once.

OIL PUMPS

Oil pumps are of two general types — the meshed-gear and the rotor type. The meshed-gear type, shown in Fig. 6, consists of a driven gear and an idler gear enclosed in a housing. The two gears are rotated by a shaft that is usually coupled to the camshaft. In some instances, the oil pump shaft is an extension of the distributor shaft. Maximum oil pressure is regulated by means of a pressure-regulator valve. Oil is drawn into the pump through a screened intake which prevents any foreign material from entering the circulating oil system. As a safety precaution, some means is provided to bypass the screen if it should become clogged. This pickup screen assembly is designed to float in some cars to prevent its picking up any sludge or sediment that may settle to the bottom of the oil pan.

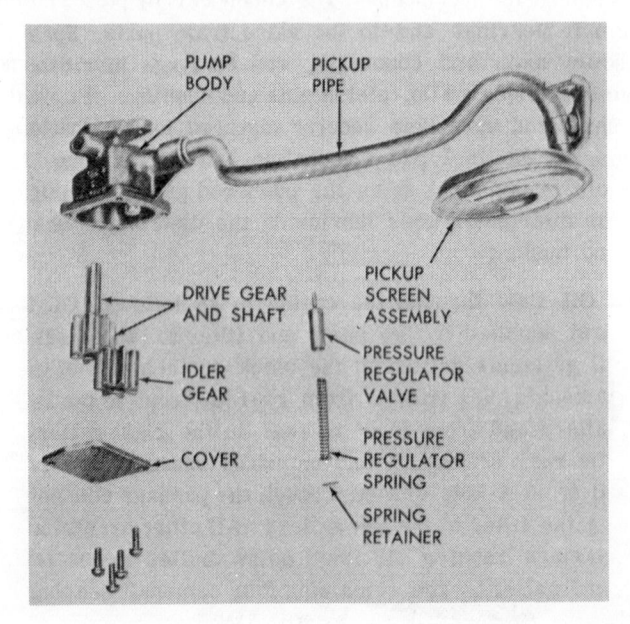

Courtesy Pontiac Motor Div., General Motors Corp.
Fig. 6. A meshed-gear type oil pump.

ENGINE LUBRICATING, EMISSION CONTROL, AND EXHAUST SYSTEMS

The rotor-type oil pump (Fig. 7) differs very little from the meshed-gear type. An off-center inner rotor is the driven element, and as it turns, it causes an outer rotor to rotate. This action draws oil into the pump and forces it out into the oil circulating system. A pressure relief valve and inlet oil strainer is also included.

To service either type of oil pump requires the removal of the oil pan on all but a few models of cars. The inlet screen should be cleaned at this time and any worn parts in the oil pump replaced. The entire meshed-gear assembly or the rotor assembly should be replaced, even though only one part is worn or defective. Always use new gaskets when reassembling the pump. Refer to the manufacturer's instructions for removal and reassembly.

OIL-PRESSURE INDICATORS

Two different types of oil-pressure indicators are in use on automobiles. The most common type is the oil-pressure warning light that comes on only if the oil pressure drops below a predetermined level. In this system, a pressure-sensitive switch is wired in series with the ignition switch, the warning bulb, and the car battery. With no or with low oil pressure, this switch is closed and the bulb lights. As pressure builds up, the switch opens and the warning light goes out. Thus, when the ignition switch is turned on, the warning light comes on. After the

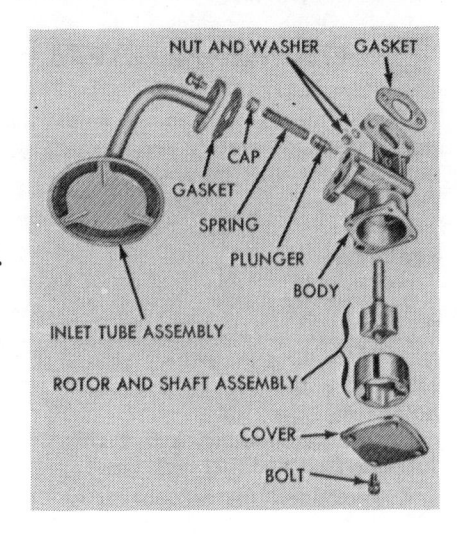

Fig. 7. A rotor-type oil pump.

engine starts, the oil pressure increases and opens the pressure-sensitive switch, and the light goes out. On some cars, the warning light may come on at slow idle speeds. This may be normal and does not necessarily indicate a malfunction of the oil pressure system.

The other type of oil-pressure indicator is a gauge actuated by a pressure-sensitive sending unit located somewhere in the oil circulating system. The resistance of the sending unit varies according to the amount of pressure in the engine lubricating system, causing the gauge to indicate the comparative pressure existing. The gauge is calibrated either in pounds per square inch or some other comparative units to indicate the relative pressure with which the oil is being forced through the system.

CRANKCASE VENTILATION

When an automotive engine is in operation, a certain amount of the fuel and exhaust fumes pass by the piston rings and into the crankcase. These fumes, called *blow-by*, must be removed to prevent serious contamination of the engine oil. Until the mid 1960s these fumes were removed through a road-draft tube leading from the crankcase (Fig. 8). Most engines also had a fresh-air inlet on the oil fill pipe. Movement of the vehicle created a slight vacuum at the draft tube outlet under the car and a slight pressure of air under the hood around the oil fill cap. These pressure differences drew in fresh air sufficient to ventilate the crankcase and exhaust the contaminated air from the crankcase.

To insure that exhaust contaminants to the atmosphere are held to a minumum, the *Positive Crankcase Ventilation* system was developed. The PCV system recycles the engine blow-by fumes back into the engine combustion chambers where the hydrocarbons are reburned (Fig. 9). In the state of California, where the problem of air pollution first reached national prominence, laws were passed requiring all cars sold in that state be equipped with the pollution control device.

Further evidence of the effectiveness of the PCV system is the fact that all domestic cars are now so equipped. While the road-draft tube did a good job of removing blow-by fumes, the system had three disadvantages:

1. At low speeds (including idling), air does not move through the system with enough velocity or often enough to properly ventilate the crankcase.

Engine Lubricating, Emission Control, and Exhaust Systems

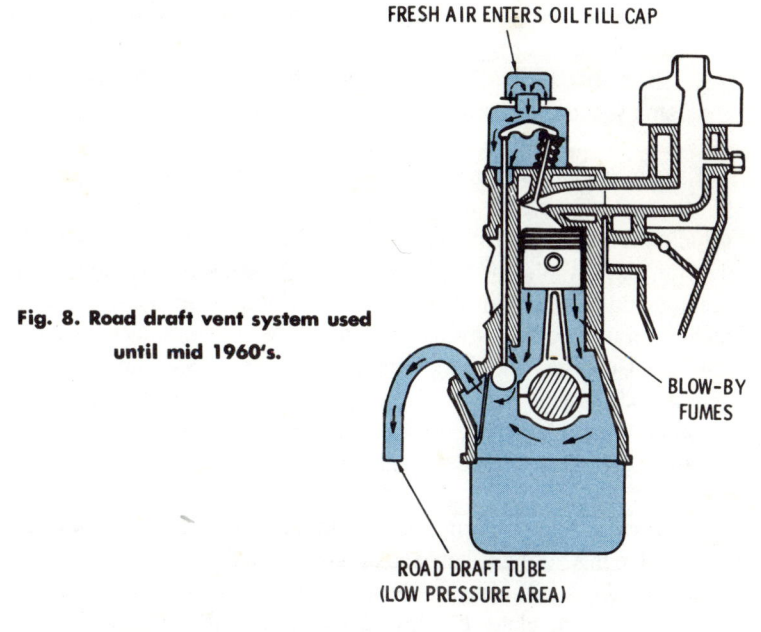

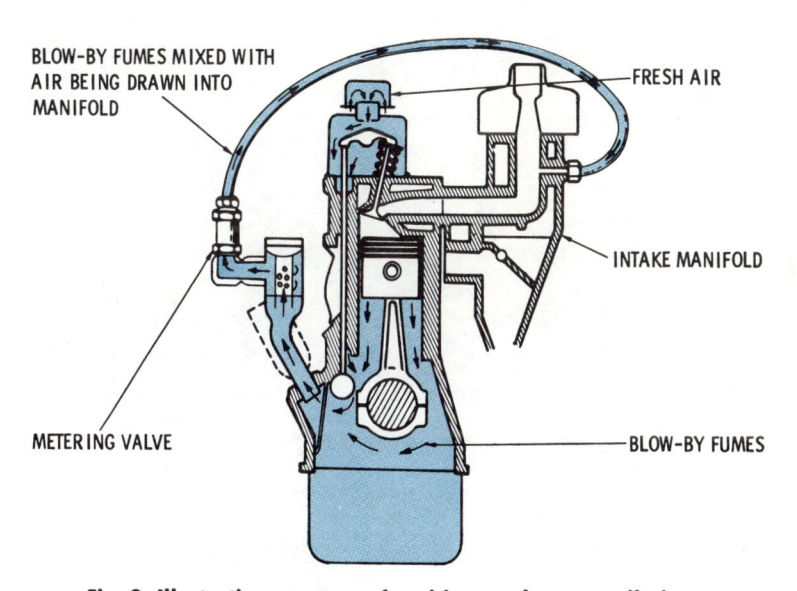

Fig. 8. Road draft vent system used until mid 1960's.

Fig. 9. Illustrating one type of positive crankcase ventilation.

261

Automobile Guide

2. The unburned gases vented into the atmosphere at higher speeds contribute to air pollution.
3. The unburned portion of the blow-by fumes are wasted in the atmosphere, reducing the vehicle's potential miles per gallon.

The disadvantages of the road-draft tube system are eliminated by the PCV system. Unlike the road-draft tube system, PCV does not rely on vehicle movement, but maintains a positive movement of air through the crankcase at idle and at all engine speeds. This greatly reduces the accumulation of harmful deposits when driving in heavy stop-and-go traffic. An unexpected advantage of the PCV system is increased fuel mileage. Unburned fuel fumes from the crankcase are drawn into the engine and burned, rather than being lost to the atmosphere.

At the present time, the various types of PCV systems installed as original equipment can be classified as follows:

1. Systems with metering valves, installed in most cars, have the valve in a hose line between the crankcase and the intake manifold (see Fig. 10). The metering valve, controlled by the engine vacuum, regulates the flow of air through the line (see Fig. 9). Fresh air is introduced through the oil fill cap.

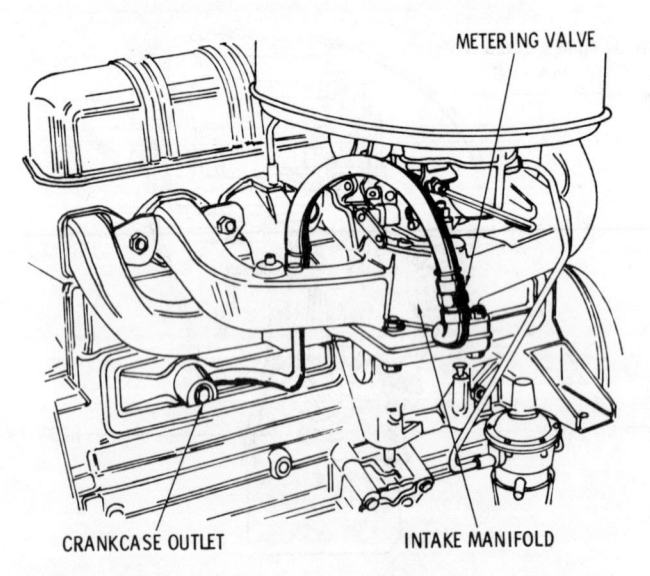

Fig. 10. A typical PCV valve installed in the return hose.

Engine Lubricating, Emission Control, and Exhaust Systems

2. Systems without valves utilize a large diameter hose which connects the crankcase outlet to the carburetor air cleaner (see Fig. 11). This system does not incorporate a valve, and therefore the service required is reduced. This system is used on many imported cars and several domestic cars.
3. Closed systems which may or may not have a metering valve will all have a sealed-type oil fill cap in place of the usual ventilated type. Air enters the crankcase through a hose connected to the carburetor air cleaner.

In all open systems, the oil fill cap (see Fig. 12), serves as a fresh air breather, which is a basic function of the PCV system. For closed systems, either the carburetor air-cleaner element or a separate element is used to filter the crankcase ventilating air.

PCV systems require regular service. If the breather opening becomes obstructed, or the valve becomes clogged with varnish-like deposits and fails to operate, many things can happen:

1. Excessive air flow in the PCV system can unbalance the engine's air/fuel ratio. This will result in rough idling of the engine or even prevent it from idling.

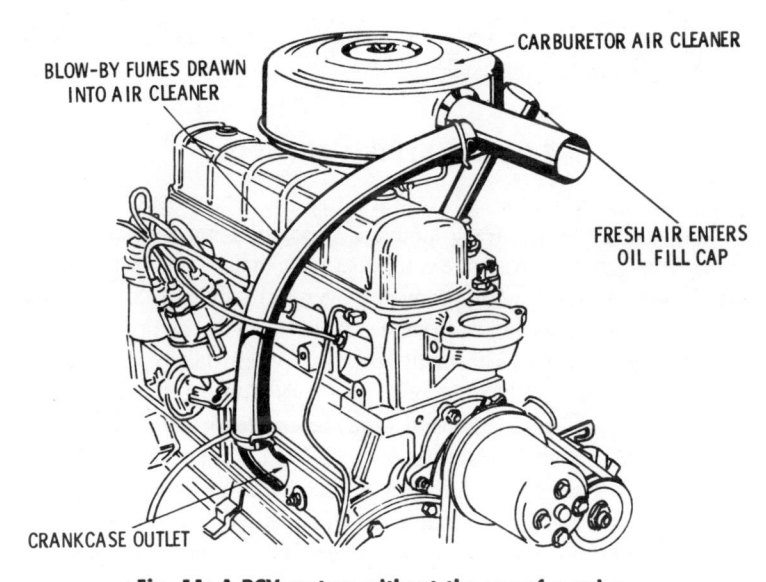

Fig. 11. A PCV system without the use of a valve.

263

Fig. 12. A ventilator type oil filler cap.

WIRE GAUZE FILTER ELEMENT

2. Too rapid air movement may pull oil out of the crankcase. The result could be engine failure because the car owner might not expect the engine oil level in the crankcase to drop so rapidly.
3. Too little air flow will not carry off the blow-by fumes and the crankcase oil will quickly become contaminated, resulting in rusting and corrosion of engine parts. Such a condition definitely shortens engine life due to the wear of moving parts.
4. Should the vent valve and breather filter become completely plugged, the build-up of blow-by fumes will create a pressure in the crankcase. This pressure can force oil out of the dipstick hole and the crankshaft seals, perhaps causing extensive damage.

PCV service is comparatively simple. The important point is to be sure that service is not neglected.

EXHAUST SYSTEM CONTROLS

For several years, the state of California has been passing legislation regarding the control of automotive hydrocarbon emission. The emissions from automobile engine crankcase and exhaust systems have acted as air pollutants and smog-producing agents. In addition to the smog-producing emissions vented from the crankcase, it has been decided that unburned hydrocarbons from the exhaust system tail pipe were also offending agents. California now has laws limiting the amount of smog-producing hydrocarbons that may be emitted from the tail pipe of motor vehicles sold in California.

Since other states are expressing an interest in air pollution control, all cars sold in the United States are equipped with a built-in exhaust emission control device in addition to the PCV system. An interesting explanation of the nature of air pollution and smog has been offered by

Engine Lubricating, Emission Control, and Exhaust Systems

the *Chrysler Corporation*. In general, it states that when we talk about smog, we are not talking about smoke. Smoke is an air pollutant of another type. Smog results from the action of sunlight on two invisible gases, partially burned hydrocarbons and oxides of nitrogen. All of these invisible gases are present in relatively small amounts in the normal automobile engine exhaust. In the atmosphere, and in the presence of sunlight, they react to form an eye-irritating haze referred to as smog. These are the elements that the new exhaust emission control systems have been designed to reduce to acceptable proportions.

Emission Control

To conform to California's requirements on pollution control, the car manufacturers have been submitting various exhaust emission control devices to California for approval. In 1965, California's Motor Vehicle Pollution Control Board officially certified *General Motors Corporation's* smog control system to be installed on 1966 model cars built for sale in California. At the same time, the MVPCB also certified the exhaust fume control systems for the 1966 car models of the *Ford Motor Company* and *American Motors Corporation*. The Board had previously approved the *Cleaner Air Package* designed by *Chrysler Corporation* for all 1966 *Chrysler* built cars for sale in California.

Chrysler calls their exhaust emission control device the *Air Injection System*. *General Motors* calls theirs the *Air Injection Reactor* system, *Ford Motor Company* calls their device the *Thermactor* system, and the *American Motors* unit is called the *Air Guard*. All of these systems have much in common. The heart of each of these systems is a high-speed, high-volume, low-pressure air pump. The pump is much the same in size and shape as an alternator. The pump is front mounted on the engine and is driven by a belt the same as other accessories.

AIR INJECTION REACTOR SYSTEM

The 1968 Federal Law required all standard shift, as well as some high-performance automatics, to be equipped with emission control. Though the device takes two or three horsepower from the engine, Federal Law prohibits disconnecting or removal for any purpose.

All automobiles sold in the United States currently are equipped with an exhaust emission control system. One system by *General Motors* known as the *Air Injection Reactor* (A.I.R.) has been designed to reduce air pollution, caused by engine exhaust tailpipe gases, by

Automobile Guide

"treating" the unburned hydrocarbons and carbon monoxide as they are expelled from the combustion chambers into the exhaust manifolds. A sealed-bearing pump, driven by the engine; compresses, distributes and injects clean, filtered air at the exhaust port of *each* cylinder. Here it combines with the unburned hydrocarbons and carbon monoxide at high temperatures in a chemical reaction, producing a "treated" exhaust that is below the maximum allowable level for air pollution from the source. This does not reduce the danger of inhaling any concentration of carbon monoxide in a confined area. In order to obtain maximum benefits from the A.I.R. system, it is necessary that other normal tune-up items receive careful and thorough attention.

The elements of the A.I.R. system include: A specific engine air cleaner, a belt-driven air injection pump, air check valves, related connecting tubes and hoses, and a bypass valve. A special calibrated carburetor and, in some cases, distributor, and vacuum-advance valve plus the component parts of the closed circuit PCV system are also used in conjunction with the A.I.R. System.

Operation

The air injection pump (Fig. 13) receives clean air by means of a hose, connected to a fitting on the underside of the carburetor air cleaner. This rotary vane-type pump has been designed to draw the air in and compress it to produce maximum air flow with quiet operation. The air injection pump is mounted on the engine and is driven by a belt.

On all V-8 engines, an air line from the injector pump is connected to the bypass valve which routes the fresh air through two pipes and a check valve to each cylinder head. The bypass valve is controlled by manifold vacuum and is required to prevent exhaust-system backfire on coast down. Upon deceleration, the mixture in the intake manifold becomes too rich to burn completely and will ignite if combined with the fresh air injected into the hot exhaust manifold.

To correct this condition, the bypass valve momentarily diverts the fresh air into the atmosphere through a porous bronze silencer located in the side of the valve.

On 6-cylinder engines, the air line from the pump is connected to the bypass valve which routes the fresh air via a check valve to the injection pipes and on into the exhaust manifold (Fig. 14). The check valves installed in the system are to prevent exhaust gas from entering the air pump in the event exhaust manifold pressure is greater than air injection pump pressure, or in the case of an inoperative pump.

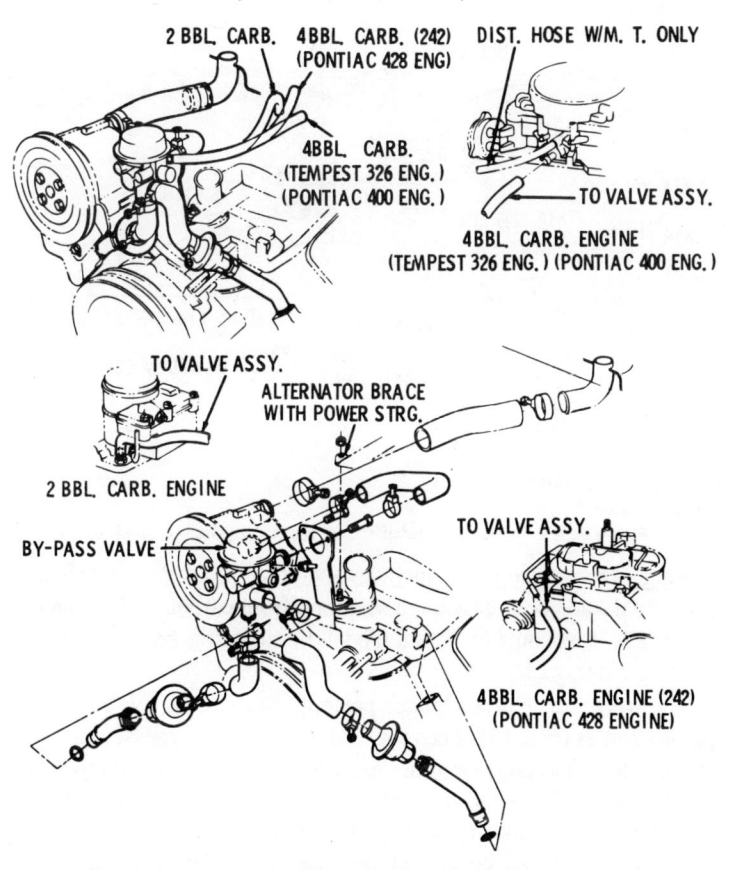

Fig. 13. Air injection installation on a V-8 engine.

AIR INJECTION PUMP

The major components of the air injection pump are enclosed in a die cast aluminum housing with a cast-iron end cover. The rotor shaft, drive hub, relief valve, and intake and exhaust tubes are visible on the pump exterior (Fig. 15).

On the inside of the pump are found a rotor, three vanes, six carbon shoes, and three shoe springs. These parts make up the rotating unit of the pump. This simple design produces maximum air flow with quiet operation.

The die-cast aluminum housing has cavities for air intake, compression, and exhaust (Fig. 16), and has a bore for mounting the front

Automobile Guide

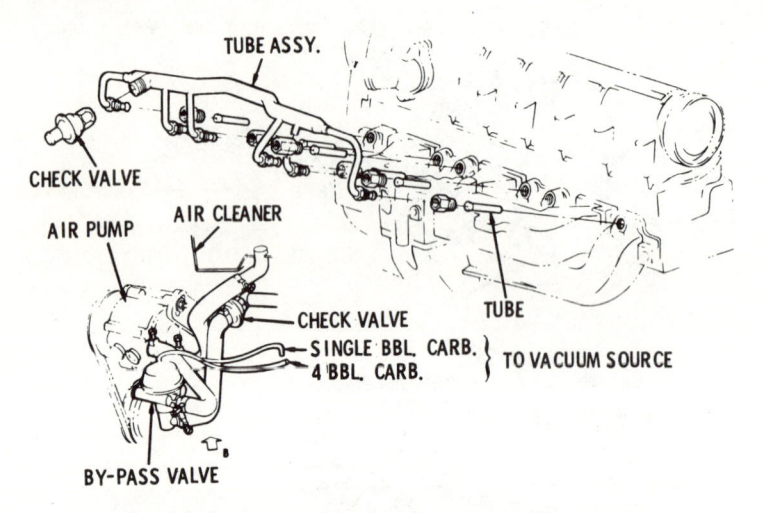

Fig. 14. Air injection installation on a 6-cylinder engine.

bearing. The housing also includes metering grooves that reduce the noise intake and compression, a seat for a front carbon seal, and a relief valve hole (two on 6-cylinder models). Mounting bosses are on the housing exterior.

The front seal (carbon plate) prevents the passage of air from the pump cavities (Fig. 15). The relief valve assembly is pressed into a hole in the side of the housing at the exhaust cavity. This valve relieves the air flow when the pump pressure reaches a predetermined value. The front bearing, secured by a snap ring, supports the rotor shaft.

The cast iron end cover supports the vane pivot pin, rear bearing inner race, and intake and exhaust tube. The end cover is correctly positioned by the two dowel pins that are pressed into the housing, and it is fastened to the housing by 4 bolts.

The rotor positions and drives the three vanes. It also supports the carbon seals, carbon shoes, and shoe springs (Fig. 16). Each of the three plastic vanes is riveted to the hubs. The hubs support bearings that rotate on the pivot pin. The pulley drive hub is pressed on the rotor shaft and 4 bolt holes in the hub provide for attachment of the air pump pulley.

Operation

The rotor is located in the center of the pump and is belt-driven by the engine. The vanes rotate freely about the off-center pivot pin and follow

ENGINE LUBRICATING, EMISSION CONTROL, AND EXHAUST SYSTEMS

the circular-shaped housing bore. The vanes create 3 chambers in the housing; intake, compression, and exhaust. Each vane completes a pumping cycle with every revolution of the rotor. The vane tips make no contact with the housing walls, but pass extremely close. The vane tips wear away to conform to the housing during initial run-in of the pump.

Air is drawn into the intake cavity through the intake tube from the air cleaner as the rotor is rotated. The air is sealed between the vanes as the rotor moves it into a smaller area — the compression cavity. After this air is compressed, the vanes pass it on into the exhaust cavity where this air exits through the exhaust tube and on through hoses to the cylinder heads. Next, the vane passes a part of the housing called the stripper,

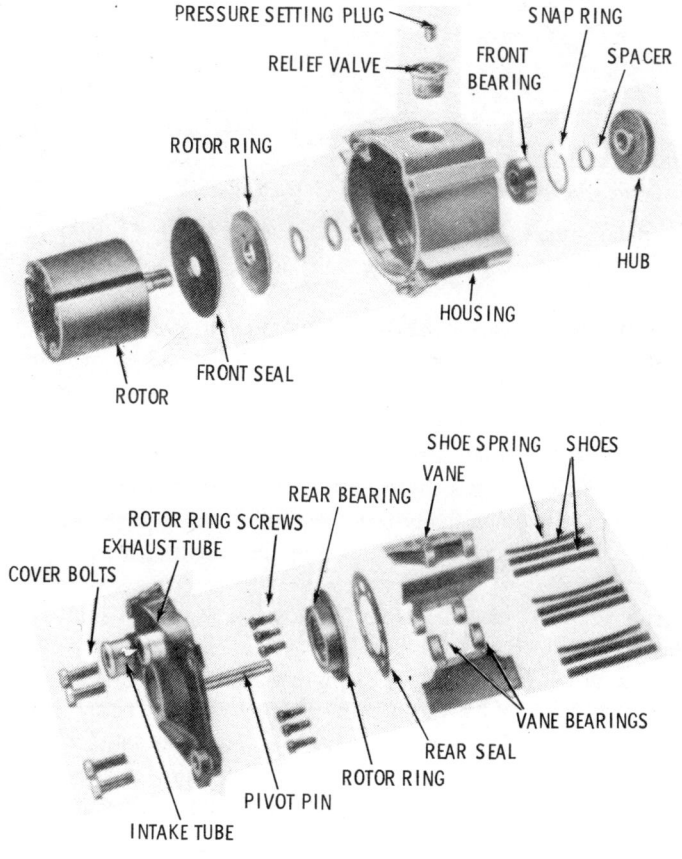

Fig. 15. An air injection pump.

269

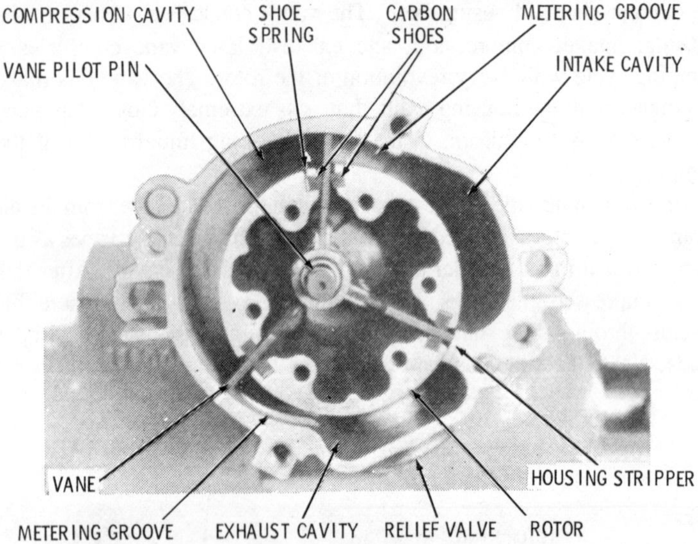

AUTOMOBILE GUIDE

Fig. 16. Air injection pump with end cover removed.

which separates the exhaust and intake cavities (Fig. 16). Continuing the cycle, the vane once more enters the intake cavity to repeat its pumping cycle.

Explanation of the vane rotation and pump cavities does not completely describe the air pump operation. The relief valve, metering grooves, and seals, also influence the cycle. The relief valve is located in the exhaust cavity, and has been pressed into the housing wall. The valve body encloses a preloaded spring, a seat, and a pressure setting plug. If air pressure exceeds the pre-set value, the spring-loaded valve seat is forced up, opening the orifice which relieves the pressure. The pressure at which it opens is determined by the length of the pressure setting plug.

Metering grooves, machined into the housing wall, are located in both the intake and exhaust cavities. Their purpose is to provide a quiet transition of air between the intake, compression, and exhaust cavities.

Carbon shoes support the vanes from slots in the rotor. The shoes are designed to permit sliding of the vanes and to seal the rotor interior from the air cavities. Leaf springs which are behind the follower-side of the shoes compensate for shoe wear and vane articulation. Air leaking into the rotor is exhausted through two small holes in the end cover. The rotor is further sealed by flexible carbon seals which are attached to each

Engine Lubricating, Emission Control, and Exhaust Systems

end. The plates also seal off the housing and end cover to confine the air to the pump cavities. Air that leakes by the front carbon seal is exhausted through a small hole in the housing.

Completing the rotating unit is a steel ring (Fig. 15) bolted to the rotor end. This ring prevents the rotor from spreading at high r/min, and also positions and holds the rear bearing and the carbon seal. The front and rear bearings which support the rotor are of two types. The front bearing uses ball bearings and the rear bearing uses needle bearings. The hub bearings are the needle-bearing type. All bearings are sealed in grease for the life of the bearing.

Chrysler Corporation's Cleaner Air Package, called CAP, employs slight modifications to existing engine components as a means of controlling smog. CAP components are a modified carburetor, a slightly altered distributor and a sense valve to control spark advance during periods of deceleration. The function of the CAP is to burn the air/fuel mixture more completely in the engine's combustion chambers, thereby reducing the unburned hydrocarbons in the exhaust.

The carburetor modifications include a choke that opens more quickly during the warm-up cycle to lean the air/fuel mixture sooner; an idle adjustment that is set to a leaner mixture combined with a slightly increased throttle opening at idle; and main jets are set to operate close to the lean setting to provide a lean mixture that burns more efficiently at cruising speeds. The only alteration to the distributor is a greater range of breaker plate travel to acquire a substantial spark retard at idle while retaining the same maximum spark advance for cruising as is designed into the conventional distributor. The sensing valve, the only new unit in the system, is a vacuum-sensitive device that is located in the vacuum circuit between the distributor and the carburetor. It functions only during closed throttle deceleration when it advances the spark timing to improve combustion during this period.

Regardless of the type of emission control system employed on an engine, it is imperative that the engine be expertly tuned at least once a year. Included in the tune-up should be the proper inspection and servicing of the PCV and exhaust emission control devices. The following are PCV and emission control system maintenance requirements that have been approved by California's motor vehicle pollution control board.

General Motors Corporation Air Injection Reactor System — As an annual service:

Automobile Guide

1. Replace the crankcase ventilation valve in the PCV system.
2. Check the condition of the air pump belt and adjust the belt tension as required.
3. Service the air pump air filter on those vehicles employing a separate air cleaner unit.

Ford Motor Company Thermactor System — As an annual service:

1. Replace crankcase ventilation valve.
2. Service the air pump air filter element.
3. Inspect the condition of the air pump drive belt and adjust tension as required.

American Motors Corporation Air Guard System — As a 12,000 mile interval service:

1. Replace the crankcase ventilation valve.
2. Service the *Air Guard* air filter.
3. Inspect the condition of the air pump drive belt and adjust tension as required.

Chrysler Corporation states that the tune-up requirements of California engines equipped with CAP require only the same adjustments recommended for all *Chrysler Corporation* cars. The only additional operation required during tune-up for a CAP equipped car is the checking of the sensing valve located between the distributor and carburetor.

A CAP equipped engine has its initial spark timing set at 5 degrees *after* TDC, at 600 r/min idle speed. This is contrary to the popular before TDC setting. The retarded ignition timing at idle speed is an aid to more complete combustion of the air/fuel mixture in the cylinders. In addition to improved combustion at idle, the new distributor design also provides optimum timing for all driving ranges above idle.

The vacuum sensing valve used in the CAP system functions in the following manner. With the engine idling, the vacuum in the manifold port is not strong enough to overcome the spring pressure of the sensing valve. This makes the valve inactive and the vacuum-advance unit on the distributor functions as it does on a conventional engine. When the car is decelerating with the throttle closed, the high manifold vacuum created by the engine overcomes the spring in the sensing valve and

ENGINE LUBRICATING, EMISSION CONTROL, AND EXHAUST SYSTEMS

opens the alternate vacuum line to the distributor vacuum-advance unit. The spark timing is thereby advanced during deceleration to permit maximum burning efficiency of the air/fuel mixture in the engine's combustion chambers.

At all other periods of engine operation, the sensing valve does not function, and the standard vacuum control unit on the distributor operates in the usual manner. The changes in the CAP carburetor permit the use of a specific amount of air over and above the normal air intake.

Basically stated, *Chrysler's* CAP emission control system functions through the precise control of ignition timing and carburetion. If you operate your shop in California it is imperative that you understand the state's requirements relative to crankcase and exhaust emission control testing and servicing. Or, it may be that the only California cars that you will be tuning are those that are driven into your area by tourists. In either event, it pays to be informed since some form of exhaust emission control device is now built into every engine.

THE EXHAUST SYSTEM

The exhaust system in the modern car, in addition to its obvious purpose, has two other very important functions; driver and passenger *comfort* and *safety*. The exhaust system is, however, one of the most neglected systems of the car from the standpoint of periodic inspection.

Driver and passenger comfort is aided by the muffler of the system in that it deadens (muffles) engine combustion noises to the point they are hardly heard. Safety is provided by the system in that deadly exhaust gases, the products of combustion, are safely expelled to the rear of the car and away from its occupants.

There are four major parts of the exhaust system; the exhaust manifold, exhaust pipe, muffler, and tail pipe. In those systems having a resonator there are six major parts; the exhaust manifold, exhaust pipe, muffler, intermediate pipe, resonator, and tail pipe. Fig. 17 shows a dual exhaust system without resonator while Fig. 18 shows a single exhaust system with a resonator.

Inspection of the exhaust system is most important. A leaking connection or component can allow exhaust gas to enter the driver/passenger compartment of the car *undetected by the occupants*. This gas, the product of combustion, is *deadly* carbon monoxide (CO). Depending on quantity, carbon monoxide causes headaches, drowsiness, nausea, unconsciousness, — and death.

AUTOMOBILE GUIDE

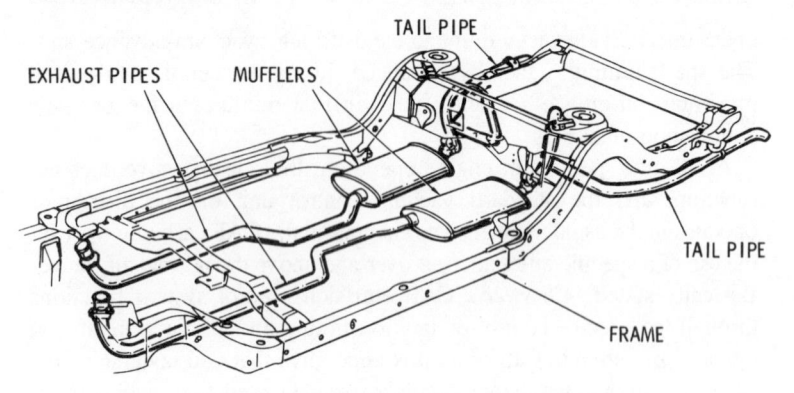

Fig. 17. Typical dual exhaust system.

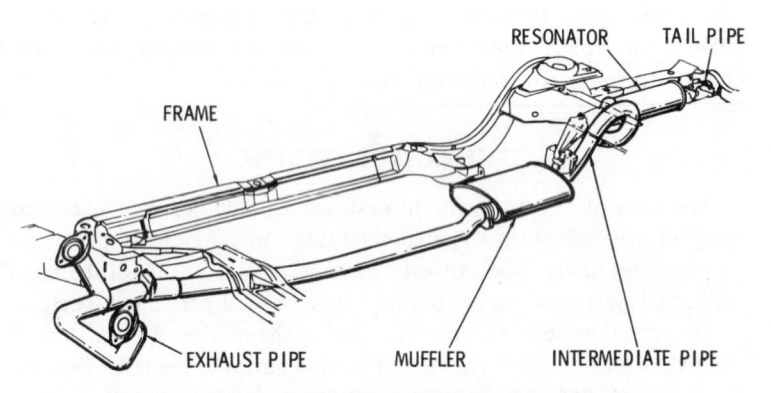

Fig. 18. Typical single exhaust system with resonator.

The exhaust system is carefully inspected by inspection stations of those states that require periodic vehicle inspection. Most *do not* allow any type "patch" repairs to mufflers or pipes. Studies indicate that five percent of all cars have passenger compartment carbon monoxide levels sufficient to cause drowsiness.

THERE ARE NO SHORTCUTS TO EXHAUST SYSTEM SAFETY. IF A COMPONENT IS DEFECTIVE OR LEAKING — REPLACE IT!

The *Catalytic Converter*, shown in Fig. 19, replaces the muffler as required by Federal Legislation in recent years. The purpose of the catalytic converter is to reduce hydrocarbon (HC) and carbon monoxide

Engine Lubricating, Emission Control, and Exhaust Systems

(CO) exhausts to the atmosphere. The catalytic converter, if properly operating, combines HC and CO with oxygen (O_2) to form two harmless elements, water (H_2O) and carbon dioxide (CO_2).

As noted in Fig. 19, the catalytic converter is located in the system between the exhaust pipe and intermediate pipe, where the muffler was located in the early system. The muffler is moved to the rear where the resonator was located in the early system. Because of higher operating temperatures, some catalytic converters require the use of heat shields to protect chassis components and passenger compartment (floor) from excessive heat or heat damage.

The catalytically-active materials, often platinum, can tolerate only very small amounts of leaded fuels without permanently reducing its effectiveness. For this reason, unleaded fuels are mandatory for cars equipped with catalytic converters. Small-diameter fuel tank filler tubes prevent fuel pump nozzles of leaded gas pumps from being used. The fuel pump nozzles of unleaded gas pumps are equipped with smaller fill-pipes which fit the fuel tank filler tube.

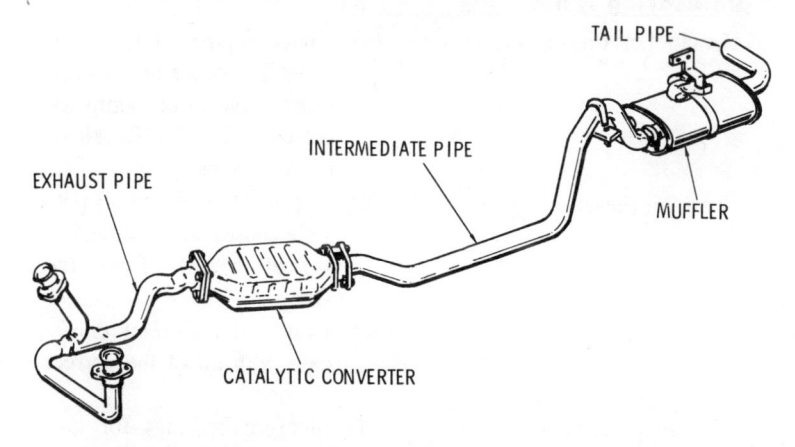

Fig. 19. Typical single exhaust system with catalytic converter.

LUBRICATING-SYSTEM TROUBLES AND REMEDIES

Symptoms and Possible Causes *Possible Remedies*

Oil-Pressure Drop
(a) Low oil level.

(a) Fill crankcase to correct level.

AUTOMOBILE GUIDE

Symptoms and Possible Causes

(b) Faulty oil-pressure sending unit or oil warning-light switch.
(c) Thin or diluted oil.

(d) Relief valve in oil pump stuck.
(e) Oil-pump suction tube loose or cracked.

(f) Clogged oil filter.
(g) Excessive bearing clearance.

Main Bearing Noise
(a) Insufficient oil supply.

(b) Low oil pressure.

(c) Thin or diluted oil.

(d) Excessive bearing clearance.

(e) Excessive end play of crankshaft.

(f) Main-bearing journal(s) out-of-round or worn.
(g) Loose flywheel or torque converter.

Possible Remedies

(b) Install new sending unit or warning-light switch.

(c) Drain oil and refill crankcase with oil of the correct viscosity.
(d) Remove valve, and clean and repair as necessary.
(e) Remove oil pan and install new tube or oil-pump assembly as necessary.
(f) Install new oil filter.
(g) Measure bearing for correct clearance and repair as necessary.

(a) Check engine oil level and add oil if necessary. Check relief valve in oil pump for correct operation. Repair or replace as necessary.
(b) Check oil level and all possible causes under preceding symptom **(Oil-Pressure Drop).**
(c) Drain oil and refill crankcase with oil of the correct viscosity.
(d) Measure bearings for correct clearance and repair as necessary.
(e) Check main bearings for flange wear. Correct as necessary.
(f) Remove crankshaft and regrind journal(s).
(g) Tighten to the correct torque.

Engine Lubricating, Emission Control, and Exhaust Systems

Symptoms and Possible Causes	Possible Remedies
Connecting-Rod Noise	
(a) Insufficient oil supply.	(a) Check oil level and correct as necessary. Check relief valve in oil pump for correct operation, and repair or replace as necessary.
(b) Low oil pressure.	(b) See preceding symptom **(Oil-Pressure Drop)**.
(c) Thin or diluted oil.	(c) Drain oil and refill crankcase with oil of the correct viscosity.
(d) Excessive bearing clearance.	(d) Measure bearing clearance and correct as necessary.
(e) Connecting-rod journal(s) out-of-round.	(e) Remove crankshaft and regrind journal(s).
(f) Connecting rod bent.	(f) Replace defective rod.

Noisy Valves

(a) High or low oil level.	(a) Add or remove oil to bring to the correct level.
(b) Thin or diluted oil.	(b) Drain and refill with oil of the correct viscosity.
(c) Low oil pressure.	(c) See preceding symptom **(Oil-Pressure Drop)**.
(d) Dirt in valve tappets.	(d) Clean valve tappets.
(e) Bent push rod(s).	(e) Replace defective push rod(s).
(f) Worn rocker arm(s).	(f) Replace defective rocker arm(s).
(g) Worn tappets.	(g) Install new tappets.
(h) Worn valve guides.	(h) Ream guides and install new valves with oversize stems, or replace guides and valves as necessary.
(i) Excessive run-out of valve faces or seats.	(i) Grind the valve faces and seats.

AUTOMOBILE GUIDE

Symptoms and Possible Causes   *Possible Remedies*

Oil Pumping at Rings

(a) Worn, scuffed, or broken piston rings.
(b) Carbon in oil-ring slots.
(c) Rings fitted too tight in grooves.

(a) Hone cylinders and install new rings.
(b) Clean slots and install new rings.
(c) Remove rings and check the groove width. If too narrow, replace the piston.

CHAPTER 12

Cooling Systems

Most automobiles are equipped with a liquid-type cooling system. The principle of operation is the same for all cars and the actual construction features differ only slightly. The cooling system is necessary because of the high temperature generated during engine operation. Efficient combustion requires a relatively high temperature, but it is not possible to use all of the heat generated without harming the engine. The melting point of iron is between 2100°F. and 2450°F. and the temperature within the combustion chamber rises as high as 4500°F. It is easy to see that something must be done to remove much of the heat generated in the combustion chamber to prevent damage to the engine. If the engine is not cooled during operation, valves will burn and warp, lubricating oil will break down, pistons and bearings will overheat, and pistons will seize in their cylinders.

COOLANTS

Water is universally used as the coolant in most automobiles. Only clean soft water should be used. Hard water contains minerals which form a scale on the inside surfaces of the cooling system, reducing its efficiency. Inhibitors are available to reduce or prevent the formation of scale and rust, and serve as a lubricant for the water pump. An additive of some type should always be used when only water is used as the coolant.

The main objection to using water alone is its relatively high freezing point of 32°F. Automobiles in most sections of the country will be operated in temperatures below this point at some time during the year, making the use of water alone impractical.

Additives

Besides the inhibitors used to prevent scale and rust, the most well-known additive is antifreeze. The most common antifreeze solutions are methyl alcohol, ethyl alcohol, and ethylene glycol. The first two are the least expensive, but are subject to evaporation caused by boiling at temperatures at which the engine operates most efficiently. Ethylene glycol, however, has a boiling point (330°F.) well above normal operating temperatures, and so is well suited for engine cooling purposes. It is noncorrosive, has no appreciable odor, and offers complete protection from freezing when used in the proper amount. The maximum protection from freezing is obtained with a mixture of approximately 40% water and 60% ethylene glycol.

This mixture offers protection from freezing at temperatures down to −65°F. A higher concentration of ethylene glycol will only raise the freezing point of the mixture. In fact, pure ethylene glycol has a freezing point that is not much below that of water alone. Methyl and ethyl alcohol do not show this increase in their freezing point, however, as the concentration is increased. Methyl alcohol has a freezing point of −144°F., while ethyl alcohol will freeze at −174°F.

Most antifreeze solutions now available contain an inhibitor. This is not permanent protection against scale and rust formation, however, and the antifreeze solution should be drained and discarded each spring. The system should be flushed and cleaned, and fresh summer coolant added. As the first freezing weather approaches, this coolant should be drained and discarded, the system flushed and cleaned, and new antifreeze added to fresh water for the winter driving.

Coolant Flow

The basic automobile cooling system consists of a radiator, coolant (water) pump, flexible hose, fan, thermostat, and a system of passages and water jackets in the cylinder head and cylinder block through which the coolant circulates. This is shown in Fig. 1. Cooling of the engine parts is accomplished by keeping the coolant circulating and in contact with all of the metal surfaces to be cooled.

The pump draws the coolant from the bottom of the radiator, forces it through the passages and water jackets in the engine, and ejects it into

COOLING SYSTEMS

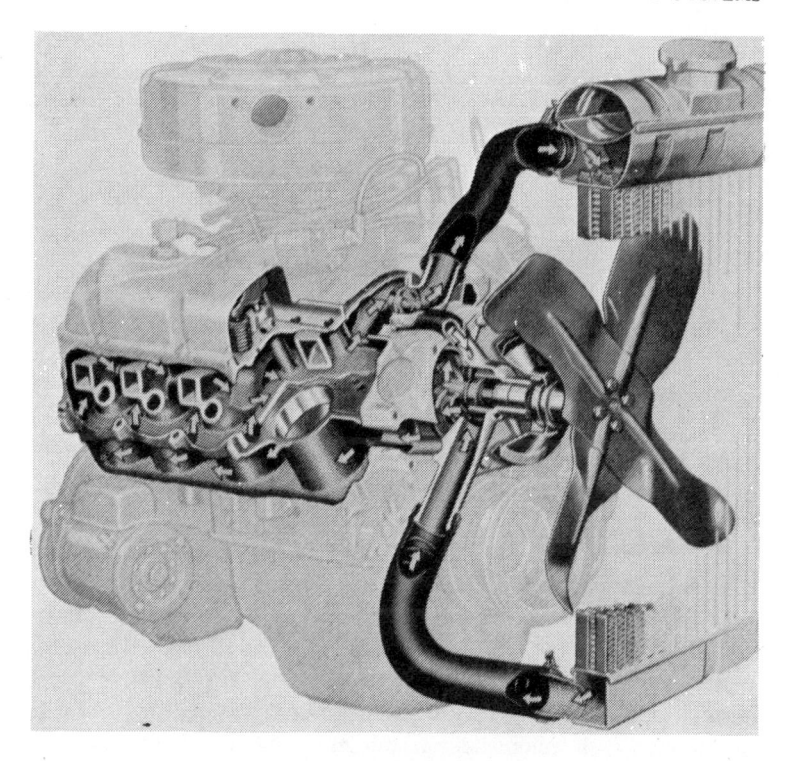

Fig. 1. The cooling system on a FORD CHALLENGER 289 V8 engine is typical of all cooling systems.

the tank at the top of the radiator. From here, the coolant passes through tubes to the bottom of the radiator and is again circulated through the engine by the water pump. A fan draws air over the outside surfaces of the radiator tubes and cools the liquid as it travels through them.

WATER JACKETS

The water passages in the cylinder block and head form the engine water jacket. In the cylinder block, the water jacket completely surrounds all the cylinders along their full length. In addition, narrow passages are provided between the cylinders for coolant circulation. In L-head engines, still other passages are provided in the cylinder block around the valve seats and any other hot parts that might be present.

281

In the cylinder head, water passages surround the combustion chambers. If the engine is of the overhead-valve type, passages around the valve seats will also be provided. The coolant flows from the cylinder block up into the head through openings called water transfer ports. A tight seal at the ports between the cylinder block and head is very important. This seal must be watertight at the ports and gas tight at the combustion chamber openings, and is obtained by using a single large gasket, called the head gasket.

RADIATORS

Automobile radiators consist of two general types — the vertical-flow (Fig. 2) and cross-flow (Fig. 3). Both types contain two tanks with cores between them to form the radiating portion. The inlet tank contains an opening with a fitting to which is attached a flexible inlet hose. This tank is at the top of the radiator (on vertical-flow types) and usually contains a baffle located above the inlet opening. Most radiators of this type also have a filler neck located on the inlet tank. An overflow pipe is generally a part of the filler neck.

The outlet tank also has an opening and a fitting to which the flexible outlet hose is connected. In addition, a drain cock is provided in the bottom of this tank for draining the radiator. The radiators on later model cars with automatic transmissions will also have oil-cooler connections in the outlet tank. Transmission fluid is pumped through pipes to a coil inside the outlet tank to dissipate some of the heat built up in the automatic transmission. The radiator connections for cooling the transmission fluid in a 1964 *Ford* 289 V8 is shown in Fig. 4, and is typical of many cars so equipped.

The inlet tank collects the incoming coolant and distributes it across the top of the radiator cores (or along the side in cross-flow radiators). The baffle helps distribute the coolant and also prevents the coolant from being forced up into the filler neck and out the overflow pipe.

The overflow pipe provides an opening for the escape of coolant or steam that might otherwise cause excessive pressure which could rupture the thin metal walls of the radiator.

The radiating portion of the radiator consists of many water tubes to which are attached air fins. The passage in the tubes is divided into many very thin columns, which exposes a larger radiating surface to the cooler air passing through the radiator than a single large passage would provide.

COOLING SYSTEMS

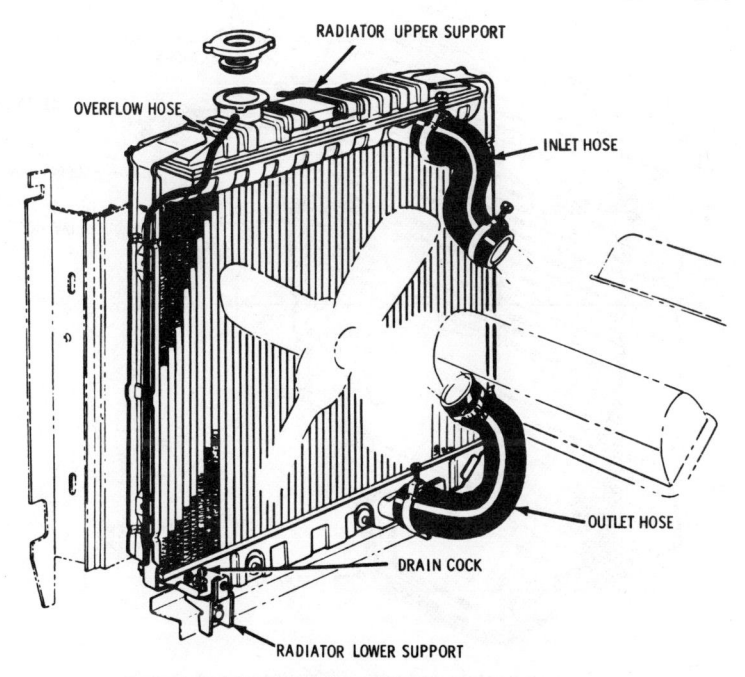

Fig. 2. A typical vertical-flow radiator.

WATER PUMPS

The water pumps on all domestic cars are very similar in operating principles and construction. The pump is usually located at the front of the engine block and powered by the same shaft as the fan. Coolant from the lower part of the radiator is drawn into the pump through the lower radiator hose, and is forced through the water jacket into the upper part of the radiator.

The pump is a centrifugal type, having an impeller with blades which force the coolant outward as the impeller rotates. The impeller may be made of metal or plastic.

A cross-sectional view of a typical water pump is shown in Fig. 5. The bearings shown are ball bearings and are permanently lubricated. Some water pumps on older-model cars have sleeve bearings that require periodic lubrication with a special water-pump grease. A seal assembly around the shaft prevents the coolant from leaking out around the shaft. Should any liquid escape, however, a slinger rotating with the shaft throws the leakage away from the shaft by centrifugal force and it

AUTOMOBILE GUIDE

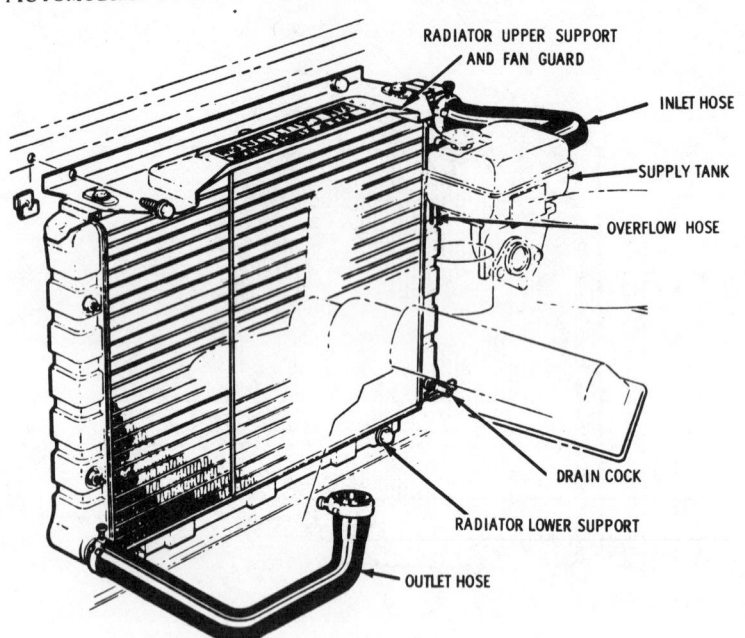

Fig. 3. A cross-flow radiator with a separate supply tank.

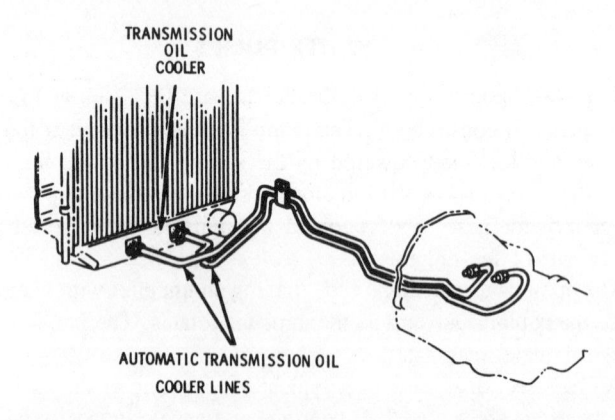

Fig. 4. Typical connections for cooling automatic transmission fluid.

drains out of the pump body through a hole provided for this purpose. Thus, any coolant leaking past the seal assembly is prevented from entering the bearings where it could cause damage. Excessive leakage indicates the need for a new seal assembly.

COOLING SYSTEMS

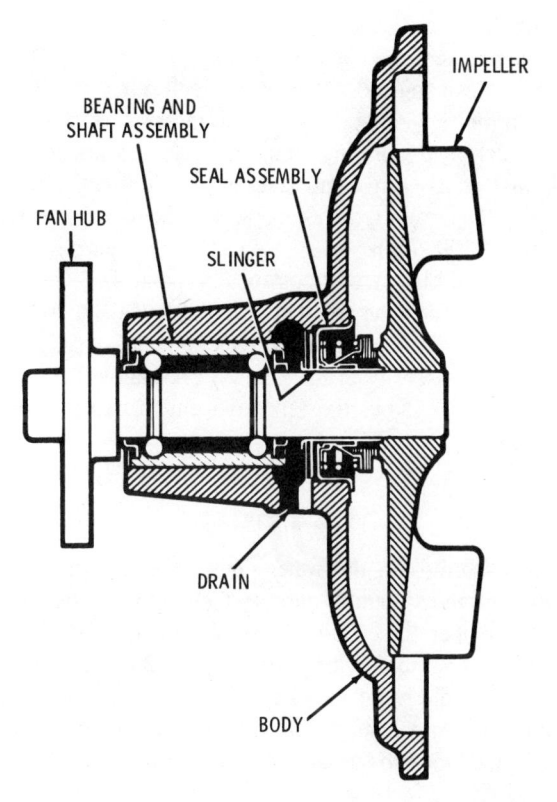

Fig. 5. The construction features of this water pump is similar to all late model pumps.

Courtesy Pontiac Motor Div., General Motors Corp.

FANS

The fan circulates a large amount of air through the radiator core to rapidly dissipate the heat carried by the coolant. In addition to removing heat from the radiator, this flow of air also provides some direct air cooling of the engine. Fans may have from four to eight blades, the number depending somewhat on the size of the engine and whether or not the car has air conditioning.

Late model air conditioned cars are often equipped with a fan driven by a torque and/or temperature sensitive clutch. The thermostatically controlled clutch consists of a driving member (connected to the water pump shaft) and a driven member (connected to the fan), a thermosta-

Automobile Guide

tically controlled valve and silicone fluid. The rotating members are independent of each other and have lands and grooves machined in them, which mesh (but do not contact) each other.

During normal engine operation, with radiator air at approximately 135°F., rotation of the driving member forces the silicone fluid out of the lands and grooves and into a reservoir. A small amount of fluid remains in the lands and grooves and allows the driven member (fan) to rotate at about 800 r/min. When the radiator air temperature exceeds approximately 160°F., a thermostatically controlled valve opens to allow the fluid to enter the area between the lands and groves, causing the fan to rotate at the same speed as the engine to a maximum of about 2600 r/min. The viscosity of the fluid will not allow the fan to exceed 2600 r/min. Fig. 6 shows the fan drive clutch that is used on some automobiles.

THERMOSTATS

Without a thermostat, the water pump would start circulating the coolant through the system as soon as the engine is started, no matter how low the temperature. Thus, a thermostat is included in the cooling system of an automobile to insure rapid warmup and to prevent overcooling in cold weather. The thermostat regulates the engine temperature by automatically controlling the amount of coolant flowing from the engine block to the radiator core. With the thermostat closed,

Fig. 6. A typical fan-drive clutch installation.

Cooling Systems

water circulates through the engine block and head, but not through the radiator. This is possible because of a bypass through which the coolant returns directly to the water pump for recirculation when the thermostat valve has the circulation blocked through the radiator.

Two general types of thermostats are in use today — the bellows type and the pellet type. The bellows type may be found in some older-model cars and consists of a flexible metal bellows attached to a valve. The sealed bellows, which is expandable, is filled with a highly volatile liquid, such as ether. When this liquid is cold, the bellows chamber is contracted and the valve is closed. When heated, the liquid vaporizes and expands the chamber, opening the valve.

The pellet-type thermostat is found in nearly all late-model cars. This type of thermostat uses a pellet containing a paste. As the temperature rises, the paste turns to a liquid, expanding the pellet and opening the valve against the tension of a spring. A typical unit of this type is shown in Fig. 7.

Thermostats are available to maintain the engine at various operating temperatures. When nonpermanent antifreeze is used, a low-temperature thermostat should be installed. This type of thermostat usually starts to open in the range of 150°-160°F. For more efficient operation of the engine and heater, permanent antifreeze should be used and a high-temperature thermostat installed. This type of thermostat usually starts to open in the range from 180°-190°F.

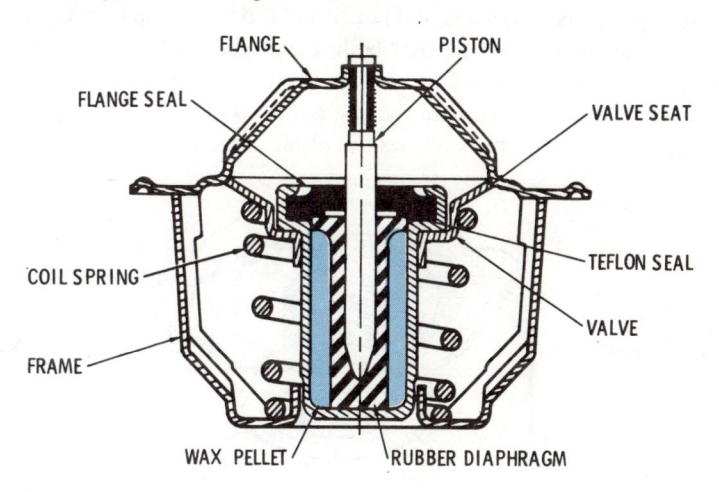

Fig. 7. A pellet-type thermostat.

AUTOMOBILE GUIDE

A thermostat may fail either in the closed position (most unlikely) or the open position (most likely). When it fails closed, engine overheating, loss of coolant, and eventual engine damage will result. When it fails open, slow engine warmup, low engine efficiency, and poor heater operation will result. *A defective thermostat cannot be repaired. Always replace with a new unit.*

RADIATOR CAPS

The cooling system on most all late-model cars is pressurized and requires a pressure radiator cap similar to the one in Fig. 8. A pressure of from 7 to 15 lbs. is maintained in the cooling system during the time the engine is operating normally. This pressure is maintained in order to raise the boiling point of the coolant, allowing the engine to operate at a higher temperature without overflow and loss of coolant.

The cap contains two valves, shown in Figs. 8 and 10, which are normally closed, sealing the system. The pressure-on blowoff valve is the larger of the two, and acts as a safety valve to relieve the pressure in the system if it should increase above the safe level. The smaller valve opens only when the pressure in the system becomes less than the atmospheric pressure as the system cools off. When this vacuum valve opens, air is drawn into the system through the overflow pipe (Fig. 9).

Care should be taken when removing the cap from a pressurized system while the coolant is still hot. If the cap is removed too rapidly, the coolant may suddenly start boiling and gush out the filler neck, resulting in serious burns to the individual. To properly remove this type of cap, either wait until the engine has cooled, or rotate the cap counterclockwise to the stop, wait until the pressure has been relieved

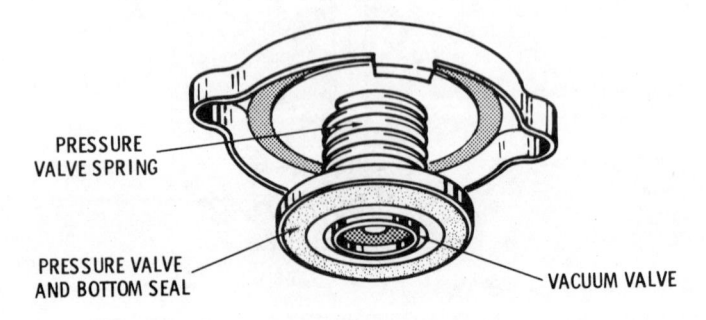

Fig. 8. A typical pressure- type radiator cap.

COOLING SYSTEMS

through the overflow pipe, then turn again counterclockwise until the cap is released.

OVERFLOW TANKS

Overflow or radiator supply tanks are provided on some cars, such as some Ford V8's (Fig. 11). A pressure-type radiator cap is placed on the supply tank instead of the radiator. The radiator itself may or may not have a separate cap — usually it does not.

The use of an overflow or supply tank is made necessary on some engines having a larger-than-normal coolant capacity to offer greater protection for prolonged high-speed driving at high temperatures.

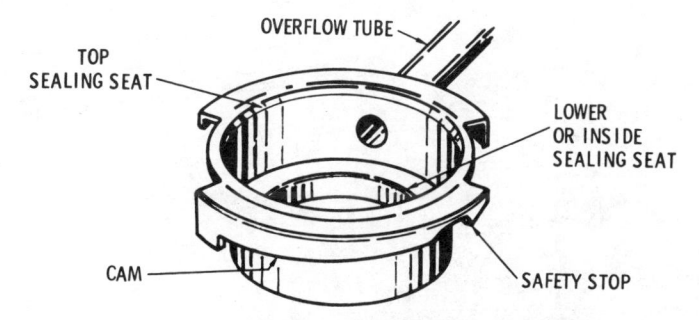

Fig. 9. Typical radiator filler neck.

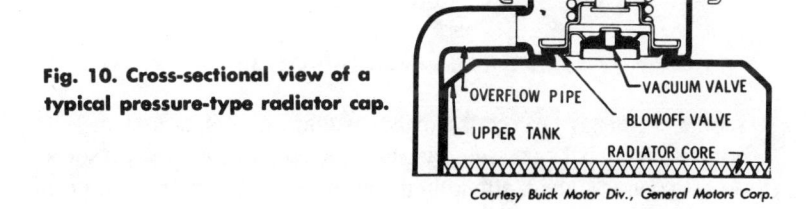

Fig. 10. Cross-sectional view of a typical pressure-type radiator cap.

Courtesy Buick Motor Div., General Motors Corp.

COOLANT RECOVERY SYSTEM

Some cooling systems in late model cars have a storage tank for excess coolant. This is often referred to as a reservoir. The coolant recovery system, Fig. 12, may be easily installed if the car is not so equipped. With this type system, the entire cooling system is "sealed" from atmospheric pressure.

Automobile Guide

Fig. 11. A radiator supply tank is provided on some makes and models of automobiles.

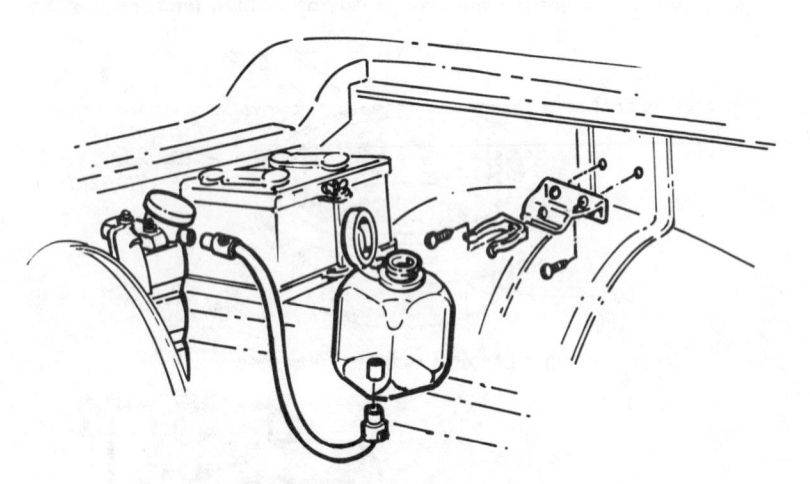

Fig. 12. Coolant recovery system.

As the coolant is heated, it expands within the coolant system and overflows, through the pressure cap, into the reservoir. As the coolant is cooled it contracts and the fluid in the reservoir is drawn back into the radiator by vacuum.

Because of this expansion and contraction of the coolant, the radiator is filled to capacity at all times with the use of a coolant recovery system. This, in turn, results in increased cooling efficiency.

Since the coolant recovery system is a "closed" system, a special cap is used to prevent easy removal, as the finger grips have been removed. Service to the system is required only if the liquid level is not adequate in the reservoir during indicated "hot" and "cold" coolant checks.

COOLING SYSTEMS

DRAINING THE SYSTEM

If it is found necessary to completely drain the cooling system of coolant to prevent damage by freezing, special precautions must be taken. The drain cock located at the bottom of the radiator does not completely drain the entire system in most cars. Drain plugs are provided on the side of the engine block to completely drain the water jackets in the engine. Most four- and six-cylinder in-line engines will have one drain plug, while V-type engines usually have two — one on each side of the engine.

If the car is equipped with a heater, it will be necessary to disconnect the heater hose on some cars to drain the coolant that remains even after the rest of the system has been completely drained.

COOLING-SYSTEM TROUBLES AND REMEDIES

Symptoms and Possible Causes   *Possible Remedies*

External Leakage

(a) Loose hose clamp.
(b) Hose leaking.
(c) Radiator leaking.

(d) Worn or damaged water pump.
(e) Loose freeze or core-hole plug.
(f) Damaged gasket (dry gasket if car has been stored).
(g) Cylinder-head bolts loose or tightened unevenly.

(h) Leak at heater connection.

(i) Leak at water temperature sending unit.
(j) Leak at the water pump attaching bolts.

(a) Tighten or replace clamp.
(b) Replace hose.
(c) Repair or replace radiator as required.
(d) Replace water pump.

(e) Replace with new plug.

(f) Replace gaskets as necessary.

(g) Replace cylinder-head gasket and tighten head bolts in the correct sequence.
(h) Clean the heater connections and replace hose and clamps as necessary.
(i) Tighten sending unit.

(j) Torque bolts to specifications.

291

AUTOMOBILE GUIDE

Symptoms and Possible Causes

(k) Leak at exhaust manifold stud.
(l) Cracked thermostat housing.
(m) Dented radiator inlet or outlet tube.
(n) Leaking radiator core.
(o) Warped or cracked water-pump housing.
(p) Cracked cylinder block.
(q) Cracked or warped cylinder head.
(r) Sand holes or porous condition of head or block.

Internal Leakage

(a) Defective head gasket.
(b) Crack in head into valve compartment.
(c) Cracked valve port.
(d) Crack in block into pushrod compartment.
(e) Cracked cylinder wall.
(f) Leaking oil cooler.

Poor Circulation

(a) Low coolant level.
(b) Collapsed radiator hose. (Bottom hose may collapse at driving speeds only).
(c) Fan belt glazed, oil soaked or loose.
(d) Air leak through bottom hose.

Possible Remedies

(k) Torque bolts to specifications.
(l) Replace housing.
(m) Straighten tube as necessary.
(n) Repair or replace radiator core.
(o) Replace water pump assembly.
(p) Replace block.
(q) Replace head.
(r) Replace head or block as necessary.

(a) Install new gasket.
(b) Replace head.
(c) Replace head or block as required.
(d) Replace block.
(e) Replace block.
(f) Repair or replace oil cooler.

(a) Fill radiator to correct level.
(b) Replace hose and internal spring if so equipped.
(c) Tighten or replace fan belt as required.
(d) Reposition hose clamps or replace hose.

Symptoms and Possible Causes

(e) Defective thermostat.
(f) Broken or loose water-pump impeller.
(g) Water passages in radiator clogged.
(h) Water jackets in engine clogged.

Possible Remedies

(e) Replace thermostat.
(f) Replace impeller assembly.
(g) Reverse flush and clean radiator.
(h) Reverse flush and clean cooling system.

Overheating (Apparent or Actual)

(a) Low coolant level.
(b) Air passages in radiator blocked.
(c) Incorrect ignition timing.
(d) Engine oil level low.
(e) Incorrect valve timing.
(f) Faulty temperature gauge.
(g) Overflow tube clogged.
(h) Defective pressure radiator cap.
(i) Heat control valve stuck.
(j) Brakes dragging.
(k) Prolonged engine idling.
(l) Coolant frozen.
(m) Defective fan drive unit.
(n) Defective temperature sending unit.
(o) Defective fan drive clutch.
(p) Defective air conditioner.
(q) Bugs, dirt, etc., blocking air flow.

(a) Fill radiator to correct level.
(b) Blow air passages out with compressed air.
(c) Time ignition system.
(d) Add oil to correct level.
(e) Correct valve timing.
(f) Replace temperature gauge.
(g) Remove restriction in overflow tube.
(h) Replace cap.
(i) Free up heat control valve.
(j) Adjust brakes.
(k) Stop engine.
(l) Thaw cooling system and add antifreeze as required.
(m) Repair or replace fan drive unit.
(n) Replace unit.
(o) Replace fan drive clutch.
(p) Repair air conditioner as required.
(q) Clean from air conditioner condenser or radiator.

Symptoms and Possible Causes

Radiator Overflows

(a) Radiator overfilled.

(b) Coolant foaming.

(c) Air leak at bottom radiator hose.
(d) Blown head gasket.
(e) *Defective pressure cap.*
(f) *Improper pressure cap.*
(g) Engine overheating.

Corrosion

(a) Use of water that is too hard.
(b) Low coolant level.

(c) Insufficient inhibitor.

(d) Prolonged use of antifreeze.

(e) Air leak at bottom radiator hose.

Low Engine Temperature

(a) Defective thermostat.
(b) Defective temperature gauge.
(c) Defective temperature sending unit.
(d) No thermostat.

Possible Remedies

(a) Adjust coolant to correct level.
(b) Flush cooling system and add antifreeze or inhibitor as required.
(c) Reposition hose clamp or replace hose.
(d) Replace head gasket.
(e) *Replace with cap of proper pressure.*
(f) *Replace with proper cap.*
(g) Determine cause and correct. See preceding section: *OVERHEATING.*

(a) Use only clean soft water.

(b) Fill radiator to correct level.
(c) Fill with fresh antifreeze or inhibitor as required.
(d) Drain cooling system and replace with fresh antifreeze.
(e) Reposition hose clamps or replace hose.

(a) Replace thermostat.
(b) Replace gauge.

(c) Replace unit.

(d) Install thermostat.

COOLING SYSTEMS

Symptoms and Possible Causes   *Possible Remedies*

Noisy Water Pump

(a) Defective seal.

(b) Defective bearing.

(a) Replace seal and lubricate as required.

(b) Replace bearing or pump assembly as required.

CHAPTER 13

Engine Tune-Up

Wear, heat, and vibration gradually change the clearances between the engine parts and the adjustments within the electrical, fuel, and other systems. These changes cause a gradual falling off of engine performance which may not be noticeable at any given moment because the deterioration has been slow.

Periodic car servicing should include engine tune-ups, preferably every spring and fall, and more often if necessary or justified by the car's mileage (usually every 10,000 to 12,000 miles). A good tune-up follows a definite sequence of tests and adjustments that will restore the car's original performance, power and economy as completely as possible. In addition to improved performance, a good tune-up reduces major repair bills, since minor parts failure or defective adjustments are often caught before major engine trouble can result.

This chapter details the steps to be followed for a satisfactory tune-up. It is important to perform the tests and adjustments in a logical and orderly sequence such as listed here. Failure to follow such a sequence may cause some troubles to be overlooked, make additional work necessary, or make it impossible to correctly perform a check or adjustment. For example, making carburetor adjustments while the ignition timing is incorrect is a waste of time. It cannot be done satisfactorily.

Tuning the modern automotive engine requires the following:

1. A knowledge of how to do the job.
2. Dependable test instruments and equipment; such as a voltmeter, ammeter, compression tester, hydrometer, timing light (or test

Engine Tune-up

lamp), tachometer, dwell tester, feeler gauges, and necessary hand tools.
3. Accurate test specifications.
4. Quality replacement parts installed in a workmanlike manner.
5. A recommended tune-up procedure.

An engine with poor compression or with uneven compression between cylinders cannot be properly tuned. Therefore, many checks start with a compression test. This test requires that the engine be cranked with the starter at sufficient r/min to indicate the maximum engine compression. This cannot be done if the battery is low in charge; therefore, start the tune-up tests and adjustments in this manner:

1. Inspect and test the battery:
    (a) Look for a cracked or bulged battery case; acid, dirt, or corrosion on top of the battery; plugged cap vents; loose battery clamp; and loose, corroded, or frayed cables or connections. Clean, tighten, or replace as necessary. A saturated solution of sodium bicarbonate (baking soda) will neutralize acid on battery tops. Be careful not to get this solution in the battery electrolyte.
    (b) Test the specific gravity of the battery electrolyte with a hydrometer — a temperature-corrected reading of less than 1.215 for a 12-volt battery indicates that the battery should be recharged. Variations of more than .025 between individual cell readings indicates a defective battery, or that it is nearing the end of its useful life. Refer to Table 1 for temperature correction chart for specific gravity reading, or review Chapter 4. When the specific gravity is satisfactory, test the battery capacity under load with a suitable battery-starter tester.

2. Test engine compression:
    Provided the battery has sufficient charge, make an engine compression test as follows:

    (a) Run the engine until normal operating temperature is reached. Shut off the engine, clean the dirt from around spark plug ports, and remove the plugs. Remove the air cleaner and block the throttle plate wide open.

AUTOMOBILE GUIDE

- (b) Using a short "jumper" lead, ground the distributor side of the coil.
- (c) Insert the compression tester firmly in a spark plug hole, and crank the engine with the starter for at least four compression strokes to obtain the maximum compression reading. Record the reading.
- (d) Repeat the test for all cylinders, cranking the engine the same number of strokes for each cylinder.
- (e) Compression should be uniform for all cylinders (less than a 10% variation) and greater than the minimum listed in the car manufacturer's specifications.

Low compression must be corrected before any tune-up can be performed. When the compression is low in only one cylinder, look for valve or ring leakage in that cylinder; if it is low in two adjacent cylinders, suspect a cylinder head-gasket leak between these two cylinders.

To determine whether the valves or the rings are at fault, squirt about a tablespoon of heavy oil into the combustion chamber. Crank the engine to distribute the oil and repeat the compression test. The oil will stop leakage past the rings temporarily. If the same low reading is obtained, the rings are satisfactory, but the valves are leaking. If the compression reading has increased by more than ten pounds, the rings are leaking.

If, during a compression test, the pressure fails to increase steadily but remains the same during two consecutive strokes, and then increases on later strokes, a valve is sticking.

3. Visually check electrical connections:
    Make a visual inspection of the battery, starter, generator or alternator, voltage regulator, ignition switch, and coil primary wiring and connections. Tighten the connections if required. If any of the cables are frayed or appear doubtful, use a voltmeter to check for excessive voltage drop between the connections.
4. Make mechanical checks:
    Tighten to the manufacturer's specified torque all:

    - (a) Cylinder head cap screws or bolts (be sure to follow the correct sequence for tightening).
    - (b) Intake and exhaust manifold bolts. Look for any external evidence of gasket leaks.

Engine Tune-up

    (c) Carburetor attaching nuts at the mounting base and any attaching screws at the carburetor air horn.
    (d) Fuel and vacuum line connections at the carburetor, fuel pump, and distributor.
    (e) Check the manifold heat control valve for free operation and free it if it is stuck.
    (f) Check all vacuum lines for cracks or breaks.

5. Check fan belt:
   Check belt(s) for fraying, cracks, or glaze, and replace as necessary. Check the fan-belt deflection as recommended by the manufacturer. If the specifications are not available, a deflection of about ⅜" to ½" in the center of the longest unsupported section of the belt under moderate hand pressure is usually satisfactory.

6. Service the air cleaner:
   A partially clogged, dirty air cleaner can reduce the engine air intake to a point where the air/fuel mixture is made richer regardless of the carburetor adjustment. A reduction of air intake will also cause loss of power. Always service the air cleaner as a part of the engine tune-up. Oil-wetted, oil-bath, and dry-element air cleaners require different service procedures. Follow the recommended servicing procedure for the type used.
   Check the thermostatic control device of the air cleaner to assure proper damper action. Check the manifold vacuum at the sensor element and the vacuum hose for deterioration. Make sure that the heat stove is properly located and secure and that the connector hose (stove to snorkel) is not damaged. *Do not overtighten the air cleaner wing nut. Overtightening may cause binding of the choke valve.*

7. Service the spark plugs:
   When servicing the spark plugs, the spark-plug covers and cables should also be checked. Look for cracks, burns, or other damage to the insulation. Also check the cables for loose connections, both at the plug ends and at the distributor-cap tower.
   Remove the spark plugs and inspect them carefully before cleaning and regapping any serviceable plugs. The condition of the spark plugs can indicate the source of some engine troubles. For example, the wet, black deposits of an oil-fouled plug indicate oil

pumping due to worn piston rings, pistons, or cylinders; a soft, dry, black deposit indicates gas fouling caused by excessive fuel in the combustion chambers. Burned plugs may indicate an overheating condition, or they may show that a plug of too hot a heat range is being used in the engine. Review Chapter 4 for spark plug diagnosis. Clean any serviceable plugs. File the electrode surfaces until they are clean and flat, and until parallel surfaces are obtained between the two electrodes. Adjust the gap to the manufacturer's specifications by bending the outer electrode only. Use a round-wire gauge to check the gap.

8. Service the distributor:
Remove the distributor cap; clean and inspect the cap and rotor. Make sure that the condenser connections are secure and that the lead is not frayed. Carefully examine the breaker points for burning, pitting, or misalignment, and replace if unserviceable. Check the breaker-point spring tension and correct if necessary. Lubricate the cam with high-temperature grease, and lubricate the other distributor areas specified; *do not overlubricate.* Any lubricant getting on the points will cause arcing and will shorten their life. Set the point gap to the correct specification and check the dwell angle to verify the setting.

9. Service the fuel system:
Clean the carburetor sediment bowl. Clean or replace fuel filters or screens. Check the action of the choke. Adjust the linkage, if necessary, on mechanical chokes. For an automatic choke, make sure the heat-riser tube is not clogged or burned out, and check the settings and action of the choke mechanism. Check the fuel-pump pressure and volume output. If an electric fuel pump has been installed, check the electrical connections and the condition of the contact points.

0. Make final electrical checks:
If the diagnosis or tune-up indicates electrical trouble, the following electrical checks should be made: Check alternator output. When the output is low or unsteady, look for a slipping fan belt, or loose wires. When the voltage reading is high, check the regulator. On the regulator, check the cutout-relay closing voltage and opening current, the voltage regulator, and the current regu-

ENGINE TUNE-UP

lator. Check for excessive starting-motor current. Check the ignition coil for primary and secondary circuit resistance, leakage, and output capacity.

11. Check valve clearance:
    Check the valve-stem clearance with the appropriate feeler gauge and adjust to specifications. Note carefully whether the adjustment is to be made with the engine hot or cold.

1 Service cooling and exhaust systems:
    Check both the radiator and heater hoses for cracks, loose connections, or soft spongy hose. Tighten the hose clamps. Blow debris from the radiator core with an air hose, blowing from the side opposite the normal flow of air. Check the water pump if the engine has been running hot. Check the thermostat and the radiator pressure cap. Check the exhaust manifold, muffler, and tailpipe. Carefully inspect the catalytic converter for visual damage. Dents in the outer cover may indicate damage to the converter.

13. Check Emission Control:
    Visually inspect all hoses and lines to insure that none are misrouted, damaged, or kinked. Inspect all hoses for cracks or deterioration. Check pump belt(s) for looseness or fraying. System check valves should be tested for proper operation (one should be able to blow through the check valve in one direction, but not the other). Check the pressure-side of the system for leaks with soapy water — if there is a leak, bubbles will appear. A product, called *Snoop*, is excellent for this test, but any good sudsing detergent may be used. If the unit is inoperative check for a blown fuse or broken wiring.

14. Road test:
    The final step in a good tune-up should be a road test, which can be used to verify all the checks and adjustments on the basis of actual performance.
    Operate the car at minimum speed in high gear, then accelerate rapidly. The engine should accelerate smoothly and evenly. If the engine misses or hesitates, recheck the electrical system. If there are "flat spots," recheck the ignition timing, which may be overadvanced.

Automobile Guide

A road test also provides an opportunity to check the brakes, steering, clutch and/or transmission, instruments, and accessories. On completion of the road test, recheck for any oil, water or fuel leaks, and correct all troubles that may have been found. Check "Troubles and Possible Remedies" section of applicable chapters in this book for specific "Troubles" and "Remedies" to the following problems.

TUNE-UP TROUBLES AND POSSIBLE REMEDIES

Symptoms

(a) Engine will not start.
(b) Hard starting when hot.
(c) Hard starting when cold.
(d) Engine stalls.
(e) Misfires at low speeds.
(f) Misfires at high speeds.
(g) Lack of power.
(h) Rough idle.

Refer to Chapter(s)

(a) 2, 3, 4, 5, and 6.
(b) 2, 5, 6, and 15.
(c) 2, 5, 6, and 11.
(d) 3, 6, and 10.
(e) 3, 4, 5, 6, and 10.
(f) 3, 4, 5, 6, and 10.
(g) 3, 4, 6, 10, 20, 21, and 28.
(h) 4, 5, 6, and 10.

CHAPTER 14

Troubleshooting

In every car ever built, the engine and chassis parts are subjected to abrasive and corrosive wear, heat, vibration, and other factors that cause constant deterioration. In time, hard starting or failure to start, poor engine performance, low gas mileage, and other minor or more serious troubles may result from wear, broken parts, or changes in adjustments.

A car's trouble symptoms may be simple and have an easily identified source; or they may be complex — for example, loss of engine power resulting from a *combination* of ignition-system troubles.

One can save much time, wasted effort, and money by using a *planned procedure* for troubleshooting that will:

1. Quickly isolate the system responsible for the trouble.
2. By elimination, determine the particular part or adjustment responsible for the trouble.

The clues for troubleshooting are provided by the performance of the engine or other components and the appearance and *variation* of parts from the manufacturer's specified wear limits or adjustments.

When using the troubleshooting check lists, it will be helpful to keep the following points in mind:

1. Any troubleshooting check list can only tell *what* to check. A knowledge of engine components, systems, and functions, plus some practical experience is necessary if one is to know *how* to do the job.

Automobile Guide

2. When troubleshooting, always check the obvious first — is the ignition on, car out of gas, overheated?
3. Don't quit too soon. Find and fix the cause of the trouble, not just a symptom. For example, recharging a battery without finding and fixing a low-drain short in the wiring that caused the battery to become discharged is only a temporary and expensive solution.

The remainder of this chapter lists the most commonly experienced troubles. Their most probable causes are listed under each symptom in the order in which they most frequently occur.

Once the probable cause has been identified, refer to the index to locate the chapter covering the particular component or function. Individual chapters in this book cover specific details on the repair and adjustment procedures for American cars produced in the last ten years.

1. **STARTER DOES NOT CRANK AND STARTING RELAY DOES NOT "CLICK"**

    Probable cause:

    (a) Neutral (or parking) safety switch on cars equipped with automatic transmission. Gearshift lever not in Neutral (or Park).
    (b) Loose or broken battery- or starter-cable connections or an undercharged battery.
    (c) Defective starter solenoid or remote switch (relay).
    (d) Defective ignition starter switch or loose connections.

2. **STARTER DOES NOT CRANK BUT STARTING RELAY DOES "CLICK"**

    Probable cause:

    (a) Loose or broken battery- or starter-cable connections or an undercharged battery.
    (b) Starter drive gear and flywheel ring gear locked.
    (c) Loose starter mounting bolts.
    (d) Water in cylinders or engine locked.

3. **STARTER ROTATES BUT DOES NOT CRANK ENGINE**

    Probable cause:

    (a) Starter drive improperly adjusted.
    (b) Starter drive stuck or broken.

4. ENGINE CRANKS TOO SLOW TO START

Probable cause:

(a) Undercharged battery.
(b) High resistance in battery or starter cables due to corrosion, dirt, or loose connections.
(c) Defective starter.
(d) Oil of too high viscosity (in cold weather) or upper cylinder gum and sludge condition. Oil contaminated with permanent antifreeze.
(e) Mechanical causes — high engine friction from tight bearings or similar causes.

5. ENGINE CRANKS NORMALLY BUT DOES NOT START

It is first necessary to determine whether the electrical or the fuel system is the cause of the trouble. Make certain that the car is not out of gas (don't trust the gauge), then proceed as follows: Disconnect the high-tension cable at any spark plug. Place an adaptor in the cable terminal (a paper clip will do). Hold the adaptor about ¼ of an inch from the engine block or the manifold. Have someone turn on the ignition and crank the engine. No spark or a weak spark from adaptor to ground indicates that the trouble is in the ignition system. A good spark indicates that the trouble is probably with the fuel system.

It is well to remember that three things are essential for an engine to run: spark, fuel, and compression — and all at the right time.

5A. Engine Cranks Normally, But Does Not Start — Has No Spark or a Weak Spark (from test)

Probable cause:

(a) Burned, pitted, or dirty ignition points.
(b) Points not opening — worn cam rubbing block or weak point-spring tension.
(c) Distributor cap cracked or has corroded terminals or carbon tracks in the cap.
(d) Distributor rotor burned, cracked, broken, or excessively worn.
(e) Defective condenser or coil.
(f) Moisture in distributor cap or on high-tension cables.

AUTOMOBILE GUIDE

(g) Loose or broken primary-wiring connections.
(h) Defective ballast resistor or resistance wirings.

There are two more electrical possibilities to consider before troubleshooting the fuel system. Although a plug cable may provide a good spark against the block, the spark plugs may be fouled or have incorrect gap settings. Therefore, check the spark plugs for the correct gap and good condition. The car may have an electric fuel pump installed. These pumps have wiring connections that can become loose or can break, and electrical contact points that can pit, corrode, or fail. Remember to check these possible electrical troubles when troubleshooting the fuel system.

5B. **Engine Cranks Normally and Has a Good Spark, But Does Not Start**

Probable cause:

(a) Clogged fuel lines or screens.
(b) Choke sticking shut.
(c) Fuel pump inoperative or not delivering sufficient fuel.
(d) Fuel pump sediment bowl not seated against its gasket (leaking air).
(e) Carburetor float valve stuck or set at wrong level.
(f) Air leaks at intake manifold or carburetor gaskets.
(g) Low compression from worn rings, burned or sticking valves, blown head gasket, etc.
(h) Valve tappets too tight.
(i) Valves out of timing.

6. **HARD STARTING**

First determine whether the engine is hard to start at all times, only when cold, only when hot, or only on quick restart. As a rough rule (to which there are a number of exceptions), hard starting only when the engine is cold often indicates electrical trouble, while hard starting when the engine is hot or on quick restart indicates fuel-system troubles. Regardless of the condition under which hard starting occurs, if the engine cranks slowly, check the reason for this first.

Probable cause:

(a) Loose or corroded battery or ground cables or connections.
(b) Battery undercharged or of low capacity.

TROUBLESHOOTING

(c) Defective starting motor, solenoid, or relay circuit.
(d) Loose starting motor mounting bolts.
(e) Engine oil viscosity too high.
(f) Ignition problems (see Spark Test). Spark plugs fouled or improperly gapped. Ignition points pitted, corroded, or with improper gap. Weak condenser. Loose primary wiring connections causing high resistance. Weak coil. Corrosion or poor connections in the high-tension cables.
(g) Fuel system problems. Partial clogging of fuel lines or filters. Choke sticking shut or inoperative automatic choke on cars so equipped. Carburetor float valve sticking. Improper idle speed or mixture adjustment. Fuel pump providing insufficient pressure or fuel volume. Air leaks. Vapor lock when engine is hot. Improper synchronization of carburetors on multiple carburetor installations.
(h) Low engine compression, which may be caused by any of the following: a blown or leaking head gasket; worn piston rings with or without worn or out-of-round cylinders; burned or sticking valves; excessive clearances between valve stems and guides; air leaks (loss of vacuum) at intake manifold or carburetor gaskets. *Note: Low compression is more likely to cause hard starting when the engine is hot than when the engine is cold.*

7. ENGINE STALLS

Probable cause:

(a) Fuel system problems: wrong idle or mixture adjustments; choke not operating properly; carburetor float setting incorrect; defective fuel pump; dirt or water in fuel system.
(b) Ignition system problems: bad or improperly gapped points; defective coil or condenser; worn distributor rotor or defective ignition wiring.
(c) Insufficient valve lash.

8. ENGINE MISSES

There are many possible causes for engine missing. Six conditions of engine missing have been selected that can easily be identified. It is useful to determine which type of missing is involved, since this information will help determine the system responsible for the troubles.

AUTOMOBILE GUIDE

8A. **Steady Missing At All Engine Speeds**

Probable cause:

(a) Ignition difficulties are usually responsible. Check: plug gap and condition; plug cables, especially the terminal ends; distributor cap, rotor, and contacts.

(b) Low compression.

8B. **Uneven Missing At All Engine Speeds**
(Most often caused by fuel system troubles.)

Probable cause:

(a) Dirt or water in fuel system, clogged fuel filter, sticking choke, sticking float valve.

(b) Ignition system troubles: malfunction of plugs, points, coil, condenser, or cables.

(c) Excessive back pressure caused by exhaust system restrictions such as crimped exhaust or tail pipes, rusted muffler baffles, etc.

(d) Air leaks at carburetor or intake manifold gaskets.

8C. **Engine Misses Only At Idling Speed**

Probable cause:

(a) Ignition point gap too close (excessive dwell angle).

(b) Improper idle speed or mixture adjustment. Dirty carburetor.

(c) Air leaks in fuel intake system.

(d) Manifold heat control valve stuck open.

(e) Other ignition troubles, such as: defective coil, condenser, rotor, cap, wiring or plugs.

(f) Low compression.

(g) Improper valve lash.

8D. **Engine Misses Only At High Speed**
(This complaint is most often traced to ignition troubles.)

Probable cause:

(a) Spark plug condition and gap, or plugs of improper heat range.

(b) Poor condition or alignment of ignition points, or wrong gap setting, causing dwell to be incorrect. Improper timing.

TROUBLESHOOTING

    (c)   A weak coil, condenser leaky or loosely connected, worn distributor shaft bearings, or distributor poorly grounded.
    (d)   Fuel pump pressure low or restrictions in fuel lines or filters.
    (e)   Carburetor power valve sticking or not operating properly.
    (f)   Dirty or clogged air cleaner causing reduced air intake at the time of high air intake requirement.
    (g)   Gas tank vent clogged.
    (h)   Sticking valves.
    (i)   Overheated engine.

8E. **Steady Missing Only During Acceleration**
    Probable cause:
    (a)   Dirty or fouled spark plugs or cracked insulators.
    (b)   Trouble with points, condenser, coil, or plug cables.
    (c)   Weak fuel pump.
    (d)   Carburetor troubles.
    (e)   Defective resistance wiring (ballast resistor).

8F. **Momentary Missing (Flat Spot) During Acceleration** (usually caused by carburetor troubles.)
    Probable cause:
    (a)   Defective accelerator pump. Low float level setting.
    (b)   Choke sticking (cold engine).
    (c)   Manifold heat control valve stuck open (cold engine).
    (d)   Low fuel pump pressure or volume.
    (e)   Ignition defects: fouled spark plugs or incorrect gap, weak coil, high resistance in plug cables.

9. **ENGINE STARTS BUT WILL NOT RUN**
    Probable cause:
    (a)   Defective ignition switch.
    (b)   Defective coil.
    (c)   Defective ballasts (or resistance wiring).

10 . **INSUFFICIENT POWER OR POOR HIGH-SPEED PERFORMANCE**
    Probable cause:
    (a)   *Fuel-system troubles*
        (1)   Air cleaner dirty; restriction in fuel lines or filters.
        (2)   Fuel pump pressure and/or volume low.

       (3)   Choke partially closed or carburetor linkage does not allow throttle to be opened fully.
       (4)   Carburetor power circuits or high-speed jets not functioning properly.
       (5)   Uneven synchronization of multiple carburetors.

(b) *Ignition-system troubles*
       (1)   Improper ignition timing, weak coil, or leaky condenser. Points burned or improperly gapped. Mechanical or vacuum advance mechanisms not functioning properly. Ignition polarity reversed.
       (2)   Spark plugs fouled or improperly gapped, or plugs of wrong heat range.

(c) *Mechanical causes*
       (1)   Low compression caused by: incorrect valve lash or timing; worn or sticking valves; excessive valve stem-to-guide clearance; leaking head or manifold gaskets; worn piston rings; etc.
       (2)   Manifold heat valve stuck closed.

(d) *Overheating*
       (1)   Loose or broken fan belt; leaks at radiator hoses or clamps; water pump defective; radiator or cooling system partially clogged; thermostat defective; defective radiator cap, insufficient coolant.
       (2)   Carburetor air/fuel mixture wrong; automatic choke stuck.
       (3)   Excessive friction. Friction may be in the engine or anywhere in the drive train back to the wheels at the ground; tight engine bearings (especially connecting-rod bearings); excessive expansion resulting in decreased clearances and increased friction; oil viscosity too high; clutch or propeller-shaft misalignment; improperly adjusted or lubricated wheel, pinion, differential, or transmission bearings; brakes dragging; underinflated tires; front end out of alignment.

11. COOLING-SYSTEM TROUBLES

High engine temperature is the major clue that indicates cooling-system troubles.

Probable cause:

(a)   Loss of coolant, either external or internal.

- (b) Reduction in air flow.
- (c) Reduction of heat transfer because of clogging of the radiator or deposits in the water jacket.
- (d) *Coolant loss not evident.*
    - (1) Loose, worn, or broken fan belt.
    - (2) Defective radiator pressure cap.
    - (3) Defective thermostat or one installed upside down.
    - (4) Partially clogged radiator. Check for cool spots, which indicate clogging.
    - (5) Defective water pump.
    - (6) Deposits in water jackets.
- (e) *Coolant loss evident*
    - (1) Cracked or leaking radiator hose or loose hose connections.
    - (2) Radiator leaks.
    - (3) Leaks at welch (freeze) plugs.
    - (4) Defective pressure cap.
    - (5) Improper pressure cap.

When there is a *gradual* loss of coolant, but no evidence of external leaks, suspect internal coolant loss. Look for water in the lubricating oil. If water is present in the oil (more than normal condensation), check for a leak in the head gasket or for a cracked block. When the coolant contains permanent-type (ethylene glycol) antifreeze, internal coolant leaks will quickly cause the buildup of gum, sludge, and lacquer deposits that can ruin the engine.

12. ELECTRICAL CHARGING-SYSTEM TROUBLES

The battery, alternator, and regulator work together in the charging system and all three components must be considered when troubleshooting the charging system. For example, when the regulator is out of adjustment (set too high) the alternator output will be high, overcharging the battery. This condition *could* damage the alternator or battery.

Probable cause:
- (a) *Alternator fails to charge*
    - (1) Belt(s) loose or broken.
    - (2) Brushes or slip ring worn.
    - (3) Alternator defective:
        - a. Defective rotor.

AUTOMOBILE GUIDE

        b. Defective stator.
        c. Defective diode(s).
    (4) Regulator defective.
(b) *Low charging rate*
    (1) Loose belt(s).
    (2) Defective or improperly adjusted regulator.
    (3) Defective alternator (see above).
    (4) Excessive resistance in circuit.
        a. Loose connection(s).
        b. Poor ground.
        c. Defective wiring.
(c) *Excessive charging rate.*
    (1) Defective or improperly adjusted regulator.
    (2) Defective alternator.

Note: *If not equipped with an ammeter, excessive charging rate may be noted by the frequent need to add water to the battery.*

13. EXCESSIVE FUEL CONSUMPTION

The fuel consumption for every car is determined by:

(a) Driving conditions — city or country, low or high speeds, winter or summer.
(b) Driving habits — slow or fast acceleration, low or high speeds.
(c) Mechanical condition of the engine. Determine the actual rate of fuel consumption in order to obtain a basis for comparison for any improvement in economy made by mechanical changes or adjustments.

Probable cause:

(a) Carburetor float valve too high or needle valve not closing fully on its seat.
(b) Fuel mixture excessively rich.
(c) Carburetor power valve not operating properly or jets worn or wrong size.
(d) Defective choke operation.
(e) Partially clogged air cleaner (air/fuel mixture richer).
(f) Spark plugs fouled, wrong gap, or otherwise defective.
(g) Defective ignition breaker points or improper ignition advance.

TROUBLESHOOTING

- (h) Incorrect ignition timing.
- (i) Low engine compression.
- (j) Excessive rolling resistance — dragging brakes, tight bearings, low tires, towing trailer or boat, etc.
- (k) Leak in fuel system — tank, lines, pump, carburetor, etc.
- (l) Improper operation of emission control system.

14. EXCESSIVE OIL CONSUMPTION

Oil can be lost from an engine through external leaks, internal leaks, faulty accessories, through the valve guides, or past the pistons and rings.

Probable cause:

- (a) *External oil leaks*
    1. Valve cover or fuel pump gasket.
    2. Timing gear cover.
    3. Oil pan gasket or drain plug.
    4. Front or rear main bearing oil seals.
    5. Loose oil filter or defective gasket.
    6. Rear camshaft welch (freeze) plug defective.
- (b) *Internal oil leaks*
    1. Defective positive crankcase ventilation (PCV) valve.
    2. Defective gasket:
        - a. Separating an internal oil passage and a cylinder.
        - b. Separating an internal oil passage and an internal water passage.
    3. Defective vacuum section of double-action fuel pump (if equipped).
- (c) *Oil losses through the valve guides*
    1. Excessive valve stem-to-guide clearance.
    2. Faulty valve-stem oil seals.
- (d) *Oil loss past pistons and piston rings*
    1. Worn, scuffed, scored, or broken piston rings. Oil rings clogged or stuck in their grooves by deposits. Directional-type piston rings installed upside down. Rings installed in excessively worn piston grooves.
    2. Cylinder bores worn beyond allowable limits or out-of-round.

AUTOMOBILE GUIDE

(3) Cylinder block distorted because wrong sequence and/or torque used to tighten cylinder head cap screws.

15. ENGINE KNOCK OR PING

Normal engine combustion proceeds at a controlled rate for a predetermined time. Combustion knock is abnormal combustion that proceeds at an uncontrolled rate. It is always associated with high temperature. Knock causes high combustion chamber temperature and pressure as well as a noticeable loss of power. This condition can vary widely in severity from an annoying light ping to a severe detonation or preignition, which can break piston rings, cause scuffing or scoring, or even burn holes through piston heads or otherwise cause complete engine failure.

Probable cause:

(a) *Detonation*
   (1) Fuel mixture too lean.
   (2) Fuel of too low an octane value.
   (3) Overadvanced ignition timing.
   (4) Excessive carbon deposits on pistons and cylinder heads.
   (5) Engine compression increased (by milling cylinder head or using thinner gasket).

(b) *Preignition*
   (1) Carbon deposits that stay incandescent.
   (2) High valve temperatures.
   (3) Hot spots caused by poor cooling, especially in the jacket area around the valves.
   (4) Spark plugs of too high a heat range or with broken or cracked porcelain insulators.
   (5) Detonation or any of its causes.
   (6) Sharp edges in the combustion chamber.

Symptoms and Possible Causes are covered in the text of this chapter. For additional *Symptoms and Possible Causes* and their *Possible Remedy* refer to the chapter most applicable in this book.

CHAPTER 15

Ignition Testing

The ignition system in a modern car consists of a primary (low-voltage) and a secondary (high-voltage) circuit, as shown in Fig. 1. The primary circuit consists of the:

1. Battery.
2. Ignition switch.
3. Primary circuit resistance wire (or resistor).
4. Primary winding of the ignition coil.
5. Breaker points.
6. Condenser.

The secondary circuit consists of the:

1. Secondary winding of the ignition coil.
2. Distributor rotor.
3. Distributor cap.
4. High-tension wires.
5. Spark plugs.

Ignition Switch — The ignition switch on most modern cars serves two purposes. It provides a means of energizing the ignition system, and also of energizing the starter motor. After the engine has started, the switch returns to the run position when it is released, disconnecting the starter motor and connecting a resistance in series with the ignition coil and breaker points. This resistance is connected in the circuit on some

AUTOMOBILE GUIDE

cars by contacts on the ignition switch. In other cars, the resistance is switched in and out of the circuit by contacts on a relay (usually the starter solenoid) controlled by the ignition switch.

Primary Circuit Resistance Wire (or Resistor) — A resistance wire or an actual resistor is placed in the primary circuit of the ignition system of most makes and models of automobiles. The purpose of this resistance is to limit the amount of current flow through the breaker points at low speeds when they are closed for longer periods of time. This resistance also protects the coil and points when the engine is stopped but the ignition switch has been left on.

During engine starting, this resistance is bypassed to provide increased voltage (9 to 10 volts) to the ignition coil during the time the starter has lowered the battery voltage. The bypass action is accom-

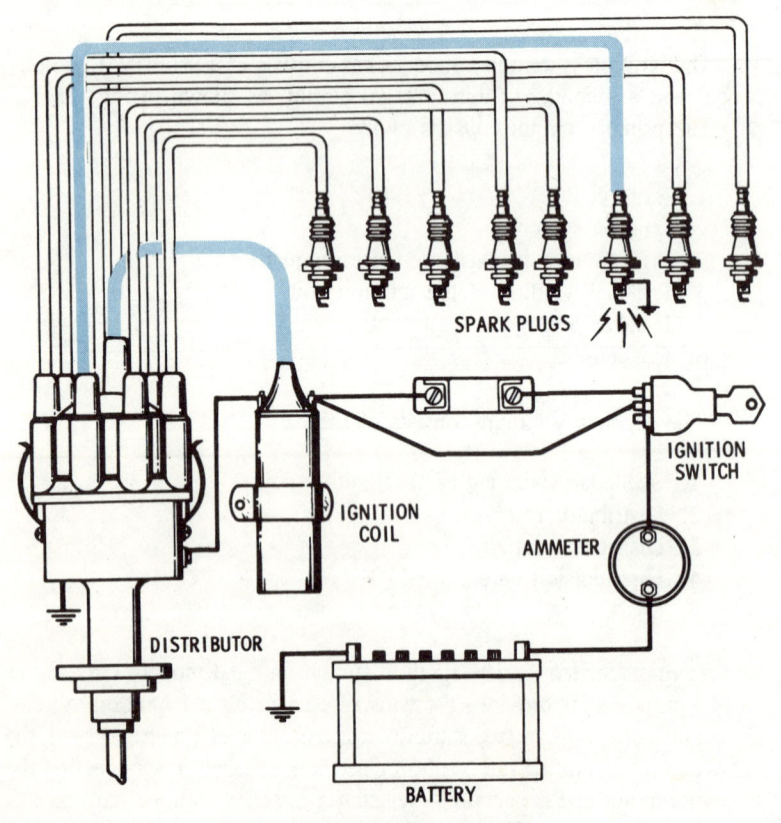

Fig. 1. Typical ignition system.

316

Ignition Testing

plished either by contacts on the starter relay (solenoid) or by contacts on the ignition switch assembly.

Ignition Coil — The ignition coil consists of a primary winding of a few hundred turns of relatively heavy wire plus a secondary winding of many thousands of turns of very fine wire. Both windings are assembled around a soft iron core and enclosed by a case, one end of which contains the terminals. Fig. 2 shows a sectional view of a typical ignition coil.

Distributor — The distributor performs several functions in the ignition system: (1) It closes and opens the primary circuit to produce the magnetic buildup and collapse. (2) It times these actions so the resultant high-voltage surges from the secondary occur at the right time. (3) It directs the high-voltage surges to the proper spark plug at the proper time. Fig. 3 shows an exploded view of a typical distributor. The illustration in Fig. 4 is the top view of a distributor with cap and rotor removed.

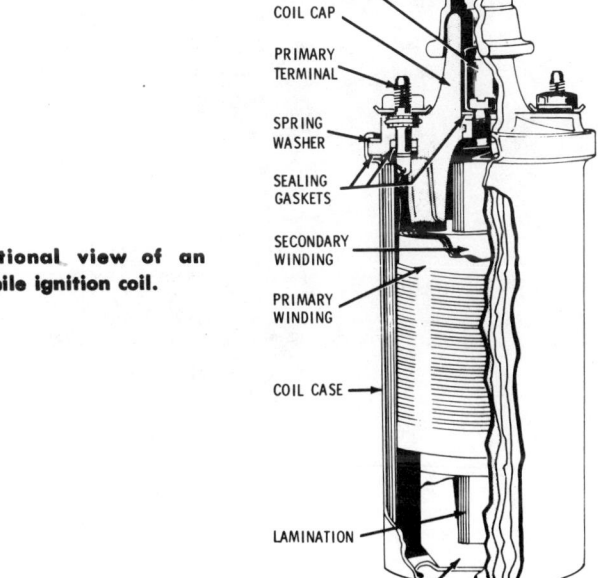

Fig. 2. Sectional view of an automobile ignition coil.

317

Automobile Guide

Breaker Points — The breaker points are located in the distributor. They are closed by spring pressure and opened by a cam on the distributor shaft. The distributor shaft is rotated at one-half engine speed, by a gear on the camshaft or oil pump of the engine.

The purpose of the breaker points is to open and close (break and make) the ignition coil primary circuit. This action produces a high-voltage ignition secondary circuit, necessary to "fire" the spark plugs.

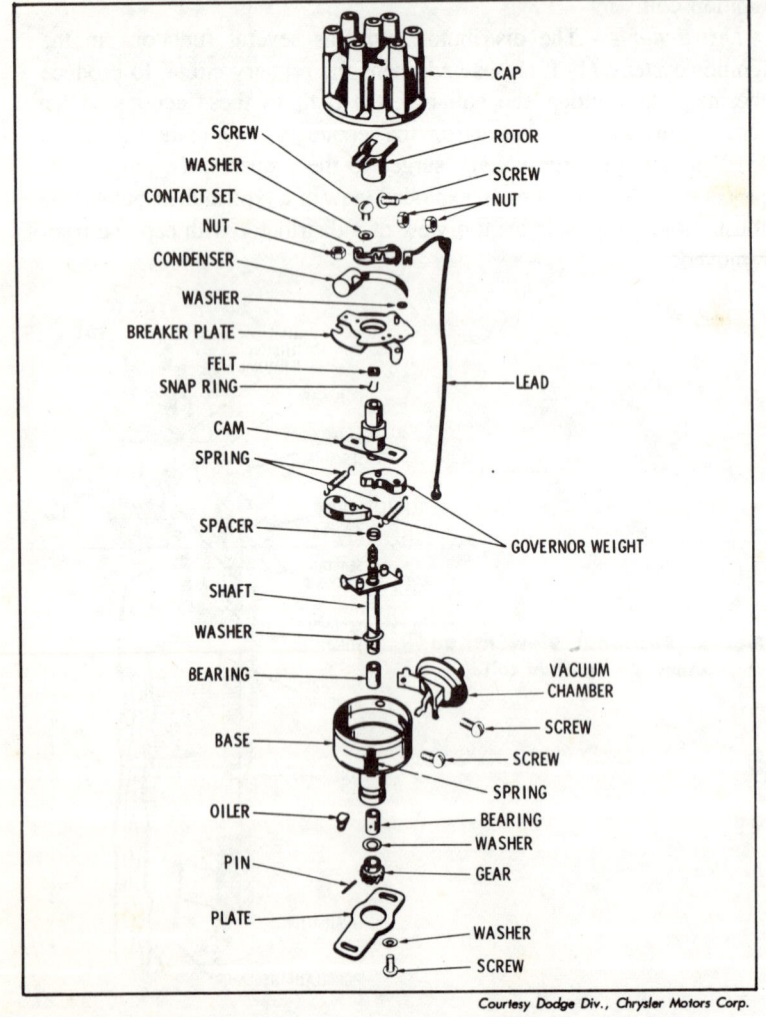

Courtesy Dodge Div., Chrysler Motors Corp.

Fig. 3. Illustrating component parts of a distributor assembly.

318

IGNITION TESTING

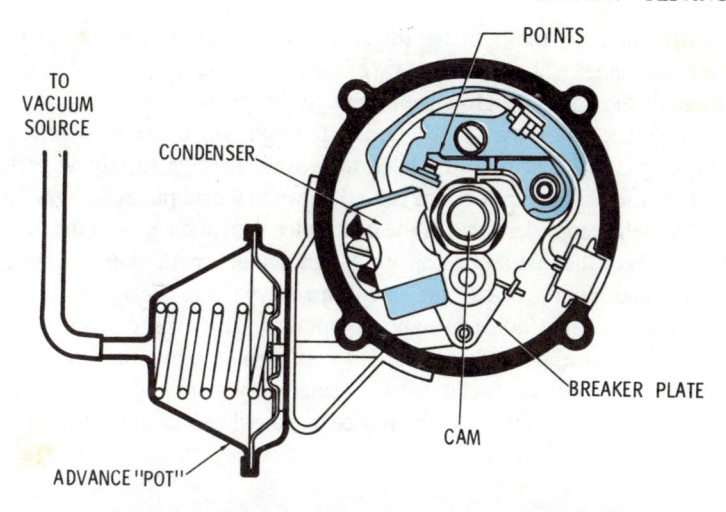

Fig. 4. Distributor (top view) with cap and rotor removed.

Condenser — The condenser in a conventional ignition system serves a dual purpose. It protects the contacts by suppressing the arc that results when the points open the circuit to the primary winding of the ignition coil. In addition, the condenser hastens the collapse of the magnetic field, thus increasing the high-voltage output from the secondary of the ignition coil.

Distributor Rotor — The distributor rotor switches the high-voltage surges from the secondary winding of the ignition coil to the proper spark plug at the proper time. The rotor fits on the end of the distributor shaft and is keyed in such a way as to prevent installing it incorrectly. Thus, it rotates with the distributor shaft and is synchronized with the opening and closing of the breaker points.

The high-voltage surges from the ignition coil enter the center terminal of the distributor cap and make contact with the rotor. The surges travel through the rotor to a small metal tip on the outside edge of the rotor. This small metal tip passes very close to, but does not quite touch, the terminals around the inside of the distributor cap. These terminals are connected to the spark plug wires inserted in the distributor cap.

With this arrangement, and if the ignition system is functioning properly, the metal tip on the rotor is directly under one of the terminals on the inside of the cap at the instant the breaker points open. Thus, the high-voltage surge from the ignition coil enters through the center of the distributor cap, through the rotor, jumps the short distance to the terminal under which the metal tip of the rotor is positioned, and travels through the correct high-tension wire to the proper spark plug.

High-Tension Wire — All wiring through which the high-voltage surges travel are heavily insulated to prevent leakage to ground or to other wiring. This type of wire is used between the output of the ignition coil and the center terminal of the distributor cap, and between the outer terminals of the distributor cap and the individual spark plugs. On most makes and models of car this is resistance-type wire, designed to help eliminate ignition noise in radio equipment. This type of wire is not actually a wire at all, but a carbon-impregnated cord. Standard type wiring may still be found used as secondary wiring on some cars, however suppression-type should be used whenever replacement is necessary.

BASIC OPERATING PRINCIPLES

When the breaker points are closed, the low-voltage (primary circuit) current flows from the battery, through the ignition switch to the primary winding of the coil, and then to ground through the closed contacts of the breaker points. This primary current flow causes a magnetic field to build up around the primary winding in the ignition coil. When the breaker points open, this magnetic field collapses and moves through the secondary winding of the ignition coil. This action produces a high-voltage current in the secondary.

The high-voltage current, which is produced each time the breaker points open, flows from the coil through the high-tension lead to the distributor cap. The high-tension lead is connected by a rotating contact to the rotor inside the distributor cap. As the rotor turns, it distributes the high-voltage current to the correct spark-plug terminal in the distributor cap. From this terminal, the high-voltage current flows through the high-tension spark-plug wire to the proper spark plug. Thus, the spark plug fires and ignites the air/fuel mixture in the cylinder at the proper time. This process is repeated for every power stroke of the engine.

The demands placed on the ignition system in late-model, high-compression, high-speed engines are enormous. For example, the breaker points in the ignition system of a 6-cylinder engine turning at 3000 r/min will make and break 9000 times every minute, or 540,000 times an hour. Not only must the points make and break at this high rate, but they must do so at very precise times if satisfactory engine performance is to be acheived. Thus, it is apparent that the ignition system must be maintained in first-class operating condition by a thorough, systematic and periodic testing and adjustment routine.

TROUBLE ISOLATION

Ignition system troubles are caused either by a failure in the primary and/or secondary circuit, or by incorrect ignition timing. If an engine trouble has been traced to the ignition system, the trouble can be found by performing a series of tests using individual hand-held instruments, or by using specialized test equipment that has been designed expressly for overall engine analysis and adjustment.

Trouble in the ignition system can usually be isolated to the primary or secondary ignition circuit without the use of instruments, as follows:

1. Remove the coil high-tension lead from the distributor cap.
2. Hold the high-tension lead approximately 3/16" from some convenient point on the motor block or head.
3. Turn the ignition switch on, crank the engine, and check for a spark. If the spark is good, the trouble is in the secondary circuit. If there is no spark, or if it is weak, the trouble is in either the primary circuit, the coil-to-distributor high-tension lead, or the coil.

PRIMARY-CIRCUIT TESTS

A breakdown or loss of energy in the primary circuit can be caused by:

1. Defective primary wiring or corroded and/or loose terminals.
2. Burned, shorted, sticking, or improperly adjusted breaker points.
3. A defective coil.
4. A defective condenser.

A complete test of the primary circuit consists of checking the circuit from the battery to the coil, the circuit from the coil to ground, and the starting ignition circuit. Excessive voltage drop in the primary circuit will reduce the output from the secondary of the ignition coil, resulting in hard starting and poor performance.

When making the following tests, keep in mind that the readings for different makes and models of automobiles may vary somewhat from

AUTOMOBILE GUIDE

those given. Always consult the manufacturer's specifications when in doubt.

TEST 1

Connect a voltmeter between the positive battery terminal and the battery-side primary terminal of the ignition coil, as shown in Fig. 5. Observe the meter reading while cranking the engine. The voltage at this point should not exceed 1 to 1.5 volts. *Note: The maximum allowable voltage at this point may vary, depending on the make and model of automobile. Always consult the car manufacturer's specifications for the exact voltage.*

Possible Troubles

If the voltage exceeds the specifications, the following are possible troubles:
1. Open circuit from the battery side of the coil to the ignition switch.
2. Ignition switch not closing the circuit to the ignition coil in the start position.
3. Ground in the circuit from the ignition coil to the ignition switch.
4. Ground in the coil.

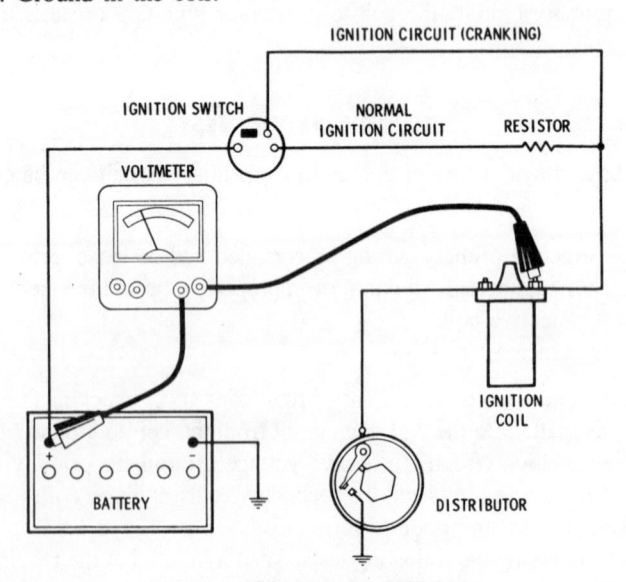

Fig. 5. Ignition system TEST 1.

IGNITION TESTING

TEST 2 (Points open)

Connect the voltmeter between the battery-side primary terminal of the ignition coil and ground, as in Fig. 6. Turn the ignition switch to the ON position, and make sure the breaker points are open. (If the points are closed, jog the starter until they open.) The voltage at this point should be the normal battery voltage.

Possible Troubles

If the voltage is less than the normal battery voltage, the following are possible troubles:

1. Battery not fully charged.
2. Points not open.

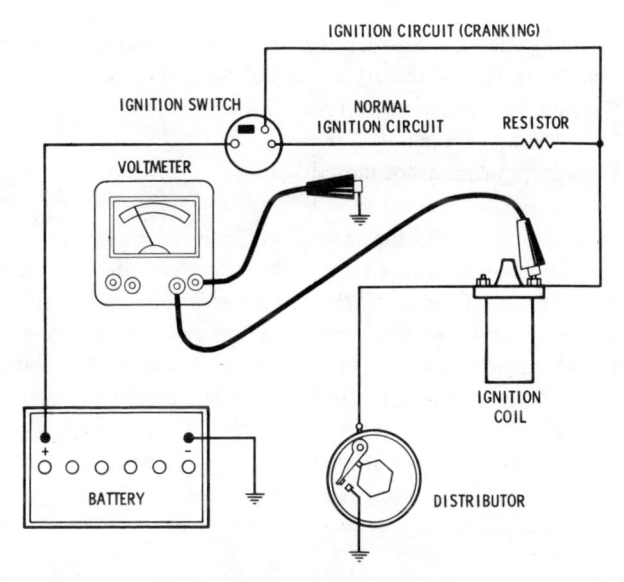

Fig. 6. Ignition system TEST 2.

3. Ground in the circuit from the ignition coil to the distributor.
4. Ground in the distributor.
5. Ground in the coil.
6. Ground in the circuit to the ignition switch or to the resistor.

TEST 2 (Points closed)

The voltmeter remains connected as in Fig. 6. Close the breaker points by jogging the starter. Turn the ignition switch to ON. The voltage at this point should be between 5 and 7 volts.

Possible Troubles

If the meter reads less than 5 volts, the following are possible troubles:

1. Loose connection from the resistor through the ignition switch circuit to the battery.
2. Loose connection between the resistor and the ignition coil.
3. The resistor is open or has too much resistance.

If the meter reads more than 7 volts, the following are possible troubles:

1. Loose connection between the ignition coil and the distributor.
2. Resistor out of the circuit because of shorted or incorrect wiring.
3. Resistor has decreased in resistance.
4. Coil primary is open.
5. Breaker points are not closed.

The primary winding of the ignition coil can be checked for an open condition by means of a resistance test. To perform this test, turn the ignition switch OFF. *Caution: If the ignition switch is not turned off, the ohmmeter may be damaged.* Connect an ohmmeter across the primary terminals of the coil. The resistance of the primary winding should be from 0.3 to 9 ohms, the exact value depending on the make and model of automobile.

Check the manufacturer's specifications for the exact resistance value. If the resistance reading is infinite, the primary winding is open.

TEST 3

The breaker points are closed as in the last part of **TEST 2**. Turn the ignition switch ON. Connect the voltmeter between the primary distributor terminal and ground, as in Fig. 7. The meter reading at this point should not exceed 0.2 volt.

Possible Troubles

If the meter reads more than 0.2 volt, the following are possible troubles:

IGNITION TESTING

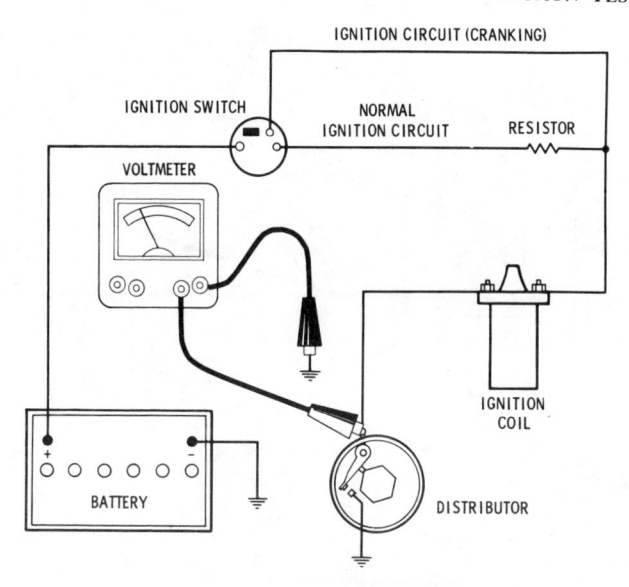

Fig. 7. Ignition system TEST 3.

1. Breaker points not closed.
2. Loose connections in the distributor.
3. Distributor not grounded to the engine.
4. Faulty breaker points.

TEST 4

The breaker points are closed as for **TEST 3**. Turn the ignition switch ON. Connect the voltmeter between the ignition switch-side of the resistor and the positive battery terminal, in the manner shown in Fig. 8. The meter reading at this point should not exceed 0.7 volt.

Possible Trouble

If the meter reads more than 0.7 volt at this point, look for a loose connection or broken wire from the resistor through the ignition switch circuit to the battery.

SECONDARY-CIRCUIT TESTS

A breakdown or energy loss in the secondary circuit can be caused by:

AUTOMOBILE GUIDE

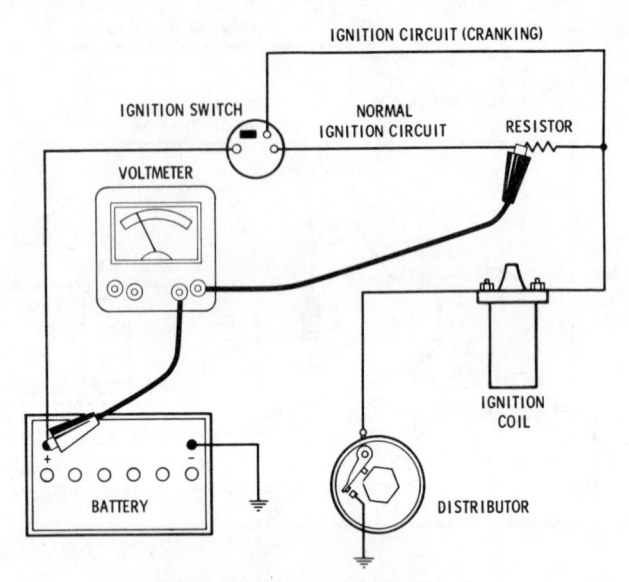

Fig. 8. Ignition system TEST 4.

1. Fouled or improperly adjusted spark plugs.
2. Defective high-voltage wiring.
3. High-voltage leakage across the coil, distributor cap, or rotor.
4. Open secondary winding in the ignition coil.

The following procedure is used to test the secondary circuits of the ignition system:

1. Remove the high-tension lead between the coil and distributor, and remove the spark plug wires from both the plugs and distributor cap. Make sure the location of each plug wire in the distributor cap is known so they can be replaced correctly. (Draw a diagram if in doubt.) Inspect the wire terminals for looseness and corrosion. Inspect the wires for breaks and cracked or oil-soaked insulation. Replace any defective wires.
2. Clean both the inside and outside of the distributor cap and inspect it for cracks, burned contacts, permanent carbon tracks, and a defective center electrode. Remove any dirt or corrosion from the sockets. Replace the cap if defective.
3. Inspect the rotor for cracks and for burned or pitted contacts. Clean thoroughly. Replace the rotor if it is found to be defective. Fig. 9 shows a typical "button" type rotor.

IGNITION TESTING

4. Check the high-tension wires. Using an ohmmeter, measure the resistance of the individual wires.

Caution: Do not puncture the insulation of the wire while making a resistance test. To do so may cause separation of the conductor. Measure only from the ends of the wire, as shown in Fig. 10.

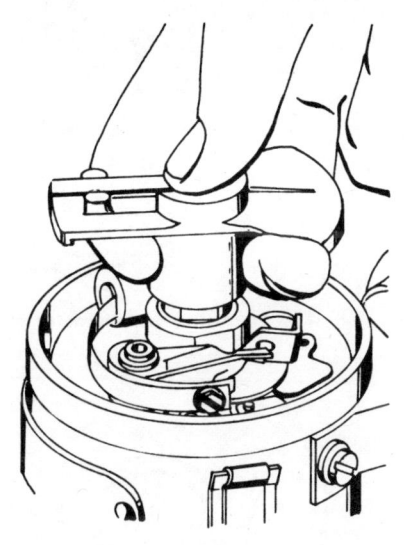

Fig. 9. Typical button push-on type rotor.

When removing the wires from the spark plugs, grasp the molded cap only, as shown in Fig. 11. Do not pull on the wire because to do so may separate the wire connection inside the cap or damage the weather seal.

Resistance type wire should read no more than 30,000 ohms. If it exceeds 30,000 ohms it should be replaced. Standard type wire should have a resistance reading of just over zero ohms. Excessive resistance reading indicates that the wire is defective and should be replaced. As a rule of thumb, all secondary wires should be replaced if two or more are found to be defective.

Ignition Coil — To test the secondary winding of the ignition coil, disconnect the high-tension lead from the coil tower. Connect an ohmmeter between the coil tower and either of the primary terminals on the coil. If the resistance reading is infinite, an open secondary winding is indicated. The correct resistance reading will depend on the make and model of automobile, but will range between 5000 and 15,000 ohms. Check the manufacturer's specifications for the correct resistance. A

AUTOMOBILE GUIDE

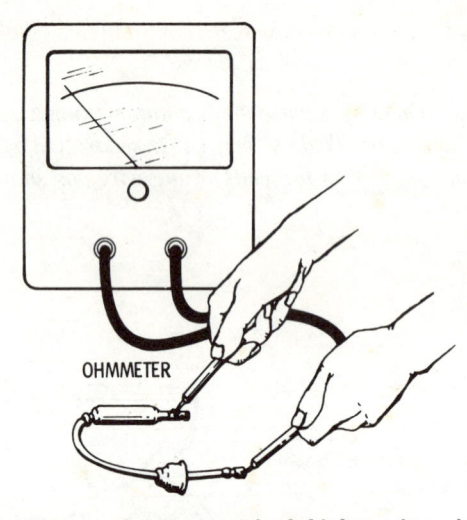

Fig. 10. Using an ohmmeter to check high tension wires.

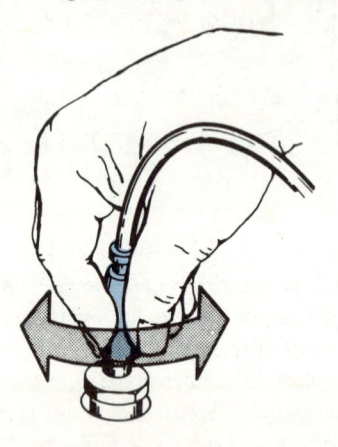

Fig. 11. Grasp the molded cap when removing spark plug wires.

reading of less than the specified resistance indicates an internal short within the coil.

Spark Intensity — Disconnect the wire from one of the spark plugs, and check the spark intensity by holding the loose end of the wire approximately 3/16" from the engine block or head. (To conduct this test, crank the engine with a remote starter switch.) The spark should jump the gap regularly. Perform the same test with each of the remaining spark plug wires, one at a time.

If the spark intensity of all spark plug wires is good, the coil, condenser, rotor, distributor cap, and high-tension wires are probably satisfactory.

If the spark is good at some wires, but poor at others, perform a high-resistance test of the faulty leads.

If the spark is weak or intermittent at all wires, check the ignition coil, distributor cap, rotor, and high-tension wire from the distributor to the coil.

Spark Plugs — Clean, inspect, and gap the spark plugs according to specifications. If specifications are not available, set the gap at .030-.035. Replace any plugs which show signs of excessive wear, corrosion, or deposits.

Ignition Timing — Incorrect ignition timing can cause hard starting, spark knock, loss of power, poor fuel economy, engine overheating, and/or failure to start. Some of the most common causes of incorrect timing are:

1. Timing incorrectly adjusted.
2. Distributor bushing worn, or the distributor shaft is worn or bent.
3. Defective vacuum-advance system.
4. Defective centrifugal-advance system.

Any of the above troubles are best detected by using instruments.

TRANSISTOR IGNITION SYSTEMS

Transistor ignition systems are now available on many new cars as standard equipment. There are also several transistor ignition kits on the market that can be installed in practically any car. This new type of ignition system will no doubt become standard equipment on *most* cars before many years have passed. The basic principles of operation of all transistor ignition systems are the same, even though their circuits and parts values may differ widely.

The schematic of one type of transistor ignition system is shown in Fig. 12. This system is used on some *Fords* and *Mercurys*. The primary of the ignition coil in this system is designed to draw a peak current of 12 amperes (or approximately 5.5 amperes of average current) to provide a high spark-plug voltage at the higher engine speeds.

The transistor in this system acts as a heavy-duty switch, except that it has no moving parts. Consequently, there is practically no time lag in opening and closing the primary circuit. The transistor is connected

Automobile Guide

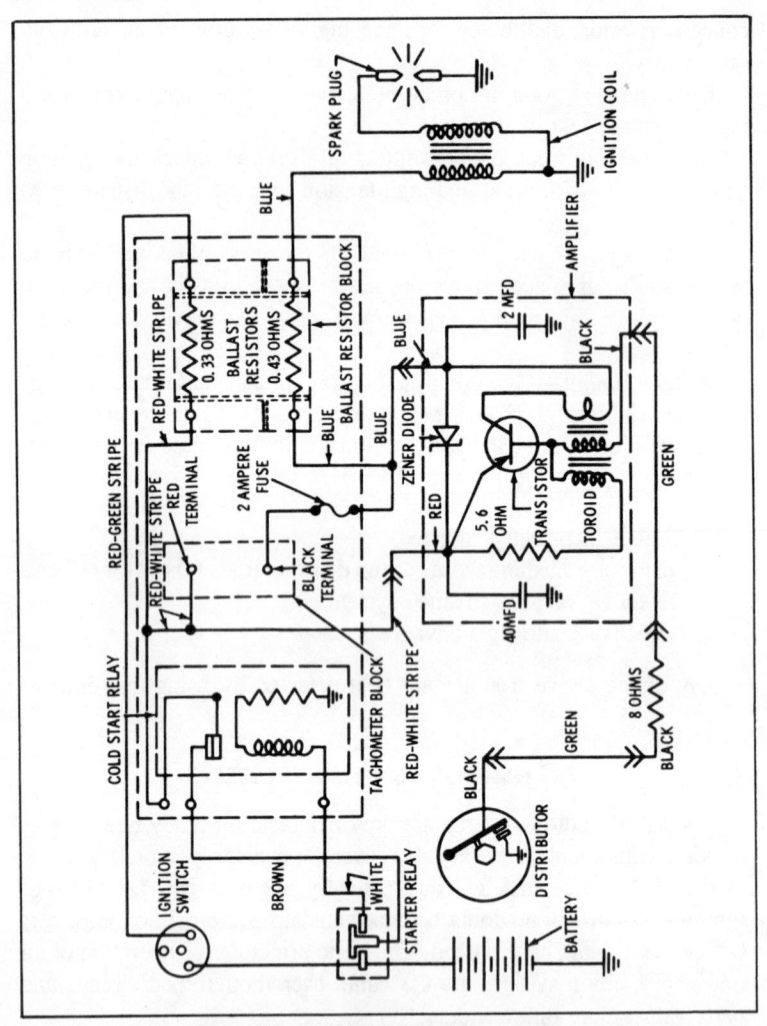

Fig. 12. Transistor ignition system.

between the battery and the ignition coil, and is used to make and break the primary circuit of the ignition coil.

The breaker points in the distributor control the transistor. The 2-watt, 8-ohm resistor connected in the wiring harness between the distributor and the transistor, limits the transistor control current (and breaker point current) to 0.5 ampere. This low current through the breaker points reduces point pitting and increases their life.

IGNITION TESTING

The condenser placed across the breaker points in a conventional ignition system is no longer needed in this location in the transistor system. Instead, its value has been increased to 2 mF and is now located in the amplifier assembly. Here, this condenser performs the function of absorbing the high inductive energy when the breaker points open. However, it no longer has any effect on the points because it is isolated from them by the transistor.

The amplifier portion of this system is assembled in a separate unit (Fig. 13) and is mounted under the instrument panel to protect the parts from the engine heat.

The ballast resistors, a tachometer-connecting block, and a cold-start relay are enclosed by a fiber cover and mounted in the engine compartment. A 2-ampere fuse in the lead from the tachometer block to the collector of the transistor in the amplifier protects the transistor from damage if other than normal testing instruments are used.

The contacts of the cold-start relay are normally closed, being opened only during the start cycle. When the starter relay is energized, the cold-start relay is actuated and its contacts open. If, during starting, the available voltage drops below 10.5 volts, the relay contacts will close, bypassing the 0.33-ohm ballast resistor, thus applying full available voltage to the system.

The tachometer block is used to connect a tachometer or dwell meter into the circuit. *Do not connect a tachometer or dwell meter in any other manner. To do so may result in inaccurate readings and possible damage to the transistor.*

The schematic of a slightly different type of transistor ignition system is shown in Fig. 14. This type is available in certain models of the *Pontiac Tempest*, and features a specially designed distributor, a control

Fig. 13. Transistor ignition amplifier assembly.

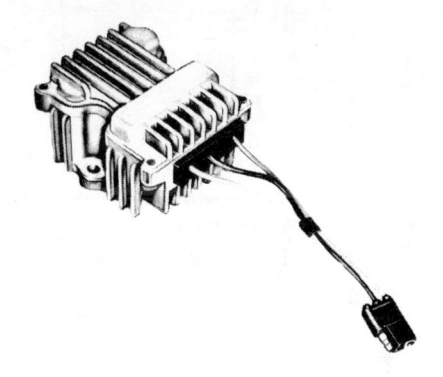

unit (ignition pulse amplifier), and a special coil. The other units in the system are standard items as used with conventional ignition systems.

The external appearance of the distributor resembles a standard unit, but the internal construction, as shown in Fig. 15, is quite different. An iron timer core and a steel pole piece are used instead of breaker points. These two parts have the same number of projections, or teeth, as there are engine cylinders. The timer core rotates inside a magnetic pickup assembly which replaces the conventional breaker plate, breaker points, and condenser.

The magnetic pickup assembly is mounted over the main bearing of the distributor housing, and can be rotated by the vacuum control unit to provide vacuum advance. The timer core can be rotated about the distributor shaft by centrifugal advance weights to provide centrifugal advance.

The electronic control unit consists primarily of transistors, resistors, diodes, and condensers mounted on a printed circuit board. This unit contains no moving parts.

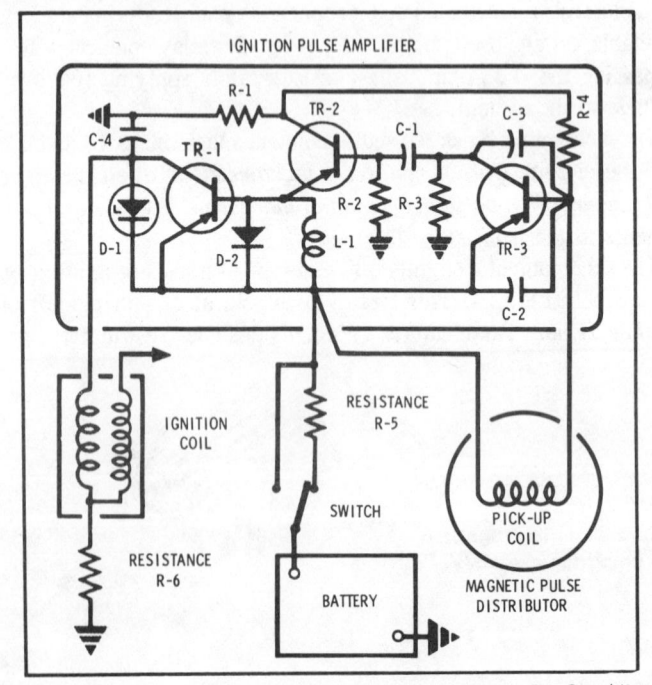

Fig. 14. Schematic of the PONTIAC TEMPEST transistor ignition system.

IGNITION TESTING

Fig. 15. Internal view of a PONTIAC TEMPEST distributor used with a transistorized ignition system.

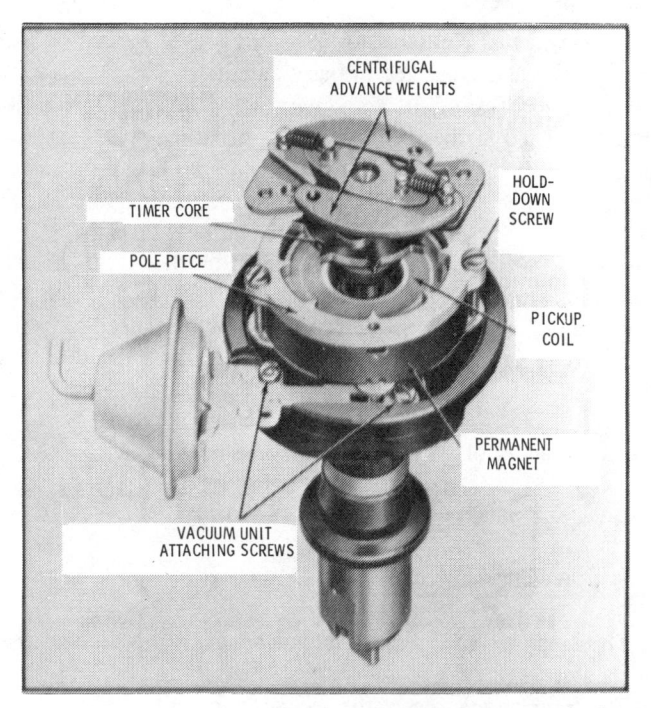

Courtesy Pontiac Motor Div., General Motors Corp.

The operation of this type of transistor ignition system is similar to the one just described, except for the distributor action. In the previous system, breaker points in the distributor control the amplifier unit. In the *Tempest* system, however, the teeth or vanes on the timer core pass by the teeth on the pole piece. At the instant of their passing, a magnetic path is established between them, causing a voltage pulse to be induced in the pickup coil. This voltage pulse causes *TR*-3 in the amplifier to conduct. This action turns *TR*-2 and *TR*-1 off, which interrupts the current flowing through the primary winding of the ignition coil. Thus, a high-voltage surge is produced in the coil secondary to fire the proper spark plug.

Troubleshooting

Finding remedies in a transistor ignition system follows the same general procedures as used for a conventional ignition system. Keep in

333

mind, however, that the transistor amplifier is used instead of breaker points to make and break the primary circuit.

Procedure for Testing Ford and Mercury Transistor Ignition — If trouble is isolated to the primary circuit, make the following tests to locate the defective item. *Do not use any other procedure or short cut, nor connect test equipment in any other manner than described. To do so may seriously damage the transistor ignition system.*

Remove the cover from the ballast-resistor block and *disconnect the cold-start relay.* Connect a dwell meter to the tachometer block. Connect the red lead to the red terminal and the black lead to the black terminal. Turn the ignition switch on, and observe the dwell-meter reading.

A dwell reading of 0° indicates:

1. Breaker points are dirty or are not closing.

A dwell reading between 0° and 45° indicates:

1. The amplifier and primary circuit are both functioning as they should.
2. The troubles may be in the secondary circuit.

A dwell reading of 45° indicates:

1. No power from the ignition switch.
2. Breaker points are closed and are not opening.
3. Defective amplifier assembly.

To determine which of the three listed items is causing the trouble, use the following procedure:

Disconnect the high-tension lead to the distributor and crank the engine. If the dwell meter reading is 0°, the distributor points are not opening. If 45° dwell is indicated, either the amplifier is defective or there is no power to it from the ignition switch.

Use a voltmeter or test lamp to determine if the transistor in the amplifier is defective. Connect the voltmeter or test lamp between the red-green lead terminal of the ballast resistor and ground. Crank the engine. If a steady voltage is indicated, the trouble is in the amplifier. If no voltage is indicated, there is an open circuit or no power between the

IGNITION TESTING

ignition switch and the amplifier. This condition could be caused by an open ballast resistor. Replace with a known good resistor and repeat the test.

If the tests indicate a defective amplifier unit, replace with a known good unit and proceed as follows:

Connect the high-tension lead to the distributor. Crank the engine and observe the dwell meter. A reading of less than 45° indicates satisfactory ignition. This means that the original amplifier was defective.

If the dwell reading is still 45°, the wiring between the amplifier and coil (through the ballast resistor) is defective. Replace the defective item.

Procedure for Testing Transistor Ignition — If trouble has been isolated to the primary circuit of the ignition system, make the following checks:

Check the pickup coil in the distributor by separating the harness connector and connecting an ohmmeter across the coil. The resistance of the coil should be from 550 to 650 ohms. (Check the car manufacturer's specifications for the particular make and model car being checked to insure the correct resistance value.) If the resistance is infinite, the coil is open. If the reading is below the specified value, the coil is shorted. (The resistance of the coil will increase slightly as the temperature rises.)

The pickup coil may be tested for grounds by connecting the ohmmeter between either coil lead and the distributor housing. The reading should be infinite — if it is not, the coil is grounded.

The centrifugal- and vacuum-advance mechanisms can be checked on a conventional distributor tester (*CHAPTER 3: DISTRIBUTORS*) designed to accommodate this type of distributor.

The primary of the ignition coil can be checked for an open condition by connecting an ammeter across the two primary terminals. An infinite reading indicates an open primary windings.

The secondary of the ignition coil can be checked by connecting the ohmmeter from the high-tension center tower to either primary terminal. An infinite reading indicates an open winding.

The repair of the amplifier unit in any transistor ignition system requires special technical knowledge and the use of special instruments. For this reason, repair of these units should be attempted only by qualified persons having the necessary instruments and proper instructions.

IGNITION TIMING

Correct timing of the spark, with relation to the position of the pistons in the cylinders, must be made for efficient engine operation. Most engines have a timing mark or marks (located either on the flywheel or the crankshaft vibration damper) that are used to correctly set the ignition timing. These marks must align properly with a pointer or marks on an adjacent stationary portion of the engine at the instant a spark occurs at the No. 1 spark plug. Fig. 16 shows the timing marks on a typical automobile.

The proper alignment of the timing marks is determined by the gap setting of the breaker points, and the time at which the cam lobes open the breaker points. The gap setting can be adjusted by means of a feeler gauge or a dwell meter, and the opening time can be adjusted by rotating the distributor housing.

Two common methods of setting ignition timing are the test light method and the timing light method. With the test light method, a low-voltage light is connected across the breaker points. The engine is then cranked, with the ignition switch on, until the breaker points just begin to open as the No. 1 piston is in the firing position (both intake

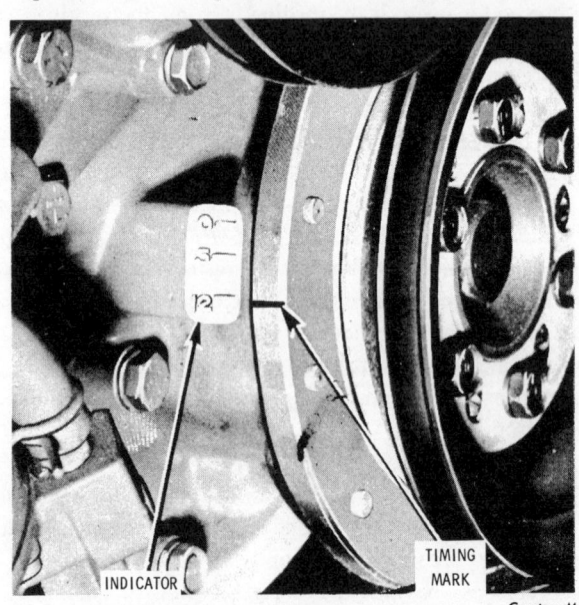

Fig. 16. Ignition timing mark and indicator.

IGNITION TESTING

and exhaust valves closed and piston near the top of the cylinder). The timing marks should align just as the test light comes on (indicating breaker point opening).

The second timing method consists of using a timing light connected to the No. 1 spark plug terminal. The light will flash each time the No. 1 spark plug fires, so that if the light is directed at the flywheel or vibration damper markings, they will appear to stand still. With this method, the engine is running at idle speed (usually about 550 r/min). Fig. 17 shows a timing light being used on a typical engine. Fig. 18 shows various timing markings on other engines.

With either method, the distributor is loosened in its mounting and turned one way or the other until the correct alignment of the timing marks, as specified by the manufacturer, is accomplished.

If the distributor has a vacuum advance mechanism, it must be disabled before setting the ignition timing with a timing light. This is done by removing the vacuum line from the vacuum advance unit. The vacuum line should be plugged (in most cases) so as not to affect engine speed.

The breaker points should be examined and adjusted before the final timing takes place. If a smudge line appears on the point support and

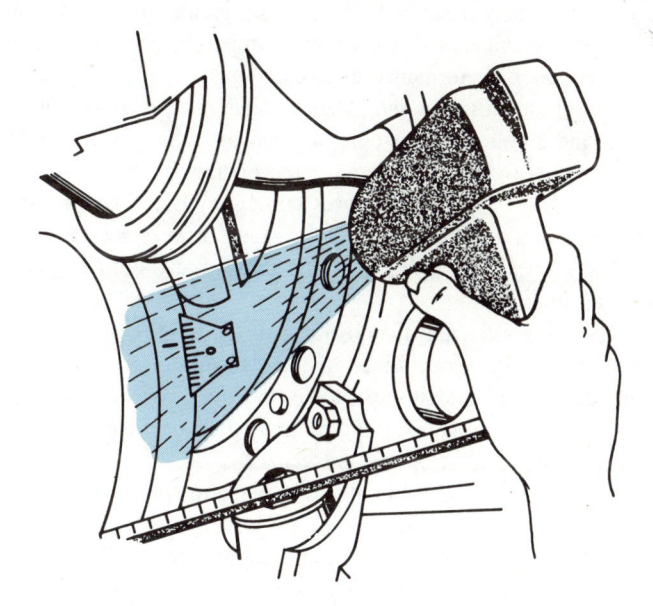

Fig. 17. Illustrating the timing mark and the use of a timing light.

breaker plate, burned points are very probable. Points that have been in service for several thousand miles will have a rough surface, but this does not necessarily mean that the points should be replaced with new ones. The roughness on each of the points matches and thus maintains a large contact area. If dirt or scale is present, however, the points should be cleaned with a few strokes of a clean, fine-cut, contact file. Do not attempt to remove all roughness nor try to dress the points down smooth. *Never use emery cloth or sandpaper to clean the points.*

If the points are excessively burned or pitted, they should be replaced. The cause of this condition should be found and corrected. If the cause is not corrected, the new points will also pit and burn in a short time.

The breaker point gap should be set to the manufacturer's specifications (usually .016″ to .020″) before the final timing adjustments are made.

ENGINE TESTERS

Special engine testers are available from several manufacturers. These units make possible more rapid trouble diagnosis than with the methods previously described. In addition, greater precision of adjustment is also possible which is of great importance in the later model high-speed, high-performance engines.

Most of these units test and make possible precise adjustment on the ignition and carburetion systems, as well as indicating other troubles that hinder the overall efficiency of the engine.

Fig. 19 shows a engine analyzer computer. Based on programmed "facts" about a particular engine, this type of analyzer automatically reads engine systems "problems" and prints a read-out of system tests indicating malfunctions.

Another computerized diagnostic analyzer is shown in Fig. 20. In addition to regular scope functions, the results of a seven-step programmed engine diagnosis sequence is displayed on a large screen. The computer section has a 3500 word program that is permanently stored in a memory bank with a 64,000 bit capacity.

Many smaller testers are available to perform checks on only certain systems in the automobile. For example, Fig. 21 shows a unit for checking dwell, primary voltages, and engine speeds. This instrument is transistorized, making possible greater accuracy in checking dwell on some of the modern ignition systems.

IGNITION TESTING

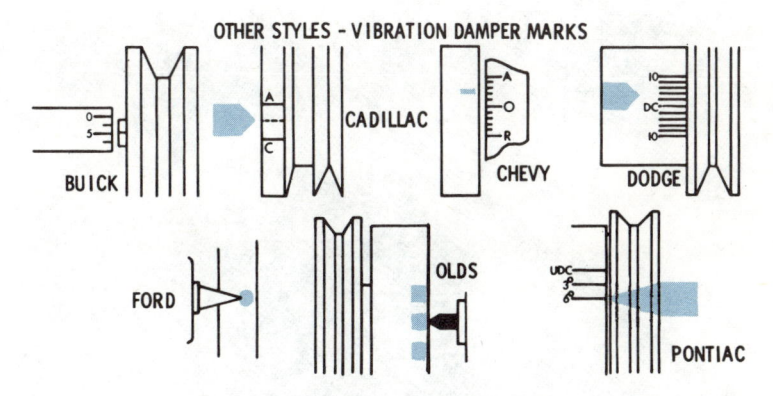

Fig. 18. Illustrating various timing marks.

Another example of a smaller tester is the unit in Fig. 22. This instrument can be used to test the entire ignition system, including the mechanical condition of the distributor. Besides ignition tests, it can also be used to measure the generator or alternator voltage and cranking current.

IGNITION TESTING WITH A TYPICAL ENGINE TESTER

Testing and adjusting the ignition system of a modern automobile can be made with greater accuracy and speed by using one of the many engine testers now available. In addition to checking the ignition system, these testers are designed to also check other functions of the automobile. Some of these tests are outlined in other chapters of the guide.

The final choice of which tester, or analyzer to use, is, of course, at the discretion of the user. It will be found that some have features that may not be found on others. Before making a decision, it is wise to consider several different models and manufacturers.

The ignition system tests described in this section are made with the *Sun Electric* model *TUT-1015 Tune-Up Tester*, shown in Fig. 23. These tests are generally representative of tests that may be made with similar testers of various manufacture.

Before making any tests, it is important that the equipment be calibrated and adjusted according to procedures outlined in the operator's manual for that particular unit. As a matter of safety and to protect the equipment, cables used to hook the unit up to the engine should be kept clear of belts, pulleys, fan, and exhaust manifolds.

Automobile Guide

Courtesy Bear Manufacturing Co.

Fig. 19. Typical engine analyzer computer.

A systematic approach to troubleshooting is essential for the proper diagnosis of system function or malfunction. A seven-step testing procedure recommended by *Sun*, when used with manufacturer's specifications, results in a step-by-step GO/NO-GO determination based on the results of each test. In this process, a customer complaint may be validated, while at the same time insuring that there is no more than one problem causing the customer complaint.

The tester is connected to the engine electrical and vacuum system according to the diagram in Fig. 24. Certain HEI, BID, and CD systems may require a different hookup. It is therefore important that specific instructions of the tester manufacturer's Operator's Manual be followed.

The seven-step testing procedure with *GO/NO-GO* analysis recommendations are: Cranking Tests, Charging Tests, Idle Tests, 1200 r/min Low Cruise Test, Cylinder Power Balance Tests, Snap Acceleration Test, and 2500 r/min High Cruise Test.

IGNITION TESTING

Cranking Test

Before holding the cranking test, insure that the tester is properly connected to the engine electrical and vacuum systems. Insure that the cable is free from the path of moving parts.

1. Disable the ignition system by disconnecting the secondary wire from the distributor cap. To disable HEI ignition systems push *engine kill* button so it shows red.
2. Turn off all lights and accessories.
3. Observe indications of tester instruments while cranking the engine.

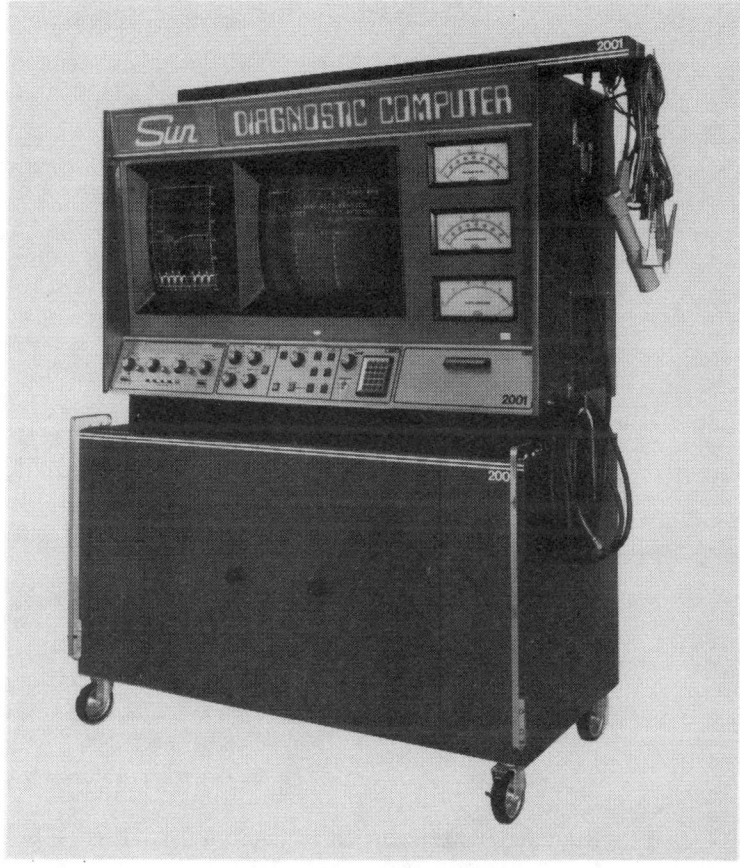

Courtesy Sun Electric Co.

Fig. 20. Typical computerized diagnostic analyzer.

AUTOMOBILE GUIDE

a. Read cranking coil output (in kilovolts) on the 50 kV scale of the scope. This test is not valid when using the engine kill button (as with the HEI system).
GO — Scope pattern height reaches or exceeds specified minimum height, Fig. 25.
NO-GO — Scope pattern height is below specified minimum height.

(1) Low battery voltage.
(2) Dwell too low.
(3) Defective bypass circuit.
(4) Primary ignition current low.
(5) Defective condenser.
(6) Defective coil.
(7) Defective coil/distributor cap wire.

b. Read the cranking starter current on the 500 ampere scale of the ammeter.
GO — Starter current draw is not more than specified maximum, Fig. 26.
NO-GO — Starter current draw is more than specified maximum.

(1) Discharged battery.
(2) Defective battery.
(3) Defective battery cables.
(4) Defective starter motor.
(5) Tight engine.
(6) Engine overheated.
(7) Defective starter solenoid.

c. Read the cranking battery voltage on the 20 volt scale of the voltmeter.
GO — Cranking battery voltage is at, or above, specified minimum, Fig. 27.
NO-GO — Cranking battery voltage is below specified minimum.

(1) Battery discharged.
(2) Battery defective.
(3) Battery cable(s) defective.
(4) Starter motor defective.
(5) Engine too tight.
(6) Overheated engine.
(7) Starter solenoid defective.

d. Read the cranking engine vacuum on the vacuum gauge, Fig. 28.
GO — Vacuum reading steady at normal level.

IGNITION TESTING

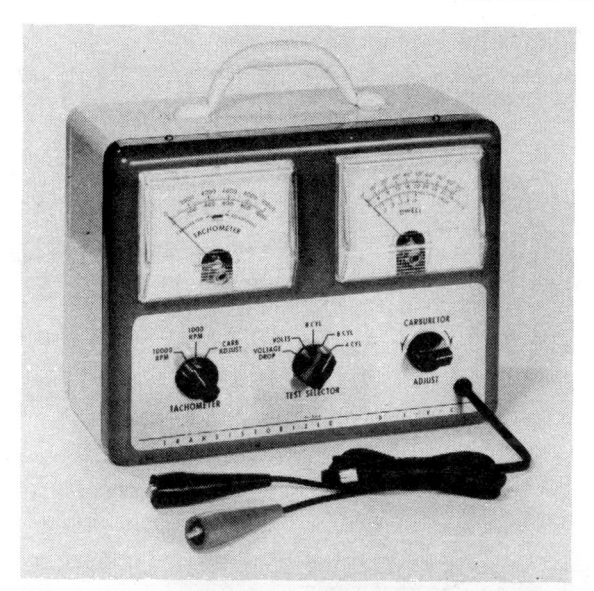

Fig. 21. The ALLEN-TRONIC Model 27-83 engine analyzer.

Fig. 22. The DYNA-TUNE Model T-200S engine analyzer.

AUTOMOBILE GUIDE

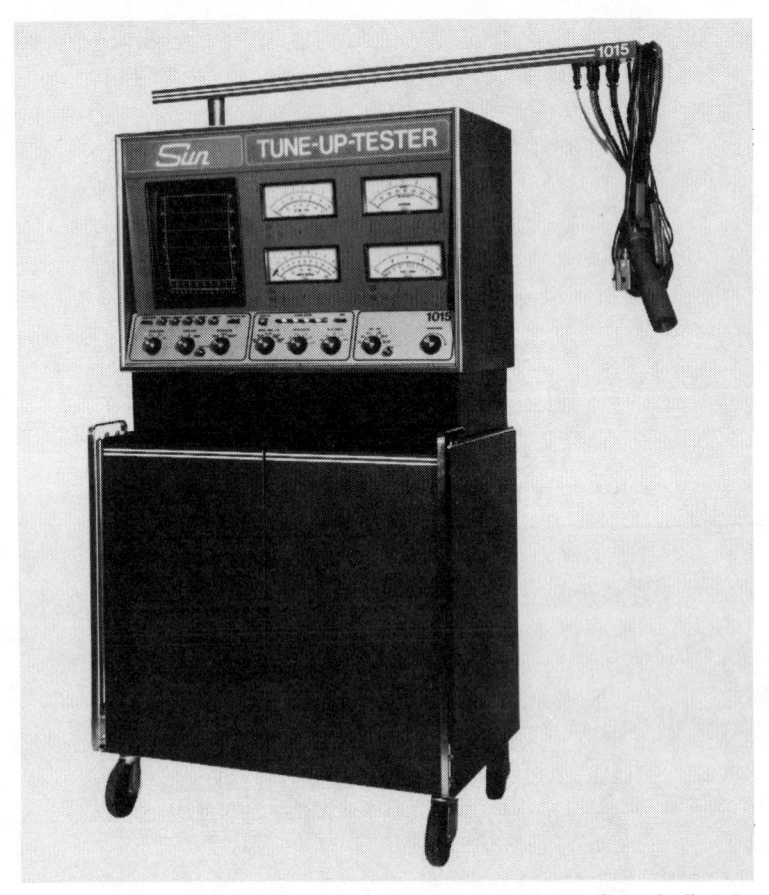

Courtesy Sun Electric Co.
Fig. 23. Sun Electric's Tune-Up Tester, Model TUT-1015.

NO-GO — Vacuum reading unsteady or lower than normal.

(1) Vacuum leak in hoses, emission control, or accessories.
(2) Vacuum leak at engine manifold, carburetor, power brake unit, etc.
(3) Engine mechanical problem; valves, rings, head gasket, etc.

Charging Test

Before making the charging test insure that the tester is properly

IGNITION TESTING

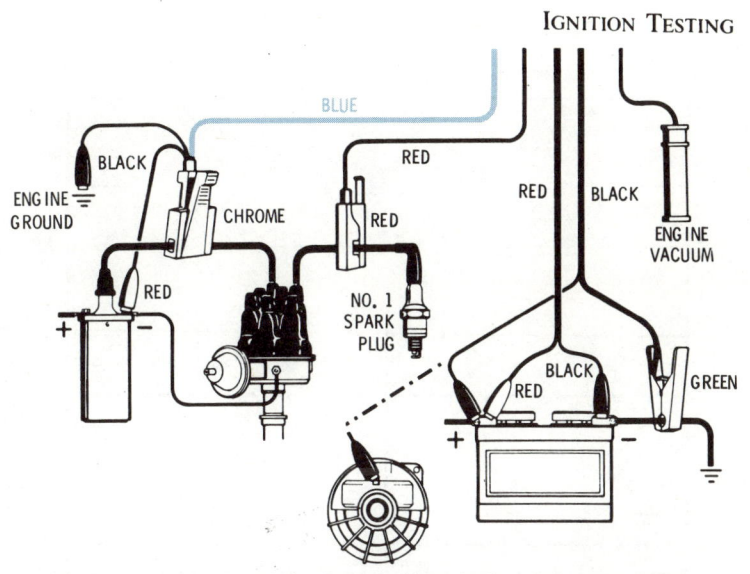

Fig. 24. Tune-Up Tester hook-up to electrical and vacuum systems.

connected to the engine electrical and vacuum system. Insure that the cable is free of the manifold and moving engine parts.

1. Set function switches and controls as outlined in the manufacturer's operation manual. Prepare engine to run; enable ignition system or release engine kill button.
2. Start engine and adjust speed to 2000 r/min.

   a. Note alternator output on 100 ampere scale of ammeter.
   GO — Ammeter indicates alternator output is at least half of rated output.
   NO-GO — Ammeter indicates alternator output below half of rated output (or no output at all).

   (1) Loose belt(s).
   (2) Broken belt(s).
   (3) Defective alternator.
   (4) Excessive electrical load.
   (5) Defective regulator.

   b. Note pattern on scope.
   GO — Scope shows even ripple, Fig. 29.
   NO-GO — Scope shown uneven ripple, Fig. 30.

   (1) Defective diode(s)
   (2) Defective stator

345

AUTOMOBILE GUIDE

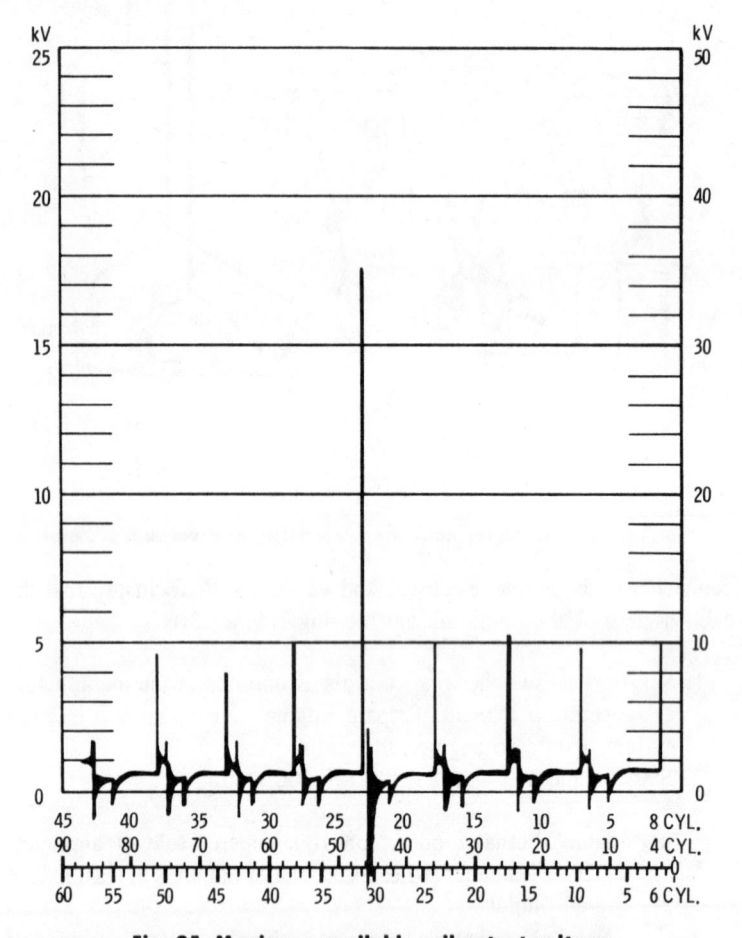

Fig. 25. Maximum available coil output voltage.

Idle Test

Insure that the tester is properly connected to the engine electrical and vacuum system. Insure that the cable is free of the manifold and moving engine parts.

1. Set function switches and controls as outlined in the manufacturer's operation manual.
2. Start engine and let it warm-up until the choke is open and the engine is at normal idle speed.

IGNITION TESTING

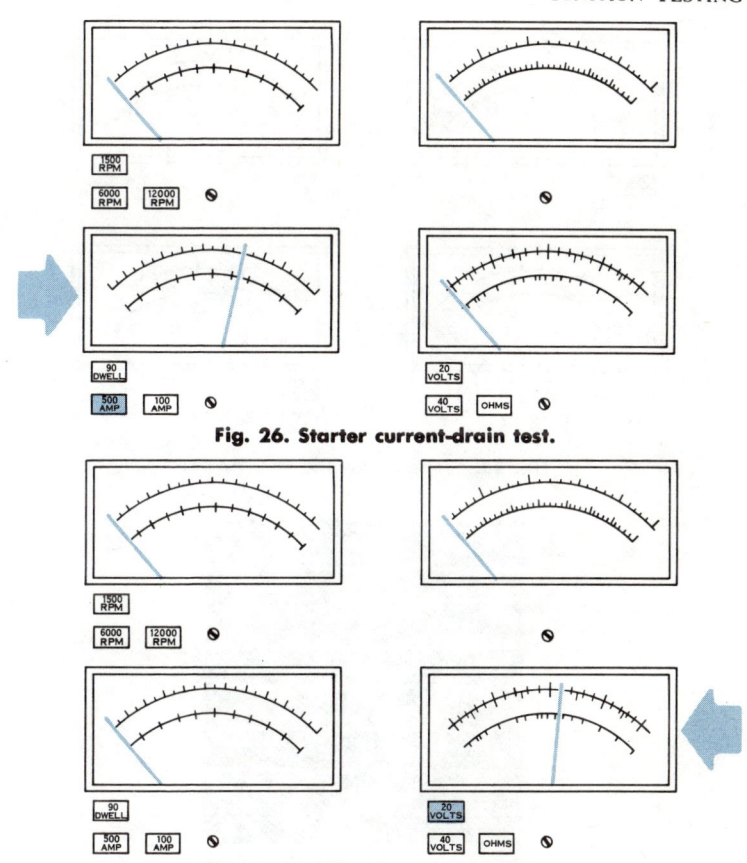

Fig. 26. Starter current-drain test.

Fig. 27. Cranking battery voltage test.

a. Read idle speed on 0-1500 r/min scale of the tachometer.
GO — Idle speed according to manufacturer's specifications.
NO-GO — Idle speed not according to manufacturer's specifications (too fast or too slow).

(1) Idle speed screw(s) out of adjustment.
(2) Idle mixture screw(s) out of adjustment.
(3) Engine malfunction (plugs, wiring, etc).
(4) Choke not fully open.
(5) Choke sticking.
(6) Idle solenoid out of adjustment (if equipped).
(7) Emission control problems (EGR valve, etc.)

Automobile Guide

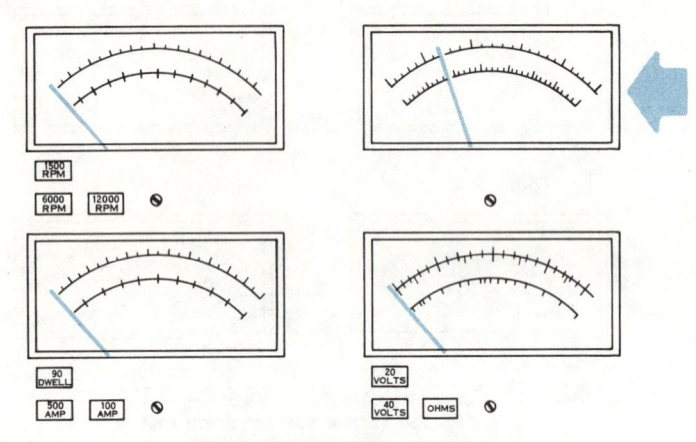

Fig. 28. Cranking engine vacuum test.

Fig. 29. Normal alternator scope pattern.

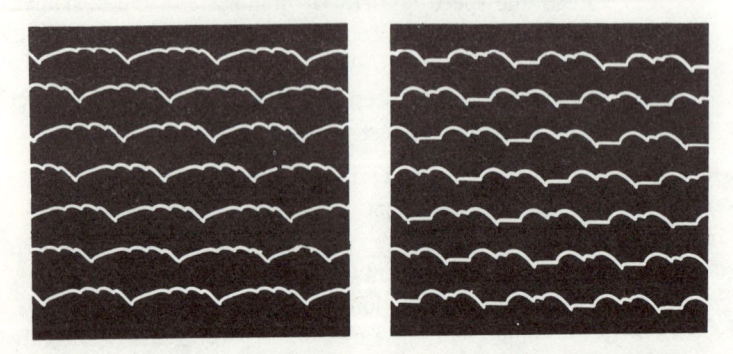

Fig. 30. Alternator open-diode and shorted-diode scope patterns.

Ignition Testing

b. Read dwell on dwell meter scale.
GO — Dwell is within manufacturer's specifications.
NO-GO — Dwell is incorrect (too high or too low).

(1) Defective points
(2) Points improperly adjusted.
(3) Defective distributor.

c. Check timing with timing light (Fig. 31).
GO — Timing set to specifications.
NO-GO — Timing is incorrect (too early or too late).

(1) Improper adjustment.
(2) Defective advance mechanism.
(3) Engine not running at correct speed.
(4) Vacuum retard not disconnected (if required).

d. Read engine manifold vacuum on vacuum gauge.
GO — At or above specified minimum and steady.
NO-GO — Below specified minimum and/or unsteady.

(1) Vacuum leak in hoses, emission control, or accessories.
(2) Engine mechanical problem; valves, rings, head gasket, etc.

e. Test PCV valve according to manufacturer's recommended procedures.
GO — Engine r/min and/or vacuum changes, as specified, when PCV valve is plugged.
NO-GO — Engine r/min and/or vacuum does not change when PCV valve is plugged.

(1) PCV valve plugged.
(2) Hose or vacuum source plugged or broken.
(3) Defective PCV valve.
(4) Incorrect PCV valve.

Low Cruise Test

With tester properly connected to the engine electrical and vacuum systems, be sure that the cable is free of the manifold and moving engine parts.

AUTOMOBILE GUIDE

Fig. 31. Using a timing light to check ignition timing.

Courtesy Sun Electric Corp.

1. Set function switches and controls as outlined in the manufacturer's operation manual.
2. Start engine and adjust speed to about 1200 r/min for the following scope tests:

   a. Check coil polarity.
   GO — Pattern right side up, Figs. 32 and 33.
   NO-GO — Pattern inverted, Fig. 34.

       (1) Reversed battery polarity.
       (2) Incorrect coil.
       (3) Reversed coil primary connections.

   b. Check spark-plug firing voltage.
   GO — Voltages about even and normal, Fig. 35.
   NO-GO — Voltages vary more than 3 kV (high or low), Fig. 36.

       (1) Incorrect spark plug gap.
       (2) Defective rotor.
       (3) Defective distributor.
       (4) Incorrect fuel mix.
       (5) Defective resistor-type spark plugs.

IGNITION TESTING

    (6) Defective distributor cap.
    (7) Incorrect timing.
    (8) Incorrect advance.

c. Check maximum coil output (available voltage).
GO — Meets or exceeds minimum specifications.
NO-GO — Output is less than minimum, Figs. 37 through 42.

    (1) Dwell too low.
    (2) Low primary voltage.
    (3) Defective coil.
    (4) Defective condenser.
    (5) Excessive resistance in primary circuit(s).
    (6) Defective insulation in secondary circuit(s).

d. Check for secondary insulation problems.
GO — Secondary waveform proper (down spike equal to about one-half upward spike) *NOTE: Check operator's manual for information regarding high output systems, such as HEI.*
NO-GO — Coil output is less than 25 kV and down spike is missing, or intermittent, Fig. 43.

    (1) Defective wires.
    (2) Defective cap.
    (3) Defective rotor.
    (4) Defective coil.

e. Check for secondary resistance problems.
GO — Slope and length of spark lines normal for engine.
NO-GO — One or more spark lines slant and is too short. Indicates excessive resistance in:

    (1) Spark plugs.
    (2) Rotor.
    (3) Coil tower.
    (4) Plug wires.
    (5) Cap.

f. Check for condition of coil and condenser.
GO — Proper number and size of oscillations in intermediate section of pattern.
NO-GO — Oscillations missing or diminishing in intermediate section of pattern.

    (1) Defective coil.
    (2) Loose wiring.
    (3) Defective condenser.
    (4) Loose parts in distributor

Automobile Guide

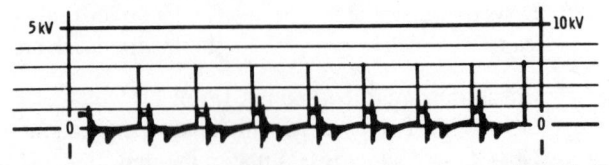

Fig. 32. Normal secondary ignition display for a typical 8-cylinder engine.

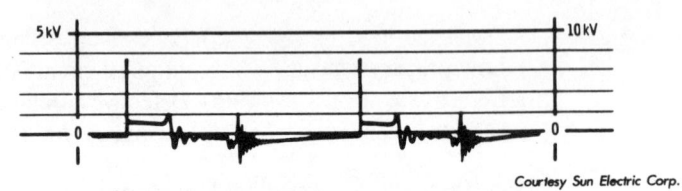

Fig. 33. Normal ignition coil output display.

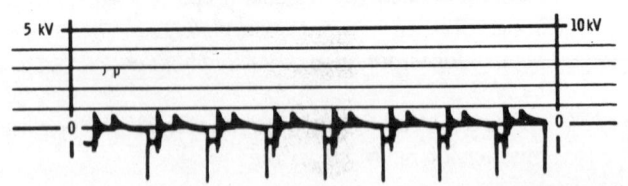

Fig. 34. Inverted pattern caused by incorrect polarity.

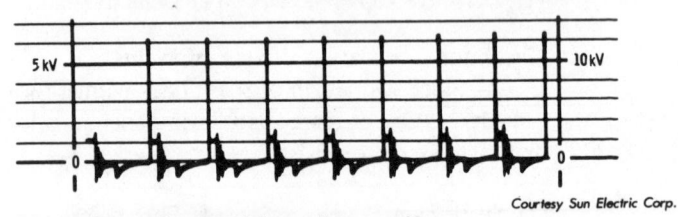

Fig. 35. Firing voltage uniform.

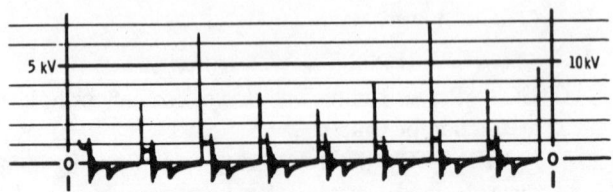

Fig. 36. Uneven firing voltages.

    g. Check for breaker point condition.
         GO — Point opening and closing signal normal.

IGNITION TESTING

Fig. 37. High secondary resistance affecting all cylinders.

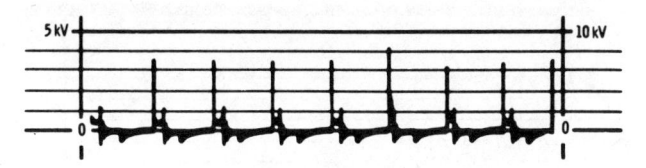

Fig. 38. High resistance in the secondary circuit affecting one or more cylinders, but not all.

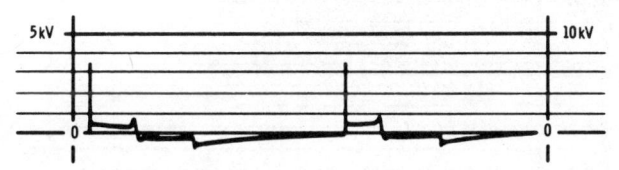

Fig. 39. Waveform indicating a defective ignition coil or condenser.

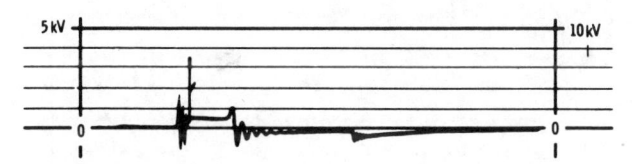

Fig. 40. Scope display showing breaker-point bounce.

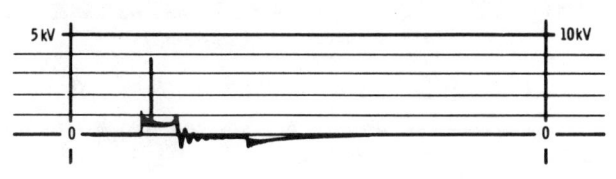

Fig. 41. Scope display showing effect of weak breaker-point spring tension.

NO-GO — Point opening and closing signal arcing or irregular.

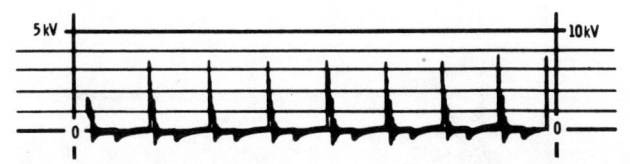

353

AUTOMOBILE GUIDE

Courtesy Sun Electric Corp.
Fig. 42. Abnormal pattern caused by burned or dirty breaker points.

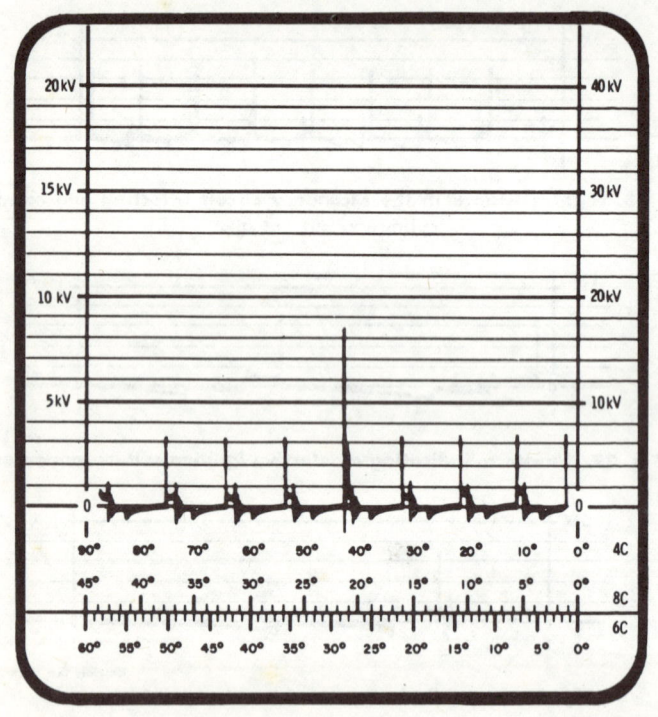

Courtesy Sun Electric Corp.
Fig. 43. The missing lower portions of the waveforms indicate trouble in the secondary insulation.

    (1) Defective points.
    (2) Incorrect coil.
    (3) Defective ballast resistor or wiring.
    (4) Dwell too high.
    (5) Incorrect charging voltage.

  h. Check cylinder timing accuracy.
      GO — Point opening signals within specifications.
      NO-GO — Point opening signals vary more than +2°.

IGNITION TESTING

(1) Cam defective.
(2) Worn bushing(s).
(3) Worn breaker plate.
(4) Engine problems.

Cylinder Power Balance Test

Insure that tester is properly connected to the engine electrical and vacuum system and that cable is free of manifold and moving engine parts.

1. Set function switches and controls as specified in the manufacturer's operation manual.
2. Start and operate engine at desired test speed. Record r/min.
3. Press "cylinder select" buttons, one at a time. Note and record r/min of engine as each cylinder is shorted.

GO — Engine r/min dropped about the same as each cylinder was shorted.

NO-GO — Engine r/min changes little or none as one or more cylinders are shorted.

(1) Engine problems (check compression and cylinder leakage).
(2) Vacuum leak.
(3) Ignition problems
(recheck Low Cruise Test).
(4) Fuel mixture problems (check carburetor adjustment).

Snap Acceleration Test

With tester properly connected to engine electrical and vacuum system, insure that cable is free of manifold and moving engine parts.

1. "Jab" accelerator throttle to about 2500 r/min and then release while observing spark plug firing lines on scope.

GO — Firing lines increase slightly and evenly. Firing voltage does not exceed maximum specifications.

NO-GO — Firing lines do not increase evenly, and/or firing voltages exceed maximum specifications, Fig. 44.

(1) Defective plug(s).
(2) Lean fuel mixture.
(3) Plug gap too wide.

High Cruise Test

With tester properly connected to engine electrical and vacuum system, adjust engine speed to about 2500 r/min. Make sure that tester cable is free of manifold and moving parts.

355

AUTOMOBILE GUIDE

1. Check timing advance with timing light.

    GO — Timing advance is correct.
    NO-GO — Timing is too advanced or too retarded.

    (1) Vacuum advance chamber is defective (leaking).
    (2) Defective mechanical advance.
    (3) Vacuum line clogged or disconnected.
    (4) Incorrect distributor for engine.

2. Check dwell on dwell meter.

    GO — Dwell change from idle is correct.
    NO-GO — Dwell change from idle is incorrect.

    (1) Defective advance in distributor.
    (2) Defective distributor.

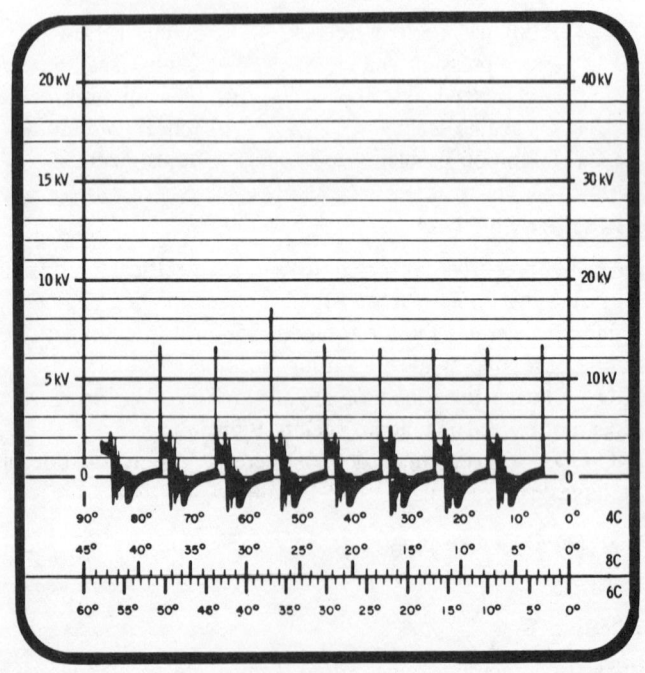

Courtesy Sun Electric Corp.

Fig. 44. Scope pattern showing the effect of wide plug gap, open plug resistor, or bad electrodes.

IGNITION TESTING

3. Check charging voltage on 20V scale of voltmeter.

GO — Voltage reading is correct with specifications.
NO-GO — Voltmeter reading too high or too low.
  (1) Defective alternator. (2) Defective regulator.

4. Check engine manifold vacuum on vacuum gauge.

GO — Reading is steady and higher than at idle speed.
NO-GO — Reading unsteady and/or lower than at idle speed.
  (1) Engine problems (recheck Cylinder Power Balance Test).
  (2) Restriction in exhaust system.
  (3) Timing not advancing.

BASIC SCOPE PATTERNS

An oscilloscope (scope) provides a convenient means of observing the performance of an ignition system. A scope does this by displaying on a screen an easily interpreted graph-like pattern of all phases of the ignition cycle at the instant at which they occur. The displayed "picture" permits the technician to actually see, in detail, the results of the many factors which affect the performance of the ignition system.

To interpret patterns of an ignition scope into test results it is important that the basic scope patterns be thoroughly understood by the technician. There are but two basic patterns, called *waveforms*. They are the *secondary waveforms* and *primary waveforms*.

In studying scope patterns, they should be considered to be graphs of voltage with respect to time. The vertical displacement of the scope trace from the zero line (either up or down, depending on polarity) represents voltage at any instant along the zero line.

Secondary Waveform Interpretation

Each part of the waveform represent a specific phase of operation of the ignition system. For purposes of explanation and better understanding, the scope pattern is divided into three sections — *Firing, Intermediate,* and *Dwell*.

The Firing Section — This part of the waveform is called the firing section because it is during this period that the actual firing of the spark plug takes place. This portion of the pattern is composed of only two lines:

The firing line, a vertical line indicating the voltage required to overcome the plug and rotor gaps.

The spark line, a horizontal line indicating the voltage required to maintain the spark.

Point *A* in Fig. 45 represents the instant at which the breaker points have separated. The resultant high voltage is indicated by the vertical rise from *A* to *B*. The height at point *B* shows the voltage required to fire the plug and rotor gap.

Once the plug fires, there is a noticeable drop in secondary voltage to point *C*. As the spark continues across the gaps, the spark voltage remains at a fairly constant lower value until the spark extinguishes at point *D*.

The Intermediate Section — This part of the waveform immediately follows the firing section, and is seen as a number of gradually diminishing oscillations which disappear, or nearly so, by the time the dwell section begins. Starting at point *D*, the remaining coil energy dissipates itself as an oscillating current which gradually dies out as it approaches point *E*. The oscillations result from the combined effect of the coil and condenser in dissipating this energy.

The Dwell Section — This part of the waveform represents the period in the ignition cycle during which the breaker points are closed. The dwell section starts at point *E* when the breaker points close. This closure causes a short, downward line followed by a series of small, rapidly diminishing oscillations. The dwell section continues until the breaker points open at the beginning of the next waveform (point *F*).

Primary Waveform Interpretation

Since any voltage in the primary circuit of the ignition system will be reflected in the secondary, it is seldom necessary to view the primary pattern for general ignition testing. Most ignition scopes, however, have provisions for viewing the primary waveform when necessary.

Although the primary and secondary patterns resemble each other, it should be noted that the voltage values represented in the primary patterns are much lower than those represented in the secondary patterns. For example, the scales on the *Sun 820* ignition scope indicate a maximum primary voltage of either 40 or 400 volts instead of 20,000 or 40,000 volts indicated for secondary patterns.

The primary pattern (Fig. 46) has the same basic sections as the secondary pattern.

IGNITION TESTING

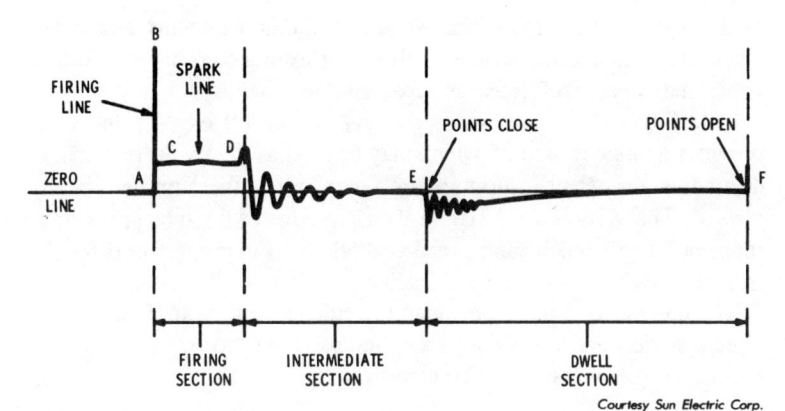

Fig. 45. Basic secondary waveform obtained at the high-tension tower of the ignition coil.

Courtesy Sun Electric Corp.

The Firing Section — This section displays the series of rapid oscillations occurring in the primary circuit during the time the spark plug is firing. Point A in Fig. 46 represents the instant at which the breaker points open.

The vertical rise from A to B, and the diminishing oscillations which follow, represent the initial and repeated charge and discharge of the condenser and the induced voltage surges in the primary circuit while the spark plug is firing. As the spark jumps the gap and energy is being drained from the coil, the size of these oscillations will decrease until the spark ends (point C).

The Intermediate Section — The intermediate section contains a series of gradually diminishing oscillations which disappear, or nearly so, by the time the breaker points close. Beginning with point C, the energy remaining in the coil will dissipate itself as an oscillating current which gradually dies out as it approaches point D.

The Dwell Section — The breaker points close and cause a faint downward line from point D to point E. The dwell section is represented by the horizontal line extending from point E to point F. It is during the dwell section that the breaker points remain closed.

THE ANALOG OSCILLOSCOPE

The analog scope features a screen of sufficient vertical display capabilities to present better readability of the raster display. Additionally, the scope has the facilities for displaying special waveforms for

AUTOMOBILE GUIDE

testing alternators, regulators, electronic ignition systems and other electronic systems. It provides methods for testing conventional, transistor, and capacitive-discharge type ignition systems.

Note Fig. 47. The vertical scale (A) on the left edge of the tube provides a range of 0 to 25 which may be read as 0-25 volts or 0-25kV depending on whether primary or secondary waveforms are being viewed. The vertical scale (B) on the right edge of the tube provides a range of 0 to 50 which can be read as 0-500 volts in primary or 0-50 kV in secondary.

The horizontal scale (C) reads in increments of 1° from 0° to 45° for eight cylinders and 0 to 60° for six cylinders. The 0° to 90° scale for four cylinder engines reads in increments of 2°.

HIGHWAY SAFETY — DIAGNOSTIC TESTING

An ever increasing number of vehicles are entering this nation's highways each year. Car registrations are increasing at the rate of about five percent annually. Truck registrations are up about 40% during the past five years, and the number of motorcycle registrations have more than doubled over the same period of time.

In 1976 over 1.39 trillion vehicle-miles were logged — resulting in 47,100 deaths and over 1 million injuries. In addition to deaths and injuries more than 1.5 billion dollars are lost in automobile accidents *each month.*

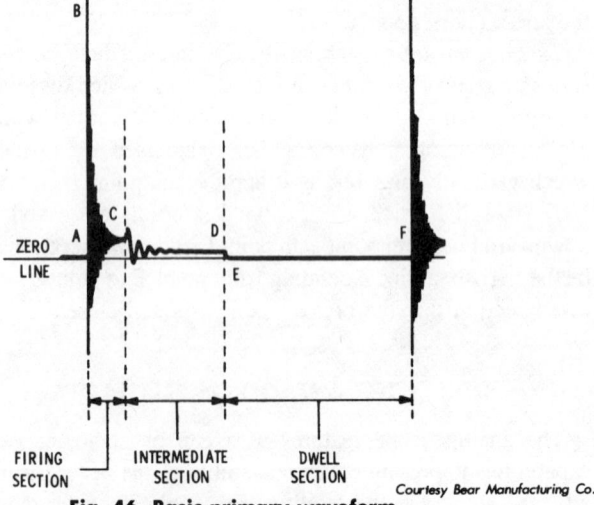

Courtesy Bear Manufacturing Co.
Fig. 46. Basic primary waveform.

360

IGNITION TESTING

In the late 60's and early 70's, concerted efforts to reduce highway deaths and injuries through the use of new and improved safety devices were initiated. These efforts, and the reduction of maximum speed limits, proved effective. In 1968 over 54,800 people were killed. This figure was reduced over 7700 to 47,100 deaths in 1976 (1.39 trillion vehicle miles) though vehicle miles increased almost 35 percent.

No figures are available on the number of deaths and injuries as a result of vehicle equipment failure — but the percentage must be considerable. Vehicle accidents have decreased, in most cases, in states that have instituted mandatory periodic vehicle inspection.

Some interesting facts about automotive safety show that of those states that have a mandatory vehicle inspection (annually or semiannually), it has been found that 25 percent (that's 1 out of 4) of all cars less than 2 years old are rejected. Forty percent (four out of ten) of all

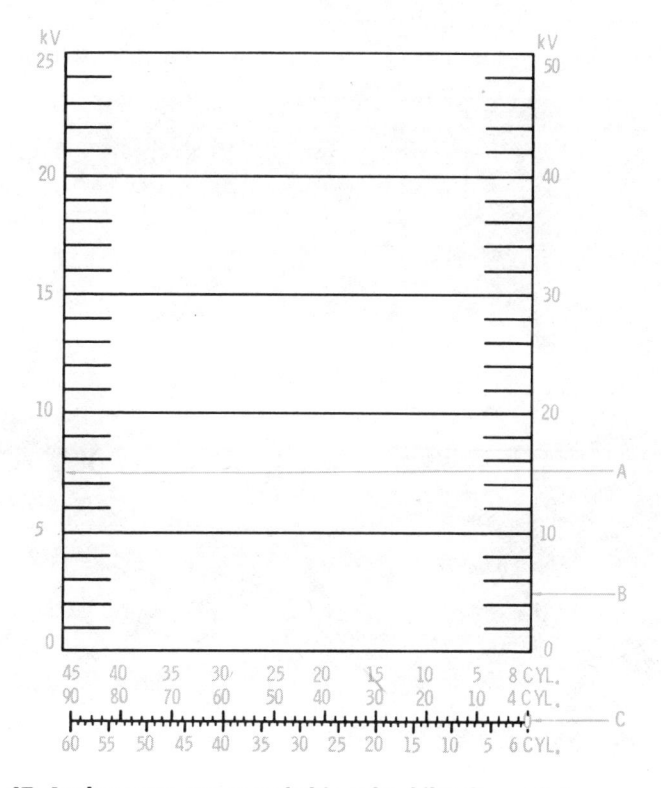

Fig. 47. Analog scope screen scaled in volts, kilovolts and degrees.

361

cars 2 to 5 years old are rejected; and 51 percent (over half) of all cars 6 to 10 years old are rejected.

It seems then, to save our own "necks," we should all be concerned with vehicle safety. It would also seem that if a car was inspected periodically it should be a safer car. Many states have a mandatory inspection; others have a spot-check inspection, while others have no inspection program at all.

In some areas, motorists have their cars checked voluntarily. Voluntary inspection, even in states that require regular inspection, has certain advantages. As well as determining any unsafe condition, an inspection can point out other problems affecting improper performance. Diagnostic lanes are generally used for this type inspection. Diagnostic lanes are reasonable, fast, and dependable.

Diagnostic Lanes

Diagnostic lanes, though not new, are "springing" up all around the country. A diagnostic lane offers, among many other things, a good

Courtesy Bear Manufacturing Co.

Fig. 48. Car being tested on an AUTOROL.™

Ignition Testing

way to determine car performance and safety. A car standing still, with its brakes locked, in gear and its engine speeded up, produces a torque at the driving (rear) wheels. It produces no horsepower, however, since its drive wheels are not turning.

A diagnostic lane, having a device such as the *Autorol*™, Fig. 48, provides a safe indoor method of testing that can closely duplicate actual road conditions. Road tests at wide open throttle with the car under full load can only be safely made on a closed track. Today's sophisticated, high performance, cars demand testing methods approximating actual driving conditions.

An *Autorol*™, in addition to providing a means to determine specifications of power output, can also be used to troubleshoot engine and mechanical drive line problems under various load conditions; problems such as engine missing at certain speeds or load conditions. Drive shaft and transmission malfunctions can also be checked under any given driving condition.

Fig. 49. Oscilloscope and console used with diagnostic lane.

AUTOMOBILE GUIDE

Complete ignition and carburetion operation can be analyzed using an oscilloscope (Fig. 49), timing light, exhaust gas analyzer, and other testing equipment. These tests can be made under virtually any road speed and load condition.

Mechanical performance of the many accessories and prime devices in the car can be tested and investigated. Transmission "up" and "down" shift points can be checked. The speedometer can be checked for accuracy. Driveshaft and drive axle can be checked with the car stationary and in actual running condition.

Exhaust systems, cooling systems, fuel lines, filters and pumps, and the many auxillary systems need analysis while the engine is operating under load. As a practical quality control tool, the *Autorol** (or any other such device) can be used as a quality control device to check engine tune-up work to insure efficient performance after corrective engine repairs have been made.

Fig. 50. Layout of typical diagnostic lane.

364

Ignition Testing

As mentioned earlier, the diagnostic lane, Fig. 50, is used to check many other things that add to the comfort and safety of the driver and passengers.

A visual inspection is made under the hood for defective hoses, belts, wiring, and for oil and fuel leaks. A visual inspection is also made around the car for defective or burned out lights.

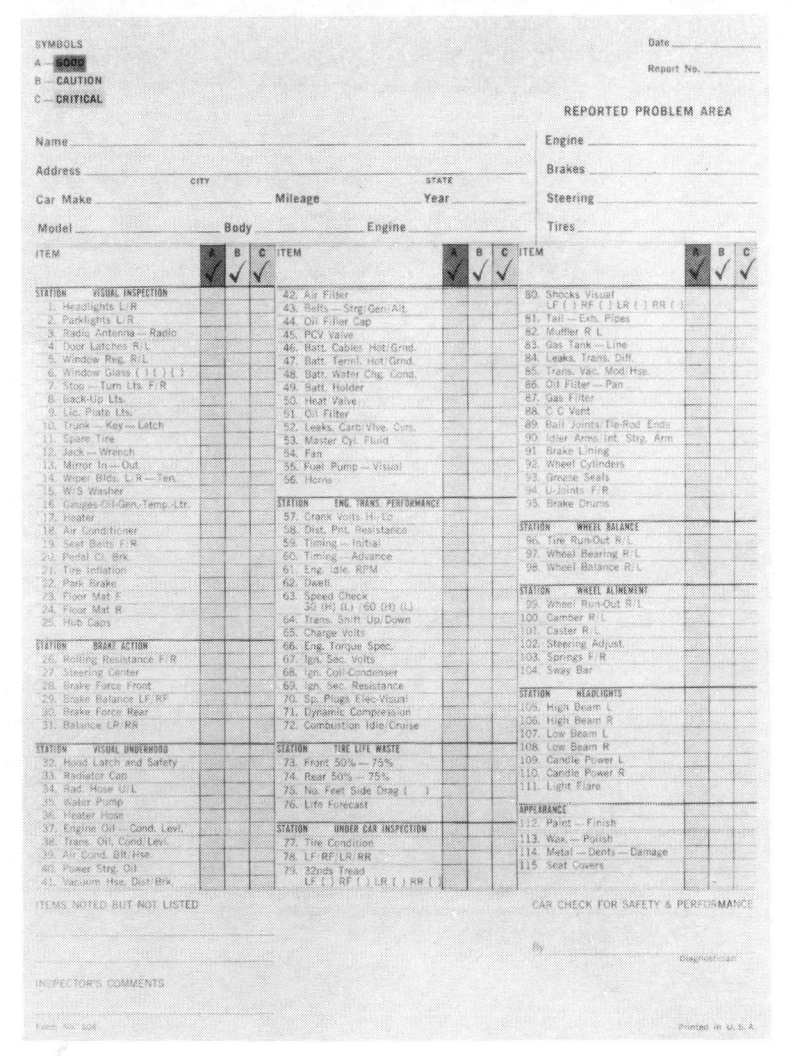

Fig. 51. Diagnostic report forms.

In the diagnostic lane, under-the-hood electronic analysis includes; cranking voltage, secondary voltage, charging voltage, battery condition, timing, dwell, compression, and resistance (to name a few).

Under-car inspection includes exhaust and frame inspection, brake lining wear and efficiency. Wheel balance, front-end alignment and wear, as well as sway bars and shock absorbers are also checked.

Finally, a general check should be made of the appearance of the car. It should be checked for rust, nicks, dents, poor paint, upholstery, etc. Problems that affect car safety are easily pointed out in a diagnostic

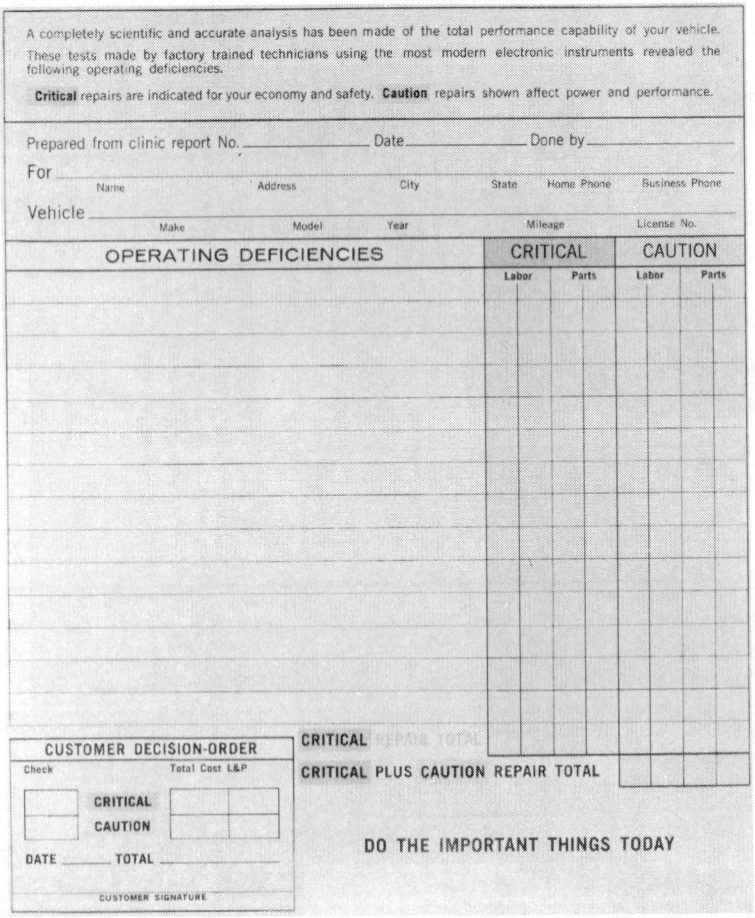

A completely scientific and accurate analysis has been made of the total performance capability of your vehicle. These tests made by factory trained technicians using the most modern electronic instruments revealed the following operating deficiencies.

Critical repairs are indicated for your economy and safety. **Caution** repairs shown affect power and performance.

Prepared from clinic report No. ______ Date ______ Done by ______

For ______
Name Address City State Home Phone Business Phone

Vehicle ______
Make Model Year Mileage License No.

OPERATING DEFICIENCIES	CRITICAL		CAUTION	
	Labor	Parts	Labor	Parts

CUSTOMER DECISION-ORDER
Check / Total Cost L&P
CRITICAL
CAUTION
DATE ______ TOTAL ______
CUSTOMER SIGNATURE

CRITICAL REPAIR TOTAL

CRITICAL PLUS CAUTION REPAIR TOTAL

DO THE IMPORTANT THINGS TODAY

Fig. 52. Typical report form for performance capability of vehicle.

IGNITION TESTING

lane. A written record or report can easily be given the customer by using a form such as the one shown in Fig. 51. Specific complaints may be reported by using a form such as the one shown in Fig. 52.

Remember, it is a fact that at least one out of every four cars on our highways needs service directly related to vehicle safety. Of 100 cars tested by *Bear Manufacturing Company*, 147 defective or worn out parts were discovered. That is an average of almost 1.5 defective parts per car. That is not counting 479 wheel weights that had to be used on the 100 cars tested. Table 1 shows that those parts discovered to be defective related directly to car safety.

NOTE: This chapter gives a systematic check of the ignition system giving "Symptoms and Possible Causes" as well as "Possible Remedies." Refer to other chapters of this book as applicable for more specific information for a particular problem whose "Remedy" is not given in this chapter.

Table 1. Number of Worn Parts in 100 Cars Checked

Part	Count	Part	Count
Center control steering set	2	Radiator hose	1
Lower control arm bushing	2	Radius arm set	2
Upper control arm bushing	6	Rear grease seals	2
Front springs	10	Left axle shaft	1
Lower control arm set	38	Shocks and brackets	4
Upper control arm set	43	Upper control arm and bushings	8
Lower control rubber bumper	2	Idler arm pin and bushings	4
Shocks	72	Wheel cylinder cups	22
Weights	479	Brake lining	2
Tie rod ends	41	Dimmer switch	1
Upper control arm	23	Left front bearing	2
Pivot shaft bushings	78	Stabilizer link	1
Pivot shaft set	1	Center tie bolt	1
Grease fittings	3	Spring shackles	1
Rear main leaf	1	Inner upper shaft	5
Shims	17	Radius arm bushings	2
Master cylinder kit	2	Steering knuckle supports	2
Lower arm set	56	Tie rod and sleeve	1
Brake fluid	9	Spring leaves	3
Steering worm and tube	1	Headlight lens	1
Steering sector shaft	1	Headlight gasket	1
Kingpin and bushings	32	Pitman arm bushings	5
Drag links	4	Brake rod pins	3
Steering Pitman arm	5	Steering jacket bushings	2

CHAPTER 16

Starters and Alternators

The starting and charging systems on the modern automobile have much in common. Though the alternator is not similar in construction, its purpose is the same as its predecessor, the generator — that is, to convert mechanical motion into electrical energy.

STARTERS

The starter used to crank the engine on all modern automobiles is actually a direct current (dc) motor capable of developing a high torque (twisting force). The electric current supplied to the starter is furnished by the storage battery.

A cross section of a typical starting motor is shown in Fig. 1. The starter cranks the engine through a pinion gear which is attached to the armature shaft. This pinion gear is brought into mesh with teeth on the rim of the engine flywheel through the action of an overrunning clutch (Fig. 2). With this arrangement, the pinion gear is moved into mesh by a lever actuated by the starter solenoid when the ignition switch is in the start position. As soon as the engine starts, the speed of the flywheel becomes greater than the speed of the pinion gear, causing the pinion to be pulled out of mesh with the flywheel gear through the action of spiral splines on the armature shaft. The pinion gear will also be pulled out of mesh by the solenoid shift lever whenever the solenoid is de-energized, whether the engine has started or not.

STARTERS AND ALTERNATORS

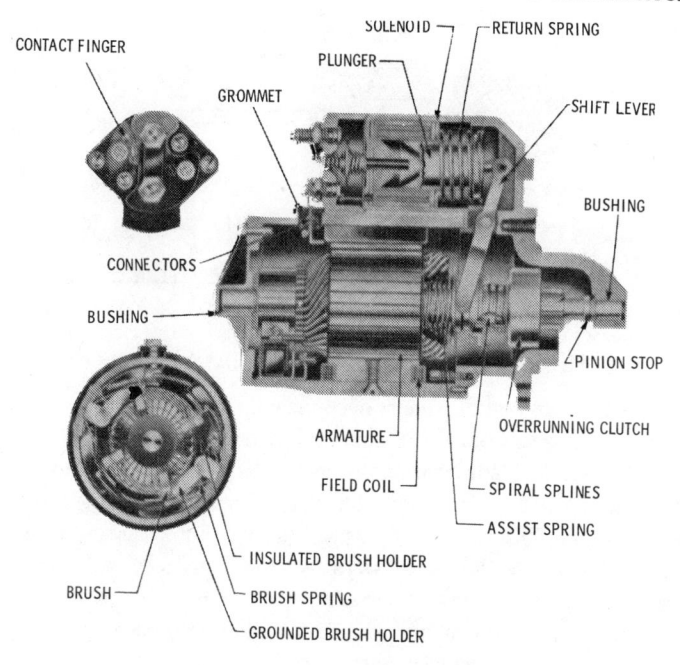

Fig. 1. Starting motor details.

STARTER BRUSHES

The brushes used on 12-volt starting motors are made of a high metal content material for good conductivity and excellent starting torque, with sufficient graphite for good commutation and brush life. When new brushes are installed, the spring tension should be checked to make sure the brushes will ride firmly on the commutator. The brushes should be *seated* properly. A piece of fine sandpaper (never emery cloth) can be attached to the commutator, so that the rough side of the sandpaper shapes the brushes to the commutator when the starter armature is manually rotated.

STARTER DRIVES

In order to develop sufficient torque to crank an engine, gear reduction must be used between the starting motor drive and the engine flywheel. This ratio is usually from 15:1 to 20:1. Therefore, it is necessary to have a drive mechanism which can engage the starter to the

369

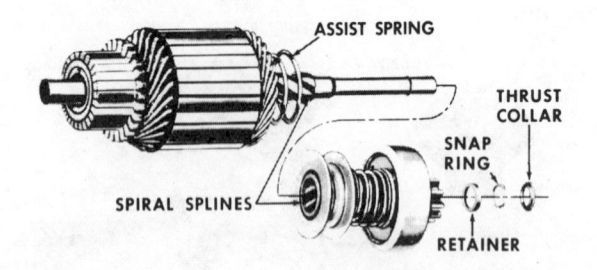

Automobile Guide

Fig. 2. Armature and overrunning clutch assembly.
Courtesy Pontiac Motor Div., General Motors Corp.

engine, crank it, and disengage once the engine starts. This requirement is obvious if one would consider the fact that if disengagement of the starter motor does not occur after the engine has started and the engine accelerated to, say, 4000 r/min, the starter could be driven to a possible 60,000 to 80,000 r/min. At this speed, the windings of the starter armature would be thrown outward by centrifugal force and the starter would be ruined.

Although there are many types of starter drive mechanisms, all are based on two fundamental types — the *Bendix* drive and the *overrunning clutch* drive.

The Overrunning Clutch

In an overrunning clutch-type starter drive, the drive pinion is attached to the collar, Figs. 1 and 2. The entire assembly is connected to the starter drive motor by means of a splined drive shaft.

Whenever the starter switch is "closed" by the driver, the solenoid immediately pulls in the plunger which in turn pulls the upper leg of the shift lever away from the flywheel. The lower leg, or yoke, of the shift lever then moves toward the flywheel and with it, the overrunning clutch assembly. This action engages the gears of the clutch with the gears of the flywheel.

When the pinion is fully engaged, electrical contact is made to the starter motor and it starts to spin, thereby cranking the engine. When the engine starts, the starter pinion is driven to very high speeds. But due to the overrunning clutch arrangement, the starter armature cannot be driven to speeds higher than those due to electrical action. In this manner the armature is protected from the destructive speeds mentioned earlier. When the engine starts, the electrical connection is broken to the

STARTERS AND ALTERNATORS

STARTER GEAR
10 TOOTH

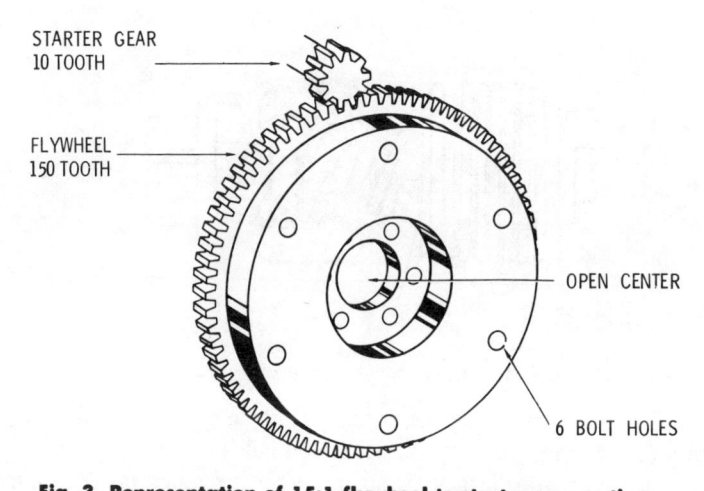

FLYWHEEL
150 TOOTH

OPEN CENTER

6 BOLT HOLES

Fig. 3. Representation of 15:1 flywheel-to-starter gear ratio.

DRIVE PINION & SLEEVE   SPRING   DRIVE HEAD

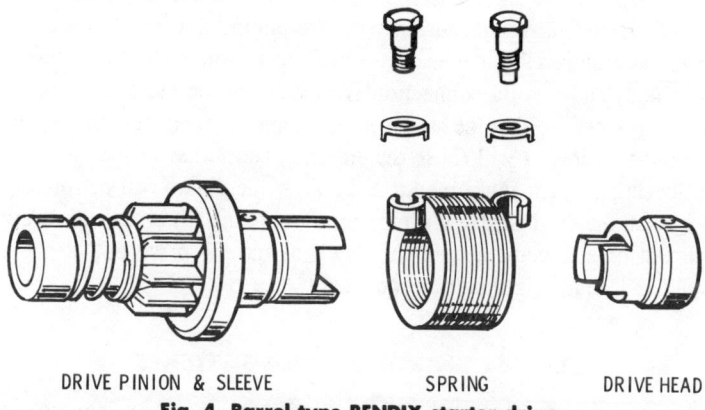

Fig. 4. Barrel-type BENDIX starter drive.

motor and the overrunning clutch assembly is allowed to slide out of engagement with the flywheel.

Two popular types of the *Bendix* drive are the *barrel-type*, Fig. 4, and the *folo-thru type*, Fig. 5. Either type drive utilizes a lead screw on the starter motor shaft as a connection between the starter drive pinion and the starter drive shaft. Whenever there is a relative motion between the pinion and the starter drive shaft, the starter pinion will move back and forth on the starter shaft due to this screw action. The direction of travel, back or forth, will depend on whether the starter motor is turning slower than, or faster than, the starter drive pinion.

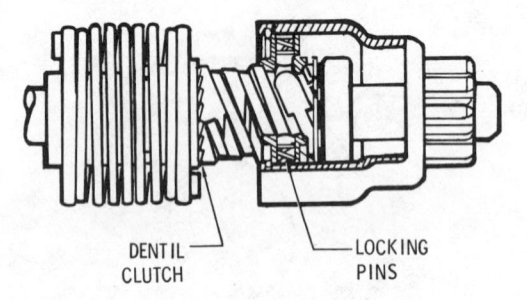

Fig. 5. Follow through-type of BENDIX starter drive.

In this type of drive, the starter motor starts to spin rapidly when it is energized. The inertia of the starter pinion holds it stationary for just a moment, and for this instant the starter motor is running faster than the pinion. This causes the starter pinion to move along the length of the drive shaft and move into mesh with the engine flywheel. When the starter has engaged the flywheel, it is prevented from further lengthwise movement, and a solid connection is made between the starter motor and the flywheel so that the starter motor cranks the engine. As soon as the engine rotates, it will cause the pinion to accelerate very rapidly. In considering the gear ratios mentioned above, the pinion will be rotating faster than the drive shaft. With the pinion running faster, it will screw itself out of engagement with the flywheel and the drive between the starter and engine is thus disconnected.

REMOTE CONTROL STARTER SWITCHES

Two types of magnetically operated switches are in common use in present-day starting systems. One of these is a magnetic starter switch, the function of which is to close heavy contacts that are capable of carrying large amounts of starter current. The other type is a solenoid starter switch which, in addition to performing the operation of the magnetic starter switch, magnetically operates the necessary linkage to engage the starter motor with the flywheel of the engine.

Magnetic Starter Switch

The magnetic starter switch consists mainly of two large copper contacts, a large copper contact washer, and an energizing winding.

Starters and Alternators

This type of starter switch may or may not contain the coil resistor bypass contact. All of these switches are basically the same; however, there are a variety of electrical connections used in conjunction with the magnetizing winding. Various types of winding connections are shown in Fig. 6.

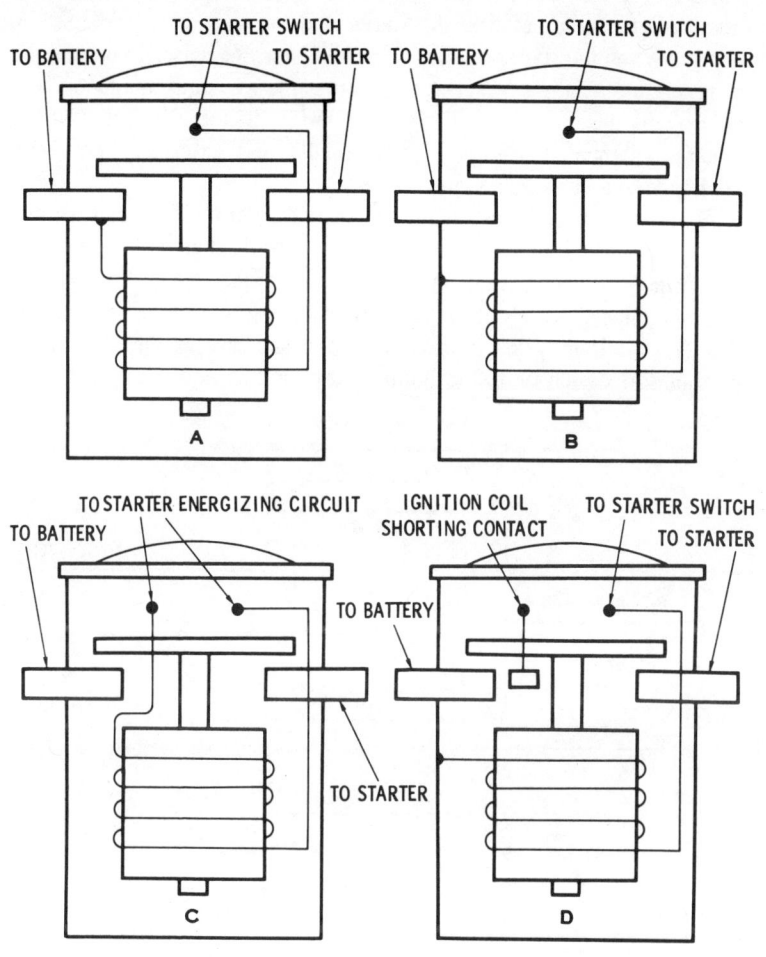

Fig. 6. Various types of magnetic starter switch diagrams; (A) Externally grounded magnetic; (B) Internally grounded magnetic; (C) Starter switch with independent energizing studs; (D) Internally grounded starter switch with coil resistor bypass contacts included.

AUTOMOBILE GUIDE

When the starter button is closed on any of the circuits shown in Fig. 6, the battery voltage pushes current through the energizing winding. The magnetic field produced by the winding pulls the iron core down in the solenoid, closing the circuit between the heavy copper contacts by means of the copper contact washer. When these contacts are closed, the circuit is completed to the starter and the starter motor begins to rotate. When the starter button is released, current ceases to flow in the magnetizing winding. A spring overcomes the weakened magnetic field and opens the contacts to the starter motor. In the schematic wiring diagram shown in Fig. 7, the internally and externally grounded magnetic starter switches are shown.

By tracing through the schematic wiring diagrams, it can be seen that when the starter button is closed, current flows through the magnetizing winding. When the magnetizing winding is strong enough to close the starter contacts, current flows from the battery to the starter motor. The starter switch may be located on the dashboard in the form of a pushbutton switch or in the ignition key lock assembly.

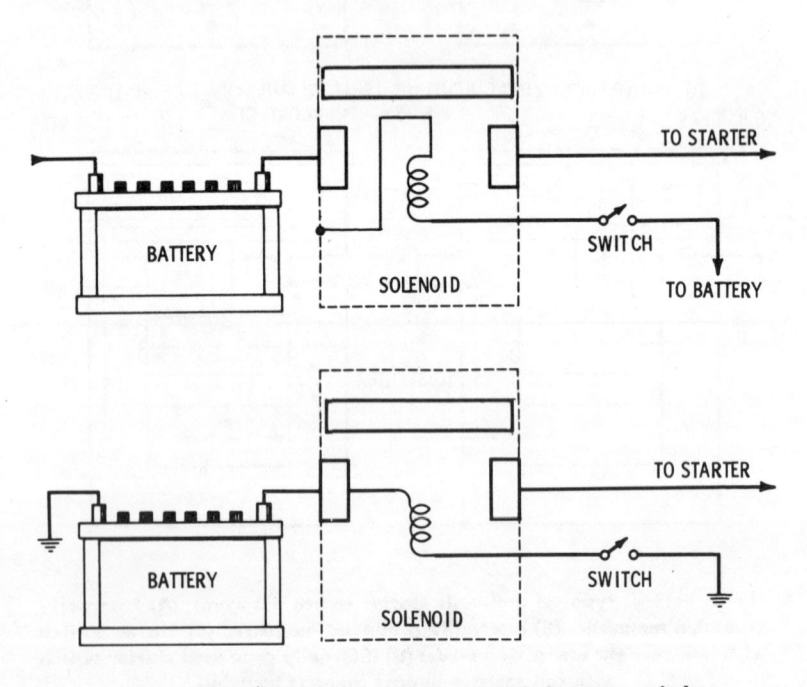

Fig. 7. Internally and externally grounded starter switches.

Solenoid Starter Switch

The solenoid starter switch (Fig. 8) functions electrically the same as the magnetic starter switch; however, in this type of switch there are two magnetizing windings. When the starter switch is closed, current flows through the *pull-in* and the *hold-in* windings.

The magnetic pull of the two windings closes the large starter contacts, allowing starter current to flow. In addition, the closing of the solenoid contacts shorts out the pull-in winding and this winding loses its magnetic ability. The hold-in winding remains energized until the starter switch is released, at which time current ceases to flow in the winding and a return spring opens the solenoid contacts. The heavy steel core is attached to the appropriate linkage, so that when the core is drawn into the center of the solenoid, the gear end of the starter motor is forced out to engage the gear with the flywheel of the engine. This type of solenoid frequently contains a coil-resistor bypass contact.

Remote Control Starter Switch

When using a remote control starter switch, *follow the hook-up instructions* that came with the switch to avoid the possibility of damaging the starter control circuit on the vehicle. For example, if the remote control switch lead is clipped to the solenoid terminal of the transmission neutral switch, the neutral switch will be burned out when the remote control switch is actuated.

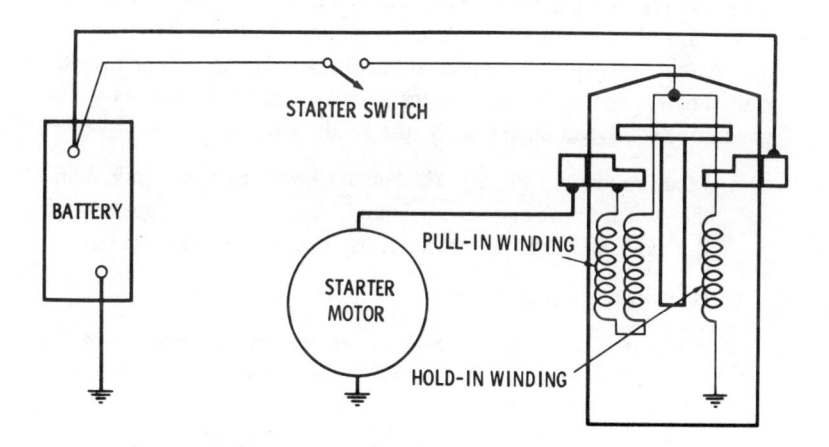

Fig. 8. A schematic diagram of a typical starter solenoid.

Starter Circuit Tests

Whenever the starter motor turns over slowly, or not at all, or the solenoid fails to engage the starter with the flywheel, excessive resistance in the starter circuit may be the cause.

The following checks for excessive resistance can be performed with the starter motor on the car:

1. Test the battery and charge it if necessary.

CAUTION: To prevent the engine from starting during the following tests, either ground or remove the distributor primary lead. Do not operate the starting motor continuously for more than 30 seconds to avoid overheating.

While cranking the engine:

2. Measure the voltage drop (V-1) between the positive battery post and the battery terminal of the solenoid, in the manner shown in Fig. 9.
3. Measure the voltage drop (V-2) between the battery terminal and motor terminal of the solenoid.
4. Measure the voltage drop (V-3) between the negative battery post and the starter-motor frame.

If the voltage drop in any of the last three checks exceeds 0.2 volt, excessive resistance is indicated in that part of the starting circuit being tested. Locate and correct the cause.

Solenoid Tests — If the solenoid fails to pull in, the trouble may be caused by excessive resistance in the solenoid circuit. To check for this condition, crank the engine as before, and:

1. Measure the voltage drop (V-4) between the battery terminal and the switch terminal of the solenoid. A voltage drop greater than 2.5 volts indicates excessive resistance in the solenoid circuit.

If the voltage drop is less than 2.5 volts:

2. Measure the voltage (V-5) between the switch terminal of the solenoid and ground. The solenoid should pull in with 8.0 volts present at this point.

If 8.0 volts or more is present and the solenoid does not pull in, remove the starter-motor assembly and check the solenoid. To check the

STARTERS AND ALTERNATORS

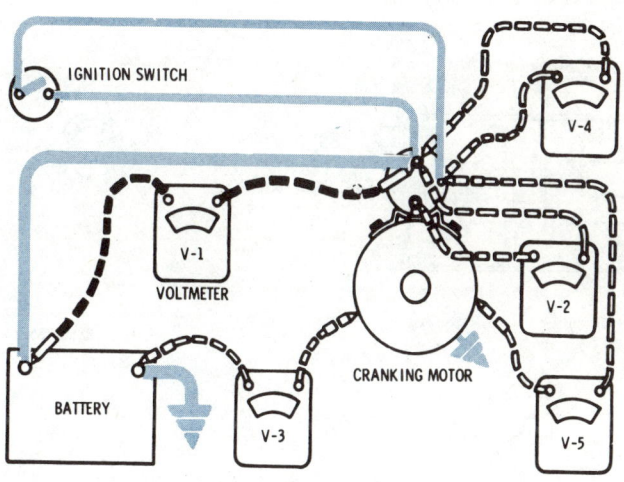

Fig. 9. Starter circuit tests.

solenoid without removing it from the starter housing, disconnect the strap between the solenoid terminal and the starter.

Complete the following tests as rapidly as possible to prevent overheating the solenoid.

To check the hold-in winding:

1. Connect an ammeter and variable resistor in series with a 12-volt battery and the switch terminal of the solenoid, as shown in Fig. 10.
2. Connect a voltmeter between the switch terminal of the solenoid and ground, as shown.
3. Adjust the variable resistor until the voltmeter reads 10 volts, and note the ammeter reading. The correct reading will depend on the make and model of automobile. The service manual should be consulted for the particular automobile under test.

To check both solenoid windings:

1. Connect the voltmeter, ammeter, and variable resistance as in the previous test.
2. Ground the motor terminal of the solenoid.
3. Adjust the variable resistance until the voltmeter reads 10 volts, and note the reading of the ammeter. The correct reading in this test also depends on the make and model of automobile.

Automobile Guide

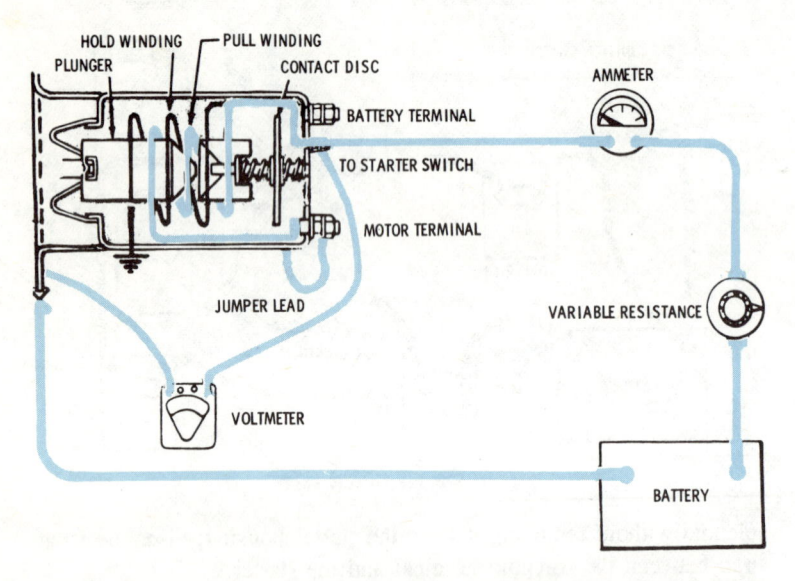

Courtesy Oldsmobile Div., General Motors Corp.

Fig. 10. Testing solenoid windings.

Current readings that are higher than the specifications indicate shorted turns or a ground in the solenoid windings. In this case, the solenoid must be replaced. Current readings that are lower than the specifications indicate excessive resistance. Check all solenoid connections, then replace the solenoid if necessary.

Neutral Safety Switch — Automobiles with automatic transmissions have a neutral safety switch in series with the solenoid to prevent starting the engine with the transmission in gear. The engine of these cars can be started only if the selector lever or pushbutton is in the neutral or park position.

Bench Test of the Starting Motor

The starter motor on most automobiles must be removed for brush replacement and to correct other troubles that may be present. The procedure for removing the starter varies with different makes and models of automobiles and is included in their service manuals.

Before disassembling the starter motor, remove the cover band (if equipped) and examine the brushes to make sure they are free in their holders. Replace brushes if they are defective or excessively worn.

STARTERS AND ALTERNATORS

Some manufacturers recommend checking the tension of each spring with a pull scale, as shown in Fig. 11. A typical spring tension is from 3 to 3½ lbs. Check the manufacturer's specifications for the exact tension for specific automobiles.

If trouble is still indicated in the starter motor after the brushes have been examined and/or replaced, the unit must be disassembled for further tests. Follow the recommended procedure as outlined in the service manual. This procedure varies for different makes of automobiles.

The following checks should be made on the starter motor after it is removed from the engine:

1. Test the action of the overrunning clutch. The pinion gear should turn freely in the overrunning direction. Check the teeth of the pinion for chips, cracks, and excessive wear. Replace the assembly if necessary. Badly chipped teeth on the pinion gear may indicate chipped teeth on the ring gear. Inspect the ring gear for this condition if the pinion is chipped, and replace if necessary.
2. Check the brush holders to see if they are deformed or bent. Make sure they hold the brushes in the proper position against the commutator. Repair or replace if necessary.
3. Check the fit of the armature shaft in the brushing of the drive end housing, commutator end housing, and (if equipped) the center bearing plate. The shaft should fit snugly, but be free turning. If either fit is loose, or appears to be worn, the bushing should be replaced. If the starter is equipped with a center bearing plate, replacing the plate is simpler than replacing the bushing alone.
4. The overrunning clutch, armature, and field coils should not be cleaned in a degreasing tank or with any grease dissolving solvents. The clutch mechanism on most starters is permanently lubricated and the solvent will dissolve the grease, leaving the unit without lubrication. The solvent will also damage the insulation on the armature and field coils. It is suggested that all parts, except the clutch, be cleaned in mineral spirits with a brush. The clutch can be wiped clean with a cloth.
5. Inspect the commutator, and if it is dirty, clean it with No. 00 sandpaper. *Never use emery cloth on the commutator.* If the commutator is worn, pitted or burned, out of round, or has high insulation between the bars, the armature should be placed in a lathe and the commutator cut down.

AUTOMOBILE GUIDE

It is advisable that the commutator be trued (cut) in a commutator lathe whenever the brushes are replaced. A slight "egg-shaped" or "flat-spot" condition of the commutator may not be noticeable to the eye, but will be obvious during truing operations.

Fig. 12 shows a tool which can be used for turning down the commutator. To use this instrument, the armature is placed in a vise having soft jaws to prevent damage to the armature laminations. Care must be taken to tighten the vise only enough to keep the armature from turning. The cutting tool is positioned on the commutator end of the armature shaft as shown in the illustration. The cutter is adjusted to remove only enough stock to clean up the commutator.

After the armature has been turned down, the insulation between the commutator bars may have to be undercut. This can be done with a regular undercutting tool, or with a hacksaw blade if care is taken. The insulation should be undercut approximately 1/32-inch deep and 1/32-inch wide. The slots thus formed should be carefully cleaned out to remove any trace of dirt or copper dust. As a

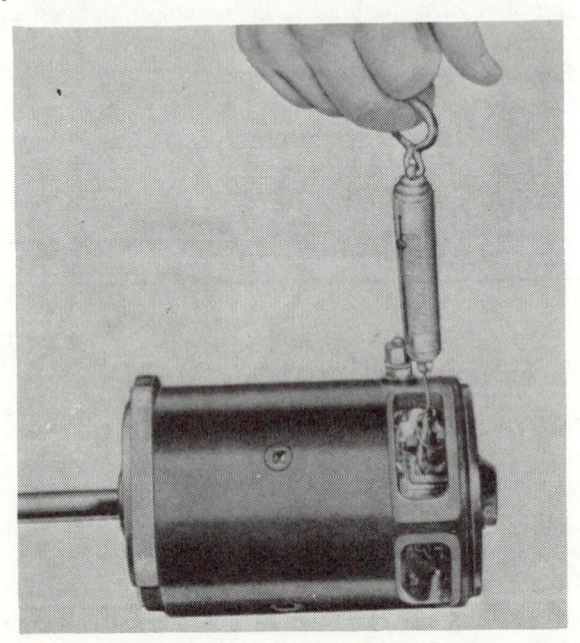

Fig. 11. Checking brush spring tension of a starter motor.

STARTERS AND ALTERNATORS

final step in this procedure, the commutator should be lightly sanded with No.00 sandpaper to remove any burrs left as a result of the undercutting process.

6. Check the armature for opens, shorts, and grounds.

Opens — The most likely place for an open to occur is at the commutator bars as a result of excessive cranking periods. Inspect the connections where the armature conductors are joined to the commutator bars. Loose connections here will cause arching and burning of the commutator bars as the starting motor is used. If the bars are not too badly burned, they can usually be repaired by resoldering the armature leads in the affected bars (with rosin core solder), and turning down and undercutting the commutator, as outlined previously, to remove the burned material.

Shorts — Short circuits in the armature are located by the use of a growler (Fig. 13). Rotate the armature slowly, holding a steel strip or hacksaw blade above it. When a shorted winding is under the steel strip, the strip will vibrate. Shorts between commutator bars are often caused by brush dust or copper particles. These shorts are eliminated by carefully cleaning the slots between the bars. Recheck after cleaning, and if the steel strip still vibrates, replace the armature.

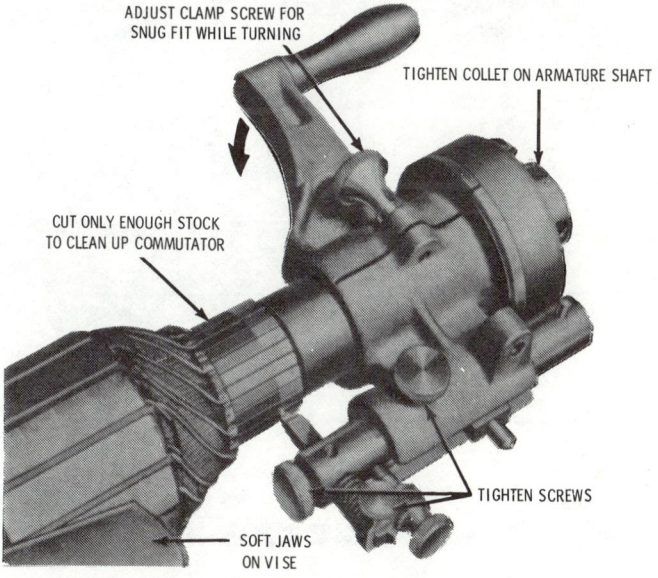

Fig. 12. Turning down the commutator of an armature.

Automobile Guide

Grounds — Grounds in the armature can be detected by means of a 110-volt test lamp and test leads. If the lamp lights when one test lead is placed on a commutator bar and the other test prod is placed on the core or shaft, the armature is grounded. Grounds are often caused by failure of the insulation brought about by overheating that occurs when the starter motor is used for excessively long cranking periods. Another cause of grounds is an accumulation of brush dust between the commutator bars and the steel commutator ring.

7. The field windings can be checked for an open or a ground as follows:

Opens — Touch one test lamp lead to an insulated brush, and the other test lead to the field terminal (Fig. 14). If the lamp does not light, the series field coils are open and should be replaced.

To check the shunt coil or coils, the ground of each coil should be disconnected. Place the test lamp leads across the shunt coil to

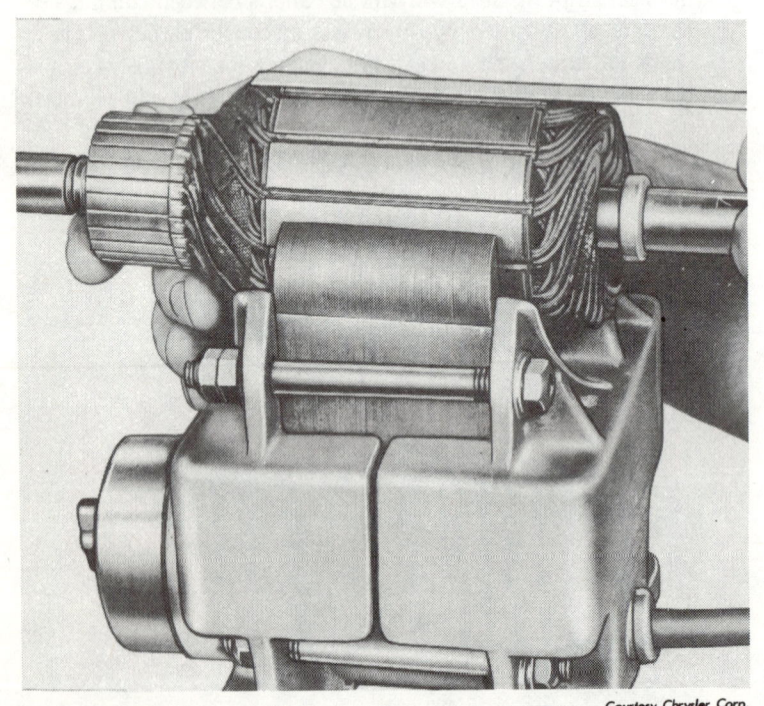

Courtesy Chrysler Corp.

Fig. 13. Using a growler to test for a short circuit in an armature.

STARTERS AND ALTERNATORS

be tested. If the lamp does not light, the coil is open and should be replaced.

Grounds — Disconnect all shunt field coils before making this test. Place one test lamp lead on the grounded brush or on the case of the starter motor (Fig. 15). Place the other test lead on the connector strap or field terminal. If the lamp lights, a grounded coil is indicated which must be repaired or replaced.

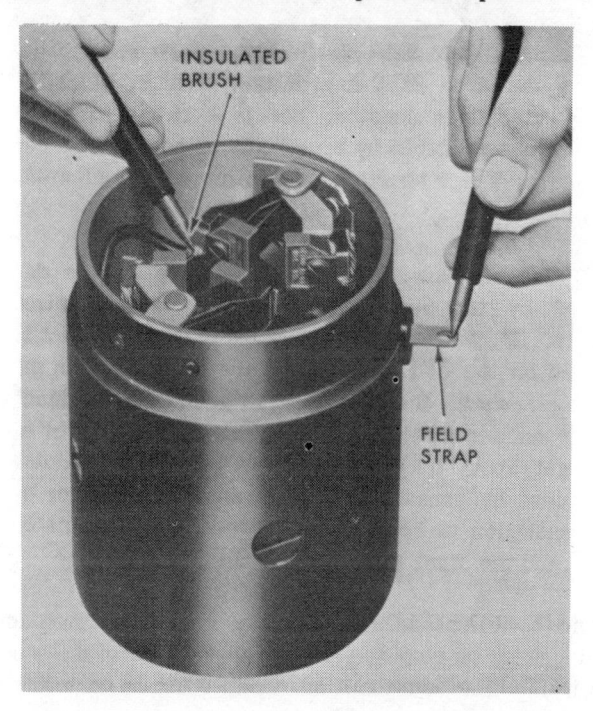

Courtesy Pontiac Motor Div., General Motors Corp.
Fig. 14. Testing the field coils for an open.

GENERATORS

The charging system of the automobile consists of three major components — the generator, the regulator, and the battery. The generator, driven by the engine, converts mechanical energy into electrical energy to be used for ignition, lights, accessories, and to keep the battery in a charged condition. Electrical energy is stored in the battery in chemical form, and is available for starting the engine and for

AUTOMOBILE GUIDE

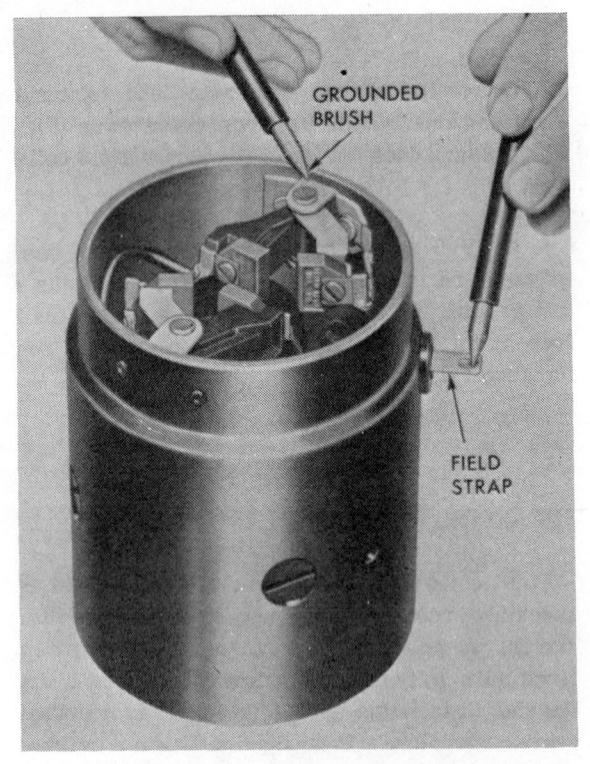

Courtesy Pontiac Motor Div., General Motors Corp.
Fig. 15. Testing the field coils for a ground.

operating the various electrical accessories when the generator is not delivering sufficient output. A cross-sectional view of the generator is shown in Fig. 16. Note the similarity in construction to the starting motor, shown previously in Fig. 1.

The regulator controls the output of the generator according to the needs imposed upon it such as, state-of-charge of the battery and electrical loads of the lights, air conditioner, or any of the other accessories. A typical generator regulator is shown in Fig. 17.

Prior to the early 1960s, a direct current (dc) generator was used. The dc generator, generally shunt wound (armature and field connected in parallel) had two brushes "riding" a commutator. Maximum output of the dc generator was about 35 amperes.

Beginning in about 1962 some cars equipped with air conditioners were also equipped with an alternating current (ac) generator. Within the following two years the ac generator was "standard equipment." The ac generator, Fig. 18, is commonly called an *alternator*.

ALTERNATORS

The alternator, unlike the generator, delivers an output voltage at low idle speed and considerably more output voltage at low operating speeds. Thus, an alternator meets the demands of stop-and-go city driving and increased accessory loads much better than did the generator.

The output of an alternator is alternating current (ac), which means that half the total output current flows in one direction and the other half flows in the opposite direction. The electrical circuits of the automobile, however, can use only current flowing in a single direction, which means the alternator output must be changed to direct current (dc). This is done by passing the alternating current through diode rectifiers which allow the current to flow in only one direction.

Construction

A typical alternator consists of a stator, a rotor, two slip rings, two brushes, and six diodes. In addition, of course, is the necessary end frames, pulley, fan, etc. A cross-sectional view of an alternator is shown in Fig. 18. An exploded view is shown in Fig. 19.

The stator consists of a number of windings on the inside of a laminated core that is attached to the frame of the alternator. It is from these windings that the output of the alternator is taken.

The field coil is wound on the rotor, which revolves within the stator. Two brushes, each riding on a slip ring, are located at one end of the rotor shaft. One slip ring is electrically connected to one end of the field coil, and the other slip ring is connected to the opposite end of the coil.

The stator windings are connected to the diodes in such a way that the alternating output of the stator is converted (rectified) to direct current. The diodes also prevent the battery from discharging through the alternator when the engine is stopped. Thus, a cutout relay in the regulator is not needed.

Servicing Precautions

Greater care must be taken in servicing an alternator system than in servicing a dc generator system. Precautions are:

Automobile Guide

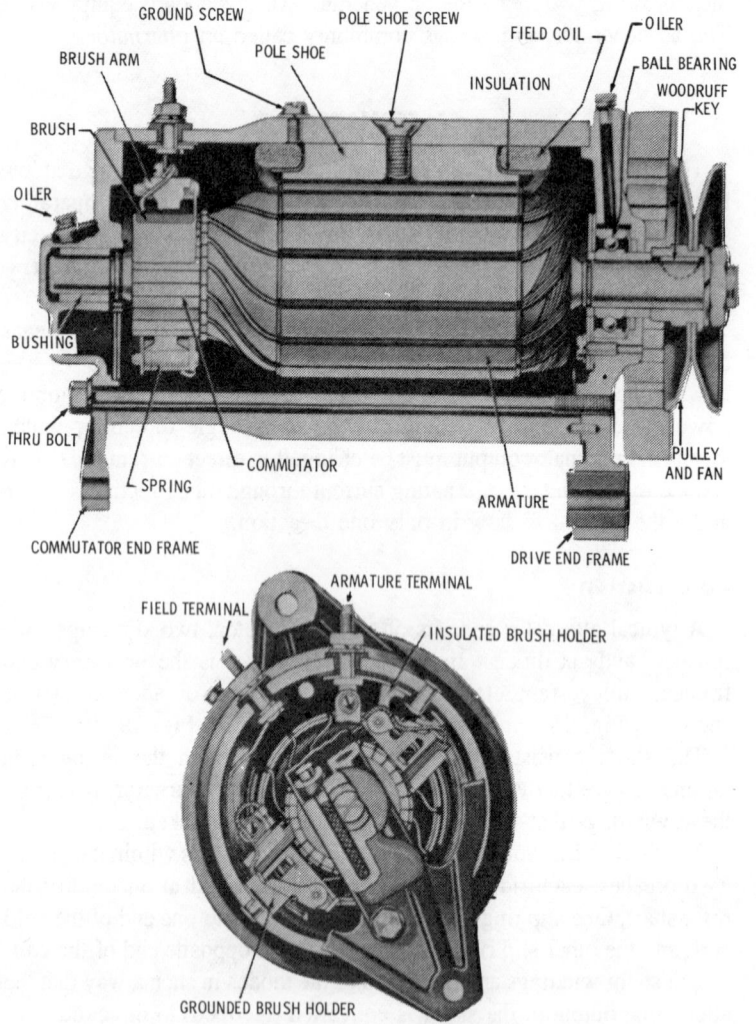

Fig. 16. Cross section of a typical automobile generator.

1. Observe correct polarities. Never reverse the battery leads as this may damage the diodes and/or the wiring.
2. Do not short or ground any of the terminals on the alternator or regulator.
3. Do not operate the alternator unless it is connected to a load. If the alternator operates with its output open, extremely high voltages

386

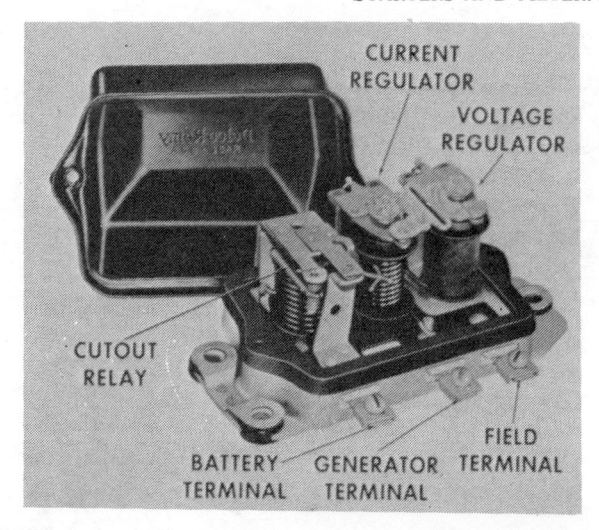

STARTERS AND ALTERNATORS

Fig. 17. A typical generator regulator showing the major components and terminals.

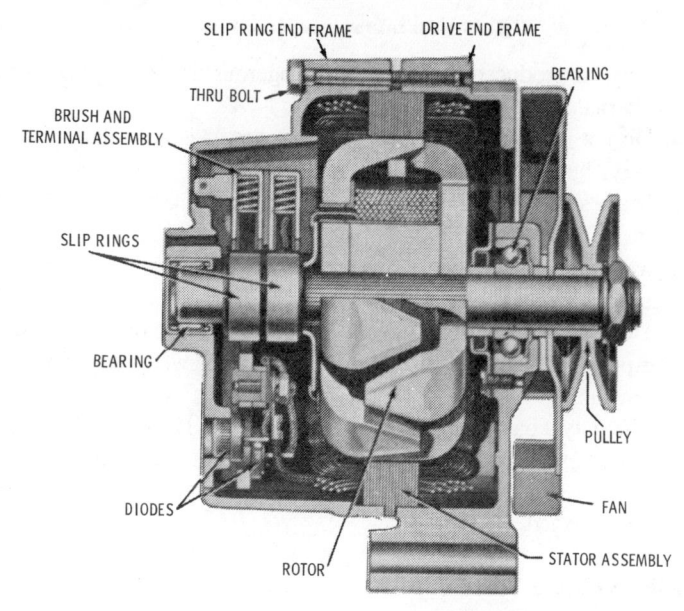

Courtesy Buick Motor Div., General Motors Corp.

Fig. 18. Cross section of a DELCOTRON alternator.

Courtesy Oldsmobile Div., General Motors Corp.

Automobile Guide

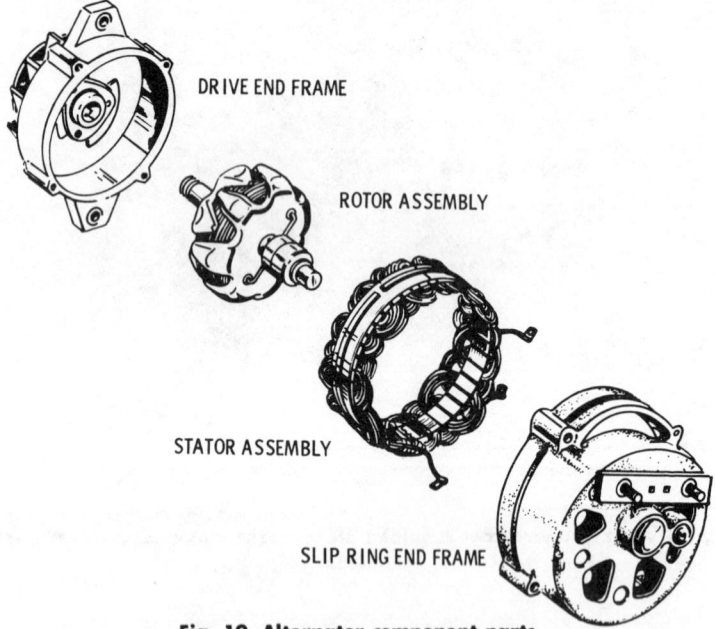

Fig. 19. Alternator component parts.

may be produced that are both dangerous and damaging to the alternator.

4. Do not attempt to polarize an alternator. It is not only unnecessary, but may damage the unit.
5. Make sure that any battery charger or booster battery is connected in the proper polarity.
6. Make sure the belt tension is proper. An alternator is more critical in this respect than a dc generator.
7. Do not apply pressure to either of the end frames of an alternator. Apply pressure only to the center portion when applying belt tension.
8. Use only a battery that is known to be good. The lower the charge condition of the battery, the higher the output of the alternator. If the battery is too low and remains so too long, the alternator may be damaged.

On-the-Vehicle Tests

The following tests can be made with the alternator and regulator in the automobile.

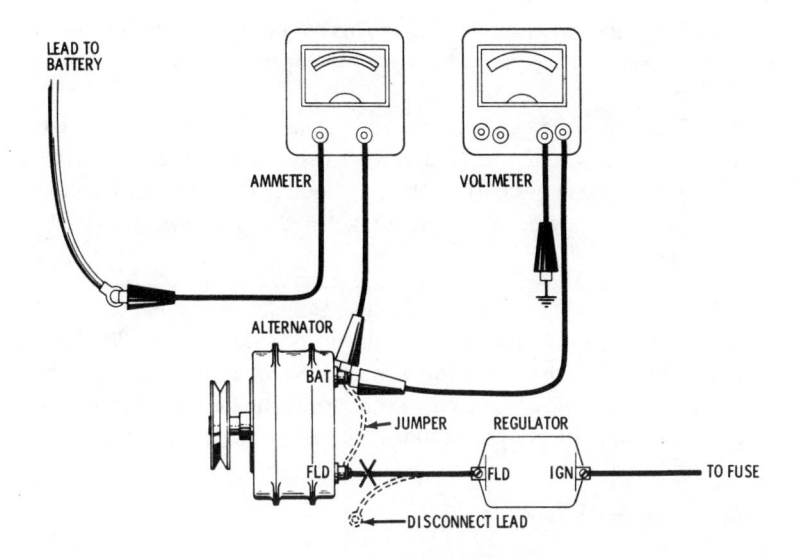

Fig. 20. Meter connections for testing an alternator.

Output Test — The output of most alternator charging systems can be checked by using a voltmeter and ammeter connected as shown in Fig. 20. In addition, a tachometer is used to accurately indicate the engine r/min. Connections to some alternator systems cannot be made as shown in Fig. 20. Therefore, the type of system must be determined before the proper connections can be made. Always follow the recommendations of the manufacturer for systems that differ from the one shown. The output test most frequently made is as follows:

1. Connect the positive lead of the voltmeter to the output terminal of the alternator, and the negative lead to ground.
2. Disconnect the lead from the output terminal of the alternator (usually labeled BAT). Connect the positive lead of the ammeter to the output terminal of the alternator, and connect the negative lead to the disconnected lead. Turn on the automobile lights and all accessories.
3. Connect a tachometer between the primary distributor terminal and ground.
4. Start the engine and gradually increase its speed to the r/min specified for the particular system being tested (usually between 1250 and 2000 r/min).

Automobile Guide

5. Note the ammeter reading. This is the output current of the alternator and should be within the specified limits for the unit being tested.
6. Note the voltmeter reading. The voltage should be slightly higher than the normal charging voltage (usually from 12.5 to 15 volts for a 12-volt system). If the rated output current is obtained at a voltage between 12.5 and 15 volts, the alternator is operating correctly.

If the rated output cannot be obtained, stop the engine and remove the field connection from the alternator. Connect a jumper from the F to the BAT terminal on the alternator. Restart the engine and see if sufficient output current is now obtained. If it is, the regulator is defective. If the current is still below specifications, the alternator is at fault.

Test Conclusions

If the alternator does not meet the output current and/or voltage specifications as listed by the manufacturer, any one of several troubles may exist. Check "Symptoms and Possible Causes" at the end of this chapter. The alternator must be removed from the automobile and disassembled for the following tests:

Stator Tests — To test the stator for opens, connect an ohmmeter or a 12-volt test lamp between one pair of stator leads, as shown in Fig. 21. If the ohmmeter reading approaches infinity or the test lamp does not light, the winding is open. Repeat this test for each of the stator windings.

To test the stator windings for a ground, connect an ohmmeter or test lamp from any stator lead to ground. If the ohmmeter reads near zero or if the test lamp lights, the stator is grounded.

Testing the stator windings for a short circuit is difficult because of the low resistance of the windings. If the other tests prove normal, and the alternator still does not produce the specified output, shorted stator windings may be the cause.

A stator that fails any of the tests just outlined should be replaced.

Rotor Tests — To test the rotor for opens, connect an ohmmeter or 12-volt test lamp to each slip ring, as shown in Fig. 22. If the ohmmeter reading is near infinity or the lamp fails to light, the field winding on the rotor is open.

Starters and Alternators

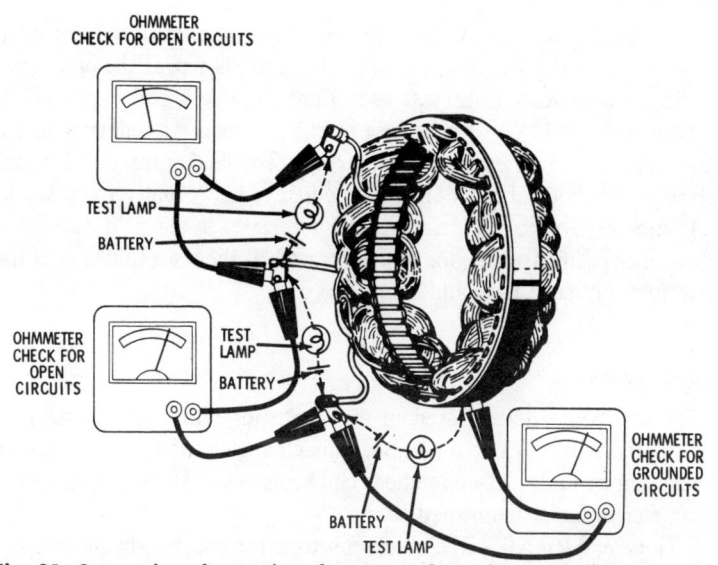

Fig. 21. Connections for testing the stator of an alternator for opens and grounds.

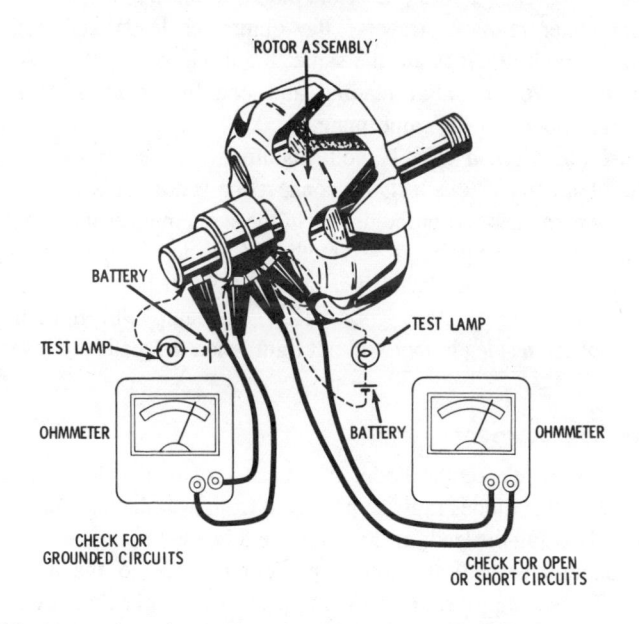

Fig. 22. Connections for testing the rotor of an alternator for opens and grounds.

Automobile Guide

To test the rotor for grounds, connect an ohmmeter or the test lamp between either slip ring and the rotor shaft, as shown. If the ohmmeter reading is near zero or the test lamp lights, the field coil is grounded.

To test the field coil for a short circuit, connect an ammeter and a 12-volt battery in series with the slip rings. The field current at standard temperature should be within the specified range (usually from 1.9 to 2.3 amperes) for the particular unit under test. If the field current is above the specified value, the coil is shorted. If the rotor fails any of the tests just outlined, it should be replaced.

Diode Tests

The rectifiers (diodes) used in the alternator allow current to flow through them in only one direction. This characteristic makes it easy to check their condition. Two methods can be used to test the diodes — the ohmmeter and test lamp methods.

Ohmmeter Method — The ohmmeter used for this test should employ a 1.5-volt cell. To make the test, disconnect the stator leads and connect the ohmmeter leads across one of the diodes as shown in Fig. 23. Note the ohmmeter reading. Reverse the ohmmeter leads and note the reading. If both readings are the same, the diode is defective. A good diode will give one high reading and one low reading. Test the remaining diodes in the same manner.

Test-Lamp Method — A 12-volt (maximum) test lamp is substituted for the ohmmeter in this test. Disconnect the stator leads and connect the test lamp across one of the diodes in the same manner the ohmmeter was connected in the previous test method. If the test lamp lights in both positions of the test leads, or if it fails to light in both positions, the diode is defective. With a good diode, the lamp will light in one position of the test leads, but will not light when the leads are reversed.

Diode Replacement

To replace a defective diode, it is necessary to unsolder the diode leads. The other diodes must be protected from heat damage during this process. Holding the leads of the defective diode with pliers will usually allow enough heat dissipation to prevent damage to the remaining diodes. The same procedure is used to protect the replacement while its leads are being soldered. Most alternators require special tools to press individual diodes in position. Still other alternators require the replace-

STARTERS AND ALTERNATORS

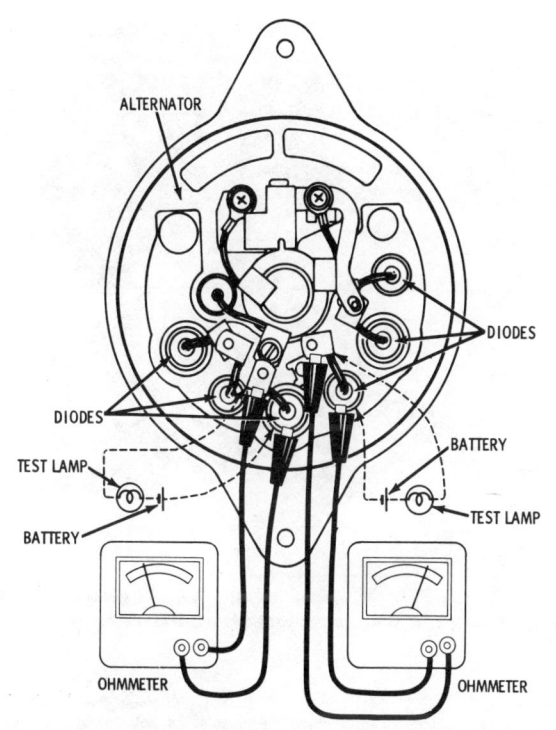

Fig. 23. Connections for testing the diodes in an alternator.

ment of an assembly unit containing three diodes mounted on a plate (called a *heat sink*). Check the instructions of the manufacturer for removal and replacement procedures. Make certain the correct diode is used for replacement. Positive diodes are usually identified by a (+) or red marking, and a negative diode by a (−) or black marking.

ALTERNATOR REGULATORS

There are three basic types of alternator regulators — the double-contact type (Fig. 24), the single-contact transistorized type (Fig. 25), and the all-transistorized type (Fig. 26). A cutout relay is not needed because the diodes in the alternator prevent a reverse-current flow. A current regulator is not required either, because the alternator is self-limiting in current output as long as voltage control is maintained.

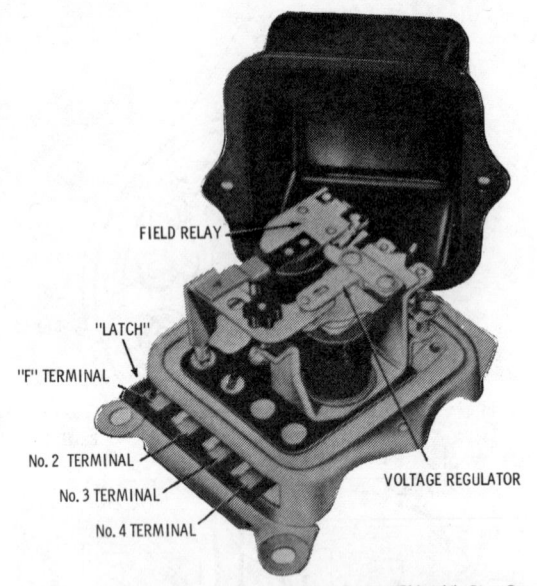

AUTOMOBILE GUIDE

Fig. 24. A double-contact alternator regulator.

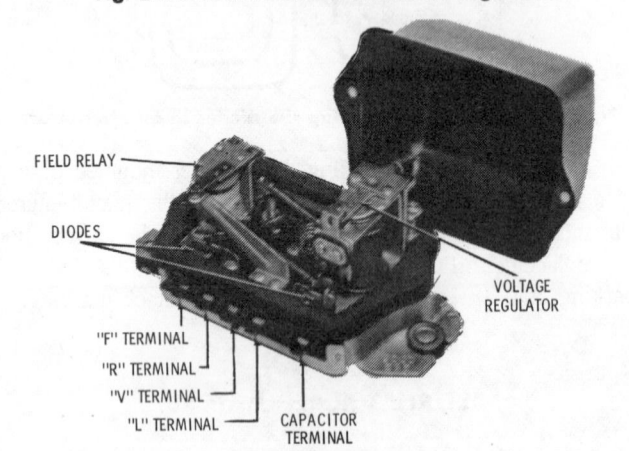

Fig. 25. A single-contact transistorized alternator regulator.

Relay-Type Regulators

The double-contact and single-contact types of alternator regulators contain two major components — a field relay and a voltage regulator relay.

STARTERS AND ALTERNATORS

Fig. 26. An all-transistorized alternator regulator.

Courtesy American Motors Corp.

Field Relay — The field relay serves two purposes. It controls the charging-indicator lamp, turning it out when the alternator has an output current. In addition, it controls the amount of current through the field to allow the alternator to start its charging action as soon as the engine starts and to increase this charging action to full output at speeds past idle.

Voltage-Regulator Relay — This relay regulates the output voltage of the alternator to a predetermined value to protect the alternator from an excessive current output.

All-Transistorized Regulators

The all-transistorized regulators do not contain any moving parts, such as relays or contacts. Instead, transistors control the alternator output. Some regulators of this type provide an output voltage adjustment. Others are completely sealed and must be replaced if the output voltage is not within the specified limits.

Regulator Servicing

The servicing of alternator regulators is seldom necessary. However, the contacts may need cleaning and the air gap need adjusting from time to time. The voltage setting may also require adjustment due to a variation in electrical load caused by changing weather conditions.

A sooty, discolored condition of the voltage regulator relay contacts after only a short operating period is normal and does not indicate a need for cleaning. However, they should be cleaned if the output voltage is measured and found to be unsteady. The contacts should be cleaned with a fine grade of silicon carbide paper followed by a bath of alcohol or trichlorethylene to remove the residue Never use a point file to clean the voltage regulator relay contacts.

A fine-cut, thin, flat file can be used to clean the contacts of the field relay. Remove only enough material to clean the contacts. *Never use sandpaper or emery cloth to clean either the voltage regulator or field-relay contacts.*

Double-Contact Regulators — Both the voltage regulator and field-relay require three adjustments — contact opening, air gap, and voltage setting.

The contact opening of the voltage regulator relay is measured between one set of contacts with the other set just touching (Fig. 27). Adjustments are made either by bending one of the contact arms, or by loosening a screw and adjusting the upper contact as required (Fig. 28). Check the manufacturer's specifications for the correct contact opening.

The air gap of the voltage regulator relay is checked by measuring the space between the relay armature and core (Fig. 29). If the air gap is not correct, turn the adjusting nut, or loosen the screw holding the contact bracket (Fig. 30), and adjust to obtain the specified gap for the unit being serviced.

The voltage setting of the voltage regulator relay can be checked by connecting a ¼-ohm, 25-watt resistor and an ammeter in series between the positive terminal of the battery and the BAT terminal of the alternator. This resistor will limit the output of the alternator to 10 amperes, which is a requirement for this test. Connect a 50-ohm variable resistor between the F terminal of the alternator and the F terminal of the regulator. Connect a voltmeter between the BAT terminal of the alternator and ground. Connect a jumper between the BAT terminal of the alternator and the regulator as shown in Fig. 31.

The regulator must be operated with the cover on for approximately 15 minutes at 1500 r/min in order to bring the surrounding temperature up to the proper level. After the warm-up period, adjust the 50-ohm variable resistor to its lowest resistance setting and increase the engine speed to 2500 r/min. Note the voltmeter reading at this speed. This reading should be within the voltage range specified by the manufacturer for the particular temperature at which the regulator is operating.

If the voltage is outside the specified range, adjust the voltage setting on *Delco-Remy* units by turning the adjusting screw (Fig. 32). On *Ford* and *Chrysler* regulators (Fig. 33), adjustment is made by bending the spring hanger down to increase the voltage and up to decrease it. With the engine speed still at 2500 r/min, increase the resistance of the

STARTERS AND ALTERNATORS

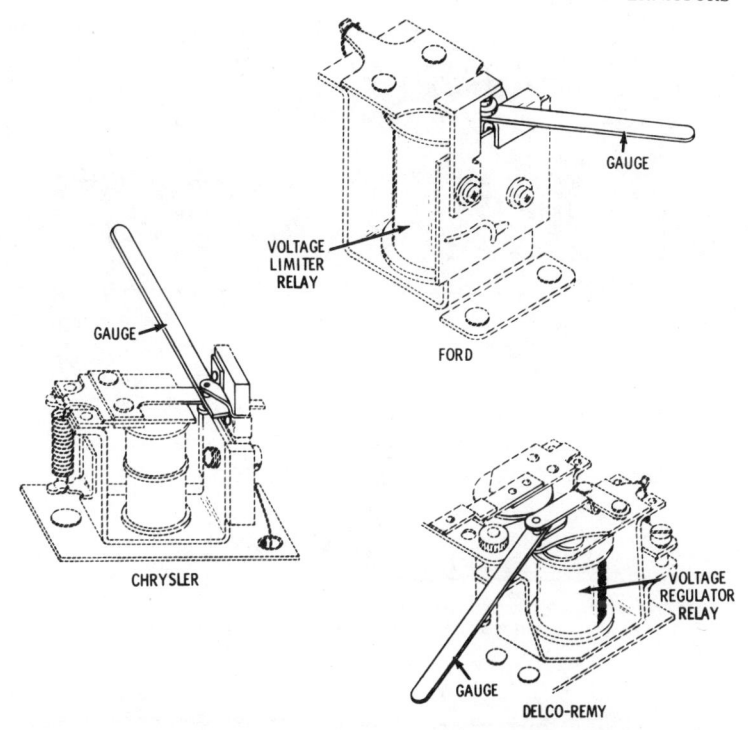

Fig. 27. Checking the contact opening on the voltage-regulator relay.

50-ohm variable resistance. The regulator should now be operating with the lower set of contacts closed. Readjust the relay to bring the voltage within the specified range.

NOTE: On **Delco-Remy** *units, the final setting of the adjustment screws must be made by turning it clockwise to insure that the screwhead is seated against the spring holder. Always take the final voltage reading with the regulator cover in place.*

The field relay contact opening is measured by inserting a feeler gauge of the correct size between the contacts, as shown in Fig. 34. If adjustment is necessary, gently bend the armature stop, or loosen the screw and raise or lower the stop assembly. (When it is necessary to make an adjustment on a unit having an adjustable armature stop, the field relay air gap must be checked and adjusted first).

The field relay air gap is checked by measuring the spacing between the armature and the relay core (Fig. 35). If adjustment is necessary,

397

Automobile Guide

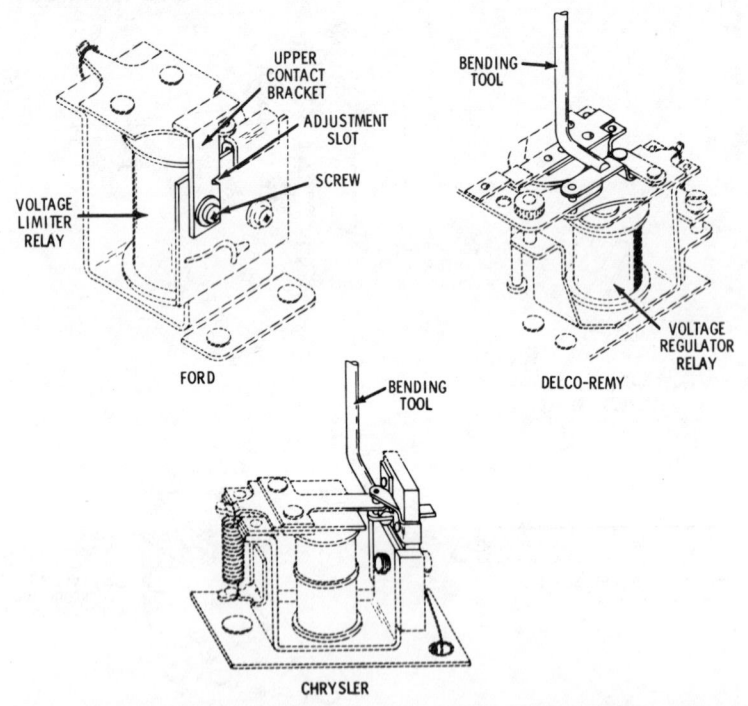

Fig. 28. Adjusting the contact opening on the voltage-regulator relay.

bend the flat contact spring carefully, or loosen the screw and move the contact mounting assembly.

The closing voltage of the field relay may be checked by connecting a 50-ohm variable resistor between the positive terminal of the battery and the coil of the field relay. Also connect a voltmeter between the coil of the field relay and ground. Set the variable resistor to its highest value, and turn the ignition switch off. Slowly decrease the resistance, and note the voltmeter reading at the instant the field relay closes. This voltage can be set to the specifications of the manufacturer by bending the heel iron of the relay or by bending the spring hanger, in a manner similar to that shown in Fig. 36.

Single-Contact Transistorized Regulators — To adjust the air gap of a single-contact transistorized type of voltage-regulator relay, press the armature (not the contact) down against the proper size feeler gauge inserted between the armature and relay core. The contacts should just touch under this condition. Adjust, if necessary, by loosening the contact support bracket screws and moving the bracket up or down.

STARTERS AND ALTERNATORS

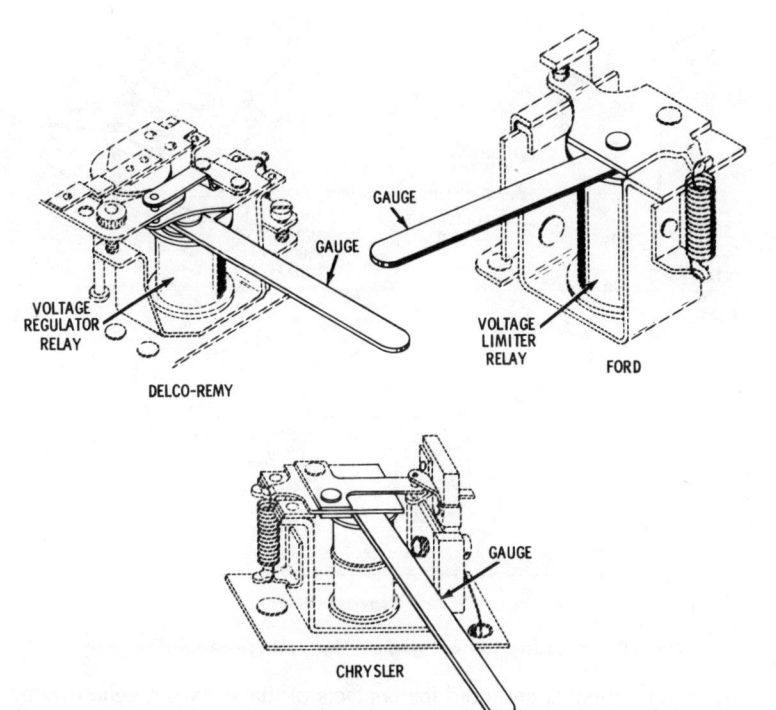

Fig. 29. Checking the air gap on the voltage-regulator relay.

The field relay air gap should be checked in exactly the same manner and adjusted by bending the flat contact support spring to provide the gap specified by the manufacturer.

The contacts of the voltage regulator may be cleaned when necessary in the same way prescribed for the double-contact regulator.

The diodes in this type of regulator may be checked with an ohmmeter that uses a 1.5-volt cell. Unsolder the diode leads and connect the ohmmeter across them, first in one direction and then with the leads reversed. If both readings approach either zero or infinity, the diode is defective and must be replaced. A good diode will give a high and a low reading for the two ohmmeter connections.

The transistor can be checked by connecting a voltmeter between the F terminal of the regulator and ground. A voltmeter reading of 9 volts or more with the ignition switch *on* indicates the transistor is satisfactory. If the meter reading is less than 9 volts, either the transistor is defective or a regulator resistor is open. To determine which is defective, remove

399

AUTOMOBILE GUIDE

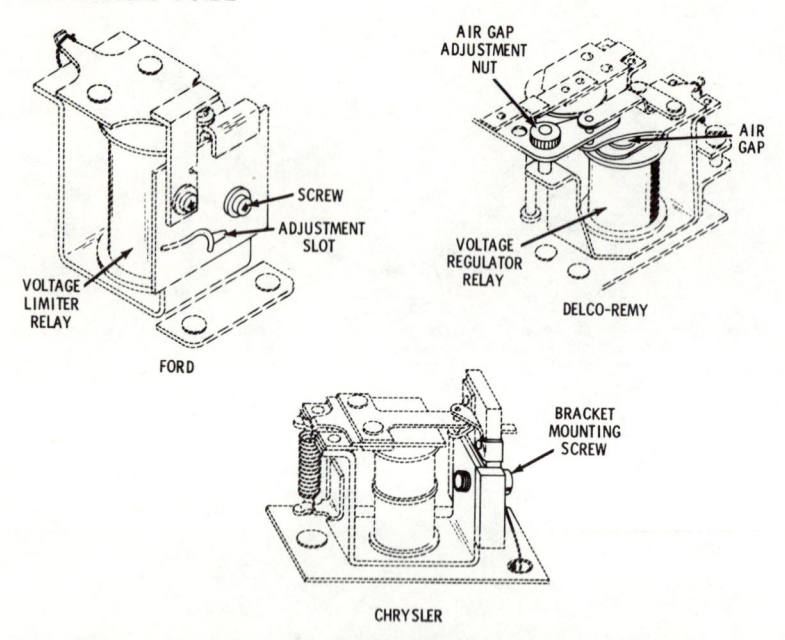

Fig. 30. Adjusting the air gap on the voltage-regulator relay.

the regulator cover and hold the contacts of the voltage regulator relay apart. If the voltmeter now reads more than 9 volts, the transistor is defective and must be replaced. If the meter reading is still less than 9 volts, a resistor is open and must be replaced.

All-Transistorized Regulator — This type of regulator has no moving parts, but some units do provide an output voltage adjustment. If the output voltage cannot be brought within range with this adjustment, the entire unit must be replaced. If the output voltage of the non-adjustable type is outside the specified range, the unit must be replaced.

INTERNAL SOLID-STATE REGULATOR

Some alternators have a solid-state regulator, using an integrated circuit (IC), built into the end frame. There is no external regulator with this system. A typical schematic is shown in Fig. 37. That part inside the dashed line is *inside* the alternator.

Aside from the internal regulator, basic construction features are the same as previously discussed. Bench testing of individual components; rotor and stator, is the same as for the externally regulated type.

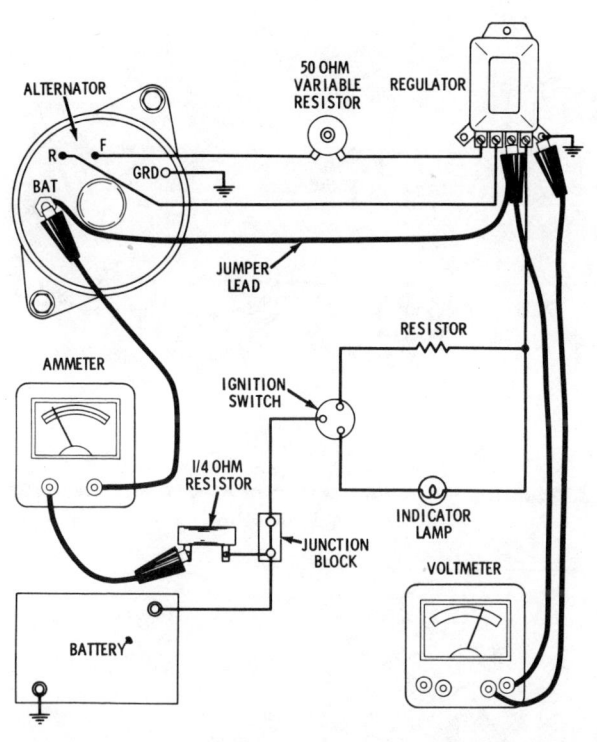

STARTERS AND ALTERNATORS

Fig. 31. Connections for checking the voltage setting of the voltage-regulator relay.

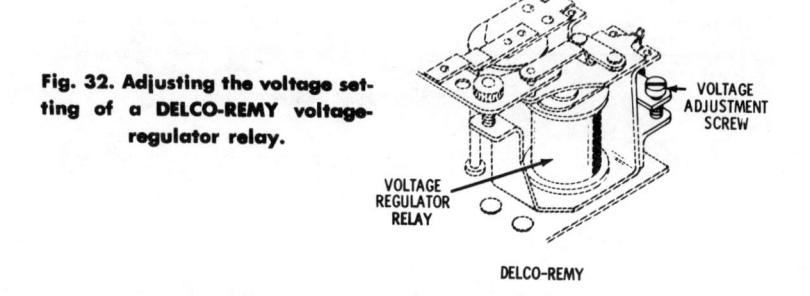

Fig. 32. Adjusting the voltage setting of a DELCO-REMY voltage-regulator relay.

DELCO-REMY

The following quick-check procedures should be considered "typical." Manufacturers specifications and recommendations should be followed for specific testing.

401

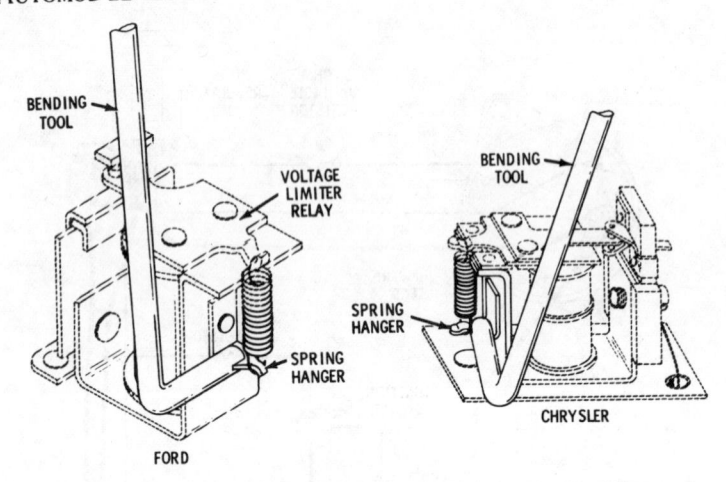

Fig. 33. Adjusting the voltage setting of a FORD and CHRYSLER voltage-regulator relay.

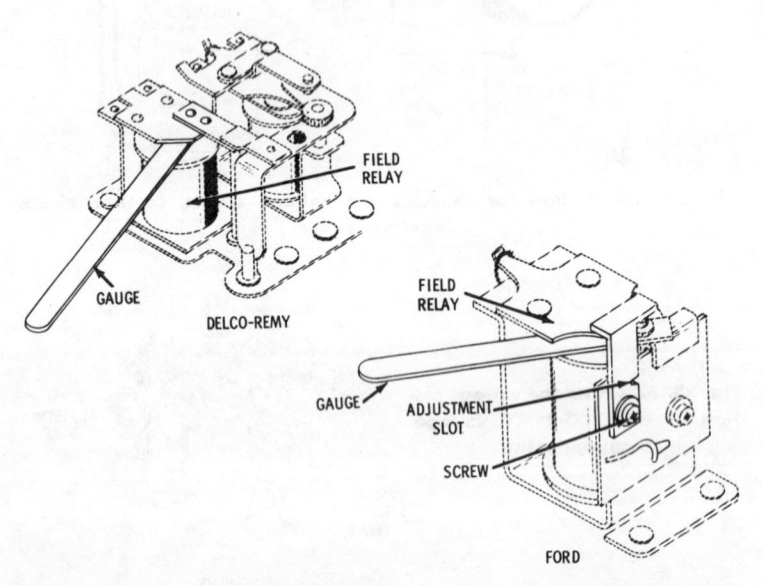

Fig. 34. Checking and adjusting the contact opening of the field relay.

Static Check

"Static" means, of course, the engine is not running and the ignition switch is *off*. Make sure the drive belt is tight and all mounting bolts are

STARTERS AND ALTERNATORS

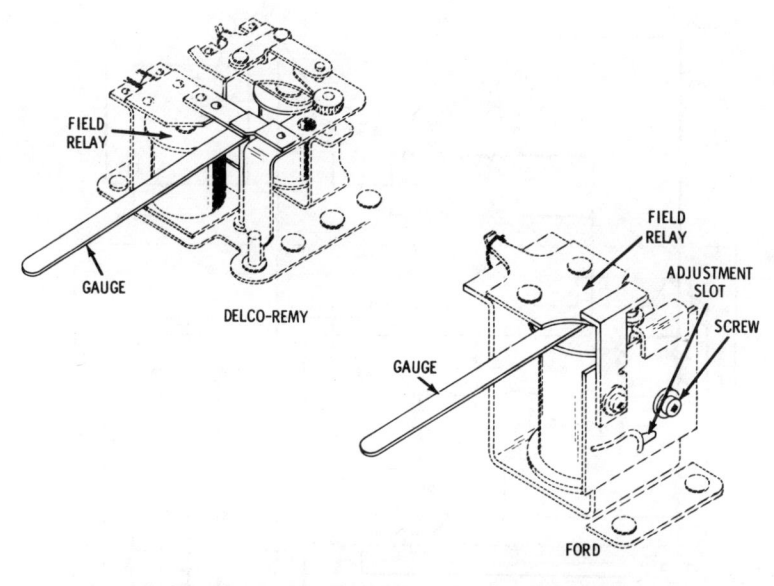

Fig. 35. Checking and adjusting the air gap of the field relay.

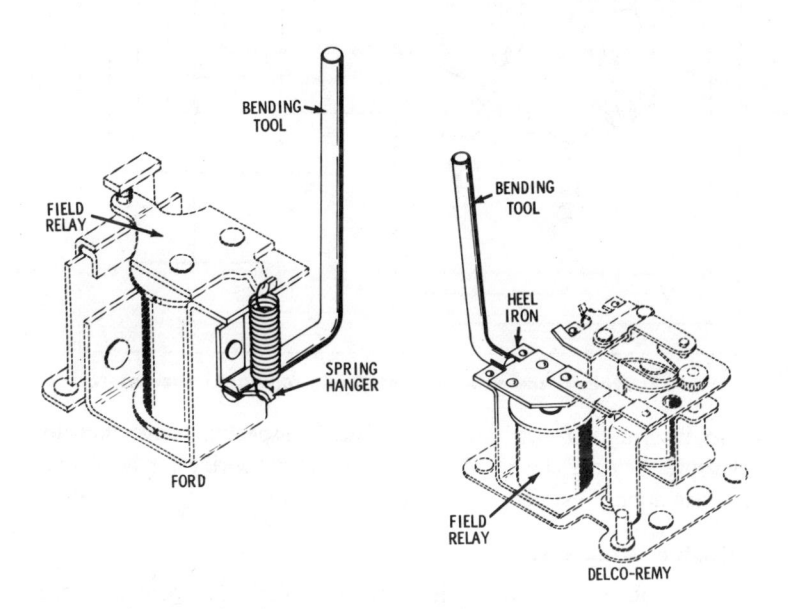

Fig. 36. Adjusting the closing voltage of the field relay.

403

AUTOMOBILE GUIDE

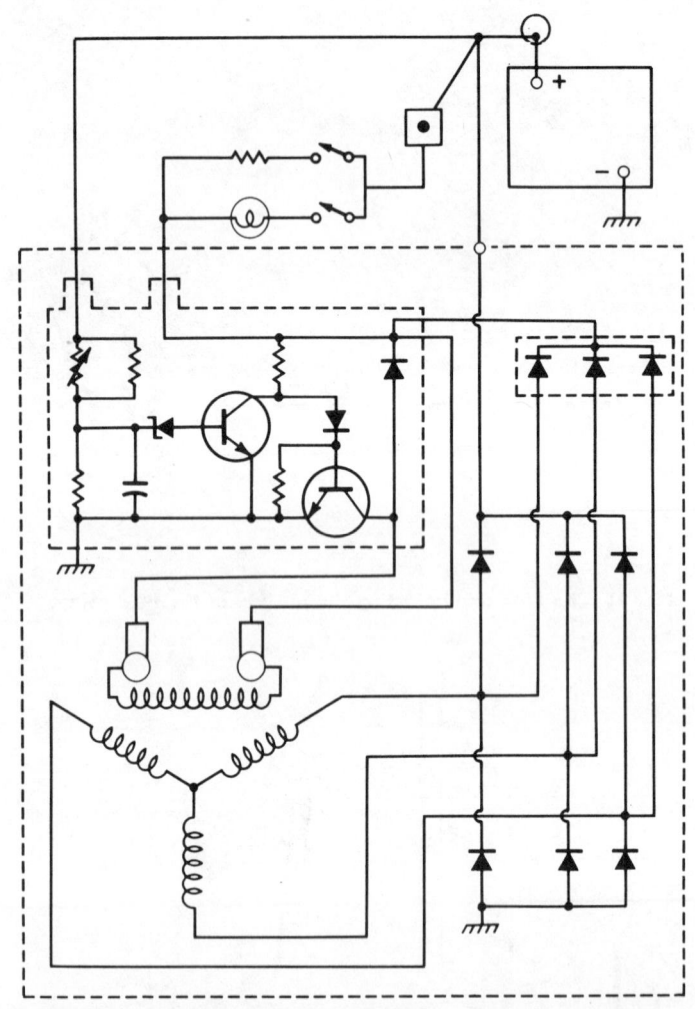

Fig. 37. Typical schematic of a internally-regulated alternator.

secure, insuring a proper "ground." Visually inspect all connections to make sure they are clean and secure. Inspect all wiring for breaks or poor insulation. Test battery to insure it is in a full-charge condition.

Indicator Lamp Check

Refer to the conditions and indications of Table 1. There are three normal and three abnormal conditions. Refer to the procedure indicated.

STARTERS AND ALTERNATORS

TABLE 1. Indicator Lamp Check of an Alternator

Ignition Switch	Indicator Lamp	Engine Condition	Test Procedure
Off	Off	Stopped	OK
Off	On	Stopped	One
On	On	Stopped	OK
On	Off	Stopped	Two
On	Off	Running	OK
On	On	Running	Three

Procedure One — Disconnect the two leads from terminals 1 and 2. If the lamp stays on, there is a short between the two leads. Repair as necessary. If the lamp goes out, replace the rectifier bridge. This condition causes an undercharged battery.

Procedure Two — This condition can be caused by the condition listed in procedure one, by terminal leads 1 and 2 being reversed, or by an open in the circuit. To determine cause, proceed as follows:

(a) Connect a voltmeter from terminal 2 of alternator to ground. If reading is zero there is an open circuit between terminal 2 and the battery. If there is a voltmeter reading, proceed with step b.
(b) With ignition switch "on" and with terminal leads disconnected, momentarily ground terminal lead 1. *Do not ground terminal lead 2.*
(c) If lamp does not light, check for a blown fuse, defective bulb or socket, or open in terminal 1 lead between alternator and ignition switch.
(d) If lamp lights replace the regulator.

Procedure Three — This condition indicates alternator output low or nil. Check alternator output as prescribed in manufacturers service manual.

(a) If output is within ten percent of specification replace regulator.
(b) If output is *not* within 10 percent of specification, check the field winding, diode trio, rectifier bridge, and stator.

STARTER, GENERATOR AND ALTERNATOR TROUBLES AND REMEDIES

Symptoms and Possible Causes   *Possible Remedies*

Current Flow to Battery Insufficient

(a) Glazed or burned generator commutator.
(b) Slipping drive belt on generator or alternator.
(c) Voltage regulator improperly adjusted.
(d) Regulator fuse blown.
(e) Grounded stator windings in alternator.
(f) Shorted or open diodes.

(a) Clean commutator and install brush set.
(b) Tighten belt.
(c) Adjust voltage regulator.
(d) Repair or replace fuse.
(e) Repair or replace stator.
(f) Replace diodes.

Starter Rotates Slowly or Won't Rotate

(a) Low battery.
(b) Loose, dirty, or corroded connections.
(c) Starter or starter circuit shorted.
(d) Starter pedal or switch stuck.
(e) Starter switch defective.
(f) Starter solenoid defective.
(g) Neutral safety switch defective or out of adjustment (on automatic transmission cars).
(h) Armature windings of starter open, shorted, or damaged.
(i) Starter brush lead grounded.
(j) Field coil(s) open or shorted.
(k) Brushes worn out or broken.

(a) Recharge battery.
(b) Clean and/or tighten as necessary.
(c) Correct as necessary.
(d) Repair or replace as necessary.
(e) Replace switch.
(f) Replace or rebuild solenoid.
(g) Adjust or replace neutral safety switch.

(h) Replace armature and brush set.

(i) Insulate brush lead.
(j) Repair or replace field coil(s).
(k) Replace brushes.

STARTERS AND ALTERNATORS

Symptoms and Possible Causes

(l) Bent or broken brush holder.
(m) Sticking brush.
(n) Commutator corroded or dirty.
(o) Commutator out of round.
(p) Starter misaligned, or loose.
(q) Defective starter drive.
(r) Damaged flywheel gear.
(s) Engine problem; too tight, incorrect oil, excessive friction, etc.

Possible Remedies

(l) Repair or replace holder.
(m) Free brush and/or replace spring.
(n) Clean commutator and install new brush set.
(o) True commutator and install new brush set.
(p) Align and/or tighten starter.
(q) Replace drive.
(r) Replace gear as necessary.
(s) Correct as necessary (refer to other chapters of this book for possible remedies.)

Starter Turns but Won't Engage Flywheel

(a) Starter drive stuck or binding.
(b) Starter drive spring or bolt broken.
(c) Starter drive pinion or flywheel gear has several teeth missing.
(d) Armature shaft broken.
(e) Starter end housing cracked or broken.
(f) Defective starter drive.

(a) Clean starter shaft and/or repair as necessary.
(b) Replace starter spring or bolt, or replace drive.
(c) Replace starter drive or flywheel gear as necessary.
(d) Replace armature.
(e) Replace end housing.
(f) Replace drive.

Starter Drive Pinion Jammed into Flywheel Gear

(a) Result of engine kick-back.
(b) Starter misaligned or loose.
(c) Burred or damaged teeth on flywheel gear.

(a) Loosen starter to free drive then retighten.
(b) Free drive then align and/or tighten starter.
(c) Repair or replace as necessary.

407

AUTOMOBILE GUIDE

Symptoms and Possible Causes *Possible Remedies*

(d) Burred or damaged teeth on drive pinion.
(d) Replace drive.

Starter Drive Pinion Won't Release or Releases Slowly

(a) Dirty armature shaft.
(b) Bent armature shaft.
(c) Stuck release pin.
(d) Solenoid defective or out of adjustment.

(a) Clean shaft.
(b) Replace armature.
(c) Replace drive.
(d) Replace or repair solenoid.

Generator Not Charging

(a) Drive belt slipping or broken.
(b) Defective or damaged commutator.
(c) Brushes or brush holder assembly stuck or broken.
(d) Cutout relay fails to close.
(e) Defective regulator.
(f) Regulator out of adjustment.
(g) Dirty, burned or corroded wiring.
(h) Open or shorted field(s).

(a) Tighten or replace.
(b) Replace commutator.
(c) Replace brushes and/or brush holders.
(d) Adjust cutout or replace regulator.
(e) Replace regulator.
(f) Adjust regulator.
(g) Clean and correct as necessary.
(h) Repair or replace as necessary.

Alternator Not Charging

(a) Drive belt slipping or broken.
(b) Brushes worn or sticking.
(c) Diode(s) open.
(d) Defective regulator or fuse.
(e) Open circuit in stator or rotor.

(a) Adjust or replace belt.
(b) Replace brushes.
(c) Replace diode(s).
(d) Replace regulator or fuse as necessary.
(e) Repair or replace as necessary.

Symptoms and Possible Causes *Possible Remedies*

Low Alternator Output

(a) Defective voltage regulator.
(b) Shorted diode(s).
(c) Stator grounded.

(a) Adjust or replace regulator.
(b) Replace diode(s).
(c) Repair or replace stator.

Excessive (high) Alternator Output

(a) Defective voltage regulator.
(b) Diode(s) open.

(a) Adjust or replace regulator.
(b) Replace diodes.

Regulator Problems

(a) Points oxidized.

(b) Points burned.
(c) Coil windings in regulator burned.
(d) Points stuck.

(a) Poor ground, improper air gap setting, regulator set too high, or shorted field in alternator.
(b) Regulator setting too high.
(c) Regulator setting too high.
(d) Poor ground between alternator and regulator.

CHAPTER 17

Lighting Systems

In general, an automobile lighting system includes those lights required by law: headlights, tail lights, license plate light, stop lights, turn-signal lights, parking lights, and side marker lights. Additionally, an automobile lighting system may include lights that may be considered "convenience" lights, such as: underhood, trunk, map compartment, interior, courtesy, instrument lamps, etc.

The lighting system includes the various lamps, wiring harness, switches, fuses or circuit breakers, and other controls. When working on the lighting system, consult the manufacturer's service manual or wiring diagram for the particular automobile being serviced. A typical wiring diagram is shown in Fig. 1.

HEADLIGHTS

The modern sealed-beam unit has its filaments, reflector, and lens sealed to form a single unit. Such a unit has a glass reflector sprayed with vaporized aluminum. This provides a reflecting surface almost as bright and much less expensive than silver.

For many years the advantages of a four-lamp system has been recognized. As long as the same reflector and lens must be used for both upper and lower beams, as in the old system (still used on two-lamp systems), it was necessary to compromise. With four lamps, the upper and lower beams could be provided with specific optical systems best suited for each. There were practical difficulties in adopting such a system, however, and it was not until 1957 that these were overcome and four headlights became an accepted thing throughout the industry.

Lighting Systems

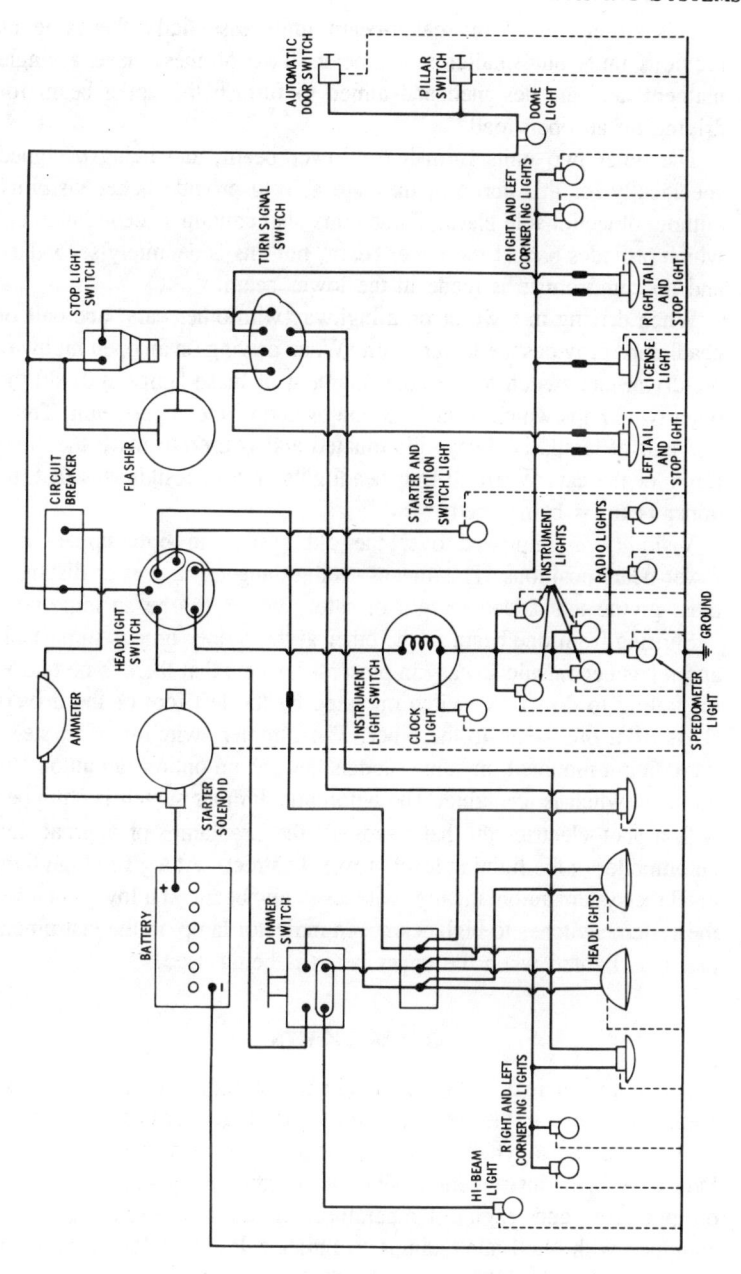

Fig. 1. A typical lighting-system wiring diagram.

This system has four sealed-beam units essentially the same as previous units but smaller in diameter. Two of these have a single filament, and are designed and aimed to furnish the upper beam for driving on an open road.

The other two units furnish the lower beam, and being designed specifically for this purpose, they are able to provide better visibility without objectionable glare. These units also contain a second filament which provides part of the upper beam, but this is definitely secondary and no compromise is made in the lower beam.

When driving in town or on a highway with other cars, one pair of headlamps provides the lower beam. When driving on an open highway the driver can switch to the other filament of these lamps and add the other two lamps which furnish the major part of the upper beam. Thus, one pair of lamps is always illuminated and is used to mark the outer limits of the car. When all four headlights are on, it indicates that the upper beam is being used.

Visibility is improved over the old system in both upper- and lower-beam positions. This means seeing danger at a greater distance, thus, giving that added margin of safety which can be so important.

Shifting from one beam to the other at the proper time is important, and it has been made so easy in present-day cars that there is no reason for failing to do so. A switch operated by the left foot of the drivers shifts from one beam to the other. The dimmer switch may be steering-column mounted on some models and, as an option, an automatic dimmer switch is available. The automatic dimmer switch is equipped with a photoelectric cell that "senses" the headlamps of approaching automobiles or the lighting level of well-lit streets. At a given high light level the system automatically switches to low beam; at a low light level the system switches to high beam. An indicator lamp, in the instrument panel, is lighted when the upper beam is being used.

OTHER LIGHTS

Many do not realize the large number of lights, other than those mentioned, used in the modern automobile. Fig. 2 points out most of the major units, to which must be added all those small lamps used as indicators on the instrument panel — turn signal, high beam, alternator, oil pressure, and engine temperature. In addition, some cars are equipped with "tell-tale" lamps to indicate low fuel level, door not fully closed, trunk lid not closed, etc.

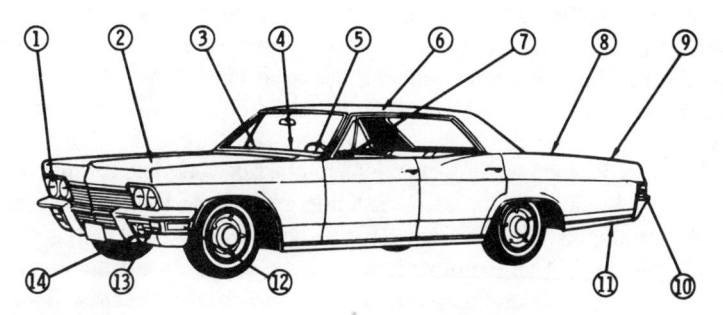

LIGHTING SYSTEMS

Fig. 2. Other lights and signals typical on most automobiles.

1 HEADLAMPS
2 UNDERHOOD LAMP
3 GLOVE COMPARTMENT LAMP
4 MAP LAMP
5 INSTRUMENT LAMPS
6 DOME OR INTERIOR LAMPS
7 COURTESY LAMPS
8 TRUNK LAMP
9 LICENSE LAMPS
10 TAIL-STOP-TURN SIGNAL LAMPS
11 BACK-UP LAMPS
12 CORNERING LAMPS
13 TURN SIGNAL AND PARKING LAMPS
14 FOG LAMPS

Probably the most important of these many lights are the tail lights, stop lights, and turn signals, and these are planned and engineered just as carefully as the headlights. Being seen is as necessary for highway safety as seeing, and your tail lights are designed to perform this function most efficiently. Light from a low-candlepower bulb is concentrated and projected through a red lens in a beam which can be seen for a long distance. The outside shape of the lens may be complicated for styling reasons, but the illuminating engineer has designed prisms into it so that the light is directed to the rear and to the side. In addition, the lens may have a retroreflector section which will reflect light from the headlights of an overtaking car and thus provide a measure of protection even if the tail light bulb is not burning.

The stop lights which go on when the brakes are applied may use the same bulbs and lenses as the tail lights or may be separate units. When they use the same bulbs however, a different filament of higher candlepower is brought into play, so a much stronger beam results. This beam, which gives many times as much light, is necessary so that it can be seen in the daylight and also to distinguish the stop signal from the tail light at night.

Turn signals are operated by the driver to let traffic know when he is about to make a turn, or when he is going to move from one lane to another. The turn signal is turned on manually by the driver but turns off automatically on completion of the turn. Small lights on the instrument panel or on the front fenders (or both) indicate when it is in operation. The signal lamps are located so they can be seen from either the front or rear of the car — generally, amber in the front and red in the rear. Turn signals are flashing to attract attention and to distinguish them from other lights on the car.

These lights for signaling intentions to other drivers, and for making the car visible in the dark, are as extremely important to the car owner as the headlights. They do not have to be as carefully aimed as the headlights do, but on the other hand, are not so obvious to the driver when they are not operating properly. It pays to check all of these lights often to make sure they are working, that the lenses are clean and the beam is bright enough for its purpose.

Most of the other lights are primarily for convenience, although some of them, such as back-up lights and cornering lights, also make a definite contribution to safety. They are all useful, as we soon discover when any of them are not functioning properly.

TURN SIGNALS

A turn signal is used to indicate, to other motorists, when a turn is about to be made. The signal lights are operated by a small control lever mounted on the left side of the steering column housing, just below the steering wheel.

When you intend to turn right, a right turn is signaled by pushing the lever up. Pushing the lever downward indicates a left turn. The turn signal filament of the front parking light and the brake light filament of the rear bulb(s), as well as the indicator light on the dash, will flash automatically in the direction to be turned at a rate of 80 to 100 flashes per minute.

Some turn signal systems are equipped with "sequential" rear lights. In the sequential system, there are usually three lights in the rear of the car on each side for signaling. If, for instance, a left turn is signaled; the in-board light will be illuminated first, then the middle, then the outboard light — then all three will cancel. The sequence will then be repeated until the turn is completed.

Fig. 3 shows a wiring diagram for the conventional turn signal system and Fig. 4 shows the wiring diagram for a sequential turn signal system. Fig. 5 shows the details of a typical conventional turn signal switch. Troubleshooting procedures will be found at the end of this chapter for both types of systems.

LIGHTING SYSTEMS

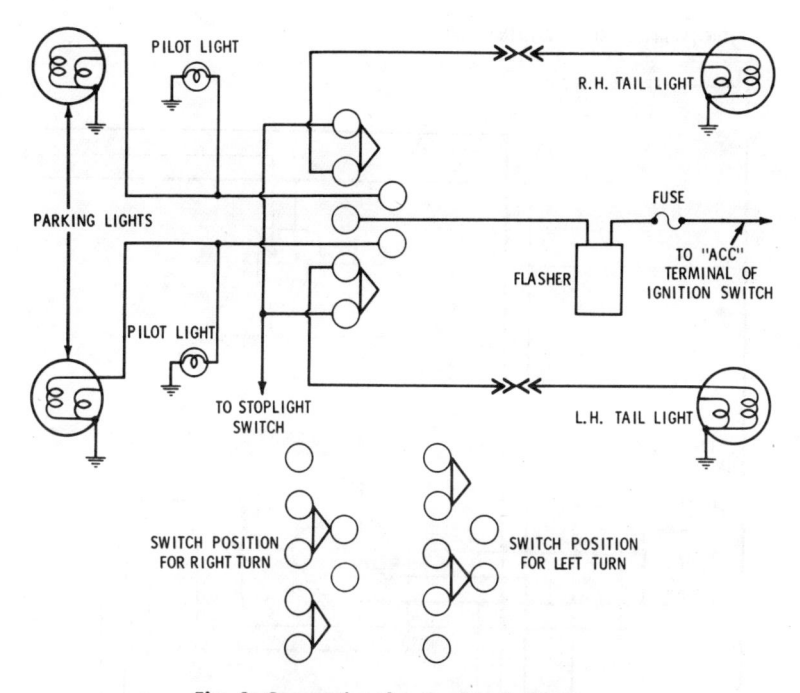

Fig. 3. Conventional turn signal diagram.

The most common causes of trouble with the turn signals are; defective flasher, burned out bulb(s), blown fuse, defective switch or defective wiring.

HEADLIGHT SWITCH AND CIRCUIT BREAKER

Though there are some lever-type switches, the pull-type headlight switch is the most common. The switch, regardless of type, is conveniently mounted on the instrument panel. The first "OUT" position of the knob turns on the parking lights. This includes the front park lights, taillights, corner marking lights, and the instrument lights. On many models the ignition switch is illuminated when the headlight switch is in the first position.

The headlight switch is usually equipped with a courtesy light switch and dash-light rheostat. With this type switch, rotating the knob to the left turns on the courtesy light(s). Rotating the knob to the right gradually dims the instrument-panel lights.

Automobile Guide

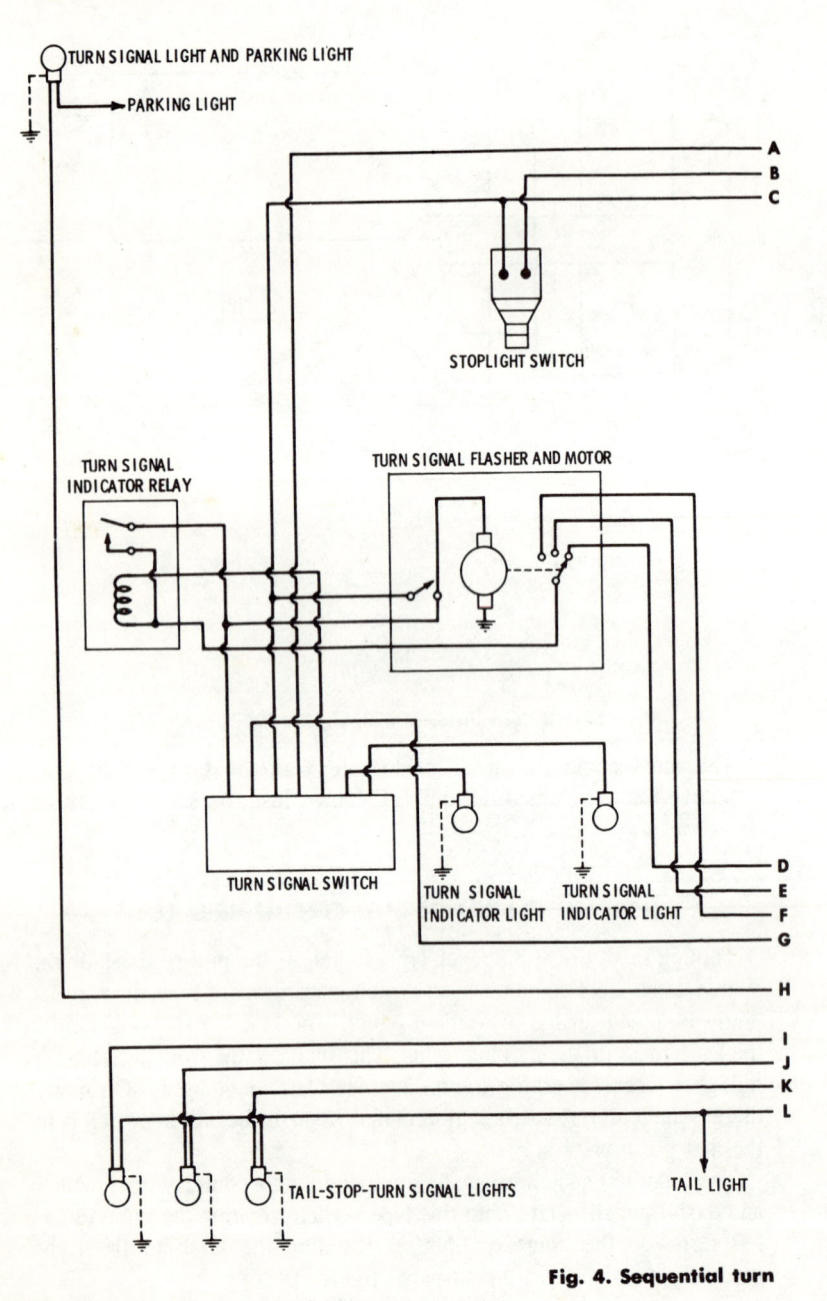

Fig. 4. Sequential turn

Lighting Systems

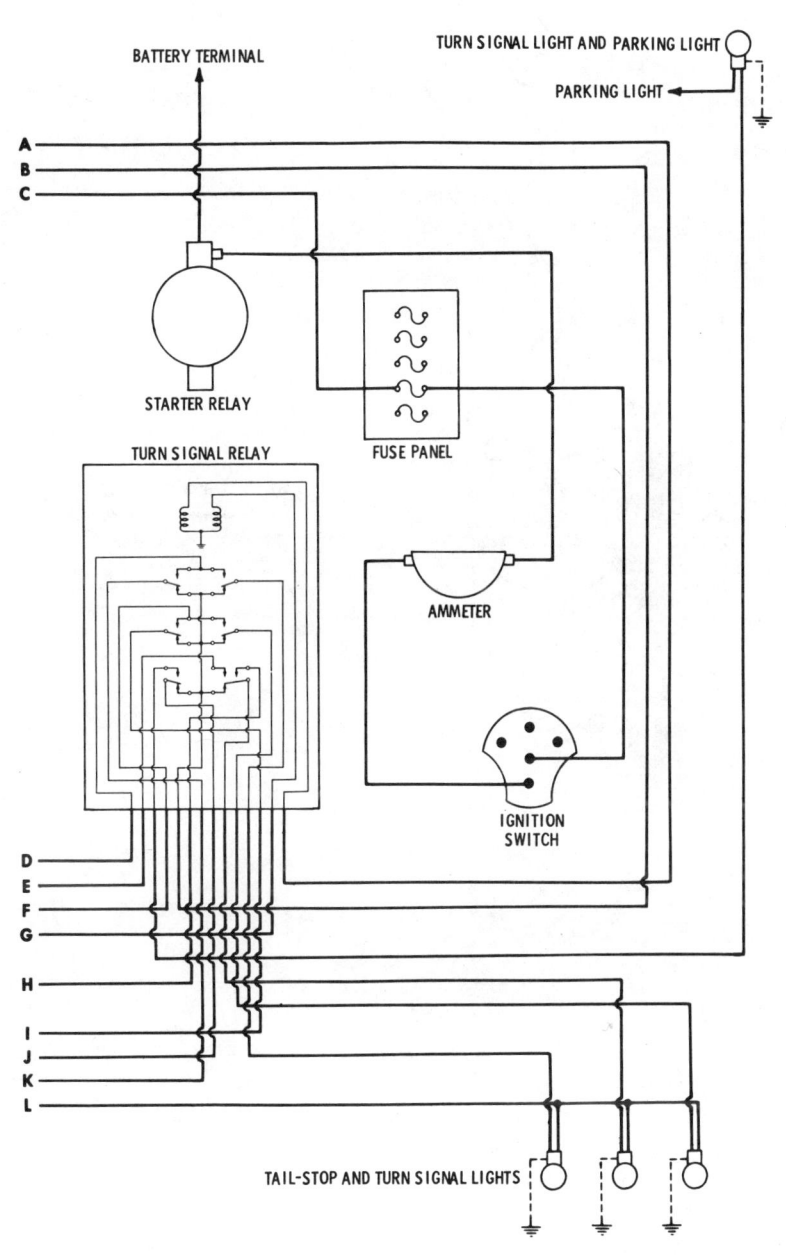

signal wiring diagram.

AUTOMOBILE GUIDE

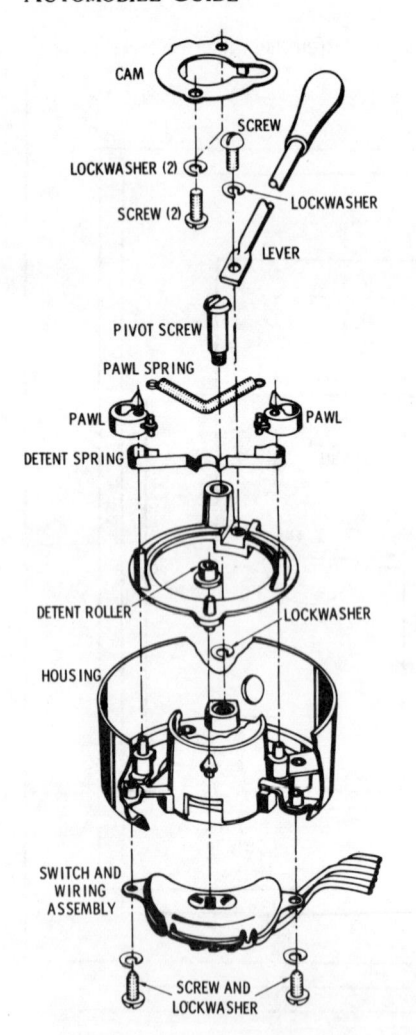

Fig. 5. Details of typical turn signal construction.

Built into the headlight switch is an overload circuit breaker. Since the headlights draw a large amount of current, this is an effective safety feature. An overload through the switch, such as that caused by a grounded or short-circuited cable or wire, causes heating of a bimetallic element of the circuit breaker which causes the separation of the contact points, stopping the flow of current.

As soon as the temperature of the bimetallic elements falls, the points snap together again, closing the circuit. In this regard, the circuit breaker acts like a flasher unit, causing the headlights to go on and off until the cause is corrected.

Some cars are equipped with hidden headlights. On a few models, the headlights themselves are retractable while on most cars, a cover hides the headlights when not in use. In either case, a vacuum or electric motor is used to actuate the headlights, or covers. A separate switch may be used to uncover the headlights, but generally pulling the headlight switch "ON" will automatically uncover them.

A headlight "ON" warning buzzer and/or light is used in many systems. The purpose of this device is to warn the driver that he has left his headlights "ON" after turning off the ignition switch, or starting to leave the car. Troubleshooting headlights will be discussed at the end of this chapter.

AIMING THE HEADLIGHTS

Modern sealed-beam headlights have been designed to make it very easy for you to maintain your lights in good condition for safe driving. The sealed unit protects the reflector against tarnishing. The filaments are designed to give long service on the car. Proper focus between filaments, reflector, and lens is a built-in feature and your unit remains in focus throughout its life.

There is one highly important thing, however, which the owner must take care of to keep his lights at their maximum efficiency. He must see that his headlights are properly aimed. It has been estimated that 50 percent of all the cars on the road have headlights that need aiming, and the only cure for this is for the owner to have them checked periodically.

Two methods are generally used for aiming headlights. One method uses special aiming equipment which mounts on the headlight lens by means of suction cups and small glass pedestals or alignment points molded into the lens surface. The other method uses the patterns made by the beams themselves on a wall or screen.

Using Aiming Equipment

Sealed-beam headlamp units are provided with aiming lugs (Fig. 6) for the alignment of aiming equipment such as the one shown in Fig. 7. This can be used to correctly aim headlights without turning them on.

The aimer consists of a circular base which attaches to the sealed-beam unit by means of a plunger-operated suction cup. Attached to the front of the base and extending perpendicular to it is an L-shaped arm.

Automobile Guide

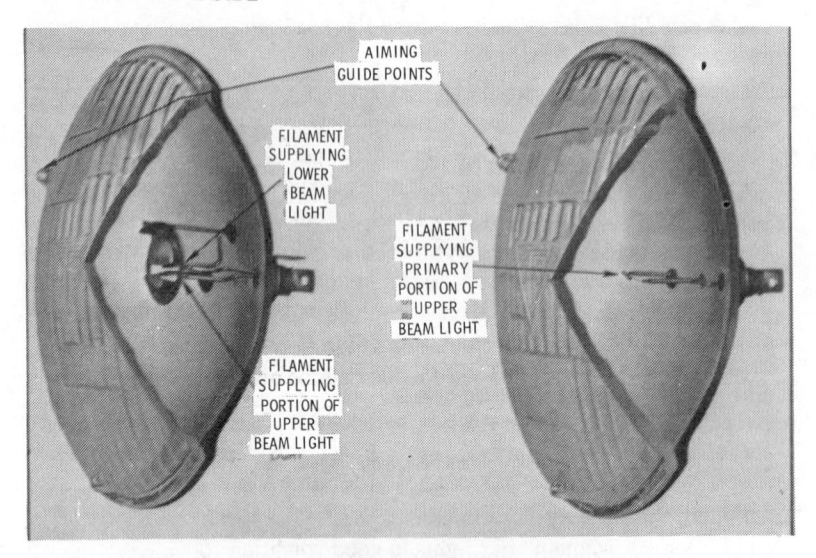

Fig. 6. Details of sealed-beam unit.

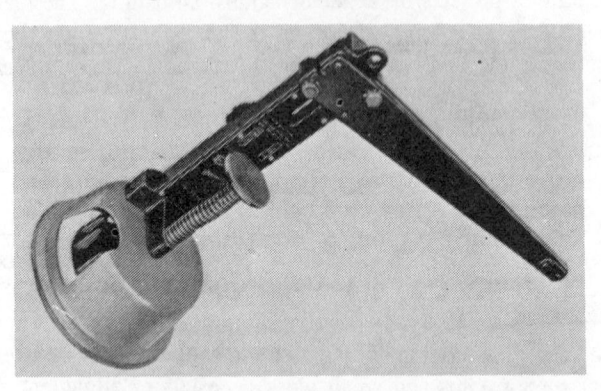

Fig. 7. One type of headlight aiming equipment.

When the aimer is mounted on the lamp, this arm points to the center of the car and is parallel to the ground. Mounted in the arm between the base and cross arm is a bubble level which may be adjusted for variations in the floor.

The various manufacturers specify different conditions of vehicle loading during headlight aiming. They may specify that the gasoline tank should be empty, full, or half full; that the driver (or a substitute weight) should or should not be behind the wheel; that the spare tire should or should not be in the trunk. Always follow the vehicle

Lighting Systems

manufacturer's specification and/or state regulations for the conditions of the vehicle.

Always bounce the car several times to allow springs and shock absorbers to settle normally. Remove the headlight trim to expose the adjustment screws (Fig. 8). Install an aimer on each headlight to be aimed. Most manufacturers specify that the inboard pair of four-headlamp cars be aimed first. These sealed-beam lamps have a numeral "1" molded into the lens and have only one filament. They are used in conjunction with the high beam of the outboard lamps for highway driving. The outboard lamps have a "2" molded in the lens and have two filaments — a low beam and a high beam.

Position the aimer over the lens with the aiming lugs engaging the proper points on the aimer. Push the lever that forces the suction cups onto the lens. Mount another aimer on the other lamp of the pair to be aimed. Rotate the crossarms so that they are approximately horizontal and pointing toward the center of the car. Knot both ends of the elastic string provided with the aimers, and stretch it between the two aimers, using the slots provided. The installation should appear as in Fig. 9.

Horizontal Adjustment — Turn the horizontal aiming screw on one lamp until the string is positioned over the crossarm centerline. Always turn the screw *clockwise* while making the final adjustment to insure that all free play in the headlamp mechanism is taken up. Repeat the adjustment on the other lamp.

Vertical Adjustment — Most state regulations require a 2- or 3-inch drop of the headlight beams at a distance of 25 feet from the vehicle.

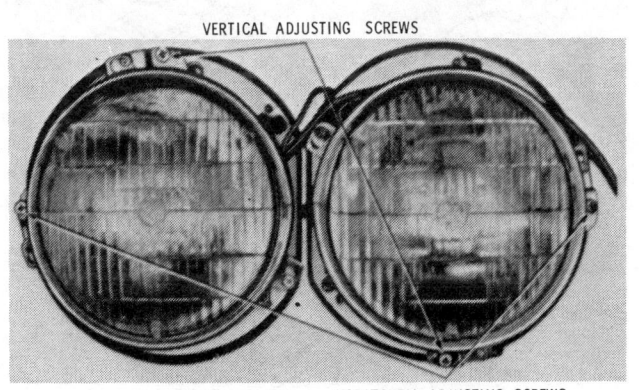

Fig. 8. Headlight aiming screws.

Courtesy Dodge Div., Chrysler Motors Corp.

AUTOMOBILE GUIDE

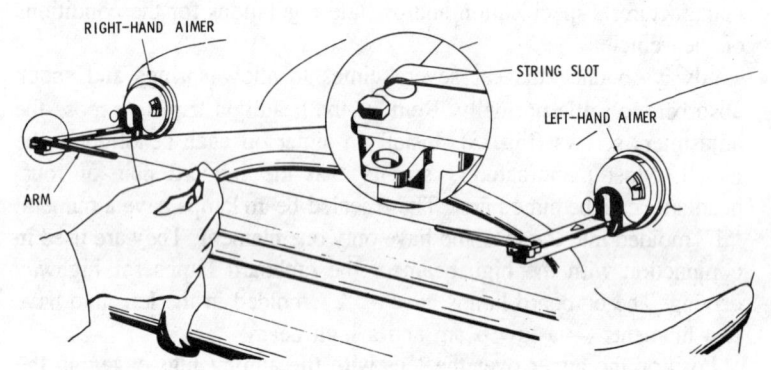

Fig. 9. Aimers and string installed on number 1 headlights.

Check your state regulations. The aimer provides an up-and-down adjustment (Fig. 10) to compensate for floor level. On a level floor, both the UP and DOWN view windows will show a zero.

To set the vertical aim of the headlights, set the aimer for a "2" or a "3" in the DOWN window. Turn the vertical aiming screw on one lamp counterclockwise until the bubble is at the end of the level. Then turn the screw *clockwise* until the bubble is centered. Repeat the operation on the other lamp.

The outboard, or No. 2 lamps are aimed in the same manner.

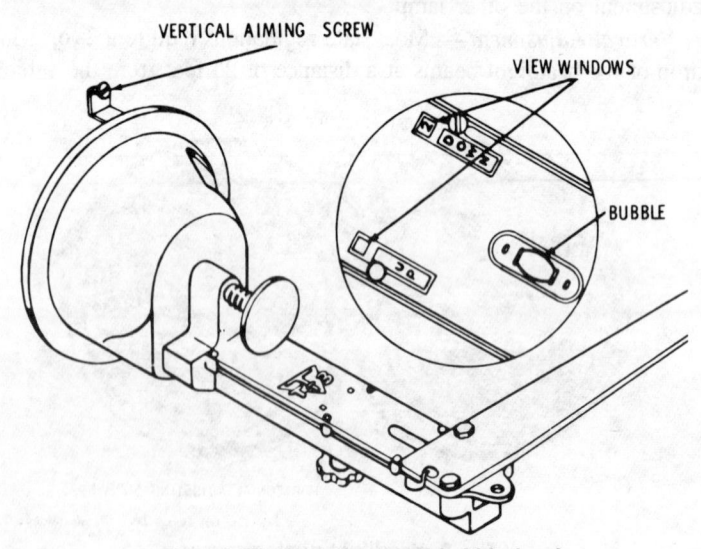

Fig. 10. View windows and bubble level.

422

Using a Wall or Screen

There are many ways of aiming headlights by means of a wall or screen. The method described does away with the need for an exactly level floor and establishes beam height correctly regardless of floor slant.

Select a location in which the vehicle can be positioned with the front surface of the headlamps exactly 25 feet from a vertical wall. The wall should preferably be painted white with a nonreflective surface.

Construct two uprights, or stands, exactly alike and 20" high. Position these on one side of the vehicle and sight across the tops of the two uprights. Have an assistant mark the spot on the wall where the line of vision intersects. Repeat on the other side of the vehicle and draw a line on the wall connecting the two points. This operation establishes a reference line exactly 20" above the floor (Fig. 11).

Measure the distance from the floor to the center of one lamp. Subtract 20 inches from this dimension and add the difference (dimension "B" in Fig. 12A) to the 20-inch line on the wall. Repeat this operation on the other lamp. Connect these points to form the horizontal center line of the lamps. Draw another horizontal line 2 inches (3 inches in some states) below and parallel to this center line (Fig. 12A). Mark the center line of the front and back windows of the vehicle with tape and sight past these to mark the center line of the vehicle on the wall. Measure the distance between the headlight centers (dimension "A" in

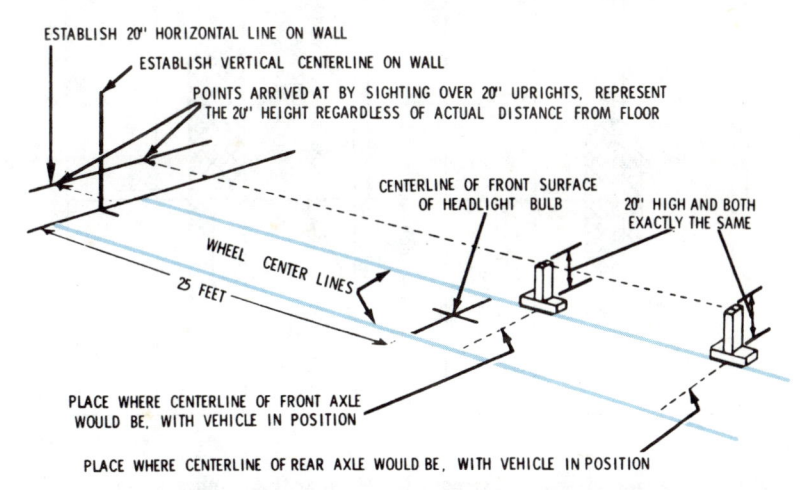

Fig. 11. Floor and wall layout for visual aiming of headlight.

Automobile Guide

Fig. 12A) and mark the center lines of the left and right headlights on the wall. Again, the inboard (No. 1) lights are to be adjusted first.

Turn the headlights on bright (high beam) and cover the outboard or No. 2 lights. Adjust the No. 1 lights horizontally and vertically until the light patterns on the wall are positioned as in Fig. 12A.

Turn the headlights on dim (low beam) and remove the covers. Adjust the No. 2 lights to position the light patterns as in Fig. 12B. Note that the lines of reference for the No. 2 lights are the vertical and horizontal centerlines of the No. 2 lights.

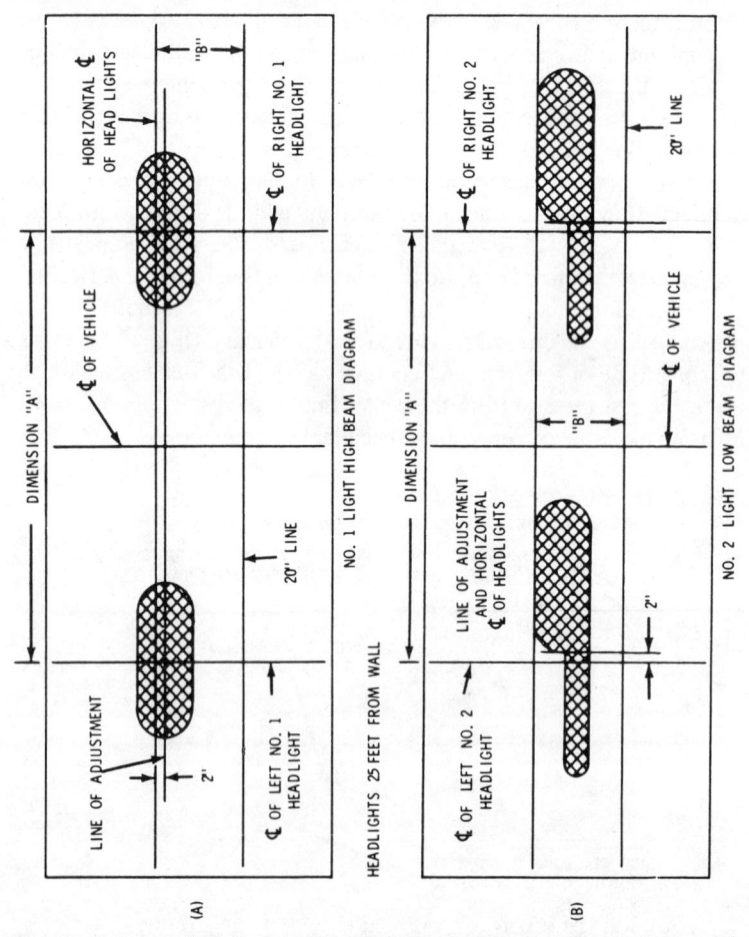

Fig. 12. Layout of wall or screen; (A) Number 1 on inboard lights; (B) Number 2 or outboard lights on low beam.

LIGHTING SYSTEMS

CONVENTIONAL TURN SIGNAL TROUBLES AND REMEDIES

Symptoms and Possible Causes   *Possible Remedies*

Dash Indicator Light Burns Steadily

(a) Burned out parking lamp.   (a) Replace parking lamp.
(b) Burned out stop lamp.   (b) Replace stop lamp.
(c) Defective flasher.   (c) Replace flasher.

Dash Indicator Light Flashes Rapidly

(a) Burned out parking lamp.   (a) Replace parking lamp.
(b) Burned out stop lamp.   (b) Replace stop lamp.
(c) Defective flasher.   (c) Replace flasher.
(d) Incorrect flasher.   (d) Replace with correct flasher.

Dash Indicator Light Fails to Light

(a) Burned out indicator light. (a) Replace indicator light.
(b) Defective flasher.   (b) Replace flasher.
(c) Defective wiring.   (c) Repair or replace wiring.

Switch Fails to Cancel

(a) Defective switch.   (a) Replace switch.
(b) Broken switch part(s).   (b) Replace part(s) or replace switch

SEQUENTIAL TURN SIGNAL TROUBLES AND REMEDIES

No Sequential Effect

(a) Bulb(s) do not light.   (a) Replace bulb(s).
(b) Defective printed circuit.   (b) Repair or replace printed circuit.
(c) Defective wiring.   (c) Repair or replace wiring.

Bulbs Flash Dimly and Together in Either Turn Position

(a) Defective turn signal indicator relay.   (a) Replace turn signal indicator relay.
(b) Open circuit (defective wiring.   (b) Repair or replace as necessary.

425

Symptoms and Possible Causes　　*Possible Remedies*

(c) Defective turn signal switch.
(c) Repair or replace switch.

(d) Open circuit in instrument cluster printed circuit.
(d) Repair or replace as necessary.

Bulbs Flash Dimly, but in Proper Side and Sequence

(a) Poor contact of bulb or socket to common ground in the instrument cluster printed circuit.
(a) Inspect for improper installation, foreign material, etc., and repair as necessary.

(b) Resistance ground circuit disconnected or broken.
(b) Repair as necessary.

Bulbs Flash on Opposite Side of Turn Selected

(a) Defective turn signal indicator relay.
(a) Replace relay.

(b) Open circuit (defective wiring).
(b) Repair or replace wiring.

(c) Defective turn signal switch.
(c) Repair or replace as necessary.

(d) Defective wiring assembly in steering column.
(d) Repair or replace as necessary.

Bulbs Glow Steadily on Side of Turn Selected

(a) Defective turn signal indicator relay.
(a) Replace relay.

(b) Short in wiring to the indicator bulb feed circuit.
(b) Repair or replace wiring as necessary.

No Set Pattern of Sequence — Indicators Flash Erratically Between the Two Bulbs

(a) Defective turn signal indicator relay.
(a) Replace relay.

(b) Improper connection in the indicator bulb system.
(b) Check bulbs, connectors, printed circuit, and ground for improper connection. Correct as necessary.

Lighting Systems

Symptoms and Possible Causes

One Bulb Does Not Light

(a) Defective bulb.
(b) Bulb or socket not making proper connection with printed circuit.
(c) Open circuit (wiring or printed circuit).

Bulbs Will Not Light

(a) Defective bulbs.
(b) Bulbs or sockets not making proper contact with printed circuit.
(c) Open circuit (wiring, ground wire or printed circuit).
(d) Defective turn signal indicator relay.

Possible Remedies

(a) Replace bulb.
(b) Inspect for improper installation, foreign material, etc., repair as necessary.
(c) Repair as necessary.

(a) Replace bulbs.
(b) Inspect for improper installation, foreign material, etc., repair as necessary.
(c) Repair as necessary.

(d) Replace relay.

LIGHTING TROUBLES AND REMEDIES

Light Does Not Burn

(a) Defective bulb.
(b) Defective wiring.
(c) Defective light switch.
(d) Loose connection.
(e) Discharged battery.

(a) Replace bulb.
(b) Repair or replace wiring.
(c) Replace switch.
(d) Correct as necessary.
(e) Recharge battery.

Light(s) Flicker

(a) Loose connection(s).
(b) Poor ground at socket(s).

(a) Repair as necessary.
(b) Repair as necessary.

Bulbs Burn Out Frequently

(a) High charging rate.

(a) Adjust regulator or correct as necessary.

Automobile Guide

Symptoms and Possible Causes

(b) Poor ground at light socket.
(c) Incorrect type of bulb.

Possible Remedies

(b) Repair as necessary.
(c) Replace with correct bulb.

CHAPTER 18

Instrument Panel

The instrument panel is not as complex as it seems when broken down into individual components. It is in the instrument panel that all of the gauges and indicators are located so that the driver can tell if his car is functioning properly. Basically, the instrument panel can be broken down into five major items, as follows:

SPEEDOMETER

The speedometer is a device that is used to indicate, in miles-per-hour, the speed of the car. The speed is shown by a pointer and face dial. A speedometer assembly will also contain an odometer to record the distance, in miles, the car has traveled. The smallest unit of measurement of an odometer is one-tenth of one mile. Many speedometers, in addition to the regular odometer, will have a smaller odometer (referred to as a "trip odometer") that is used to record trip mileage. The small odometer will record up to 999.9 miles before resetting itself to zero. It may, however, at any time, be reset to zero by the driver. The large odometer, referred to as a "season" or "total" odometer cannot be reset by the driver. The "total" odometer will record to 99,999 miles before resetting itself to zero.

Most speedometers are mechanically driven. Only in some special applications will there be found an electric speedometer. A mechanically driven speedometer is operated from the transmission by a cable and casing assembly. The cable and casing need not always run from the transmission directly to the speedometer, however. In some applications, such as cars equipped with cruise control, the cable and casing will run from the transmission to the cruise control unit. From the cruise control unit to the speedometer will be found a second cable and casing assembly.

Even though the internal parts of various speedometers differ in construction and appearance, they all incorporate the same basic components and operate on the same principle.

The speed indicator, shown as A in Fig. 1, operates on a magnetic principle. It includes a revolving permanent magnet which is driven by the cable and casing assembly from the transmission or cruise control unit.

Around this magnet (B in Fig. 1) is a stationary field cup. Between the revolving magnet and stationary field cup (Fig. 1) is a speed cup (C). The speed cup is magnetic. A part of the speed cup is the spindle and hair spring (D). The pointer of the speed indicator is attached to the spindle.

The revolving magnet sets up a rotating magnetic field which exerts a pull (or magnetic drag) on the speed cup, making it move in the same direction. Its movement, however, is retarded and held steady by the hair spring. The hair spring also serves to "zero" the pointer whenever the rotating magnet is not turning.

There is no mechanical connection between the magnet, speed cup, or field cup. As the speed of the magnet increases due to increased car speed, the magnetic drag on the speed cup also increases, pulling the speed cup further around to indicate a faster speed on the face of the speedometer. The magnetic field is constant. The amount of speed cup deflection is, at all times, proportional to the speed at which the magnet is revolving.

The odometer is driven through a series of gears; the first of which is a spiral gear cut on the magnet shaft. This gear, known as the first gear, drives an intermediate second gear, and in some cases, a third gear, which is connected to a fourth gear at the odometer. This arrangement is shown in Fig. 2. The final gear turns the odometer through a series of star pinion gears which are found between each number wheel. The odometer is so constructed that whenever each wheel to the right makes one complete revolution the wheel immediately to its left turns one-tenth revolution.

Generally, speedometer repair is not accomplished by the average auto repair shop. Repair and calibration require special tools and equipment. It may be found, however, that in many cases the cable and

INSTRUMENT PANEL

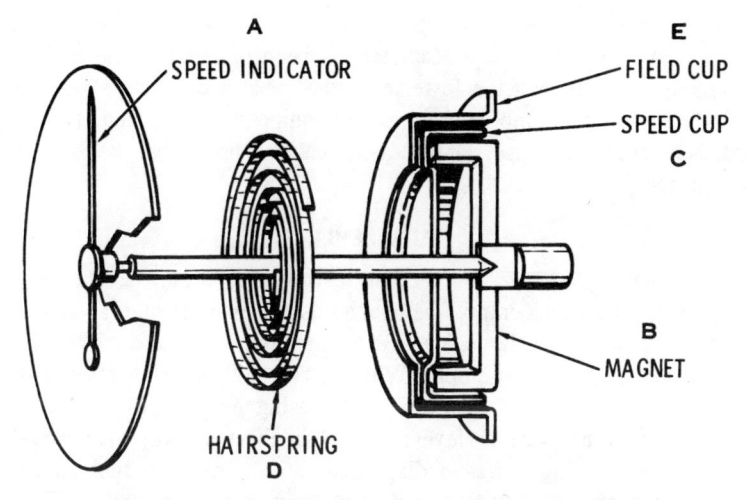

Fig. 1. Speedometer head assembly; (A) Speed Indicator; (B) Magnet; (C) Speed Cup; (D) Hairspring; (E) Field cup.

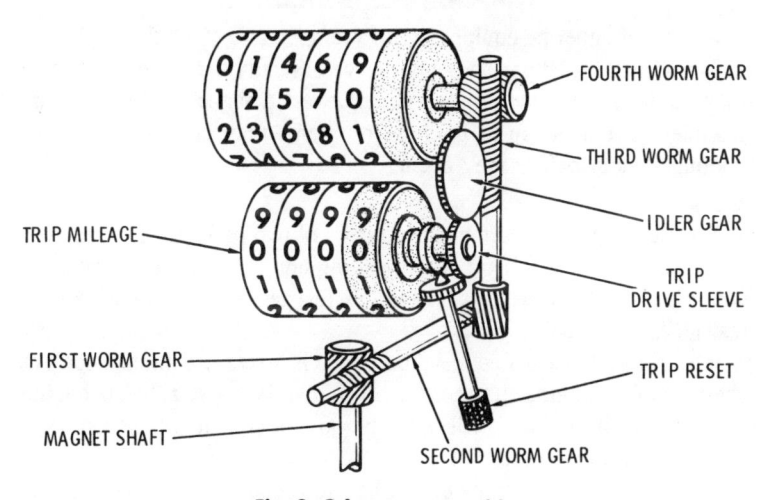

Fig. 2. Odometer assembly.

casing are at fault causing an incorrect indicated speed, in which case you may use the following procedure.

Disconnect the speedometer cable and casing from the rear of the speedometer. Pull the cable from the casing and inspect for breaks. If the cable seems "twisted" and broken at the extreme lower end, it is

431

usually due to a defective speedometer. The cable core should be replaced only after the speedometer has been repaired. If the cable is broken anywhere but the lower end, the cable and casing should be replaced as an assembly. If the car is equipped with an intermediate device, such as cruise control, both cables should be checked for breakage.

FUEL LEVEL

The fuel level gauge is a variable resistance-type unit, as shown in Fig. 3. With the tank empty, the float holds the slide rheostat (a variable resistance device in the tank unit), to maximum resistance. This will cause the gauge to read empty. With the tank full, the slide rheostat is moved to the minimum resistance point causing the gauge to read full. It can be seen that various levels of fuel in the tank will give varied resistance, causing corresponding readings on the dash fuel gauge. Testing procedures will be found at the end of this chapter.

TEMPERATURE INDICATOR

A car will either be equipped with a temperature "telltale" light or a gauge. For the most part they both serve basically the same purpose. It may be determined from this test, however, that the gauge is a more reliable instrument, since possible problems may be detected in the cooling system before they occur.

Gauge

The electric temperature gauge consists of two parts; the sending unit and the dash unit. The heart of the sending unit is a "sintered" material which has a characteristic of having low resistance when hot and a high resistance when cold.

It is enclosed in a sealed metal bulb which is screwed into the coolant chamber of the engine. It is positioned so that the resistor, located at the extreme end of the bulb, will be in the flow of coolant whose temperature is to be measured.

The high resistance in the unit, when surrounded by cold coolant, as shown in Fig. 4, causes the indicator to read on the cold end of the dial. The unit has low resistance (Fig. 5) when surrounded by hot coolant, causing the indicator to read on the hot end of the scale.

Telltale Light

Some cars are equipped with two temperature lights; a green one that is lighted whenever the ignition switch is turned ON and the engine cold,

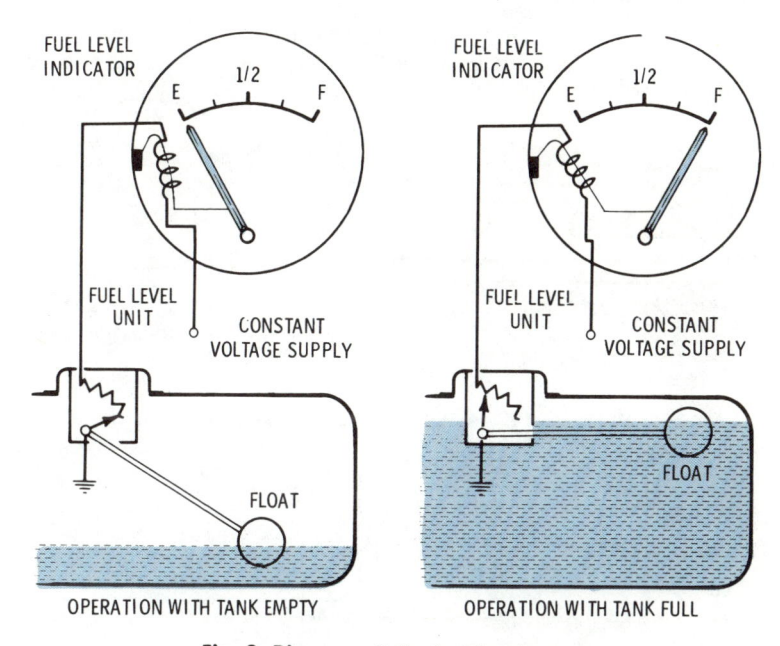

Fig. 3. Diagram of the fuel level gauge.

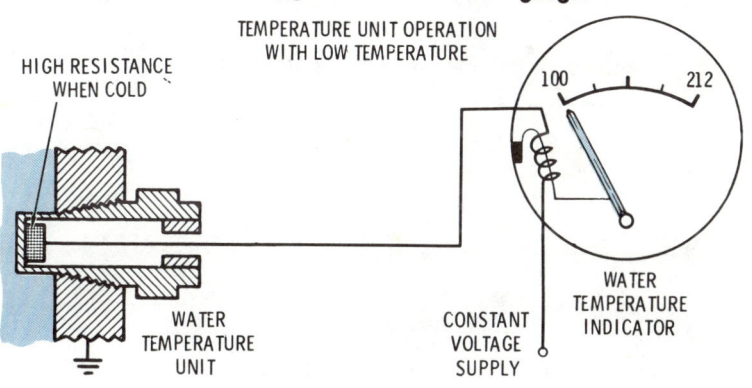

Fig. 4. Diagam of the temperature gauge (at low temperature).

and a red one when the car is overheating. Others are equipped with only one light: a red one that is lighted whenever the engine is nearing its overheat limit. Both types of unit operate basically in the same manner. Fig. 6 shows a schematic of a unit with both hot and cold lights. Fig. 7 shows a unit with only the hot-indicator light.

433

AUTOMOBILE GUIDE

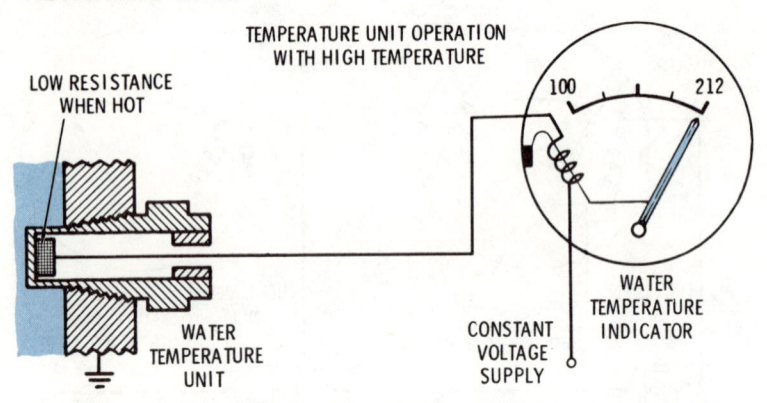

Fig. 5. Diagram of the temperature gauge (at high temperature).

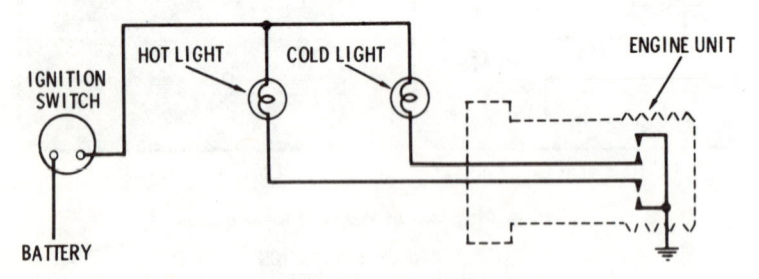

Fig. 6. Hot and cold warning light diagram.

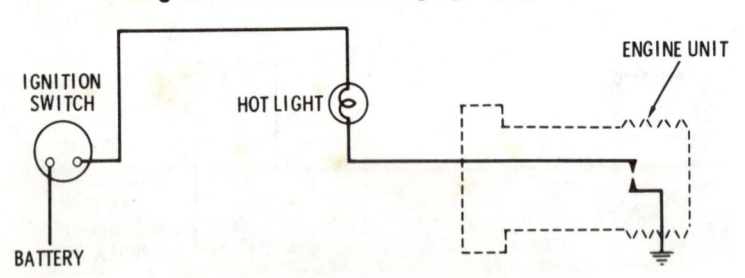

Fig. 7. Hot warning light diagram.

The sending unit is equipped with bimetallic sensing elements that react differently to hot and cold. This unit is enclosed in a sealed metal bulb which is screwed into the coolant chamber of the engine in a position so that the element will be in the stream of coolant whose temperature is to be measured.

The "cold" switch is normally closed whenever coolant temperature is below 165°F. to 180°F. Whenever the engine coolant reaches this

434

INSTRUMENT PANEL

temperature, generally only a few minutes if the car is equipped with a thermostat (see CHAPTER 12: COOLING SYSTEMS), the contact points open and the green light goes out.

The "hot" switch is normally open and does not close until the coolant reaches 235 F. to 250 F., depending on the design. Whenever the switch closes, the red light is lighted on the instrument panel indicating cooling system problems. Since it is obvious that the "hot" light does not come on until coolant reaches temperatures well above the boiling point of water (212 F.), a review of the chapter on cooling systems will explain how these temperatures are reached without the engine boiling over.

CHARGING INDICATOR

The car may be equipped with either an ammeter or a "telltale" light. With an ammeter, the driver is able to determine the rate (in amperes) of charging, or discharging. With a "telltale" light the driver is only able to determine whenever the system is not charging, generally only after a problem has occurred. Fig. 8 shows a charging circuit equipped with a "telltale light" and Fig. 9 shows a charging circuit equipped with an ammeter.

Basically, the purpose of either type of indicator is to tell if the generator or alternator, is charging the battery. A review of CHAPTER 16: STARTERS AND ALTERNATORS will give a better understanding of the operation of this unit.

OIL PRESSURE

Again, the car may be equipped with either a gauge or a "telltale" light. The oil-pressure indicator light is designed with a pressure sending switch that is normally closed. It is opened at about 5 psi pressure. The modern engine requires oil pressures upward to about 35 psi — it is easily seen that the gauge is the better of the two warning devices. For instance, the car could operate for months with only 10 psi oil pressure and the light would not indicate any danger.

The oil gauge operates on the same principle as does the gas gauge except it is not equipped with a float. The oil pressure sending unit consists of a spring loaded diaphragm and a variable resistance unit. The electrical circuit for the oil-pressure system grounds through a pin in the diaphragm. The gauge-system sending unit is shown in Fig. 10.

AUTOMOBILE GUIDE

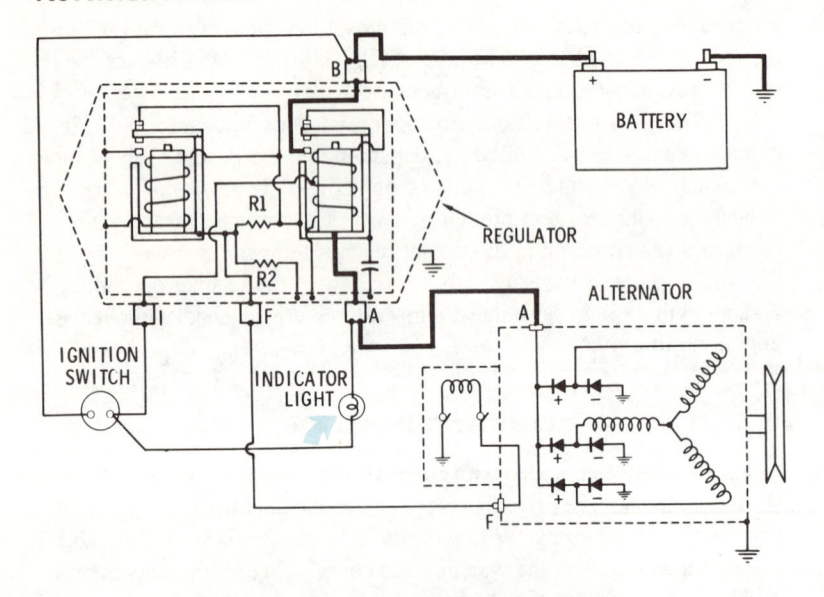

Fig. 8. Charging circuit with light indicator.

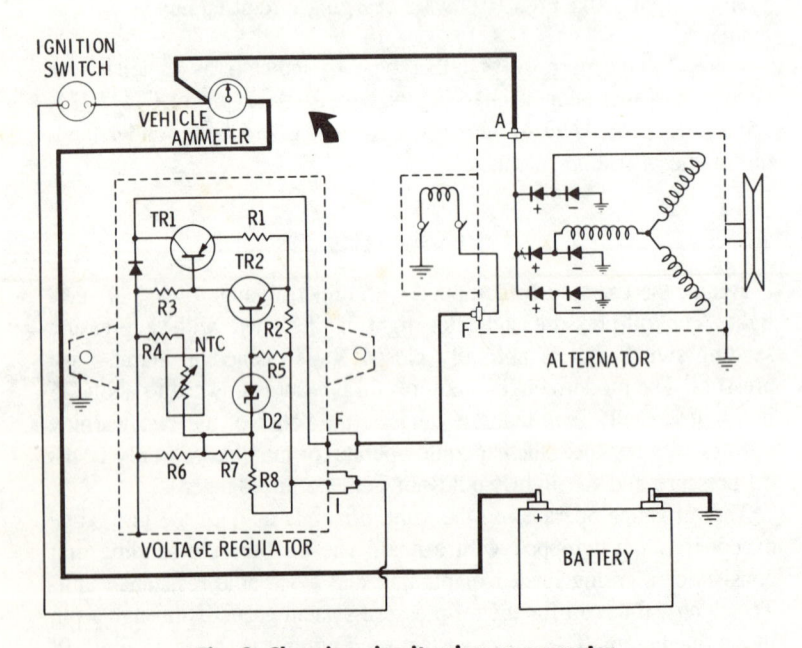

Fig. 9. Charging circuit using an ammeter.

436

INSTRUMENT PANEL

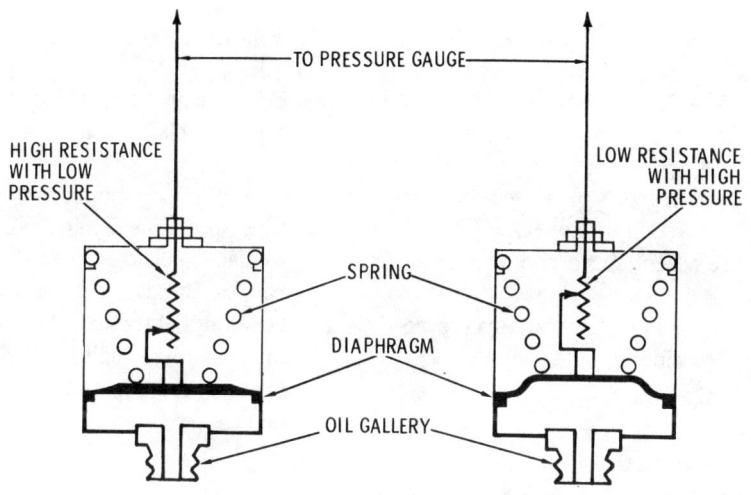

Fig. 10. Oil pressure sending unit.

INSTRUMENT VOLTAGE REGULATOR

The function of the voltage regulator (sometimes referred to as constant voltage regulator) is to regulate the variable voltage available from the car battery or charging system to produce a constant voltage, generally about 5.0 volts to the gauges.

This regulator is a simple device operating with a bimetallic heater in conjunction with a pair of contacts. It is temperature compensating to produce a correct, constant voltage for the gauge(s). If input voltage falls below the rated output voltage, the result will be proportionately low gauge indications.

SPEEDOMETER TROUBLES AND REMEDIES

Symptoms and Possible Causes   *Possible Remedies*

Pointer Fluctuates (Waves)

(a) Defective main frame.

(b) Excessive end play in magnet shaft.

(a) Replace speedometer or have repaired.

(b) Tighten collar on end of magnet shaft.

437

Symptoms and Possible Causes

(c) Dirt, grease, or foreign matter on magnet and/or speed cup.
(d) Speed cup rusted or corroded at jewels.
(e) Bent speed cup spindle.
(f) Field plate improperly positioned.

Possible Remedies

(c) Clean magnet and speed cup with clean cloth.
(d) Clean ends of spindle, or have speedometer repaired.
(e) Replace speedometer or have repaired.
(f) Position field plate. Spacing should be uniform between speed cup and field plate.

Pointer Does Not Return to Zero

(a) Weak hairspring.
(b) Broken hairspring.
(c) Hairspring improperly adjusted.
(d) Upper (front) jewel too tight.
(e) Dirt or grease in mechanism.
(f) Pointer improperly set.
(g) Broken or distorted hairspring regulator.

(a) Replace hairspring, calibrate speedometer.
(b) Replace hairspring, calibrate speedometer.
(c) Adjust hairspring, calibrate speedometer.
(d) Adjust upper jewel.
(e) Have speedometer cleaned and calibrated.
(f) Remove pointer and reposition to zero on dial.
(g) Replace field plate assembly or regulator. Calibrate speedometer.

Incorrect Speed Indication

(a) Incorrect drive gear at transmission.
(b) Mechanism dirty or grease filled.
(c) Out of calibration.

(a) Replace with correct drive gear.
(b) Have speedometer cleaned and repaired. Calibrate.
(c) Have recalibrated.

INSTRUMENT PANEL

Symptoms and Possible Causes　　*Possible Remedies*

Excessive Noise

(a) Excessive end play in magnet shaft.
(b) Worn gears.
(c) "Kinked" cable and casing assembly.

(a) Tighten collar on end of magnet shaft.
(b) Replace gears.
(c) Straighten cable and casing assembly.

Odometer Inoperative

(a) First gear stripped.

(b) Second gear end play excessive.
(c) Second and/or third gears stripped.
(d) Odometer bound (seized).

(a) Replace magnet and first gear. Calibrate speedometer.
(b) Adjust to proper end play.
(c) Replace second and/or third gears.
(d) Replace odometer. Replace damaged gears. Calibrate speedometer.

Odometer Records Incorrectly

(a) Improper second and/or third gear.
(b) Improper transmission drive gear.
(c) Improper odometer.

(a) Replace with correct gear(s).
(b) Replace with correct gear.
(c) Replace odometer.

FUEL GAUGE TROUBLES AND REMEDIES

Gauge Does Not Read "FULL" With Full Tank When Ignition Is On

(a) Tank unit float arm bent.

(b) Defective tank unit.
(c) Pointer sticking on dial of dash gauge.

(a) Repair or replace tank unit.
(b) Replace tank unit.
(c) Carefully bend pointer to relieve binding.

439

Automobile Guide

Symptoms and Possible Causes *Possible Remedies*

(d) Defective dash gauge.
(e) Defective constant-voltage supply.

(d) Replace dash gauge.
(e) Replace voltage regulator.

Gauge Does Not Read "EMPTY" With Empty Tank and Ignition On

(a) Tank unit float arm bent.
(b) Defective tank unit or defective dash gauge.
(c) Pointer sticking on dial of dash gauge.

(a) Repair or replace tank unit.
(b) Replace tank unit or dash gauge as necessary.
(c) Carefully bend pointer to relieve binding.

Gauge Does Not Read "EMPTY" With Empty Tank and Ignition Off

(a) No problem.

(a) Dash gauge needle may read anything with ignition off.

Gauge Does Not Indicate Proper Fuel Level Of Tank

(a) Defective tank unit or bent float arm.
(b) Defective dash gauge or bent pointer.
(c) Defective constant-voltage supply.

(a) Replace tank unit to repair float arm.
(b) Replace dash gauge or carefully bend pointer to correct.
(c) Replace voltage regulator.

Gauge Does Not Move With Ignition Switch Turned On

(a) Defective wiring.
(b) Blown fuse (if equipped).
(c) Defective dash gauge or tank unit.

(a) Replace or repair.
(b) Replace fuse.
(c) Replace dash gauge or tank unit as required.

INSTRUMENT PANEL

TEMPERATURE INDICATOR TROUBLES AND REMEDIES

Symptoms and Possible Causes *Possible Remedies*

Gauge Constantly Reads Too Hot

(a) Engine overheating.
(b) Defective engine unit.
(c) Defective dash gauge.
(d) Defective constant-voltage supply.

(a) Isolate problem and correct.
(b) Replace engine unit.
(c) Replace dash gauge.
(d) Replace voltage regulator.

Gauge Constantly Reads Too Cold

(a) Defective engine unit or dash gauge.
(b) Defective constant-voltage regulator.
(c) High resistance in wiring.

(a) Replace unit or gauge as required.
(b) Replace voltage regulator.
(c) Replace or repair wiring.

Gauge Does Not Read Correctly

(a) Defective engine unit.
(b) Defective dash gauge.
(c) Defective constant-voltage regulator.

(a) Replace engine unit.
(b) Replace dash gauge.
(c) Replace regulator.

Telltale Light Stays Lit

(a) Engine overheating.
(b) Defective engine unit.
(c) Defective wiring.

(a) Isolate problem and correct.
(b) Replace engine unit.
(c) Repair or replace wiring as necessary.

Telltale Light Stays Off

(a) Burned out bulb.
(b) Defective engine unit.
(c) Defective fuse.

(a) Replace bulb.
(b) Replace engine unit.
(c) Replace fuse.

Symptoms and Possible Causes | Possible Remedies

Telltale Light Flashes On-Off

(a) Engine nearing overheat range.
(b) Defective engine unit.
(c) Defective wiring.

(a) Isolate problem and correct.
(b) Replace engine unit.
(c) Repair or replace wiring as necessary.

CHARGING INDICATOR TROUBLES AND REMEDIES

Charging Rate Too High

(a) Defective dash gauge or bent pointer.
(b) Voltage regulator improperly adjusted.

(a) Replace gauge or repair as necessary.
(b) Adjust regulator.

Charging Rate Too Low

(a) Defective dash gauge or improperly set.
(b) Voltage regulator improperly adjusted.
(c) Defective generator or alternator.

(a) Replace gauge or repair as necessary.
(b) Adjust regulator.

(c) Repair or replace generator or alternator as necessary.

Telltale Light Stays Lit

(a) Defective alternator or generator.
(b) Defective regulator.
(c) Improperly adjusted regulator.

(a) Repair or replace as necessary.
(b) Replace regulator.
(c) Adjust regulator.

Telltale Light Does Not Light

(a) Burned out bulb.
(b) Defective fuse (if equipped).
(c) Defective wiring.

(a) Replace bulb.
(b) Replace fuse.

(c) Repair or replace wiring.

INSTRUMENT PANEL

OIL PRESSURE INDICATOR TROUBLES AND REMEDIES

Symptoms and Possible Causes   *Possible Remedies*

Gauge Constantly Reads Too High Pressure

(a) Incorrect grade of oil in engine.
(b) Defective engine unit.
(c) Defective dash gauge.
(d) Defective constant-voltage regulator.

(a) Replace with proper grade of oil.
(b) Replace engine unit.
(c) Replace dash gauge.
(d) Replace regulator.

Gauge Reads Zero, or Constant Low Pressure

(a) Low oil level.
(b) Defective oil pump.
(c) Defective engine unit.
(d) Defective dash gauge.
(e) Incorrect grade of oil in engine.
(f) Defective constant-voltage regulator.
(g) Blown fuse, if equipped.

(a) Check and correct oil level.
(b) Repair or replace oil pump.
(c) Replace engine unit.
(d) Replace dash gauge.
(e) Replace with proper grade of oil.
(f) Replace regulator.
(g) Replace fuse.

Telltale Light Stays Lit

(a) Low oil level.
(b) Defective oil pump.
(c) Defective engine unit.
(d) Defective wiring.
(e) Incorrect grade of oil in engine.

(a) Check and correct oil level.
(b) Repair or replace oil pump.
(c) Replace engine unit.
(d) Correct or replace wiring.
(e) Replace with proper grade of oil.

Telltale Light Stays Off

(a) Burned out bulb.
(b) Blown fuse, if equipped.

(a) Replace bulb.
(b) Replace fuse.

Symptoms and Possible Causes *Possible Remedies*

(c) Defective engine unit.
(d) Defective wiring.

(c) Replace engine unit.
(d) Repair or replace wiring.

Telltale Light Flashes On-Off

(a) Low oil level.

(b) Defective engine unit.
(c) Defective wiring.

(a) Check and correct oil level.
(b) Replace engine unit.
(c) Repair or replace wiring.

CHAPTER 19

Tire Servicing

Servicing automobile tires includes not only the repair of punctures, blowouts, and other tire damage, but also includes wheel balancing, tire rotation and, in many cases, wheel alignment. Higher driving speeds, increased engine horsepower, and heavier loads make tire servicing more exacting today than in the past. Tire manufacturers have kept pace with the changes in driving habits and automotive design by constantly improving and changing their product. Thus, the methods of tire repair and service have also changed.

TIRE MAINTENANCE

Inflation

The weight of an automobile is supported by the air in the tires. Proper inflation is one of the most important facts in insuring satisfactory and long tire life. Fig. 1 shows the appearance of a tire in different stages of inflation on an automobile.

Too little air pressure allows an abnormal distortion of the tire body and causes the tread in the shoulder area to wipe and scuff on the road. Extra strain is placed on the cords in the tire which increases the chances for fabric injury and separation. Excessive flexing of the tire causes internal temperatures to increase which softens the rubber tread resulting in rapid wear.

Too much air pressure is equally bad. Overinflation reduces the tire distortion from normal and causes the tread to wear faster in the center portion than on the outside portion. Overinflated tires are also much more susceptible to fabric breaks.

The following rules will be helpful in preventing tire failure due to improper inflation.

1. Inflate tires to the pressure recommended by the manufacturer for the load and driving conditions to be encountered. Check the tire pressure at regular intervals and inflate only when the tire is cool.
2. Keep the valve caps screwed on finger tight.
3. Inspect and replace any damaged or worn valve cores or stems.
4. Check for slow leaks if air must be added at frequent and regular intervals.
   Repair all leaks promptly to prevent permanent tire damage that will result from under-inflation.
5. Check air pressure only while tire is cool. Do not bleed the tire (reduce the air pressure) when it is found the tire has a few pounds of extra pressure after being run. Bleeding will cause excessive flexing of the sidewalls resulting in abnormally high internal tire temperatures. Besides, the tires will be badly underinflated when they cool off.

Abnormal tire wear resulting from underinflation is shown in Fig. 2. Overinflation also causes uneven tread wear such as that shown in Fig. 3. Other types of abnormal tire wear will sometimes be encountered promptly before the tire is ruined. For example, excessive speed on curves and around corners will cause the condition illustrated in Fig. 4. A combination of underinflation and unbalance may cause a tire to wear similar to the one in Fig. 5. Incorrect wheel camber can cause the condition shown in Fig. 6, while misalignment resulted in the peculiar tread wear illustrated in Fig. 7.

TIRE TYPES

In recent years, several improved tire types, (Fig. 8), have been developed for the domestic car. They have been given the names "Bias Ply," "Bias Belted," and "Radial Ply." Cording used for "plies" in the early type tires were nylon or rayon. Cordings now used include nylon, rayon, fiberglass, and steel.

Cord layers of a bias-ply tire run from side to side at an alternate angle of about 35 degrees to the centerline. Bias-belted tires are similar except that additional plies of rayon, fiberglass, or steel cord encircle

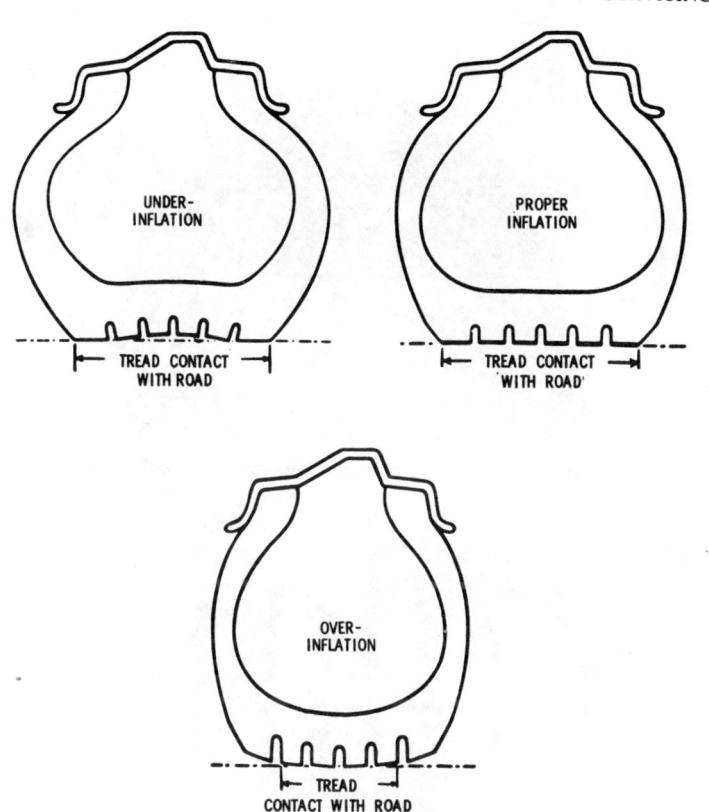

Fig. 1. Appearance of a tire in various stages of inflation.

the tire under the tread. The cord layers of a radial ply tire cross the tread at about 90 degrees. In addition, two or more belts encircle the tire directly under the tread.

Servicing or repairing the "new" type tires are generally the same as with the "older" type tire. There are, however, some precautions relating to their use (or misuse) on some cars.

The Rubber Manufacturers Association (RMA) recommends that the mixing of conventional bias tires with wide-tread bias belted or cross bias tires be done only in pairs, and only when mounted on the same axle. Tires should never be mixed in any other way. For example; Mount 2 in the front or 2 in the rear, never 2 of one type on one side and 2 of another type on the other side.

AUTOMOBILE GUIDE

Fig. 2. Abnormal tread wear due to underinflation.

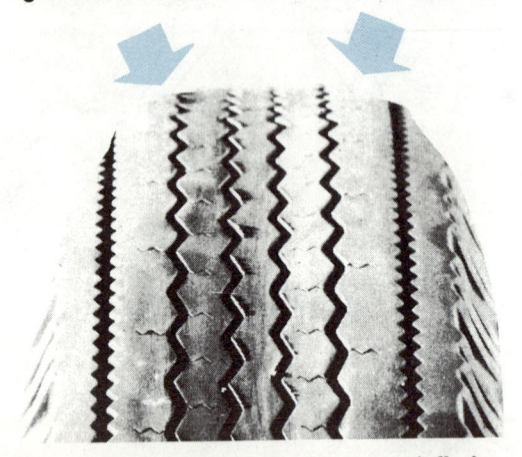

Fig. 3. Abnormal tread wear due to overinflation.

Radial ply tires should never be installed on older model cars. The older car suspension systems are "tuned" for conventional bias ply tires. The use of radial ply tires will cause a rougher ride, steering problems, and even (in some cases) brake chatter. In other words; The newer type tires are not compatible with the older type suspension systems.

Radial ply tires are not recommended (by the auto manufacturer) for use on some late model cars. If, however, radial ply tires are desired by the customer, tire sizes and wheel diameters must be changed in order to

TIRE SERVICING

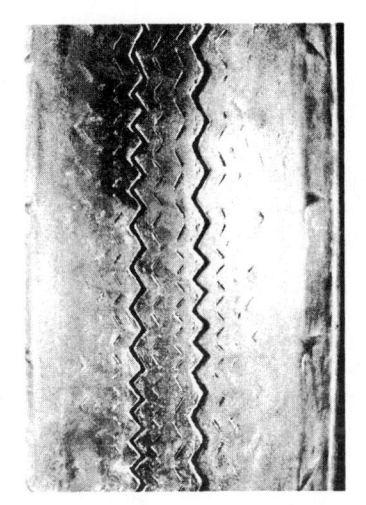

Fig. 4. Tire wear due to fast driving on curves and around corners.

Fig. 5. A single worn spot or a series of cuppings around the tire may be caused by underinflation and/or mechanical irregularities.

maintain proper ground clearance and load capacities that is equivalent to the original minimum specified tire specifications.

Radial ply tires should always be used in sets of 4 (or 5 for rotation), and under no circumstances should they be used only in the front. If snow tires are installed on the rear of a car equipped with radial ply

AUTOMOBILE GUIDE

Fig. 6. Tire wear as a result of incorrect camber.

Fig. 7. Feathered edges on the tread of this tire are caused by wheel misalignment.

tires, then bias belted or cross bias tires must be installed on the front. All tires should also be of the same width. Not insuring that tires are "matched" will result in oversteering and could very possible cause spins on wet or icy roads. The policy is: **Never mix radial ply tires with bias belted or cross bias tires.**

Tire Servicing

Fig. 8. Cord arrangement of three types of tire: (a) Bias Ply (b) Bias belted and (c) Radial ply.

There are many ply designs and types used on the modern tire. Two- and four-ply tires will generally be found on passenger cars. There may be some 6-ply tires found on the rear wheels of station wagons. A tire may have all 2-ply, all 4-ply, or have 2-ply sidewalls with a 4-ply tread. Two-ply tires, found as original equipment on many cars, have a rating equal to 4-ply tires. They are claimed by some to be superior. Both 2-ply and 4-ply tires meet safety requirements, so the choice is generally up to the driver.

Tire Wear Indicator

Original equipment car tires have a built-in tread wear indicator (Fig. 9) as an aid in determining when tires are nearing the end of their useful life, or are considered unsafe. These indicators are molded into the bottom of the tread grooves and will appear as bands across the tread.

When the depth of the tread is 1/16" or less (as indicated by the bands) there is an appreciable decrease in antiskid and traction properties. The majority of tire failures will occur during the last 10% of tire life. The tire tread wear indicators are now a part of many passenger car tires and should be, as a safety measure, noted to the customer whenever noticed while servicing the car.

Rotation

The tires on an automobile all wear differently, even under normal driving conditions, because each does a different kind of work. This is especially true of the front and rear tires. For example, the front tires: (1) withstand the forces exerted in steering the car; (2) hold the car straight on rough roads; (3) absorb bad driving habits and braking wear; and (4) are subject to misalignment and other mechanical irregularities. The rear wheels: (1) propel the car; (2) absorb "jack rabbit" starts and

AUTOMOBILE GUIDE

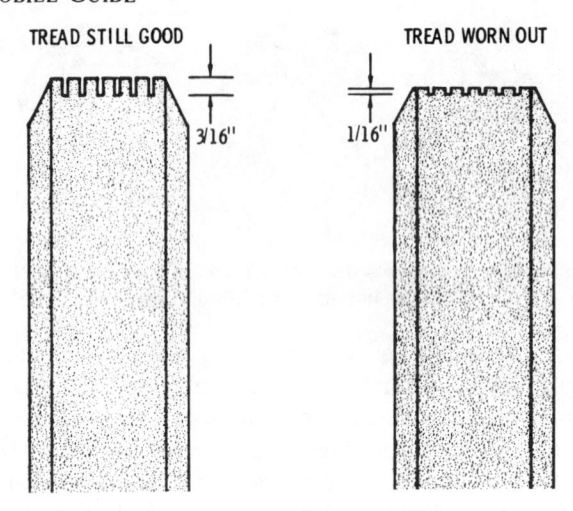

TREAD STILL GOOD 3/16"   TREAD WORN OUT 1/16"

Fig. 9. Tire tread wear indicator.

stops; (3) help hold the car on curves; (4) absorb the normal driving and stopping forces; (5) absorb spinning and slippage during starting and on curves; and (6) are subject to reverse camber and other mechanical irregularities.

To equalize the wear on all tires (including the spare) they should be rotated and run on different wheels at regular intervals as specified by the manufacturer. When tires wear unevenly (especially front tires) and are not rotated to different wheel positions, the uneven wear becomes worse and will cause such disturbances as shimmy, vibration, noise, thumps, bumps, and/or rough riding. Periodic rotation of the tires according to the diagram in Fig. 10 will materially lengthen tire life and contribute to greater driving comfort and safety.

Under normal operating conditions it is recommended that all tires, especially the wide tread and fiberglass belted type, should be rotated no later than every second oil change and should be in correct balance to obtain the most uniform tread wear. Tire inspection at every oil change is recommended if irregular tread wear is evident. Be sure to always adjust tire pressures after rotation, especially on station wagons. Follow rotation pattern shown in Fig. 9.

Uneven tire wear is often the cause of tire-induced noises which are attributed to rear axle gears, bearings, etc. Unnecessary work is often performed on other chassis components in an effort to correct tire noises.

TIRE REPAIR

Tubeless Tires

The repair of tubeless-type tires requires methods and techniques that differ somewhat from those used for tube-type tires. Sidewall and tread should be examined for damage or extraordinary wear. Look for leaks around the rim and valve stem. Discourage the repair of a puncture in a tire with:

1. Ply separation.
2. Broken or damaged bead.
3. Flex breaks.
4. Chafed fabric injuries.
5. Loose cords on the band ply or evidence of tire having been run flat.
6. Tread separation.
7. Wear below 1/16" depth in major grooves.
8. Any open liner splice which shows exposed fabric.
9. Cracks which extend into the tire fabric.
10. Any tire with a liner showing evidence of having been run underinflated or under excessive overload.

The following procedure should be followed for repairing a leak in a tubeless-type tire:

1. Locate leak by inflating the tire to its normal pressure and dip into a water tank. If a tank is not available, apply a soapy solution and look for bubbles or foam evidence of leaks.
2. Mark the location of the leak with chalk or crayon.
3. If the leak appears at the valve stem, or around the rim, mark both the tire and the rim. The tire will have to be removed from the rim if this type of leak is found. Procedure under **Demounting and Mounting** should be followed.
4. If the leak is found to be caused by a cut or puncture, one of the following methods of repair are recommended:

    a. *Hot Patch (Vulcanizing Patch) Method* — Demount the tire from the rim, and on the inside of the tire, locate the punctured area, then:

453

AUTOMOBILE GUIDE

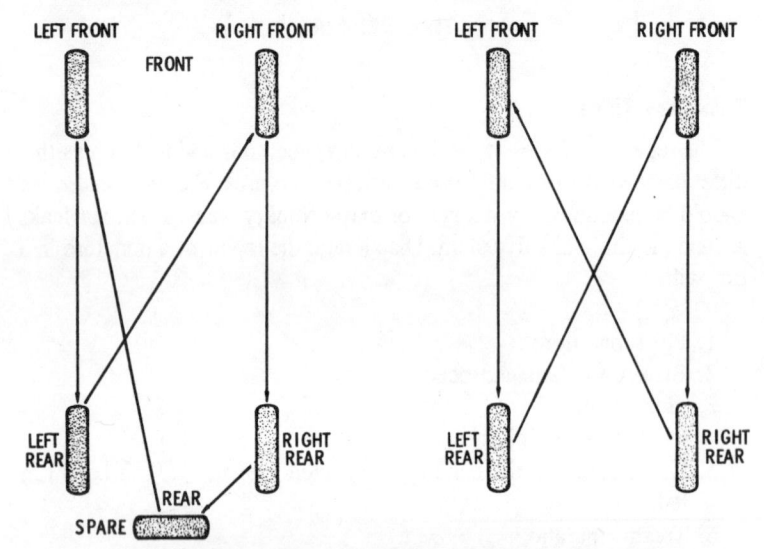

Fig. 10. Suggested rotation pattern to equalize tire wear.

(1) Using a clean cloth and an oil-free solvent, thoroughly clean a large area around the injury.
(2) Thoroughly buff an area 1/4" larger than patch. For large holes or tears, fill with vulcanizing rubber or rubber from the patch.
(3) Apply the patch. Remove backing from patch and center it over the injury. Do not touch raw rubber with fingers.
(4) Install clamp with spider over the patch. Hold with one hand while tightening with the other.
(5) Ignite fuelboard and keep the patch under clamp pressure until cool enough to touch the tire (about five minutes).
(6) The tire is now ready to remount and check for leaks.

b. *Chemical Patch or Boot Method* — Demount the tire from the rim, and on the inside of the tire, locate the punctured area, then:
(1) Remove puncturing object and mark area with crayon.
(2) Using a clean cloth and an oil-free solvent, clean a large area around the injury.

TIRE SERVICING

(3) Thoroughly buff an area 1/4" larger than the patch or boot. For large holes or tears, fill with vulcanizing rubber or rubber from patch.

(4) With the brush cap, apply cement to the buffed area. Work well into the pores of the rubber. Allow cement to dry thoroughly.

(5) Remove backing from patch or boot and center it over the damaged area. Do not touch raw rubber with fingers.

(6) Starting at the center and working toward the edges, stitch down the patch or boot.

(7) The tire is now ready to remount and check for leaks.

c. *Rubber Plug Method* — There are several types of rubber plugs available for tubeless tire repair. Follow the instructions furnished with the repair kit you are using. The following instructions are for the *Camel Perma Strip Patch* method:

(1) Remove puncturing object if still in the tire (tire is not dismounted from the rim).

(2) Fill tire with air to 30 psi. Dip probe into cement, insert it into injury and work up and down to lubricate injury.

(3) Grasp each end of patch. Stretch and roll center of patch into eye of needle. Remove protective covering from both sides of the patch, being careful not to touch raw rubber.

(4) Dip *Perma Strip Patch* into cement, making sure that all surfaces are coated.

(5) Insert patch slowly and steadily into injury, up to handle. Then turn needle 1/4 turn and remove.

(6) Without stretching the patch, cut it 1/8" from the tread.

(7) Inflate to proper pressure. Tire is now ready for service.

d. *Other Methods* — There are other methods of repairing tubeless tires and a variety of tubeless tire repair kits. Consult your tire supplier or automotive parts house for information on their availability.

Demounting and Mounting

Most wheels on the modern automobile now have reduced rimwell width and depth dimensions. This reduction was made necessary to provide for new safety features and new brake drum clearances. These new wheel construction features have made necessary some changes in standard demounting and mounting procedures. (Some tire-changing machines may need adapters to handle tires on the newer-type rims.) These new tire-changing methods may be used for older-type rims as well as for tube-type tires (except for insertion of the tube).

IMPORTANT: In both mounting and demounting, always start with the narrow bead ledge.

Demounting — Use this method for removing the tire from the rim:

1. Place the tire and rim on the tire changer or on the floor with the narrow bead ledge up, as shown in Fig. 11 and 12.
2. Brush on a liberal amount of approved rubber lubricant on the tire beads.
3. Actual removal of the tire must be done carefully. Do not attempt to force the bead into the drop-center portion of the rim at only one spot. Instead, "inch" the bead into the drop center a little at a time, working progressively around the tire to prevent damage to the bead area.

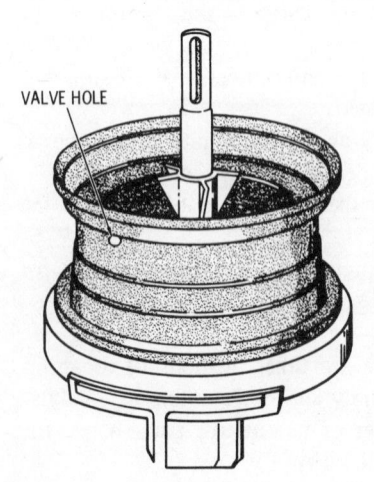

Fig. 11. Proper position of the rim is with the narrow ledge up. In this type, the valve is on the narrow ledge side.

TIRE SERVICING

Rim Preparation— After the tire is removed, the rim should be thoroughly examined and corrective measures taken, as necessary.

1. Examine the rim flanges for sharp dents. Remove any dents with a hammer (Fig. 13), after which the hammer dents must be smoothed out with a file. If it is impossible to straighten the rim in this manner, have a rim-and-wheel service dealer do the job.
2. Clean the rim flange and bead seats with emery cloth or coarse steel wool (Fig. 14) to remove all foreign matter. Use a wire brush to remove any rust. Pitted areas may be smoothed with a file.
3. Inspect the butt-weld for any grooves or high spots in the bead area. Grooves or high spots may be removed with a file (Fig. 15).

Valve Installation — After the rim has been prepared, the valve is installed as follows.

1. Clean the area around the valve hole, both inside and outside the rim, with steel wool (Fig. 16). Remove any burrs or rough metal with a file.
2. Install the valve. There are two types of tubeless-tire valves available — the metal clamp-in type and the rubber snap-in type.
    a. To install the metal clamp-in type (Fig. 17), place the larger rubber washer (oval or round, depending on the shape of the hole in the rim) over the valve base and insert the valve in

Fig. 12. Proper position of a rim in which the valve hole is on the wide ledge side. Note that the narrow ledge of the rim is up.

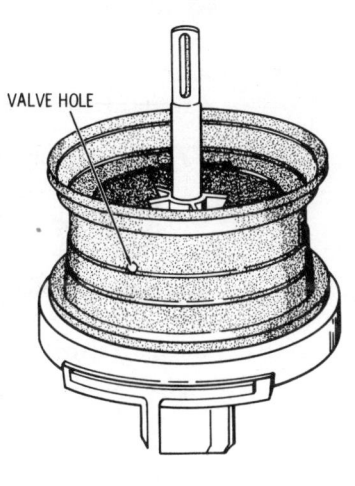

AUTOMOBILE GUIDE

the hole. Slip the smaller rubber washer over the valve stem, followed by the metal washer with the raised center facing up. Screw on the metal nut and tighten it until the small rubber washer is flush with the edge of the metal washer.

Fig. 13. Dents in the rim should be removed with a hammer.

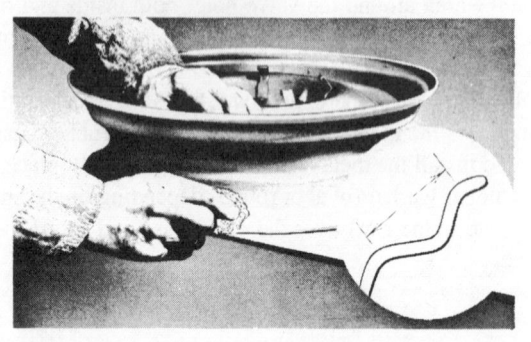

Fig. 14. The rim flange and bead seats must be clean. Steel wool or emery cloth is used in the area shown in the circle.

    b.   To install the rubber snap-in type of valve (Fig. 18), first lubricate the valve with rubber lubricant. Insert the valve through the valve hole in the rim. Apply pressure to the base of the valve with a valve inserting tool until the valve snaps into place and is firmly seated against the rim surface. If an inserting tool is not available, the valve can be inserted by using a valve fishing tool to pull the valve into position.

NOTE: Rubber snap-in valves should not be used in oval-shaped holes. Metal clamp-in valves should be used instead.

TIRE SERVICING

Fig. 15. Butt-weld grooves or high spots must be removed in the bead area to prevent air leaks.

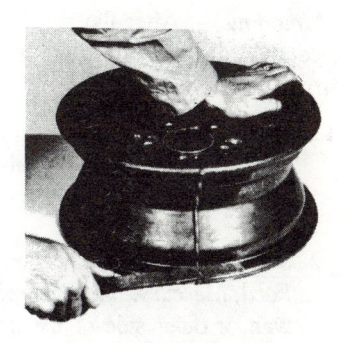

Fig. 16. The area around the valve hole must be cleaned both inside and outside the rim before installing the valve.

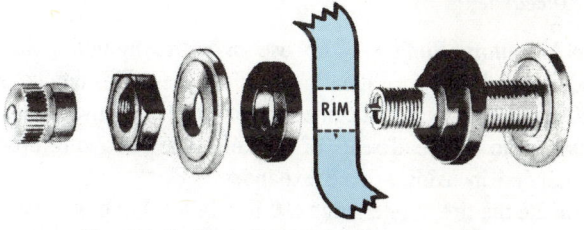

Fig. 17. A clamp-in metal valve assembly.

Fig. 18. A rubber snap-in type valve.

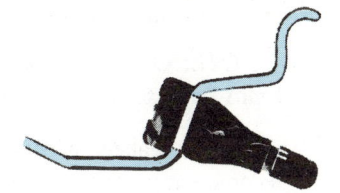

459

Automobile Guide

Mounting — After the rim is prepared and the proper valve is in place, the following procedure is recommended to mount the tire on the rim.

1. Lubricate the tire beads, rim flanges, and bead-ledge areas with a liberal amount of rubber lubricant. Properly lubricated beads will seat themselves quickly and easily with a minimum of air pressure.
2. Start the mounting procedure with the narrow ledge of the rim up. *Ford, Mercury, and Chevrolet* wheels require mounting the white wall or outer side of the tire first.
3. Inflate the tire to *no more than 40 lbs. pressure.* Use an extension gauge and clip-on chuck, as shown in Fig. 19, for safety. If 40 lbs. pressure will not seat the beads properly, deflate the tire, relubricating the beads, center the tire on the rim, and reinflate. After the beads have seated, deflate the tire to the recommended operating pressure.

CAUTION: If a tire is not centered properly on the rim, inflation beyond 40 lbs. of pressure may break a bead with an explosive force, resulting in serious injury or death. DO NOT STAND OVER THE TIRE WHILE INFLATING IT. Lock the wheel down when using a tire changing machine. Check the pressure frequently to be absolutely sure the 40-lb. limit is never exceeded.

Tire Mounting Band — The use of a tire mounting band (bead expander) is helpful when inflating tubeless tires. This device, shown in Fig. 20, contracts the tread center-line of the tire, which helps to force the beads onto the bead seats of the rim. The following procedure is recommended in using a bead expander.

1. Inflate the tire only enough (10 lbs. or less) to move the tire beads out to make contact with the bead seats on the rim. Remove the expander for safety.
2. Increase the air pressure as needed (up to 40 lbs.) to fully seat the tire beads on the rim (Fig. 21).

NOTE: On a safety or hump-type rims, make sure the tire beads have snapped over the hump and are fully seated.

3. Check for leakage and, if none, reduce the air pressure to the recommended level.

TIRE SERVICING

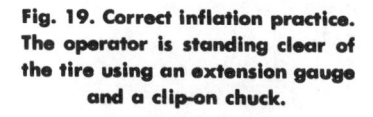

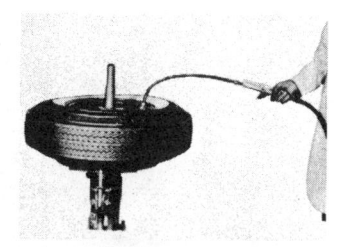

Fig. 19. Correct inflation practice. The operator is standing clear of the tire using an extension gauge and a clip-on chuck.

Fig. 20. A bead expander being used to help force the tire beads into their proper position.

461

Automobile Guide

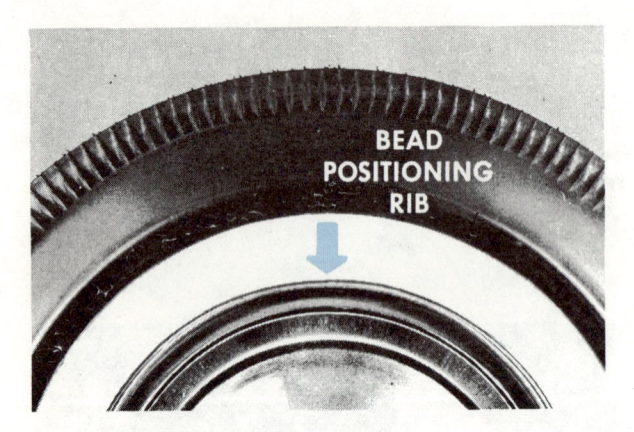

Fig. 21. When the beads are properly seated, the bead-positioning rib on the tire will be visible and evenly spaced around the entire rim.

WHEEL BALANCING

Modern suspension systems and higher driving speeds have made it necessary that the wheel and tire assembly be in balance if maximum driving and riding comfort, maximum safety, and maximum tire life are to be realized. Front wheels are more sensitive to an unbalanced condition than the rear wheels, but all four should be balanced to prolong tire life.

A wheel and tire assembly can be unbalanced in two ways — statically and dynamically. Static imbalance is indicated by an up-and-down hopping or pounding action, often called "wheel tramp." Dynamic imbalance will cause the wheel to wobble or shimmy. Either type of imbalance can exist without the other, although both types are usually present at the same time.

Wheel balance should be checked at regular intervals, and always after a tire has been repaired, retreaded, or recapped. Wheels which have not been balanced should be placed on the rear axle where an unbalanced condition does not affect the performance of the automobile as much as when they are placed on the front. Any unbalanced condition may be destructive and dangerous, reducing not only the life of the tires, but also the life of other vital parts of the automobile. Wheel balance is the equal distribution of the weight of the wheel, tire (and tube, if used), brake drum, and hub around the axis of rotation. The

Tire Servicing

complete wheel assembly should be balanced both statically and dynamically.

Static Balance

A wheel assembly may be considered to be in static balance when it will remain at rest in any position to which it is revolved on its axis. A wheel that is not statically balanced (Fig. 22) causes the tire to bounce at each revolution. The effect of static imbalance increases with the speed of the automobile.

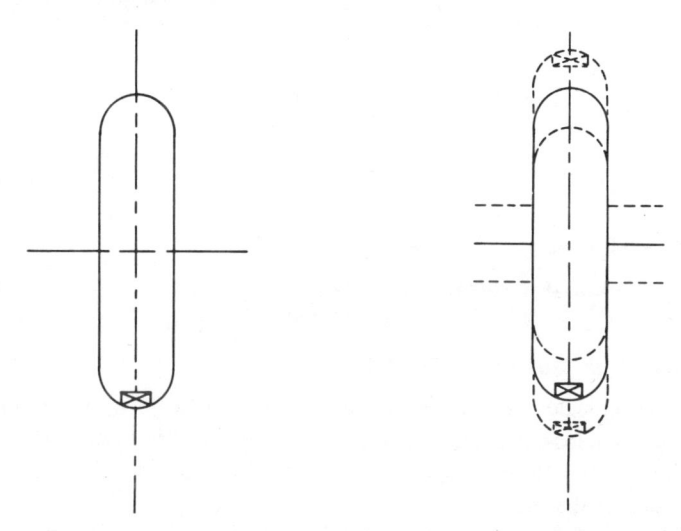

Fig. 22. A wheel assembly with an uneven distribution of weight at right angles to the axis of rotation is statically unbalanced. When the wheel is rotated, the heavy side causes the assembly to move up and down, producing "wheel tramp."

Dynamic Balance

Perfect static balance does not mean that the wheel assembly is in perfect balance. It must still be dynamically balanced.

A wheel that is dynamically out of balance does not have its weight distributed evenly in a plane perpendicular to its axis of rotation. This type of imbalance causes the wheels to vibrate rapidly from side to side as they rotate. The reason for this vibration, or wobble, is the attempt the wheel is making to align the heavy spots in a plane that is at right angles to the axis of rotation (Fig. 23). As the speed of the automobile

Automobile Guide

increases, the wobble increases, and steering becomes more difficult. This causes excessive wear of the tires, wheel bearings, king pins, ball joints, steering connections, etc.

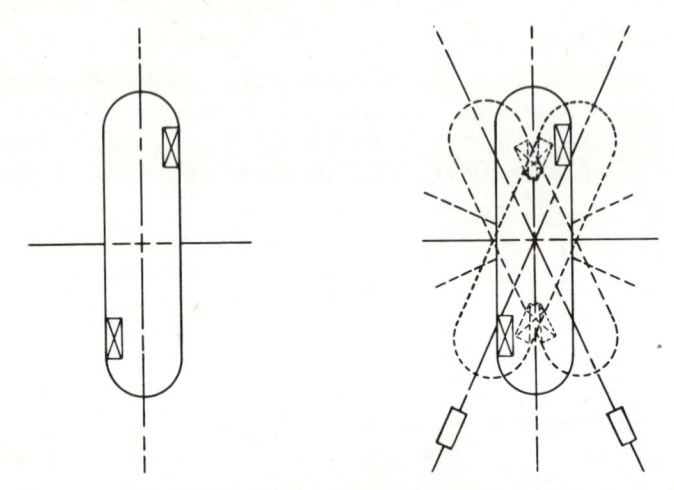

Fig. 23. A wheel assembly that is dynamically unbalanced will wobble when rotated.

Wheel Run-Out and Eccentricity

A wheel should always be checked for run-out (wobble) and eccentricity (roundness) before balancing the wheel and tire assembly. The run-out should not exceed 1/16" as measured on the side of the rim at the base of the tire.

Excessive run-out can be caused by a bent wheel, an improperly mounted wheel, and worn knuckle bearings or steering connections. These parts should always be checked and corrected whenever excessive run-out is encountered.

The wheel should also run concentric within 1/16" as measured on the tire-bead seat of the rim with the tire removed. This is a check of the roundness of the wheel. Any wheel that is out-of-round by more than the specified amount should be replaced with a good unit.

Balancing Methods

Static balancing can be carried out on a locally-made balancing fixture, if necessary. However, dynamic balancing requires special equipment to determine the amount and location of weights to correct the condition without disturbing the static balance. Several types of

TIRE SERVICING

wheel balancers are available for both static and dynamic balancing. One such model is shown in Fig. 24. The specific instructions provided

Courtesy Bear Div., Applied Power Inc.

Fig. 24. A wheel balancer for performing static and dynamic balancing of an automobile tire and wheel assembly.

by the manufacturer of the particular balancer being used should always be carefully followed.

Static Balance — If a special wheel balancer is not available, static balance can be corrected as follows:

1. Remove the wheel and hub from the spindle as a unit.
2. Clean all grease from the wheel bearings and races.
3. Clamp a clean spindle in a bench vise, or clean the spindle on the car carefully.
4. Mount the wheel on the spindle and adjust the bearings loosely so the wheel is just held in position and is practically frictionless.

Automobile Guide

5. Make sure the tire is inflated to the correct pressure.
6. Spin the wheel by hand and allow it to stop by itself. The wheel will stop with heavy side at the bottom.
7. Mark the heaviest point and also the lightest point, which will be diametrically opposite.
8. Install two wheel weights, one on the inside and one on the outside of the rim, and both opposite the heavy point on the wheel.
9. Move these two weights equally in opposite directions toward the heavy side until the wheel is in balance.
10. Repack the wheel bearings, and reinstall the wheel according to the manufacturer's specifications.

Static imbalance can be corrected by the use of special balancing equipment. Some of this equipment requires that the wheel be removed from the car. Other makes of wheel balances, however, allow correcting imbalance without the necessity of removing the wheel from the automobile. Fig. 25 shows a balancer being used to balance the wheel on the automobile.

Fig. 25. An on-the-car wheel balancer. Spinning at high speeds; the tire, wheel, and brake drum or disc is balanced as an assembly.

Tire Servicing

Dynamic Balance — Special balancing equipment is necessary to balance a wheel dynamically. The instructions of the equipment manufacturer should be carefully followed. The general procedure is as follows:

1. Attach the wheel to the balancer, or the balancer to the wheel, depending on which type of unit is being used. In either case the wheel assembly should be clean, with no accumulation of mud or grease.
2. Spin the wheel at high speed.
3. Determine the size of weights needed.
4. Determine the points on both sides of the rim where the weights must be attached and attach them.
5. Recheck the static balance to see that it hasn't been disturbed.

An unbalance of up to one ounce can usually be tolerated without affecting the driving and riding qualities of the automobile.

TIRE TROUBLES AND REMEDIES

Symptoms and Possible Causes   *Possible Remedies*

Rapid Tire Wear

(a) High speed driving.

(b) Over or under-inflation.

(c) Rapid starts and/or stops.
(d) Front end misaligned.

(e) Tire(s) out of balance.
(f) Vehicle overloaded.

(g) Unfavorable road conditions; sand, gravel, etc.

(a) Correct driving habits if speed excessive (tires normally wear faster at high speeds).

(b) Correct as necessary for proper inflation.

(c) Correct driving habits.
(d) Repair and align as necessary.

(e) Balance tire(s).
(f) Reduce load or replace tires with those of a higher load rating.

(g) Change route, if possible, for better (surfaced) roads.

467

AUTOMOBILE GUIDE

Symptoms and Possible Causes   *Possible Remedies*

"Spotty" or "Cupping" Tire Wear

(a) Front-end misaligned.
(b) Tire(s) underinflated.
(c) Tire(s) out of balance.

(a) Repair and align as necessary.
(b) Inflate to proper pressure.
(c) Balance tire(s).

CHAPTER 20

Standard and Power Brakes, Drum and Disc Types

No other part of an automobile, except perhaps the steering system, contributes more to safe operation than the brakes. The brakes must not only be able to stop a moving automobile, regardless of speed, they must also stop it in the shortest distance possible.

Because the brakes are expected to decelerate an automobile at a faster rate than the engine can accelerate it, the brakes must be able to control a greater amount of power than that developed by the engine. For this reason, the brakes on a modern high-powered automobile must be well designed and kept in top-notch operating condition by regular inspection, adjustment, and repair.

Hydraulic brakes are used on all domestic cars and trucks. Power-assisted brake systems are standard on many "luxury" cars, and available as optional equipment on most all other models. Self-adjusting brakes are "standard equipment" on all cars manufactured during the past several years.

Two types of brakes are found on cars; drum-type and disc-type. Cars are equipped with drum-type brakes in front and rear; disc brakes in front with drum brakes in rear; or disc brakes in front and rear. Both of these types of brakes will be covered in this chapter.

DRUM TYPE

All drum type brakes are generally the same type of brake assembly, known as the internal-expanding type. An example of this type of brake

AUTOMOBILE GUIDE

is shown in Fig. 1. Though typical of the internal expanding type, this particular unit is not self-adjusting. Notice the hydraulic cylinder which furnishes the power to move the brake shoes outward until they contact the brake drum.

A self-adjusting brake assembly is pictured in Fig. 2. As the brake linings wear, the brake shoes must travel a greater distance to come in contact with the brake drum. When this distance exceeds a predetermined amount, and the car is driven in reverse and the brakes applied, the automatic adjusting lever engages the star wheel and turns it as the brakes are released. This action tightens the brakes and will continue each time the car travels in reverse, until the adjusting lever no longer

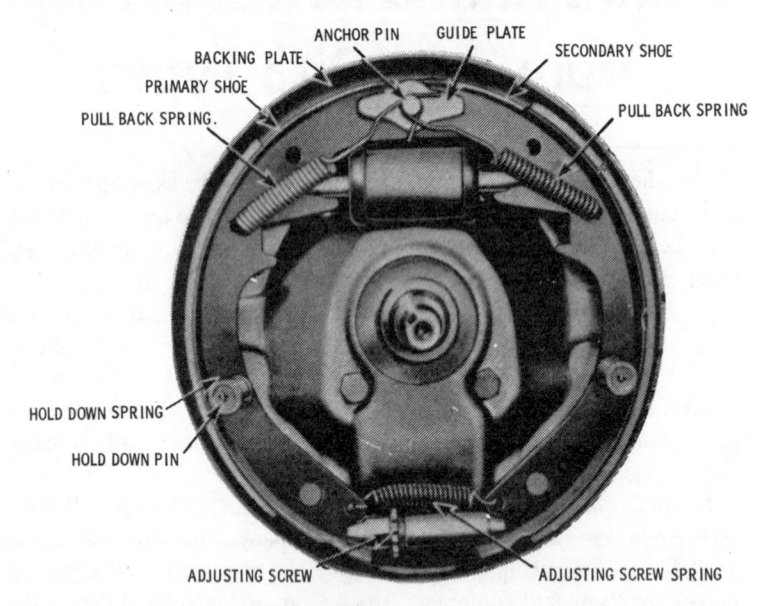

Fig. 1. A typical brake assembly of the internal-expanding type.

moves far enough to engage the next tooth on the star wheel. Thus, the brakes are automatically adjusted whenever the car is backed up and the brakes applied.

DISC TYPE

Disc-type brakes are standard equipment on all four wheels on the *Corvette,* and are also standard equipment on the front wheels of many

470

Standard and Power Brakes, Drum and Disc Types

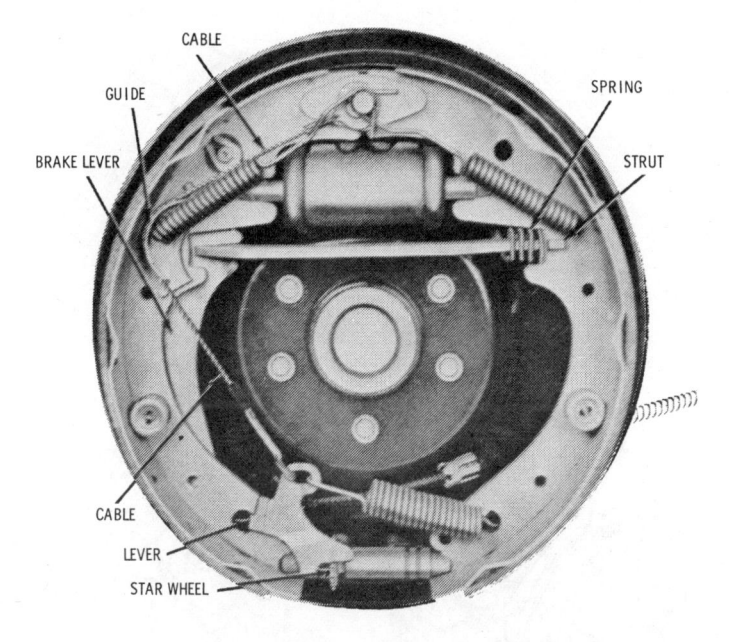

Courtesy Dodge Div., Chrysler Motors Corp.

Fig. 2. An example of a self-adjusting brake assembly.

cars equipped with the power-brake option. Disc-type brakes are also optional equipment for most makes and models of cars.

Fig. 3 shows 5 typical disc brake assemblies that are used on various domestic passenger cars. Each assembly consists of a rotating disc, a caliper, and 2 shoe and lining assemblies. The floating-caliper type caliper contains 1 cylinder and 1 piston, while the other types contain 4 hydraulic cylinders and 4 piston assemblies.

A sectional view of a typical disc brake assembly is shown in Fig. 4. It consists of a fixed caliper, splash shield, mounting bracket, and rotating disc. A seal and dust boot are provided on each piston to protect it from foreign matter. A guide pin extends through each caliper half and both shoes. This holds the shoes and linings in position on the caliper. Machined surfaces within the caliper prevents the shoe and lining assembly from rotating with the brake disc when pressure is applied.

The cast iron braking disc has cooling fins (or air louvers) that are integrally cast between the two machined braking surfaces. When the

AUTOMOBILE GUIDE

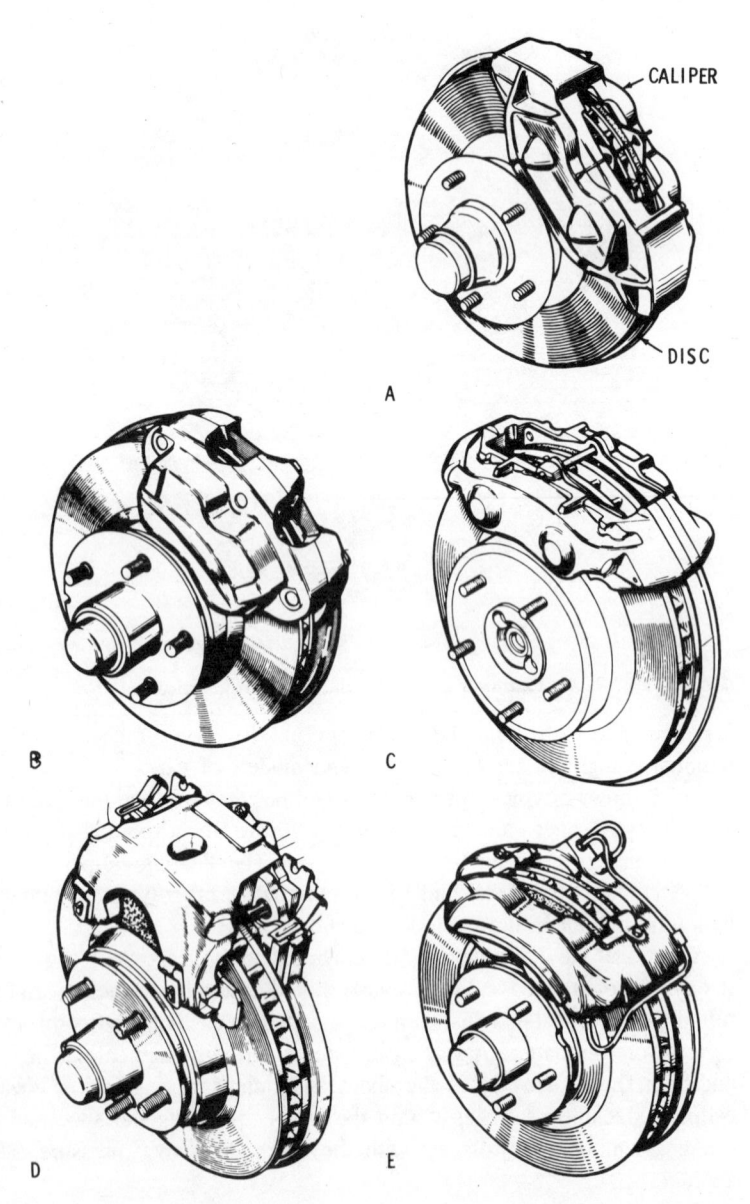

Fig. 3. Typical disc brake types; (A) BUDD design; (B) BENDIX; (C) DELCO-MORAINE: (D) Floating caliper; (E) KELSEY-HAYES.

Standard and Power Brakes, Drum and Disc Types

Fig. 4. Sectional veiw of a disc brake assembly.

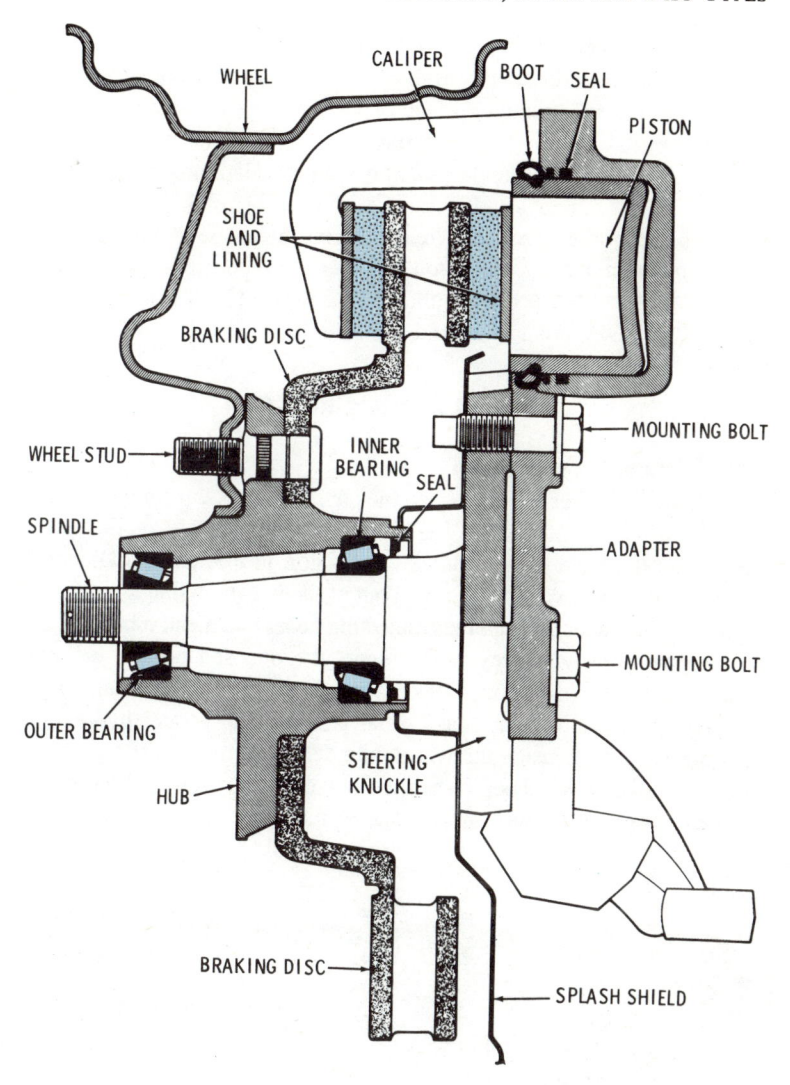

Courtesy Chrysler Motors Corp.

wheel is in motion, the rotation of the disc cooling fins creates air circulation between the braking surfaces. This allows for the disc to stay cool and prolongs the life of the lining. A shield is provided on the inboard side of the braking disc to protect it from road splash by the tire.

473

Automobile Guide

As the brake pedal is depressed, hydraulic pressure is applied against the piston(s). This force is transmitted to the inboard brake shoe lining and to the inboard braking surface of the disc. As the force increases against the disc from the inner lining, the caliper assembly moves inboard, sliding on the guide pins, providing a clamping force on the disc.

When the brake pressure is released, the piston seal returns to its normal position, pulling the piston back to released position, while the 2 positioners force the caliper outboard to create a slight running clearance between the outer shoe and the disc.

DRUM BRAKE CIRCUIT

The Hydraulic System

Automobile brakes are controlled by a hydraulic system similar to the one shown in diagram form in Fig. 5. When the brakes are applied, the force from the brake pedal operates the piston in the master cylinder. This action forces the hydraulic fluid out of the master cylinder and into each wheel cylinder through the connecting hoses and metal tubing. The fluid entering the wheel cylinders forces the opposed pistons farther apart, thus moving the brake shoes outward against the brake drums. As the pressure applied to the brake pedal is increased, greater hydraulic pressure is built up inside the wheel cylinders, and they exert a greater pressure to the brake shoes. When the brake pedal is released, springs on the brake shoes return the pistons in the wheel cylinders to their normal position, forcing the hydraulic brake fluid back into the master cylinder.

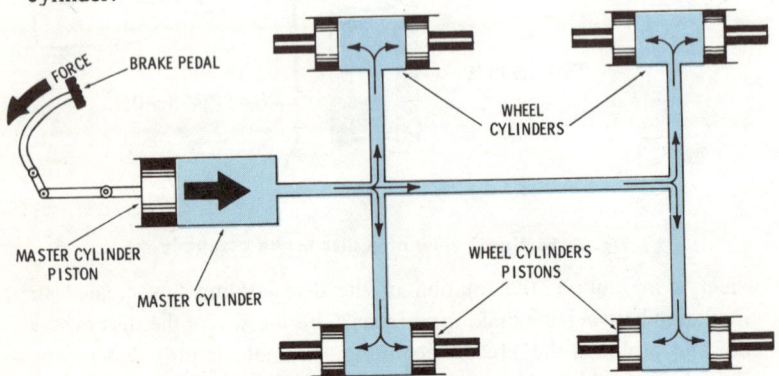

Fig. 5. Diagram of a hydraulic brake system.

Standard and Power Brakes, Drum and Disc Types

Parking Brakes

The parking brake, more commonly called "emergency brakes," are independent of the regular brake system. The parking brake system shown in Fig. 6, is mechanically operated. The parking brakes on most cars utilize the brake shoes in the rear brake assembly, actuating them by means of a cable connected to the parking-brake lever through a mechanical linkage. On some *Chrysler*-built cars, however, a completely independent parking-brake system attached to the rear of the transmission will be found. With this type of parking brake, if the car has an automatic transmission, the brake assembly will be of the internal-expanding type, while with a manual transmission, an external-contracting type is used.

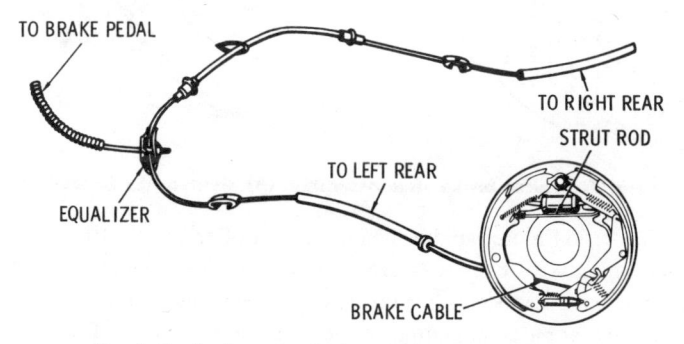

Fig. 6. Typical mechanical parking brake system.

Brake Shoes

Brake shoes may be made of malleable iron, cast steel, drop-forged steel, pressed steel, or cast aluminum. Most passenger automobiles have brake shoes made of steel because of ease and cost of manufacture. In addition, steel shoes expand at about the same rate as the brake drums when heat is generated by braking drum and brake shoe.

A friction lining is riveted or bonded to the face of the brake shoe, Fig. 7, and is used to make contact with the brake drum to provide braking action. Bonded linings (Fig. 7b) are secured to the shoe with a special cement and then baked to set the cement.

Brake Drums

Brake drums are usually made of pressed steel, cast iron, or a combination of the two. Cast iron drums dissipate the heat generated by

Automobile Guide

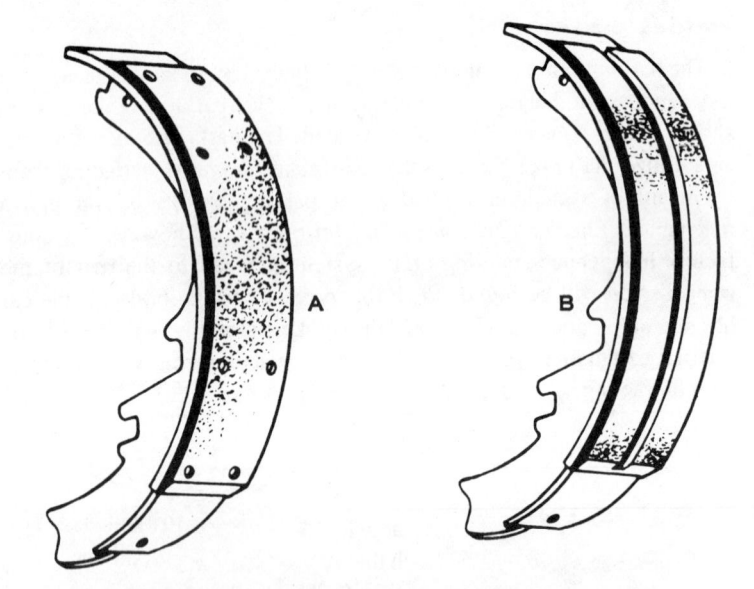

Fig. 7. Typical brake shoe assembly; (A) Riveted; (B) Bonded.

braking action more rapidly than steel, and offer greater friction to the brake lining. However, cast iron drums having sufficient strength are much heavier than steel. For this reason, many automobiles have brake drums that are a combination of the two types of metal. Brake drums that are a combination of cast iron and cast aluminum are sometimes used.

Some automobiles, especially the newer models having higher horsepower engines, have cooling ribs or fins around the brake drum. These ribs or fins offer a greater surface area to the surrounding air, thus allowing the heat generated by braking action to be dissipated more rapidly. Some cars even have slots cut in the wheel covers in such a way as to force air over the surface of the brake drums to increase the cooling effect.

MAINTENANCE AND ADJUSTMENTS

When servicing any brake system, it is very important that absolute cleanliness be observed. Any foreign matter that enters the hydraulic system may clog the lines, ruin the rubber cups in the master and wheel cylinders, cause inefficient operation, or even cause complete failure of

Standard and Power Brakes, Drum and Disc Types

the braking system. Dirt or grease on a brake lining may cause that brake to grab when the brakes are first applied, and then fade as heavier brake application is made.

Hydraulic System

Each make and model of automobile may require certain specific procedures for the maintenance and adjustment of the hydraulic system. When such adjustment or maintenance is necessary, the manufacturer's service manual should be referred to for the proper procedure. The following instructions, however, will be adequate in the majority of cases.

Hydraulic Brake Fluid — Only an approved brake fluid should be used when it is necessary to add fluid or to bleed the brakes. An approved fluid will give satisfactory performance at any atmospheric temperature that will be encountered. In addition, it will have a high boiling point to prevent evaporation and vapor lock, and will remain fluid at the lowest temperature at which the car will be driven. Its chemical composition will be such that it will not deteriorate the rubber gaskets, pistons, valves, and lines in the braking system.

To determine if the brake fluid is contaminated with mineral oil, the following tests can be made.

1. Drain a small amount of the suspected brake fluid into a small glass jar. If the fluid separates into two distinct layers, mineral oil is present.
2. Add 1 part of water to 2 parts of the contents and shake. If the contents turn milky, oil may be present. If the contents remain clear, no oil is present. Discard any fluid drained or bled from the system. Do not reuse, as such fluid may contain particles of dirt or other contamination that might be harmful to the brake system.

In the event that improper fluid has been added to the system, the following procedure will be necessary.

1. Drain the entire system and flush with 90 percent pure methanol or a suitable brake system cleaning fluid.
2. Replace all rubber parts of the system, including brake hoses.
3. Refill the brake system with an approved hydraulic brake fluid.
4. Bleed the system according to the manufacturer's instructions, or the instructions as follows.

Bleeding the Hydraulic System — The hydraulic brake system of an automobile must be bled whenever a pipe line or any part of the system has been disconnected, whenever a leak has allowed air to enter the system or whenever the fluid level in the master cylinder has become too low. The system must be absolutely free of air at all times.

The hydraulic system can be bled manually, or by using pressure bleeding equipment. To bleed the system, proceed as follows:

1. To bleed the brakes manually, check the fluid level in the master-cylinder reservoir and, if necessary, add approved fluid. KEEP THE RESERVOIR AT LEAST HALF FULL DURING THE BLEEDING OPERATION. To bleed the brakes with pressure equipment (Fig. 8), connect the pressure tank to the master cylinder reservoir and increase the pressure to the point recommended by the manufacturer.
2. Attach a bleeder tube to the bleeder valve of the wheel to be bled. (Fig 9). The bleeder tube must be kept submerged in a clean container partially filled with approved brake fluid throughout the entire bleeding operation.

NOTE: *Most car manufacturers specify the order in which the wheel cylinders should be bled. Check the service manual for the correct order. Usually, the wheel farthest from the master cylinder is checked first.*

3. Unscrew the bleeder valve approximately three-quarters of a turn with a suitable wrench. If pressure equipment is used, watch the flow of liquid from the bleeder tube. When air bubbles stop appearing, close the bleeder valve.

    If the brakes are being bled manually, the brake pedal must be pumped during this operation to force the fluid from the bleeder hose. To do this, open the bleeder valve, fully depress the brake pedal, and then close the valve. Slowly release the pedal until it has returned to its normal position. Continue operating the pedal and opening and closing the bleeder valve until all air bubbles stop emerging from the bleeder tube. (This operation, of course, calls for the services of two men, one to operate the brake pedal on signal, and the other to open and close the bleeder valve.)
4. Close the bleeder valve and remove the bleeder tube.

Standard and Power Brakes, Drum and Disc Types

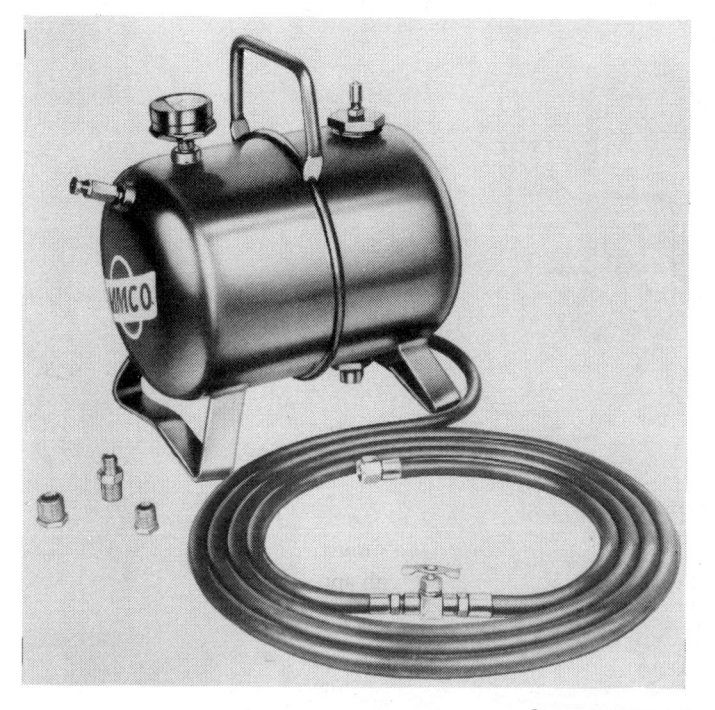

Courtesy AMMCO Tools Corp.

Fig. 8. Typical pressure brake bleeder.

5. Repeat the preceding steps on the remaining wheel cylinders, making sure the fluid in the master cylinder is maintained at the proper level at all times.
6. After the bleeding operation is complete, check the fluid level in the master cylinder and replenish if necessary.
7. Discard all brake fluid removed from the system by the bleeding operation. *Do not reuse.*

MASTER CYLINDER

The purpose of the master cylinder is to transmit mechanical pressure (when the brake pedal is depressed) through the brake lines as a hydraulic pressure to each individual wheel cylinder. The operating principles of most master cylinders are similar though construction

Automobile Guide

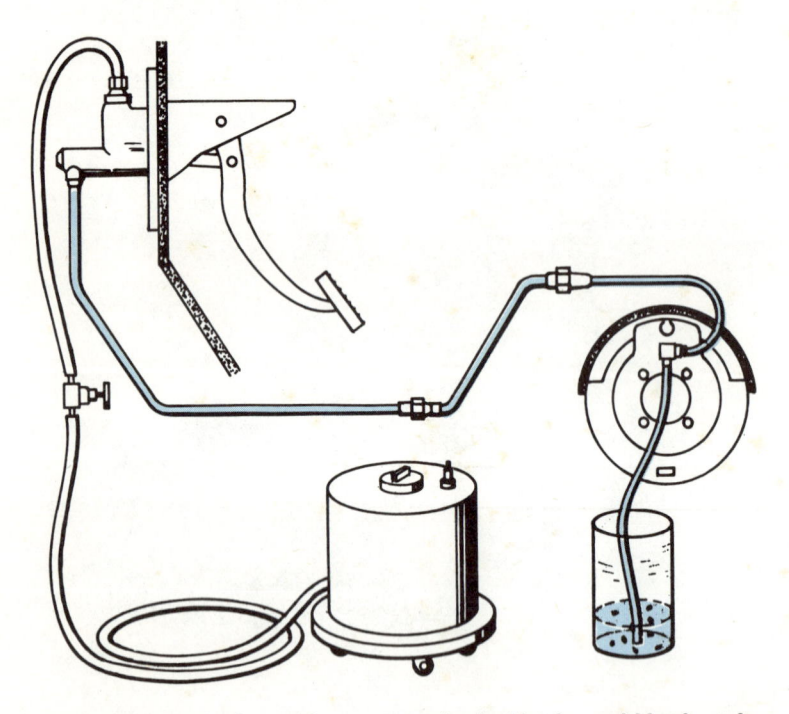

Fig. 9. Bleeding brakes with a pressure brake bleeder and bleeder tube.

features and appearance may differ, depending on the make and model of the car. Earlier model cars used a standard single master cylinder, however, late model cars are all equipped with a dual master cylinder.

Single Master Cylinder

The single master-cylinder, shown in Fig. 10, was used in cars until recent years. As shown in Fig. 11, its purpose was to supply a hydraulic pressure to each of the 4 wheels for slowing or stopping the car. These pressures may be as high as 800 psi to the wheel cylinders, which actually requires very little effort on the part of the driver. The use of power brakes makes the effort of stopping a car almost nil.

Dual Master Cylinders

The dual master cylinder is used on all late model cars. These cars have a split brake system. That is, the front brakes are totally indepen-

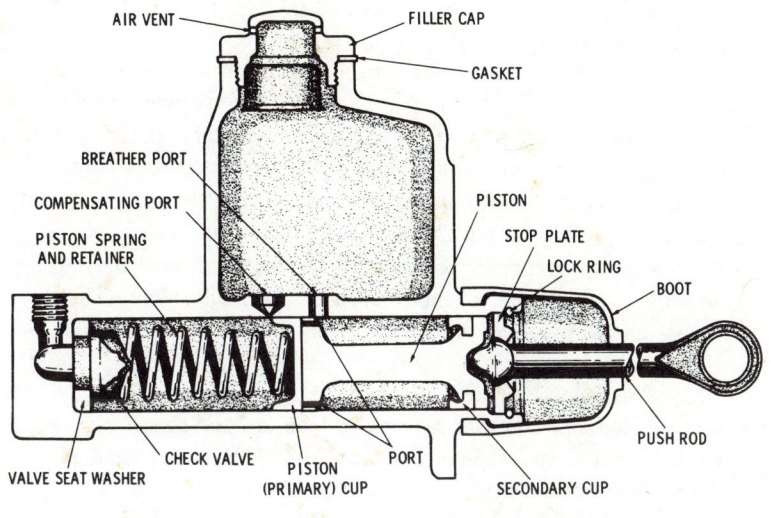

Standard and Power Brakes, Drum and Disc Types

Fig. 10. Cross-section of a typical master cylinder.

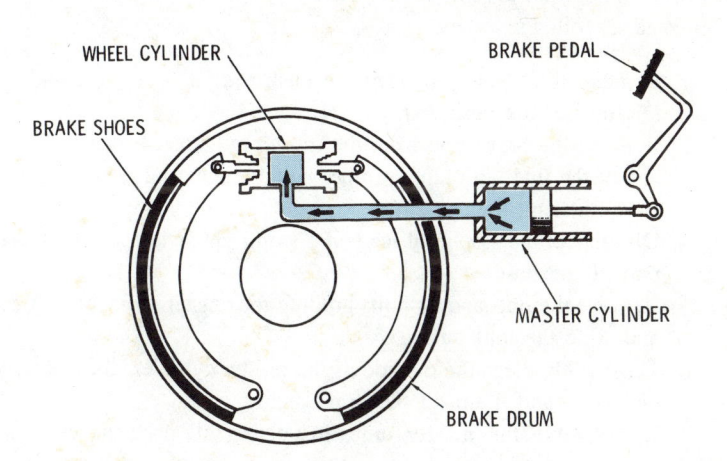

Fig. 11. Hydraulic pressure is applied to the wheel cylinder by the master cylinder when the brake pedal is depressed.

dent from the rear brakes. If a wheel cylinder or brake line should fail in either the front or rear system the other system will still function allowing the driver to still be able to bring the car to a controlled stop — though it will take longer to do so.

The dual master cylinder, as shown in Fig. 12, has two entirely separate reservoirs and outlets in a common body casting. The front reservoir and outlet is connected to the front wheel brakes, while the rear reservoir and outlet is connected to the rear wheel brakes. A common filler cap is usually found on the dual master cylinder, allowing inspection of the fluid level in both reservoirs at the same time.

An incorrectly adjusted brake pedal can keep the master cylinder piston from fully returning to its released position, which may cause brake drag or lock up. Brake drag may also be caused by improper adjustment of the brake shoes during shoe adjustment. Therefore, always check the free pedal movement before making brake shoe adjustments.

Misadjustment, binding, or lack of lubrication of the master cylinder push rod can also cause brake drag or lock up, and should be checked before making brake shoe adjustment. The push rod on some automobiles cannot be adjusted, so binding or lack of lubrication will be the only thing that will prevent the foot pedal (and master cylinder piston) from returning to its normal position.

If it is necessary to remove the master cylinder for repair or overhaul, proceed as follows:

1. Remove the clevis pin from the push rod.
2. Disconnect the push rod.
3. Remove the brake line from the master cylinder. Cover the open end of the line with tape or other suitable material to prevent dirt from entering the system.
4. Disconnect the stop light leads if a stop light switch is an integral part of the unit.
5. Remove the nuts and/or bolts holding the master cylinder in place and slide the unit out.
6. Thoroughly clean the outside of the master cylinder, then remove the cover and drain all the brake fluid.
7. Disassemble the master unit, inspecting all parts as they are removed.
8. Inspect the piston for scoring and corrosion. If either condition is excessive, replace with a new piston. New piston cups and valve assembly should be used with a new piston.
9. Light scratches or slight corrosion on the cylinder walls can usually be removed by cleaning carefully with crocus cloth. *Never use emery cloth.* Heavier scratches or scoring can some-

Standard and Power Brakes, Drum and Disc Types

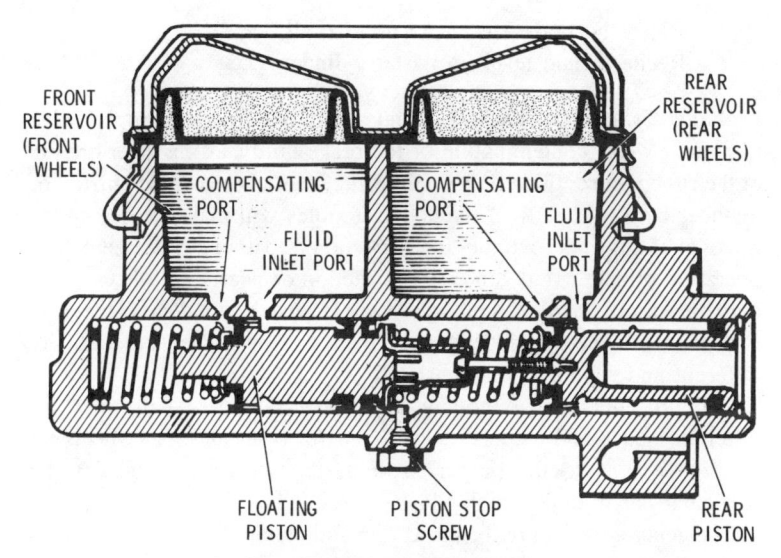

Fig. 12. Dual master cylinder.

times be removed by honing, although some manufacturers do not recommend this practice. If a cylinder is honed, the bore must not be increased by more than a specified amount (see manufacturer's maintenance manual). Honing will often cause rapid wear of the piston and rubber cups, and an increased pedal pressure necessary to apply the brakes.

10. Use extreme care in cleaning the master cylinder after reconditioning. Remove all dirt, dust, and grit by flushing with alcohol. *(CAUTION: Do not use antifreeze-type alcohol, gasoline, kerosene, or any other cleaning fluid that might contain even a trace of oil.)* Wipe dry with a clean lintless cloth and reflush with alcohol. Dry the assembly with compressed air, and flush with clean, approved brake fluid. (Make sure the compensator port in the master cylinder is open.)
11. Immerse the piston, cups, and valve assembly in approved brake fluid before assembly.
12. Reassemble the master cylinder and install it. Make sure all connections are tight and the push rod (if adjustable) is adjusted properly.
13. Fill the master cylinder reservoir to the required level with approved brake fluid.

AUTOMOBILE GUIDE

Bleed the brake system to remove all air.
Recheck fluid level in master cylinder.

Wheel Cylinders—A wheel cylinder may not function properly due to natural wear, contamination of the brake fluid causing deterioration of the rubber cups, broken or weak spring, scored or corroded piston or cylinder bore, etc. Any of the above troubles will make necessary the removal of the wheel cylinder for inspection, repair or replacement. The operating principle and general construction of nearly all wheel cylinders are similar. An example of a typical wheel cylinder is shown in Fig. 13. The wheel cylinder for the front and rear wheels are usually different and cannot be interchanged.

The procedure for removing the wheel cylinders will vary for different makes and models of cars, and for front and rear wheels. If doubt exists as to the proper method, the service manual for the particular car in question should be consulted.

The general procedure for inspection and repair of wheel cylinders is as follows.

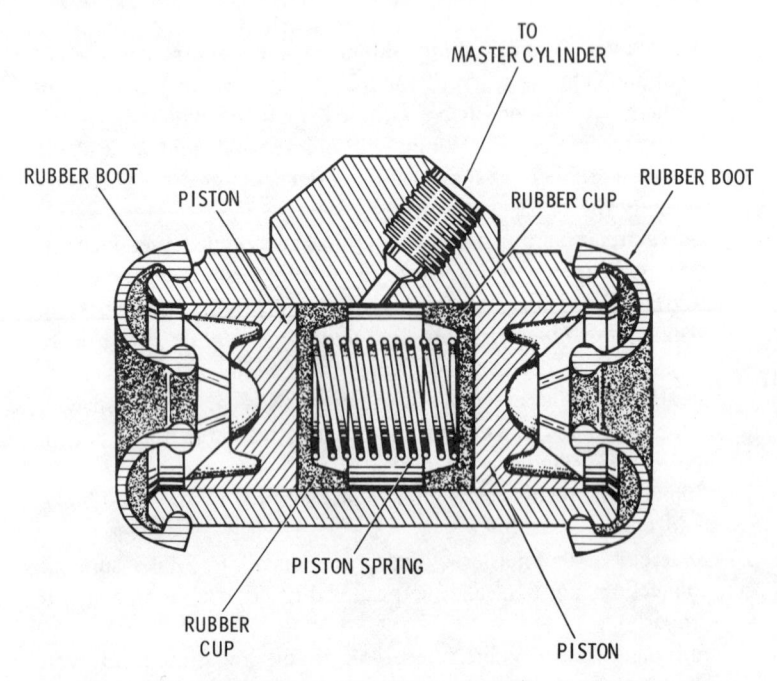

Fig. 13. Sectional view of a typical wheel cylinder.

484

Standard and Power Brakes, Drum and Disc Types

1. Remove the brake drum.
2. Remove the brake shoe pull-back spring. (On some cars, it is also necessary to remove the brake shoes. Consult the service manual for specific instructions.)
3. Disconnect the brake line or hose from the wheel cylinder. Tape the end of the line to prevent entrance of dirt.
4. Remove the wheel cylinder retaining bolts and lift the wheel cylinder free.
5. Remove the links and rubber boots from the cylinder.
6. Remove the pistons, cups, expanders, and spring.
7. Wash all metal parts in alcohol or brake flushing fluid and blow out all passages with compressed air.
8. Inspect the cups for swelling or distortion. If the cups are swollen, contamination of the brake fluid should be suspected, and the entire hydraulic system should be flushed, all rubber parts in the system should be inspected, including the flexible brake hose. Replace any damaged parts.
9. Inspect the wheel cylinder bore for scratches, scoring, rust, pits, or etches. Any such condition should be corrected if possible. Light scratches, scoring, or corrosion can sometimes be removed by using crocus cloth or by honing. *(NOTE: Some manufacturers recommend replacement instead of any attempt to polish or hone the cylinder bore.)* If honing is performed, the cylinder bore should not be increased beyond the limits specified by the manufacturer. If the diameter should be increased beyond the specified limit the entire wheel cylinder assembly should be replaced. A wheel cylinder hone is shown in Fig. 14.

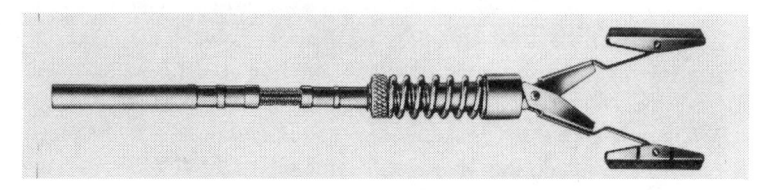

Courtesy AMMCO Tools Corp.

Fig. 14. A wheel cylinder hone.

10. Check the fit of the pistons in the cylinder bore as shown in Fig. 15. The clearance should be within manufacturer's specifications, usually as follows: Cylinders under one-inch in diameter by more than .005 inch. Cylinders one-inch in diameter and over must not

exceed the standard diameter by more than .007 inch. Replace the cylinder if the clearance is not within the specified limits.

11. Shake the excess cleaning fluid from the wheel cylinder and lubricate the bore with approved brake fluid. *(NOTE: Some manufacturers recommend assembling the wheel cylinder without lubricating any of the parts with brake fluid. Consult the service manual to determine if this is true for the car being serviced.)*
12. Install the spring, expanders, cups, and pistons in the cylinder bore.
13. Install the boots and links.
14. Install the assembly on the wheel.
15. After the installation is complete, bleed the system to remove any air.

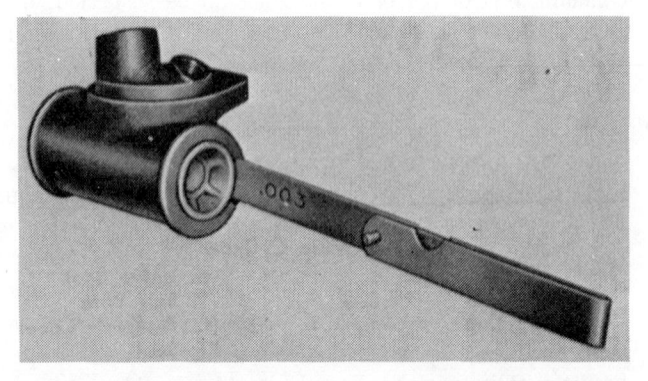

Fig. 15. Checking the piston clearance in a wheel cylinder.

Brake Lines and Hoses— Brakelines and hoses are made of special material to withstand the high pressure that exists when the brakes are applied. Only approved line and hose should be used for replacement. *Do not use copper tubing as a replacement.*

When replacing metal brake tubing, it is important to use the proper flaring tool to flare the ends of the tubing to fit the compression couplings. The tubing should be double flared with a suitable flaring tool, such as the one shown in Fig. 16. This type of tool produces a double-lap flare on the end of the tube that is necessary for a strong and leakproof joint, as shown in Fig. 17.

Proper bending tools should be used to bend the tubing to fit the underbody or rear axle contours. If an attempt is made to bend the tubing without tools (especially short-radius bends), there is danger of

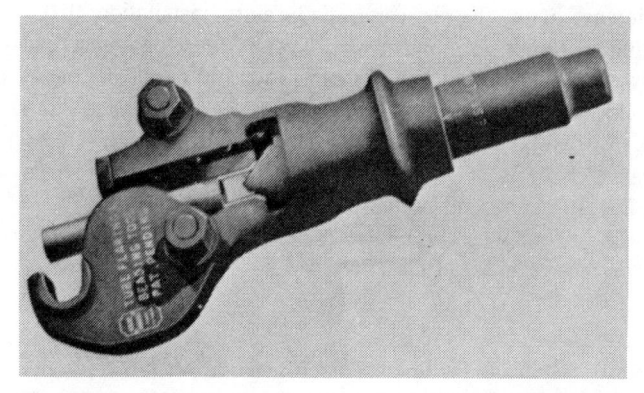

Fig. 16. A double-flaring tool used to flare the ends of hydraulic brake lines.

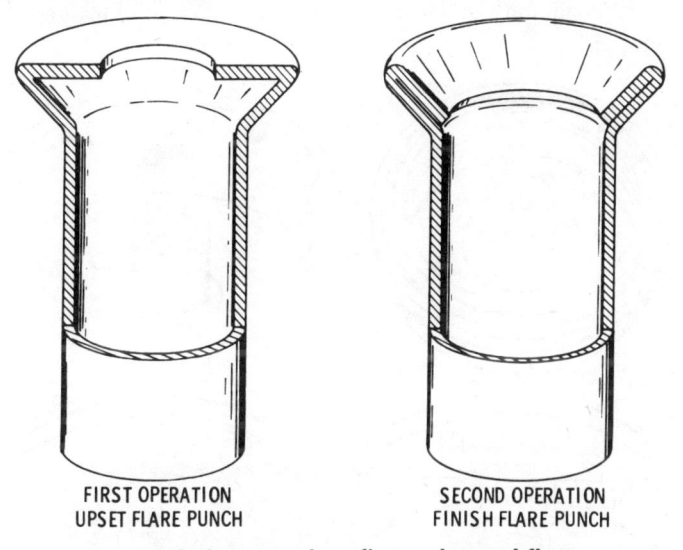

FIRST OPERATION
UPSET FLARE PUNCH

SECOND OPERATION
FINISH FLARE PUNCH

Fig. 17. Flaring operation—first and second flare.

the tubing kinking and collapsing. New tubing should be cleaned and flushed with alcohol before final installation.

The new tubing should be routed carefully to prevent interference with any moving part of the vehicle, such as springs, shock absorbers, exhaust pipes, etc. Contact with any of these parts will result in abrasion of the tubing and eventual failure.

Brake hoses should be inspected whenever any brake service is performed. They should be checked for cracks, scuffing, worn spots,

Automobile Guide

interference with chassis parts, and faulty installation that causes twisting, pulling, and contact with wheels, tires, or chassis parts.

Always use approved replacement hose, and check mating surfaces for nicks and burrs. Position the new hose to avoid contact with chassis parts, especially the exhaust pipe and shock absorbers. Check the clearance of the front brake hoses throughout the entire steering range with the normal weight of the car on the wheels.

Bleed all four wheel cylinders if either wheel cylinder, connecting line, or master cylinder has been opened for inspection, repair, or replacement.

Brake Drums — Whenever the brake drums are removed, they should be inspected for cracks, deep grooves, scoring, or any other condition that would lead to their early failure, such as in Fig. 18. Any abnormal condition should be corrected to restore full braking safety and efficiency.

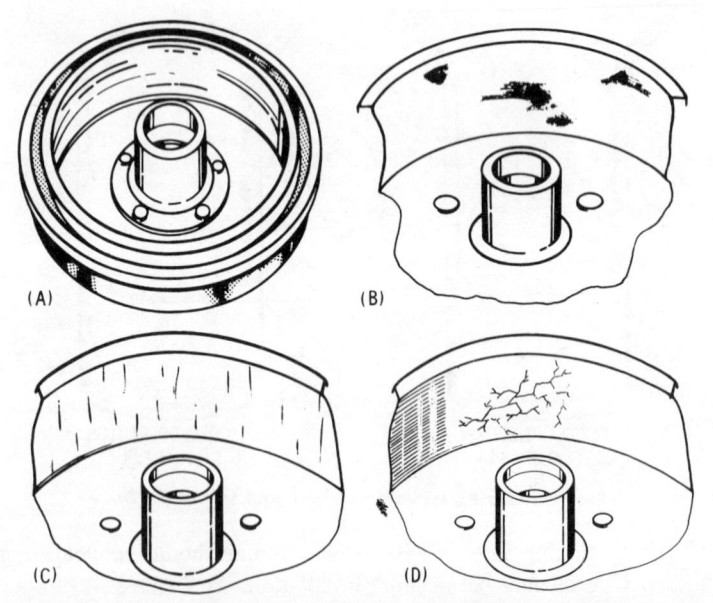

Fig. 18. Inspection of brake drums may reveal (A) Heavy scoring, (B) Hot spots, (C) Checks, or (D) Cracks.

Cracked brake drums should be replaced. Slight scoring can usually be eliminated by rubbing with fine emery cloth. Deep grooves and/or an out-of-round condition can only be corrected by turning. A brake drum

STANDARD AND POWER BRAKES, DRUM AND DISC TYPES

can be checked for an out-of-round condition by measuring the inside diameter at two points at right angles to each other with an inside micrometer fitted with extension rods. The amount of variation between the two readings will depend on the size of the brake drum. Consult the car's service manual for the correct specifications.

Brake drums may be resurfaced either by turning on a lathe or by grinding. The best brake performance is usually obtained by turning, using a very fine lathe feed.The braking surface must be smooth and free of tool or chatter marks. Drums that are to be used with standard size brake linings should have only a small amount of metal removed. If this is not sufficient to correct the condition, then the drum must be rebored to accommodate oversize linings. Check the specifications to determine the new diameter to which the drum should be rebored. Most car manufacturers specify .06 inch as the maximum amount over the standard diameter. Drums rebored to more than this specified amount will not dissipate the heat properly and will be subject to distortion.

New linings may be riveted or molded on. In either case, the new linings should be ground down on a machine having a cylindrical grinding wheel. The maximum amount they should be ground is specified on the manufacturer's service manual, but usually is from .010 to .025 inch under the diameter of the brake drum. Some replacement linings are preground and, of course, do not require this operation.

A preliminary adjustment should be made whenever new linings have been installed. This is done by using a gauge that is set to the diameter of the brake drum (Fig. 19). The gauge is then turned over and the other side is fitted to the brake shoes by turning the star-wheel brake adjustment until the gauge just slides over the lining (Fig. 20). The gauge is then rotated around the brake shoe surface to assure that proper clearance is present.

NOTE: *Whenever it is necessary to back off the brake shoe adjustment on self-adjusting brakes, the adjusting lever must be held away from the sprocket (star wheel).*

Care must be taken during any operation in which the brake linings are exposed that grease, oil, or dirt does not come in contact with the braking surfaces of the brake drum and brake shoes.

Brake Adjustment

Specific procedures for adjusting the brakes are given in the service manual for each make and model of car. The following general

AUTOMOBILE GUIDE

Fig. 19. Checking the brake drum diameter with a brake-shoe clearance gauge.

Fig. 20. Checking the brake shoe diameter for proper clearance.

STANDARD AND POWER BRAKES, DRUM AND DISC TYPES

procedure, however, will be satisfactory for adjusting the brakes on most cars manufactured by *American Motors, General Motors, and Ford Motor Company.* Some late-model *Chrysler*-made cars also use this procedure.

1. Raise the car until the wheels are off the floor. If a frame-contact hoist is used, disconnect the parking-brake cables to prevent the rear-wheel sag from partially applying the rear brakes.
2. Remove the adjusting hole cover in the brake flange plate. *(NOTE: Some General Motors cars have the adjusting hole in the brake drum, as shown in Fig. 21. This type requires the brake-adjusting tool to be moved in a direction opposite that when the access hole is in the brake flange plate.)*
3. Expand the brake shoes (tighten the brakes) by inserting a brake-adjusting tool through the adjusting hole (Fig. 22) and turning the star wheel until a light uniform drag is felt on the brake drum. This is accomplished on most cars by moving the end of the adjusting tool downward while it is engaged with the star wheel. (The end of the tool is moved upward when the adjusting hole is in the brake drum.)
4. Turn the adjusting screw back 10 notches, or more if drag is still felt on the brake drums. Always back the adjusting screw off the same number of notches on all four wheels.

CAUTION: On self-adjusting brakes, it is absolutely necessary to hold the adjuster lever away from the star wheel while backing off the adjusting screw (Fig.23). Failure to do so will damage the adjusting mechanism.

5. Repeat operations 3 and 4 at each wheel and replace the hole covers.
6. Reconnect the parking brake cables and adjust the parking brakes if necessary.
7. Road test the brakes.

The following procedures should be used to adjust the brakes on *Chrysler*-made cars that have cam-adjusted brakes similar to the one shown in Fig. 24. Whenever the brake shoes have been replaced or reinstalled for any reason, always apply pedal pressure before making a brake adjustment. This is necessary to center the brakeshoes in the brake drum to permit proper adjustment.

Automobile Guide

Fig. 21. Some makes and models of GENERAL MOTORS cars have the brake-adjusting hole in the brake-drum assembly.

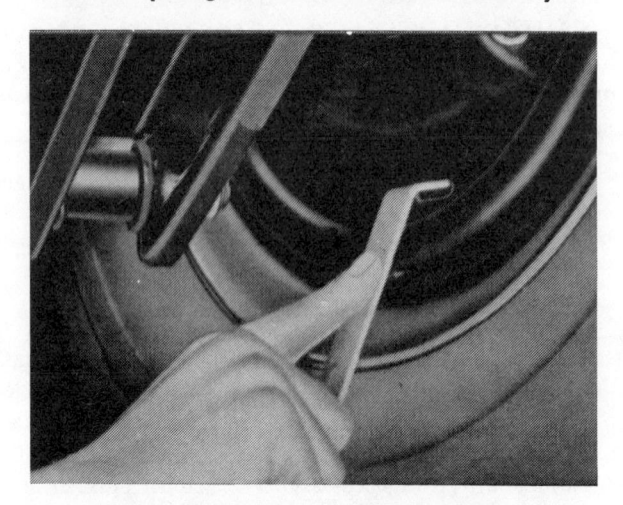

Fig. 22. Adjusting the service brake.

Standard and Power Brakes, Drum and Disc Types

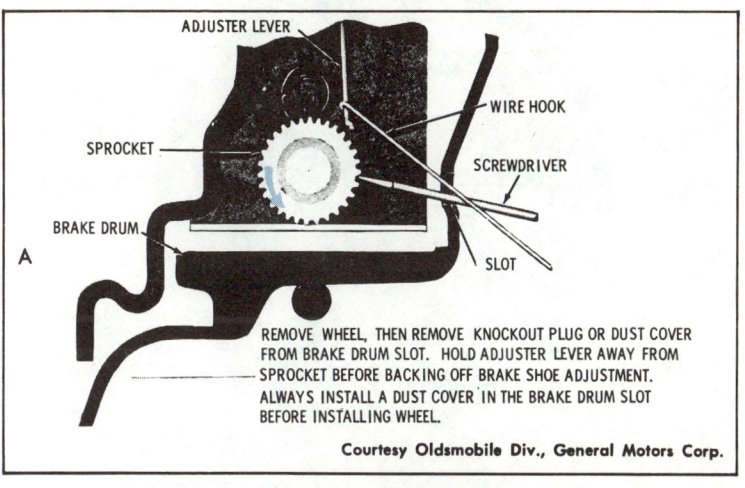

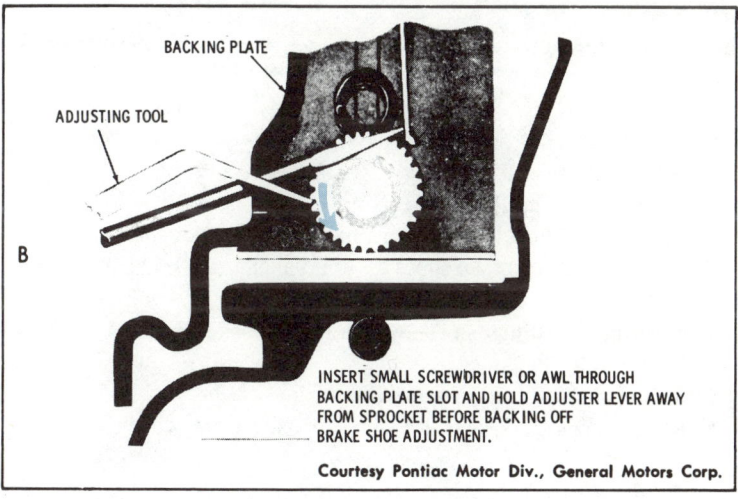

A — REMOVE WHEEL, THEN REMOVE KNOCKOUT PLUG OR DUST COVER FROM BRAKE DRUM SLOT. HOLD ADJUSTER LEVER AWAY FROM SPROCKET BEFORE BACKING OFF BRAKE SHOE ADJUSTMENT. ALWAYS INSTALL A DUST COVER IN THE BRAKE DRUM SLOT BEFORE INSTALLING WHEEL.

Courtesy Oldsmobile Div., General Motors Corp.

B — INSERT SMALL SCREWDRIVER OR AWL THROUGH BACKING PLATE SLOT AND HOLD ADJUSTER LEVER AWAY FROM SPROCKET BEFORE BACKING OFF BRAKE SHOE ADJUSTMENT.

Courtesy Pontiac Motor Div., General Motors Corp.

Fig. 23. Holding the adjustor lever away from the star wheel to back off the brake adjustment; (A) Adjusting hole in brake drum; (B) Adjusting hole in the brake flange plate.

AUTOMOBILE GUIDE

CYLINDER ASSEMBLY

ADJUSTING CAMS

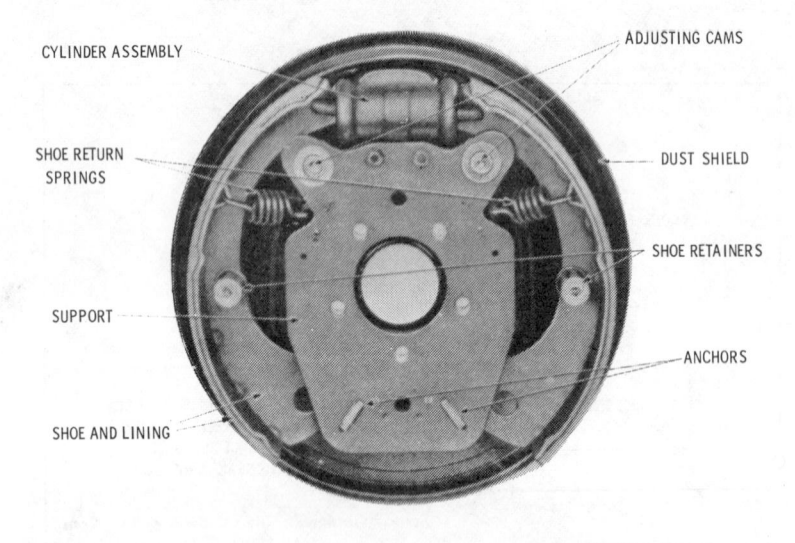

SHOE RETURN SPRINGS

DUST SHIELD

SHOE RETAINERS

SUPPORT

ANCHORS

SHOE AND LINING

Courtesy Dodge Div., Chrysler Motors Corp.

Fig. 24. Some CHRYSLER made cars use brakes that have adjusting cams instead of a star wheel adjustment.

1. Raise the car until the wheels are off the floor.
2. Turn one of the adjusting cams in the direction of forward wheel rotation until the brake shoes are solid against the brake drum and the wheel is locked. Refer to Fig. 25.
3. Turn the adjusting cam slowly in the opposite direction until no drag is felt.
4. Repeat the operation on the other cam.
5. Repeat steps 2, 3, and 4 on the opposite front wheel.

Rear-Brake Adjustment

1. Turn the forward adjusting cam in the direction of forward wheel rotation (See Fig. 25) until the wheel is locked.
2. Turn the adjusting cam slowly in the opposite direction until no drag is felt.
3. Turn the rearward adjusting cam in the direction opposite to forward wheel rotation until the wheel is locked.

Standard and Power Brakes, Drum and Disc Types

4. Turn the adjusting cam slowly in the opposite direction until no drag is felt.
5. Repeat steps 1, 2, 3, and 4 on the opposite rear wheel.
6. Road test the brakes.

LEFT FRONT

RIGHT FRONT

LEFT REAR

RIGHT REAR

Courtesy Dodge Div., Chrysler Motors Corp.

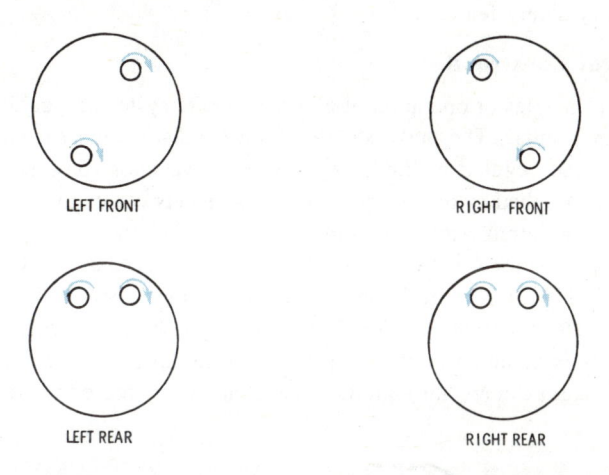

Fig. 25. Brake adjusting diagram for cam-adjusted brakes used on some CHRYSLER made cars.

POWER BRAKES

Power brakes are available, as optional equipment, for all domestic cars. Power brake units may be factory installed or may be added by the dealer or garage to a car having a standard brake system. Although usually an option, some makes and models of cars in recent years have the power brake system as standard equipment.

The wheel brake assemblies are the same on cars having power brakes as on cars with standard brakes. The power brake unit merely provides a lighter pedal pressure with a reduced pedal travel making possible a brake pedal height near that of the accelerator pedal.

The power to operate the power brakes is obtained from the vacuum produced in the intake manifold. This means, of course, the engine must be running in order to provide the vacuum. A vacuum reserve, however, is maintained either in the unit itself or in a separate vacuum

Automobile Guide

tank which permits power assist for three to ten normal power brake applications after the engine stops running.

The brakes can always be applied manually even though the power unit is malfunctioning. This requires extra pedal effort, but is a necessary safety feature.

General Construction

The principles of operation of all power brake systems, regardless of type, are similar. The brake shoe to drum (or disc) contact is engaged through the regular hydraulic system with vacuum (power) assist. *Power* is supplied by the difference in pressure between engine manifold vacuum and atmospheric pressure.

A cross-sectional view of a single vacuum assist master cylinder is shown in Fig. 26. Figure 27 shows a cross-sectional view of the double vacuum assist master cylinder. The master cylinder and vacuum assist assembly is mounted on the engine side of the firewall. The operating rod (linkage) extends through the firewall and is connected to the brake pedal.

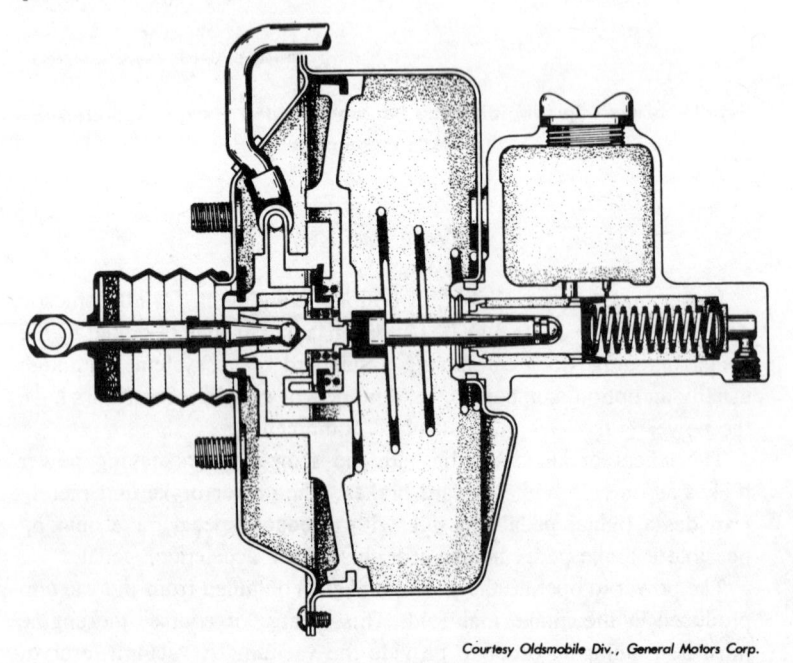

Courtesy Oldsmobile Div., General Motors Corp.

Fig. 26. Cross-section of BENDIX power-brake unit.

Standard and Power Brakes, Drum and Disc Types

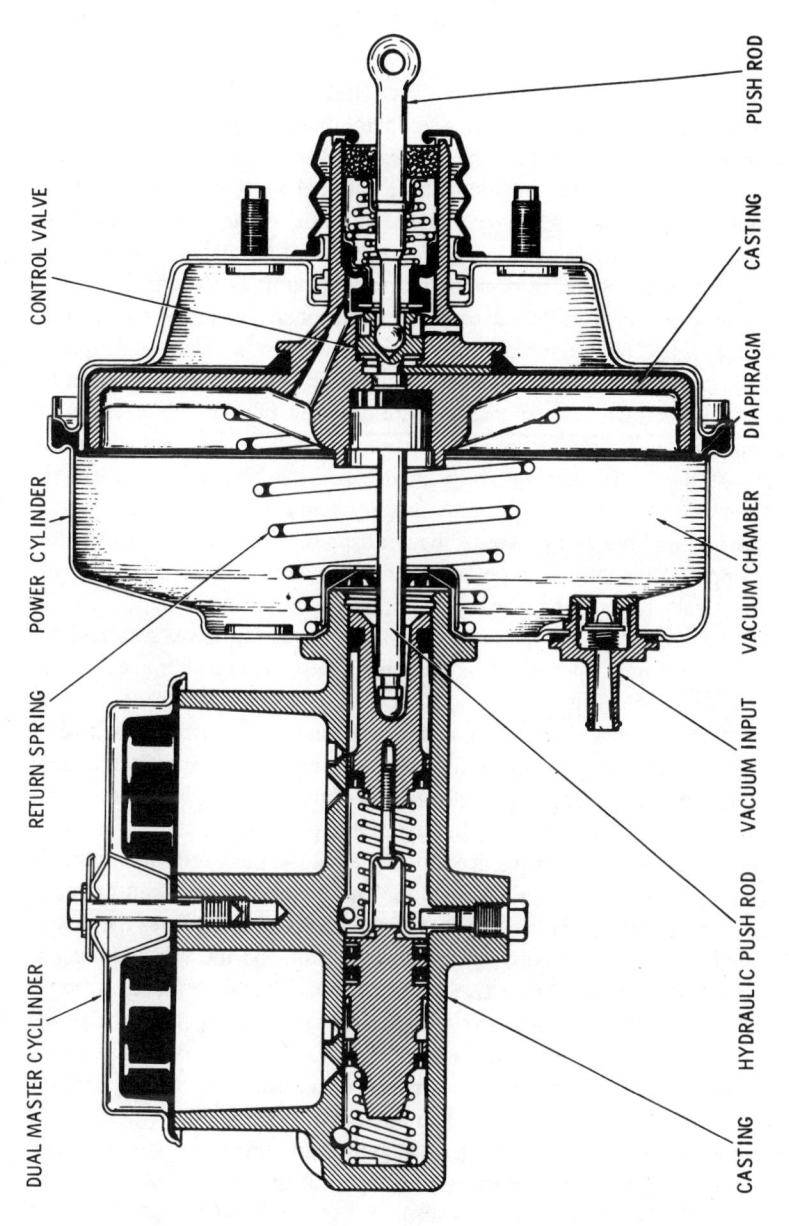

Fig. 27. Cross-sectional view of a dual master cylinder power-assisted brake.

Operating Principle

The operating principle may differ slightly between different makes and models of power brakes. The operation of a typical unit, however, will aid in understanding the general operation of all power units.

Fig. 28 shows the position of the internal parts in the power-brake unit used on some *Mercury* models. With the engine running, and the brakes released, vacuum is applied to the unit but cannot evacuate the power-piston chamber because the vacuum port is closed. The atmospheric port is open, however, so the atmosphere is free to enter through the port and on into the chamber ahead of the piston. Thus, atmospheric pressure is present on both sides of the piston and it is suspended in the position shown. Under these conditions, the push rod is exerting no pressure on the master-cylinder piston, so the brakes are not energized.

As the brake pedal starts to move when the brakes are applied, the operating rod moves forward, slightly compressing the valve return spring, and brings the seat of the atmospheric valve in contact with the poppet valve, closing the atmospheric valve. As the operating rod continues to move forward as the brake pedal is further depressed, the poppet valve is moved away from the vacuum-valve seat and the vacuum port is opened. Thus, vacuum enters the chamber ahead of the power piston (Fig. 29).

With vacuum ahead of the piston and atmospheric pressure behind it, a force is developed which moves the power piston, the hydraulic push rod, and the hydraulic piston forward. This forces hydraulic fluid into the wheel cylinders. As the hydraulic pressure starts to increase, however, a counter force is exerted against the push rod, attempting to move it back to its original position. This counter force is transmitted to a rubber reaction disc at the rear of the push rod and causes the disc to distribute the force between the power piston and the valve plunger in proportion to their respective contact areas. This action tends to move the valve plunger backward a slight amount with respect to the power piston to close off the vacuum port (Fig. 30). A part of this rearward force reacts through the valve plunger and operating rod against the driver's foot, providing a certain amount of braking effort "feel." The amount of this reaction force increases in direct proportion to the amount of hydraulic pressure developed in the brake system.

With both vacuum and atmospheric ports closed, a partial vacuum exists in the chamber ahead of the power piston and the unit will hold the brakes at the degree of brake application present at that moment,

Standard and Power Brakes, Drum and Disc Types

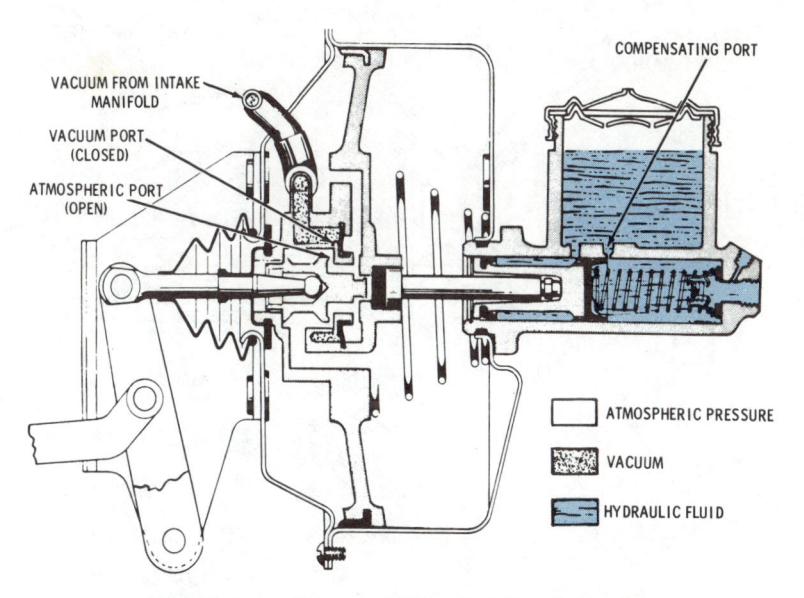

Fig. 28. Power-brake unit in the released position.

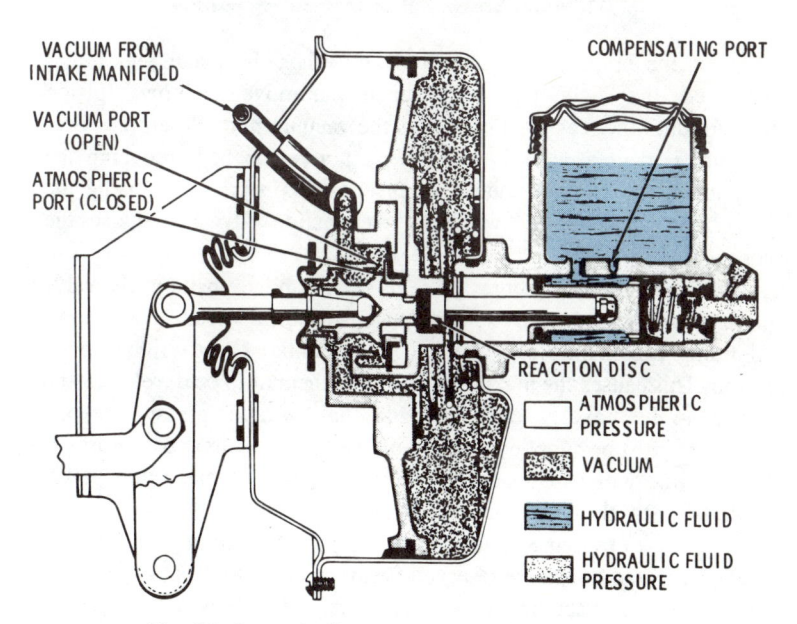

Fig. 29. Power-brake unit in the applied position.

499

AUTOMOBILE GUIDE

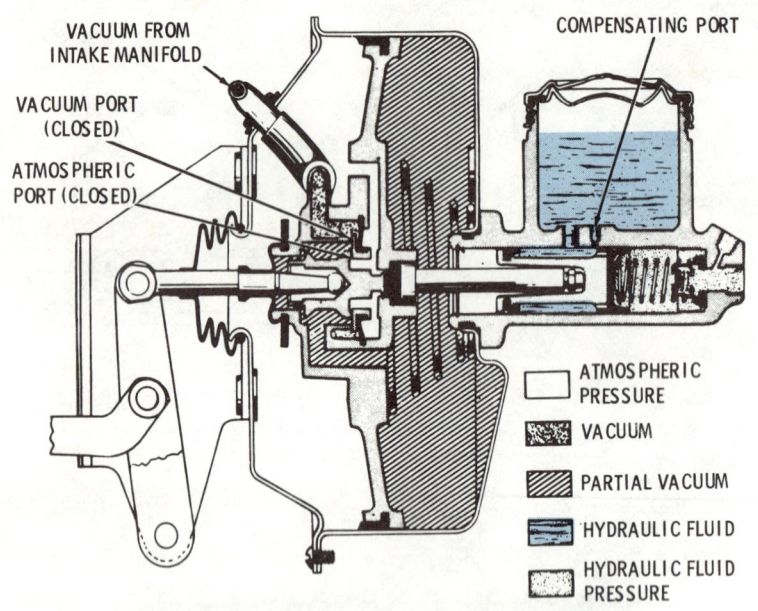

Fig. 30. Power-brake unit in the holding position.

provided the brake pedal is not moved. When the pedal pressure is increased, the vacuum port will open and move the power piston forward until the reaction disc closes the vacuum port. When the pedal pressure is decreased, the atmospheric port is opened, reducing the vacuum in the chamber ahead of the power piston and causing the power piston to move backward until the reaction valve again closes the port.

If the brake pedal is depressed to its fully applied position, the valve plunger will hold the valve poppet away from the vacuum-valve seat, admitting full manifold vacuum to the chamber ahead of the power piston. This causes the maximum power of the unit to be developed and applied to the brake system. Any additional hydraulic pressure beyond this point must be supplied entirely by the physical effort of the driver. Wheel slide will usually occur below the point of maximum power application by the power unit, however.

In the case of engine failure and consequent loss of engine vacuum, the vacuum in the separate reservoir is sufficient for several power-brake applications. If vacuum is lost completely, the brakes can still be applied in the conventional manner, except that more effort is required.

Standard and Power Brakes, Drum and Disc Types

It must be remembered that all power brakes do not use the same principle of operation. For example, in some units, vacuum exists on both sides of the power piston when the brakes are released. When the brakes are applied, atmospheric pressure is permitted to enter the chamber behind the piston, forcing it forward. Also, many units are designed to operate without a separate vacuum reservoir tank. Therefore, for the exact operating principle of a particular make and model power-brake assembly, the manufacturer's shop manual should be consulted.

POWER BRAKE TESTING PROCEDURE

The following tests are applicable to all power brake systems and are useful in determining which part of the system is causing trouble.

1. Road test the brakes by applying the brakes while moving about 20 mph to determine if the automobile stops evenly and quickly. If the pedal feels spongy, air may be present in the hydraulic system. Bleed the system to remove the air.
2. With engine stopped and transmission in neutral, apply the brakes several times until all vacuum in the system is depleted. Depress the foot pedal and hold it with a light foot pressure. Start the engine. If the vacuum system is operating, the pedal will tend to fall away, and less foot pressure will be required to hold the pedal in a given position. If no action is felt, the vacuum is not functioning. Check for a broken, kinked, or collapsed vacuum hose, defective check valve, or a leak in the vacuum reservoir or power brake vacuum diaphragm.
3. Stop the engine and again apply the brakes until all vacuum is depleted. Depress the foot pedal and hold with considerable pressure. If the pedal gradually falls away, the hydraulic system is leaking.
4. Start the engine. With the brakes off, run the engine up to medium speed and turn off the ignition, releasing the accelerator immediately. This builds up vacuum. Wait several minutes (the system should hold vacuum for an extended period of up to 12 hours) before trying brake action. If vacuum assist is not present for several slow brake applications, the vacuum system is leaking. Always check for an external leak before blaming the power unit itself. If no vacuum is present, the problem may be due to a

disconnected, broken, kinked or collapsed vacuum hose. The problem may also be due to a leaking vacuum reservoir.

CLEANING, INSPECTION, AND OVERHAUL

If trouble is indicated in the power brake unit, it should be disassembled according to the procedure listed in the manufacturer's service manual. After disassembly, follow these steps:

1. Wipe the fluid from all rubber parts and inspect them for nicks, cuts, or other damage. If any are found defective, discard all the rubber parts.
2. Thoroughly clean the remaining parts of the power unit in diacetone alcohol or clean brake fluid.

    CAUTION: Do not use antifreeze-type alcohol, gasoline, kerosene, or any other cleaning fluid that might contain even a trace of mineral oil. To do so may cause serious damage to the rubber parts.

3. Examine the cleaned parts for nicks, burrs, stripped threads, damage, or excessive wear. Replace any parts or housings that are damaged or show signs of excessive wear. If the inside of the vacuum power chamber is rusted or corroded, polish with fine steel wool or fine emery cloth. Replace the chamber if it is scored.
4. Make certain the small compensating port in the master cylinder (if part of the power unit) is clear.
5. If the outer surface of the air valve shows abrasion, polish out light scores with crocus cloth, then wash and dry thoroughly.
6. Inspect the master cylinder (if part of the power unit) and correct any defects in the manner prescribed for the master cylinder used with standard brakes.
7. If any parts indicate that heavy corrosion or abrasive action has caused the brake fluid to be contaminated, replace the damaged parts and thoroughly flush the hydraulic system.
8. Repair kits are available for the overhaul of most power brake units, and contain all the necessary replacement parts. Use all the new parts contained in the kit, even though the old parts appear satisfactory. In addition, replace any other parts which appear to be unfit for use.

STANDARD AND POWER BRAKES, DRUM AND DISC TYPES

9. Reassemble the power unit according to the procedure outlined in the manufacturer's service manual.

BRAKE LIGHT WARNING SYSTEM

All domestic cars are equipped, by law, with a brake light warning system. A lamp, in the instrument panel, is lit by the action of a grounding-type pressure differential switch, Fig. 31, located in a junction block near the master cylinder.

It is a common practice for the car owner to disconnect the wire at the switch if the dash lamp remains lit and the brakes *seem* to be in good order. The truth is — if the dash lamp is lit *there is a problem* in the braking system. The problem should not be ignored although braking action may seem to be adequate.

Note the cross-sectional view of the pressure differential switch in Fig. 32. As long as the front and rear brakes are balanced, switch contact is not "made" and the dash lamp will not light. If, for any reason, there is an imbalance in either front or rear brakes, the piston

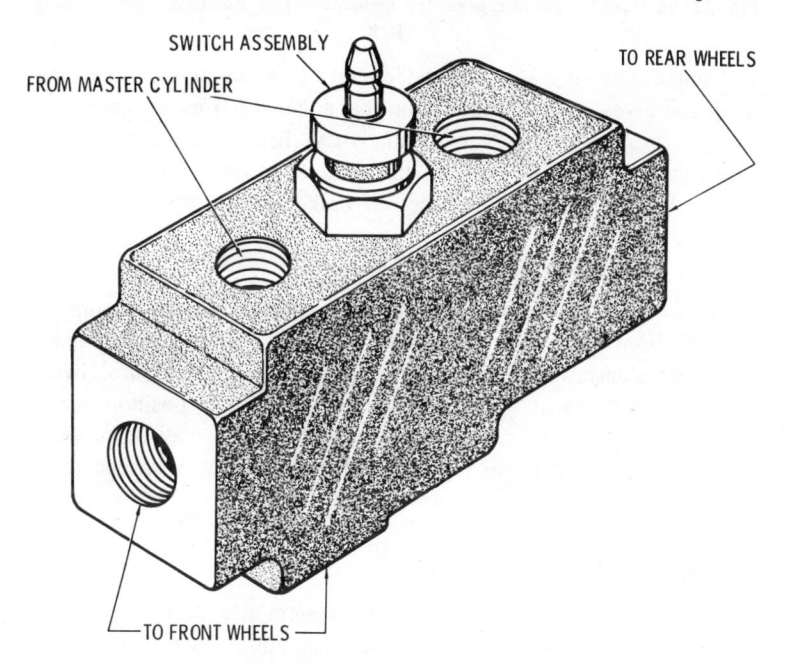

Fig. 31. Pressure differential-type brake light warning switch.

AUTOMOBILE GUIDE

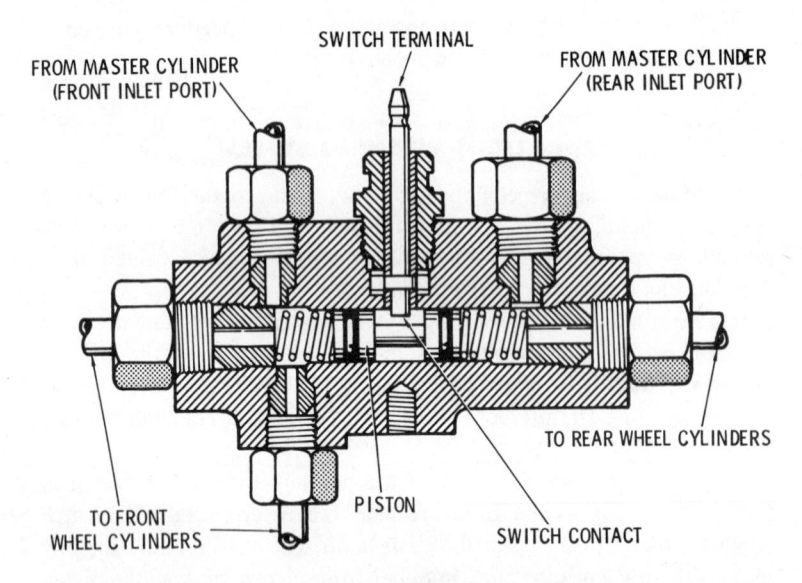

Fig. 32. Sectional view of a pressure differential-type brake light warning switch.

will move "making" the ground circuit. This action lights the dash lamp and gives a definite indication that either the front or rear brakes are not operating to maximum efficiency. Inspection of the master cylinder would probably reveal that one of the reservoirs was below normal level — another indication of brake malfunction.

Switch Operation

The pressure differential switch is designed to constantly compare rear and front brake system pressures from the master cylinder and to energize the dash warning lamp in the event of unequal pressure. Switch design is such that it will remain in the "warning" position once a malfunction has occurred. The only way the lamp may be properly turned off is to first repair the malfunction (electrical or mechanical), then reset the switch.

Testing and Resetting Switch

After the malfunction of the brake system has been located and repaired (or for routine testing) the instructions given by various manufacturers should be followed. Instructions given here may be

Standard and Power Brakes, Drum and Disc Types

considered "typical" for information only. They are *not* for any particular type of system.

Electrical Testing — First, determine if the indicator lamp is defective (burned out). The lamp may be removed from the socket and tested on a bulb checker, or as follows:

1. Disconnect lead wire from the pressure differential switch terminal.
2. Attach a jumper wire from the disconnected wire to a good ground.
3. Turn ignition switch to "on." The dash lamp should light. If not lit in step 3 a defective bulb or wiring is indicated. Replace bulb or repair wiring.
4. Turn ignition switch to "off," remove the jumper wire and replace wire on switch.

Testing Pressure Differential Switch — The following procedure is typical for insuring proper operation of the pressure differential switch for both rear and front brakes. If improper operation is noted the switch is usually replaced as an assembly.

1. Test electrical circuit as outlined in "Electrical Testing."
2. Insure that master cylinder reservoirs are filled to proper level.
3. Attach a bleeder hose to either rear brake bleed screw and immerse the other end into a container partially filled with clean brake fluid.
4. Turn ignition switch to "on."
5. As assistant applies moderate pressure to the brake pedal, open bleeder screw.
6. Dash warning lamp should light.
7. Close bleeder screw *before* assistant releases brake pedal.
8. Recheck fluid level at master cylinder.
9. As assistant applies heavy pressure to brake pedal again open bleeder screw.
10. Dash warning lamp should go out.
11. Again, close bleed screw *before* assistant releases brake pedal.
12. Recheck fluid level at master cylinder.
13. Repeat steps 3 through 12 with bleeder hose attached to either front brake as outlined in step 3.

AUTOMOBILE GUIDE

14. Turn ignition switch to "off."
    If test results are negative for steps 6 or 10 (front or rear), the switch is probably defective and should be replaced.

BRAKE-SYSTEM TROUBLES AND REMEDIES

Many brake-system troubles that occur with power brakes are the same as those that occur with standard brakes. Therefore, before checking the power-brake system for the source of trouble, refer to the troubles and remedies chart for standard brakes. After these possible causes have been eliminated, check for power-brake troubles.

Some of the troubles and remedies listed are not applicable to all power brake units. Instead, the list includes the troubles and remedies for power brake units in general. For specific instructions, the manufacturer's service manual should be consulted for the particular type of unit being serviced.

STANDARD BRAKES

Symptoms and Possible Causes   *Possible Remedies*

Pedal Goes to the Floor (or nearly so)

(a) Fluid low in master cylinder.
(b) Excessively worn brake linings.
(c) Improperly adjusted brake shoes.
(d) Leaking wheel cylinders.

(e) Loose or broken brake line.
(f) Air in hydraulic system.

(g) Leaking or worn master cylinder.

(a) Fill and bleed the master cylinder.
(b) Reline and adjust brakes.
(c) Adjust brakes.

(d) Recondition or replace wheel cylinders and replace linings.
(e) Tighten all brake fittings or replace broken line.
(f) Bleed and fill hydraulic system.
(g) Recondition or replace master cylinder and bleed the hydraulic system.

506

Standard and Power Brakes, Drum and Disc Types

Symptoms and Possible Causes *Possible Remedies*

(h) Self-adjusters not working.
(h) Clean and free-up all threaded areas of adjuster mechanism. Replace the thrust washer if necessary.

Pedal Spongy

(a) Air in hydraulic system.
(a) Bleed hydraulic system and fill master cylinder.

(b) Improper brake fluid (low boiling point).
(b) Drain, flush, and refill with approved brake fluid.

(c) Excessively worn or cracked brake drums.
(c) Replace defective drums.

All Brakes Drag

(a) Incorrect brake adjustment.
(a) Adjust brakes and check fluid.

(b) Parking brakes engaged.
(b) Release or adjust parking brakes.

(c) Wheel cylinder sticking.
(c) Recondition wheel cylinder.

(d) Weak or broken brake shoe return spring.
(d) Replace return spring.

(e) Brake pedal binding.
(e) Free-up and lubricate pedal and linkage.

(f) Master cylinder cup sticking.
(f) Recondition master cylinder.

(g) Incorrect master cylinder push rod adjustment.
(g) Adjust push rod.

(h) Mineral oil in system.
(h) Flush entire brake system, replace all rubber parts, and refill with approved brake fluid.

(i) Compensating port in master cylinder restricted.
(i) Overhaul master cylinder.

Symptoms and Possible Causes	Possible Remedies

One Brake Drags

(a) Loose or damaged wheel bearings.
(b) Weak, broken, or unhooked brake shoe return spring.
(c) Brake shoes adjusted too close to brake drum.
(d) Brake shoe bent and binding on backing plate.
(e) Brake drum out of round.

(a) Adjust or replace wheel bearings.
(b) Replace return spring.
(c) Adjust brakes correctly.
(d) Replace shoes.
(e) Turn brake drum down.

Pedal Applies Brakes but Slowly Goes to Floor

(a) External leaks.

(a) Check master cylinder, wheel cylinder, and all lines for leaks. Repair as necessary.

Uneven Braking

(a) Grease on linings.

(b) Tires improperly inflated.
(c) Incorrect brake adjustment.
(d) Brake drums out of round.
(e) Bent brake shoes.
(f) Restricted brake hose or line.
(g) Unmatched brake lining.
(h) Front end out of alignment.

(a) Remove drums and clean and dry linings, or replace if necessary.
(b) Inflate tires to the recommended pressure.
(c) Adjust brakes correctly.
(d) Turn or replace brake drums.
(e) Replace defective shoes.
(f) Replace plugged hose or line.
(g) Match lining on all wheels.
(h) Align front end.

Standard and Power Brakes, Drum and Disc Types

Symptoms and Possible Causes

(i) Broken rear spring.
(j) Brake drum scored.

Possible Remedies

(i) Replace spring.
(j) Grind or replace defective drum.

Hard Pedal

(a) Incorrect brake lining.
(b) Incorrect brake adjustment.
(c) Frozen brake pedal linkage.
(d) Restricted brake hose or line.
(e) Grease, brake fluid, mud or water on brake linings.
(f) Full surface of linings not contacting brake drum.
(g) Scored brake drums.

(a) Install matched and approved linings.
(b) Adjust brakes correctly.
(c) Free-up and lubricate linkage.
(d) Replace defective hose or line.
(e) Clean, dry, or replace linings. Correct cause of grease or fluid.
(f) Free-up shoe linkage, grind linings, or replace shoes.
(g) Turn or grind drums and replace linings.

Wheel Locks

(a) Loose or torn brake lining.
(b) Incorrect wheel bearing adjustment.
(c) Wheel cylinder cups sticking.
(d) Loose backing plate.

(a) Replace brake lining.
(b) Clean, pack, and adjust wheel bearings.
(c) Recondition or replace wheel cylinder.
(d) Tighten backing plate.

Brakes Grab

(a) Grease or brake fluid on lining.
(b) Scored drums.

(a) Clean or replace linings. Find and correct grease or fluid leak.
(b) Grind or replace drums.

AUTOMOBILE GUIDE

Symptoms and Possible Causes

(c) Loose backing plate.

(d) Drums out of round.

Possible Remedies

(c) Tighten or replace backing plate.

(d) Grind or replace drums.

Brakes Chatter

(a) Rough or scored brake drum.
(b) Loose backing plate or shoe support.
(c) Bent support plate.
(d) Bent brake shoe.
(e) Machine grooves in contact face of brake drum.
(f) Saturated brake lining.
(g) Loose front suspension system.
(h) Poor lining-to-drum contact.

(a) Grind or replace brake drum.
(b) Tighten the backing plate.
(c) Replace support plate.
(d) Replace brake shoe.
(e) Grind or replace brake drum.
(f) Replace linings.
(g) Overhaul front suspension system.
(h) Grind lining to correct contour, replace lining, or replace brake shoe.

Brakes Do Not Self-Adjust

(a) Adjuster screw frozen.

(b) Adjuster screw corroded at the thrust washer.
(c) Automatic-adjuster mechanism broken or bent.

(a) Clean and free-up all thread areas.
(b) Clean the threads and replace thrust washer.
(c) Repair automatic-adjuster mechanism as necessary.

POWER BRAKES

See note of introduction to "Brake System Troubles and Remedies" regarding power brakes.

Symptoms and Possible Causes

Hard Pedal

(a) Faulty vacuum check valve.

Possible Remedies

(a) Replace valve.

Standard and Power Brakes, Drum and Disc Types

Symptoms and Possible Causes	Possible Remedies
(b) Collapsed or leaking vacuum hose to manifold or reserve tank.	(b) Replace hose.
(c) Plugged vacuum fittings.	(c) Clean or replace fittings.
(d) Leaking vacuum reservoir tank.	(d) Replace tank.
(e) Vacuum check valve stuck closed.	(e) Free-up or replace. **Do not oil.**
(f) Internal vacuum hose loose or restricted.	(f) Tighten, clear, or replace as necessary.
(g) Jammed vacuum cylinder piston.	(g) Free-up or replace and correct cause of jam.
(h) Loose piston plate screws.	(h) Tighten screws.
(i) Faulty vacuum cylinder piston seal.	(i) Replace piston. Check cylinder for scoring.
(j) Restricted air filter element.	(j) Replace element.
(k) Faulty rubber stop in reaction diaphragm.	(k) Replace faulty part.
(l) Tight pedal linkage.	(l) Adjust linkage.

Brakes Fail to Release

(a) Blocked passage in power piston.	(a) Clear passage and replace defective parts if necessary.
(b) Air valve stuck closed.	(b) Free-up or replace. **Do not oil.**
(c) Broken air valve spring.	(c) Replace spring.
(d) Tight pedal linkage.	(d) Adjust and lubricate as necessary.
(e) Restricted air filter element.	(e) Replace element.
(f) Restricted air passage.	(f) Clear passages and replace parts if needed.
(g) Sticking vacuum valve.	(g) Free-up or replace. **Do not oil.**

AUTOMOBILE GUIDE

Symptoms and Possible Causes *Possible Remedies*

(h) Incorrect push rod adjustment.
(i) Leak in rear housing of power unit.
(j) Diaphragm out of location in housing.
(k) Sticking or unseated actuating valve assembly.

(h) Adjust push rod.

(i) Locate and correct leak.

(j) Reposition the diaphragm.

(k) Free-up and seat properly.

Grunting Noise in Power Unit

(a) Air in hydraulic system.
(b) Valve plunger dry.
(c) Fluid low in master cylinder.

(a) Bleed brakes.
(b) Lubricate valve plunger.
(c) Add brake fluid.

CHAPTER 21

Front Suspension, Chassis, Springs, and Shocks

Correct operation and alignment of the front suspension and chassis is of the utmost importance in an automobile. Proper attention to the springs and shocks aid in riding comfort, road handling ability, ease of steering, and longer tire life.

A regular schedule of maintenance, inspection, and adjustment should be followed to keep these important parts of the car in first-class condition. They are too often neglected by the average car owner. Neglect of minor problems often develop into major problems — saving a few cents today can cost many dollars tomorrow.

STANDARD SUSPENSION

Passenger cars presently being manufactured in the United States have independent front-wheel suspension similar to that shown in Fig. 1. It should be noted, however, that *Chrysler*-made cars use a torsion bar instead of the coil spring shown.

Some older cars and certain makes of light trucks have a solid-type front axle, somewhat like the one shown in Fig. 2. One of the main disadvantages of the solid axle, as compared to independent suspension, is that the up-and-down motion of one front wheel will affect the camber of the opposite wheel. In other words, as one wheel raises in going over a bump, for example, the opposite wheel is tilted outward, tending to cause the vehicle to turn in the direction of the tilt. Independent wheel suspension removes this tendency, because the vertical movement of one wheel is not transferred to the opposite wheel. Thus, steering stability is improved.

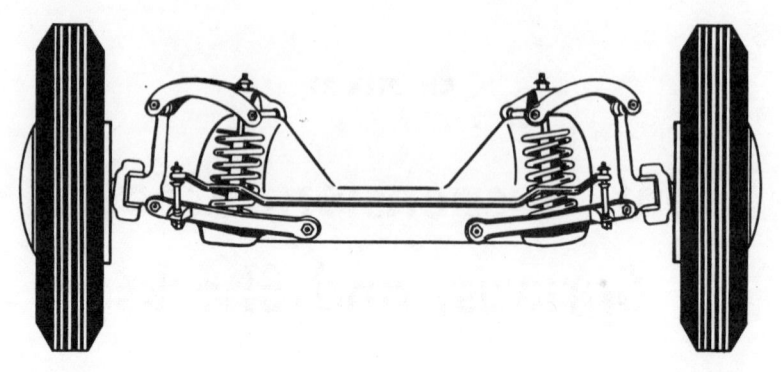

Fig. 1. Independent front suspension as used on most domestic automobiles.

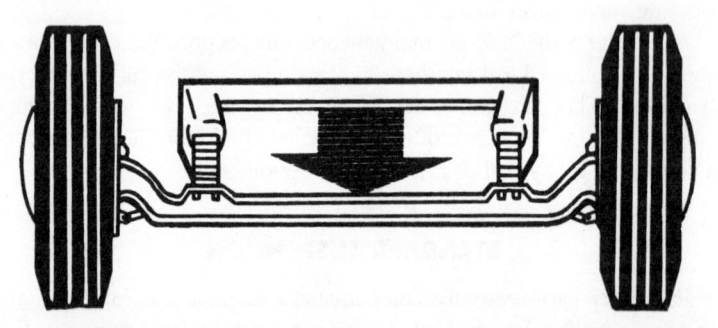

Courtesy Hunter Engineering Co.

Fig. 2. Solid-axle type of front suspension system.

Courtesy Hunter Engineering Co.

Ball Joints

All automobiles manufactured in recent years have some form of ball joint suspension instead of the individual kingpin shown in Fig. 3. The use of ball joints reduces the transmission of road shock to the steering wheel and improves the steering stability. A typical front-wheel suspension employing the ball-joint principal is shown in Fig. 4. It will be found that most cars, regardless of make, have this type of suspension, with only minor differences in construction features.

FRONT SUSPENSION, CHASSIS, SPRINGS, AND SHOCKS

Courtesy Moog Industries, Inc.

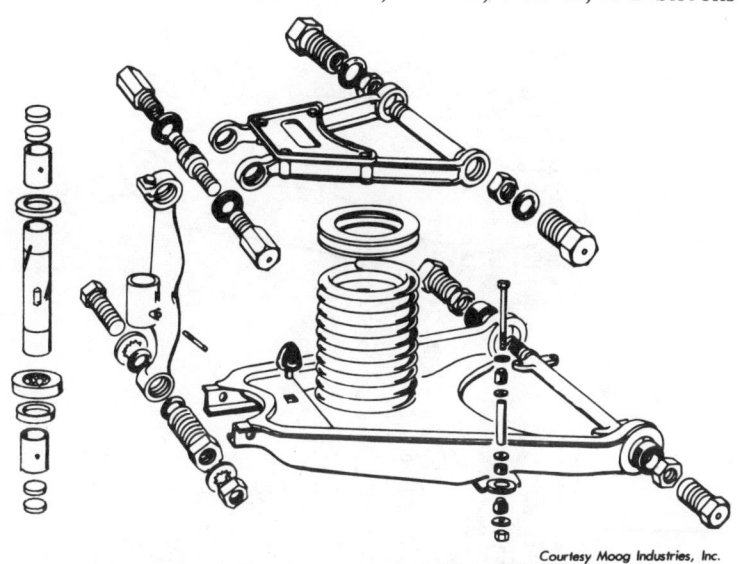

Fig. 3. Kingpin type front suspension system.

Stabilizer (Sway) Bar

Notice in Figs. 1 and 5 that a stabilizer bar is fastened to the lower control arm by means of a rubber-mounted fixture. This bar reduces the tendency for the car to roll and sway, and helps minimize differences in spring action between the two front wheels.

Brake Reaction Rods

A brake reaction rod will be found on some front suspension assemblies. As shown in Fig. 5, this rod is positioned between the lower control arm and the front of the frame side rails. The forward end of the rod is rubber-mounted to the frame bracket and held secure by a castellated nut and cotter pin. This reaction rod maintains the position of the lower control arm and helps to resist torsional roll characteristics.

Shock Absorbers

A shock absorber is part of each front suspension assembly. The upper stem of the shock is secured to the frame by rubber grommets and retainers held in place by a nut. The lower stem of the shock is fastened to the lower control arm and is also insulated with rubber bushings to prevent metal-to-metal contact. The shock absorber is usually posi-

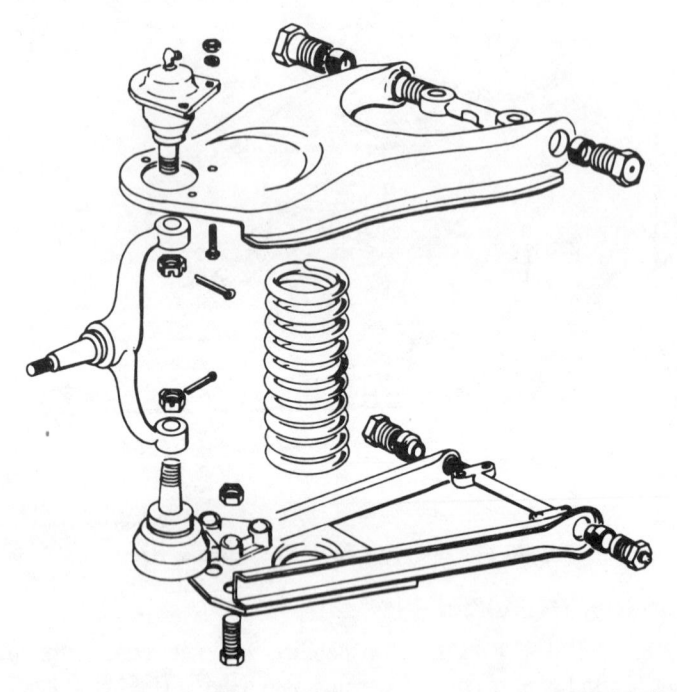

Automobile Guide

Fig. 4. Ball-joint type front suspension system.

tioned inside the coil spring except on those cars equipped with torsion bars, see Fig. 6.

Coil Springs

Many cars have a coil spring positioned between the upper and lower control arm, as shown in Fig. 7. Others have the spring positioned between the upper control arm and car frame, while some may be positioned between the lower control arm and the frame. Regardless of their positioning, the coil spring serves the same function. They are used for springing stresses only, and are a one-piece steel coil of a special alloy. If no coil spring is found in the general area of the control arm(s), the car is equipped with a torsion bar.

Torsion Bars

Some *Chrysler*-made automobiles, especially the later models, have a torsion bar instead of a coil spring in the suspension assembly. One

Front Suspension, Chassis, Springs, and Shocks

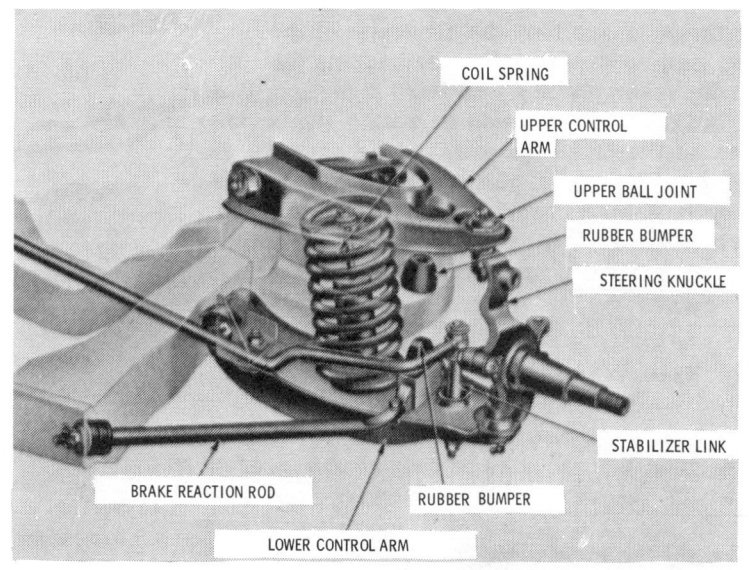

Fig. 5. Front suspension system of a typical BUICK.

end of this bar is anchored to the frame some distance back from the front wheels. The other end of the bar is connected to the lower control arm. The torsion bar is twisted as the control arm moves upward, and offers a resistance that attempts to return the arm to its normal position in the same manner as a coil-spring arrangement. Torsion bars are designed to be twisted in one direction only, so care must be taken when one is replaced to make sure the correct bar is used. The general location of the torsion bars on an automobile is shown in Fig. 8.

Rubber Bumpers

Rubber bumpers are positioned at the upper and lower limits of travel of the control arms or suspension assembly. Their purpose is to prevent metal-to-metal contact when the limits of vertical travel of the assembly is reached, such as may be the case when hitting a deep rut or ditch.

SERVICE PROCEDURES

It is impractical to list the service procedures for all makes and models of automobiles, since each will be slightly different. Instead,

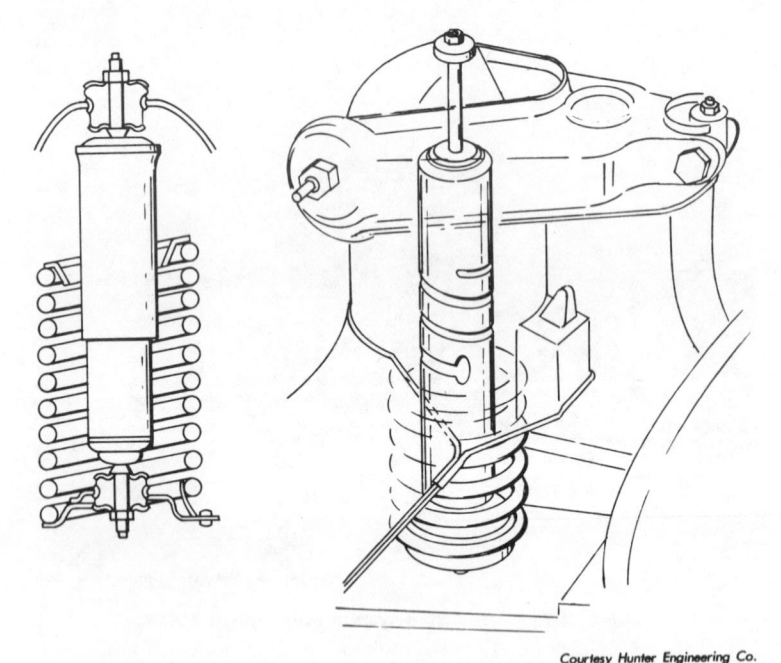

Fig. 6. Location of shock absorber on most cars equipped with coil springs.

Courtesy Hunter Engineering Co.

typical examples are given. Where specific information is desired, the service manual for the particular make and model of car involved should be consulted.

IMPORTANT: Whenever any part of the front suspension has been removed and installed, front wheel alignment must be checked.

Servicing Ball Joints

The upper and lower ball joints shown in Fig. 9, are typical of those used on most cars. It should be noted, however, that some ball joints have a plug instead of a grease fitting (Fig. 10). This type is sealed and requires lubrication only at widely-spaced intervals of 25,000 to 35,000 miles, or as specified by the manufacturer.

The ball joints should be checked periodically for wear. This can be done on most cars by raising the front end until the wheels are hanging free and shaking each wheel by grasping it at the top and bottom. Any

Fig. 7. Typical position of coil spring.

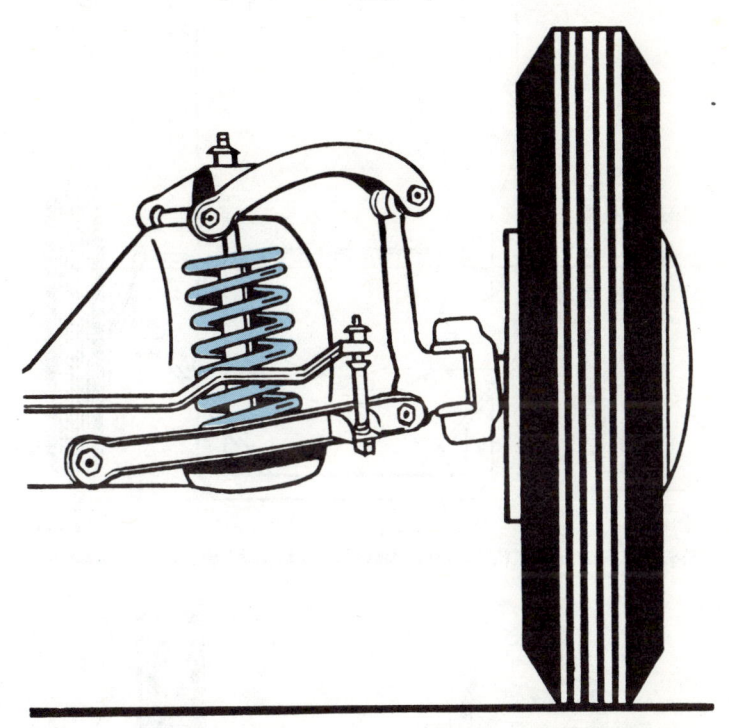

Courtesy Hunter Engineering Co.

ball joint showing excessive wear should be replaced, following the procedure outlined in the manufacturer's service manual.

Replacement of the ball joints on most cars require special tools. Care must be taken when replacing ball joints to prevent any damage to the new parts being installed. Always follow the manufacturer's procedure outlined in the service manual. For example, on certain cars, completely removing the stud nut on either the upper or lower ball joint may result in a sudden release of the coil spring. Since the coil spring is under heavy tension, serious injury can result.

Remember: Always follow the correct procedures.

Stabilizer-Bar Servicing

When replacing the stabilizer bar or support bushings, no oil or grease must be used. Either install the bushings on the bar dry, or use

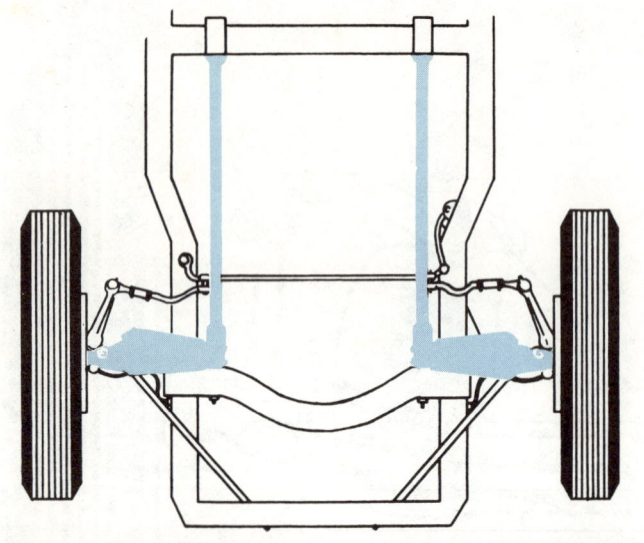

AUTOMOBILE GUIDE

Fig. 8. Location of the torsion bars on a typical domestic automobile.

UPPER BALL JOINT

LOWER BALL JOINT

Courtesy Buick Motor Div., General Motors Corp.

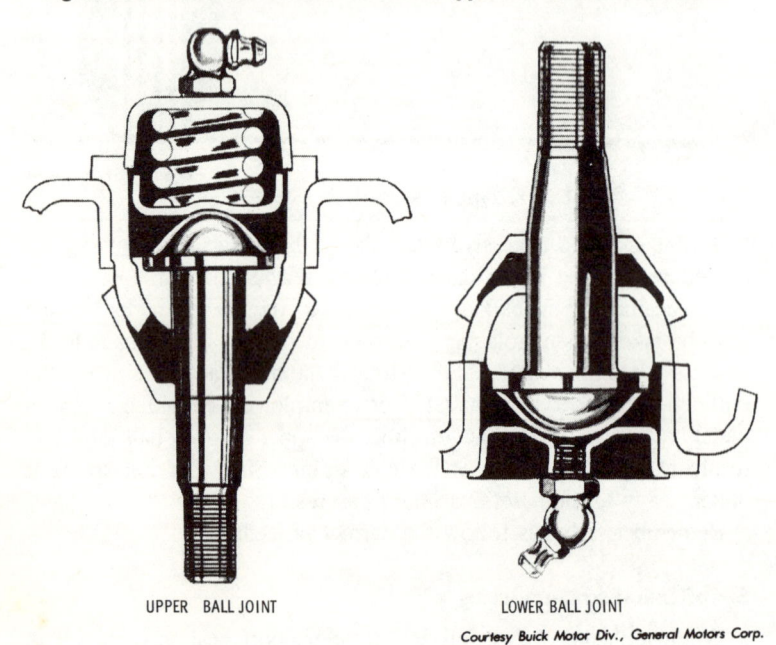

Fig. 9. Typical upper and lower ball joints.

520

FRONT SUSPENSION, CHASSIS, SPRINGS, AND SHOCKS

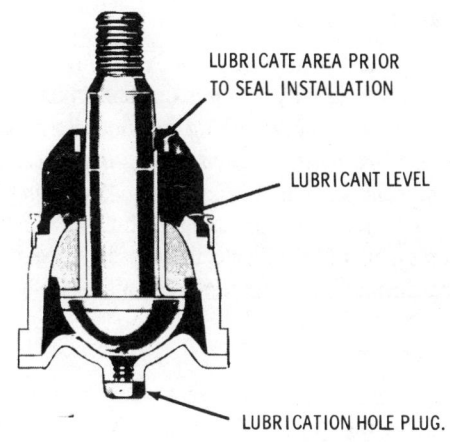

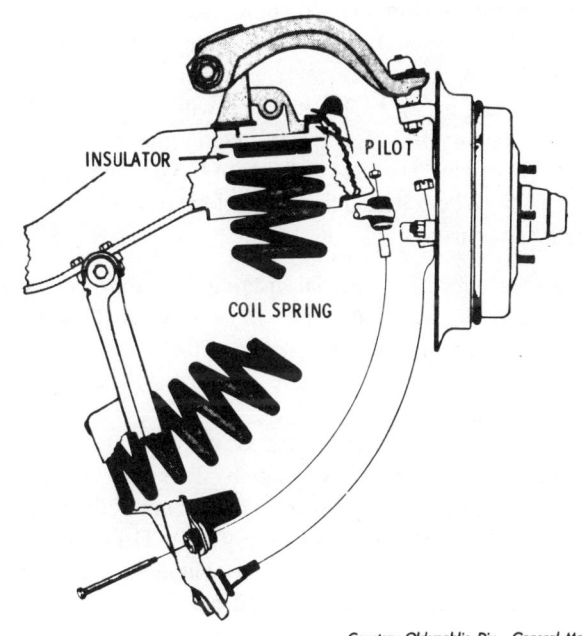

Fig. 10. A typical sealed ball joint.

Fig. 11. Coil spring installation.

water to make their installation easier. Grease or oil will cause these parts to deteriorate rapidly.

521

Coil-Spring Replacement

The coil springs must be replaced if they become weak or if they are broken. This operation usually requires disconnecting the lower control arm at the lower ball joint and swinging the control arm down to free the spring (Fig. 11). *Care must be taken during this operation to prevent the coil spring from suddenly releasing and causing injury to the mechanic.* The manufacturer's procedure should be carefully followed. These procedures generally indicate the use of a special tool to compress the spring during this operation, such a tool is shown in Fig. 12.

Torsion-Bar Service

Late-model *Chrysler*-made cars use torsion bars for the front suspension instead of coil springs. These bars are provided with adjustments which make it possible to raise or lower the suspension height of the car. Fig. 13 shows this adjustment feature which is located at the rear end of the torsion bar. Turning the adjusting bolt clockwise increases the suspension height, and turning the bolt counterclockwise decreases the height.

The front suspension height must be within the specified limits to provide satisfactory tire life. The following procedure can be used to measure this height. The tires must be at the recommended pressures, the gas tank must be full, and the car must have no load in the passenger compartment or trunk.

1. Clean all foreign material from the bottom of the ball-joint assembly on each side of the car. Also clean the bottom of each lower control-arm bushing between the flanges.
2. Bounce the car several times, releasing it on the downward motion.
3. Measure the distance from the lowest point on one of the lower control-arm bushing housings to the floor (measurement A in Fig. 14), and from the flat portion on the bottom of the lower ball joint to the floor (measurement B in Fig. 14). The difference between measurement A and B should be within ⅛-inch of the reading specified for the particular model being serviced.
4. Measure the other side in the same manner. The difference between the two sides should not exceed ⅛-inch.
5. Adjust the torsion bars, if necessary, until the readings for each side of the car are within the specifications and within ⅛-inch of one another.

FRONT SUSPENSION, CHASSIS, SPRINGS, AND SHOCKS

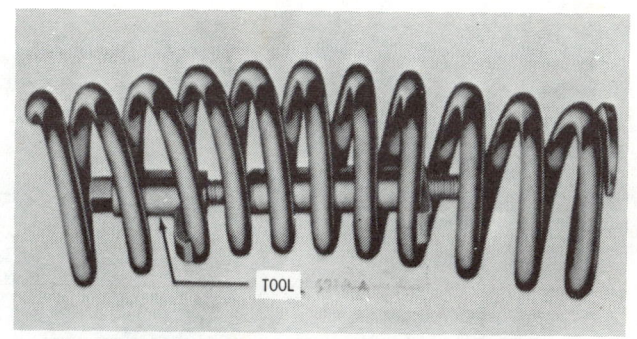

Fig. 12. A coil spring compressed for installation.

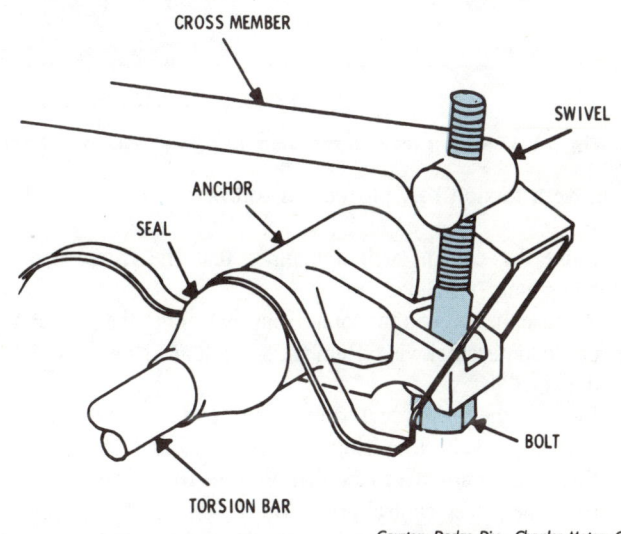

Fig. 13. Torsion-bar adjustment assembly.
Courtesy Dodge Div., Chrysler Motors Corp.

6. Bounce the car after each adjustment before rechecking the measurements. Both sides should be measured, even though only one side has been adjusted.

It will be necessary to install a new torsion bar if it is impossible to bring the suspension to the correct height by the torsion-bar adjustment or if the torsion bar is broken. The torsion bars are not interchangeable side for side. They are marked either right or left by an "R" or an "L" stamped on one end of the bar.

AUTOMOBILE GUIDE

Courtesy Dodge Div., Chrysler Motors Corp.

Fig. 14. Checking front suspension on a CHRYSLER made car.

To remove a torsion bar, proceed as follows:

1. Raise the car in such a manner that the front suspension is completely unloaded.
2. Release the load on the torsion bar by turning the anchor adjusting bolt counterclockwise. Remove the bolt and swivel, and discard if damaged.
3. Remove the plastic seal from the rear end of the torsion bar anchor and remove the lock ring. See Figs. 15 and 16.
4. Slide the torsion bar to the rear until the forward end is disengaged from the lower control arm. Slip the rear anchor balloon seal off the anchor and forward along the torsion bar, being careful not to damage the seal.
5. Remove the torsion bar either by sliding it forward and down until it is clear of the rear anchor, or by sliding it out through the rear of the rear anchor.

To install the torsion bar, proceed as follows:

1. Inspect the balloon seal for damage and replace if necessary.
2. Inspect the torsion bar for scores and nicks. Dress down all scores and nicks to remove the sharp edges, then paint the repaired area with rust preventive.

Front Suspension, Chassis, Springs, and Shocks

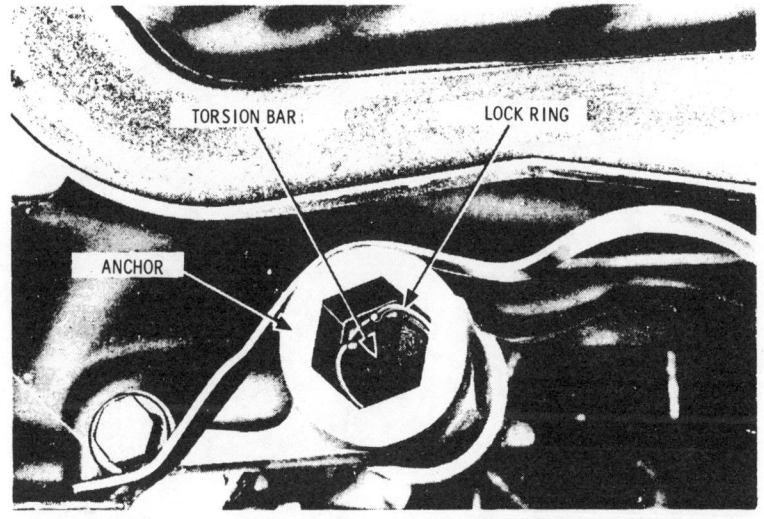

Fig. 15. View of the torsion-bar anchor assembly.

3. Slide the balloon seal over the torsion bar with the cupped side toward the rear anchor.
4. Apply a thick coating of chassis lubricant around each end of the torsion bar.
5. Slide the rear of the torsion bar into the rear-support assembly and turn until the adjusting lug is positioned approximately 120° down from the frame.
6. Engage the front end of the bar in the hex opening of the lower control arm. If the adjusting lug on the rear anchor is not in the position described in step 5, it will be impossible to adjust the front suspension to the correct height.
7. Center the bar so that full contact is obtained at both the rear anchor and the control arm.
8. Install the lock ring, making sure it is seated firmly in its groove.
9. Pack the opening in the forward end of the rear anchor full of multi-purpose lubricant. Position the lip of the balloon seal in the groove in the anchor hub. Install the plastic seal into the rear end of the torsion bar anchor.
10. Position the adjusting bolt swivel and install the adjusting bolt and seat. Tighten the adjusing bolt until approximately 1 inch of thread is showing out of the swivel. This is an approximate

AUTOMOBILE GUIDE

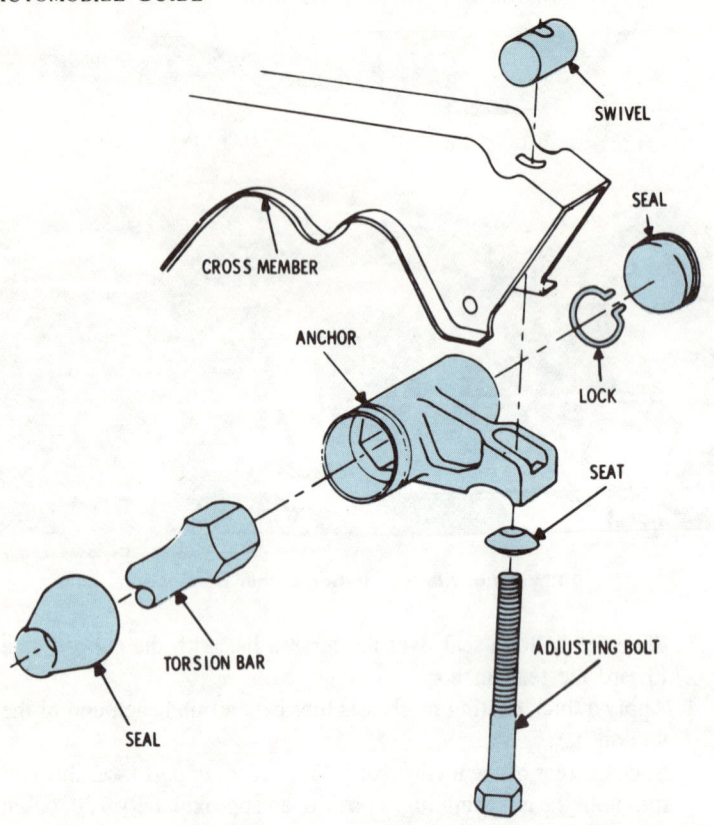

Courtesy Cadillac Motor Car Div., General Motors Corp.
Fig. 16. Exploded view of the torsion-bar anchor assembly.

setting used as a starting point to adjust for the correct suspension height. This setting also places a load on the torsion bar before lowering the vehicle to the floor.
11. Lower the vehicle to the floor, and measure and adjust the suspension height as required.

AIR SUSPENSION

An air-suspension system that replaces the coil springs is used on some automobiles. This system incorporates leveling valves to control the riding qualities and maintain the car at a constant height regardless of the amount of load it is carrying. Most air-suspension systems, while

FRONT SUSPENSION, CHASSIS, SPRINGS, AND SHOCKS

differing somewhat in overall design according to the make and model of car, generally consist of the following units:

1. Air spring (bellows) units.
2. Height control (leveling) valves.
3. Air compressor.
4. Air storage tank (accumulator).
5. Manual control valve.

A diagram of a typical air-suspension system is shown in Fig. 17.

Air-Spring Units — Air springs are located in the same general position as the coil springs on cars with standard suspension. Each air-spring unit (Fig. 18) consists generally of a barrel or dome shaped air chamber into which a rubber diaphragm or bellows is positioned. This diaphragm is compressed by a specially-shaped plunger, the lower end of which is fastened to the axle or lower control arm. The air chamber is fastened to the frame of the car. Thus, the plunger pushes against the diaphragm, attempting to collapse it into the air chamber.

The normal air pressure in the chamber is 100 lbs. or more per square inch. If the car load weight is increased, however, the leveling valve

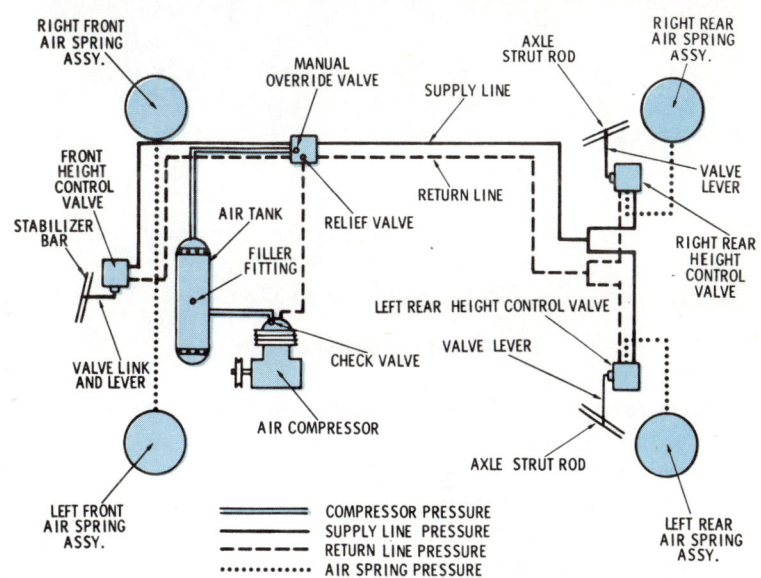

Fig. 17. A diagram of a typical air suspension system showing the air-line connections between the various units.

527

Automobile Guide

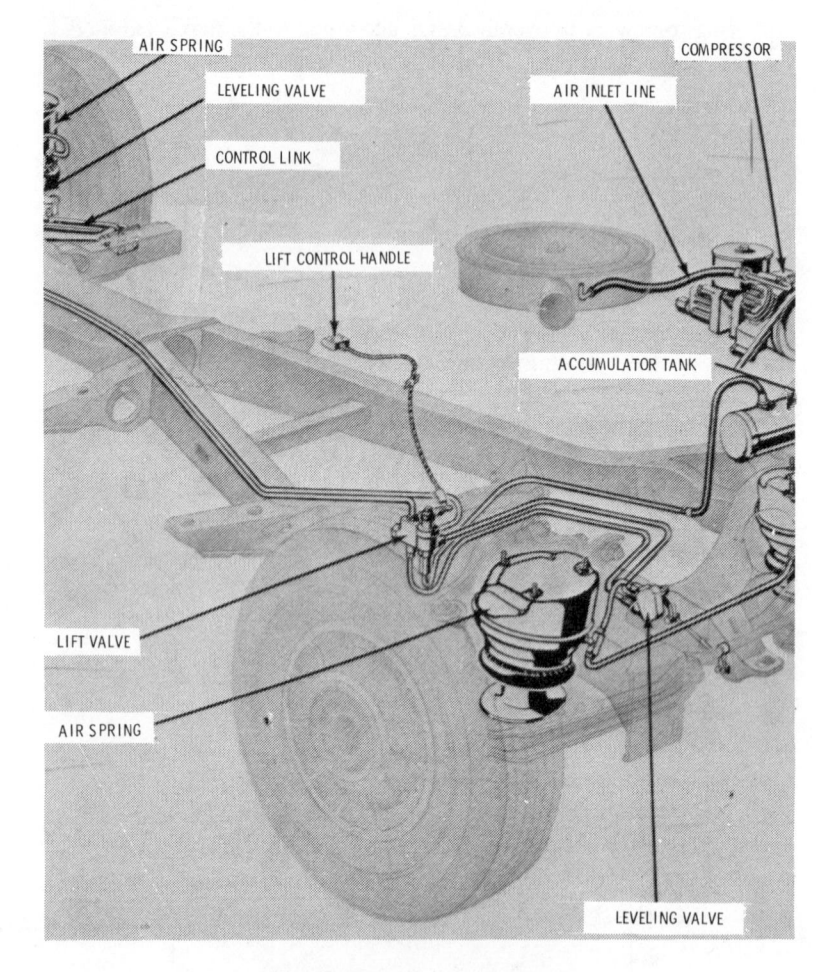

Fig. 18. A front air-spring unit.

causes more air to enter the chamber, increasing the pressure. Thus, the trim height is adjusted to maintain a constant level. A reverse action takes place when the load weight of the car is decreased.

Normal bumps and road vibrations cause no leveling-valve action to take place. Therefore, the air spring units function very much like conventional coil springs during normal driving.

Height-Control Valves — Most cars equipped with air suspension have three height-control valves, one at the front and two at the rear.

Front Suspension, Chassis, Springs, and Shocks

Through the use of these three valves, a constant relationship is maintained in the distance between the spring weight (frame and body) and the ground, regardless of any variations in car loading.

The function of these leveling valves is to control the flow of air to and from the air spring units at each of the four wheels as required to maintain the level of the body parallel to and at a fixed distance from the ground. The leveling valve assemblies are secured to some portion of the car frame, and each actually consists of two valves in one unit. One valve allows air to enter the air domes, and the other valve allows air to escape to the lift valve and then to the atmosphere.

The front leveling valve assembly is mechanically actuated by a link connected to the stabilizer bar. Each of the rear leveling valve assemblies is mechanically actuated by a link connected to some point on the rear-axle assembly.

A dashpot is included in each of the leveling valves to delay the valve action for approximately one second. This prevents the leveling valves from operating as the wheels move rapidly up and down over rough roads. Thus, the leveling system is essentially inactive under most conditions when the car is in motion.

Air Compressor — An air compressor driven by a belt from the crankshaft pulley furnishes the compressed air to operate the air-suspension system. A pressure of approximately 250 lbs. per square inch is maintained in the air storage tank by this compressor. When the pressure of the air in the storage tank equals the capacity of the compressor, the inlet and exhaust valves in the compressor cannot operate and no additional air is supplied.

The compressor unit is usually lubricated by the oil from the car engine and, therefore, needs no manual lubrication when this method is employed. Clean air is drawn into the compressor either through a filter furnished as part of the equipment, or through the carburetor air cleaner.

Air Storage Tank — Compressed air for the system is stored in an air storage tank, sometimes called an accumulator. Its function is to store enough high-pressure air to re-level the car from its curb weight to a normal passenger load without the need for additional air from the compressor. In addition to storing air, the accumulator traps any dirt, oil, or water that might enter the system through the compressor. A drain valve is usually provided in the bottom of the tank to permit draining any accumulated dirt or water. This should be done at regular intervals, such as each time the car is lubricated.

A tire-type valve, located on top of the tank, is also usually provided to introduce air from a service station hose in case the air supply is exhausted while working on the system. Air pressure can also be checked at this valve.

A high-pressure relief or blow-off valve is also located on the tank or at some point in the high-pressure line leading from the tank. This valve is spring-loaded to open if the air pressure should exceed a specified limit, usually 300 to 400 psi. This valve will close automatically after the pressure falls below the specified limit.

A check valve to prevent leakback of air from the accumulator tank when the compressor is not running is located at the port of the tank.

Manual Control Valve — A manual control or lift valve is usually located in an accessible position in the engine compartment. This valve normally contains two major units — a pressure regulator valve, and an override valve.

The pressure regulator valve controls the amount of air pressure from the air storage tank through the leveling valves to the air spring units. The maximum pressure that is allowed to reach the leveling valves and air spring units is predetermined by a factory adjustment of the regulator screw.

The purpose of the override valve is to supply the air springs with regulated air pressure if conditions require that the car body be raised above its normal standing height. The valve is actuated manually at the unit, or, in some cases, by means of a cable-connected handle located on the dash panel. Pulling the control handle out shifts the air pressure into the return air lines from the leveling valves and, at the same time, blocks the exhaust port to the atmosphere. Since the regulated air pressure is greater than the exhaust pressure, the air flow from the air springs through the return lines is reversed, and air enters the air springs, raising the car up to the rebound bumpers. The car will remain at this height until the control handle is pushed back in.

NOTE: Some air suspension systems do not contain a manual control valve as previously described. Instead a manual shut off valve is included which, when closed, prevents the complete exhaust of air from the system. This valve is used when the car is to be hoisted by other than drive-on, ramp-type hoists, or when the frame will be disturbed in relation to the wheel position, such as jacking up one side of the frame, etc.

Front Suspension, Chassis, Springs, and Shocks

FRAME

The frame of most automobiles is a base to which the body and other units are fastened. The most important requirement of the frame is stiffness which must be sufficient to withstand unusual twisting under load, to absorb road shocks, and to keep the attached units in correct alignment.

The plan and construction of the frame differ somewhat in various automobiles, but most consist of side rails, cross members, and gussets, riveted or welded into some form of "A," "X," "Y," or "K" in order to gain maximum stiffness with minimum weight. This type of frame is shown in Fig. 19. Most of the stiffness of the frame is obtained from the steel body structure. One manufacturer does not include a separate frame, as such. Instead, the body forms the principal supporting structure to which the wheels and other units are attached. In this type, shown in Fig. 20, the underbody and sills are welded together to form one single unit. The body is then welded to this assembly, which results in the required stiffness.

Another manufacturer uses two partial frames, one at the front and one at the rear (Fig. 21), welded to the car underbody.

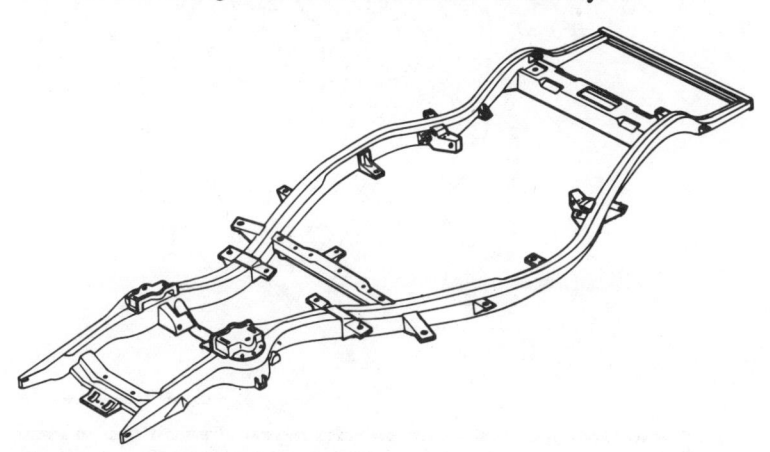

Fig. 19. A typical automobile frame. The body of the car is bolted to this base, the combination forming a rigid unit.

Checking Frame Alignment

Regardless of the type of construction, any misalignment in the frame structure can affect the front wheel alignment and cause improper

531

Automobile Guide

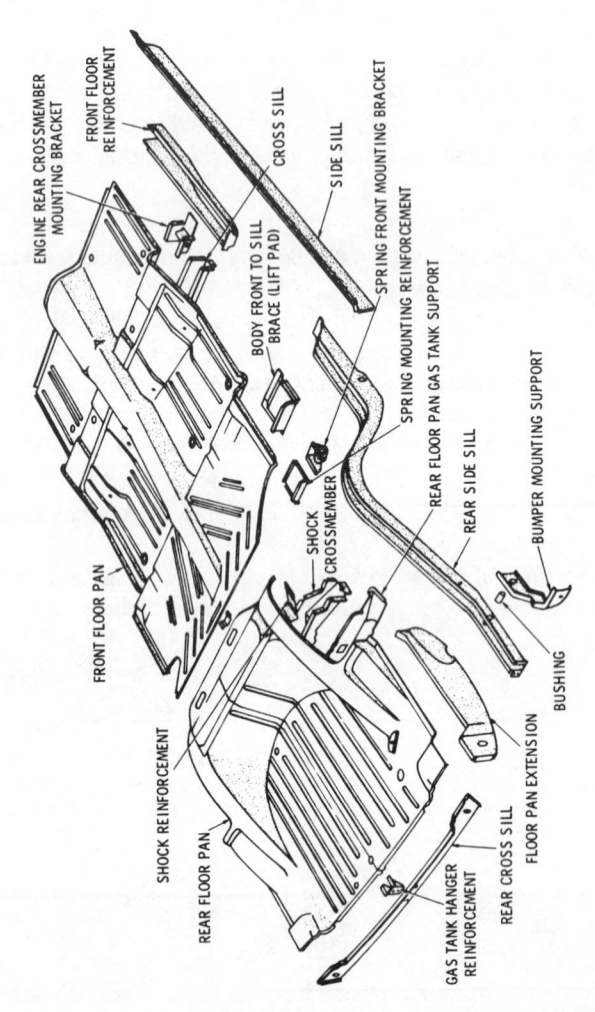

Courtesy American Motors Corp.

Fig. 20. A welded-type construction provides the required stiffness in some automobiles.

operation and abnormal wear of the chassis parts. Cracked window glass, poor fitting and hard-to-close doors, trunk lids, and hoods, are often the result of a bent or twisted frame.

Before checking frame alignment, inspect the frame for damage and loose parts. Inspect all frame members for cracks, twists, and bends.

Front Suspension, Chassis, Springs, and Shocks

FORE-STRUCTURE ASSEMBLY UNDER-BODY OUTER RAILS

UNDER-BODY FLOOR PAN

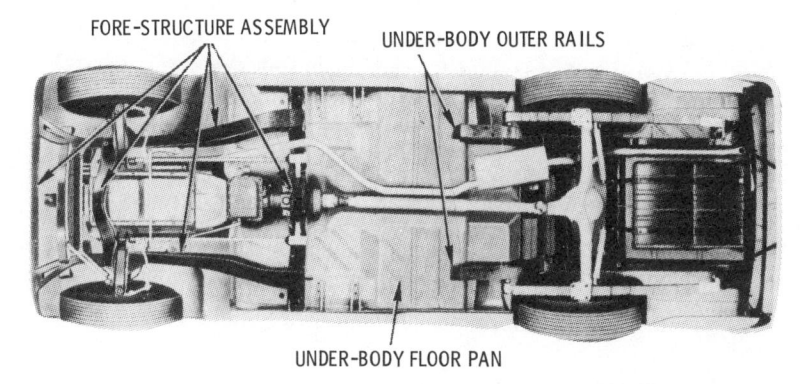

Courtesy Dodge Div., Chrysler Motors Corp.

Fig. 21. Front and rear semi-frame welded to the underbody of the car is used by one automobile manufacturer

Check all welded connections for cracks. Inspect all rivets, bolts, and body support brackets for looseness. Make any necessary repairs or replacements. Fig. 22 shows some typical frame misalignments due to collision or a broken spring hanger.

Several types of commercial frame alignment equipment are available, with complete instructions for their use. If such equipment is not present, however, an adequate job of alignment can usually be accomplished with portable equipment found in most shops. The following procedure outlines a convenient method of checking the frame alignment.

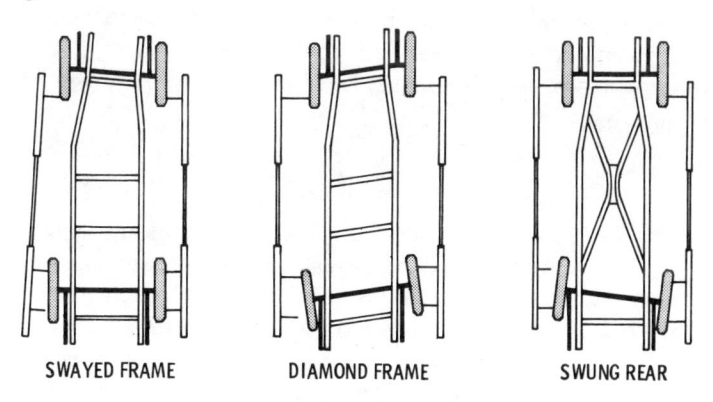

SWAYED FRAME   DIAMOND FRAME   SWUNG REAR

Fig. 22. Frame misalignement problems.

533

AUTOMOBILE GUIDE

1. Place the car on a clean level floor and set the parking brake.
2. Select several points along one frame side member (or along one side of the underbody if the car has no frame) and very carefully transfer these points to the floor by means of a plumb bob.
3. Locate the corresponding points along the opposite side of the frame (or underbody) and carefully transfer these points to the floor in the same manner.
4. Move the car away from the marks on the floor, and measure between points. The corresponding diagonal measurements should be within ⅛-inch of each other. If the measurements differ by more than ⅛-inch, realignment of the frame is indicated.

Frame Repair and Replacement

Misalignment of the frame can be corrected by straightening the defective parts, or by replacing the cross members, braces, or brackets, if they are badly damaged.

To prevent internal stresses in the metal, frame straightening should be limited to those parts which are not severely bent. If heat is needed to straighten a frame member, keep the temperature below 1200°F. This is the temperature at which the metal will glow a dull red. Excessive heat may weaken the metal and cause permanent damage.

Electric welding equipment should be used for all frame welding. Heat should be isolated to as small an area as possible to keep the hardness of the metal from being affected. When a reinforcement is to be welded to a frame side member, run the welds lengthwise along the side of the reinforcement.

If a frame member is to be replaced, use the same method of attachment as on the original member. New bolts or rivets, if required for replacement of parts, should be of the same specifications as the original bolts or rivets.

SPRINGS

The front suspension system of all domestic cars use either coil springs, as shown in Fig. 23, or torsion bars, as shown in Fig. 24. Coil springs and torsion bars were discussed earlier in this chapter.

The rear suspension system will be found to be one of two types — the coil spring, as shown in Fig. 25, or the leaf spring, as shown in Fig. 26. The coil springs used on the rear suspension are basically the same as those used on the front suspension.

Front Suspension, Chassis, Springs, and Shocks

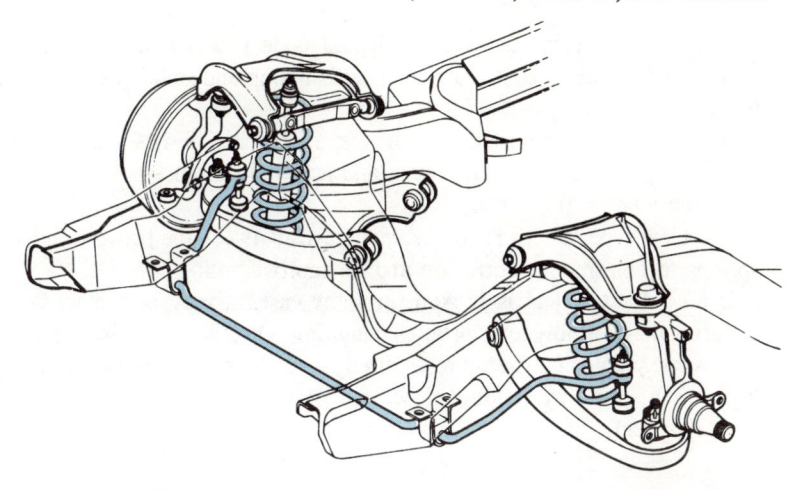

Fig. 23. A typical coil-spring type front suspension.

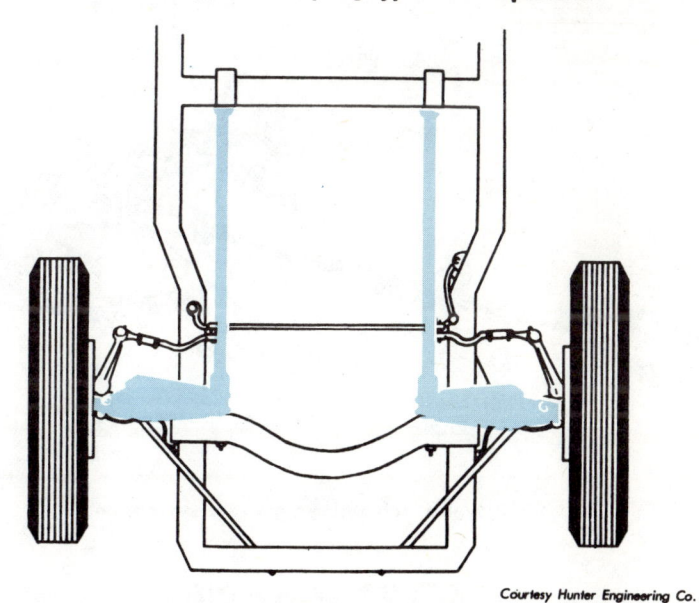

Courtesy Hunter Engineering Co.

Fig. 24. Torsion bars used in the front suspension system of some cars.

Many rear springs are of the leaf type and are designed to have little or no camber under light loads. A small amount of reverse spring camber is normal however when the load on the rear springs is increased.

AUTOMOBILE GUIDE

The flat rear spring gives better lateral (side to side) stability and reduces side sway to contribute to better handling and stability characteristics.

Rubber bushings inserted into the "eye" of each end of the main leaves (Fig. 26), serve as insulators and help reduce noise transmitted from the wheels to the body.

Most leaf type springs have zinc interleaves between the leaves of all springs to help reduce corrosion and to improve spring life.

If an individual leaf is broken, in many cases it may be replaced, restoring the assembly to its original condition. On others, a broken leaf necessitates replacing the entire assembly. No attempt should be made to repair a spring by welding, since the heat will remove the temper from the steel.

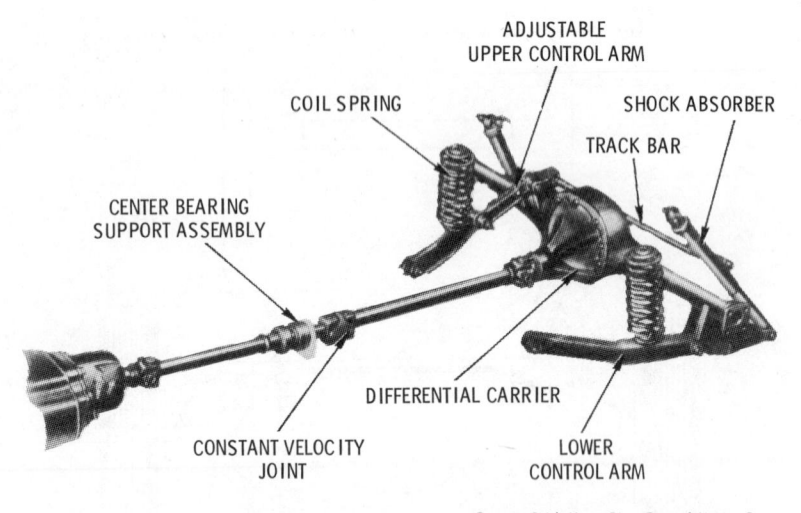

Courtesy Buick Motor Div., General Motors Corp.

Fig. 25. A typical coil-spring type rear suspension.

CHECKING REAR SUSPENSION

The coil spring type of rear suspension should be checked at regular intervals to determine the condition of the rubber bushings in the control arms. A sagging or weak spring should be replaced, following the procedure outlined in the service manual for that particular car. If the rear wheels do not track, check for a bent or misadjusted rear stabilizer

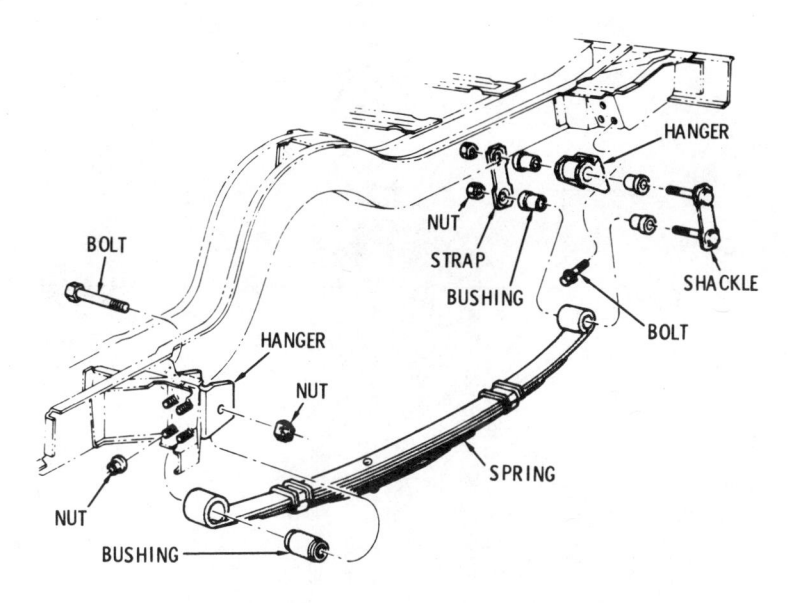

Fig. 26. Typical rear leaf spring assembly.

bar. Some cars have swing-type rear axles, in which case the toe-in of the rear wheels must be checked and adjusted at regular intervals or when abnormal steering indicates the toe-in is incorrect.

On cars with leaf-type rear springs, the rubber bushings, shackles, and hangers should be inspected periodically for wear and looseness. Any defective parts should be replaced.

Check for broken spring leaves, and for worn or missing anitsqueak inserts between the leaves. Replace any worn, broken, or missing parts. Inspect the rear stabilizer bar (if so equipped) for damage, worn grommets, or misadjustment. Repair or adjust as necessary.

SHOCK ABSORBERS

The shock absorbers for all makes and models of automobiles are very similar in construction and operation. They differ only in calibration, physical dimensions, and type of attaching bolt or lug. A cross-sectional view of a typical shock absorber is shown in Fig. 27.

All shocks are filled with a calibrated amount of fluid and sealed during construction. It is therefore impossible to refill or service them

Fig. 27. Rear shock absorber.

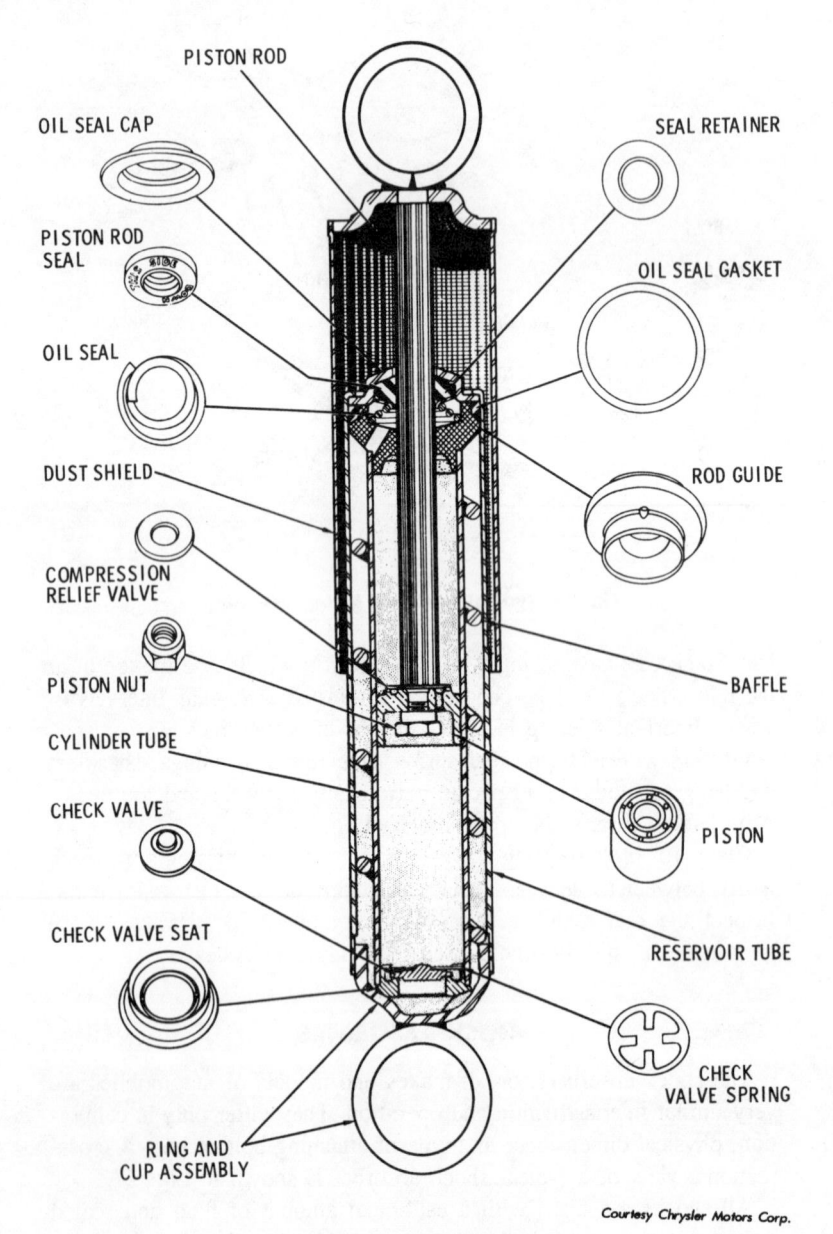

Front Suspension, Chassis, Springs, and Shocks

other than replacement of deteriorated rubber bushings or grommets on the end fittings.

The front shocks are usually mounted on the inside of the coil spring (when the car is so equipped). The upper stem is attached to some part of the frame by means of rubber grommets or bushings to prevent metal-to-metal contact. The lower stem is fastened to the lower control arm, also being insulated from the arm by rubber fittings.

The rear shocks are normally mounted at an angle, with the upper ends in toward the center of the car, to provide greater stability. The upper end is fastened to the frame or body by means of rubber grommets, bushings, or washers. The same method is used to attach the lower end to some part of the rear axle housing.

Front shock absorbers are interchangeable with respect to right or left, as are the rear shocks. However, the front and rear units are not interchangeable with each other on most cars.

Servicing

Defective shock absorbers cannot be repaired, but must be removed and replaced. However, they should only be replaced if they have lost their resistance, are damaged, or if they drip oil. A slight amount of oil moisture on the outside of the shock is not sufficient cause to warrant replacing the unit, however.

To test the shock absorber after it is removed, hold it in an upright position with the dust shield or piston rod section at the top. Extend the shock to its maximum length and turn it upside down. Now compress the shock absorber. Repeat this procedure until it is certain that all air is removed from the unit. Do not extend the shock while it is upside down or laying on its side, because air will enter the unit.

After the air has been bled from the shock, a steady resistance should be felt as the unit is extended and compressed. If no resistance is felt, replace the shock.

A new shock absorber should be bled of all air, in the manner just described, before it is installed. In addition, compressing it to its shortest length will usually be necessary in order to make the installation.

NOTE: Whenever it is necessary to replace one shock absorber, it is generally advisable to replace all four if possible. If this is not practical, it is almost essential (particularly on the front end), to replace them in pairs.

SUSPENSION-SYSTEM TROUBLES AND REMEDIES
STANDARD SYSTEM

Symptoms and Possible Causes *Possible Remedies*

Hard Steering

(a) Low tire pressure.
(b) Lack of lubrication.
(c) Improper wheel alignment.
(d) Sagging front or rear spring.
(e) Bent wheel or spindle.
(f) Defective wheel bearings.
(g) Tight ball joints.
(h) Upper or lower control arms bent.
(i) Torsion bar broken.

(a) Inflate tires to recommended pressure.
(b) Lubricate according to instructions.
(c) Align front end.
(d) Replace springs as required.
(e) Straighten or replace wheel, or replace spindle.
(f) Replace wheel bearings as required.
(g) Lubricate or replace as required.
(h) Replace control arms as required.
(i) Replace torsion bar.

Front Wheel Shimmy

(a) Underinflated tires.
(b) Broken or loose wheel bearings.
(c) Worn ball joints.
(d) Improper wheel alignment.
(e) Loose wheel lugs.
(f) Bent wheel.
(g) Wheels out of balance.

(a) Inflate tires to recommended pressure.
(b) Replace or adjust wheel bearings.
(c) Replace ball joints.
(d) Align front end.
(e) Tighten lugs.
(f) Straighten or replace wheel.
(g) Balance wheels.

Excessive Play in Steering System

(a) Worn ball joints.
(b) Front wheel bearings worn or loose.

(a) Replace ball joints.
(b) Replace or adjust wheel bearings as required.

Front Suspension, Chassis, Springs, and Shocks

Symptoms and Possible Causes

(c) Front stabilizer-bar link loose or bushings worn.

Possible Remedies

(c) Tighten link or replace bushings as required.

AIR-SUSPENSION SYSTEM

Symptoms and Possible Causes

System Will Not Hold Air

(a) Leaks in system.

(b) Compressor output low.

(c) Safety valve leaking.

(d) Drain cock leaking or open.

(e) Lift valve control handle in middle position.

Air-Spring Unit Not Functioning Properly

(a) Broken, bent, or worn leveling valve.
(b) Pinched or plugged air line to leveling valve.
(c) Ruptured bellows on air-spring unit.
(d) Leak in air dome.

Possible Remedies

(a) Check all lines, fittings, valves, reservoir, and air-spring bellows for leaks, and repair or replace as required.

(b) Check efficiency of compressor as per manufacturer's instructions.

(c) Repair or replace safety valve.

(d) Replace or close drain cock.

(e) Place handle either all the way in or all the way out.

(a) Repair or replace leveling valve.
(b) Replace line.

(c) Replace bellows.

(d) Test air dome and fittings for leaks. Install new O-ring seal and tighten fitting.

System Loses All Air When Car is Hoisted

(a) Manual shutoff valve open.

(a) Close manual shutoff valve before hoisting.

AUTOMOBILE GUIDE

Symptoms and Possible Causes	Possible Remedies

Car Raises to Full-Rebound Position

(a) Manual shutoff valve closed with compressor running.
(b) Lift control handle pulled out.
(c) Lift control valve defective.

(a) Open manual shutoff valve.
(b) Push lift control handle in.
(c) Repair or replace lift control valve.

Car Will Not Rise to Design Height With Compressor Operating

(a) Compressor discharge line not connected or broken.
(b) Accumulator drain cock open.
(c) Excessive number of leaks in system.

(a) Connect or replace discharge line.
(b) Close drain cock.
(c) Check entire system for leaks and repair as required.

Hard Riding

(a) Incorrect standing height.
(b) Insufficient air pressure in system.

(a) Check and adjust front and rear standing height.
(b) Replenish air supply and check for leaks.

Air System Too Sensitive — Excessive Leveling Action

(a) Leveling-valve dashpot does not delay valve action.

(a) Replace dashpot.

Frequent Operation of Accumulator Blow-Off (Safety) Valve

(a) Pressure too high because of carbon deposits in compressor cylinder.
(b) Defective blow-off valve.

(a) Remove compressor cylinder heads and remove carbon.
(b) Replace blow-off valve.

FRONT SUSPENSION, CHASSIS, SPRINGS, AND SHOCKS

SPRING AND SHOCK TROUBLES AND REMEDIES

Symptoms and Possible Causes   *Possible Remedy*

Springs Sag or Bottom

(a) Springs sag.
(b) Broken spring leaf.
(c) Bent or weak spring leaf.

(a) Replace spring assembly.
(b) Replace leaf or assembly.
(c) Replace leaf or assembly.

Noisy Spring

(a) Loose "U" bolt.
(b) Loose or worn "eye" bushing(s).
(c) Loose or broken hanger.
(d) Loose or broken shackle.
(e) Interliner(s) worn or missing.

(a) Tighten "U" bolt nuts to specifications.
(b) Replace "eye" bushing(s).
(c) Tighten or replace hanger.
(d) Tighten or replace shackle.
(e) Replace interliner(s).

Noisy Shock Absorber

(a) Worn bushing.
(b) Loose mounting bolt or stud.
(c) Air trapped in shock.
(d) Undercoating on reservoir.

(a) Replace bushing(s).
(b) Tighten to specifications.
(c) Purge air from shock.
(d) Clean shock.

Oil Dripping From Shock Absorber

(a) Damaged shock absorber.
(b) Worn seal.

(a) Replace shock absorber.
(b) Replace shock absorber.

CHAPTER 22

Steering System

Many different types of steering systems have been used on automobiles in the past. Constant improvements and new designs necessary to meet the demands of higher driving speeds and changed suspension, however, have resulted in one general type of system being used on nearly all U.S. cars manufactured at the present time.

CONTROL LINKAGE

The proper design and correct adjustment of the steering control linkage is of the utmost importance if satisfactory tire wear and good car-handling characteristics are to be obtained. The linkage mechanism shown in Fig. 1 is typical of that found on most domestic cars in use today, and is the result of careful design after years of research.

Turning Angles

The steering geometry designed into the steering system causes all wheels to pivot around the same center as the car is turned. When this happens, a different turning angle exists for each front wheel, as shown in Fig. 2. Notice that the front wheels are actually toed-out under this condition. The amount of this toe-out increases as the turn is shortened. In order to provide the correct toe-out when turning, the steering arms are positioned at an angle with the wheels. The angle the steering arms should make with the wheels is determined by extending an imaginary line through the plane of each arm and having the two lines intersect at the center of the rear axle (Fig. 3).

Steering System

If the steering arms were placed parallel to the front wheels, as in Fig. 4, the wheels would remain parallel on a turn and all tires would scuff. In addition, turning effort would increase.

The turning angle of the front wheels of an automobile can be checked on special wheel-alignment equipment. If, for example, one of the front wheels is turned *in* 20°, as in Fig. 5, this wheel simulates the wheel on the outside of the curve of a turning vehicle. The opposite, or inside, wheel should then be at a turned angle of *more* than 20°. The correct angles for the two wheels are listed in the specifications of the car manufacturer or in the charts supplied with the wheel-alignment equipment. Some car manufacturers specify the turning angle of the wheel on the outside of the curve when the inside wheel is turned out 20°. In this case, the specified angle of the outside wheel will be less than 20° (Fig. 6).

If the turning angle readings are different than those specified, one or both steering arms have been bent and must be replaced. Do not attempt to straighten a bent arm, either cold or hot, for to do so may cause the arm to break while the car is being driven. Therefore, always replace a bent steering arm with a new unit.

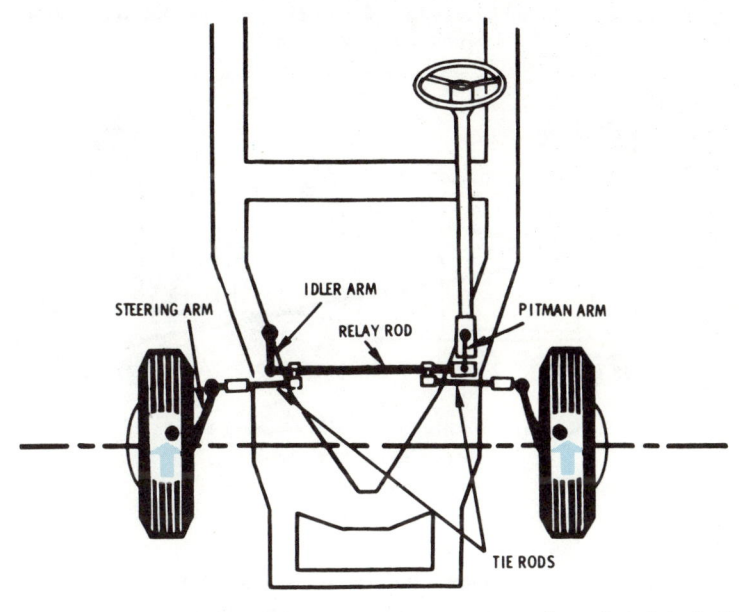

Courtesy Hunter Engineering Co.

Fig. 1. Steering control linkage of a typical automobile.

545

AUTOMOBILE GUIDE

TOE-OUT

ALL WHEELS TURN FROM THE SAME CENTER

Courtesy Hunter Engineering Co.

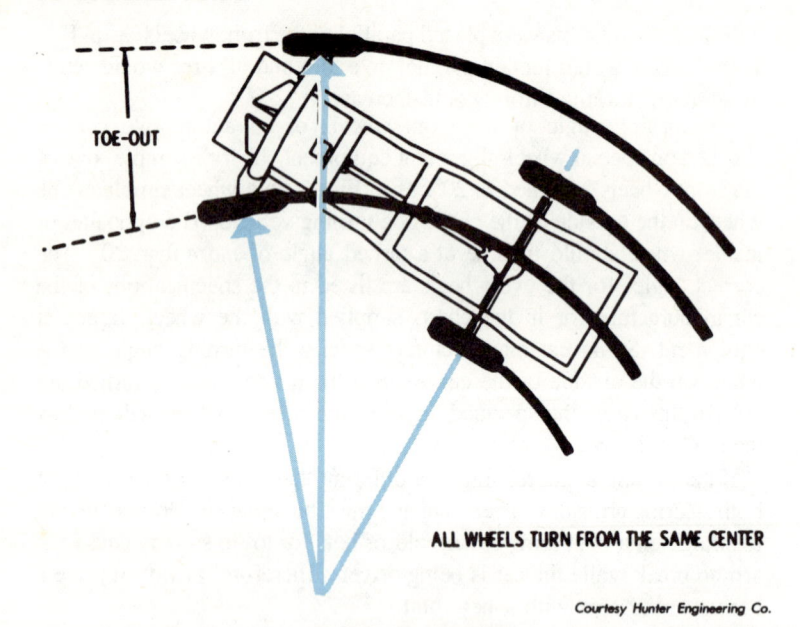

Fig. 2. All wheels of an automobile should pivot around the same center when a turn is made.

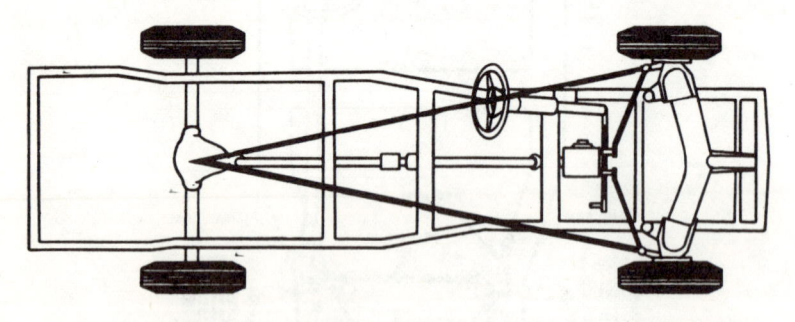

Fig. 3. Manner in which the angle that the steering arms make with the wheels is determined.

Toe-In

All four wheels of an automobile should be parallel with one another when the car is traveling in a straight line. If the wheels are not parallel, tire scuff will result. To obtain this parallel condition for average

STEERING SYSTEM

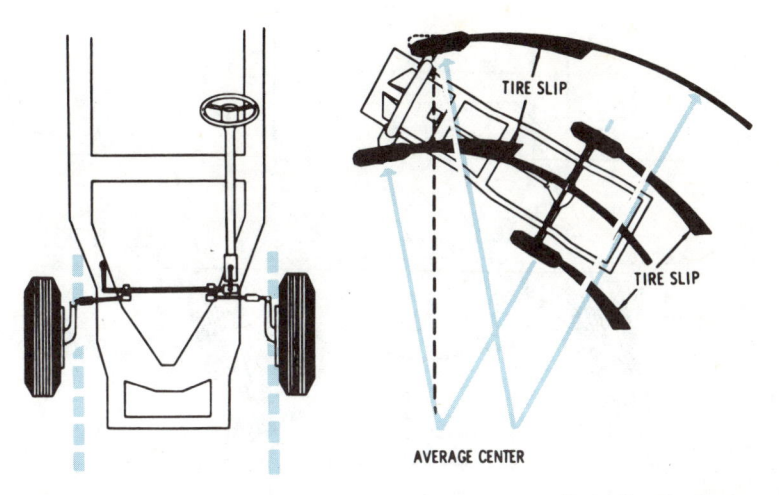

Courtesy Hunter Engineering Co.

Fig. 4. Steering arms that are parallel to the wheels cause each front wheel to pivot around a different center. This causes all tires to slip.

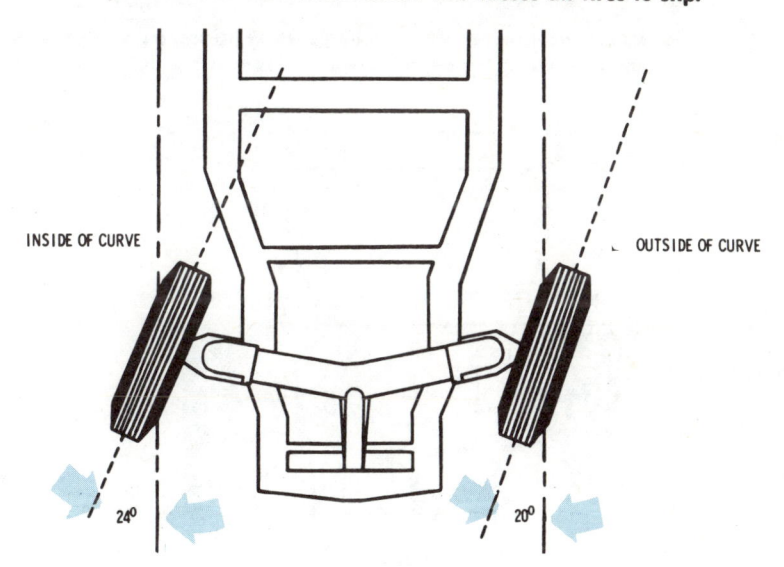

Courtesy Hunter Engineering Co.

Fig. 5. A check of the turning angle in which the wheel on the outside of the curve is turned to 20°. The inside wheel then should be at some specified angle greater than 20°.

547

Automobile Guide

INSIDE OF CURVE   OUTSIDE OF CURVE

20°   18°

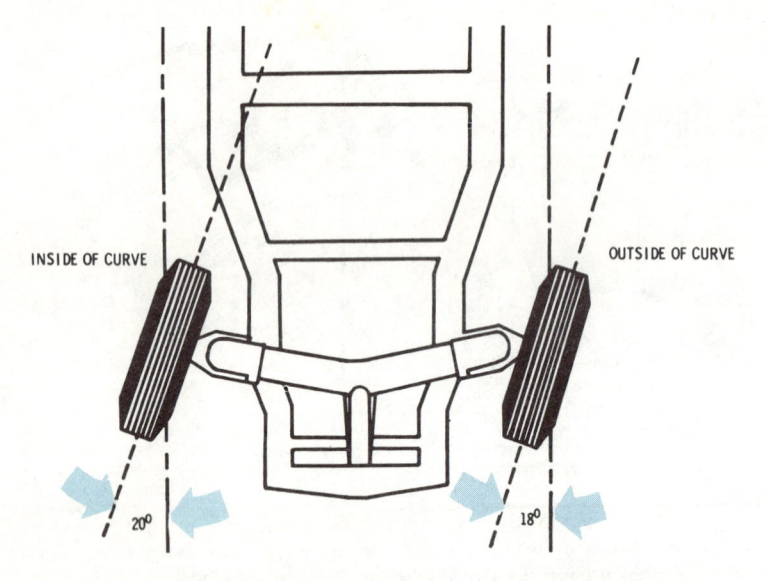

Courtesy Hunter Engineering Co.

Fig. 6. Some manufacturers specify the angle at which the outside wheel should be when the opposite wheel is turned out 20°.

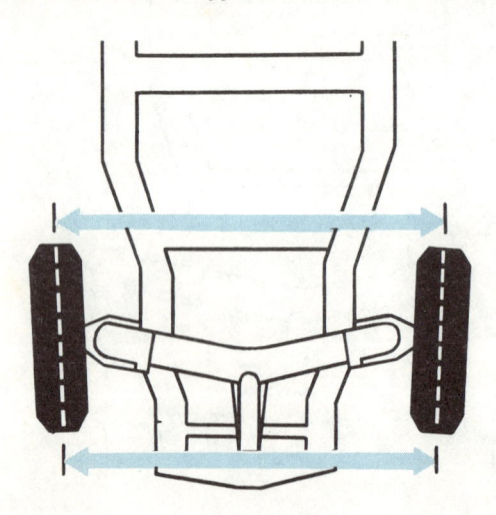

Courtesy Hunter Engineering Co.

Fig. 7. Toe-in is the amount that the front wheels are closer together at the extreme front of the tires than they are at the extreme rear.

STEERING SYSTEM

driving, it is usually necessary to set a small amount of toe-in to the front wheels when the car is stationary. As shown in Fig. 7, toe-in is the amount that the front wheels are closer together at the extreme front of the tires than they are at the extreme rear. This amount is measured in fractions of an inch.

Toe-in compensates for small deflections caused by rolling resistance and braking, which tends to spread the front of the wheels outward. The steering linkage on most cars is symmetrical, and is designed so that the path of the ball stud on the end of the tie rod is nearly the same as the path of the suspension-system geometry. This is shown in Fig. 8. Thus, the amount of toe changes very little as the car is loaded. Nevertheless, a small change does take place, and accounts for another reason for a toe-in of the wheels while the car is standing unloaded.

A small amount of running toe-out will cause no more tire wear than the same amount of toe-in. Why, then, is it necessary to have toe-in? The answer to this is that even a small amount of toe-out will tend to cause the car to wander.

Fig. 8. The steering linkage on most cars is symmetrical and designed so the path of the tie-rod ball is nearly identical to the path of suspension system geometry.

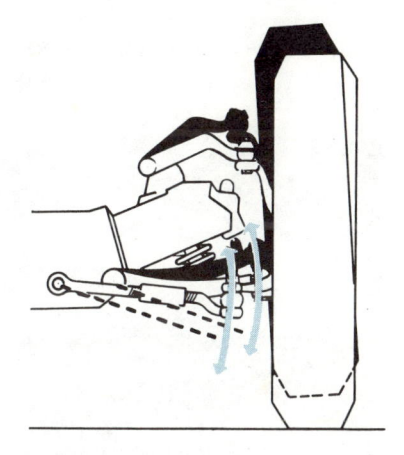

Courtesy Hunter Engineering Co.

Any wear or looseness in the steering linkage will have an unfavorable effect on the toe conditions, causing a running toe-out even though the proper toe-in setting is made while the car is stationary.

Toe-in adjustment is made by turning the sleeves located in the end of each tie rod. These sleeves are secured by clamps which must be loosened before adjustment can be made. As shown in Fig. 9, the

Automobile Guide

left-hand sleeve is turned in the direction of tire rotation when driving to *decrease* toe-in. The right-hand sleeve must be turned in the opposite direction to decrease toe-in. Whether the sleeves are turned to decrease or increase toe-in, both should be turned exactly the same amount. If one sleeve is turned more than the other, the steering wheel will not be in its normal center position, even though the correct toe-in may exist.

A commercial toe-in gauge being used to measure the distance between the extreme front of the front wheels is shown in Fig. 10. A similar measurement made at the extreme rear of the front wheels is necessary before the amount of toe-in existing can be determined.

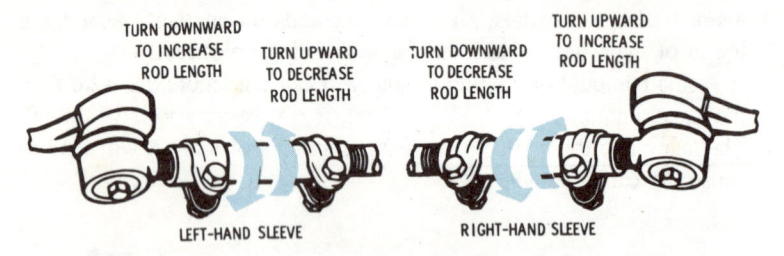

Fig. 9. The sleeve on the end of each tie rod is turned to change the length of the tie rod.

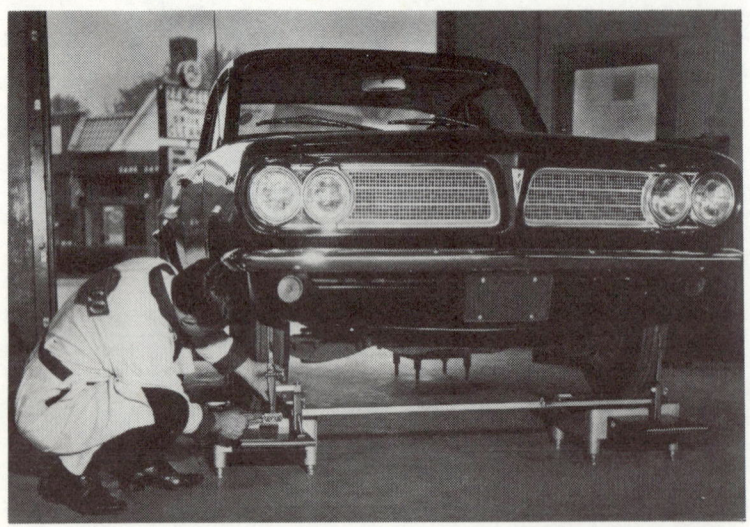

Fig. 10. A toe-in gauge being used in aligning the front wheels.

STEERING SYSTEM

Center-Point Steering

Center-point steering means that condition when the steering wheel is in its normal (level or straight-ahead) position, the worm gear is in the center of the steering worm, the pitman and idler arms are in a centered position, and each of the front wheels is at the same angle with an imaginary line drawn down through the center of the vehicle (Fig. 11). On new cars this condition can be expected to exist. Therefore, by leveling the steering wheel, the front wheels should then be in the straight ahead position necessary for measuring and correcting toe-in.

On older vehicles, or those that might have been damaged, it is recommended that the complete steering assembly be checked for center-point steering. With the car stopped (after being driven straight ahead for a short distance), turn the steering wheel completely to the right. Now turn the wheel completely to the left, counting the exact number of revolutions plus any fractions of a revolution (for example,

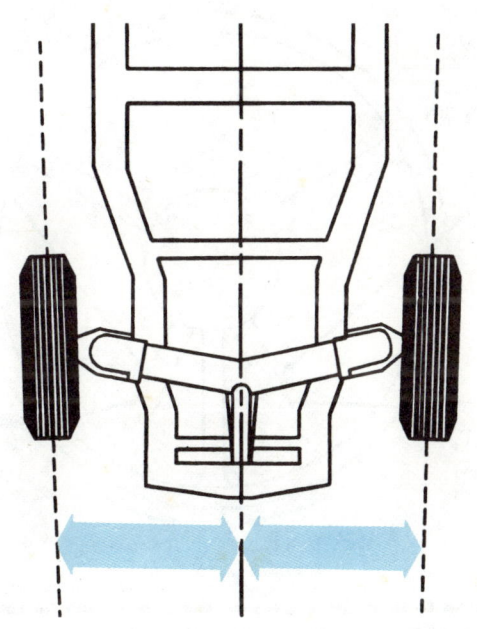

Courtesy Hunter Engineering Co.

Fig. 11. The front wheels of an automobile, when in a straight-ahead position, are not necessarily parallel. When correctly aligned, each front wheel is at the same angle with an imaginary line drawn through the center of the car.

551

Automobile Guide

three and one-half turns). Turn the steering wheel back to the right exactly half of this number of revolutions (one and three-quarter revolutions, in this case). Check the position of the pitman and idler arms. If they are not centered, it means the steering worm gear is not centered on the steering arm. In this case it may be necessary to remove the steering wheel and reposition it in a level position after setting the pitman and idler arms in a centered position. Bent parts of the steering linkage may also cause this condition. Replace such parts — **do not attempt to straighten them.**

It is sometimes possible to obtain correct center-point steering by turning the sleeves on the ends of both tie rods an equal amount in the same direction. The direction to turn the sleeves is shown in Fig. 12. When any adjustment has been made on the tie-rod ends, it is important that the sleeve clamp bolts are positioned correctly before they are tightened so as not to cause interference with any part of the car.

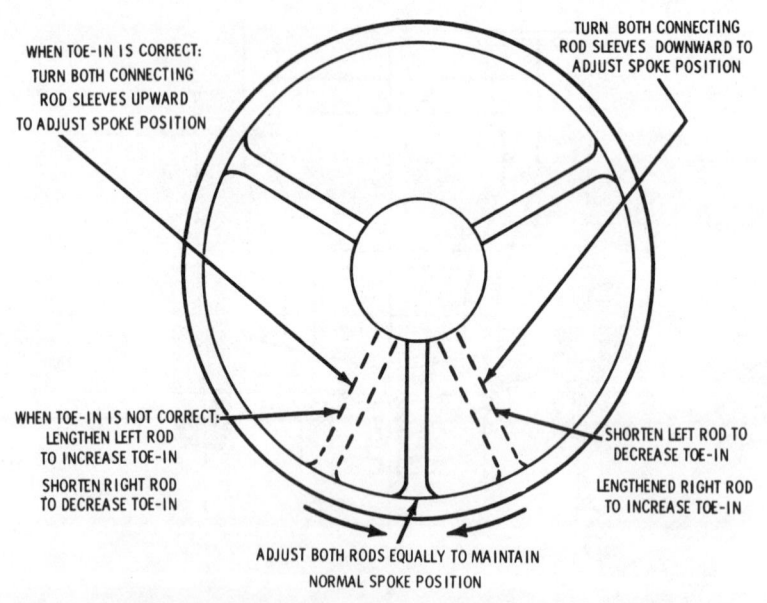

Fig. 12. Direction to turn the sleeves on the ends of the tie rods to correct toe-in or to adjust the position of the steering wheel.

Steering-Linkage Service

All parts of the steering linkage should be examined periodically or whenever steering troubles are encountered. Any part that has been bent

Steering System

or damaged should be replaced with a new part. *Do not attempt to straighten or repair any component part of the steering linkage.* Straightening a bent part or welding a damaged part will cause metal fatigue which may result in failure of that part while the car is being driven.

Ball Studs

Ball studs are used on most steering linkages (Fig. 13) to provide ease of movement and to help minimize wear. Some types of ball studs are permanently lubricated and have no provisions for additional lubricant. Other types have a plug in the ball stud that can be removed so a regular grease fitting may be installed. Still other types are equipped with a grease fitting and require lubrication at regular intervals.

Generally, the sealed-type ball stud has been designed so it does not require lubricant as long as its seals remain undamaged. If provisions for lubrication are not provided and the seals are broken the stud should be replaced.

Any ball stud showing excessive looseness should be replaced as no adjustment is provided on most cars to correct this condition. Care must be taken when tightening the nut on a ball stud that it is tightened to the torque specified by the manufacturer. **Make sure the cotter pin is installed through the castellated nut and through the bolt to prevent the nut from working loose.**

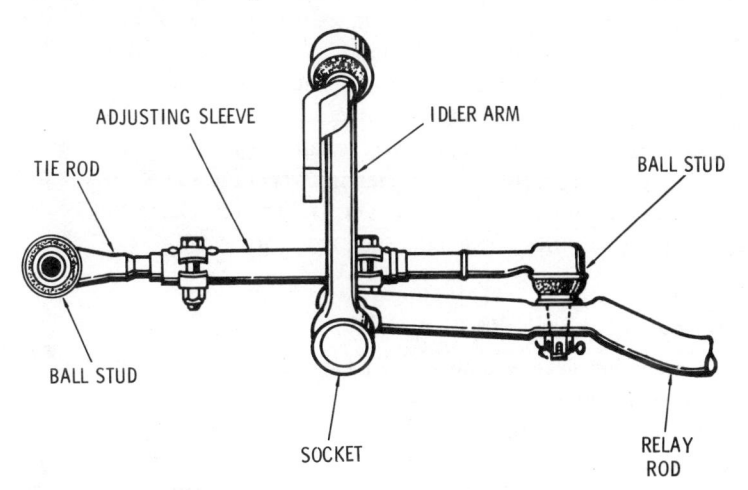

Fig. 13. Partial steering linkage detail; note the use of a castellated nut, secured with a cotter pin, to fasten the tie rod end ball stud to the relay rod.

553

Tie-Rod Ends

When new tie-rod ends are installed, make sure both ends are threaded into the tie rods an equal amount. Usually, from $\frac{1}{4}''$ to $\frac{3}{8}''$ of thread should be exposed between the tie-rod and the sleeve. This amount of exposed threads is necessary to allow adjustment for toe-in and center-point steering.

Pitman and Idler Arms

Any time either the pitman or idler arms are removed, the steering linkage should be placed in the straight-ahead position and kept there until the arm or arms have been replaced. The steering wheel should be secured in some way to prevent its turning. In addition, before removing the pitman arm, a mark should be inscribed on both the arm and pitman shaft to insure that the arm will be positioned correctly on the splined shaft when reinstalled.

Make sure the idler-arm support bracket is adjusted according to specifications, if it is the adjustable type.

STEERING GEAR

The steering gear, mounted on the end of the steering column, operates the pitman arm which moves the steering linkage. The number of revolutions the steering wheel must make to turn the front wheels from hard left to hard right is determined by the ratio of the steering sector gear to the worm gear. The ratio is different for different makes and models, and whether they have manual or power steering. An average ratio for manual steering is around 24:1, while for power steering the ratio is somewhat lower, usually around 18:1. The higher the ratio, the more revolutions the steering wheel must make to turn the front wheels from hard left to hard right, or vice versa. Generally, older cars will have a lower gear ratio than new cars.

Recirculating Ball Worm and Nut

The steering gear assembly in all *General Motors* and *Ford*-made cars manufactured in recent years are very much alike, using the recirculating ball worm and nut design. Fig. 14 shows a typical steering gear used on a modern car. Two sets of 25 balls each are used in the steering gear shown, with each set operating independently of the other. The worm on the lower end of the steering shaft, and the ball nut which

STEERING SYSTEM

Fig. 14. Cross-sectional view of a recirculating-ball type steering gear.

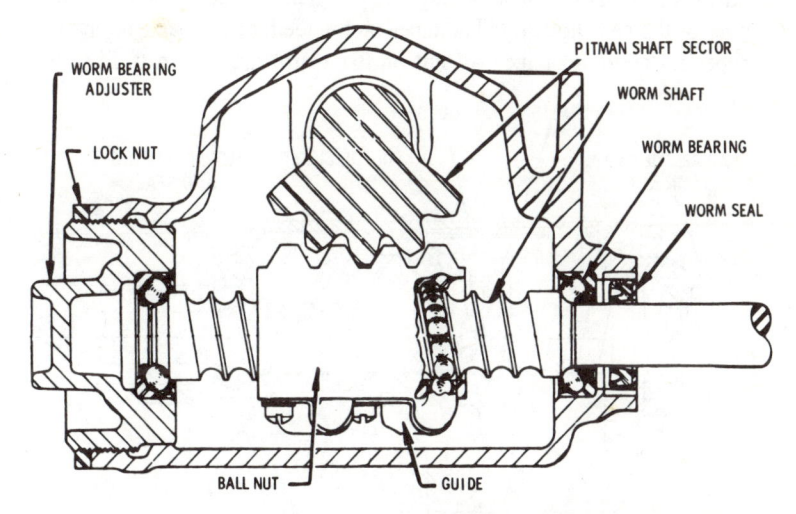

Courtesy Buick Motor Div., General Motors Corp.

is mounted on the worm have mating spiral grooves in which the steel balls circulate to provide a low friction drive between the worm and nut.

A cutaway view of a similar steering gear is shown in Fig. 15. The only appreciable difference between this unit and the one shown in Fig. 14 is the number of steel balls used. There are 27 balls, instead of 25, in each set in the gear shown in Fig. 15.

The circuit through which each set of balls circulate includes the grooves in the worm and ball nut, and a ball return guide attached to the outside of the nut. When the steering shaft turns to the left, the ball nut is forced toward the lower end of the worn by the balls which roll between the worm and ball nut. As the balls reach the outer surface of the nut, they enter the return guides which direct them across and down into the other side of the ball nut, where they enter the circuit again. When a right turn is made, the ball nut is forced toward the upper end of the worm, and the balls circulate in the reverse direction.

Teeth on the side of the ball nut mesh with the teeth of a sector gear forged on the end of the pitman shaft. The teeth on the ball nut are made so that a tighter fit exists between them and the teeth on the sector gear when the front wheels are in the straight-ahead position. In addition, the teeth of the sector gear and ball nut are slightly tapered so that the

AUTOMOBILE GUIDE

proper lash between the two can be obtained by moving the pitman shaft endways by means of an adjusting screw which extends through the side cover of the gear housing. The taper on the teeth of the ball nut and the proper installation of the ball nut on the worm are shown in Fig. 16.

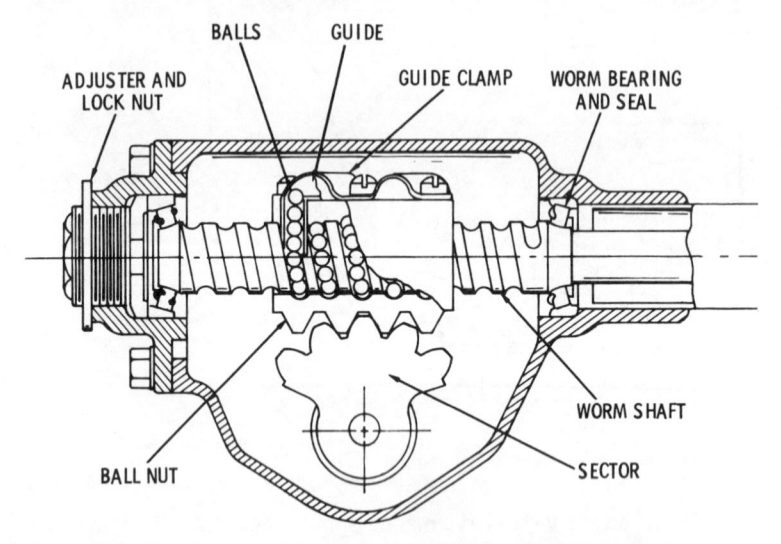

Fig. 15. Cutaway view of the recirculating-ball type gear.

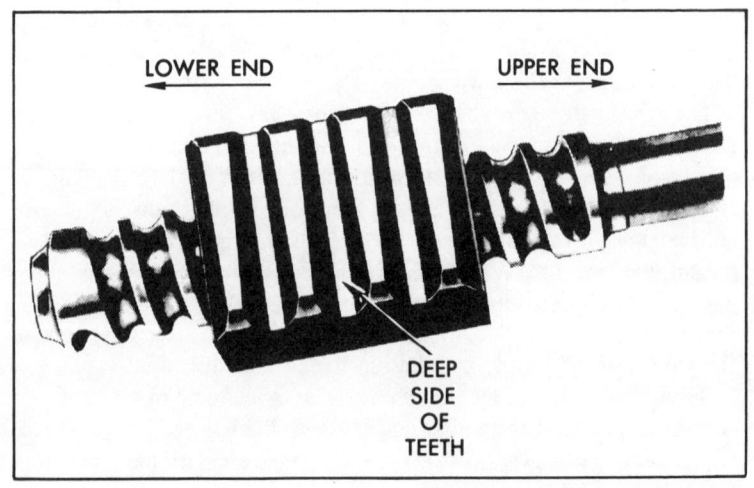

Courtesy Pontiac Motor Div., General Motors Corp.

Fig. 16. Proper installation of the ball nut on the worm of a steering gear.

556

STEERING SYSTEM

End play of the worm and the proper preloading of the upper and lower worm bearings is taken care of by an adjustment nut at either the upper or lower worm bearing. This adjustment is at the lower worm bearing on *General Motors* cars, and at the upper worm bearing on *Ford*-made cars.

Worm and Roller

Late-model *American Motors* and *Chrysler*-made cars use a worm-and-roller type manual steering gear similar to the one shown in Fig. 17. In this type of steering gear, a roller in the cross (pitman) shaft meshes with the worm on the lower end of the steering shaft. As the worm rotates, the roller actually turns, instead of sliding as with a normal

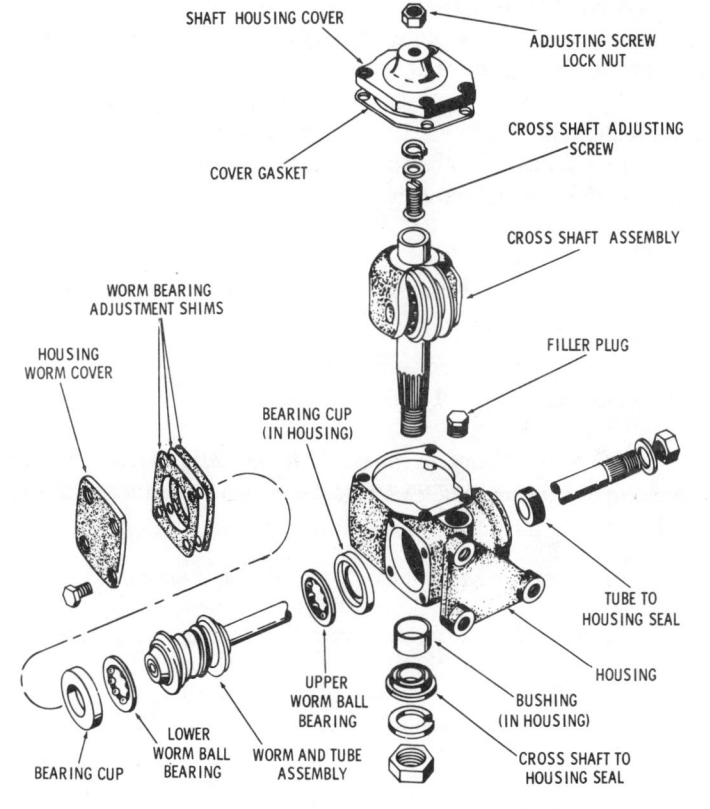

Fig. 17. Exploded view of a worm-and-roller type manual steering gear.

AUTOMOBILE GUIDE

worm and sector gear. This greatly reduces friction and the effort necessary to steer the automobile.

End play of the worm is adjusted by adding or removing shims between the worm-bearing cover and the steering housing. Proper mesh between the roller and worm is obtained by an adjusting screw at the roller end of the cross shaft.

STEERING-GEAR SERVICE AND ADJUSTMENT

Correct adjustment of the steering gear is extremely important for maximum driving comfort and safety, and to prevent damage to the steering gear components. Before any adjustments are made to the steering gear in an effort to correct conditions such as shimmy, hard or loose steering, and road shocks, a check should be made to determine that shock absorbers, ball joints, tie-rod ends, wheel balance, front-end alignment, and tire pressure are adjusted correctly and/or are operating properly. Before servicing the steering system the battery ground cable should be disconnected. Some service is performed with the horn button or ring removed and disconnecting the battery eliminates annoying horn blowing during testing and adjustments.

Recirculating-Ball Type

There are two adjustments on the recirculating-ball type steering gear:

1. Worm bearing preload adjustment.
2. Sector and ball-nut backlash adjustment.

CAUTION: It is very important that the adjustments on the steering gear be made in the foregoing sequence. Failure to do so may result in damage to the steering gear.

To adjust the worm-bearing preload, proceed as follows:

1. Disconnect the pitman arm from the steering linkage assembly.

   NOTE: Do not attempt to adjust the steering gear while it is connected to the steering linkage. The steering gear must be free of all outside load in order to make the proper adjustments.

2. Loosen the pitman arm adjusting screw lock nut and back off the adjusting screw a few turns (Fig. 14 or 15).

558

Steering System

3. Turn the steering wheel slowly from one extreme to the other. *(CAUTION: Never turn the wheel hard against the stopping point on the gear, as damage to the ball-nut assembly may result.)* The steering wheel should turn freely and smoothly throughout its entire range. Any roughness indicates faulty internal parts, requiring disassembly of the steering gear. A hard pull or binding indicates an excessively tight adjustment of the worm bearings or excessive misalignment of the steering shaft coupling. Any excessive misalignment must be corrected before the steering gear can be adjusted properly.
4. Remove the horn button or the horn ring from the steering wheel.
5. Turn the steering wheel gently in one direction until it stops. This positions the gear away from the "high-point" load that exists in the straight-ahead position.
6. Attach a in.-lb. torque wrench to the steering wheel retaining nut and check the torque required to turn the steering shaft in the range where lash exists between the ball nut and pitman sector gear.

NOTE: Take a reading while pulling the torque wrench in one direction, and then take a reading pulling the wrench in the other direction. Total both readings and take one-half of the total as the average torque.

The torque required should be within the specifications listed by the car manufacturer (usually from 5 to 10 in.-lb. Check the service manual of the car being serviced for exact figures.)

7. To correct the worm preload torque, loosen the worm-bearing adjuster lock nut with a brass drift punch and turn the adjuster to bring the torque within the limits specified by the manufacturer.
8. Retighten the lock nut when the torque is correct, and recheck as in Step 6.

To adjust the sector and ball-nut backlash, also called "over center preload," proceed according to the following steps:

1. Turn the steering wheel gently all the way to the left (or right) stop.
2. Counting the number of turns, turn the steering wheel all the way to the right (or left) stop.

AUTOMOBILE GUIDE

3. Turn the steering wheel, in the opposite direction of step 2, exactly half the number of turns counted in that step.
4. Loosen the lash adjuster screw locknut (Fig. 18).
5. Turn the lash adjuster screw clockwise (cw) to take out all lash between the ball nut and pitman shaft sector teeth.
6. Tighten the adjuster screw locknut.
7. Check the torque at the steering wheel using a torque wrench with a maximum reading of 50 in.-lb.
8. Compare highest reading of step 7 with manufacturer's recommendations (usually not more than 18 in.-lb.).
9. Replace the pitman arm.
10. Replace the horn ring or button.

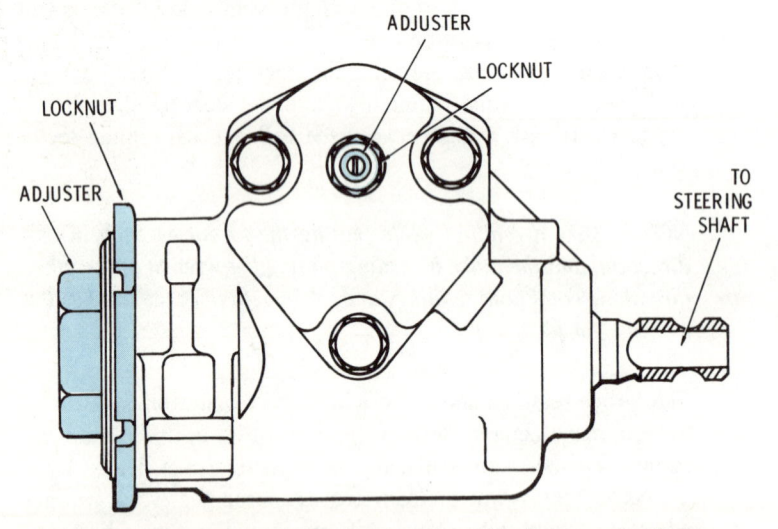

Fig. 18. Steering gearbox showing location of locknuts and adjusters.

Worm-and-Roller Type

There are two adjustments on the worm-and-roller type steering gear:

1. Worm bearing adjustment.
2. Roller-and-worm mesh adjustment.

To adjust the worm bearing end play, proceed as follows:

1. Rotate the steering wheel one turn from the straight-ahead position and secure the wheel to prevent any movement.

Steering System

2. Shake one of the front wheels sideways and note any end movement between the steering wheel hub and the steering jacket tube.

CAUTION: Make sure any movement present is not caused by looseness in the steering jacket tube bearing.

3. If end play is present, adjust the worm bearing by loosening the four cover cap screws about one-eighth inch. Separate the top shim with a knife and remove. Do not damage the remaining shims. Tighten the cover cap screws and inspect for worm bearing end play. Remove only one shim at a time to prevent adjusting the worn bearings too tight, which will cause hard steering and possible damage to the bearings.

To adjust the mesh between the roller and worm, proceed as follows:

1. Disconnect the pitman arm from the steering linkage, and turn the steering wheel to the mid-position of its turning limits.
2. Shake the pitman arm sideways and check for movement. A movement of the pitman arm in excess of 1/32-inch indicates an adjustment of the mesh between the roller and worm should be made.
3. Adjust the mesh by loosening the lock nut on the adjusting screw and turning the screw clockwise. Do not overtighten. Check for proper mesh after adjusting by shaking the pitman arm.
4. Tighten the adjusting screw lock nut while holding the adjusting screw to keep it from turning. Recheck for correct mesh.
5. Reconnect the pitman arm to the steering linkage.

NOTE: A spring scale attached to the rim of the steering wheel to measure the amount of force necessary to turn the wheel can also be used to check for proper worm-bearing and worm-and-roller mesh adjustment. Consult the car manufacturer's specifications for the correct scale readings.

POWER STEERING

Two general types of power steering are in use today. One type (Fig. 19) uses a separate hydraulic power cylinder controlled by a valve

AUTOMOBILE GUIDE

assembly coupled to the pitman arm to assist in steering the automobile. The second general type has the power cylinder and control valve as an integral part of the steering assembly, as shown in Fig. 20.

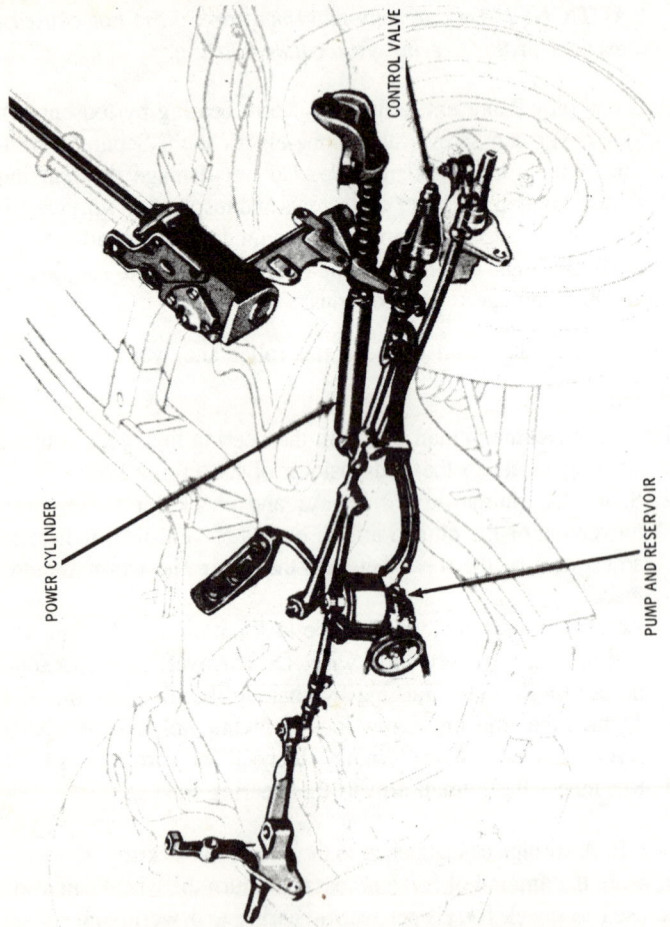

Fig. 19. Typical FORD power-steering system.

Both types of power steering systems require a fluid pump to furnish fluid under pressure to operate the hydraulic cylinder when the steering wheel is turned. This fluid pump is driven by a belt coupled to the crankshaft vibration damper.

The steering ratio on a car having power steering is usually less than in one having manual steering. The steering effort required with manual

STEERING SYSTEM

Fig. 20. A typical power-steering system in which the power unit is an integral part of the steering gear.

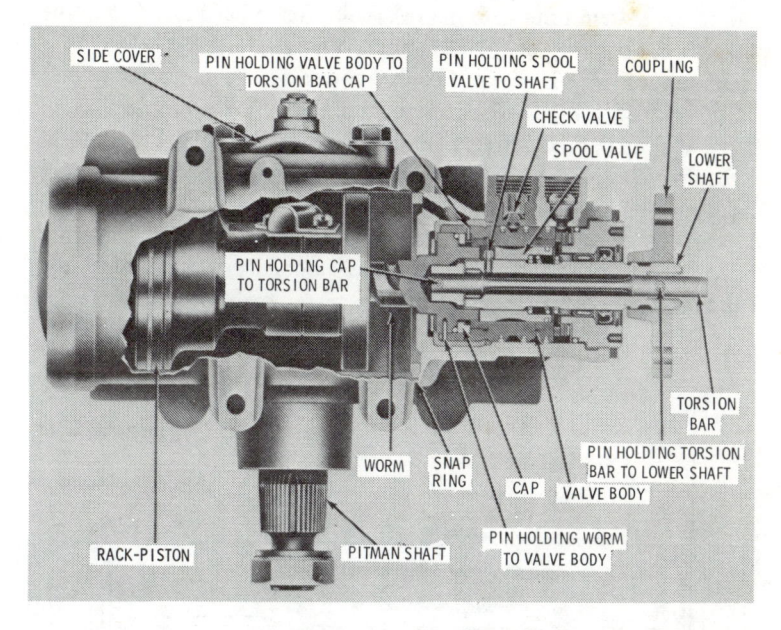

Courtesy Oldsmobile Div., General Motors Corp.

steering is reduced by increasing the steering ratio. With power steering, this ratio can be reduced because the extra effort needed is supplied by the power unit.

Both types of power steering incorporate a "fail-safe" design which permits manual steering even though hydraulic pressure is lost due to some malfunction. More effort is required to steer the car under this condition than is required to steer the same make of car with standard steering.

Linkage Type

This type of steering system includes a fluid reservoir and pump, a control valve, a power cylinder, connecting fluid lines, and the necessary steering linkage. The hydraulic pump is belt driven from the engine crankshaft, and provides fluid pressure for the system. A pressure relief valve is incorporated in the pump, and is used to govern the pressures

563

Automobile Guide

within the system according to the varying conditions of operation. The fluid in the system returns to the reservoir after it has passed from the pump to the control valve and power cylinder.

The control valve is operated by the movement of the steering wheel, and serves to direct the path and amount of the oil to the proper place in the system, and at the correct pressure necessary for the oil to perform its required task. For example, when the front wheels are in the straight ahead position and no force is applied to the steering wheel, the control valve spool is held in the center (neutral) position by its centering spring, as shown in Fig. 21. Fluid flows around the valve lands and returns to the reservoir.

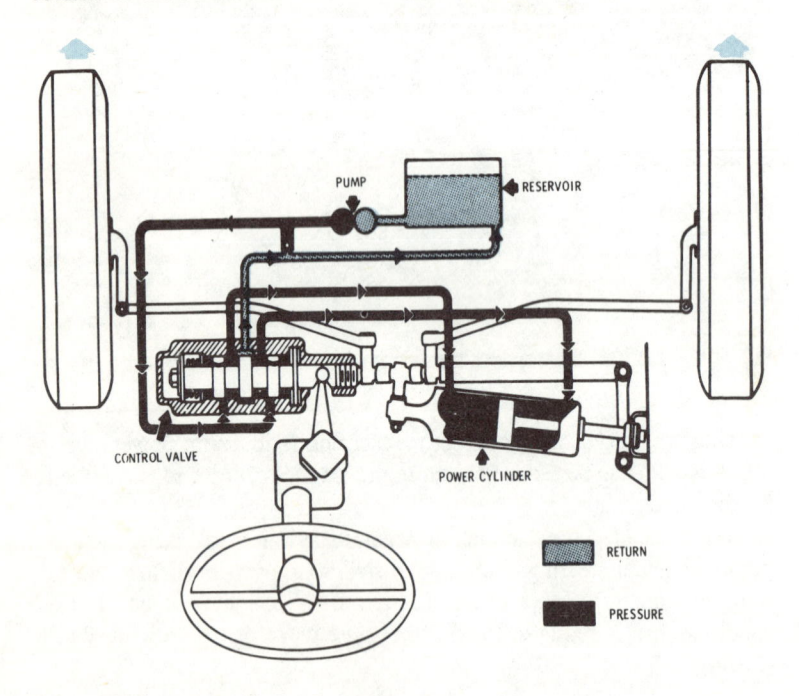

Fig. 21. Flow of fluid in a linkage type power steering system—straight-ahead position.

When a force of 4 to 7 pounds (depending on the make and model of car) is exerted at the rim of the steering wheel for a left turn, the valve spool overcomes the force of the centering spring and moves toward the right-hand end of the valve. This causes pressure to be exerted on the

Steering System

right side of the power-cylinder piston, and causes the fluid in the left side to be returned to the reservoir. This condition is shown in Fig. 22.

When the force on the steering wheel falls below the design force of 4 to 7 pounds, the valve spool centering spring forces the spool back to the center position, causing the pressure on both sides of the power piston to become equal. With the absence of operative pressure withing the power cylinder, the front wheels will tend to return to the straight-ahead position. This is a normal effect of the front-wheel alignment.

When a right turn is made, the directional forces explained for a left turn are reversed. The fluid flow for a right turn is shown in Fig. 23.

If, for any reason, the pump fails to deliver fluid pressure, the car can still be steered, but with a considerable increase in manual effort.

Road shock in this type of system causes movement of the control valve in relation to the valve spool. This movement sets up a counteracting pressure momentarily to the power cylinder, which absorbs the shock.

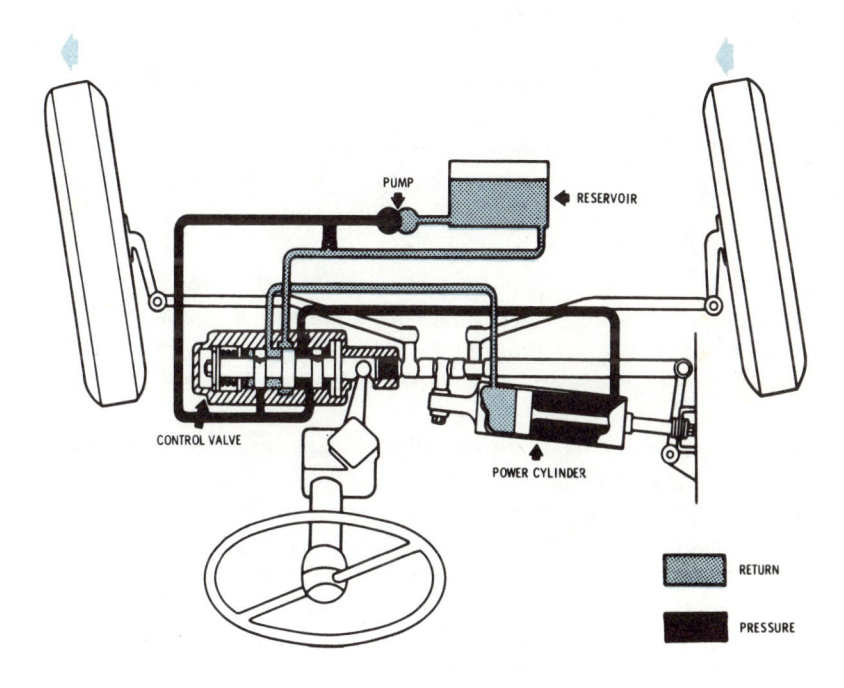

Fig. 22. Flow of fluid in a linkage-type power steering system—left turn position.

565

AUTOMOBILE GUIDE

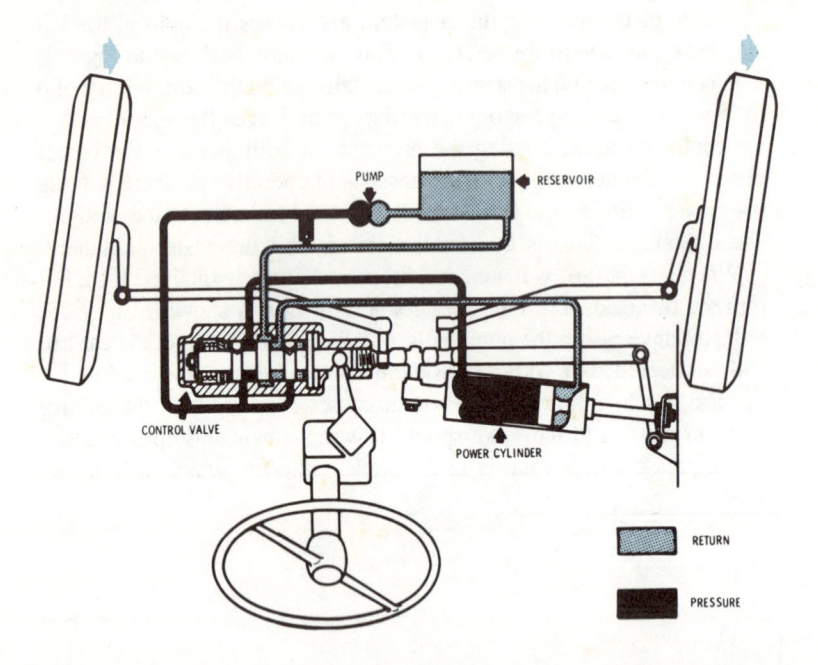

Fig. 23. Fluid flow in a linkage-type power steering system—right turn position.

Integral Type

This type of power-steering system includes a fluid reservoir and a pump driven by the engine crankshaft. The pump is connected by flexible hydraulic lines to a power piston that, along with a control valve, is an integral part of the steering gear.

With the engine running, steering is manual as long as the steering effort at the rim of the steering wheel is less than one pound. (Note: This is an approximate figure and may vary slightly depending on the make and model of car.) When a greater effort is required, the power mechanism operates to assist in turning the front wheels. The effort required increases to a maximum of from 3 to 4 pounds, above which the power assist furnishes any extra effort needed to steer the automobile. This condition will exist on normal turns and when parking. The variable feature just described gives the driver a "feel" of steering and removes the objection many drivers had to earlier types of power steering, which gave the feeling of "driving on ice."

Steering System

When the steering wheel is released to recover from a turn, the front wheels return to the straight-ahead position (in the same manner as with manual steering) without assistance or interference from the power mechanism.

When the engine is stopped, or if any part of the power mechanism is inoperative, the steering gear will operate manually. This gives the driver full control of the car at all times.

The control valve in this system is a rotary type and is located in the upper section of the gear housing. It consists of a stub shaft, a torsion bar, a valve body, a valve spool, and a valve-body cap. These parts are shown in the sectional view in Fig. 24.

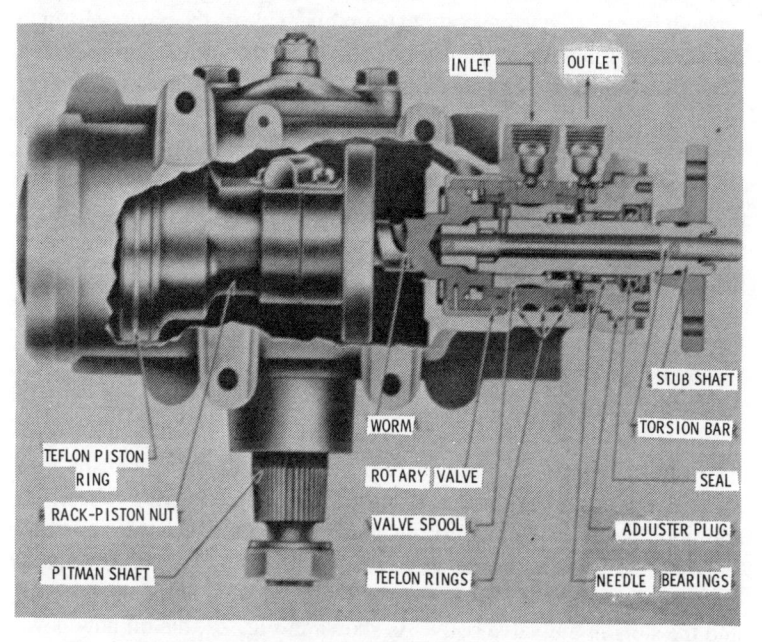

Fig. 24. Sectional view of a typical SAGINAW power-steering gear.

Basically, the valve assembly is divided into two separate sections which are fastened together by the torsion bar. One section is connected to the steering wheel and consists of the stub shaft, valve spool, and upper end of the torsion bar. A pin on the outside diameter of the stub shaft fastens the upper end of the torsion bar and stub shaft together.

The other section of the valve assembly is connected to the front wheels of the car through the steering linkage, the pitman shaft, sector

567

gear, ball-nut and piston, and the worm. This section consists of the worm, valve body, valve body cap, and lower end of the torsion bar. The worm is attached to the valve body by a pin at the upper end of the worm. A pin on the inside diameter of the valve body fastens the valve body cap to the valve body. To complete the assembly, a pin attaches the valve body cap to the lower end of the torsion bar. Thus, the steering wheel is coupled to the steering gear only through the torsion bar.

When the steering wheel is turned, the torsion bar will twist and cause the stub shaft and valve spool to rotate with the steering wheel. Thus, the relationship between the valve spool and valve body is changed, and the flow of oil is directed by slots on the valve spool through holes in the valve body to the proper side of the power piston to assist the turning action. The torsion bar can only be twisted a predetermined amount. If this limit is exceeded, as in the case of power mechanism failure, two slots in the end of the stub shaft will contact two tangs on the upper end of the worm, and steering will be manual.

The worm shaft turns in the ball nut, using the steel balls as a rolling thread. The ball groove is made shallower in the center of the worm so that a slight worm-to-ball nut preload exists in the straight-ahead position.

The straight-ahead position of the control valve assembly is shown in Figs. 25 and 26. Oil flows fron the pump into the pressure port, through the open center of the valve spool, and out the return port. There is no flow of oil to either side of the power piston, but each side is full of oil at all times. In the straight-ahead position, the pressure on both sides of the piston is equal, so it does not move. The oil acts as a cushion to absorb shocks so they are not transferred to the steering wheel. In addition, the oil serves to lubricate all internal parts of the steering gear.

When the steering wheel is turned to the right, the torsion bar is twisted, changing the relationship between the slots in the valve spool and the slots in the valve body. As shown in Fig. 27, the oil now flows into the lower chamber of the power piston, forcing it upward. At the same time, the oil in the upper chamber of the power piston is forced out through the valve and back to the reservoir. The greater the turning effort applied to the steering wheel, the more the torsion bar is twisted, and the greater will be the change in the relationship between the valve spool and body. This condition causes a greater oil pressure to be applied to the lower side of the power piston. Thus, the proper amount of power assist is supplied for variable turning conditions. Fig. 28 shows an end view of the rotary valve during a right turn.

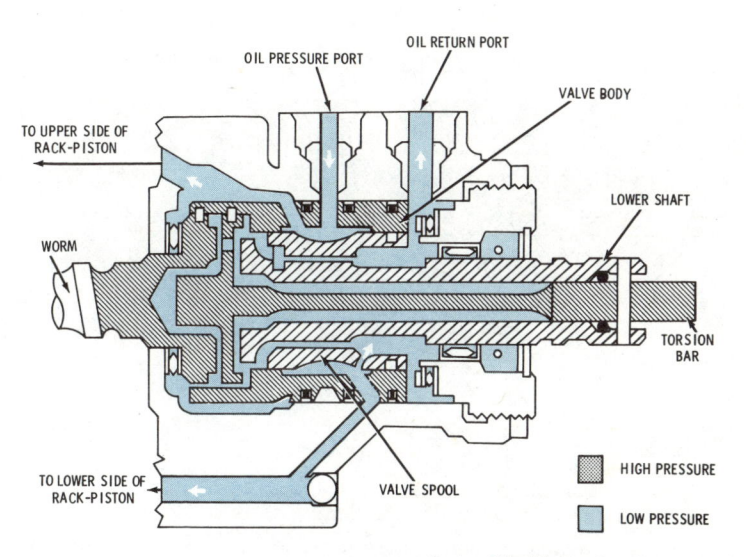

STEERING SYSTEM

Fig. 25. Cross-sectional view of the control valve in the neutral or straight ahead position.

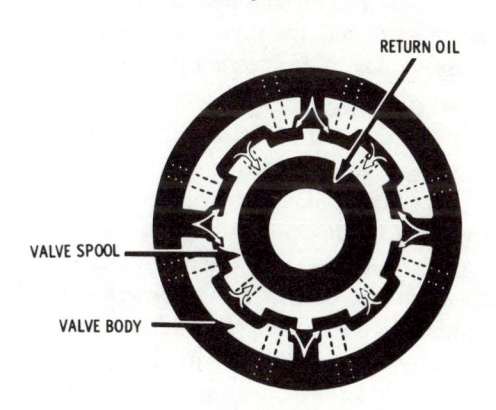

Courtesy Oldsmobile Div., General Motors Corp.

Fig. 26. End view of the control valve in the neutral position.

Courtesy American Motors Corp.

The instant this turning effort is removed from the steering wheel, the torsion bar untwists, returning the valve spool to a straight-ahead

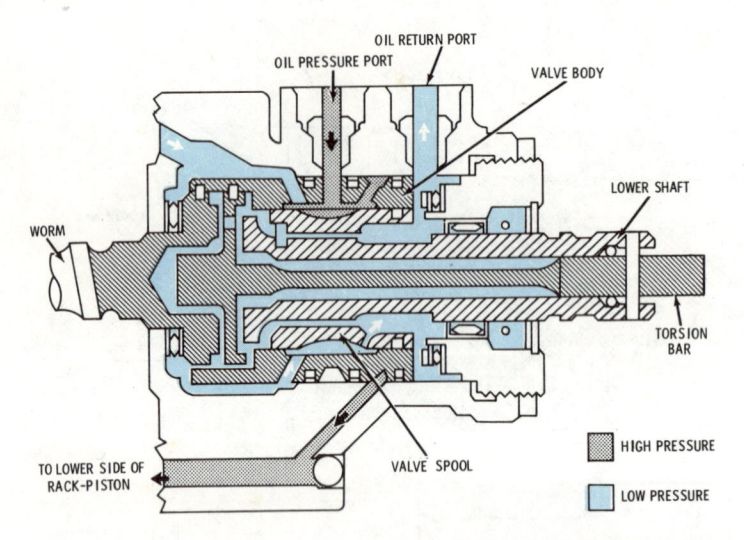

Automobile Guide

Fig. 27. Cross-sectional view of the control valve during a right turn.

position with relation to the valve body. When this happens, the oil pressure again becomes equal on both sides of the power piston, and no further power assist is present. The front wheels will now return to the straight-ahead position due to the steering geometry and wheel alignment. The reverse procedure takes place when the steering wheel is turned to the left. Oil pressure is routed to the upper chamber of the power piston, forcing it downward. Fig. 29 shows the valve and oil flow under this condition. Fig. 30 shows an end view of the valve assembly during a left turn.

The power steering used on some *Chrysler*-made cars differ somewhat from the system just described. The power piston assembly is similar in operation, but the control valve differs. Instead of a torsion bar to "sense" turning effort and control the flow of oil into the proper power piston chamber, reaction springs are used. Turning effort causes the worm to be displaced slightly, tilting a pivot lever to control the flow of oil. The reaction springs maintain the pivot lever in a center position until turning effort overcomes their resistance. With the pivot lever in the center position, equal pressure is applied to both ends of the power piston, so it does not attempt to move. Thus, the reaction springs introduce a power assist that is proportional to the amount of turning

STEERING SYSTEM

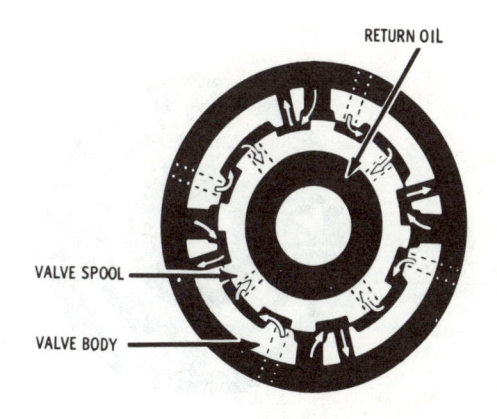

Fig. 28. End view of the control valve during a right turn.

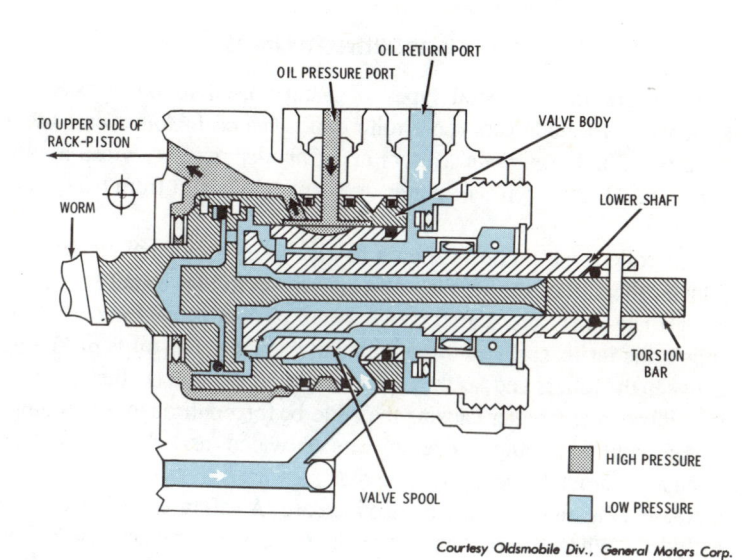

Fig. 29. Cross-sectional view of the control valve during a left turn.

effort being applied. This provides the driver with the driving "feel" necessary for safe steering. Manual steering, with increased effort, is possible if any part of the power system should fail.

571

AUTOMOBILE GUIDE

Fig. 30. End view of the control valve during a left turn.

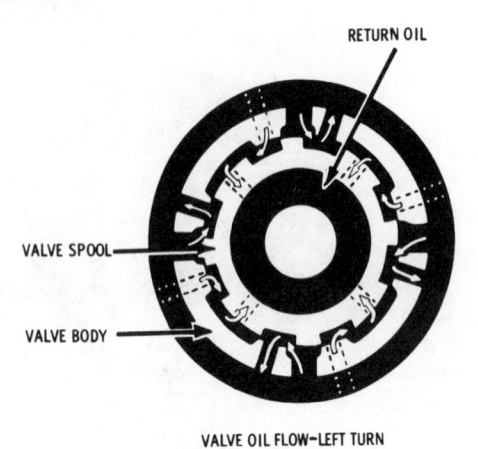

(Labels: RETURN OIL, VALVE SPOOL, VALVE BODY, VALVE OIL FLOW—LEFT TURN)

Courtesy American Motors Corp.

POWER-STEERING PUMPS

There are three general types of pumps used in power steering systems. *Ford*-made cars use a roller-type, *General Motors* cars use a vane-type, and *American Motors* and *Chrysler*-made cars use a slipper-type. All three types of pumps are driven by a belt from the engine crankshaft.

The roller-type pump is shown in Fig. 31. A rotor having slots in which rollers ride is positioned off-center in a circular chamber. As the rotor rotates, the rollers are forced outward by centrifugal force and thus follow the inside surfaces of the circular chamber. The oil is picked up between the rollers and, as they move around the chamber, the space for the oil becomes smaller causing the oil to be forced through an opening.

An input and output opening are provided and the oil is thus circulated around the system under pressure. If the engine speed increases, the oil pressure will also increase. A safety valve is therefore included. When the pressure exceeds a specified amount, the safety valve opens and bypasses the oil, preventing an excessive load on the pump.

The vane-type pump operates on the same principle as the roller-type, except that vanes instead of rollers are held in the rotor slots. Another difference is the shape of the chamber in which the rotor rotates. As

Steering System

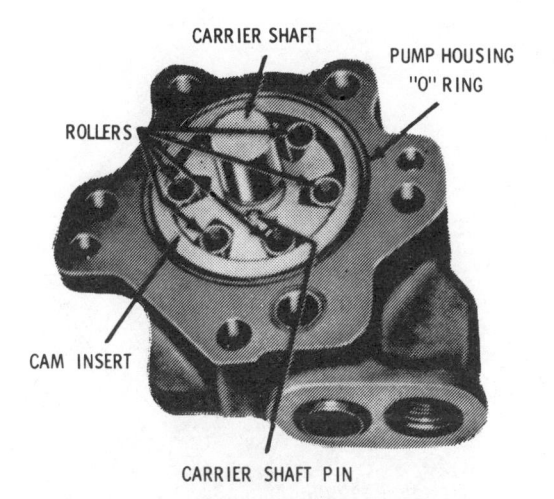

Fig. 31. A roller-type power-steering pump.

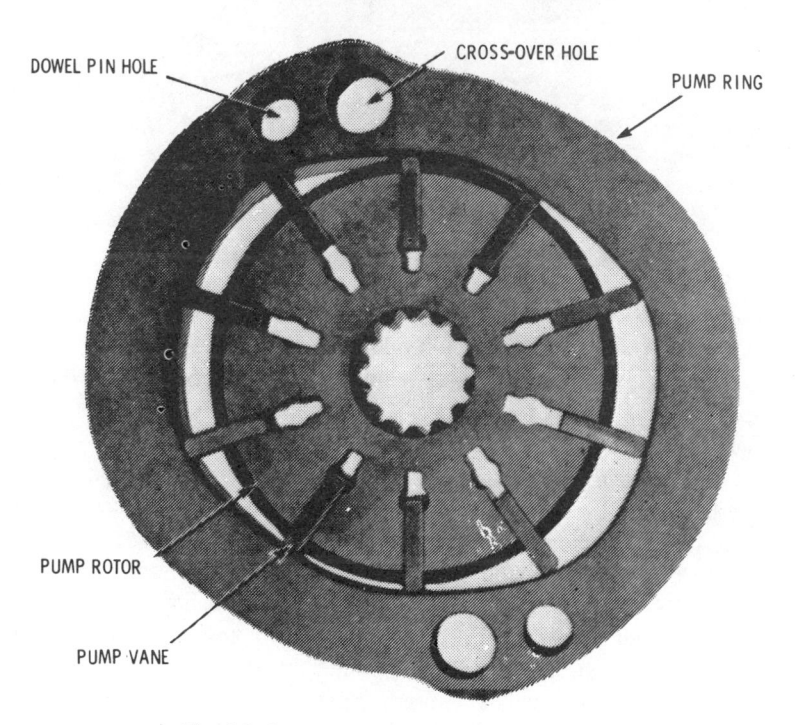

Fig. 32. A vane-type power-steering pump.

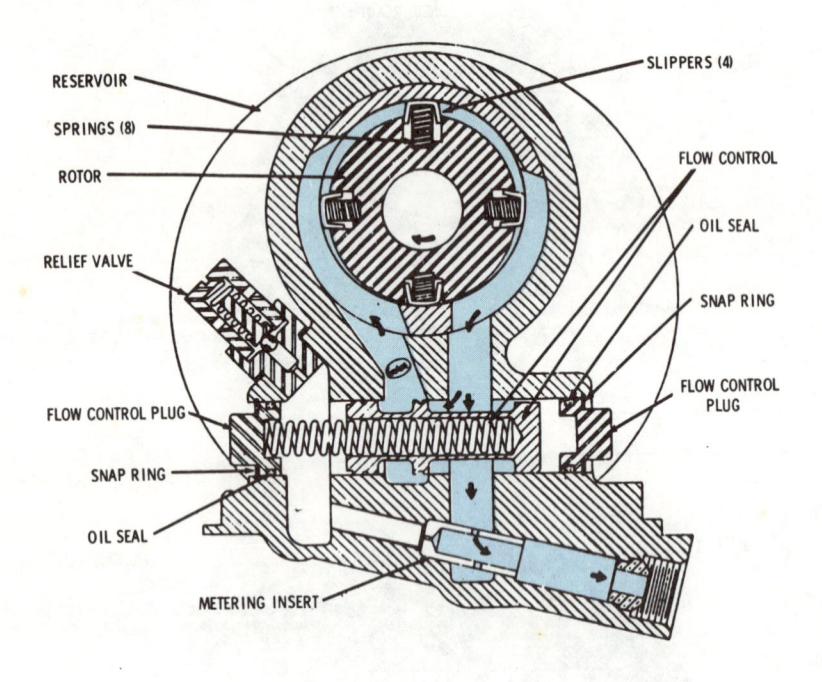

AUTOMOBILE GUIDE

Courtesy Dodge Div., Chrysler Motors Corp.

Fig. 33. A slipper-type power-steering pump.

shown in Fig. 32, the rotor is elliptical. This provides double pumping action for each revolution of the rotor.

The slipper-type pump is shown in Fig. 33. The operation of this pump is very similar to the roller- and vane-types, but uses spring-loaded "slippers" instead of rollers or vanes.

Correct belt tension to the pump is very important in any power-steering system. A loose belt may cause hard steering, jerky steering (especially when parking), noise, etc. Some manufacturers recommend the use of a gauge to adjust the belt to the correct tension. Fig. 34 illustrates one type of gauge and the method of application to measure the belt tension on some *Buicks* with a 300 cu. in. engine. Some other manufacturers list the belt-deflection method of adjusting the belt tension. When this method is used, specifications are listed for the amount the belt can be deflected when its tension is correct.

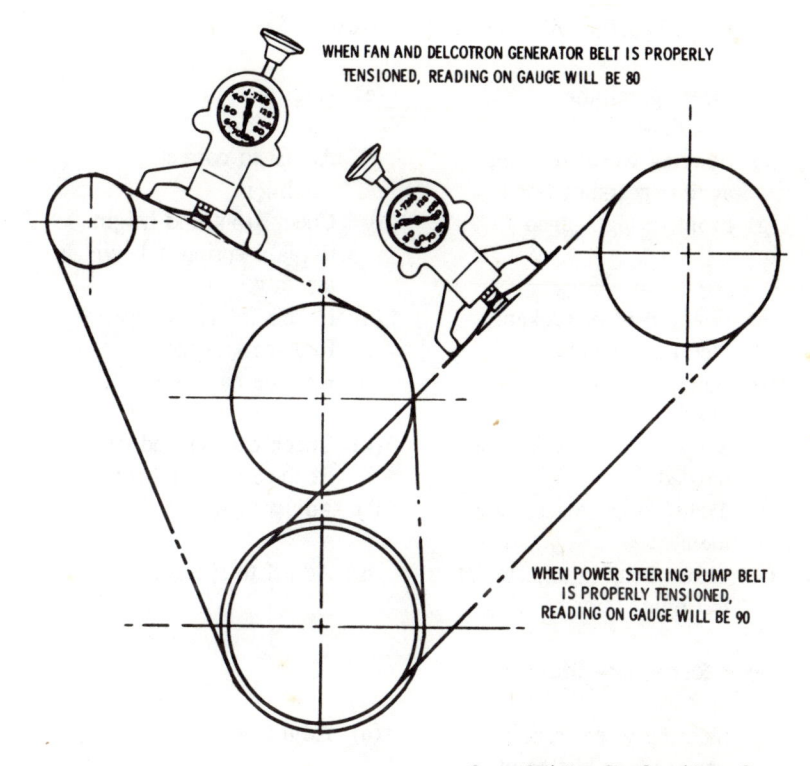

STEERING SYSTEM

Fig. 34. Typical application of a belt tension gauge.

STEERING-SYSTEM TROUBLES AND REMEDIES
MANUAL STEERING

Symptoms and Possible Causes

Hard Steering

(a) Low or uneven tire pressure.
(b) Insufficient lubricant in steering gear or linkage.
(c) Steering gear adjusted too tight.
(d) Front wheels out of line.

Possible Remedies

(a) Inflate tires to recommended pressures.
(b) Lubricate as necessary.
(c) Adjust according to instructions.
(d) Align wheels.

Automobile Guide

Symptoms and Possible Causes

(e) Steering column misaligned.
(f) Steering wheel rubbing against gearshift bowl.
(g) Front spring sagged.

(h) Frame bent or broken.
(i) Steering knuckle bent.
(j) Ball joint galled too tight.
(k) Suspension arms bent or twisted.
(l) Tight over-center adjustment.
(m) Thrust bearing adjustment too tight.

Poor Return of Steering

(a) Steering wheel rubbing against gearshift bowl.
(b) Front wheels out of alignment.
(c) Steering linkage too tight.
(d) Suspension ball joints too tight.
(e) Steering adjustment too tight.
(f) Nut and worm preload too tight.

Car Pulls to One Side

(a) Front end misaligned.
(b) Incorrect tire pressure.

Possible Remedies

(e) Align according to instructions.
(f) Adjust to correct condition.
(g) Check front end height. Replace spring if height is too low.
(h) Repair frame as necessary.
(i) Replace knuckle.
(j) Replace ball joint.
(k) Check camber and caster. Replace arms if bent.
(l) Adjust to specifications.
(m) Adjust to specifications.

(a) Adjust as necessary.

(b) Align front wheels.

(c) Lubricate and check end plugs.
(d) Lubricate.

(e) Readjust according to instructions.
(f) Remove gear and replace balls as necessary.

(a) Align front end.
(b) Inflate tires to recommended pressures.

STEERING SYSTEM

Symptoms and Possible Causes

(c) Brakes dragging.
(d) Front and rear wheels not tracking.
(e) Broken or weak rear springs.
(f) Bent suspension parts.

Posiible Remedies

(c) Adjust brakes.
(d) Adjust as necessary.
(e) Replace defective springs.
(f) Replace defective parts.

Excessive Play in Steering Wheel

(a) Lash in steering linkage.
(b) Excessive lash between sector gear and ball nut.
(c) Ball nut and worm preload incorrect.
(d) Ball joints loose.
(e) Front wheel bearings worn or incorrectly adjusted.
(f) Steering gear housing attaching bolts or nuts loose.
(g) Steering arms loose.

(a) Adjust or replace parts as necessary.
(b) Adjust to specifications.
(c) Remove gear and change balls to obtain specified preload.
(d) Replace ball joints.
(e) Replace or adjust bearings as necessary.
(f) Tighten according to specifications.
(g) Tighten according to specifications.

POWER STEERING

Troubles listed here are in addition to those listed for manual steering.

Symptoms and Possible Causes

Hard Steering

(a) Sticky spool valve.
(b) Sticking flow control valve in pump.
(c) Low oil level in pump reservoir.

Possible Remedies

(a) Remove and clean or replace valve assembly.
(b) Remove valve and clean or replace.
(c) Fill to proper level with approved liquid.

577

Symptoms and Possible Causes

(d) Pump belt loose.

(e) Faulty pump.

(f) Restriction in pump hoses.

Car Pulls to One Side

(a) Worn or damaged valve or shaft assembly.
(b) Valve body out of adjustment (*Chrysler*-made cars).

(c) Valve pivot lever damaged (*Chrysler*-made cars).

Poor Return of Steering

(a) Sticky valve spool.

(b) Faulty or damaged valve pivot lever.

Lack of Assist in One Direction

(a) Broken or worn ring on power piston.
(b) Piston end plug loose.

(c) Reaction seal missing.

Increased Effort to Turn the Wheel Fast

(a) Oil level low.
(b) Pump belt slipping.

Possible Remedies

(d) Tighten pump belt to correct tension.
(e) Check pump pressure and correct as necessary. Check for oil leaks in system and correct as necessary.
(f) Clean or replace as necessary.

(a) Replace valve or shaft assembly.
(b) Move steering valve housing up or down on the steering housing according to instructions.
(c) Remove steering gear and repair or replace as necessary.

(a) Remove and clean or replace valve.
(b) Repair or replace as necessary.

(a) Repair as necessary.

(b) Replace worm and piston assembly.
(c) Repair as necessary.

(a) Add oil to reservoir.
(b) Tighten belt to specifications.

STEERING SYSTEM

Symptoms and Possible Causes   *Possible Remedies*

(c) High internal leakage.

(d) Engine idle speed too slow.
(e) Air in system.

(c) Replace rings and seals on power piston. Replace valve as necessary.
(d) Increase idle speed to specifications.
(e) Turn steering wheel right and left several times to expel air. Add oil to proper level.

Steering Gear Hiss

(a) Normal in some units when parking or when steering wheel is turned to extreme limits.
(b) Gear loose on frame.

(a) If objectionable, replace valve and shaft assembly.

(b) Tighten bolts to specifications.

Steering Wheel Surges When Turning

(a) Loose pump belt.

(a) Tighten to specifications.

Valve "Squawks" When Turning

(a) Worn or damaged ring on valve spool.
(b) Loose or worn valve.

(a) Repair or replace.

(b) Replace valve or shaft assembly.

No Effort Required to Turn

(a) Broken torsion bar.

(a) Replace valve and shaft assembly.

Pump Noise

(a) Loose belt.
(b) Hose touching other parts of the car.

(a) Tighten belt.
(b) Relocate position of hose.

Symptoms and Possible Causes *Possible Remedies*

(c) Oil level low.
(d) Air in oil.
(e) Excessive back pressure caused by restriction in hose or valve.
(f) Scored pressure plate.

(g) Vanes, rollers, or slippers not properly installed.
(h) Scored rotor in pump.

(c) Add oil.
(d) Check oil level.
(e) Locate restriction and remove.

(f) Hone light scoring. Replace heavily scored part.
(g) Install properly.

(h) Hone light scoring. Replace heavily scored part.

CHAPTER 23

Front-Wheel Alignment

The purpose of wheel alignment is to cause the wheels of an automobile to roll without scuffing, dragging, or slipping while traveling in a straight line and around curves. This provides greater driving safety, easier steering, longer tire wear, and less strain on the parts that make up the front end of the automobile.

ALIGNMENT FACTORS

There are seven factors that are the basis of wheel alignment. These factors (shown in Fig. 1), are designed into the car by the manufacturer to correctly locate the vehicle weight on the moving parts and to make steering easier. The manufacturer specifies a range for each of these factors to permit correct adjustment when necessary. These factors must be maintained within the specified limits if correct steering and riding performance are to be expected.

Camber

Camber (Fig. 1.1), is the inward or outward tilt of the wheel at the top from the true vertical position. Camber is a tire-wearing angle and is measured in degrees. Positive camber is when the top of the wheel is tilted outward, as shown if Fig. 2. Negative camber is when the top of the wheel tilts inward. Car manufacturers indicate negative and positive camber in their specifications by the letters (N) and (P). Where a letter is not indicated, the camber is to be regarded as positive.

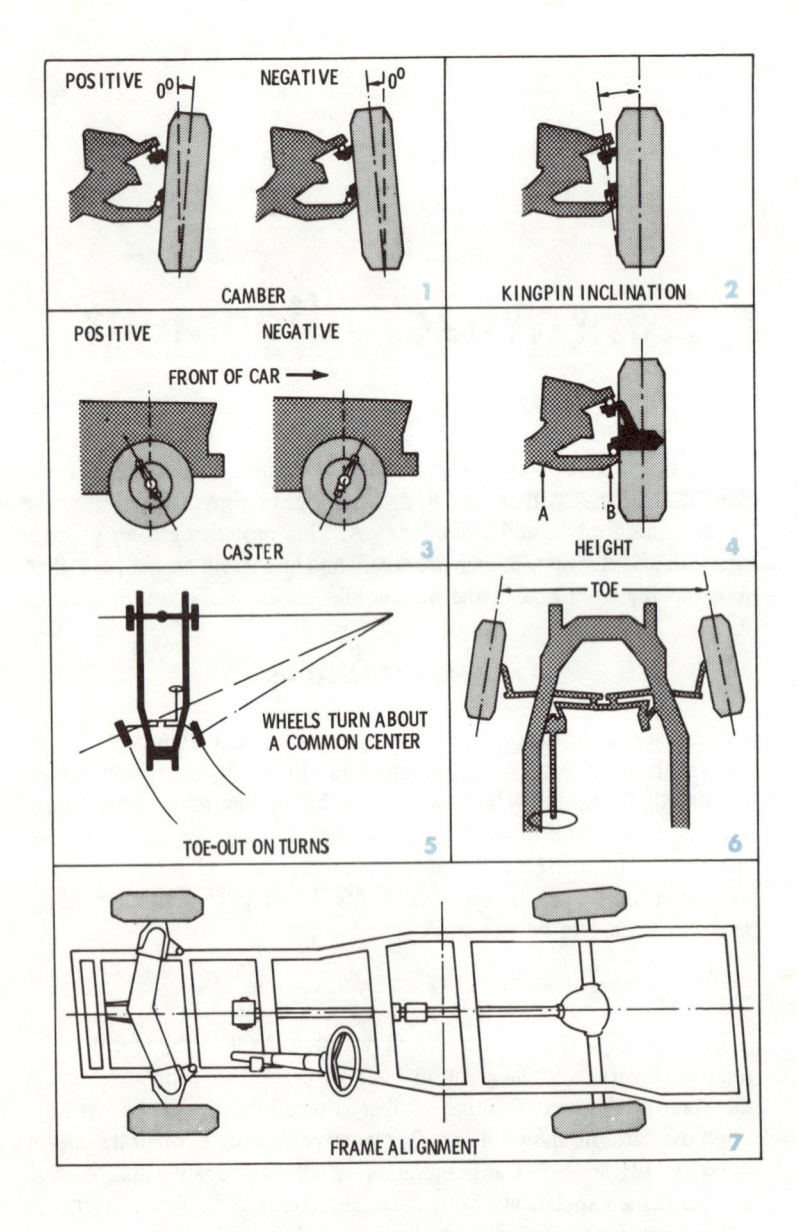

Fig. 1. Seven factors of proper wheel alignment.

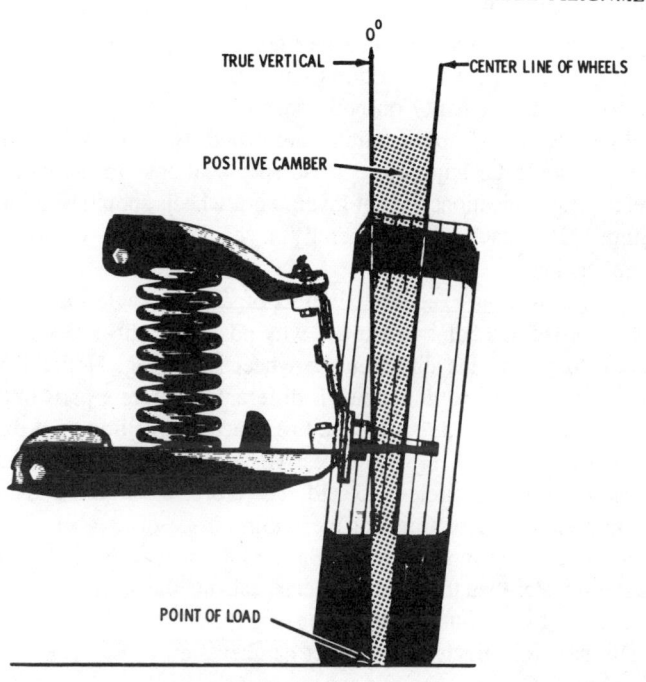

FRONT-WHEEL ALIGNMENT

Fig. 2. Camber is the amount by which the centerline of the tire is displaced from the true vertical. This illustration shows an example of positive camber and is exaggerated for clarity.

The reasons for providing camber is as follows:

1. To bring the point at which the tire touches the road more nearly under the load.
2. To cause easier steering by having the weight of the automobile borne by the inner wheel bearing and spindle.
3. To prevent excessive tire wear.

The camber of a wheel will change slightly for different load conditions and with the up-and-down movement of the wheel on rough roads. This slight change in camber is caused by the independent front-suspension design. The front-end design has been constantly improved, however, until the camber on late-model cars has been reduced to zero or nearly so.

The purpose of introducing camber to a wheel when the car is standing still and unloaded is to provide as near an average zero camber

583

Automobile Guide

as possible when the car is loaded normally and traveling down the road. Zero camber gives maximum tire life since the tire tread contacts the road surface equally on both sides of the tire.

When preferred specifications are listed by a manufacturer, the camber should be adjusted to these specifications. In the case where preferred specifications are not given, both wheels should be adjusted to within 1/2° of each other. Generally, a zero to positive camber should be maintained.

Fig. 3 shows an exaggerated effect of camber angle on tire contact with the road and helps to explain why positive camber tends to cause the car to pull in the direction the wheel is leaning. Notice from the illustration that the rolling radius is different at different parts of the tire tread. At each separate radius the tire is actually rolling on a different diameter. Thus, a wheel with excessive camber acts like part of a cone which will roll in a circle if rotated. Therefore, the wheel tends also to roll in a circle, accounting for the pulling force of camber. Since the wheel is forced to move in a straight line, the outer or smaller diameter must roll faster than the inner diameter, causing the outer tire tread to be ground off by slipping and scuffing.

The harmful effects of incorrect camber are:

1. Excessive ball joint wear.
2. Excessive wheel bearing wear.
3. Excessive tire wear (negative camber — inside tread; positive camber — outside tread).
4. Side pull of vehicle if camber is unequal.

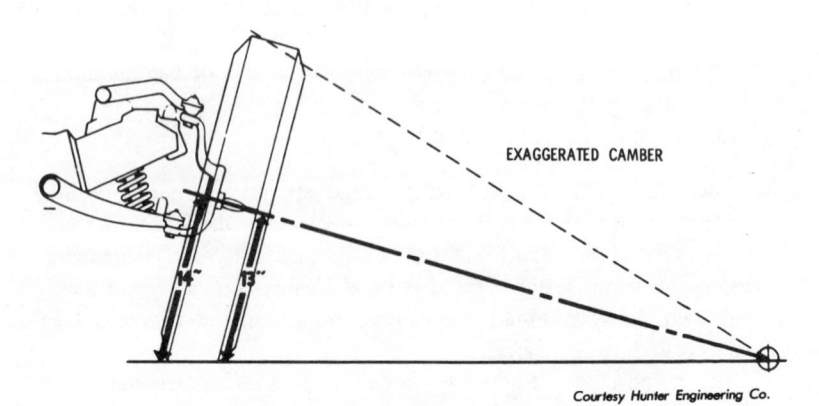

Fig. 3. Exaggerated camber.

FRONT-WHEEL ALIGNMENT

Kingpin Inclination

Kingpin inclination (Fig. 1.2) is the angle (viewed from the front of the car) between the true vertical and a line drawn through the kingpin or through the axis of the ball joints (Fig. 4). At one time, all cars were built with the kingpin axis vertical. With this arrangement, forces created by the tire hitting a bump tended to turn the wheels and caused a great amount of road shock to be transmitted to the steering wheel. To offset these effects, positive camber was introduced. It was later discovered that inclining the kingpin axis greatly reduced the lever action on bumps and allowed the camber angle to be decreased.

With the present combination of kingpin inclination and camber angle, the line through the kingpin and the line through the center plane of the wheel more nearly intersect at the road surface (Fig. 5) virtually eliminating the lever action previously described. Some specifications list the "included angle" instead of kingpin inclination. The included angle is the sum of the kingpin inclination and the camber angle. For example, with a kingpin inclination of 6° and a camber angle of negative 1/2°, the included angle is 5 1/2°.

Another advantage of kingpin inclination is the automatic steering effect it offers. As the front wheels are turned, the front of the car is actually lifted a small amount. Thus, the weight of the car actually tries to turn the wheels back to the straight-ahead position. Therefore, the wheels tend to straighten themselves after coming out of a curve.

The purposes of kingpin inclination are:

1. To reduce the need for excessive camber.
2. To distribute the weight of the car more nearly in the center of the tire tread where it contacts the road.
3. To provide a pivot point about which the wheel can turn to produce easy steering.
4. To aid steering stability.

Kingpin inclination is nonadjustable. If the angle is found to be incorrect, it will be because the spindle or spindle support arm has become bent. This condition calls for replacement of the defective part.

Caster

Caster (Fig. 1.3) is the angle (when viewed from the side of the car) between true vertical and the steering axis of the kingpin or ball joints

Automobile Guide

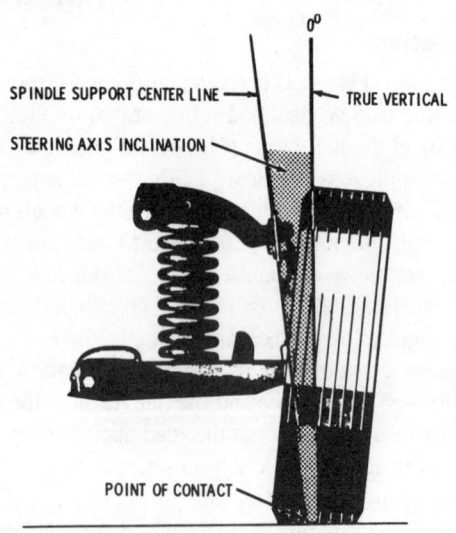

Fig. 4. Kingpin or steering-axis inclination.

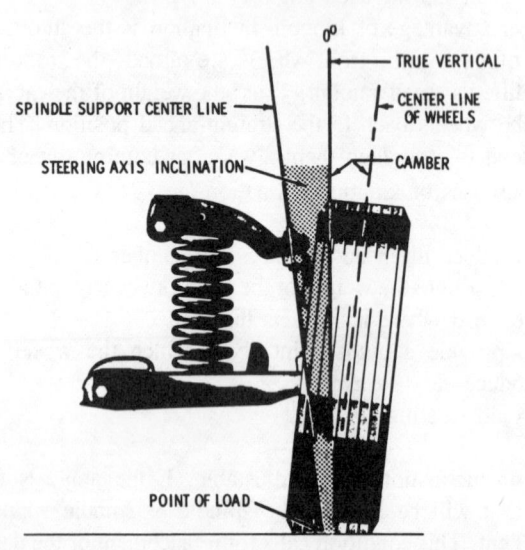

Courtesy Bear Manufacturing Co.

Fig. 5. Camber and Kingpin inclination.

Courtesy Bear Manufacturing Co.

(Fig. 6). This angle is a directional control angle and can be either positive or negative. The caster angle is positive when the spindle

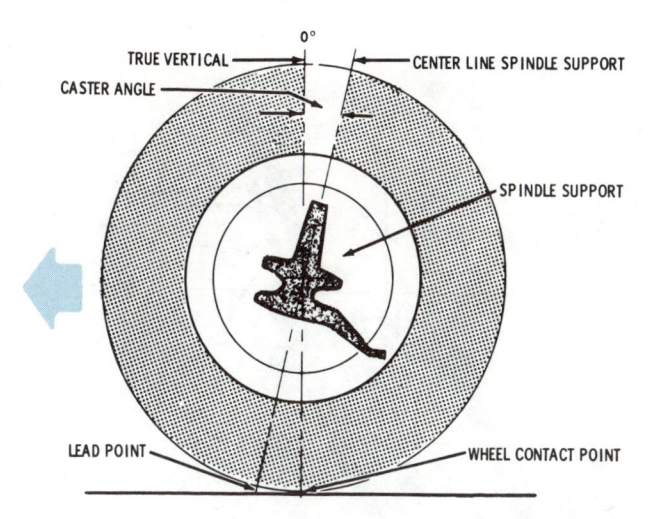

FRONT-WHEEL ALIGNMENT

Fig. 6. Caster angle.

support arm is tilted backward, as in Fig. 6, and is negative when the support arm is tilted forward. Manufacturers indicate negative and positive camber by the letters (N) and (P). Where a letter is not indicated, the caster is to be regarded as positive.

The purposes of caster are:

1. To obtain directional control of a car by causing the front wheels to maintain a straight-ahead position or to return to a straight-ahead position out of a turn.
2. To offset road crown.

Tilting the spindle support arm tends to cause the front wheels to maintain a straight-ahead position by projecting the center line of the support arm ahead, and establishing a lead point ahead of the wheel contact point on the road. The same condition exists at the front wheel of a bicycle, as shown in Fig. 7, and accounts for the fact that a bicycle can be ridden and steered without touching the handlebars.

Negative caster has been designed into some recent cars. Wider treads on tires and an increase in steering-axis inclination is responsible for maintaining directional control, even with a negative caster. On older-model cars, especially those with solid axle construction, negative caster can develop momentarily, and can prove very dangerous. As

587

AUTOMOBILE GUIDE

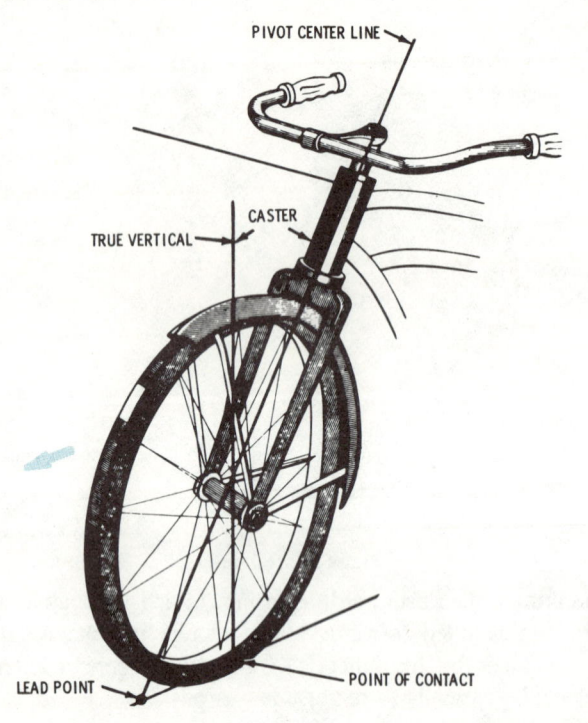

Courtesy Bear Manufacturing Co.

Fig. 7. The caster angle on a bicycle allows it to maintain a straight-ahead position without touching the handlebars.

shown in Fig. 8, a change in wheel height in relation to the vehicle will affect caster. Braking torque on the front wheels of a leaf-spring type solid axle may also develop negative caster (Fig. 9). Either of these conditions is dangerous and can throw the car completely out of control under certain combinations of driving conditions.

It is easy to see that any change in suspension height may seriously affect the steering stability of an automobile. The practice of some owners to use lowering blocks or to raise the front or rear of the car in some manner can actually be dangerous and should be discouraged in the interest of driving safety.

Caster is not a tire-wearing angle. Some manufacturers of alignment equipment, and some manufacturers of cars recommend that the right front wheel be given approximately 1/2° more positive camber than the left front wheel to offset road crown. This variation must, however, stay within the manufacturer's specifications.

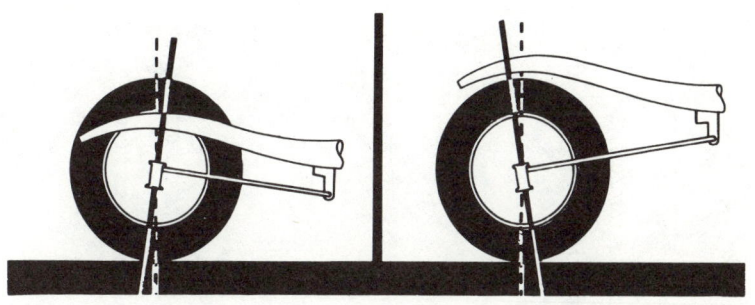

FRONT-WHEEL ALIGNMENT

Fig. 8. A change in caster angle can occur with a change in the height between the wheel and frame of the car.

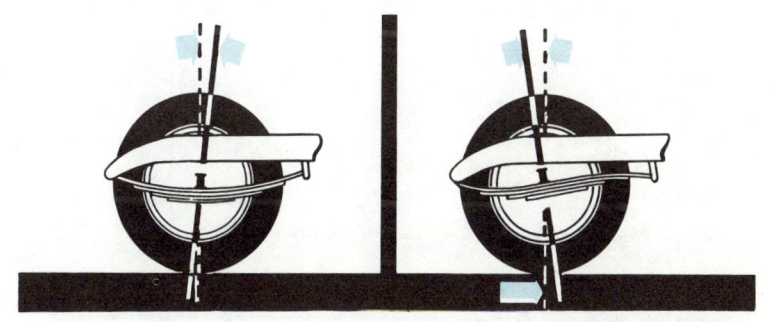

Courtesy Hunter Engineering Co.

Fig. 9. Braking torque on the wheels of a car equipped with front leaf springs may change the caster angle.

Courtesy Hunter Engineering Co.

The harmful effects of incorrect caster are:

1. Unequal caster will cause the car to pull toward the side of least positive caster.
2. Too little caster may cause wander and weave.
3. Too little caster may cause instability at high speeds.
4. Too much caster may cause hard steering.
5. Too much caster may cause road shock and shimmy.

Height

Correct height (Fig. 1.4) for the car is important for proper front end alignment. Weak or sagging coil or leaf springs (as well as torsion bars), front or rear, will affect proper alignment just as much as any other breakage. Both sides of the car should be of equal height, as

AUTOMOBILE GUIDE

shown in Fig. 10. More on car height and adjustment procedures is found in Chapter 21.

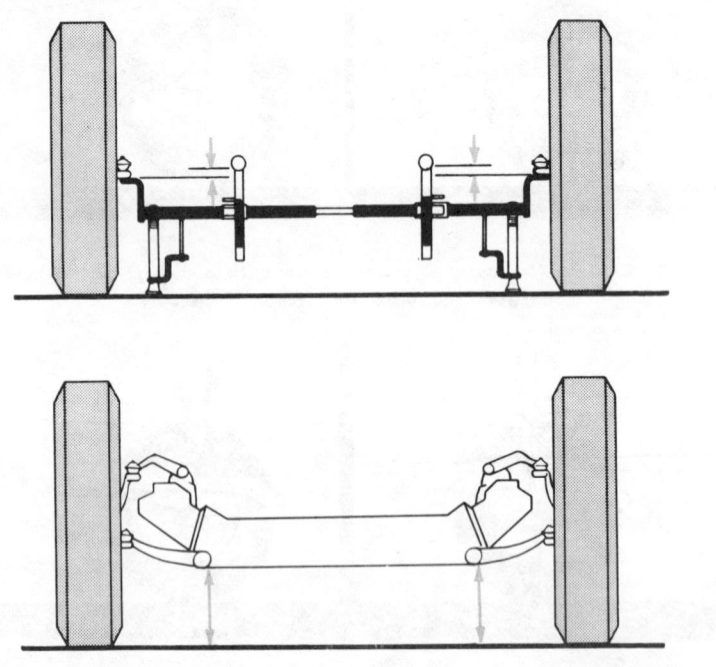

Courtesy Hunter Engineering Co.

Fig. 10. Proper wheel height is an important part of alignment.

Turning Radius Adjustment

The turning radius of a car is the result of the angle of each front wheel when the car is turning. As can be seen in Fig. 11, the inner front wheel turns shorter than the outer front wheel, resulting in a toe-out condition (Fig. 1.5) any time the car is turning. The design of the steering arms in relation to the wheelbase of the car provides the proper turning of each wheel.

Turning radius angle is a tire-wearing angle and is measured in degrees. The car manufacturer usually specifies the amount of toe-out that should exist when the wheels are turned a specific amount. Correct turning radius angle allows the front tires to roll free on turns. Incorrect turning radius will cause the tires to slip sideways, resulting in excessive tire wear. The turning radius will be correct if all other alignment angles are correct, providing the steering arms are not bent.

FRONT-WHEEL ALIGNMENT

The harmful effects of incorrect turning radius angle are:

1. Excessive tire wear on turns.
2. Squealing tires on turns, even at low speeds.

Toe-in

Toe-in (Fig. 1.6) is the amount in fractions of an inch that the front of the front wheels (line B) is closer together than the rear of the front wheels (line A). Toe-out is the amount that the front of the front wheels is farther apart than the rear of the front wheels.

Toe-in, shown in Fig. 12, is considered to be the most serious tire-wearing angle of the five alignment angles. Its purpose is to compensate for the widening influence that takes place when the car is in motion. The tire wear that occurs due to incorrect toe-in appears as a feather-edged scuff across the face of both tires. In some instances it has been found that too much toe-in will cause tire wear on the outside of the right front tire only. Conversely, too much toe-out has been found to cause tire wear on the inside of the left front tire only.

Toe-in is the last alignment to be adjusted in any wheel-alignment procedure. Adjustment is made by turning each adjusting sleeve an equal amount until the correct toe-in, as specified by the car manufacturer, exists.

The harmful effects of incorrect toe-in are:

1. Excessive tire wear due to scuffing and dragging.
2. Tendency of car to wander with toe-out.

Frame Alignment

Frame alignment, (Fig. 1.7) is also an important factor affecting front end alignment. When the front wheels are in a straight-ahead position, all wheels should be parallel with each other, as shown in Fig. 13. More on frame alignment is found in Chapter 21.

ALIGNMENT PROCEDURES

Periodic wheel alignment is necessary to provide maximum driving and riding qualities, and to prevent excessive wear of the tires and suspension components. The procedure involved in checking and correcting the various alignment angles require the use of precision equipment by qualified operators.

AUTOMOBILE GUIDE

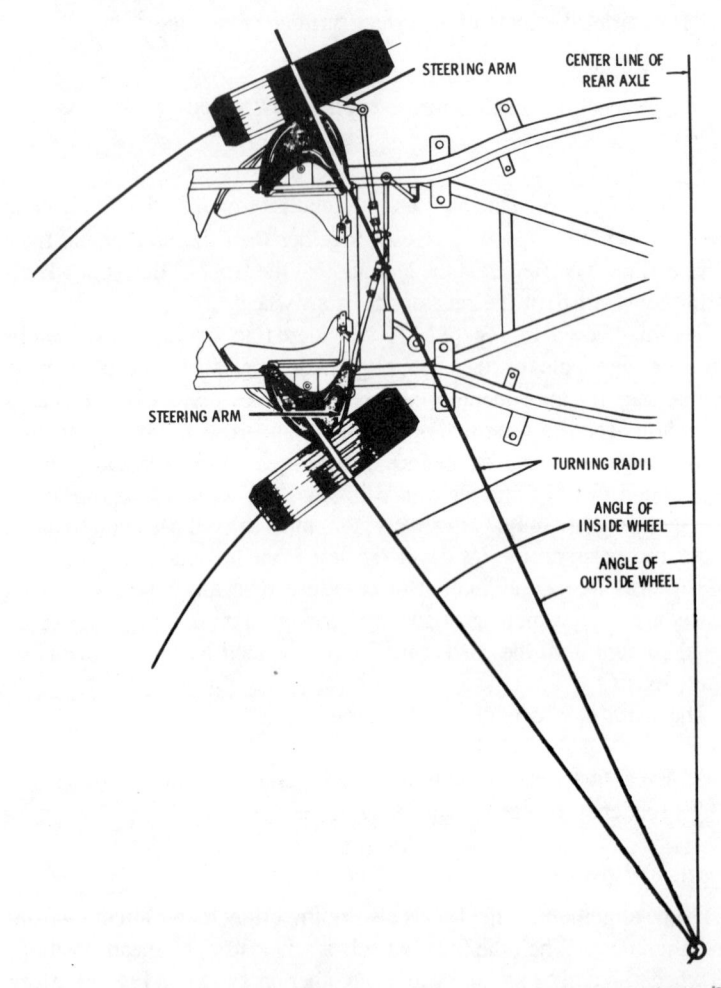

Courtesy Bear Manufacturing Co.

Fig. 11. The turning radius of a car causes toe-out on a turn, and is determined by the angle at which the steering arms are attached to the wheels.

There are several makes and types of alignment equipment available ranging from very elaborate to comparatively simple units. Regardless of the complexity or the manufacturer, each piece of equipment has been designed to accurately check the wheel alignment of any make or model of domestic automobile. Generally speaking, the more elaborate

FRONT-WHEEL ALIGNMENT

the equipment, the less time and labor is involved in making a complete and accurate alignment check.

For shops specializing in wheel alignment, a permanent pit-type installation, Fig. 14, is often used. The pit-type equipment allows floor level drive-on convenience with the feature of undercar service with a minimum of effort.

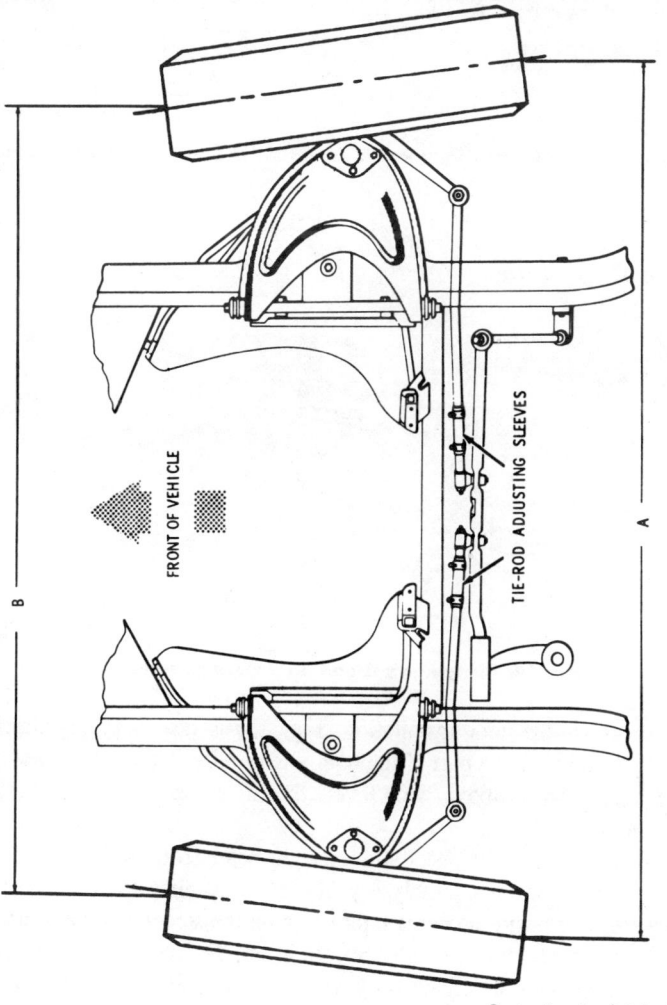

Courtesy Bear Manufacturing Co.

Fig. 12. Front wheel toe-in. The adjusting sleeves will be found on the outboard end of the tie rods on some makes of cars.

AUTOMOBILE GUIDE

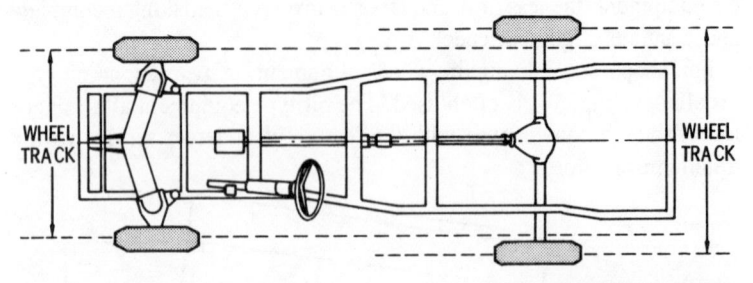

Courtesy Hunter Engineering Co.

Fig. 13. Correct frame alignment is essential for proper tracking of wheels.

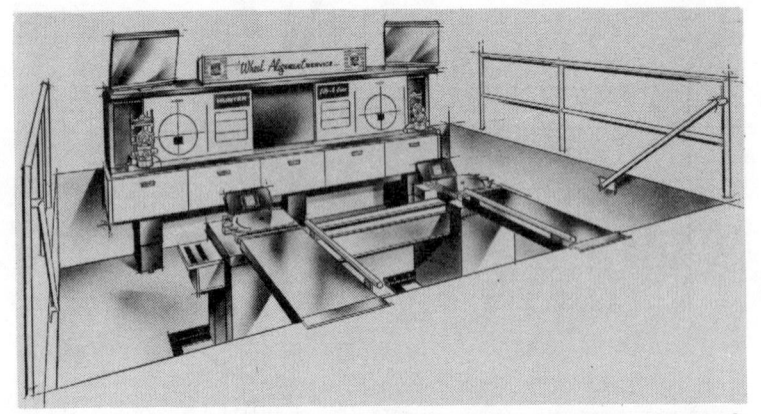

Courtesy Hunter Engineering Co.

Fig. 14. Pit-type front-end alignment installation.

An above-the-floor installation, Fig. 15, is also very popular. An air-hydraulic lift is a part of the equipment. After the car is driven onto the "rack," just above floor level, the lift raises the car to working height.

With either type of installation, a light beam from each front wheels slip-on or clamp-on assembly is projected onto calibrated screens of the console. The position of this light beam on the screen is determined by the various alignment angles existing on the car being tested. As alignment angles are changed by the technician, so does the position of the light on the screens. Thus, it is possible to determine which of the angles require adjustment, and to determine very accurately when the correct adjustments have been made.

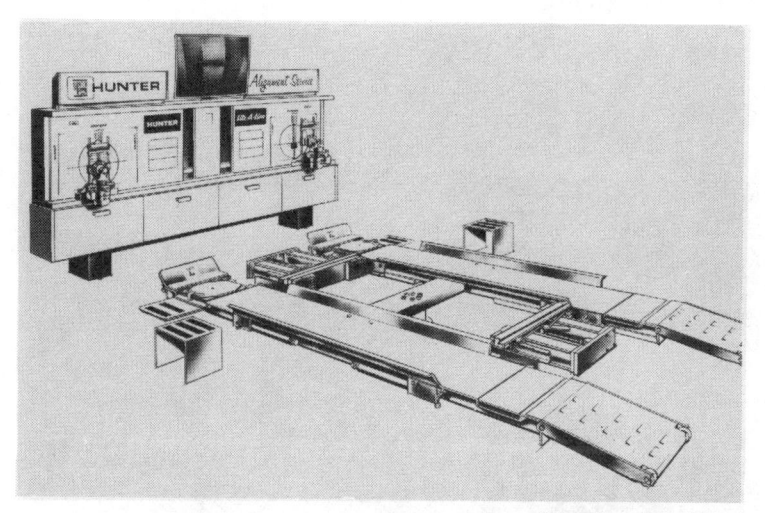

FRONT-WHEEL ALIGNMENT

Fig. 15. Above-the-floor front-end alignment installation.

Less elaborate equipment is available for the shop that has only occasional alignment work and does not have the space for a permanent installation. An example of this type of equipment is shown in Fig. 16. These portable alignment stands can be positioned in any free area that might be available. After the stands are leveled, the car is jacked up and the stands placed under the wheels. A combination camber/caster/ kingpin-inclination guage, such as the one in Fig. 17, is then used to check these three alignment angles. These alignment stands can also be used in conjunction with the gauge shown in Fig. 18 to check caster and camber. Toe-in is measured with a separate toe-in gauge, while toe-out on turns (turning radius) can be checked by reading the degree dial on each of the turntables as the front wheels are turned a specified amount.

Another type of wheel aligner is shown in Fig. 19. According to the manufacturer, this portable unit can be used anywhere on any reasonably level surface. It requires no other auxiliary equipment, and is capable of checking the five major alignment angles already discussed, plus checking center-line steering and rear-wheel track. It features a "sight-sound" system for taking toe readings. The correct toe-in reading is set on the unit and the operator makes the necessary adjustments on the tie-rod ends. When the correct adjustments have been reached, a light flashes and a buzzer is energized to give both a visual and audible indication that the correct setting has been made.

AUTOMOBILE GUIDE

Courtesy AMMCO Tools, Inc.

Fig. 16. AMMCO portable wheel-alignment stands.

This makes it unnecessary for the operator to crawl from under the car and repeatedly check the gauges to see if the setting is correct.

For the high-production specialty-shop, electronic front end equipment, such as shown in Fig. 20, is available. An array of meters replace lights and intregal computer-type circuitry automatically compensates for variables that require manual adjustment on other type equipment. On-car adjustments are made while observing the meters. Print out recorders, for shop and/or customer information is also available for this type equipment.

Obviously, the electronic front-end equipment is the most expensive. However, it offers the advantage of speed and accuracy in wheel alignment. Speed means more "jobs" per day and accuracy means fewer complaints due to human error, leading to greater customer satisfaction.

ADJUSTMENTS

All alignment checks and adjustments should be made with the car level, at curb weight, spare tire in place, normal supply of water, fuel, and oil, but with no passengers or load. All tires should be inflated to the

FRONT-WHEEL ALIGNMENT

Courtesy AMMCO Tools, Inc.

Fig. 17. A combination gauge to measure camber, caster, and kingpin (steering-axis) inclination.

recommended pressures, and the wheel assemblies balanced before alignment. Special care should be taken to check for bent wheels and out-of-round tires. Alignment should not be attempted until these conditions are corrected. Neither should alignment be made if the tires are excessively or abnormally worn, if the car frame is bent, or if any part of the suspension and/or steering system is defective.

Preliminary Inspection

Before any alignment adjustments are attempted, a systematic inspection should be made of the suspension, steering, and frame to determine if any parts are loose, broken, worn, or bent. If any of these defects exist, they must be corrected, for if they are not, alignment will be useless if not impossible.

597

AUTOMOBILE GUIDE

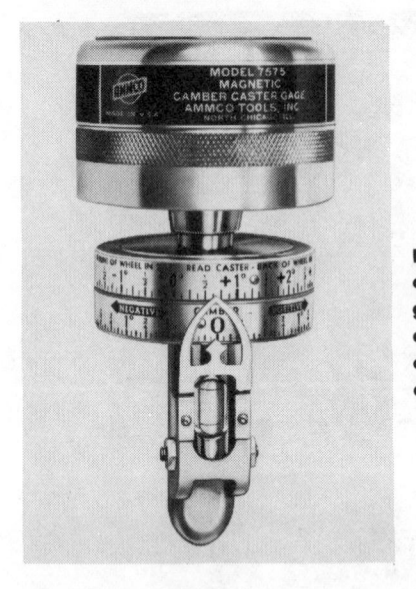

Fig. 18. A gauge used to measure caster and camber angles. This gauge is held in place by magnetic attraction and attached to the face of the wheel hub after the hub cap and dust cover are removed from the wheel.

Courtesy AMMCO Tools, Inc.

A definite step-by-step procedure should be followed for this preliminary inspection to insure that all parts are checked, and to help the operator perform his work easier and faster. An inspection report form, similar to the one shown in Fig. 21, should be filled out to aid in estimating the cost of any needed repairs. These forms are usually available from the alignment equipment manufacturers, or a similar form can be prepared by a local printer.

The following is a suggested procedure to follow in making a preliminary inspection:

1. Check with the owner of the car to determine if he has any complaints that might serve as a clue to possible trouble location. Some of the more common complaints are:

    a. Excessive tire wear.
    b. Cupping and dishing of tire tread.
    c. Front-wheel shimmy.
    d. Vehicle vibration.
    e. Car wander.
    f. Car pulls to one side when braking.

598

Front-Wheel Alignment

Fig. 19. A portable wheel aligner called the TUNE-A-LINE.

Fig. 20. Electronic front-end equipment console.

AUTOMOBILE GUIDE

Fig. 21. An Inspection Report should be filled out for each alignment job.

    g. Car pulls to one side at all times.
    h. Car steers too hard or too easy.
    i. Steering has excessive play or looseness.

From the facts given by the owner it is often possible to recognize the trouble area before a complete inspection is made.

Front-Wheel Alignment

2. Check and inflate tires to recommended pressures.
3. Examine tires for unusual or excessive wear.
   a. Excessive wear on the outside shoulder may indicate too much positive camber.
   b. Excessive wear on the inside shoulder may indicate too much negative camber.
   c. Excessive wear on both inner and outer shoulders indicate underinflation or turning corners at too high a speed.
   d. Excessive wear on the center portion of the tire indicates overinflation.
   e. Cupping or dishing indicates an out-of-balance condition.
   f. Saw-tooth wear on tread indicates improper toe-in condition.

4. Raise the front wheels with jacks placed under the lower control arms and as close to the wheels as possible.
5. Grasp each wheel, in turn, at the top and bottom and wiggle it in and out (Fig. 22). Excessive play indicates loose or worn wheel bearings. These should be tightened or replaced, as the case may be. Worn or damaged bushings should also be replaced.
6. Grasp the wheel at the front and rear, as in Fig. 23, and check for side play. Excessive play indicates worn or loose steering assembly components. Inspect for bushing wear, loose idler arms, loose or worn tie-rod ends, loose or worn ball joints, loose steering gear housing, and loose or worn pitman arm connections.
7. Check for excessive play in the ball joints by means of a dial-type indicator and pry bar, as illustrated in Fig. 24.
8. Check for wheel run-out using a dial-type indicator, Fig. 25, while turning the wheel.
9. Check the car for accident damage. Correct alignment cannot be made if the frame, steering linkage, or suspension parts have been bent.
10. If accident damage is suspected, check the wheelbase on each side of the car and compare (Fig. 26). The two measurements should be within 1/4-inch. To check for a bent frame, diagonal measurements can be made on certain parts of the frame, as shown in Fig. 26. It may be necessary to transfer the measuring points to a level floor in order to measure properly. This point transfer can be made with a plumb bob. Corresponding measurements should be

601

AUTOMOBILE GUIDE

Fig. 22. Checking for loose or worn wheel bearings.

Courtesy Hunter Engineering Co.

Courtesy Hunter Engineering Co.

Fig. 23. Checking for loose idle arms, tie-rod ends, ball joints, steering-gear housing, and pitman-arm connections.

within 1/4-inch of each other. Measurements differing by more than this amount indicate a bent frame, which should be straightened before wheel alignment is attempted.
11 . Check shock absorbers by bouncing the car up and down (Fig. 27). If the shocks are too tight, the car may not settle to a normal position. If the shocks are worn, the car will continue to bounce two or three times after the force is removed. Defective shocks

Front-Wheel Alignment

Courtesy Hunter Engineering Co.

Fig. 24. Checking ball joints with a dial indicator and prybar.

should be replaced, and always in pairs (both front shocks and/or both rear shocks).

1 2. Check the brakes for correct and even adjustment (Fig. 28).
1 3. Check for sagging springs, both front and rear, or for incorrect suspension height on cars with torsion bars. Correct before alignment.
1 4 . Check for rear-axle shift caused by loose axle clamps.
1 5 . Check rear sway bar (Fig. 29) for proper adjustment. If too tight, the rear wheels will not track.
1 6 . Check any other parts of the suspension and steering systems not listed for wear or breakage.

All of the preceding checks should be considered as a routine procedure before proceeding with any alignment adjustments. In addi-

AUTOMOBILE GUIDE

Courtesy Hunter Engineering Co.

Fig. 25. Checking wheel runout with a dial indicator.

tion, the car should be positioned on a level surface, and each time the car is jacked up and lowered, it should be bounced up and down two or three times to settle it in a normal position.

Caster and Camber Adjustments

There are only a few basic types of construction found in the different makes and models of cars for adjusting the caster and camber angles. These are:

1. Shims.
2. Eccentric bushing.
3. Eccentric pin.
4. Eccentric bolt and cam.
5. Adjustable strut rod.
6. Bolt holes in control arm shaft.

The use of shims is the most common type of caster and camber adjustment, and will be found on many *Ford* and *General Motors* cars.

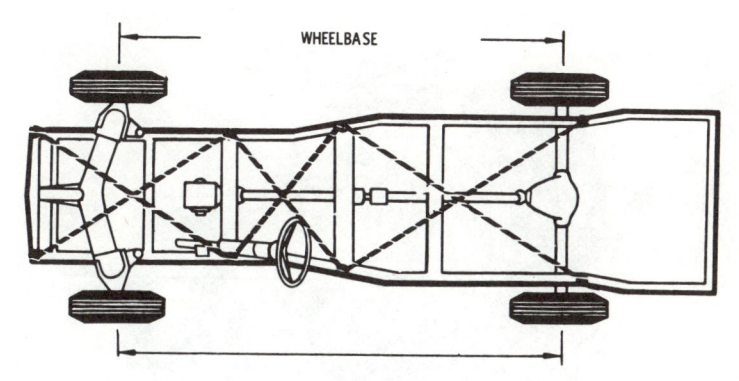

Front-Wheel Alignment

Fig. 26. Measurements made on the frame to detect incorrect rear-axle alignment or a bent frame.

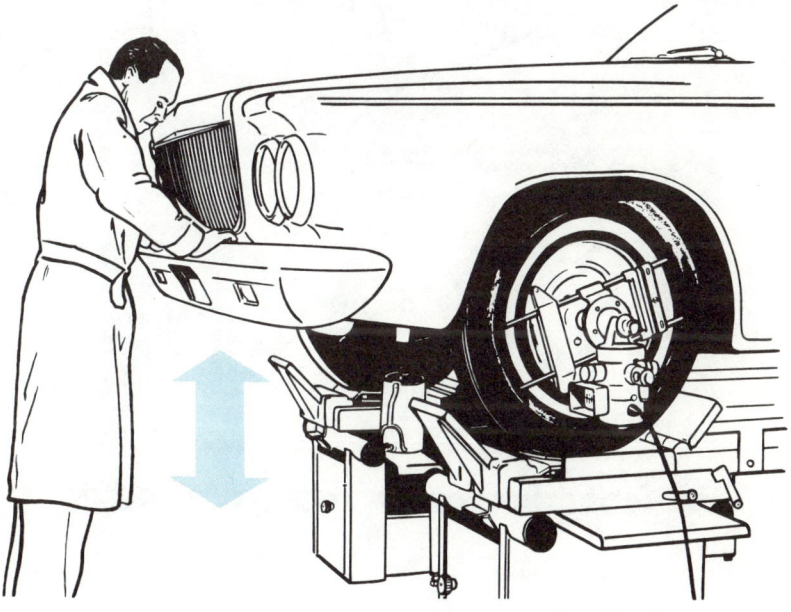

Fig. 27. Shock absorbers should be checked before wheel alignment is attempted.

The following procedures are given as typical of the various types of adjustments, as shown in Fig. 30. For specific types of adjustment on a particular car, refer to the manufacturer's service manual.

AUTOMOBILE GUIDE

Courtesy Hunter Engineering Co.

Fig. 28. A check of the brake adjustments should be made prior to wheel alignment.

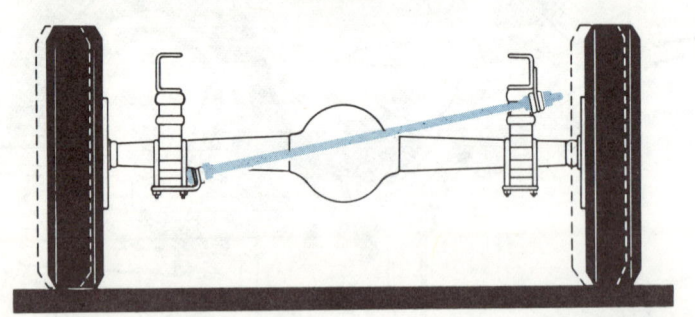

Courtesy Hunter Engineering Co.

Fig. 29. The rear sway bar should be checked for proper alignment.

Shims at Upper Control Arm and Inside the Frame — On cars having shims at the upper control arm and inside the frame (Fig. 30A), the the following procedures may be followed to adjust the caster and camber:

Both the caster and camber can be adjusted on these cars by removing or adding shims between the inner shaft of the upper suspension arm

606

FRONT-WHEEL ALIGNMENT

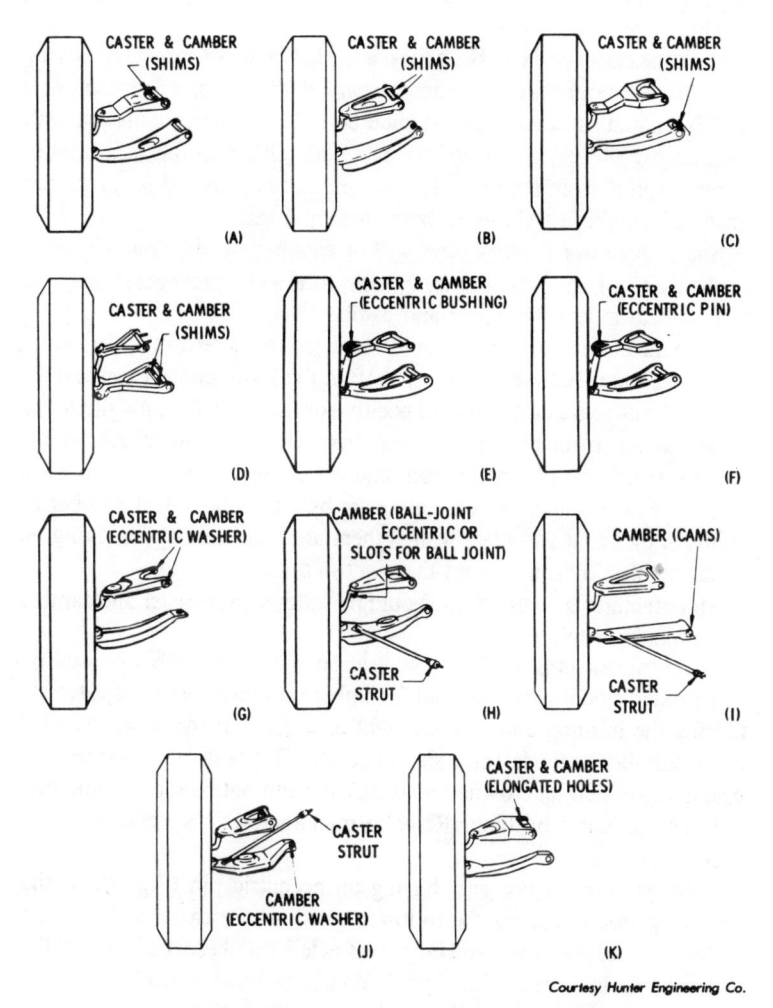

Fig. 30. Caster and camber adjustment methods.

Courtesy Hunter Engineering Co.

and the mounting bracket on the frame in the engine compartment. To increase the caster toward positive, remove shims from the front and/or add shims to the rear. To increase camber toward positive, remove an equal number of shims from both the front and rear.

Shims at Upper Control Arm and Outside the Frame — On cars having shims at the upper control arm and outside the frame (Fig. 30B), the following procedures may be followed to adjust the caster and camber:

Both the caster and camber can be adjusted on these cars by removing or adding shims between the inner shaft of the upper suspension arm and the mounting bracket on the underbody in the engine compartment. To increase the caster toward positive, add shims to the front and/or remove shims from the rear. To increase camber toward positive, add an equal number of shims to both front and rear.

Shims at Lower Control Arm — For cars having shims at the lower control arm (Fig. 30C and 30D), the following procedures may be followed to adjust the caster and camber:

Both the caster and camber can be adjusted on these cars by removing or adding shims between the inner shaft of the lower control arm and the frame. To increase caster toward positive on some cars, shims should be added to the front and/or removed from the rear; on others, shims should be removed from the front and/or added to the rear. Camber is increased toward positive on some cars by adding an equal number of shims at the front and rear; while others are increased by removing an equal number of shims from the front and rear.

Manufacturer's instructions should be followed for caster and camber adjustments in this case.

Eccentric Bushing — The eccentric bushing (Fig. 30E), is used on some older model cars. Basically, camber on these cars is adjusted by turning the bushing either to the right or to the left (no more than 1/2 turn). Camber on the left side should be set 1/2° greater than on the right side to offset pull on crowned roads. Caster can not be set on some cars with the eccentric bushing. Refer to manufacturer's specifications for specific procedures.

Eccentric Pin — For cars having an eccentric pin (Fig. 30F), the following procedures may be followed to adjust the caster and camber:

Both the caster and camber are affected on these cars when the eccentric pin is turned. Therefore, both angles must be checked simultaneously. It is necessary on some cars to average these two settings to bring each within limits.

Eccentric Bolt and Cam — Two methods of adjusting caster and camber are used on cars having an eccentric bolt and cam adjustment (Fig. 30G).

To increase camber toward the positive, some cars require turning the front cam out and the rear cam in while others the reverse is true (front cam in and rear cam out).

Still, on some cars camber is increased toward positive by turning *both* front and rear cams out — and on others by turning *both* cams in.

Adjustable Strut Rod and Eccentric Ball Joint — For cars having an adjustable strut rod to set the camber angle and an eccentric ball joint to set the caster (Fig. 30H), adjust as follows:

To increase the caster toward positive, turn the retaining nuts on the forward end of the strut rod to shorten the rod. To change the camber, loosen the ball joint stud and turn the eccentric to obtain the correct camber angle.

Adjustable Strut Rod and Eccentric Cam — On cars having an adjustable strut rod to set caster and an eccentric cam to set camber, proceed as follows (Fig. 30I):

To increase the caster toward positive, shorten the strut rod. To change the camber angle, turn the eccentric cam right or left, but no more than 1/2 turn.

Adjustable Strut Rod and Eccentric Washer — Fig. 30J shows a car having an adjustable strut to change caster and an eccentric washer to adjust the camber. The following procedure may be followed:

To increase the caster toward positive, lengthen the strut rod. To change the camber angle, turn the eccentric washer right or left, but no more than 1/2 turn.

Slotted Cross Member — Caster and camber are corrected on cars with a slotted cross member, Fig. 30K, as follows:

To increase the caster toward positive, move the front bolt outboard and the rear bolt inboard. To increase the camber toward positive, move both the front and rear bolts outboard an equal amount.

Toe-In Adjustments

The procedure for adjusting the toe condition is practically the same for all makes and models of automobiles. A typical steering linkage similar to the one found on all cars is shown in Fig. 31. Both tie-rods are adjustable as to length.

To adjust the toe-in, first check the steering wheel for a straight-ahead position. If the steering wheel is not in the correct position with the front wheels straight ahead, adjust by loosening the clamps on the tie-rod ends and shorten one tie-rod and lengthen the other and equal amount until the steering wheel position is correct.

To obtain the correct toe-in, turn the tie-rod ends to either lengthen or shorten each tie rod an equal amount until the correct toe is obtained.

AUTOMOBILE GUIDE

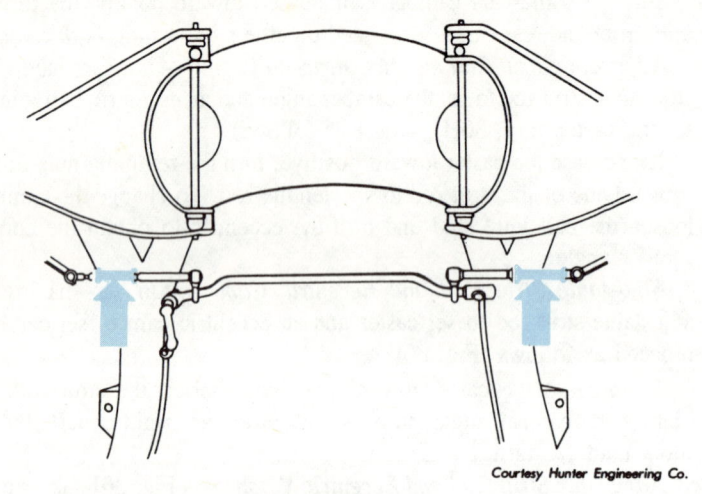

Courtesy Hunter Engineering Co.

Fig. 31. Location of toe adjustments on a typical car.

SUMMARY

Because of the specialized and often expensive equipment and tools required for front end alignment service, this "job" is often left to the professional technician.

If, however, front end equipment and tools are available, the car manufacturer's specifications should be followed. Specifications for toe-in, toe-out, caster, camber, kingpin inclination, and height differ from car to car. Specifications are usually included with, or available from, the equipment manufacturer. If not available, the car manufacturer's service manual will include this information.

WHEEL-ALIGNMENT TROUBLES AND REMEDIES

Symptoms and Possible Causes   *Possible Remedies*

Hard Steering

(a) Low or uneven tire pressures.

(b) Steering gear or connections adjusted too tightly.

(a) Inflate tires to recommended pressures.

(b) Inspect steering system for binding with front wheels

Symptoms and Possible Causes	FRONT-WHEEL ALIGNMENT Possible Remedies
	off the ground. Adjust as necessary and lubricate.
(c) Dry steering gear, kingpins, ball joints, or tie-rod ends.	(c) Lubricate as necessary.
(d) Excessive caster.	(d) Check caster and adjust.
(e) Steering knuckle or spindle bent.	(e) Replace with new part.
(f) Kingpin thrust bearings worn.	(f) Install new bearings.
(g) Suspension arms bent or twisted.	(g) Install new arms and adjust caster and camber, and check kingpin inclination.
(h) Front springs sagged.	(h) Check car spring height and replace both front springs if one is defective.
(i) Frame out of line or broken.	(i) Check car tracking and frame alignment. Repair frame as necessary.

Excessive Play in Steering System

(a) Worn kingpins and bushings or worn ball joints.	(a) Install new kingpins and bushings or new ball joints.
(b) Worn or incorrectly adjusted front wheel bearings.	(b) Adjust bearings or replace with new units.
(c) Steering gear adjusted too loosely or worn.	(c) Adjust or install new parts.
(d) Loose steering gear mounting.	(d) Tighten steering gear mounting bolts.
(e) Pitman arm loose on cross shaft.	(e) Replace worn parts or tighten cross shaft nut.
(f) Drag link loose.	(f) Adjust or replace with new parts.
(g) Tie-rod ends worn.	(g) Install new tie-rods ends.

Automobile Guide

Symptoms and Possible Causes	Possible Remedies

Erratic Steering When Brakes are Applied

(a) Low or uneven tire pressures.
(b) Brakes incorrectly adjusted.
(c) Brake linings oil or grease soaked.
(d) Front wheel bearings worn or incorrectly adjusted.
(e) Front springs and/or shock absorbers weak.
(f) Excessive caster.
(g) Steering knuckle or spindle bent.
(h) Spring U-bolts broken or loose.
(i) Spring center bolt broken.

(a) Inflate tires to recommended pressures.
(b) Adjust brakes.
(c) Replace brake linings and clean brake drum.
(d) Replace or adjust bearings.
(e) Replace with new springs and/or shock absorbers (in pairs).
(f) Check caster and adjust.
(g) Replace with new parts.
(h) Replace or tighten.
(i) Install new center bolt.

Car Pulls to One Side

(a) Low or uneven tire pressures.
(b) Brakes incorrectly adjusted.
(c) Brake linings oil or grease soaked.
(d) Incorrect or uneven caster angles.
(e) Excessive unequal camber angles.
(f) Toe-in or toe-out incorrect.
(g) Front tires scuffed.
(h) Steering knuckle or spindle bent.
(i) Spindle support arm bent.

(a) Inflate tires to recommended pressures.
(b) Adjust brakes.
(c) Replace brake linings and clean brake drums.
(d) Check caster and adjust.
(e) Adjust camber.
(f) Adjust tie-rod ends for correct toe-in.
(g) Rotate tires.
(h) Replace with new knuckle or spindle.
(i) Replace with new arm.

FRONT-WHEEL ALIGNMENT

Symptoms and Possible Causes

(j) Front springs sagged.

(k) Rear axle shifted.

(l) Frame out of line or broken.

Possible Remedies

(j) Check front spring height. Replace both front springs if one is found sagged.

(k) Check for loose spring clips or broken center bolt. Measure from the spring anchor bolts to the rear housing. This distance on both sides of the car should be equal.

(l) Check tracking and frame alignment. Correct and repair frame.

Scuffed Tires

(a) Tires improperly inflated.

(b) Incorrect toe-in.

(c) Wheels or tires out of true.

(d) Worn kingpin thrust bearings.

(e) Incorrect toe-out on turns.

(f) Worn or incorrectly adjusted front-wheel bearings.

(g) Suspension arms bent or twisted.

(h) Steering knuckle or spindle bent.

(i) Excessive speeds on turns.

(a) Inflate tires to recommended pressures.

(b) Adjust tie-rod ends for correct toe-in.

(c) Check wheels and tires for wobble. Correct condition or replace.

(d) Install new bearings.

(e) Check caster and adjust. Install new steering arms.

(f) Adjust or replace bearings.

(g) Install new arms and adjust caster and camber. Check kingpin inclination.

(h) Replace with new unit.

(i) Caution driver.

Symptoms and Possible Causes   *Possible Remedies*

Cupped Tires

(a) Tires improperly inflated.
(b) Wheels, tires, and/or brake drums out of balance.

(c) Dragging brakes.
(d) Worn or incorrectly adjusted front wheel bearings.
(e) Improper camber angle.
(f) Steering knuckle or spindle bent.
(g) Worn or loose steering linkage and suspension parts.

(a) Inflate tires to recommended pressures.
(b) Balance wheel assemblies. Check for eccentric brake drums, wheels, and tires and replace if necessary.
(c) Adjust or repair brakes.
(d) Adjust or replace bearings.

(e) Adjust camber.
(f) Replace with new knuckle or spindle.
(g) Replace defective part or parts.

Front-Wheel Shimmy

(a) Low or uneven tire pressures.
(b) Worn or incorrectly adjusted steering connections.
(c) Loose steering-gear mounting.
(d) Incorrectly adjusted steering gear.
(e) Worn or incorrectly adjusted front-wheel bearings.
(f) Out-of-balance wheels, tires, or brake drums.

(a) Inflate tires to recommended pressures.
(b) Adjust or install new parts.
(c) Tighten steering gear mounting bolts or nuts.
(d) Adjust steering gear.
(e) Adjust or replace bearings.

(f) Balance wheel assemblies. Check for eccentric brake drums, wheels, and tires.

FRONT-WHEEL ALIGNMENT

Symptoms and Possible Causes

(g) Wheels and/or tires out of true.
(h) Incorrect or unequal caster.
(i) Dead or weak shock absorbers.
(j) Worn kingpin thrust bearings.
(k) Incorrect toe-in.
(l) Steering knuckle or spindle bent.

Possible Remedies

(g) Check for wheel and tire wobble. Correct condition or replace with good units.
(h) Adjust caster.
(i) Replace with correct type. Always replace in pairs.
(j) Install new bearings.
(k) Adjust toe-in.
(l) Replace with new knuckle or spindle.

Front- or Rear-Wheel Tramp

(a) Out-of-balance wheels, tires, or brake drums.

(b) Weak front springs.

(c) Dead or weak shock absorbers.

(a) Balance wheel assemblies. Check for eccentric brake drums, wheels, or tires and replace if necessary.
(b) Replace both front springs if only one is weak.
(c) Install new units of the correct type. Always replace in pairs.

Wander

(a) Low or uneven tire pressures.
(b) Loose steering gear mounting.
(c) Worn or loose steering gear or connections.
(d) Tight steering gear or connections.

(a) Inflate tires to recommended pressures.
(b) Tighten steering gear mounting bolts or nuts.
(c) Adjust or install new parts.
(d) Inspect steering system with front wheels off ground. Adjust as necessary and lubricate.

Symptoms and Possible Causes

(e) Dry steering linkage.

(f) Worn kingpin thrust bearings.
(g) Incorrect front-wheel toe.
(h) Incorrect caster.
(i) Steering knuckle or spindle bent.
(j) Rear axle shifted.

(k) Inoperative stabilizer.

(l) Tread on rear tires better than on front tires.

Road Shocks

(a) Low tire pressure.

(b) Steering gear or connections incorrectly adjusted.
(c) Excessive caster.
(d) Dead or weak shock absorbers.
(e) Front springs weak or sagged.

(f) Wrong type or size of tires used.
(g) Steering knuckle or spindle bent.

Possible Remedies

(e) Lubricate with correct lubricant.
(f) Install new bearings.

(g) Adjust toe.
(h) Adjust caster.
(i) Replace with new unit.
(j) Check for loose spring clip or broken center bolt. Measure from the spring anchor bolt to the rear housing. This distance should be the same on both sides of the car. Correct as necessary.
(k) Inspect grommets and links, replacing worn parts.
(l) Change tires, placing best tread on front.

(a) Inflate tires to recommended pressures.
(b) Adjust steering gear and connections.
(c) Adjust caster.
(d) Replace shocks in pairs.

(e) Check car spring height. If incorrect, replace springs in pairs.
(f) Install new tires of correct type and size.
(g) Install new unit.

CHAPTER 24

Clutches, Manual Transmissions, and Overdrives

The automatic transmission, in recent years, has been preferred by most drivers. It is "standard equipment" on most top-of-the-line models of cars, and an "option" on other models.

The three-speed manual transmission is "standard equipment" on many cars offering "optional" four-speed, five-speed, or automatic transmissions. Cars equipped with either type of manual transmission are also equipped with a manual clutch.

CLUTCHES

The clutch provides a means of disconnecting and connecting the engine from the transmission. During disengagement, the clutch must completely disconnect the two units, during which time the transmission gears may be "shifted."

When engaged, the clutch must completely connect the two units to transmit full engine power to the transmission without slipping.

The manual clutch consists of three basic units, as shown in Fig 1. They are; the driving members (attached to the engine and turn with it), the driven members (attached to the transmission and turn with it), and

AUTOMOBILE GUIDE

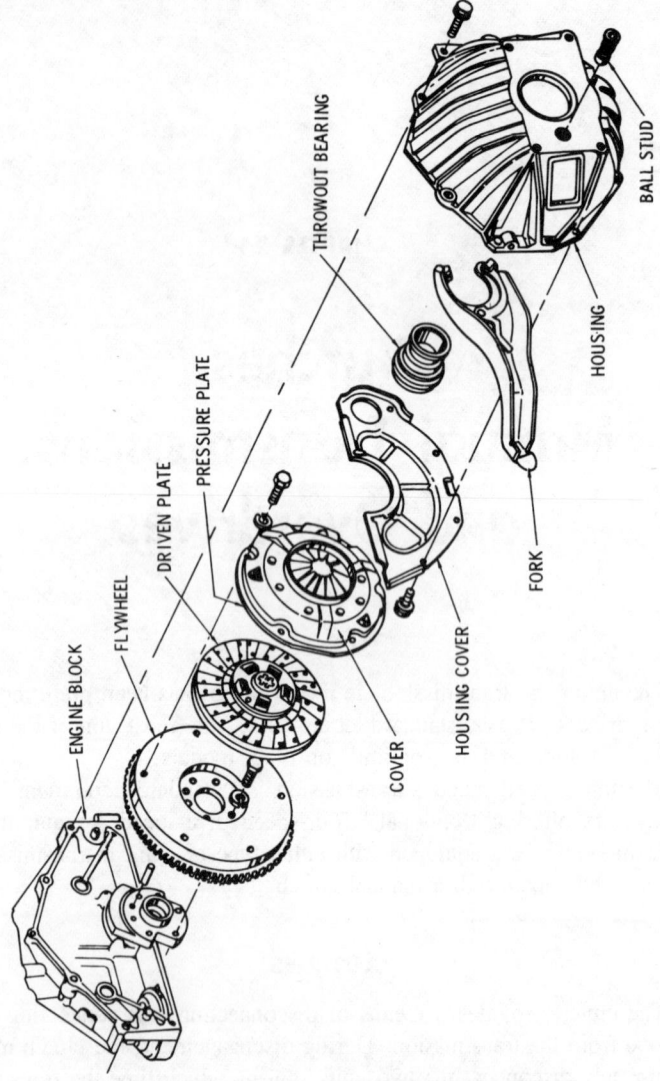

Fig. 1. Exploded view of a typical clutch assembly.

the operating members (necessary to engage or disengage the driving and driven members).

There are basically two types of dry-disc clutch — the centrifugal type (Fig. 2) and the diaphragm type. Either type is actuated by the driver by a mechanically-linked clutch pedal.

Clutches, Manual Transmissions, and Overdrives

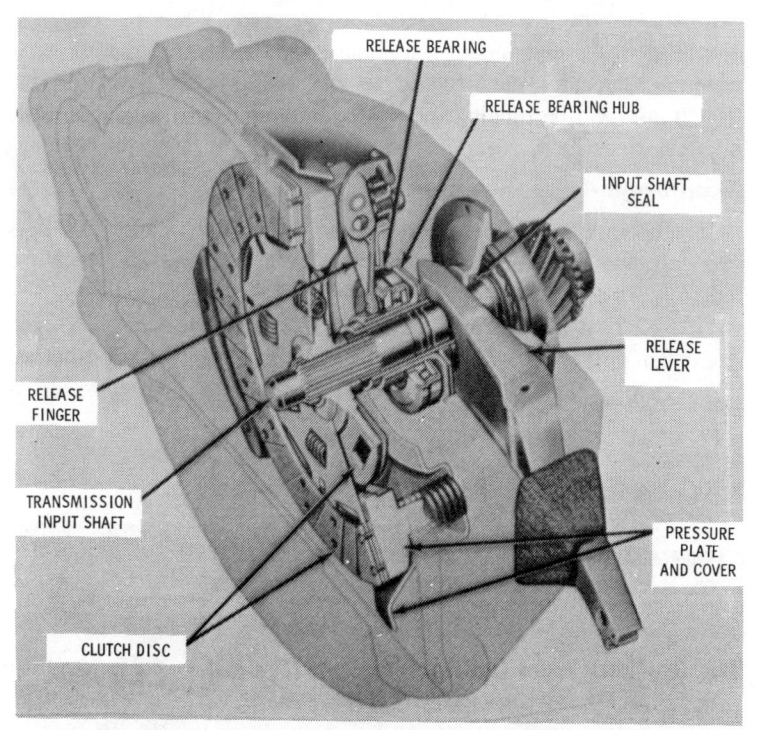

Fig. 2. A typical centrifugal-type clutch assembly.

Centrifugal-Type Clutch

With the clutch pedal in the engaged position (not depressed), the clutch disc facings are clamped between the friction surface on the engine flywheel and the face of the clutch pressure plate by the pressure of the clutch springs. When the clutch pedal is depressed, the release yoke or fork is moved on its pivot, applying pressure to the release (throw-out) bearing sleeve or collar. The rotating race of the throw-out bearing presses against the clutch release levers and moves them on their pivots. Since the outer end of the release levers are fastened to the clutch cover, the pressure plate is moved back from the clutch disc, compressing the clutch springs and allowing the engine flywheel and clutch elements to rotate independently of each other.

The throw-out yoke moves on its pivot which is fastened to the flywheel housing by means of a bracket or transverse shaft. All parts of the clutch assembly, except the throw-out bearing and collar, rotate

619

AUTOMOBILE GUIDE

with the flywheel when the clutch is engaged. When the clutch is disengaged, the clutch disc will come to rest if the transmission is in neutral or the car is standing still. If the car is in gear and moving, the clutch disc will be rotating, being driven through the transmission by the rear wheels.

Diaphragm-Type Clutch

The operating principle of a diaphragm-type clutch (Fig. 3) differs from that of the centrifugal-type only in the method by which the pressure plate is held against the clutch disc. Instead of helical clutch springs, a disc-shaped diaphragm is used to supply the pressure to hold the clutch disc against the flywheel facing. The diaphragm is positioned between the cover and the pressure plate so that the diaphragm spring is nearly flat when the clutch is engaged.

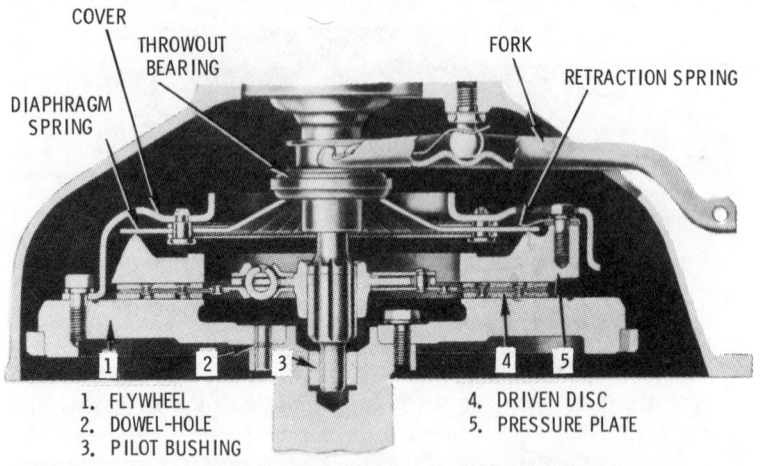

Fig. 3. A typical diaphragm-type clutch assembly.

Service

Several things can affect good clutch operation. Therefore, before performing any major clutch operations, preliminary inspections should be made to determine if the trouble is actually in the clutch proper. The following checks should be made:

1. With the engine running, hold the clutch pedal approximately ½ inch from the floor mat and shift between first and reverse gears several times. if the shifting is smooth, adjustment of the clutch is necessary.

620

Clutches, Manual Transmissions, and Overdrives

2. Check the clutch pedal bushings for binding or excessive wear.
3. Check the throw-out yoke for proper installation on the ball stud or pivot pin. Lack of lubrication on the yoke can cause it to be pulled off the ball, or can cause it to bind on the pivot pin.
4. Check for bent, cracked, or damaged crossshaft levers, support brackets, and other parts of the clutch linkage.
5. Check for loose or damaged engine mounts which may allow the engine to shift its position causing a bind in the clutch linkage. Check to make sure proper clearance is present for all parts of the clutch linkage to operate without interference.

The adjustments to be made on the clutch while it is in the vehicle are: total travel of the clutch pedal (necessary on some models only) and clutch pedal free play. Improper adjustment is one of the most frequent causes of clutch failure and can, in some cases, be one of the contributing factors to transmission failure.

The *total travel* is that distance the pedal moves from its bumper stop position to its fully depressed position. An example of the measurements to make for determining total travel is shown in Fig. 4 for some *Chevelles*. Here, measurement A is subtracted from measurement B to determine total travel. If the total travel is less than the specifications (6½" in this case), the bumper stop is trimmed until the correct travel is obtained. If the bumper stop is excessively worn or missing, the pedal will be abnormally high. Always check total travel before checking free play.

Clutch pedal free play is an adjustment that must be made from time to time on all cars equipped with a manual transmission. This adjustment is for the amount of free clutch pedal travel before the throw-out bearing makes contact with the release fingers. This measurement will vary slightly from model to model, but the usual free play specified is around ½ inch. This adjustment is made on most cars by lengthening or shortening one of the linkage rods equipped with adjusting nuts. On some makes, the rod itself is turned into or out of a threaded fitting to obtain the correct length. A locknut is provided to lock the adjustment after it is made. On other cars, the adjusting rod is threaded on one end and has two nuts, one being loosened while the other is tightened to change the length of the rods. After the correct adjustment is made, both nuts are tightened to effectively lock the adjustment.

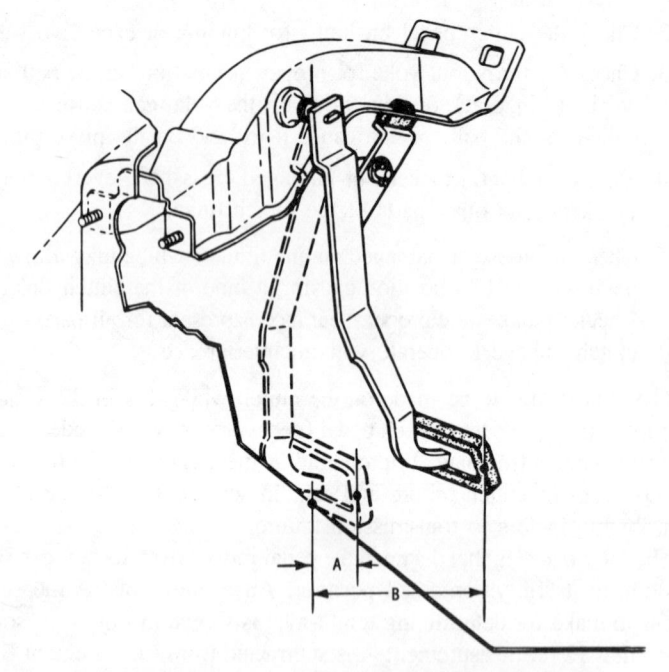

Fig. 4. Measurements to determine total pedal travel.

Fig. 5 shows an example of clutch linkage and adjustments. The total pedal travel is adjusted on this particular linkage by moving the pedal bumper and bracket up or down.

Hydraulic Clutch

On many types of vehicle, particularly on tilt-cab trucks, the clutch is operated hydraulically rather than manually. When the driver pushes the clutch pedal, hydraulic fluid (brake fluid) is forced through a line from the main cylinder (located at or near the clutch pedal) into the slave cylinder (located on or near the transmission). The slave cylinder moves a rod against the clutch fork pivoting it to move the throwout bearing against the clutch release fingers to release (disengage) the clutch.

When the clutch pedal is released the clutch fork return spring forces the fluid from the slave cylinder back into the main cylinder to engage the clutch.

The hydraulic clutch consists of pedal and push rod assembly, main cylinder, tubing, slave cylinder, clutch fork and push rod assembly, throw-out bearing, and clutch fork return spring.

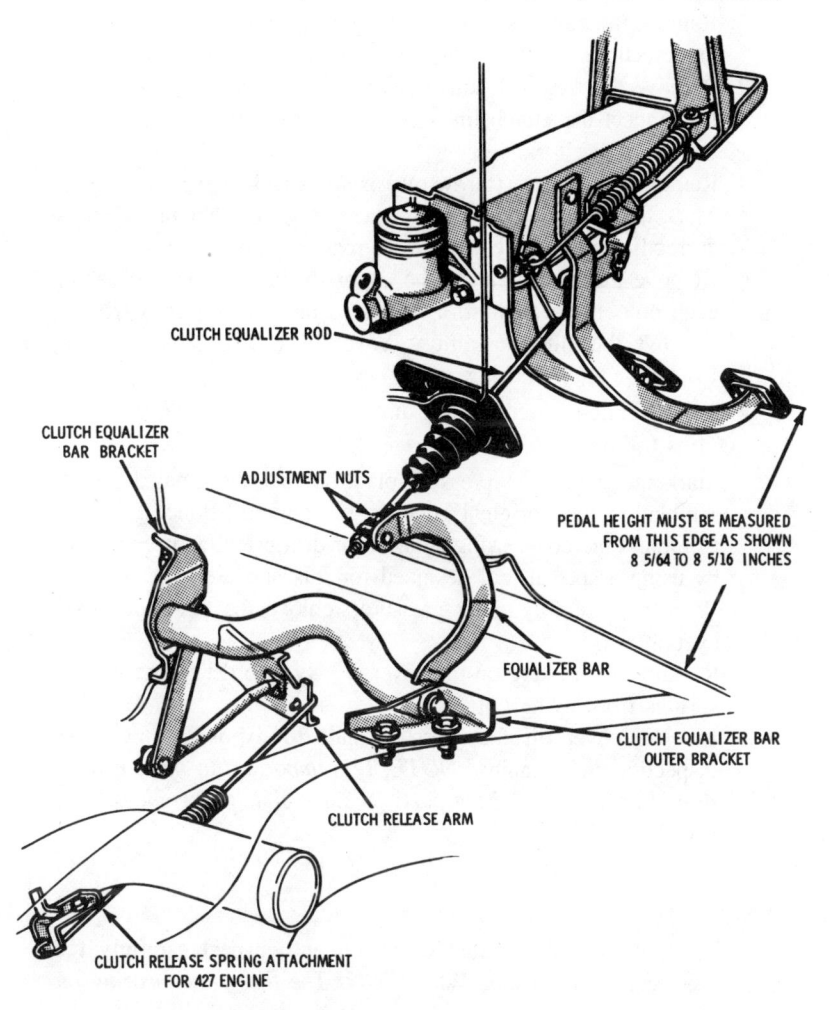

Clutches, Manual Transmissions, and Overdrives

Fig. 5. Typical FORD clutch linkage and adjustments.

A fitting is provided, usually on the slave cylinder, for bleeding air from the hydraulic system in much the same manner as is done in a hydraulic brake system.

Clutch Removal

To remove the clutch for inspection and repair, the following steps are necessary on most cars:

1. Remove the transmission, following the procedure outlined by the manufacturer for the particular car being serviced.
2. Remove the flywheel housing cover.
3. Disconnect the clutch linkage and any retracting springs at the clutch release fork.
4. Remove the release (throw-out) bearing and sleeve.
5. Mark the clutch cover and flywheel to insure that they will be correctly matched when they are reassembled.
6. Remove the bolts holding the cover to the flywheel, loosening each bolt (in succession) a few turns until the cover is free.
7. Remove the clutch assembly (cover, disc, and pressure plate) from the clutch housing.

With the clutch cover, clutch disc, and pressure plate removed, proceed as follows:

1. Mark the cover and pressure plate so that they may be reassembled in their original position to maintain balance.
2. Compress the cover using an arbor or drill press, as in Fig. 6, or by using a special tool designed for this purpose (Fig. 7).
3. With the assembly under pressure, remove the throw-out lever eyebolt nuts.
4. Release the pressure on the cover slowly in order to prevent the springs from flying out.
5. Lift the cover off the pressure plate to expose all parts for inspection and cleaning. *NOTE: It is important to make a notation of the location of the parts on some clutch assemblies. (See Fig. 8.)*

Inspection

Clean all parts with a suitable solvent and inspect carefully for excessive wear or distortion. *WARNING: The throw-out bearing on some cars is prelubricated and should not be cleaned with a solvent.* Inspect the bearing retainer for loose spring clips and rivets.

Throw-Out Bearing — Inspect the throw-out bearing assembly for burrs. If any are found, they should be removed with fine crocus cloth. Also inspect the input shaft to the transmission and remove any scoring with crocus cloth. Coat the bearing retainer with a thin film of lithium-base grease. Hold the inner race of the throw-out bearing and rotate the outer race while applying pressure to it. If the rotation is rough or noisy, replace the bearing.

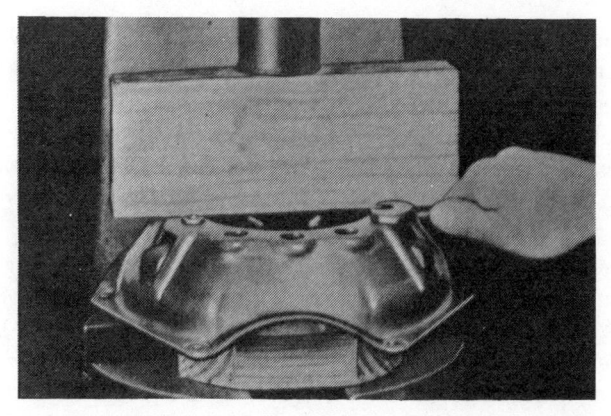

Clutches, Manual Transmissions, and Overdrives

Fig. 6. Compressing the clutch cover to permit disassembly.

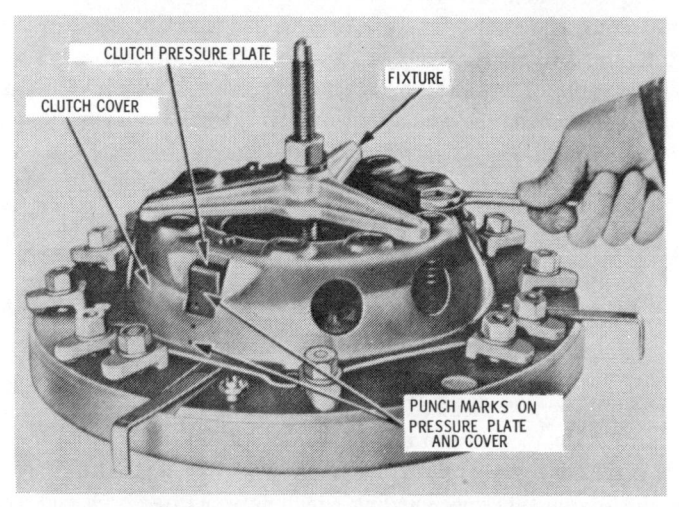

Fig. 7. Using a special tool to compress the clutch cover for disassembly.

Most throw-out bearing failures are the result of improper clutch pedal adjustments. Failure can also be caused by the throw-out lever contact points being out of plane. If one side of the throw-out bearing assembly is worn more than the other side, either the lever is bent or is not centered on the flywheel housing bracket. Misalignment between the engine and transmission can also cause throw-out bearing failure.

Pressure Plate — Inspect the pressure plate surface for burn marks, scores, or ridges. Minor imperfections can be removed if care is taken to maintain the flatness of the pressure plate. If the plate is badly heat checkered, deeply scored, or warped more than 0.005 inch, it should be replaced along with the cover assembly.

Clean the surfaces of the pressure plate and flywheel with a suitable solvent, such as carbon tetrachloride, to make sure the surfaces are free of any oil film. *CAUTION: Do not use cleaners having a petroleum base, and do not immerse the pressure plate in the solution.*

Clutch Disc — Inspect the clutch disc facings for oil or grease. *NOTE: Eliminate the source of any oil or grease before replacing the disc.* An excessive amount of grease in the pilot bushing in the throw-out bearing hub will eventually find its way to the disc facings. Too high a lubricant level in the transmission or a plugged transmission vent will force lubricant from the transmission out past the input shaft and onto the clutch facings.

Inspect the clutch disc for worn or loose facings. Check the disc for distortion and for loose rivets at the hub. Check for broken springs. Replace the disc if any of these defects are present. *CAUTION: Do not drop or contaminate the new disc with oil or grease while installing it.*

Pressure Springs — It is advisable to test the pressure springs when the clutch is dismantled after considerable service, or if there has been considerable slippage. Slippage creates heat which may cause the springs to lose their specified load. Discard any spring that does not meet the minimum requirements.

Cover Plate — Check the cover plate for distortion by laying it on a perfectly flat and smooth surface. If the cover shows signs of being warped, replace with a new unit.

Release Levers — Replace any release levers that are badly worn on the tips. Correct the cause of this abnormal wear (insufficient clutch free pedal play, damaged throw-out bearing, worn or damaged threads on eyebolts or adjusting nuts, binding which prevents free back-and-forth movement, etc.).

Reassembly

To reassemble the clutch, coat the side of the driving lugs and edges of the pressure plate openings with a thin film of lithium-base grease. *Do not apply excessive lubricant.*

Place the pressure springs in their proper place and in their proper sequence (in some clutches) to maintain the proper clutch balance. Place the cover over the springs, using an arbor or drill press (or special tool), making sure the bolts are guided through the holes in the cover.

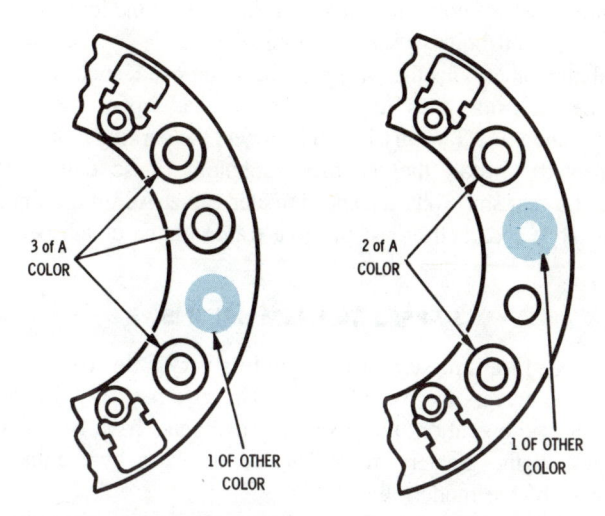

Clutches, Manual Transmissions, and Overdrives

Fig. 8. The pressure springs must be replaced in the proper order in certain CHRYSLER-made clutch assemblies.

Screw the adjusting nuts on the protruding bolts until the nuts are flush with the top of the bolts. Slowly release the pressure on the cover. Depress the throw-out levers several times to properly seat the parts.

Either torque the fastening nuts to specifications, or adjust the throw-out levers by the use of a feeler gauge and spacers. Follow the manufacturer's instructions if the clutch is the type in which the throw-out levers must be adjusted.

Before installing the clutch assembly in the car, make sure the mounting surfaces of the transmission and flywheel housing are free of dirt, paint, and burrs. Place the clutch disc and pressure plate assembly in position on the flywheel and start the attaching bolts to hold the assembly in place. **Take care not to drop the parts or to contaminate them with oil or grease.** Align the clutch disc and tighten the fastening bolts evenly to specifications.

Place the throw-out bearing and hub on the throw-out lever and coat the inside of the bearing retainer lightly with lithium-type grease. **Do not grease the bearing hub.** (Pack the throw-out bearing with grease if it is not of the prelubricated type.)

Install two guide pins in the lower mounting holes of the flywheel housing and move the transmission forward on these pins until it is tightly positioned against the flywheel housing. Install the upper mounting bolts. Remove the guide pins and install the lower mounting bolts. Torque all bolts to specifications.

Install any other bolts that may have been removed, such as those that attach the extension housing to the engine rear support. Remove the jack from under the transmission and connect the parking brake cable (if disconnected). Install the overdrive solenoid (if so equipped) and connect the gear shift rods and speedometer cable. Adjust the linkage of the gear shift rods and adjust the free travel of the clutch pedal.

3-SPEED TRANSMISSIONS

The 3-speed transmission of today differs very little from the transmission used on cars the past 30 years. They are basically the same in appearance and operation, however, improvements have been made to keep up with the greater stresses placed on them by the increased horsepower of the modern engines.

Operating principles remain basically the same; the shift pattern for the 3-speed units have not changed. Gear shift levers were first found on the floor. Styling improvements found the lever moved to the right of the steering column — then again, in some cases, back to the floor.

3-speed transmissions are available that are synchromeshed in second and third gears; or in units that are fully synchromeshed in all three gears. Synchronizing permits quicker shifts, reduced gear clash, and permits "down-shifting" for better car control. Reverse gear, of course, is not synchronized in the 3-speed transmission.

The standard 3-speed transmission may be down-shifted from third to second gear between 40 and 10 miles per hour (mph). Shifting from second to first gear is only accomplished at 0 mph.

The fully synchronized 3-speed transmission may be down-shifted from third to second gear between 45 and 15 mph; and from second to first gear between 25 and 0 mph.

Either of the 3-speed transmissions, not having a synchronizer for reverse, may be shifted into reverse only at 0 mph. A typical three-speed transmission is shown in Fig 9.

Operations

All forward-speed shifting is accomplished through the action of synchronizer sleeves (Fig. 10). These sleeves allow all forward-speed gears to be in constant mesh at all times, thus preventing one source of gear clash.

Clutches, Manual Transmissions, and Overdrives

Fig. 9. A typical 3-speed transmission.

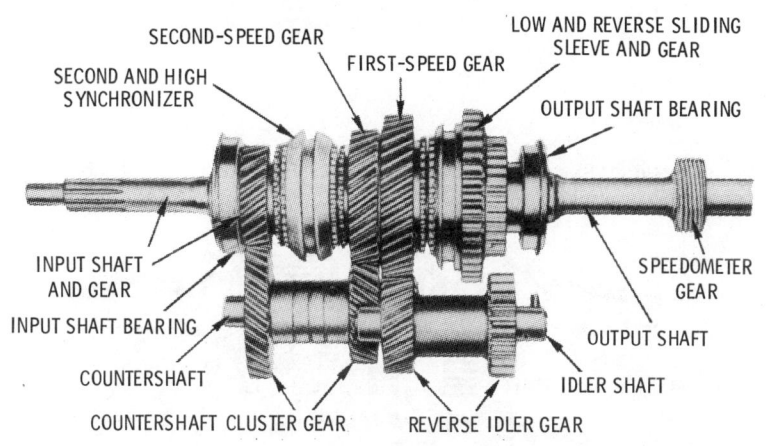

Fig. 10. Internal gear arrangement of a typical 3-speed transmission.

When the first speed is selected, the shift lever moves the reverse gear and sleeve forward and forces the conical surface of the synchronizer blocking ring against the matching cone on the first gear located on the output shaft. If the car is moving, the internal teeth of the reverse gear and sleeve will not mesh with the first gear until the speed of the first gear is increased or decreased to match the speed of the reverse gear and sleeve which are rotating with the output shaft.

The reverse gear and sleeve have internal splines that will slide over the teeth on the first gear when the speed of the two assemblies match. Since first gear is always in mesh with the countershaft cluster gear, the action just described causes the power flow to be from the input shaft (and gear), through the countershaft gear, to the first gear through the reverse gear and sleeve, to the output shaft. See Figs. 11 and 12 to follow the power flow.

Automobile Guide

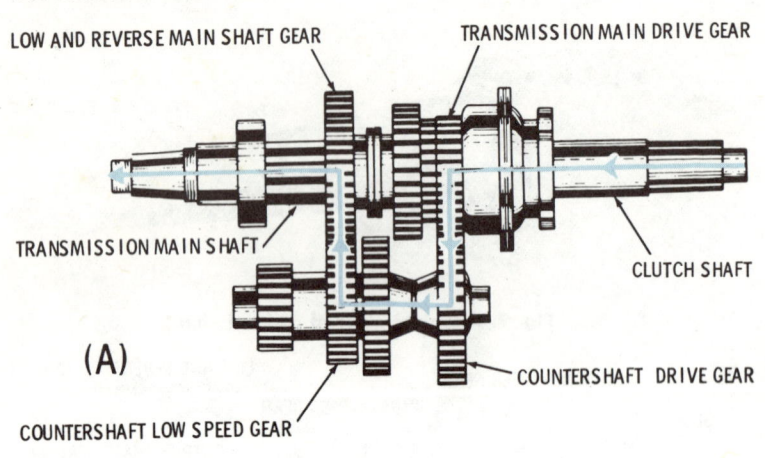

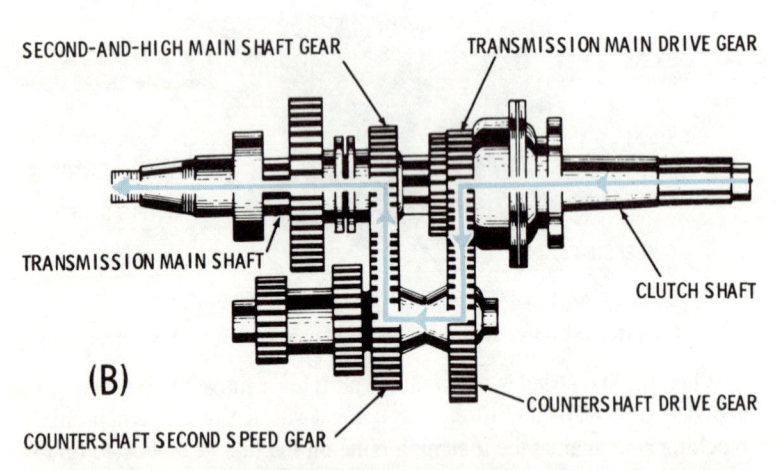

Fig. 11. Power flow in first and second gear. A. Power flow in first gear. B. Power flow in second gear.

Selection of second and third gears are similar to first, except a different synchronizer is used. This synchronizer, like the reverse gear and sleeve, is splined to the output shaft.

Those 3-speed transmissions in which first gear is not synchronized usually have only one gear for both first and reverse gears. This single gear is slipped forward or backward along the splined output shaft until it meshes with one or the other of two counter-gears. Thus, either first or reverse is selected. A system of mechanical interlocks prevents the selection of more than one gear at a time.

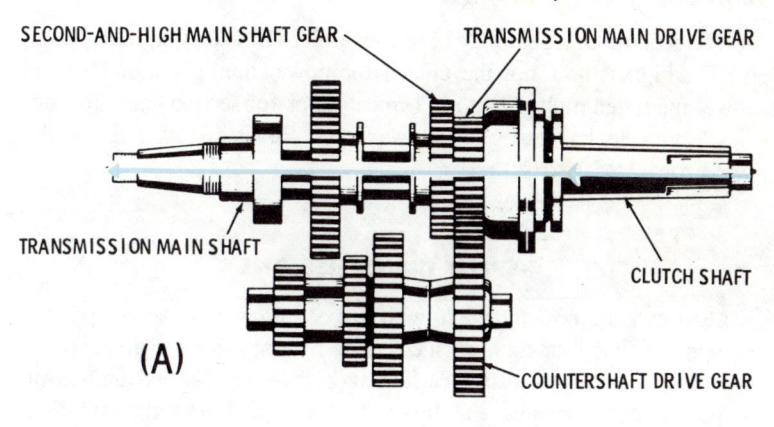

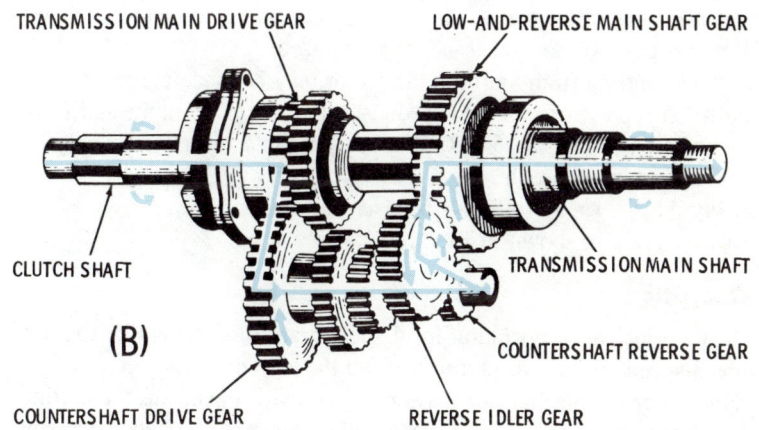

CLUTCHES, MANUAL TRANSMISSIONS, AND OVERDRIVES

Fig. 12. Power flow in third and reverse gear. A. Power flow in third gear. B. Power flow in reverse gear.

Gear Ratios

The ratio between the rotational speed of the input shaft and the output shaft in the transmission is different for each gear selected. The ratio is determined by the size of the engine, weight of the car, type of differential, size of rear tires, type of service to which the car will be subjected, etc. This means that, for a given make and model of car, the transmission gear ratios might be different depending on the size of the engine, for example. Cars of different manufacture will also likely have different gear ratios. One ratio, however, that all seem to have in common is that of third speed. Here, the ratio is always 1 to 1.

631

AUTOMOBILE GUIDE

The ratio for first gear may be as low as 2.25 to 1 to as high as 3.25 to 1. The higher the ratio, the greater the power multiplication, but the lower the speed multiplication. Typical ratios for second gear are from 1.5:1, to 1.85:1. Third gear is always 1:1. Reverse may range all the way from 2.25:1 to 4.15:1.

4-SPEED TRANSMISSIONS

Most cars are now available with 4-speed transmissions as optional equipment. The four forward speeds and reverse offer the driver more complete control and better performance than the 3-speed units. All 4-speed transmissions have all forward speeds synchronized, permitting downshifting without gear clash or the necessity of double clutching. Reverse gear, of course, is not synchronized.

Downshifting from fourth to third gear may be made at speeds from 50 to 25 mph; from third to second gear at 25 to 15 mph; and from second to first gear at 15 to 0 mph. Shifting into reverse may only be accomplished at 0 mph.

Fig 13 shows a typical 4-speed cross section. Power flow in the various gears is shown in Fig. 14.

Operation

The principal of operation for 4-speed transmissions is like that for the 3-speed types except for the fourth gear that has been added. Synchronizing ring and clutch assemblies provide the means for shifting into any forward gear at any speed without gear clash or the necessity for double clutching.

> **NOTE:** Downshifting into first gear above 45 mph, and into second above 65 mph causes extra work for the synchronizers and will require more time and force on the shift lever to complete. *There is danger of over-speeding the engine if first or second gear is used at high car speeds. It is not recommended, therefore, to downshift into first and second at speeds above 45 mph and 65 mph, respectively.*

Gear Ratios

The gear ratios in 4-speed transmissions are closer spaced than in 3-speed units. This provides a better engine-to-car speed ratio with a

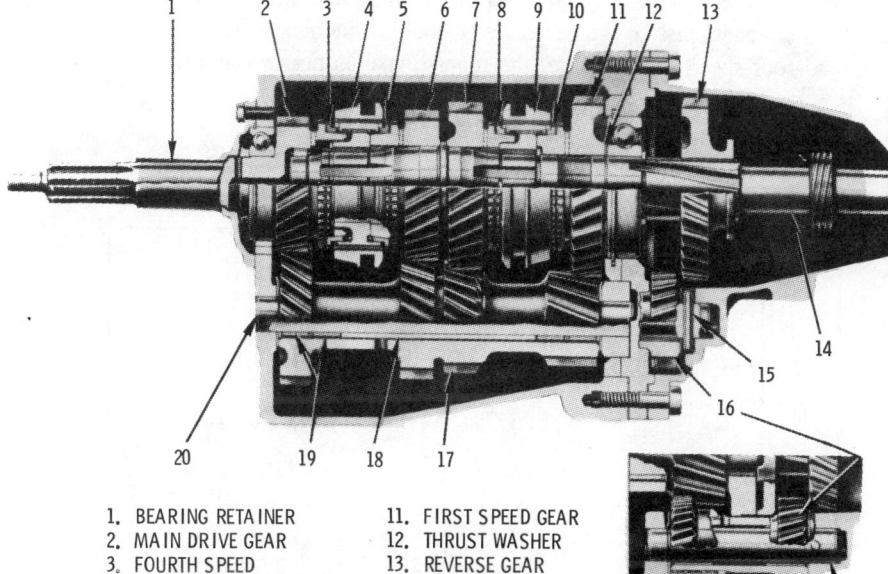

CLUTCHES, MANUAL TRANSMISSIONS, AND OVERDRIVES

Fig. 13. A typical 4-speed transmission.

1. BEARING RETAINER
2. MAIN DRIVE GEAR
3. FOURTH SPEED SYNCHRONIZING RING
4. THIRD AND FOURTH SPEED CLUTCH ASSEMBLY
5. THIRD SPEED SYNCHRONIZING GEAR
6. THIRD SPEED GEAR
7. SECOND SPEED GEAR
8. SECOND SPEED SYNCHRONIZING RING
9. FIRST AND SECOND SPEED CLUTCH ASSEMBLY
10. FIRST SPEED SYNCHRONIZING RING
11. FIRST SPEED GEAR
12. THRUST WASHER
13. REVERSE GEAR
14. MAIN SHAFT
15. REVERSE IDLER SHAFT ROLL PIN
16. REVERSE IDLER GEAR (REAR)
17. COUNTERSHAFT
18. COUNTERSHAFT BEARING ROLLER SPACER
19. COUNTERSHAFT BEARING ROLLER
20. COUNTERSHAFT
21. REVERSE IDLER GEAR (FRONT)
22. REVERSE IDLER SHAFT

TOP VIEW OF REVERSE IDLER GEARS

minimum loss of engine speed at the shift points. Typical ratios in 4-speed units are around 3:1 for first gear, 1.9:1 for second gear, 1.4:1 for third, with direct (1:1) drive in fourth. Reverse gear will always have a ratio the same as or near that of first gear.

5-SPEED TRANSMISSIONS

A five-speed transmission is now available, the helical gears engaged and disengaged by the use of synchronizers. All five forward speeds are

633

Automobile Guide

synchronized, permitting downshifting (within a limited speed range) without gear clash or the necessity of double clutching. Like the three- and four-speed transmission, the reverse gear is not synchronized.

Operation

The principle of operation of the 5-speed transmission is much like that for the 4-speed type except for the fifth gear. Like the 4-speed

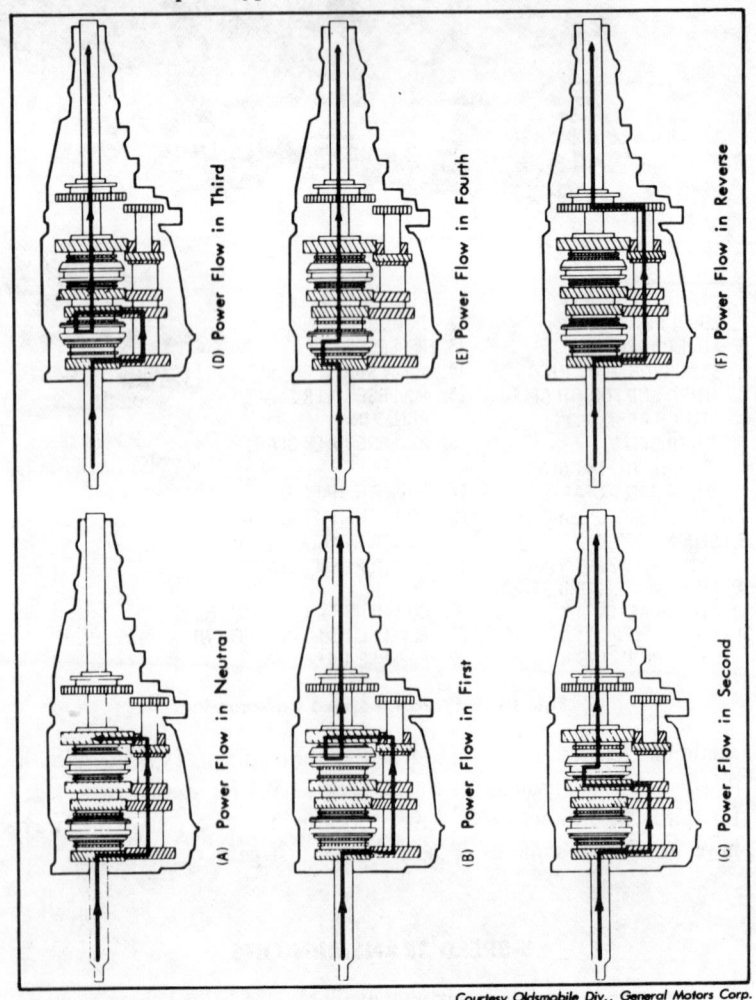

Courtesy Oldsmobile Div., General Motors Corp.

Fig. 14. Power flow in the transmission of Fig. 4.

Clutches, Manual Transmissions, and Overdrives

transmission, synchronizing ring and clutch assemblies provide the means for shifting into any forward gear at a limited speed without gear clash.

NOTE: The same precautions regarding downshifting speeds that apply to the 4-speed transmission apply to the 5-speed transmission. *Downshifting at high speeds not only cause extra work for the synchronizers, there is danger of overspeeding the engine if first or second gear is used at high speeds.*

Gear Ratios

The gear ratios of 5-speed transmissions are spaced somewhat closer together than in 4-speed units. This provides an even better engine-to-car speed ratio with a minimum loss of engine speed at the shift points. Additionally, low ratio of the fifth gear provides higher top-end road speed.

Typical ratios of a 5-speed unit are around 3.1:1 for first gear, 1.9:1 for second gear, 1.3:1 for third gear, 1:1 (direct) for fourth gear, and 0.85:1 for fifth gear. Reverse gear has the same, or near the same, as that of the first gear.

OVERDRIVES

Overdrive units are available as optional equipment on some makes of automobiles if they are equipped with 3-speed transmissions. Essentially, the overdrive unit is a two-speed planetary transmission attached to the rear of the conventional 3-speed transmission. This provides four forward speeds instead of three. In overdrive, the engine speed is approximately 30% lower at a given road speed. This is made possible by the planetary gears which provide a lower overall gear ratio than that obtained in high gear with the conventional transmission. A typical overdrive unit is shown in Fig. 15.

An electrical system controls the operation of the overdrive unit and consists of a solenoid, a relay, a speed-sensitive governor switch, a manual kickdown switch, and the circuit wiring.

Operation

When the overdrive control handle is pushed in, the power flow from the transmission up to a speed of approximately 28 mph is direct (1:1)

Automobile Guide

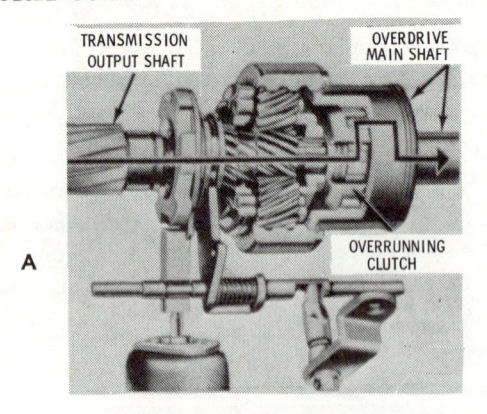

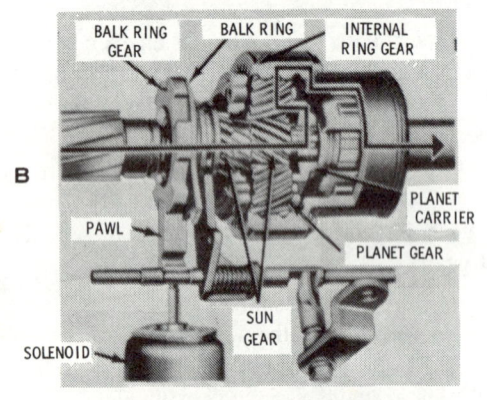

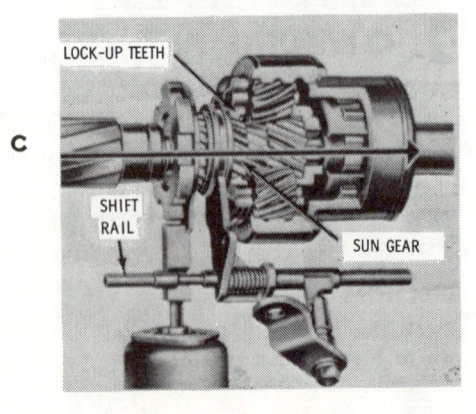

Fig. 15. A typical overdrive unit; (A) Direct (free-wheeling) drive; (B) Overdrive; (C) Lock-out drive.

Clutches, Manual Transmissions, and Overdrives

and free-wheeling (Fig. 15A). This drive is said to be free-wheeling because the overrunning clutch permits the transmission output shaft to drive the overdrive main shaft, but it does not permit the rear wheels to drive the engine.

While the overdrive unit is in the free-wheeling condition, the planetary gearing is in neutral, because the sun gear can run free. It can rotate in either direction or stand still depending on the relative speeds of the planet carrier and the internal ring gear.

At a speed of approximately 28 mph, the solenoid energizes and the pawl is pushed in against the balk ring. However, as long as the engine is driving the car, the overdrive will still not engage. This is because the balk ring is in the position shown in Fig. 16A, and will not allow the pawl to engage. All elements of the planetary gearing are revolving as a unit in a counterclockwise (from the rear) direction which rotates the balk ring against the pawl.

When the driver releases the throttle above the 28-mph speed, the main shaft of the overdrive overruns the output shaft of the transmission. When this overrun exceeds a ratio of 0.7:1, the sun gear and balk ring reverse direction, allowing the pawl to slide into the slot in the balk ring (Fig. 16B).

In this condition, the power flow is from the output shaft of the transmission to the planet carrier splined to it, through the planetary gears, and to the sun gear. With the sun gear held from rotating, the planetary gears are forced to "walk around" the sun gear and thus drive the internal ring gear. The transmission will then drive the main shaft of the overdrive unit at a ratio of 0.7:1.

The overrunning clutch is uncoupled when in overdrive because the main shaft of the overdrive is turning faster than the output shaft of the transmission. The engine can now drive the rear wheels or the rear wheels can drive the engine. There is no free-wheeling action when in overdrive.

The pawl can be disengaged under two conditions. One is when the car speed drops below approximately 22 mph. At this speed or below, the governor switch opens and de-energizes the solenoid, permitting the return spring to pull the pawl out of the slot in the balk ring. Too, the driver may shift the overdrive back to direct drive at any road speed by pressing the accelerator to the floor, thereby actuating the kickdown switch.

This action opens the circuit to the solenoid, permitting the return spring to exert a pull on the pawl. At the same time, the kickdown

AUTOMOBILE GUIDE

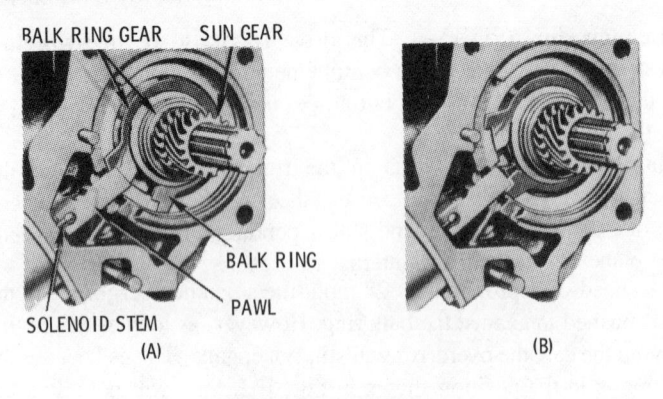

Fig. 16. Pawl and balk ring position. A. Engine driving. B. Pawl engaged. C. Coasting.

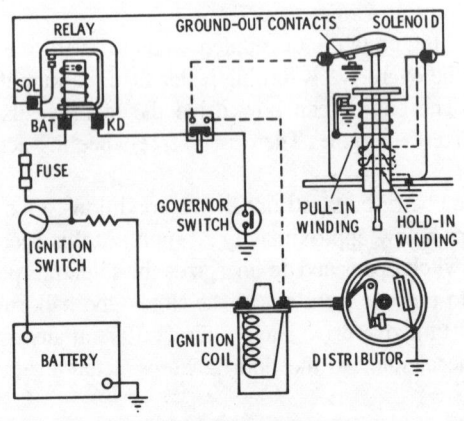

Fig. 17. Diagram of a typical overdrive electrical system used by GENERAL MOTORS CORP.

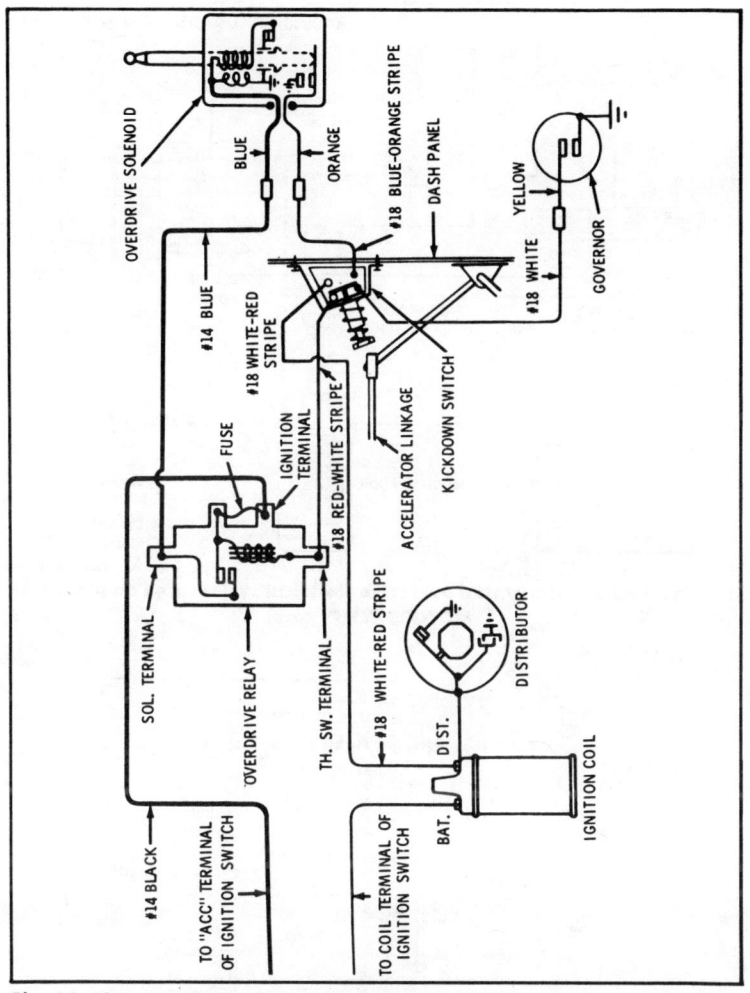

CLUTCHES, MANUAL TRANSMISSIONS, AND OVERDRIVES

Fig. 18. Diagram of a typical overdrive electrical system used on FORD and MERCURY products.

grounds the ignition system causing the engine to misfire long enough to permit the pawl to be pulled out of the balk ring. Normal ignition is restored as soon as the pawl moves out of the slot, and the car is now in direct drive. The actual time of ignition interruption is equal to that required for one revolution of the crankshaft.

If the solenoid should energize when the car is coasting up through 28 mph, with the engine idling (such as might occur on a downhill grade),

639

AUTOMOBILE GUIDE

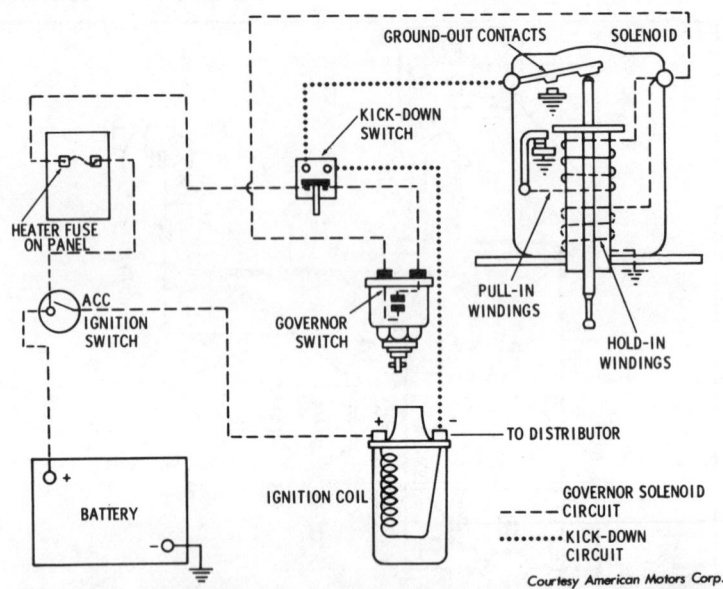

Fig. 19. Diagram of a typical overdrive electrical system used on **AMERICAN MOTORS CORP.** cars.

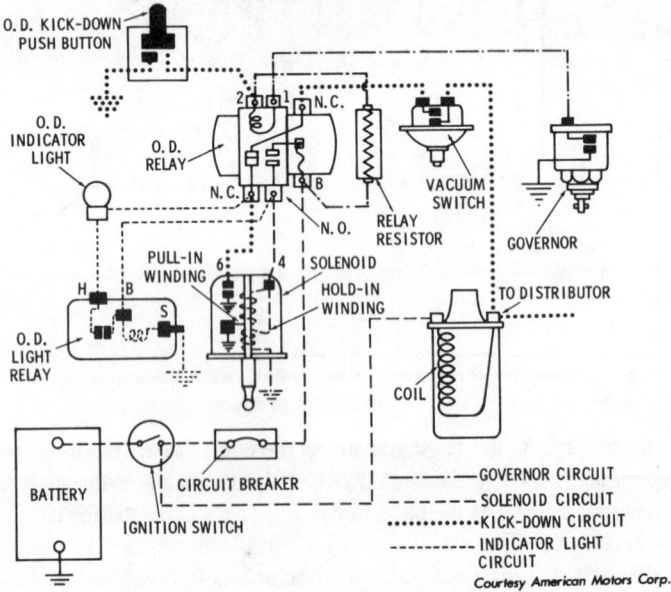

Fig. 20. Diagram of a typical overdrive electrical system used on **AMERICAN MOTORS CORP.** cars equipped with **TWIN-STICK.**

Clutches, Manual Transmissions, and Overdrives

the sun gear will be rotating clockwise (from the rear) and the balk ring will be in the position shown in Fig. 16C. The pawl cannot engage under this condition. To place the unit in overdrive, it will be necessary to speed the engine up to the point where the sun gear reverses its direction of rotation. The balk ring will then move counterclockwise, allowing the pawl to be forced into the slot.

When the overdrive control handle is pulled out, the car cannot be placed in overdrive at any speed. This lockout is accomplished by the shift rail moving the sun gear into engagement with the lockup teeth on the planet carrier (Fig. 15C). This locks the planetary gearing as one unit, mechanically connecting the output shaft of the transmission to the main shaft of the overdrive. This action is necessary to drive the car in reverse or when pushing the car to start the engine. Otherwise, the overrunning clutch would prevent power flow through the unit with the elements running backwards or with the rear wheels trying to transmit power to the engine through the drive shaft.

Service

Troubles may originate in either the mechanical portion of the overdrive unit or in the electrical control system. Therefore the control system should always be checked before disassembling the overdrive. Figs. 17, 18, 19, and 20 show the electrical systems of typical overdrive units.

When unsatisfactory overdrive operation is experienced, look at "Symptoms and Possible Causes" found at the end of this chapter. If the problem can not be found, the unit should be disassembled for inspection and repair. Follow the manufacturer's instructions for the specific unit being serviced.

CLUTCH-SYSTEM TROUBLES AND REMEDIES

Symptoms and Possible Causes   *Possible Remedies*

Clutch Chatter

(a) Worn or damaged clutch disc.

(b) Grease or oil on disc facings.

(a) Replace clutch disc.

(b) Replace clutch disc.

Symptoms and Possible Causes

(c) Improperly adjusted cover assembly.

Possible Remedies

(c) Remove and recondition.

Clutch Slipping

(a) Burned, worn, or oil-soaked facings.
(b) Insufficient pedal free play.
(c) Weak or broken pressure springs.

(a) Replace clutch disc.
(b) Adjust pedal free play.
(c) Recondition cover assembly.

Difficult Gear Shifting

(a) Excessive pedal free play.
(b) Worn or damaged clutch disc.
(c) Improperly adjusted cover assembly.

(a) Adjust pedal free play.
(b) Replace clutch disc.
(c) Remove and recondition.

Clutch Noisy

(a) Dry clutch linkage
(b) Worn throw-out bearing.
(c) Worn clutch disc.
(d) Worn release levers.
(e) Worn or dry pilot housing.
(f) Dry pressure plate lugs in cover.

(a) Lubricate as necessary.
(b) Replace throw-out bearing.
(c) Replace clutch disc.
(d) Recondition cover assembly.
(e) Lubricate or replace bushing.
(f) Lubricate lightly.

MANUAL TRANSMISSION TROUBLES AND REMEDIES

Noisy in one or more First through Third Gear Speeds (4-speed Units)

(a) First, second and/or third gear worn or damaged.

(a) Replace worn or damaged gears as necessary.

Clutches, Manual Transmissions, and Overdrives

Symptoms and Possible Causes *Possible Remedies*

(b) Counter gear worn or damaged.
(c) Counter gear bearings worn or damaged.
(d) Synchronizers worn or damaged.

(b) Replace counter gear.
(c) Replace counter gear bearing.
(d) Replace synchronizers as necessary.

Noisy in all Gear Speeds

(a) Low oil level.
(b) Wrong type of oil.
(c) Countershaft gear or bearings worn or damaged.
(d) Input shaft bearings worn or damaged.
(e) Transmission misaligned or loose.

(a) Check for leaks. Fill to proper level.
(b) Drain and fill with proper oil.
(c) Replace countershaft gear or bearings as necessary.
(d) Replace input shaft bearings.
(e) Check alignment, correct and/or tighten mounting bolts.

Noisy in High Gear

(a) Synchronizer worn or damaged.
(b) Input shaft bearing or gear worn or damaged.
(c) Output shaft bearing worn or damaged.

(a) Replace synchronizer as necessary.
(b) Replace input shaft bearing or gear as necessary.
(c) Replace output shaft bearing.

Noisy in Reverse

(a) Reverse idler or shaft worn or damaged.
(b) Reverse sliding gear worn or damaged.
(c) Shift linkage improperly adjusted.

(a) Replace reverse idler or shaft as necessary.
(b) Replace reverse sliding gear.
(c) Adjust shift linkage.

Symptoms and Possible Remedies

(d) Bent, damaged, or loose shift linkage.
(e) Shift levers, shafts or forks worn.

Possible Remedies

(d) Repair or replace shift linkage as necessary.
(e) Repair or replace parts as necessary.

Hard Shifting

(a) Clutch improperly adjusted.
(b) Clutch parts worn or damaged.
(c) Shift linkage out of adjustment.
(d) Bent, damaged, or loose shift linkage.
(e) Shift levers, shafts, or forks worn.
(f) Incorrect lubricant.
(g) Synchronizers worn or broken.

(a) Adjust clutch.
(b) Repair or replace parts as necessary.
(c) Adjust shift linkage.
(d) Repair or replace shift linkage as necessary.
(e) Repair or replace as necessary.
(f) Lubricate, using correct lubricant.
(g) Replace synchronizers as necessary.

Jumping out of Gear

(a) Shift linkage out of adjustment, worn or loose.
(b) Detent mechanism worn or springs weak or broken.
(c) Misalignment or loose transmission case or clutch housing.
(d) Worn input shaft bearing.
(e) Bent output shaft.
(f) Worn or broken high-gear synchronizer.
(g) Worn clutch teeth on input shaft and/or synchronizer sleeve.

(a) Repair, adjust, or replace as necessary.
(b) Repair or replace springs as necessary.
(c) Align and/or tighten as necessary.
(d) Replace bearing.
(e) Replace shaft.
(f) Replace synchronizer as necessary.
(g) Repair or replace defective parts.

Clutches, Manual Transmissions, and Overdrives

Symptoms and Possible Causes

(h) Bent or worn shift fork, lever, or shaft.
(i) Input shaft bearing retainer loose or broken.
(j) Shift cover loose or gasket damaged (4-speed only).

Possible Remedies

(h) Repair or replace as necessary.
(i) Inspect bearing. Repair or replace retainer. Replace bearing if necessary.
(j) Replace gasket and/or tighten cover.

Sticks in Gear

(a) Clutch not fully releasing.
(b) Burred or battered teeth on synchronizer sleeve or input shaft.
(c) Frozen synchronizer blocking ring on input shaft gear cone.
(d) Lack of lubrication.
(e) Improper lubricant.
(f) Corroded shift levers or shafts.
(g) Binding output shaft pilot bearing.

(a) Adjust clutch.
(b) Repair or replace as necessary.
(c) Repair or replace as necessary.
(d) Check for leaks, fill to proper level with lubricant.
(e) Drain and refill with proper lubricant.
(f) Clean as necessary.
(g) Replace bearing.

Gear Clash When Shifting Into Gear From Neutral With Car Not In Motion

(a) Clutch not fully releasing.
(b) Binding input shaft pilot bearing.
(c) Shifting too soon after clutch is released.

(a) Adjust clutch.
(b) Replace bearing.
(c) Correct bad habits.

OVERDRIVE UNIT TROUBLES AND REMEDIES

Symptoms and Possible Causes

Electrical

(a) Blown fuse.
(b) Loose terminal or connecting wire.
(c) Incorrect terminal locations of connecting wires.
(d) Grounded circuit.

(e) Solenoid contacts defective.
(f) Defective contacts in kickdown switch.
(g) Burned or damaged contacts in governor.

Mechanical

(a) Insufficient travel in kickdown switch.
(b) Governor shaft end play excessive.
(c) Governor control springs improperly adjusted.
(d) Rubber cover over governor damaged or missing.
(e) Shift rod out of adjustment.

Possible Remedies

(a) Replace fuse.
(b) Repair as necessary.
(c) Correct as necessary (follow wiring diagram).
(d) Check for defective wiring, water, or dirt. Correct as necessary.
(e) Repair or replace as necessary.
(f) Repair or replace as necessary.
(g) Repair or replace as necessary.

(a) Adjust or repair as necessary.
(b) Repair or adjust as necessary.
(c) Adjust governor control springs.
(d) Replace rubber cover.
(e) Adjust as necessary.

CHAPTER 25

Automatic Transmissions

Most automatic transmissions used in modern domestic cars have about the same general operating principles. Construction features are, to a great extent, similar. Parts from one type transmission cannot usually be used in a transmission of a different type, however.

Many automatic transmissions in use today are a combination of a torque converter and a two- or three-speed planetary gear system. Torque multiplication is obtained hydraulically through the converter, and mechanically through the planetary gear unit.

It would be impossible, in this text, to cover the more than thirty types and models of automatic transmissions used in today's car. One publisher of such manuals, *Motors*, covers the subject in detail. The manual — covering the last five or six years — contains 1,040 pages; each page about twice the size of the one you are now reading.

For the purpose of gaining a basic understanding of an automatic transmission, this chapter will deal with a typical torque converter/two-speed planetary gear system, as shown in Fig. 1.

The combination of the torque converter and planetary gears provides a high starting ratio for acceleration from a stop and up steep grades. The torque converter portion provides torque multiplication for proper performance and smooth operation; it functions as a fluid coupling at normal road loads, and at normal and higher speeds. The transmission consists of six (6) basic sections:

1. Torque converter.
2. Oil pump.

3. Planetary gears and controls.
4. Reverse clutch.
5. Governor.
6. Valve body.

TORQUE CONVERTER

The torque converter is connected to the engine flywheel and serves as a fluid (hydraulic) coupling through which engine torque is transmitted to the input shaft. The torque converter steps up (multiplies) engine torque whenever operating conditions are such that more torque is needed than the engine alone can supply.

The torque converter is made up of two band sections (or halves) that face each other in an oil-filled housing. These halves are welded together and serviced as an assembly.

The pump half of the converter is connected to the engine, and the turbine half of the converter is connected to the transmission.

The running engine makes the converter pumps revolve (since they are connected), sending oil against the turbine, causing it to revolve as well. The oil returns, in a circular flow, back to the converter pump, as long as the engine is running.

The torque converter, shown in Fig. 2, consists of three basic sections:

1. Converter pump.
2. Variable pitch stator.
3. Converter turbine.

Converter Pump

The function of the converter pump (Fig. 3) is to convert the power from the engine into a flow of oil to drive the converter turbine. The converter pump operates as a centrifugal type, picking up oil at its center and discharging oil at its rim.

Variable-Pitch Stator

The variable-pitch stator is supported by the stator shaft and is located between the converter turbine and the converter pump, as shown in Fig. 4. The stator is equipped with a free-wheeling (overrunning) clutch. When this clutch is held stationary, the direction of the oil flow from the turbine is changed to the proper angle for smooth entrance into the

Automatic Transmissions

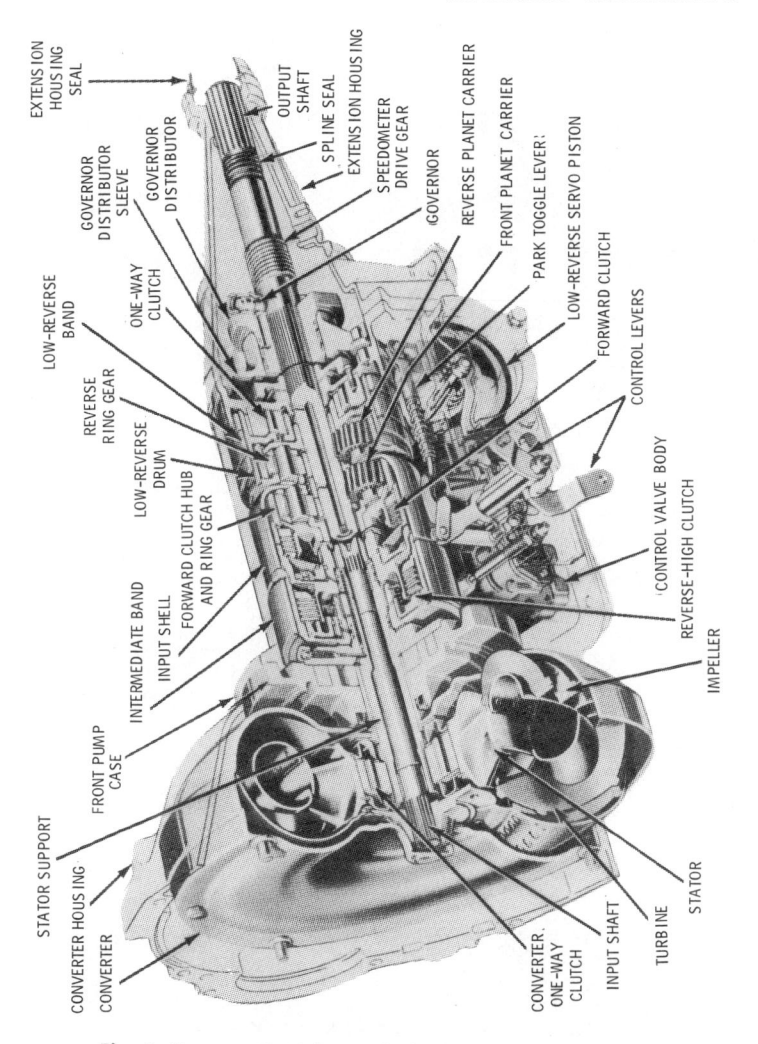

Fig. 1. Cross-section of a typical automatic transmission.

converter pump. As the speed of the turbine approaches the pump speed, the direction of the oil flow changes until it no longer opposes the pump rotation. The stator will free-wheel under this condition so that it will offer little or no interference to the flow of oil between the turbine and converter pump. For normal operation in the DRIVE range, the stator blades are at a low angle. For increased torque, the stator blades are

Automobile Guide

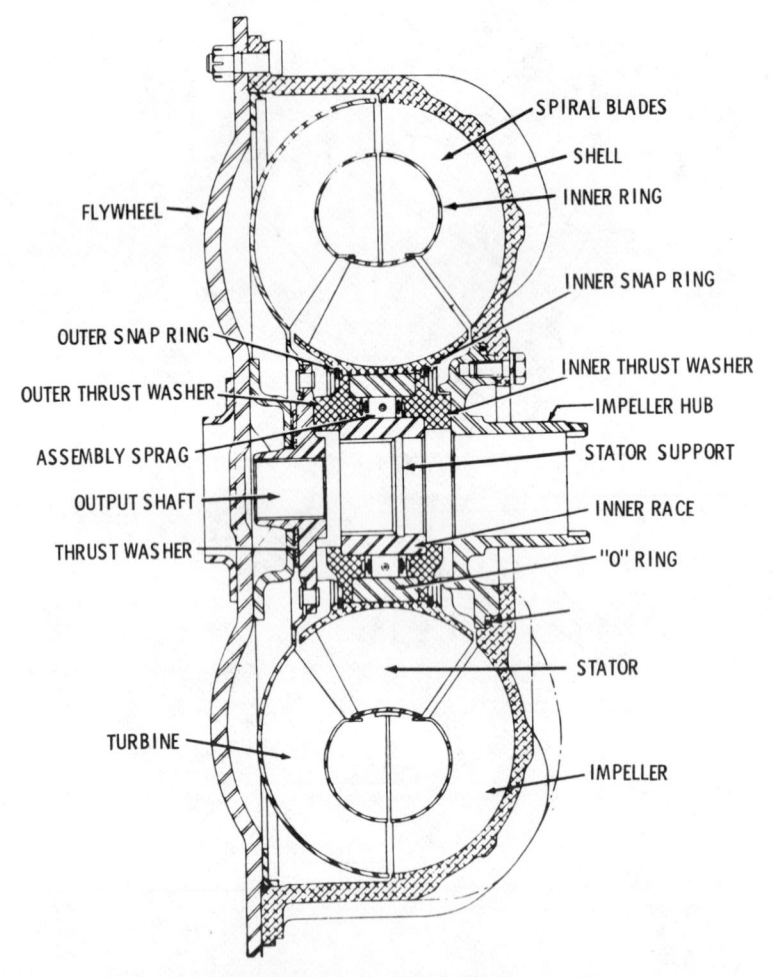

Fig. 2. Cutaway of a typical torque converter.

changed to a greater angle. This will provide more power for acceleration or increased road load.

The converter also has a smaller vaned section (called a stator) that converts oil back to the converter pump. As speed is increased the vanes close, greatly increasing the speed of the oil. This speeded up oil directs additional force through the engine-driven converter pump, multiplying engine torque.

650

Converter Turbine

The function of the converter turbine (Fig. 5) is to convert the energy present in the moving oil from the pump into torque to turn the input shaft.

Courtesy Buick Motor Div., General Motors Corp.

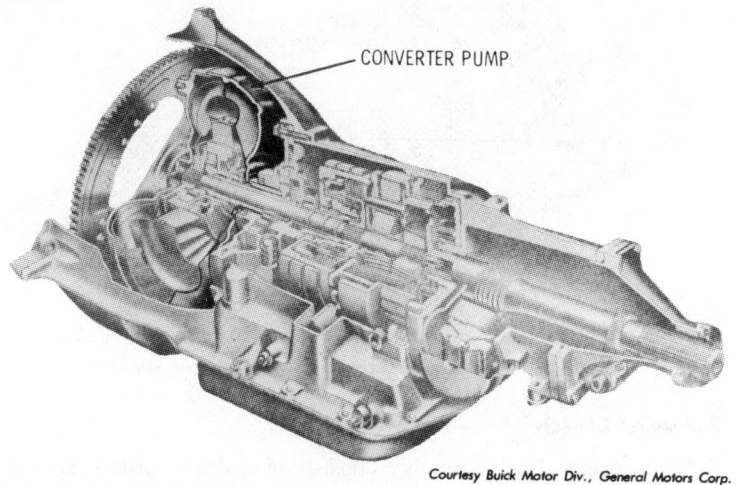

Fig. 3. The converter pump in a typical torque converter.

OIL PUMP

A gear-type oil pump, shown in Fig. 6, supplies oil to fill the converter, to operate the forward and reverse clutches, to release the low band, and to circulate the oil for lubrication and heat transfer.

PLANETARY GEARS AND CONTROLS

The planetary gear set consists of an input sun gear, low sun gear, short and long pinions, a reverse ring gear, and a planet carrier. By referring to Fig. 7, it can be seen that the input sun gear is splined to the input shaft. The low sun gear is part of the forward clutch assembly, and will revolve freely until the low band is applied. The input sun gear is meshed with three long pinions which, in turn, are meshed with three short pinions. The short pinions are meshed with the low sun gear and with the reverse ring gear.

The input sun gear and short pinions always rotate in the same direction. Application of either the low band or the reverse clutch determines whether the output shaft rotates forward or backward.

Automobile Guide

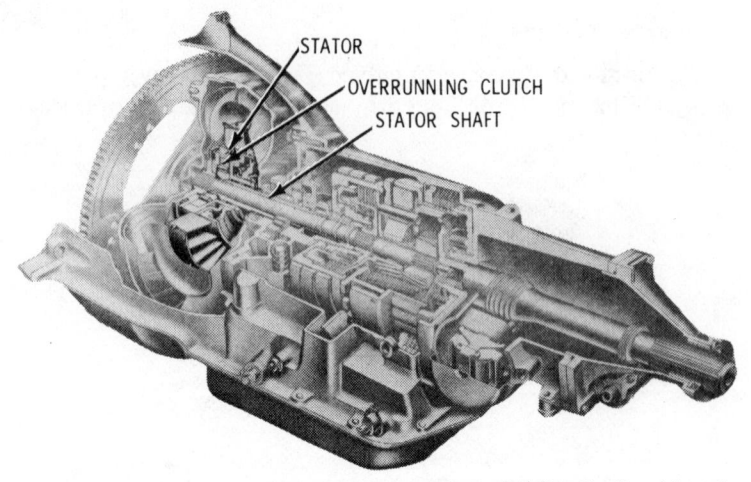

Courtesy Buick Motor Div., General Motors Corp.
Fig. 4. Variable pitch stator and supporting shaft.

Forward Clutch

The forward clutch assembly consists of a drum, piston, springs, piston seals, and a clutch pack. These parts, shown in Fig. 8, are all retained within the drum by the low sun gear and flange assembly. When oil pressure is applied to the piston, the clutch plates are forced together, connecting the clutch drum to the input shaft through the clutch hub. This action causes the low sun gear to rotate with the input shaft.

Low Band

The low band, also shown in Fig. 8, surrounds the forward clutch drum. The band is hydraulically applied by the low servo piston, and released by spring pressure.

REVERSE CLUTCH

The reverse clutch assembly (Fig. 9) consists of a piston, inner and outer seal, cushion spring, coil springs, clutch pack, and pressure plate. All these parts are retained inside the case by a retaining ring. When oil pressure is applied to the piston, the clutch plates are forced together, holding the reverse ring gear stationary. This action causes reverse rotation of the output shaft.

AUTOMATIC TRANSMISSIONS

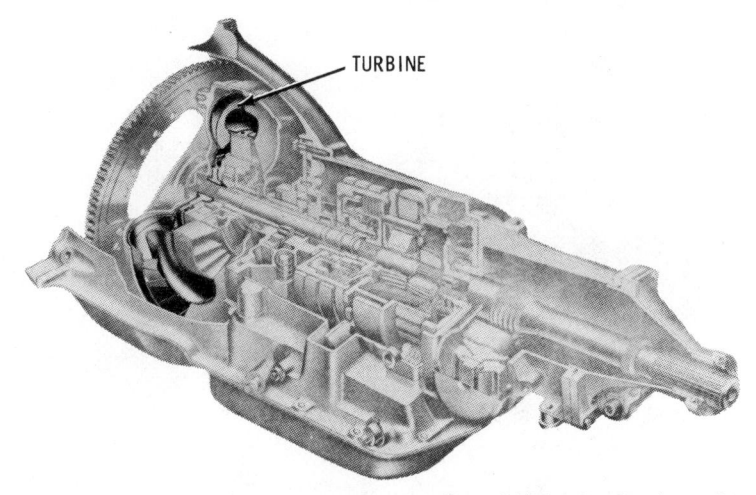

Fig. 5. The converter turbine.

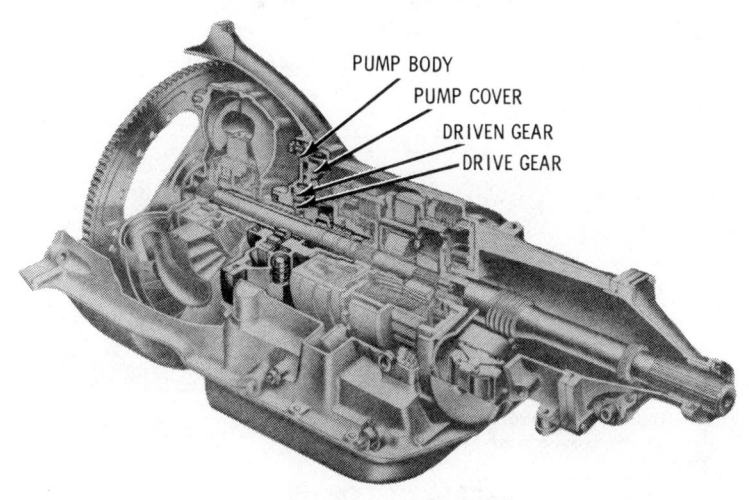

Fig. 6. The oil pump.

GOVERNOR

The governor is located to the rear of the transmission case and is driven by the output shaft. The purpose of the governor is to generate a

653

AUTOMOBILE GUIDE

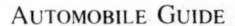

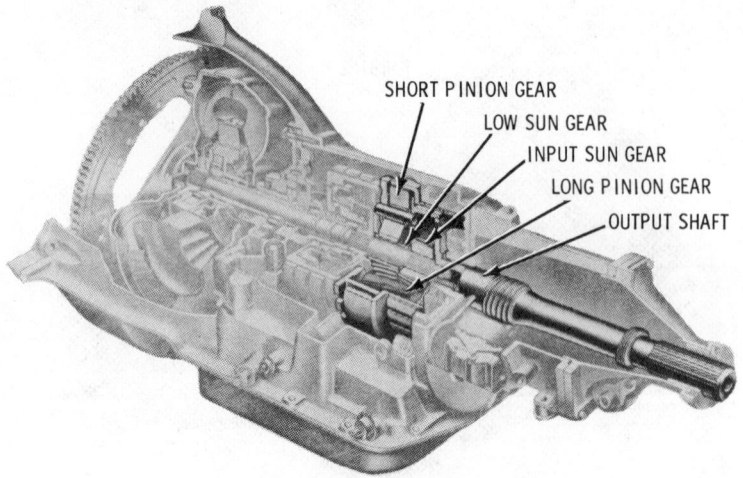

Courtesy Buick Motor Div., General Motors Corp.
Fig. 7. The planetary gear set.

speed-sensitive modulating oil pressure that increases up to a certain rotational speed of the output shaft. Thus, the governor determines or affects the shift points, main-line oil pressure, and downshift timing.

VALVE BODY

The valve body assemblies are located at the bottom of the transmission. These units can be removed from some transmissions by merely removing the oil pan. In other transmissions it is necessary to remove the entire transmission to gain access to the valve body assembly. The purpose of the valve body is to direct the pressurized oil to the proper location to actuate the various clutches, bands, etc. This is accomplished by controlling the oil flow through the passages by means of spring-loaded and mechanically-actuated valves.

GEARSHIFT CONTROLS

Selection of the desired driving range (gear ratio) is made by either a selector lever mounted on the steering column or in a floor-mounted console. Fig. 10 illustrates an exploded view of a floor-mounted console shift lever. Regardless of lever mounting location the different positions are identified generally by a single letter; "L" for low, "D" for drive, "N" for neutral, "R" for reverse, and "P" for park. The "L" or "D"

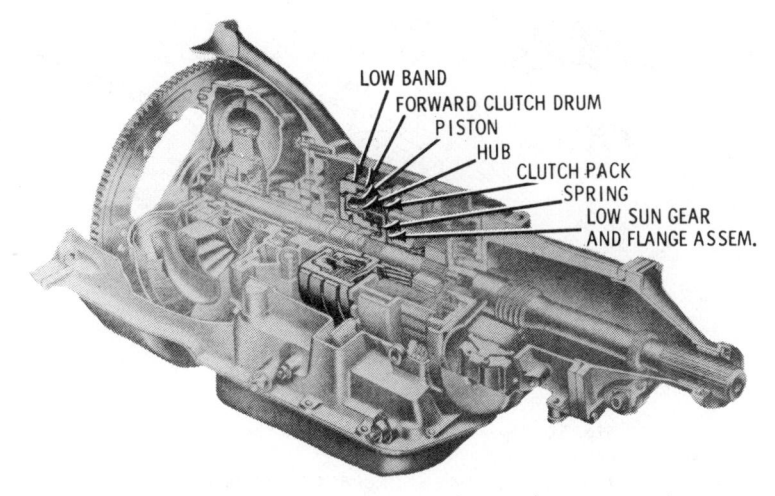

AUTOMATIC TRANSMISSIONS

Fig. 8. Forward clutch and low band assembly.

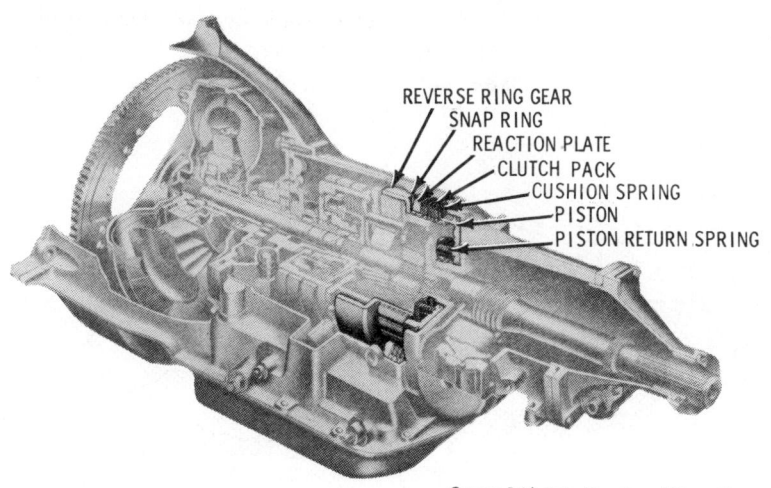

Fig. 9. Reverse clutch assembly.

range of some units may be dual range. For example "L" may be "L_1" and "L_2" or "D" may be "D_1" and "D_2". The owner's manual describes the use of these ranges.

Automobile Guide

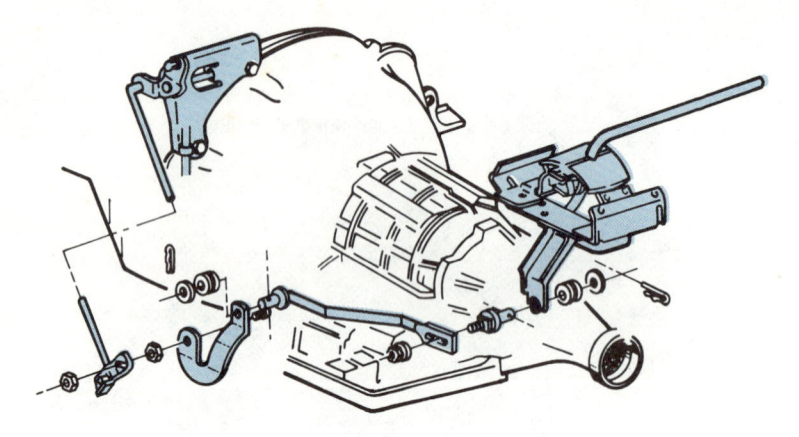

Fig. 10. Floor shift-type gearshift controls.

Generally, if properly adjusted, the car engine may be started when the selector lever is in the "N" or "P" position. This prevents car movement until the desired direction (forward or reverse) is selected. The "P" position locks the transmission and prevents the car from moving when parked. *The gear selector should only be moved to the "P" position when the car is stopped. If moved to the "P" position while the car is in motion, damage to the transmission may result.*

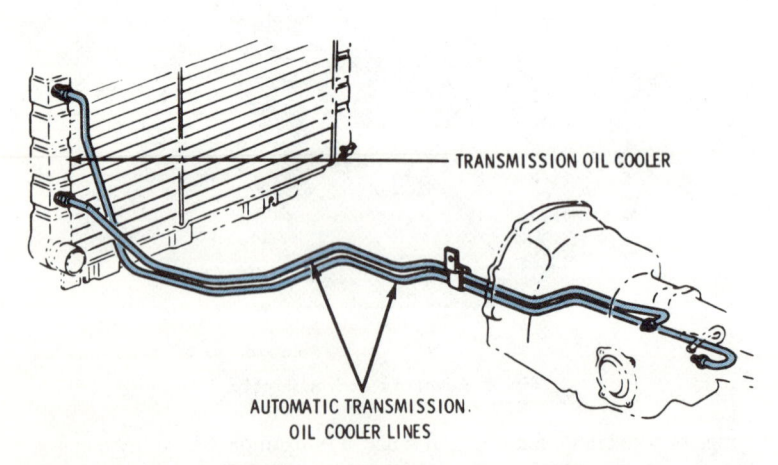

Fig. 11. Transmission fluid is circulated through a transmission oil cooler on most cars equipped with an automatic transmission.

AUTOMATIC TRANSMISSIONS
TRANSMISSION OIL COOLER

Most cars equipped with an automatic transmission have a transmission oil cooler. Transmission fluid is circulated through lines to a unit usually in the bottom of the car radiator. This unit is sometimes called a heat exchanger. Here, the heat carried by the transmission fluid, is transferred to the coolant in the radiator. Thus, the fluid returning to the transmission is at a much lower temperature. Fig. 11 shows a radiator equipped with the cooler on the side of the unit.

SERVICE

In-car service of most automatic transmissions consists of periodic checking of the fluid level, adjustment of the control linkage, adjustment of throttle and downshift linkage, and band adjustments. Due to the variations in the many makes and models of automatic transmissions, it is suggested that any service to be performed on these units follow the procedures outlined in the manufacturer's service manuals.

Transmission removal and reconditioning must be performed according to the instructions in the manufacturer's service manual.

NOTE: These units are extremely complex and only trained persons should attempt removal and repair.

STARTING AND TOWING PRECAUTIONS

Starting

Some cars equipped with automatic transmissions can be started by pushing, but most cannot. If in doubt, consult the owner's manual or service manual to determine if a particular make and model can be started in this manner. The oil circulation through most transmissions are such that the engine cannot be driven through the transmission.

It should be noted also that if the battery is "dead" the car will not start by pushing. The alternator *will not* produce an output voltage if there is no input voltage to "excite" the rotor. If this is the case there will be no electrical ignition, one of the three necessary events to start the engine. If the battery is "dead" it must be recharged or "jumped" with a good battery.

If it is determined that the car may be started by pushing, the transmission should be shifted to "L" between 20 and 35 mph for most cars (again, consult owner's manual). *Always push the car to start it — do not tow it.* The sudden surge when the car starts may cause a rear-end collision with the towing car.

Towing

Cars with automatic transmissions should be towed with the rear-end off the ground, when possible. Some makes and models can be towed for short distances with the transmission in neutral, others cannot. Check the owner's or service manual. When long distance towing is necessary, or when the transmission is faulty, *always* tow with the rear-end off the ground or with the propeller (drive) shaft removed.

Many cars may be towed up to 50 miles at a speed no greater than 35 mph with the gear selector in "N". Others may be towed "for short distances only" at speeds no greater than 25 mph. If long distance towing is required and rear-end towing is not practical due to front-end damage or no key for locked steering system the car may be towed from the front with the rear wheels on a dolly — or vice versa. If no key is available, both the steering and transmission shift mechanisms are locked.

AUTOMATIC TRANSMISSION TROUBLES AND REMEDIES

The following troubles and their possible causes and remedies are general in nature and do not necessarily apply to all makes and models. They are listed only as a possible aid in determining the cause of trouble in automatic transmissions and to suggest a possible remedy.

Symptoms and Possible Causes	Possible Remedies
Harsh Engagement	
(a) Engine idle speed too high.	(a) Adjust idle speed to recommended r/min.
(b) Hydraulic pressure too high or too low.	(b) Check fluid level. Check hydraulic pressure and adjust to specifications.
(c) Low/reverse band out of adjustment.	(c) Adjust.

AUTOMATIC TRANSMISSIONS

Symptoms and Possible Causes	Possible Remedies
(d) Faulty or leaky valve body.	(d) Perform pressure tests to determine cause. Correct as necessary.
(e) Faulty low/reverse servo, band, or linkage.	(e) Inspect servo for damaged seals or for binding. Repair as necessary.
(f) Worn or damaged front and/or rear clutch.	(f) Inspect clutches and repair or replace as required.

Delayed Engagement

(a) Low fluid level.	(a) Refill to correct level with the recommended fluid.
(b) Incorrect control linkage adjustment.	(b) Adjust control linkage.
(c) Oil filter clogged (if so equipped).	(c) Replace filter.
(d) Hydraulic pressure too high or too low.	(d) Make hydraulic pressure tests and adjust to specifications.
(e) Faulty or leaky valve body.	(e) Make pressure tests to determine cause and correct as necessary.
(f) Clutches or servos sticking or not operating.	(f) Remove valve body and make air pressure tests. Repair as necessary.
(g) Worn or faulty front and/or rear clutch.	(g) Inspect clutch and repair rear clutch.
(h) Faulty front pump.	(h) Make hydraulic pressure tests. Adjust or repair as necessary.
(i) Air bubbles in fluid.	(i) Inspect for air leaks into the suction passages of the front pump.

Runaway or Harsh Upshift or Kickdown

(a) Low fluid level.	(a) Refill to correct level with recommended fluid.

659

AUTOMOBILE GUIDE

Symptoms and Possible Causes

(b) Incorrect throttle linkage.
(c) Incorrect hydraulic pressure.

(d) Kickdown band out of adjustment.
(e) Faulty or leaky valve body.

(f) Faulty governor.

(g) Clutches or servos sticking or not operating.

(h) Kickdown servo, band, or linkage faulty.

(i) Worn or faulty front clutch.

No Upshift

(a) Low fluid level.

(b) Incorrect throttle linkage adjustment.
(c) Kickdown band out of adjustment.
(d) Incorrect hydraulic pressure.

(e) Governor sticking.

(f) Faulty or leaky valve body.

Possible Remedies

(b) Adjust throttle linkage.
(c) Make hydraulic pressure tests and adjust to specifitions.

(d) Adjust kickdown band.

(e) Make hydraulic pressure tests to determine cause and repair as necessary.

(f) Inspect governor and repair as necessary.

(g) Remove valve body and make air pressure tests. Repair as necessary.

(h) Inspect servo for sticking, for broken seal rings, for binding in linkage, or for faulty band lining.

(i) Inspect clutch and repair or replace as necessary.

(a) Refill to correct level with recommended fluid.

(b) Adjust throttle linkage.

(c) Adjust kickdown band.

(d) Make hydraulic pressure tests and adjust to specifications.

(e) Remove and clean governor. Replace if necessary.

(f) Make pressure tests to determine cause and repair as necessary.

AUTOMATIC TRANSMISSIONS

Symptoms and Possible Causes	Possible Remedies
(g) Clutches or servos sticking or not operating.	(g) Remove valve body and make air pressure tests. Repair as necessary.
(h) Faulty rear oil pump.	(h) Make hydraulic pressure tests and adjust or repair as necessary.
(i) Kickdown servo, band, or linkage faulty.	(i) Inspect servo for sticking, for broken seal rings, for binding linkage, or for a faulty band lining. Repair as necessary.
(j) Worn or faulty front clutch.	(j) Inspect clutch and repair or replace as necessary.

No Kickdown or Faulty Downshift

(a) Incorrect throttle linkage adjustment.	(a) Adjust throttle linkage.
(b) Incorrect control linkage adjustment.	(b) Adjust control linkage.
(c) Incorrect kickdown band adjustment.	(c) Adjust kickdown band.
(d) Incorrect hydraulic pressure.	(d) Make hydraulic pressure tests and adjust to specifications.
(e) Governor sticking.	(e) Remove and clean governor. Repair or replace as necessary.
(f) Faulty or leaky valve body.	(f) Make pressure tests to determine cause and repair as necessary.
(g) Clutches or servos sticking or not operating.	(g) Remove valve body and make air pressure tests. Repair as necessary.
(h) Kickdown servo, band, or linkage faulty.	(h) Inspect servo for sticking, broken seal rings, binding linkage, or faulty band lining. Repair as necessary.

661

AUTOMOBILE GUIDE

Symptoms and Possible Causes

(i) Overrunning clutch not holding.

Erratic Shifting

(a) Low fluid level.

(b) Air bubbles in fluid.

(c) Incorrect throttle linkage adjustment.
(d) Incorrect control linkage adjustment.
(e) Incorrect hydraulic pressure.

(f) Governor sticking.

(g) Oil filter clogged.
(h) Faulty valve body.

(i) Clutches or servos sticking or not operating.

(j) Faulty rear and/or front oil pump.

Possible Remedies

(i) Repair overrunning clutch as necessary.

(a) Refill with recommended fluid.
(b) Inspect for air leakage in the front pump suction linkage.
(c) Adjust throttle linkage.

(d) Adjust control linkage.

(e) Make hydraulic pressure tests and adjust to specifications.
(f) Remove and clean governor. Replace if necessary.
(g) Replace oil filter.
(h) Make pressure tests to determine cause and correct as necessary.
(i) Remove valve body and perform air pressure tests. Repair as required.
(j) Make hydraulic pressure tests and adjust or repair as necessary.

Slips in Forward Drive Positions

(a) Low fluid level.

(b) Air bubbles in fluid.

(c) Incorrect throttle linkage adjustment.

(a) Refill with recommended fluid.
(b) Inspect for air leaks in the front pump suction passages.
(c) Adjust throttle linkage.

AUTOMATIC TRANSMISSIONS

Symptoms and Possible Causes *Possible Remedies*

(d) Incorrect control linkage adjustment.
(d) Adjust control linkage.

(e) Hydraulic pressure too low.
(e) Make hydraulic pressure tests and adjust to specifications.

(f) Valve body faulty or leaky.
(f) Make pressure tests to determine cause and correct as necessary.

(g) Clutches or servos sticking or not operating.
(g) Remove valve body and make air pressure tests. Repair as necessary.

(h) Worn or faulty front and/or rear clutch
(h) Inspect clutch and repair or replace as necessary.

(i) Overrunning clutch not holding.
(i) Repair overrunning clutch as necessary.

Slips in Reverse Only

(a) Low fluid level.
(a) Refill with recommended fluid.

(b) Air bubbles in fluid.
(b) Inspect for air leakage in front pump suction passages.

(c) Incorrect control linkage adjustment.
(c) Adjust control linkage.

(d) Incorrect hydraulic pressure.
(d) Make hydraulic pressure tests and adjust to specifications.

(e) Low/reverse band out of adjustment.
(e) Adjust low/reverse band.

(f) Faulty or leaky valve body.
(f) Make pressure tests to determine cause and repair as necessary.

(g) Front clutch or rear servo sticking or not operating.
(g) Remove valve body and make air pressure tests. Repair as necessary.

(h) Low/reverse servo, band, or linkage faulty.
(h) Inspect servo for damaged seals, binding linkage, or

Automobile Guide

Symptoms and Possible Causes   *Possible Remedies*

                                                    faulty band lining. Repair as necessary.

(i) Faulty front oil pump.   (i) Make hydraulic pressure tests and adjust or repair as necessary.

No Drive

(a) Low fluid level.   (a) Refill with recommended fluid.

(b) Hydraulic pressure too low.   (b) Make hydraulic pressure tests and adjust to specifications.

(c) Oil filter clogged.   (c) Replace oil filter.

(d) Valve body faulty or leaky.   (d) Make pressure tests to determine cause and correct as necessary.

(e) Faulty front oil pump.   (e) Make hydraulic pressure tests, and adjust or repair as necessary.

(f) Clutches or servos sticking or not operating.   (f) Make pressure tests to determine cause and repair as necessary.

Drives in Neutral

(a) Incorrect control linkage adjustment.   (a) Adjust control linkage.

(b) Valve body faulty or leaky.   (b) Make pressure tests to determine cause and repair as necessary.

(c) Rear clutch inoperative.   (c) Inspect clutch and repair as necessary.

Drags or Locks

(a) Kickdown band out of adjustment.   (a) Adjust kickdown band.

(b) Low/reverse band out of adjustment.   (b) Adjust low/reverse band.

Automatic Transmissions

Symptoms and Possible Causes *Possible Remedies*

(c) Kickdown and/or low-reverse servo, band, or linkage faulty.
(c) Inspect servo for sticking, broken seal rings, binding linkage, or faulty band linings. Repair as necessary.

(d) Front and/or rear clutch faulty.
(d) Inspect clutch and repair or replace as necessary.

(e) Planetary gear sets broken or seized.
(e) Inspect gear set and replace as required.

(f) Overrunning clutch worn, broken, or seized.
(f) Inspect clutch and repair or replace as neccessary.

Transmission Overheats

(a) Low fluid level.
(a) Refill with recommended fluid.

(b) Kickdown band adjustment too tight.
(b) Adjust kickdown band.

(c) Low/reverse band adjustment too tight.
(c) Adjust low/reverse band.

(d) Faulty cooling system.
(d) Inspect transmission cooling system, clean and repair as necessary.

(e) Faulty front and/or rear oil pump.
(e) Inspect oil pump for incorrect clearance, and repair as neccessary.

(f) Insufficient clutch clearance in front and/or rear clutch.
(f) Measure clutch plate clearance and correct as necessary.

CHAPTER 26

Drive Shafts, Universal Joints, and Rear Axle Assemblies

Power from the engine to the rear wheels is coupled through the transmission, by means of the drive shaft, universal joints, and rear axle assembly (Fig. 1). Universal joints, also known as *U-joints*, are necessary because the rear wheels (and axle) move in an up and down motion in relation to the car body. The U-joint (a double-hinge type coupling) prevents the drive shaft from becoming bent or broken as the rear axle assembly moves up and down.

The rear axle assembly consists of four main parts or sub-assemblies: the axle shafts (one for each rear wheel), a differential with a ring gear, a drive pinion with carrier, and the axle housing.

The drive shaft, universal joints, and sub-assemblies of the rear axle assembly (with exception of the axle housing) can usually be serviced *on* the car without having to remove the entire assembly.

The operating principles and general construction features are similar for all domestic rear-wheel drive cars. Minor variations in design and service procedures however, make necessary the consulting of manufacturer's service manuals for specific service procedures.

Drive Shafts, Universal Joints, and Rear Axle Assemblies

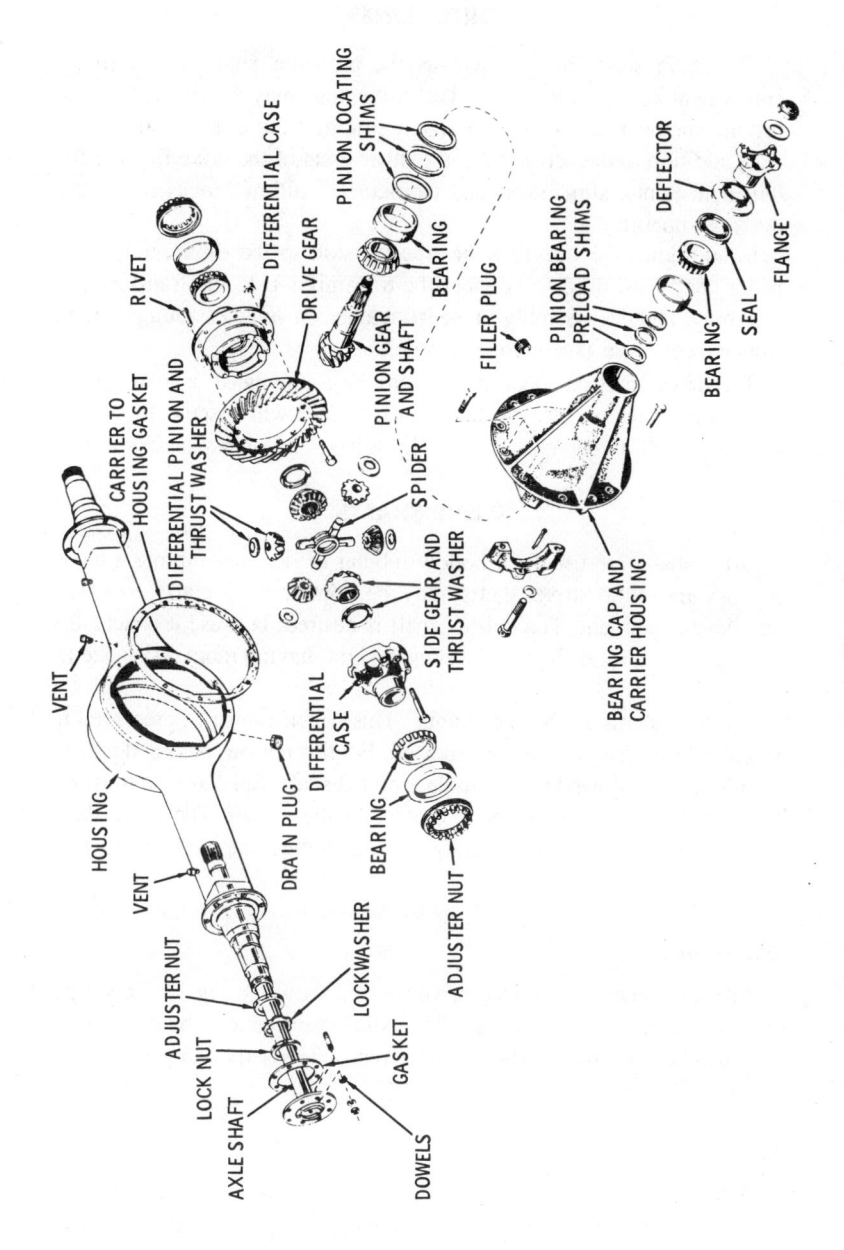

Fig. 1. Exploded view of a typical rear axle assembly.

667

DRIVE LINES

The drive shaft, also known as the propeller shaft, is the major component of the drive line. The drive line may be defined as the driving member between the transmission and the differential.

In addition to the drive shaft, the other units of the drive line are the universal joints, slip joints, and (sometimes) pillow blocks (or center bearing supports).

In addition to connecting the transmission to the differential, propeller shafts are used to connect the transmission to the transfer case assembly, and the assembly to the front axles on vehicles equipped with front wheel drive (Jeep, for example).

The drive shaft on modern cars may be a one-piece or a two-piece unit, depending on the make and model. We will discuss these two types, as well as universal joints, slip joints, and pillow blocks in this chapter.

DRIVE SHAFTS

Drive shafts are usually a hollow tubular device, resembling a large pipe. Some solid drive shafts may be found, particularly to drive auxiliary equipment. The hollow shaft is desired, because it is actually stronger than a solid shaft of the same weight, having more resistance to twist.

All drive shafts are balanced units. This balance must be preserved if vibration-free driving is to be expected. For this reason, mud and grease should not be allowed to accumulate on the shaft. Special care must be taken if the car is undercoated to protect the drive shaft. The entire shaft should be covered with paper or a cloth before the undercoating is applied.

One-Piece

An example of a one-piece drive shaft is shown in Fig. 2. This type has two universal joints and a splined slip yoke to allow the drive shaft to expand and contract endways as the rear-axle assembly moves up and down.

Two-Piece

A two-piece drive shaft is shown in Fig. 3. This type consists of a front and rear unit, a center bearing support, three universal joints, and a splined slip yoke. This type has the advantage of shorter unsupported

Drive Shafts, Universal Joints, and Rear Axle Assemblies

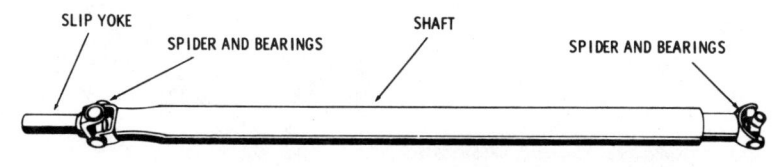

Fig. 2. Typical one-piece drive shaft.

Courtesy Oldsmobile Div., General Motors Corp.

sections of the rotating portions and thus reduces the tendency for the drive shaft to whip at high speeds.

The front and rear drive shafts are connected to each other by a slip yoke and a constant-velocity type of universal joint. The center bearing support is attached to a cross member that is fastened to the side rails of the frame or body.

UNIVERSAL JOINTS

Universal joints are used in the drive shaft to provide flexibility in the drive line so that power can be transmitted even though the differential may be moving up and down as the car goes over bumps, or the wheels drop into holes, bounces over obstructions, or as the load varies.

Universal joints are, in effect, double-hinged joints (Fig. 4), through which one shaft can drive another even though the shafts may not be in line with each other.

There are two general types of universal joints found on the domestic car. These are the cross-and-yoke type, and the constant-velocity type, Figs. 5 and 6, respectively.

In addition to being located in the driveshaft, universal joints may be found in rear axle assemblies of independently suspended rear axles, covered later in this chapter.

Cross-and-Yoke Type

The cross-and-yoke type of universal joint, as shown in Fig. 5, is found on most cars. Lubrication of this joint was necessary, at periodic intervals, in older model cars, but most late model cars are factory packed with grease to last the lifetime of the assembly. The only time they may be greased is if they are disassembled for service. Replacement cross-and-yoke universal joints are available with grease fittings, if desired.

669

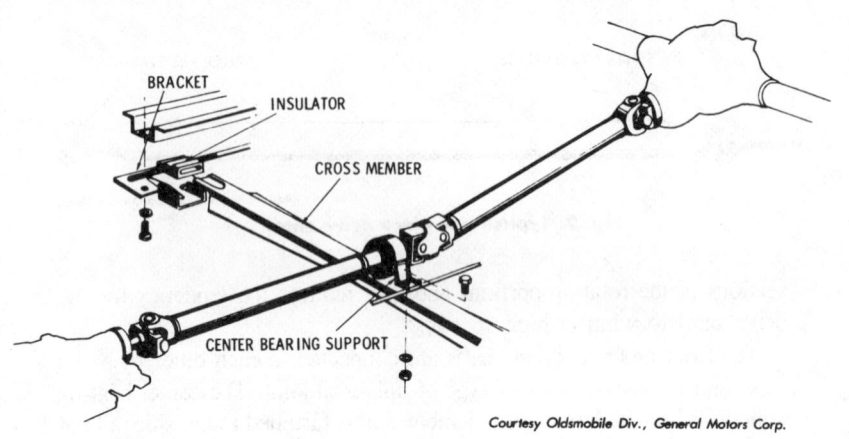

AUTOMOBILE GUIDE

Courtesy Oldsmobile Div., General Motors Corp.
Fig. 3. A two-piece drive shaft is used on many cars.

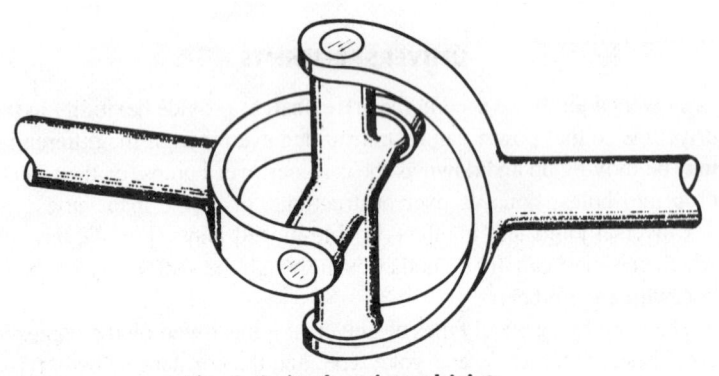

Fig. 4. A simple universal joint.

As Fig. 5 indicates, the universal joint consists of a flanged yoke, a cross journal (spider), four bearings, and a fixed yoke. It also includes necessary bushings, retainers and seals.

The two yokes are set at right angles to each other and their open ends are joined by the cross. This arrangement permits each yoke to pivot on one axis of the journal and also permits the transfer of rotary motion from one yoke to the other.

Constant-Velocity Type

A peculiarity of the conventional universal joint is that it causes the driven shaft to rotate at a variable speed with respect to the shaft doing

Drive Shafts, Universal Joints, and Rear Axle Assemblies

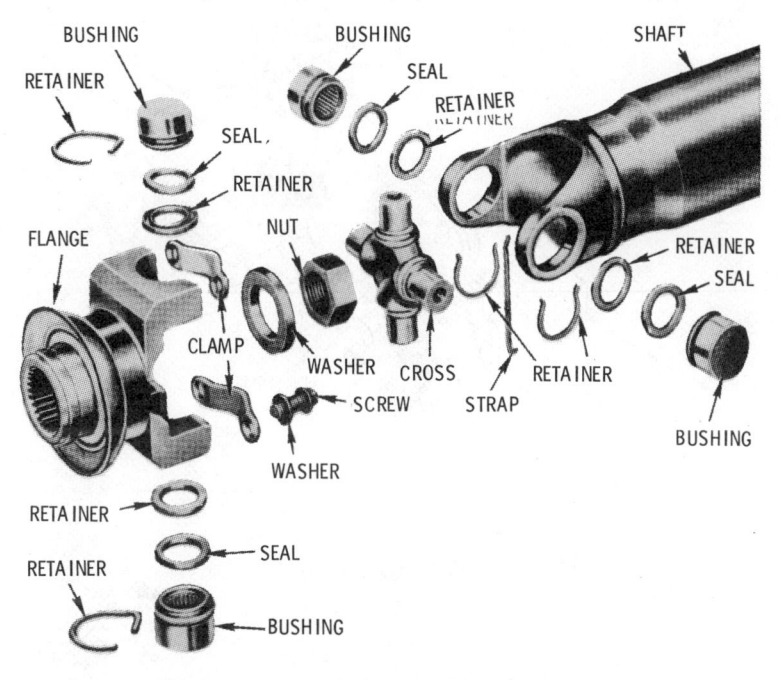

Fig. 5. A cross-and-yoke type universal joint.

the driving. This variation is in the form of an acceleration and deceleration of the rotational speed that takes place twice during each revolution of the driven shaft. The amount of such fluctuation depends on the difference in the angle of the driving shaft to the angle of the driven shaft.

This variation of rotational speed cannot be eliminated by a simple universal joint, but its effect can be minimized by using two universal joints — one at each end of the drive shaft. If only one joint were used between the transmission and rear axle, the acceleration and deceleration caused by the joint would be resisted on one end by the engine and on the other end by the inertia of the vehicle. The combined action of these two forces would place great stress on all parts of the power train and, in addition, would result in a nonuniform force being applied to the wheels. By using two universal joints, however, the second joint can compensate for the speed fluctuations caused by the first. To do this, the angle between the transmission shaft and the drive shaft must be the same as the angle between the drive shaft and the shaft into the differential.

AUTOMOBILE GUIDE

Courtesy Buick Motor Div., General Motors Corp.
Fig. 6. A constant-velocity type universal joint.

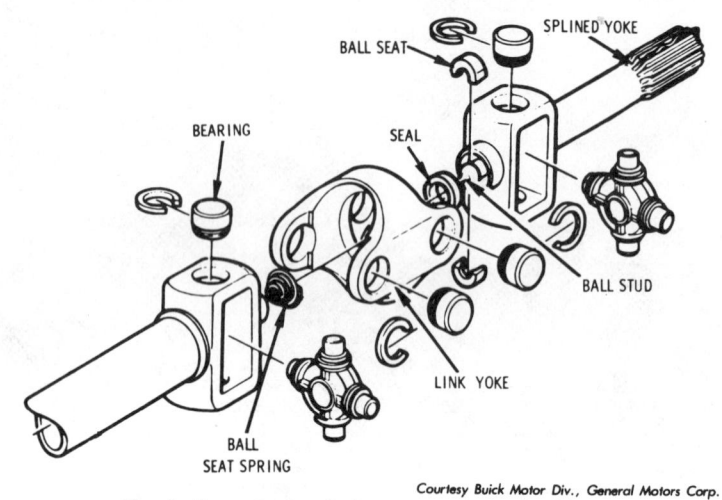

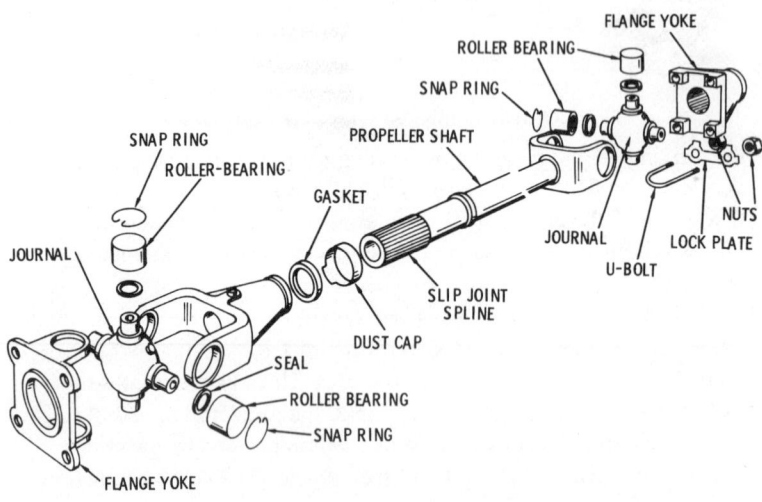

Fig. 7. Drive shaft, universal joint, and slip joint assembly.

Another requirement to minimize the speed variation is that the two driving yokes of the universal joints which are attached to the drive shaft must be displaced 90° from each other. With this arrangement, the first joint is accelerating at the same time the second joint is decelerating. This results in a nonvarying wheel speed for a given engine speed,

Drive Shafts, Universal Joints, and Rear Axle Assemblies

even though the speed of the drive shaft between the two is constantly changing.

The use of two conventional universal joints to prevent speed fluctuations is satisfactory as long as the driving angles are small. For larger driving angles, however, the constant-velocity type of joint (Fig. 6) is more satisfactory. The design of this unit is such that speed fluctuation is entirely eliminated, providing a smooth, vibration-proof ride. On most cars, these joints do not require lubrication unless disassembled for service.

Slip Joints

As shown in Fig. 7, the slip joint, by means of telescoping action, forms a variable-length connection at one end of the drive shaft. This enables the shaft to change its effective length with movement of the axle. This is necessary since the drive shaft is connected at one end to the rigidly mounted transmission and to the axle assembly at the other. The axle assembly moves up and down (and slightly forward and backward) as a result of wheel and spring movement during driving, braking, and acceleration.

The up and down motion of the rear wheel assembly either reduces or increases the distance between the transmission and axle. When the springs expand, the axle assembly moves away from the transmission. When the springs compress, the opposite occurs; the axle assembly moves closer to the transmission.

The slip-joint spline is usually found as a part of the universal joint assembly at the front end of the drive shaft (that is, closer to the transmission).

U-JOINT MOUNTING

The U-joint opposite the spline end of the driveshaft must be secured in such a manner as to support, and hold in place, the entire assembly. This is accomplished by strap-mounting or flange-mounting, as shown in Figs. 8 and 9, respectively. In either case, usually four bolts hold the assembly in place. Some are secured with two U-bolts with two lockwashers and nuts on each.

Pillow Blocks

A pillow block may be used when the distance to be spanned by a drive shaft is great, such as would be the case with a long wheelbase

AUTOMOBILE GUIDE

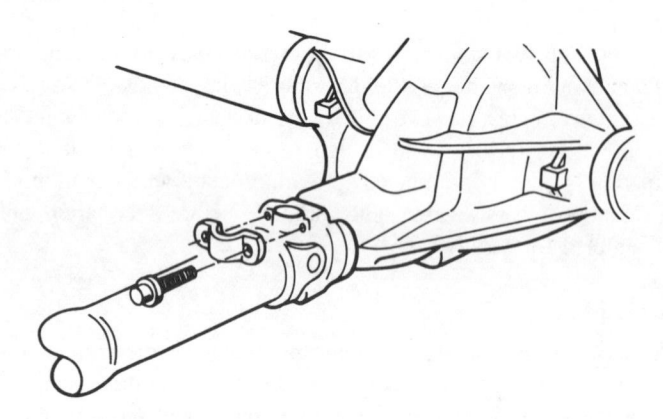

Fig. 8. Drive shaft U-joint secured with strap-type mounting.

car. The use of a pillow block allows for additional support for the drive shaft and lessens the chance for vibration of the drive line.

The pillow block is also known as a "center bearing support," or "center coupling-shaft support." A car with a two-piece drive shaft will have a pillow block and universal joint assemblies.

DRIVE-SHAFT ANGULARITY

The angles through which the universal joints on each end of the drive shaft operate must be very nearly the same. If these angles are different, operation is rough and an objectionable vibration is produced. In addition, the universal joints are designed to operate safely and efficiently within certain angles. If the design angle is exceeded, the joint may break or otherwise be damaged.

The front universal-joint angle is actually the angle between the transmission output shaft centerline and the centerline of the drive shaft which connects to it. This angle is determined by the design of the body assembly and is not likely to change. Therefore, this is not adjustable. However, the angle at the rear universal joint *can* change and must be adjusted. This adjustment is made by rotating the rear axle assembly in some way. The method used varies from car to car. Some provide a means of lengthening or shortening the upper control arms with shims at the frame bracket ends. Other cars provide adjustment with shims being placed between the rear springs and differential housing spring plates.

Drive Shafts, Universal Joints, and Rear Axle Assemblies

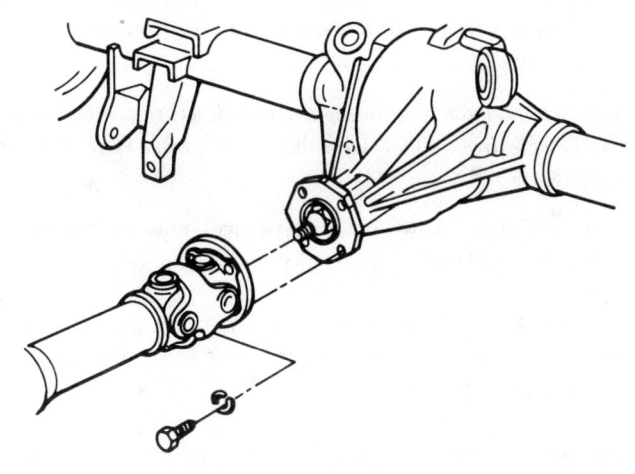

Fig. 9. Drive shaft U-joint secured with flange-type mounting.

One make of car provides cam-type adjusters located at each rear upper control arm-to-differential carrier attaching point. Refer to the manufacturer's service manual for the specific procedure for adjusting the drive shaft rear joint angle.

SERVICE

Drive shafts and universal joints require little service, other than periodic lubrication for those units that are not permanently lubricated. Failure of the joints and slip yoke does occur occasionally, and makes necessary the removal of the entire assembly to make the repair.

Drive Shaft Removal

Removal of the drive shaft can be accomplished using the following general procedures.

One-Piece Type— To remove a one-piece shaft, proceed as follows:

1. Remove both U-bolts or clamps from the pinion yoke.
2. Mark the relation of the slip yoke and the drive flange so that they may be installed in their original positions. This maintains the balance of the assembly. Some manufacturers provide a key to prevent installing in any but the correct position.

3. Disconnect the front universal joint from the transmission flange and slide the drive shaft to the rear until the front slip yoke clears the transmission housing and seal.

CAUTION: Do not allow the drive shaft to drop or hang loose on the vehicle from either joint during removal. Wire it up to the underbody.

Two-Piece Type — A two-piece drive shaft must be removed as a unit. Proceed as follows:

NOTE: During handling out of the car, the assembly must be supported in as straight a line as possible to avoid jamming or bending any of the parts.

1. Remove the bolts from the center bearing attaching plate.
2. Remove the U-bolts (or clamps) from the rear universal joint. Mark both the flange and the shaft to insure assembly in the same position.

CAUTION: If the rear universal-joint bearings are not retained on the spider (cross) by a connecting strap, use tape or wire to secure the bearings.

3. Support the rear end of the drive shaft to avoid damage to the constant-velocity joint, and slide the complete assembly to the rear until the slip yoke slides out of the splines in the transmission output shaft.
4. Protect the oil seal surface on the slip yoke by taping or wiring a cloth over the entire front universal joint.
5. Slide the entire drive-shaft assembly to the rear and out from under the vehicle. *Do not bend the constant-velocity joint to its extreme angle at any time.*

Universal-Joint Service

Consult the manufacturer's directions for special U-joint service instructions.

Cross-and-Yolk Type— To service a cross-and-yolk type of universal joint, proceed as follows:

1. Remove the retainers that hold the bearings in the yoke and drive shaft.

Drive Shafts, Universal Joints, and Rear Axle Assemblies

2. Place the joint in a vise or press.
3. Select a socket (from a socket wrench set) with an *outside* diameter slightly smaller than that of the outside diameter of the joint bearings. Select another socket with an *inside* diameter slightly larger than the outside of the bearings.
4. Place the sockets at opposite bearings so that the smaller socket becomes a bearing driver and the larger socket becomes a bearing receiver as the jaws of the vise come together (Fig. 10).

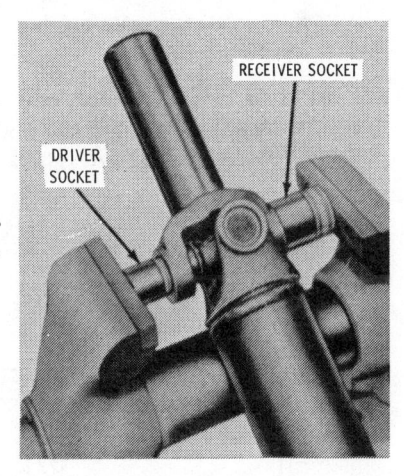

Fig. 10. Disassembly of a cross-and-roller type of universal joint.

5. Close the vise jaws until the spider (cross) contacts the yoke. Take the drive shaft from the vise and remove the one bearing with pliers.
6. Reverse the sockets and press the opposite bearing out in the same manner.
7. Remove the spider from the yoke. Remove the remaining two bearings in the same manner.
8. Clean the parts in kerosene, mineral spirits, or other suitable solvent, and dry with compressed air.
9. Inspect the bearing surfaces of the spider. The surface should be smooth and free from pits or ripples. If either are present, or if the dust seal retainers are damaged, replace the spider assembly.
10. Inspect the bearings. All bearings should have a uniform appearance and should roll freely inside the bushings. If they do not, or if they have operated on a worn spider, they should be replaced.

Automobile Guide

11. Force recommended lubricant (usually wheel-bearing grease) between the rollers in all four bushings. Fill the reservoirs (if present) in the ends of the cross.
12. Place the cross in the drive-shaft yoke and insert the roller bushing assemblies in the yoke.
13. Press the roller and bushing assemblies into the yoke while guiding the spider into both bushings.
14. Press until the bushing retainers can be installed in the grooves in the bushings.
15. Position the remaining two bushings on the spider and install the retainer strap (if so equipped) to hold them in place during installation in the vehicle.

NOTE: Some universal joints have an injected nylon or plastic bearing retainer, Fig. 11. This retainer will be sheared when the bearing is pressed out and must be replaced with a steel snap ring.

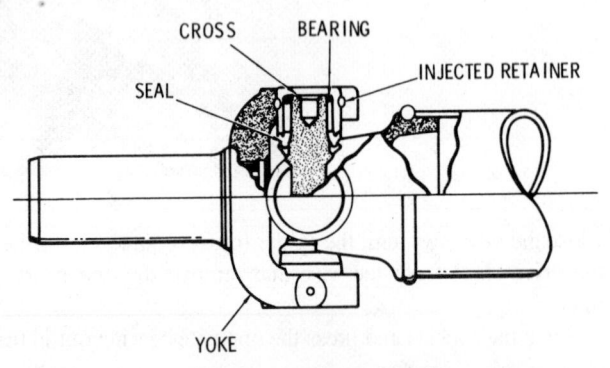

Fig. 11. Injected nylon or plastic bearing retainer.

Constant-Velocity Type — To service a constant-velocity type of universal joint, proceed as follows:

1. Mark all yokes before disassembly so they may be reassembled in their original positions to maintain proper balance. Fig. 12 shows the method of using punch marks to insure correct reassembly.

NOTE: For ease of disassembly, remove the bearings from the link yoke first.

Drive Shafts, Universal Joints, and Rear Axle Assemblies

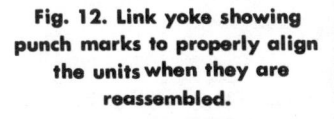

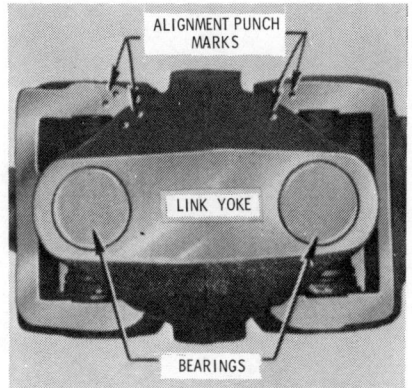

Fig. 12. Link yoke showing punch marks to properly align the units when they are reassembled.

Courtesy Buick Motor Div., General Motors Corp.

2. Remove the snap rings from the bearings. These rings are on the inside of the link yoke and can be removed with a special tool, as shown in Fig. 13.
3. Press out the bearings with a hydraulic press and special fixture as shown in Fig. 14.
4. Install a special guide through the bearing hole in the link yoke and over the journal end of the spider. This guide aligns the spider while removing the opposite bearing (Fig. 15).
5. Remove the bearing.
6. Repeat this procedure to remove other bearings until the unit is disassembled to the point desired or until the spider can be slipped out of the link yoke.
7. To remove the ball stud seat, position the drive-shaft yoke in a vise so that the seat is accessible.
8. Pry out the seal with a screwdriver, and remove the seal washer, ball seat, seat washer, and ball seat spring. See Fig. 16.
9. Inspect the ball stud and seats for scores or wear. Replacement kits are available for worn seats. A damaged ball stud requires replacement of the splined yoke, of which it is a part.
10. Clean out the seat cavity and pack with recommended lubricant.
11. Install the ball seat spring, small end first. Install seat washer, seats, and seal washer. Apply *Permatex* to the outer diameter of the seal and install the seal with its lip toward the seat.
12. Stake the seal lightly and evenly in four places. Take care not to damage or distort the seal.
13. Pack the cavity around the ball stud with recommended lubricant.

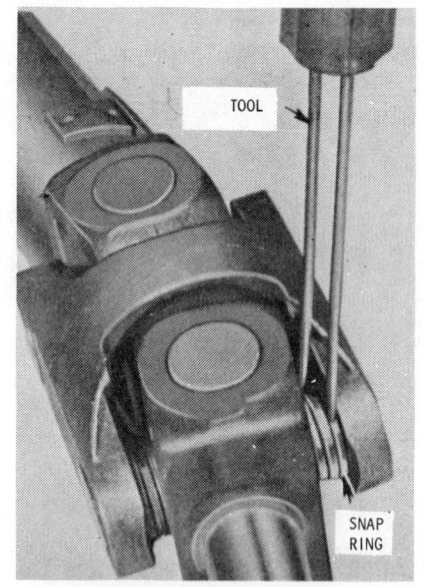

AUTOMOBILE GUIDE

Fig. 13. Removing the snap rings from a constants-velocity universal joint.

Courtesy Buick Motor Div., General Motors Corp.

Fig. 14. Pressing out a bearing.

Courtesy Buick Motor Div., General Motors Corp.

Drive Shafts, Universal Joints, and Rear Axle Assemblies

Fig. 15. Pressing opposite bearing out, using guide over spider.

Courtesy Buick Motor Div., General Motors Corp.

Fig. 16. Ball-stud seat assembly.

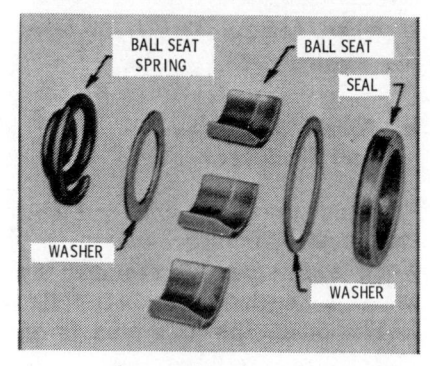

Courtesy Buick Motor Div., General Motors Corp.

14. Replace any worn or damaged parts in the constant-velocity joint. Repair kits containing a spider, four bearings, and four snap rings are available. *Always install a complete repair kit.*
15. Make certain that all the rollers are present in the bearings, that the bearings are properly packed with recommended lubricant, and that the seals are in position.
16. Reassemble the constant-velocity joint, taking care to prevent the bearing needles from becoming dislodged or burring the edge of the spider journals. Move the spider back and forth while pressing

the bearings into position to make certain the spider journals engage the bearings squarely to avoid damage and binding. If binding exists, remove the bearings and spider and examine for dislodged rollers or damaged journals.
17. Strike the yoke with a hammer to fully seat the snap rings against the yoke. Turn the spider to make certain it is free.

REAR AXLE ASSEMBLY

Rear axle assemblies are similar in construction features for all domestic cars and consist of four main sub-assemblies; the axle shafts, axle housings, differential with ring gear, and drive pinion with carrier.

Two types of rear axle is found; the standard one-piece axle assembly, shown in Fig. 17, and, in some cases, the independently suspended *axle driveshaft* assembly, Fig. 18.

Minor differences in design characteristics and service procedures require consulting the manufacturer's service manual for specific service procedures.

The rear axle suspension may be by leaf spring, Fig. 17 and 18, or by coil spring, Fig. 19. Function and service of both types of spring system is covered in Chapter 21. Rear shock absorbers, also covered in Chapter 21, are similar to those found in the front suspension system.

DIFFERENTIAL

The differential, driven off the transmission by the driveshaft, is located between the two rear axles inside the differential housing. Because of its design, it will permit one axle shaft to turn at a different speed from that of the other while, at the same time, transmitting power to both axle shafts.

The variation in axle speeds is necessary when the car rounds a corner or travels over uneven surfaces. As illustrated in Fig. 20 the inner wheel radius is 7' while the outer wheel radius is 11'. The centerline radius is, then, 9'. In this particular example the car, making a 180° turn will travel about 28'. The inside wheel will travel 22' while the outside wheel travels 34'.

Without the differential, one rear wheel should be forced to skid when turns were made. This would result in excessive tire wear and tend to make the car more difficult to control.

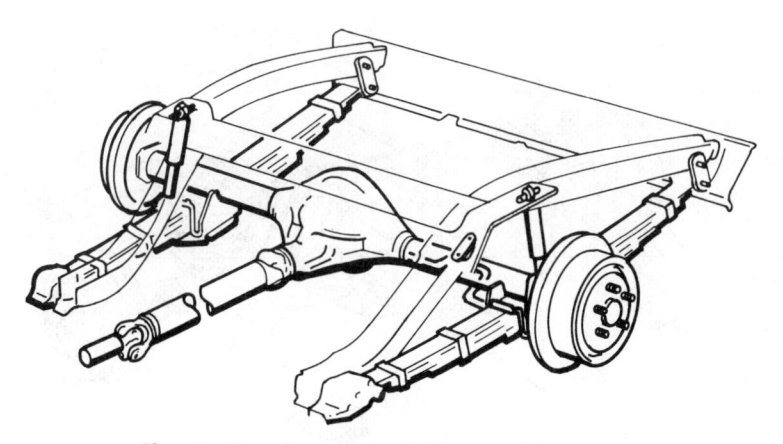

DRIVE SHAFTS, UNIVERSAL JOINTS, AND REAR AXLE ASSEMBLIES

Fig. 17. One-piece differential and axle assembly.

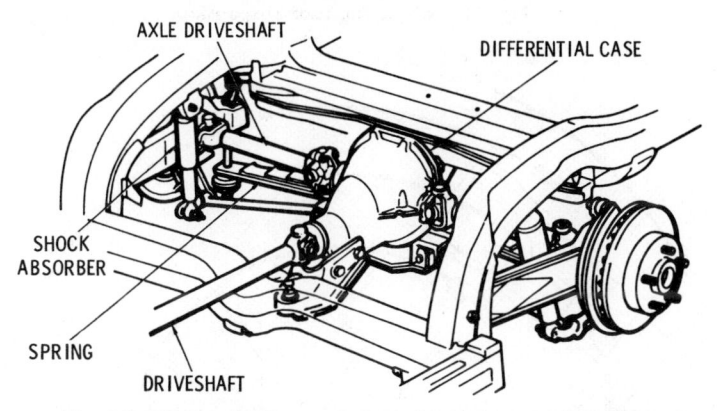

Fig. 18. Independently suspended axle-drive shaft assembly.

CONVENTIONAL DIFFERENTIAL

Fig. 21 illustrates a simple form of the working principle of a conventional type differential as used in most cars. Note that the drive is from the drive shaft through the pinion gear and then to the ring gear which has two of the differential gears attached. These two gears in turn drive two other slightly larger differential gears, one of which is splined to the inner end of each axle shaft. The two gears attached to the differential case are known as differential pinions, spur pinions, or spider gears. The two gears on the ends of the axles are called

AUTOMOBILE GUIDE

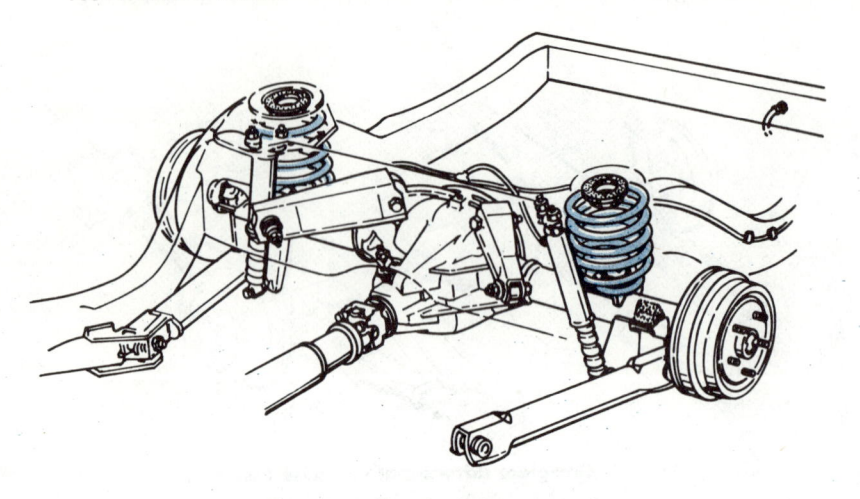

Fig. 19. Coil spring rear suspension.

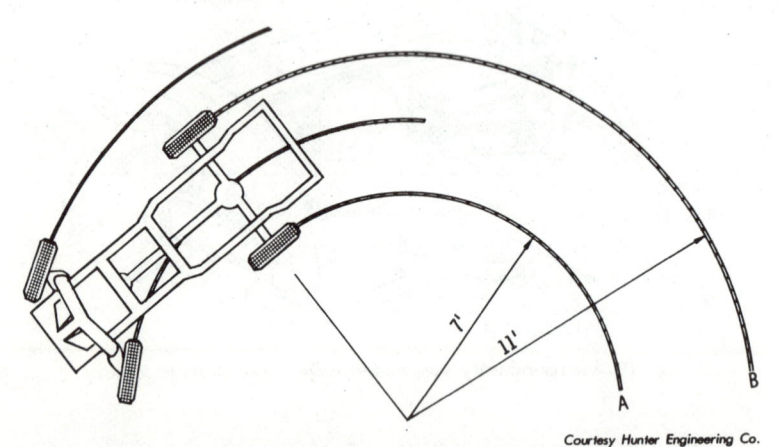

Courtesy Hunter Engineering Co.
Fig. 20. Outer wheel must travel faster (and further), than the inner wheels.

differential side gears. Were it not for the spider gears, each wheel, with its axle shaft and side gear, would be free to rotate with no connection to the ring gear. When the ring gear is rotating and both front wheels are in the straight ahead position, the differential side gears and the rear wheels are turning at the same speed as the ring gear.

When the front wheels are not in a straight ahead position, as in making a turn, the innerside gear is forced to turn slower than the other, causing the spider gears to "walk" around the slower turning side gear,

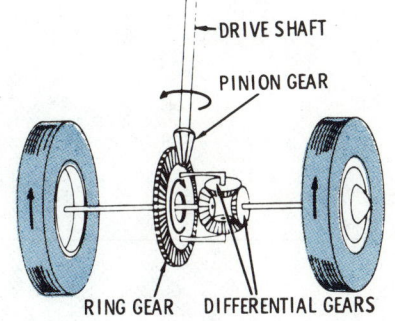

Drive Shafts, Universal Joints, and Rear Axle Assemblies

Fig. 21. Principle of a conventional differential.

forcing the other side gear to rotate faster. A cutaway view of the conventional differential is shown in Fig. 22.

LOCKING (ANTI-SLIP) DIFFERENTIAL

To overcome the inherent weakness of the conventional differential, that is its tendency for one wheel to slip (or spin) when traction is lost, the nonslip differential was developed. As mentioned earlier, the nonslip differential is available under various trade names, and is available as an option for most domestic cars.

In order to apply torque, or a driving effort, to a wheel that does not have traction (such as would be the case in mud, ice or snow), the nonslip differential, in effect, causes the spinning wheel to apply its own braking system to slow itself transferring almost an equal traction to the other wheel.

In other words, such a differential is designed to deliver only the amount of torque that the wheels can utilize without slipping and at the same time permit one wheel to rotate faster than the other when necessary, such as in turning a corner.

Locking-type differentials, Fig. 23, are also known as *Positraction, Sure-Grip, Positive Traction, No-Spin, Twin Grip, Safe-T-Track*, etc., consist of a different type of differential case assembly. Rear axle components, however, are generally the same as those used with conventional differentials.

The primary advantage of a locking differential is that it reduces the possibility of the car becoming stuck under adverse driving conditions. When only one rear wheel is on a slippery surface, the car can still move forward because both rear wheels tend to rotate at the same speed. This

AUTOMOBILE GUIDE

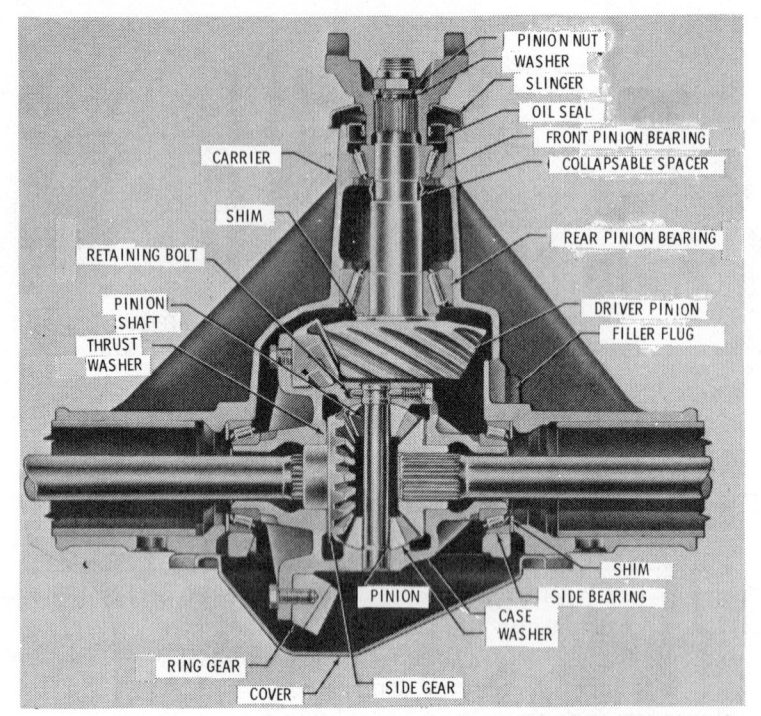

Fig. 22. The construction features of a typical standard differential.

feature allows the wheel on the dry surface to provide the necessary traction.

Another advantage of a locking differential is that bumps do not adversely affect rear wheel action. With a conventional transmission, when one rear wheel bounces clear of the road, it spins momentarily. When this rapidly spinning wheel contacts the road again, the sudden shock may cause the car to swerve. This is also hard on the entire drive train and on the tires. With a locking differential, the free wheel continues to rotate at the same speed as the wheel on the road, thereby minimizing the shock and resultant swerve.

The locking differential has pinion gears and ring gears which operate in a manner similar to those in a conventional differential. However, the locking type has clutch packs installed behind each ring gear. These clutch packs are preloaded by springs to provide internal resistance to the differential action within the case itself. The purpose of these

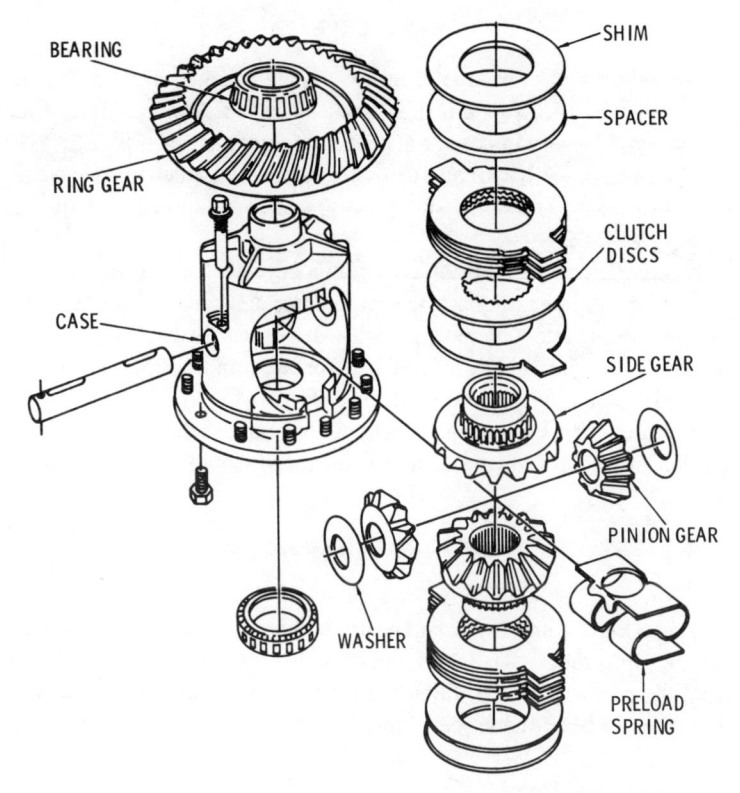

Drive Shafts, Universal Joints, and Rear Axle Assemblies

Fig. 23. Exploded view of a typical locking-type differential.

preloaded clutch packs is to hold the ring gears to the side of the case, which tends to cause the axle shafts to rotate together.

CAUTION: A car equipped with a locking differential will always have both rear wheels driving. Care must be used when servicing, because if only one rear wheel is raised off the floor, and the rear axle is driven by the engine, the wheel on the floor will drive the car off the stand or jack.

All locking-type differentials require special lubricant. *Never use lubricant other than this special kind (or its equivalent), even for adding, or a severe clutch chatter may result when turning corners.* If the wrong type of lubricant is accidentally added, it will be necessary to completely drain the differential, flush with light engine oil, then fill with the special lubricant.

REAR AXLE

The rear axle is made of heat-treated high-grade steel. Since the torsional stress of the axle is greatest at its surface, the hardness of the surface layer is very important in connection with the shearing strength. For that reason, low-carbon steel axles are case-hardened to increase their resistance to torsional stress. A typical conventional axle shaft is shown in Fig. 24.

The rear axle assembly of cars equipped with front-wheel drive is somewhat different in construction. Though it is free-wheeling much like the front axle of conventionally driven cars, its spindle is not pivoted. The rear spindle is attached (pressed and bolted) to the rear axle tube assembly, as shown in Fig. 25.

Because of the various specifications for bearing adjustment and axle service procedures, manufacturer's manuals should be consulted for service.

REAR-AXLE SERVICE

The rear axles support the weight of the car through either roller bearings (Fig. 24 and 25) or ball bearings (Fig. 26) enclosed in the outer axle-housing tubes. These bearings usually receive their lubrication from the lubricant in the differential, although it may be necessary to pack them when a new one is installed.

Rear-Axle Removal

The method of removing an axle shaft varies from car to car. Special tools are required in some cases. The procedure in general, however, is as follows:

1. Lift the car, allowing the rear-axle assembly to hang with the wheels just clear of the floor.
2. Remove the wheel and tire from the brake drum.
3. Remove the nuts or bolts that secure the brake drum to the axle flange, and remove the brake drum.
4. Remove the wheel bearing retainer plate. Take care not to disturb the brake carrier plate. One or two nuts or bolts can usually be installed to hold this unit in place.
5. Pull the axle-shaft assembly out of the housing. To remove the axle on some cars, it is necessary to install a special puller (Fig. 27). In certain other cars a "C" lock must be removed to free the

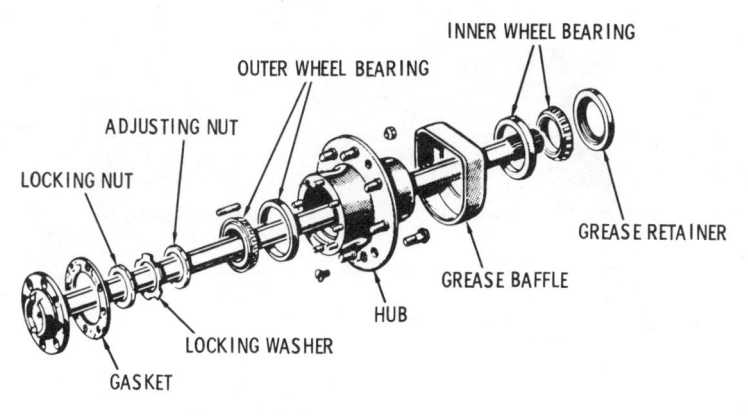

Drive Shafts, Universal Joints, and Rear Axle Assemblies

Fig. 24. A typical axle shaft assembly.

axle shaft. Check the manufacturer's service manual for specific instructions.

Wheel Bearing Replacement

The wheel bearing will come out with the axle shaft on some makes of cars, but will remain in place in the axle housing in others. The type of bearing that remains on the axle shaft can be replaced as follows:

1. Nick the bearing retainer in 3 or 4 places with a cold chisel, as in Fig. 28, to loosen it. The retainer will then slip off.
2. Press the bearing off the shaft with a special puller designed for this purpose. Take care not to damage or burr the oil-seal surface of the axle shaft. *NOTE: Whenever an axle shaft has been removed, a new oil seal should be installed.* New seals (for some cars) should be soaked in SAE 10 motor oil for 1/2 hour before installing.
3. Inspect the machined surface of the axle shaft and axle housing for rough spots or other damage which would affect the sealing action of the new seal.
4. Lightly coat the wheel bearing bores with ball joint grease, place the retainer plate on the axle and press the new wheel bearing on the axle. *Do not attempt to press both the bearing and inner retainer ring on the axle shaft at the same time.*
5. Press the inner retainer ring on the shaft until the retainer seats firmly against the bearing.

Automobile Guide

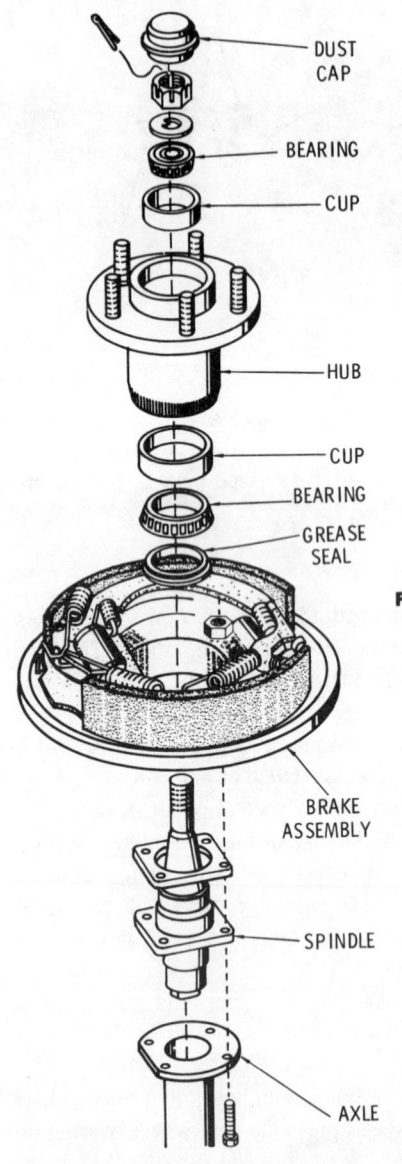

Fig. 25. Typical rear axle assembly on front-wheel drive cars.

6. Install the new oil seal. Coat the outside diameter with oil-resistant sealer before it is installed. *Do not put sealer on the sealing lip.*

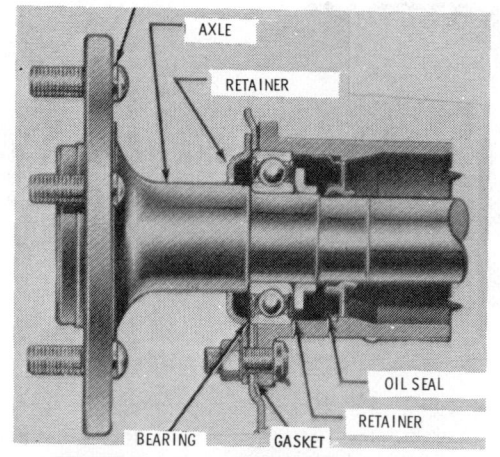

Drive Shafts, Universal Joints, and Rear Axle Assemblies

Fig. 26. A rear axle with ball bearings.

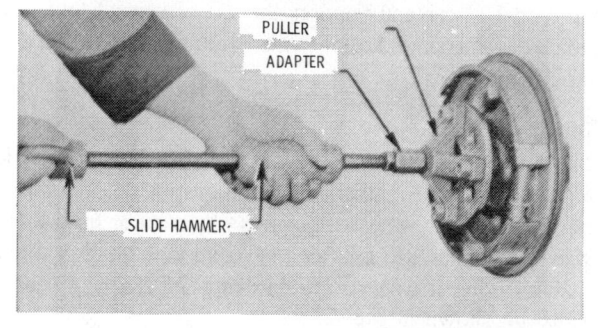

Courtesy Buick Motor Div., General Motors Corp.

Fig. 27. A special puller being used to remove an axle shaft.

7. Place new gaskets (if so equipped) on each side of the brake backing plate, and carefully slide the axle shaft into the housing. *Care must be taken during this operation so as not to damage the oil seal.*
8. Start the axle splines into the side gear of the differential, and push the shaft in until the bearing bottoms in the housing.
9. Install the bearing retainer plate and nuts (or bolts) that secure it. Tighten to specifications. (On certain cars, the axle is held in place by a "C" washer in the differential.)
10. Install the brake drum and the drum retaining nuts.
11. Install the wheel and tire on the drum.

691

AUTOMOBILE GUIDE

Fig. 28. Removing the axle shaft bearing retainer.

DIFFERENTIALS

Complete servicing of a differential is possible without removing the unit from the vehicle. The only exception to this is if the differential housing itself must be replaced. The procedure to follow varies with the make and model of car and requires the use of special tools. For this reason, the mechanic should refer to the manufacturer's service manual for specific instructions.

Gear Tooth Contact

The contact between the pinion gear teeth and the ring gear teeth is critical in all differentials. Either shims or adjusting nuts are provided to move the ring gear sideways so that it is closer to or farther from the pinion gear. Shims are also provided to move the pinion gear endways on its shaft to bring it closer to or farther from the ring gear. These adjustments are shown in Fig. 29.

Tooth contact patterns are used to determine if the contact between the teeth is correct. The pattern obtained is compared to normal and abnormal patterns and the indicated corrective adjustment is made. In order to interpret the patterns correctly, it is necessary to be familiar with the nomenclature (Fig. 30) used to identify certain portions of the gear teeth.

To check the gear tooth contact, paint the gear teeth with a suitable gear marking compound, such as a paste made with dry red lead and oil. A mixture that is too wet will run and smear, while too dry a mixture cannot be pressed out from beneath the teeth. Rotate the ring gear back and forth while holding a cloth or rope around the drive pinion flange to load the gears slightly.

Certain types of contact patterns on the ring gear indicate incorrect adjustment. Typical patterns and the necessary corrections are shown in

Drive Shafts, Universal Joints, and Rear Axle Assemblies

Fig. 31. Rear-axle noise caused by incorrect adjustment can often be eliminated or reduced by readjusting the gears.

Gear tooth runout can sometimes be detected by an erratic pattern on the teeth. However, a dial indicator should be used to measure the amount of runout, if such a condition is suspected.

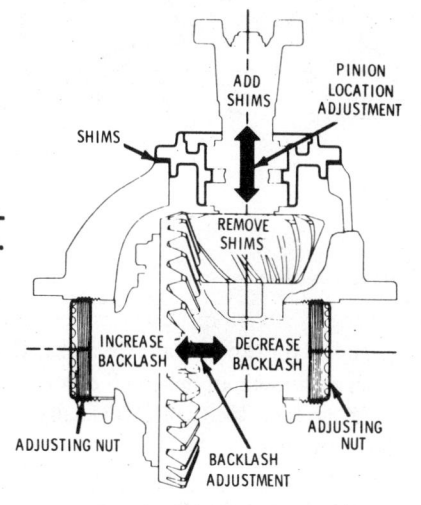

Fig. 29. Pinion and drive gear adjustments to correct tooth contact.

REAR AXLE NOISE DIAGNOSIS

Where a rear axle is suspected as being noisy, it is advisable to make a thorough test to determine if the noise is actually caused by the rear axle assembly, or if it is caused by the tires, road surface, front wheel bearings, engine, or transmission.

Tire Noise

Tire noise may easily be mistaken for rear axle noise, even though the noisy tires may be located on the front wheels. Tires worn unevenly or with saw-tooth variations may produce vibrations that seem to come from elsewhere in the vehicle.

Tire noise changes with different road surfaces — rear axle noise does not. Temporarily increase the tire pressure to 50 lbs. (for test only) and drive the car. If the noise has changed materially, the noise is caused by the tires. Rear axle noise usually disappears when coasting under 30 mph. Tire noise continues, but with a lower tone as the car speed is reduced.

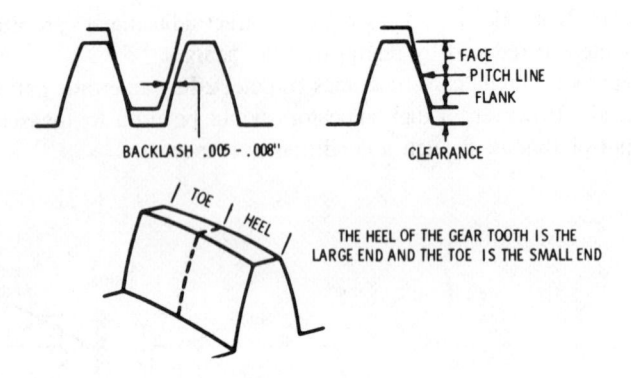

Fig. 30. Gear tooth nomenclature.

Road Noise

Brick, stone, or rough concrete roads cause noise that may be mistaken for tire or rear axle noise. Driving on a different type of road, such as smooth asphalt, will quickly show if the noise is caused by the road surface. Road noise is usually the same whether the car is driving or coasting.

Front Wheel Bearing Noise

Loose or rough front wheel bearings can cause noise that is often confused with rear axle noise. However, front wheel bearing noise does not change when comparing drive and coast.

Engine and Transmission Noise

A noise in the engine or transmission is often confused with rear axle noise. To determine which unit is actually causing the noise, observe the approximate car speeds and conditions under which the noise is most pronounced. Stop the car in a quiet place, and with the transmission in neutral, run the engine slowly up and down through the engine speeds at which the noise was formerly most pronounced. If the noise is heard under these conditions, the engine or transmission is at fault, not the rear axle.

Rear Axle Noise

If a careful test of the car shows that the noise is not caused by any of the external items just described, it is then reasonable to assume the

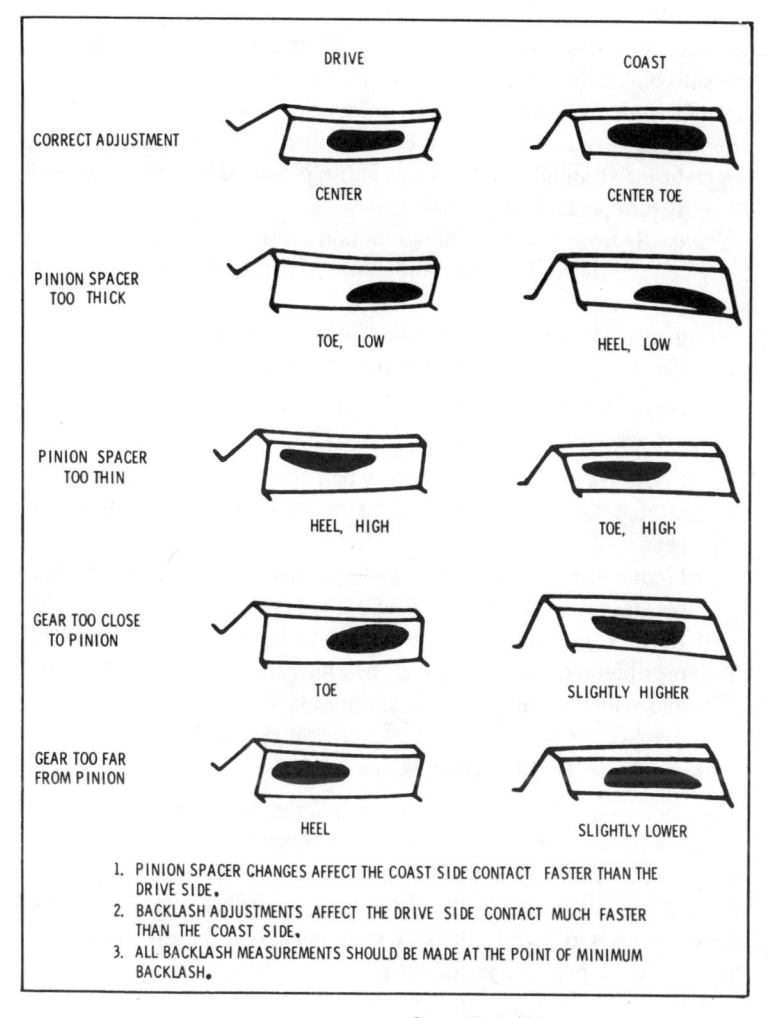

DRIVE SHAFTS, UNIVERSAL JOINTS, AND REAR AXLE ASSEMBLIES

	DRIVE	COAST
CORRECT ADJUSTMENT	CENTER	CENTER TOE
PINION SPACER TOO THICK	TOE, LOW	HEEL, LOW
PINION SPACER TOO THIN	HEEL, HIGH	TOE, HIGH
GEAR TOO CLOSE TO PINION	TOE	SLIGHTLY HIGHER
GEAR TOO FAR FROM PINION	HEEL	SLIGHTLY LOWER

1. PINION SPACER CHANGES AFFECT THE COAST SIDE CONTACT FASTER THAN THE DRIVE SIDE.
2. BACKLASH ADJUSTMENTS AFFECT THE DRIVE SIDE CONTACT MUCH FASTER THAN THE COAST SIDE.
3. ALL BACKLASH MEASUREMENTS SHOULD BE MADE AT THE POINT OF MINIMUM BACKLASH.

Courtesy Chrysler/Plymouth Div., Chrysler Motors Corp.

Fig. 31. Tooth contact pattern.

noise is from the rear axle assembly. Noise from this area may be caused by a faulty drive shaft or rear wheel bearings, faulty differential or pinion shaft bearings, misalignment between universal joints, worn differential side and/or pinion gear, or by a ring-and-pinion gear set that is either mismatched or improperly adjusted.

AUTOMOBILE GUIDE

Rear Wheel Bearing Noise — A rough rear wheel bearing produces a vibration or growl which continues with the car coasting while the transmission is in neutral.

Differential Side- and Pinion-Gear Noise — The differential side and pinion gears seldom cause noise since their movement is relatively slight during straight-ahead driving. Noise produced by these gears will be most pronounced on turns.

Pinion Bearing Noise — Rough pinion bearings cause a continuous low-pitched whirring or scraping noise starting at a relatively low speed.

Ring- and Pinion-Gear Noise — The noise produced by this set of gears usually is apparent whether driving, coasting, or floating.

(a) *Drive Noise* is most evident during constant acceleration through the speed range.

(b) *Coast Noise* is most evident when the car is allowed to coast through the speed range with the throttle closed but with the car in gear.

(c) *Float Noise* is most evident while just barely holding the car speed constant on a level road at any given speed.

(d) *Drive, Coast, and Float Noises* will be very rough and irregular if the differential or pinion shaft bearings are rough, worn, or loose, and will vary in tone with car speed.

Locking-Type Differential Noise

A chattering noise in a locking-type differential is more likely caused by a lubrication problem more than a mechanical problem, due to "dry" clutch plates. This chatter can usually be corrected by driving the car in five tight circles to the right; then five to the left. This should allow lubricant to "work" into the clutch plates. If this does not correct the condition, proceed as follows:

1. Drain or siphon lubricant from axle housing.
2. Refill with new lubricant, type and quantity as prescribed for locking type differentials.
3. Drive car for 30-50 miles to "work" in the lubricant. If chatter condition not "cured," proceed with step 4.
4. Disassemble and clean differential carrier.
5. Install new friction plates (soaked 30 minutes in special lubricant prior to assembly).

Drive Shafts, Universal Joints, and Rear Axle Assemblies

6. Reassemble differential carrier and install in car.
7. Drive car in five tight circles to the right; then to the left. If condition not corrected, proceed with step 8.
8. Drive the car for 30-50 miles, as in step 3. The chattering should now disappear.

WHEEL BALANCING PRECAUTIONS

"On car" wheel balancing is not recommended on rear wheels of locking-type differential equipped cars. *Remember, either rear wheel will "drive" if in contact with the ground — even though the other wheel is raised.*

If the only method of wheel balancing available is the "on car" type, the wheel *opposite the one being balanced* should be removed and the complete assembly should be raised.

DRIVE SHAFT AND UNIVERSAL JOINT TROUBLES AND REMEDIES

The following symptoms, their possible causes, and their possible remedies are general and do not necessarily apply to all makes and models of cars.

Symptoms and Possible Causes   *Possible Remedies*

Shudder on Acceleration

(a) Loose or missing bolt at center bearing support.	(a) Tighten bolts.
(b) Improperly adjusted rear joint angle.	(b) Adjust joint angle.
(c) Incorrect front joint angle.	(c) Shim under transmission support mount to bring to correct angle.
(d) Improper yoke phasing.	(d) Check for correct yoke phasing and correct if required.

Roughness or Vibration at All Speeds

(a) Center bearing support rubber damaged.	(a) Replace rubber.

Symptoms and Possible Causes	Possible Remedies
(b) Improper yoke phasing.	(b) Check for correct yoke phasing and correct if required.
(c) Bent shaft.	(c) Replace shaft.
(d) Dented shaft.	(d) Replace shaft.
(e) Tight universal joints.	(e) Strike yokes with hammer to free up. Replace if unable to free up or if joint feels rough when rotated by hand.
(f) Worn universal joints.	(f) Replace worn joints.
(g) Undercoating on shaft.	(g) Remove from shaft.
(h) Incorrect U-bolt torque.	(h) Torque to specifications.
(i) Incorrect rear joint angle.	(i) Check and adjust to correct angle.
(j) Tire unbalance.	(j) Balance wheels.
(k) Drive shaft unbalanced.	(k) Balance shaft or replace.
(l) Excessive grease in dust boot.	(l) Remove all grease and repack with correct amount.
(m) Worn trunnion pin.	(m) Replace pin.

Roughness on Heavy Acceleration

(a) Constant-velocity joints worn.	(a) Replace as necessary.
(b) Seat spring broken or set.	(b) Repair as necessary.

Roughness at Low Speeds and Light Loads

(a) Improperly adjusted joint angles.	(a) Adjust angles.

Whine or Whistle

(a) Defective center support bearing.	(a) Replace bearing.

Squeak

(a) Lack of lubricant or worn constant-velocity joint centering ball.	(a) Lubricate or replace ball-socket assembly.

Drive Shafts, Universal Joints, and Rear Axle Assemblies

Symptoms and Possible Causes   *Possible Remedies*

Knock or Click

(a) Joint or shaft hitting frame.
(a) Shim up or replace center bearing mount.

(b) Worn constant-velocity joint centering ball.
(b) Replace.

(c) Loose upper or lower control arm bushing bolts.
(c) Tighten bolts.

(d) Damaged center bearing support rubber.
(d) Replace rubber.

(e) Stones or gravel in frame tunnel.
(e) Remove stones or gravel.

Scraping Noise

(a) Shaft rubbing on parking-brake cable.
(a) Correctly position brake cable.

REAR AXLE TROUBLES AND REMEDIES

Intermittent Noise

(a) Loose ring gear rivets or screws.
(a) Tighten as necessary.

(b) Ring gear improperly installed.
(b) Remove gear, clean dirt and burrs from gear and case mating surfaces and re-install.

(c) Warped ring gear.
(c) Install new ring gear.

Oil Leak at Axle Ends

(a) Oil too light.
(a) Drain and install proper oil.

(b) Oil seals worn or damaged.
(b) Replace oil seals.

(c) Axle shaft bearing retainer loose.
(c) Tighten retainer.

(d) Oil level too high.
(d) Drain to proper level.

(e) Cracked or broken rear axle housing.
(e) Repair or replace housing.

(f) Vent clogged (if equipped).
(f) Unclog vent.

AUTOMOBILE GUIDE

Symptoms and Possible Causes *Possible Remedies*

Oil Leak at Pinion Shaft

(a) Oil too light.
(a) Drain and install proper oil.

(b) Oil level too high.
(b) Drain to proper level.

(c) Pinion oil seal retainer damaged or improperly installed.
(c) Install (or reinstall) new retainer.

(d) Pinion oil seal worn or damaged.
(d) Install new seal.

(e) U-joint companion flange hub damaged or distorted.
(e) Repair or replace as necessary.

(f) U-joint companion flange loose on pinion shaft.
(f) Correct as necessary.

(g) Oil return passage restricted in carrier housing.
(g) Clear restriction.

Noise on Turns

(a) Pinions or side gears damaged.
(a) Repair or replace as necessary.

(b) Pinions or side gears loose.
(b) Replace bushings and/or shaft.

(c) Backlash between pinions and side gears excessive.
(c) Correct as necessary.

(d) Axle shaft end play excessive.
(d) Correct as necessary.

(e) Pinions binding on shaft.
(e) Repair or replace shaft and/or pinions as necessary.

(f) Damaged surfaces between side gear and case.
(f) Repair as necessary.

Noise When Pulling Straight Ahead

(a) Incorrect grade of oil used.
(a) Drain and refill with proper grade oil.

(b) Oil level low.
(b) Fill to proper level.

(c) Excessive backlash on ring gear and pinion.
(c) Correct as necessary.

(d) Ring gear and pinion worn.
(d) Replace as necessary.

(e) Pinion shaft bearings worn or loose.
(e) Replace bearings or correct as necessary.

Drive Shafts, Universal Joints, and Rear Axle Assemblies

Symptoms and Possible Causes *Possible Remedies*

(f) Excessive pinion shaft end play.
(g) Ring gear warped.
(h) Ring gear rivets or screws loose.
(i) Bent axle housing or distorted case.
(j) Bearings worn or loose.

(k) Mismatch on ring gear and pinion.

(f) Correct as necessary.
(g) Replace ring gear.
(h) Replace or tighten as necessary.
(i) Replace parts (housing or case) as necessary.
(j) Repair or replace bearings as necessary.
(k) Correct. (Ring gear and pinion must be matched set.)

Noise When Coasting in Gear

(a) Ring gear and pinion meshed too tight.
(b) Pinion shaft end play excessive.

(a) Correct as necessary.
(b) Tighten pinion nut or correct adjustment.

Chatter at All Speeds (Positive Traction "Locking" Differential)

(a) Clutch plates dry.

(a) Drive car in 5 tight circles to right, then to the left. Refill with lubricant and drive 30-50 miles. Install new friction plates, new lubricant, and drive as outlined.

CHAPTER 27

Front-Wheel Drive

The front-wheel drive system, as used on *Cadillac's El Dorado* and *Oldsmobile's Toronado*, offer different and exacting requirements for servicing the front-end assembly.

Most all such service on these cars should only be attempted by an experienced mechanic. Many repairs require special tools that are not available at a regular parts house.

The torque converter and transmission are separated. The torque converter bolts onto the engine flywheel, but does not connect directly to the transmission. It is connected by a drive sprocket, link belt assembly, and driven sprocket.

The *Turbo Hydra-Matic* transmission used on *General Motors* fror wheel drive cars is fully automatic. It consists primarily of a 3-element hydro-torque converter, a dual sprocket and link assembly, and a compound planetary gear set. Three multiple clutches, a sprag unit, a roller clutch unit, and two bands provide elements required to obtain the desired function of a compound planetary gear set.

TRANSMISSION

The torque converter, dual sprocket and link, its clutches, the sprag and roller clutch, couples the engine to the planetary gears, providing 3-forward speeds and 1-reverse speed.

The torque converter, when required, will supplement the gears by multiplying engine torque. The torque converter is of welded construction and is serviced as an assembly.

Front-Wheel Drive

External connections to the transmission include:
1. Manual linkage: to select the desired gear range.
2. Engine vacuum: to operate the vacuum modulator unit.
3. Electrical system (12 volts): to operate the detent solenoid.

Gear Range — The manual linkage controls the transmission quadrant's 6 selector positions: Park (P), Reverse (R), Neutral (N), Drive (D_1), Drive (D_2), and Low (L). Drive (D_1) is used for all normal driving, Drive (D_2) is used in heavy traffic, preventing the transmission from shifting above second speed.

The gear ratio of the front-wheel drive *Turbo Hydra-Matic* is 2.5:1 for first gear, 1.5:1 for second gear, and 1.1:1 for third gear. Reverse gear ratio is 2.1:1.

Vacuum Modulator Unit — The vacuum modulator unit is used to sense engine torque input to the transmission, transmitting this signal to the pressure regulator, so that all torque requirements of the transmission are met and proper shift spacing is obtained at all throttle openings.

Detent Switch — The detent switch is activated by an electrical switch at the carburetor to cause a "downshift" (when necessary) at speeds below 70 miles per hour.

Fluid Check

To check the fluid level, the car must be on a flat surface and the fluid must be at normal operating temperature of 170° F. This temperature is obtained by at least fifteen miles of expressway driving or equivalent. To check fluid:

1. Start engine. Place foot on brake pedal and move gear selector control lever through each range.
2. Place gear selector control lever in Park (P). With engine running, immediately check fluid level on dipstick.
3. Fluid level should be at "FULL" mark on dipstick. If not, add fluid to reach this level. *CAUTION: Do not overfill.*

NOTE: *If fluid is not to normal operating temperature, and driving is not practical, the fluid may be checked at room temperature of 70°F. Fluid level should be 1/4" below the "ADD" mark on the dipstick.*

FRONT SUSPENSION

The front suspension consists of two upper and two lower control arms, a stabilizer bar, two shock absorbers, and two torsion bars (coil springs are not used) as shown in Fig. 1.

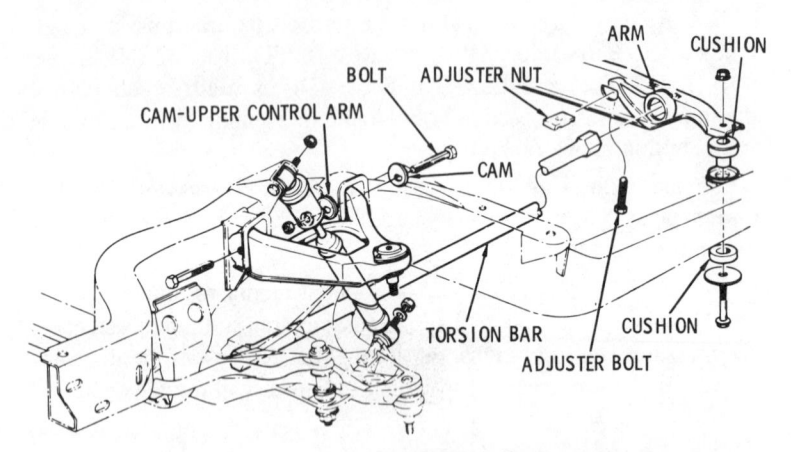

Courtesy Cadillac Motor Car Div., General Motors Corp.

Fig. 1. Typical front suspension assembly (front-wheel drive).

The standing (or carrying) height of the car is controlled by adjusting the torsion bars, the front end of which is attached to the lower control arms. This procedure is as follows:

When checking carrying heights, the car should be parked on a known level surface, gas tank full, front seat rearward, doors closed and tire pressure at specified psi. Measurements must be taken from the lower edge of rocker panel molding to door.

Carrying heights are controlled by the adjustment setting of the torsion-bar adjusting bolt. Clockwise rotation of the bolt increases the front height — counterclockwise decreases front height.

Individual components are covered in Chapters 21 through 23. Manufacturer's specifications and procedures should be followed whenever servicing the front suspension system of a front-wheel drive car.

DRIVE AXLE

Drive axles are a completely flexible assembly, consisting of an axle

FRONT-WHEEL DRIVE

shaft with a tri-pot type constant velocity joint at the inboard end and a ball-type constant velocity joint at the outboard end of the axle.

The inboard tri-pot joint is not only flexible to operate at various angles, but can also move in and out as required by the suspension while it travels through its ride motion.

TOWING

Front-wheel drive cars cannot be started by pushing. If there is something wrong with the starting system that the car cannot be started with jumper cables from another battery, it must be towed for repairs.

Towing should only be done with the front wheels off the ground. If, however, this is impractical, because of damage to the rear end of the car, it can be towed from the rear with the transmission selector in Neutral (N) up to 50 miles at speeds no greater than 35 mph. Distances greater than 50 miles and/or speeds over 35 mph may cause serious damage to the transmission. If long distance towing is required, a dolly should be used.

REAR SUSPENSION

Unlike the conventional differential-type rear axle system, the rear suspension of a front-wheel drive car consists of a solid axle, two single leaf springs, four shock absorbers (two vertical and two horizontal), and clamps and bushings, as shown in Fig. 2.

The vertical shock absorbers function in the same manner as shock absorbers of a standard suspension system (Chapter 21). The horizontal shock absorbers assist in damping the rear axle.

The rear axle is a beam-type with drop-center welded construction. The rear wheel spindles are a press fit and are bolted directly to the rear axle assembly.

Rear wheel bearings should be packed with grade-2 lithium grease. Bearings are adjusted as follows:

1. Make certain hub is seated on spindle.
2. While rotating wheel, tighten nut to 30 ft.-lb.
3. Back off nut 1/4 turn and insert cotter pin.
4. Peen cotter pin to secure it. *MAKE SURE IT IS TIGHT.*

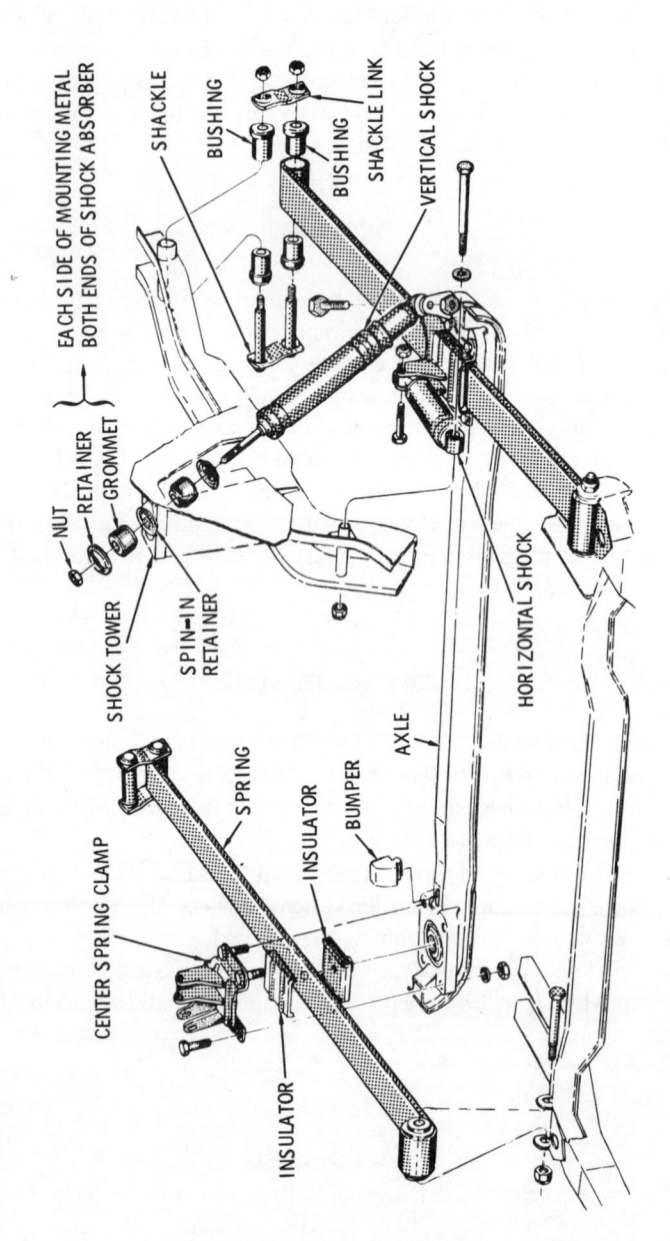

Fig. 2. Typical rear axle assembly (front-wheel drive).

TRANSMISSION TROUBLESHOOTING

Symptoms and Possible Causes   *Possible Remedies*

No Drive in "D" Range

(a) Low fluid level.

(b) Manual linkage out of adjustment.

(c) Low oil pressure.

(d) Damaged or worn parts.

(a) Check for leaks and correct fluid level.

(b) Correct alignment in manual shift lever quadrant.

(c) Determine cause and correct.

(d) Correct or repair as necessary.

No Drive in "R"

(a) Low fluid level.

(b) Linkage out of adjustment.

(c) Low oil pressure.

(d) Damaged or worn internal parts.

(a) Check for leaks and correct fluid level.

(b) Correct as required.

(c) Determine cause and correct.

(d) Correct or repair as necessary.

Slips in Reverse

(a) Same as "**No Drive in "R".**"

(a) Same as "**No Drive in "R".**"

Drives in Neutral

(a) Manual linkage out of adjustment.

(b) Forward clutch does not release.

(a) Correct adjustment and alignment in manual shift lever quadrant.

(b) Repair as necessary.

First Speed Only
(No 1-2 upshift)

(a) Governor valve sticking.

(a) Check governor valve; driven gear for looseness, damage, or wear. Check

AUTOMOBILE GUIDE

Symptoms and Possible Causes *Possible Remedies*

                                            ouput flange drive gear. Repair or replace as necessary.

(b) Control valve stuck closed. (b) Check the 1-2 shift valve train for dirt, metallic chips, or damage; blockage or leakage in governor feed channels; pipe(s) out of position; or defective gaskets. Repair or replace as necessary.

(c) Worn, broken, or misadjusted parts. (c) Repair, replace, or readjust internal assembly parts as necessary.

First to Second Speed Shift at Full Throttle Only

(a) Sticking or defective detent switch. (a) Repair or replace as necessary.

(b) Defective wiring. (b) Repair or correct as necessary.

(c) Gasket leaking. (c) Replace gasket.

First and Second Speeds Only (No 2-3 upshift)

(a) Sticking or defective detent switch. (a) Repair or replace as necessary.

(b) Control valve body; Leaking gasket or valve train stuck or dirty. (b) Clean and repair or replace necessary.

(c) Worn or damaged internal parts. (c) Repair or replace as necessary.

Slips in All Ranges

(a) Low fluid level. (a) Check for leaks and correct fluid level.

FRONT-WHEEL DRIVE

Symptoms and Possible Causes

(b) Low oil pressure.

(c) Clutches slipping.

(d) Roller clutch damaged or worn.

No Downshift

(a) Detent switch out of adjustment.
(b) Detent switch electrical problem.

(c) Solenoid defective or loose electrical connection.
(d) Valve train stuck.

Will Not Hold in Park

(a) Manual linkage out of adjustment.
(b) Parking brake lever or actuator rod defective.

Possible Remedies

(b) Determine cause and corect.

(c) Repair as necessary; replace damaged clutch plate(s).

(d) Repair as necessary; repair damaged springs, cage, or races.

(a) Adjust detent switch.

(b) Connection loose or wiring defective. Correct as necessary.

(c) Replace or repair as necessary.

(d) Repair as necessary.

(a) Correct alignment in manual shift lever quadrant.

(b) Check for proper actuator spring action; check parking pawl. Repair or replace broken or inoperative parts.

CHAPTER 28

Accessories

Automotive *accessories* to many people mean, among other things, outside rear view mirrors, deluxe wheel covers, custom trim, padded dash, or deluxe interior trim. To the automotive technician, in addition to the air conditioner (covered in Chapter 29), accessories include speed control devices, windshield wiper system, washer fluid indicator, sun roof, and theft-deterrent system. These devices are covered in this chapter. Other accessories not covered in this text, because of their highly technical nature, include the radio, tape deck, and AM/FM/Stereo systems.

SPEED CONTROL DEVICES

There are several types of automatic speed control devices used on the modern car. More commonly referred to as "Cruise Control" they all basically perform the same function. That is, to keep the car at an even, preselected speed by taking over throttle control. Within engine limitations, the cruise control will hold the car speed at a predetermined setting regardless of changing road conditions. If a speed is set at 60 mph, the cruise control will maintain this speed uphill or downhill as well as on level roads.

Generally, the lowest speed that the cruise control may be set is 30 mph. It is designed to release whenever the brake pedal is depressed. Most can also be released manually by the driver if he wishes. For safety's sake, there are usually two (or more) release switches or devices in most cruise control units. We will briefly describe two types of cruise control units in this text. One type operates with battery voltage and manifold vacuum (electro-pneumatic) and the other operates with battery voltage only (electrical).

Electro-Pneumatic

Study the wiring and vacuum diagram shown in Fig. 1 while reading the following text:

Engaging Switch — The engaging switch, generally a pushbutton, is found in many applications to be mounted at the end of the turn-signal switch lever. It becomes an integral part of the turn-signal switch lever assembly. It is used to engage the cruise control or to adjust the speed upward or downward.

To engage the cruise control, the driver accelerates to the desired speed then momentarily presses the button. After doing so, he may take his foot off of the accelerator pedal. The car will then hold the preselected speed.

If the driver wishes to slow down (but not go "off" cruise control) he simply presses the button, holding it in this position until the desired lower speed is reached. On releasing the button, the car will hold the new speed.

If, however, the driver wishes to increase his cruising speed he may do so in two ways. He may depress the accelerator until the new speed is reached then momentarily depress the button, or he may increase the car speed from 3 to 5 miles per hour by momentarily depressing and releasing the cruise control button.

Regulator Assembly — The regulator assembly contains a governor (flyball type) and a valve body and magnet assembly. The regulator is driven by a flexible cable and shaft assembly from the transmission. A second flexible cable and shaft assembly (from the regulator to the speedometer) drives the speedometer. The regulator assembly is a speed-sensing and control device, and may well be considered the heart of the system.

Vacuum Servo — The vacuum servo, just as its name implies, is connected to the throttle linkage. It is controlled by the regulator assembly. Its purpose is to control throttle speed through the accelerator linkage to the carburetor. It is actuated by a vacuum "signal" from the regulator assembly.

Release Switch — There are generally two release switches — one electric and one vacuum. The electric release switch is mounted on the brake pedal bracket or linkage assembly. Its function is to release the

AUTOMOBILE GUIDE

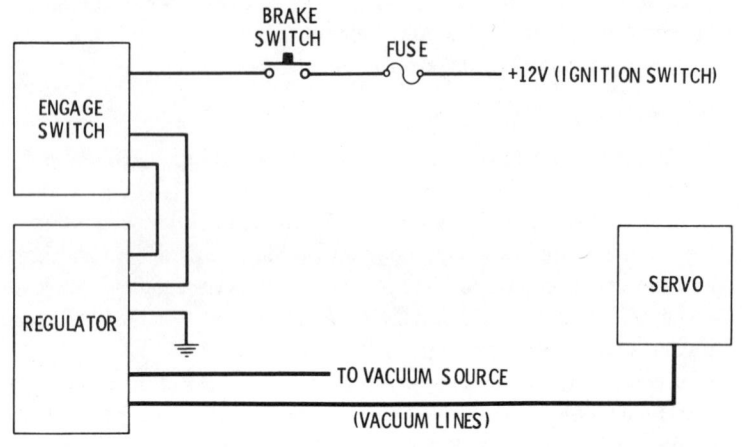

Courtesy Hayden Lynn Writing Service.

Fig. 1. Typical PERFECT CIRCLE speed control wiring and vacuum diagram.

cruise control unit electrically whenever the brake pedal is depressed. The vacuum release switch is also usually mounted on the brake pedal bracket or linkage mechanism. Its function is to release the cruise control unit whenever the brake pedal is depressed.

Electrical

Study the wiring diagram in Fig. 2 while reading the following text:

Engaging Switch — The engaging switch, generally a pushbutton (rocker type), is found in most applications to be mounted on the steering wheel. There are usually two switches: one to turn the cruise control unit on and off and the other to set the speed or release the speed. To engage the cruise control, first push the on-off button to the "ON" position. The driver then accelerates to the desired speed and momentarily presses the "set" button, After doing so, he may take his foot off the accelerator and the car will hold the preselected speed.

If the driver wishes to slow down, but not go off cruise control, he simply presses the "cruise" button, holding it in this position until the new desired speed is reached. On releasing the button the car will hold the lower speed selected.

If the driver wishes to increase his speed, he may do so in one of two ways. He may accelerate to the new speed and momentarily press the "set" button or he may (without touching the accelerator) hold the "set" button in until the new higher speed is reached. Releasing the button will hold the car at the new speed.

Amplifier Assembly —The amplifier assembly is the "brains" of the unit. It receives a signal from the sensor as to car speed and relays this information to the throttle actuator.

Sensor — The sensor is driven by a flexible cable and shaft assembly from the transmission. A second flexible cable and shaft assembly in turn drives the speedometer from the sensor. Car speed is determined by the small electrical impulses of the sensor — feeding this information into the amplifier assembly.

Throttle Actuator — The throttle actuator is connected to the throttle linkage. It is controlled by the amplifier assembly and its purpose is to control throttle speed through the accelerator linkage.

Release Switch — There are several ways of releasing the cruise control. There is an on-off switch convenient to the driver. Depressing "OFF" turns the unit off, thereby releasing the cruising speed. If either the brake pedal, horn, or turn signals are actuated the cruise condition is cancelled and must be reset if desired.

CONTROLLED CYCLE WIPER AND WASHER SYSTEM

A motor, gear box, relay control, pulse timing control, and washer unit make up the typical controlled cycle wiper/washer system. Note these components shown in the electrical schematic of Fig. 3. This schematic may be followed while reading the theory of operation.

Operation

The controlled cycle wiper system usually has a five-position control switch; *off - low - medium - high - delay*. In either the low, medium, or high speed position the wiper will operate at the selected speed until the switch is turned to the *off* position. In the delay position the wipers will stop in the "rest" position at the bottom of the windshield after a one-sweep delay wipe or a completed wash cycle.

Low-Speed — In the low-speed switch position a circuit is complete through the relay control, shunt field, and pulse relay to ground. This circuit, bypassing both resistors, causes the wiper motor to operate in low-speed only.

Medium-Speed — In the medium-speed switch position, a 13 Ω resistor, located in the control switch, is connected in parallel, with a 20 Ω resistor, between the shunt field and ground. These two resistors, in

AUTOMOBILE GUIDE

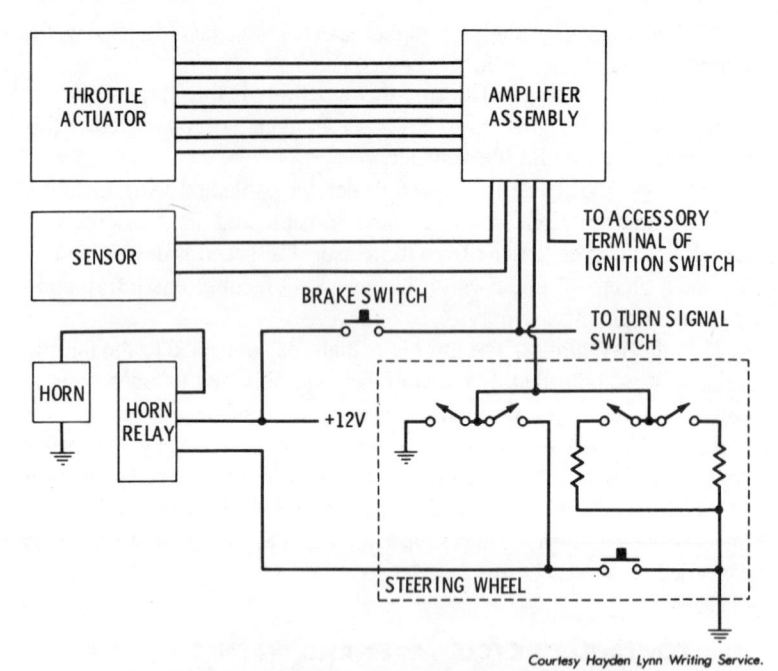

Courtesy Hayden Lynn Writing Service.

Fig. 2. Typical BENDIX speed control wiring diagram.

parallel, result in a total resistance of just under 8 Ω in the shunt field allowing less current to flow then did in the low speed. This, in turn, permits more current to flow through the armature of the wiper motor, resulting in a higher (medium) speed.

High Speed — With the control switch in the high-speed position, only the 20 Ω resistor is in the shunt circuit. With less current flowing through the shunt field, more current will flow through the armature. This will result in high-speed operation.

Delay — If the control switch is moved to the delay position, both the relay coil and shunt field are grounded (as in low-speed operation). As the switch is moved to the right a pause of 0 to 10 seconds is introduced between wipe cycles. This is accomplished by the use of a transistor and capacitor in the timing circuit, controlled by a variable resistor in the master control switch.

Washer Circuit — As the *wash* button is depressed; the relay coil, washer coil, and pulse relay are momentarily grounded. This causes the motor to operate in low speed and the washer ratchet to rotate, allowing the washer override switch to close. When the wash button is released

ACCESSORIES

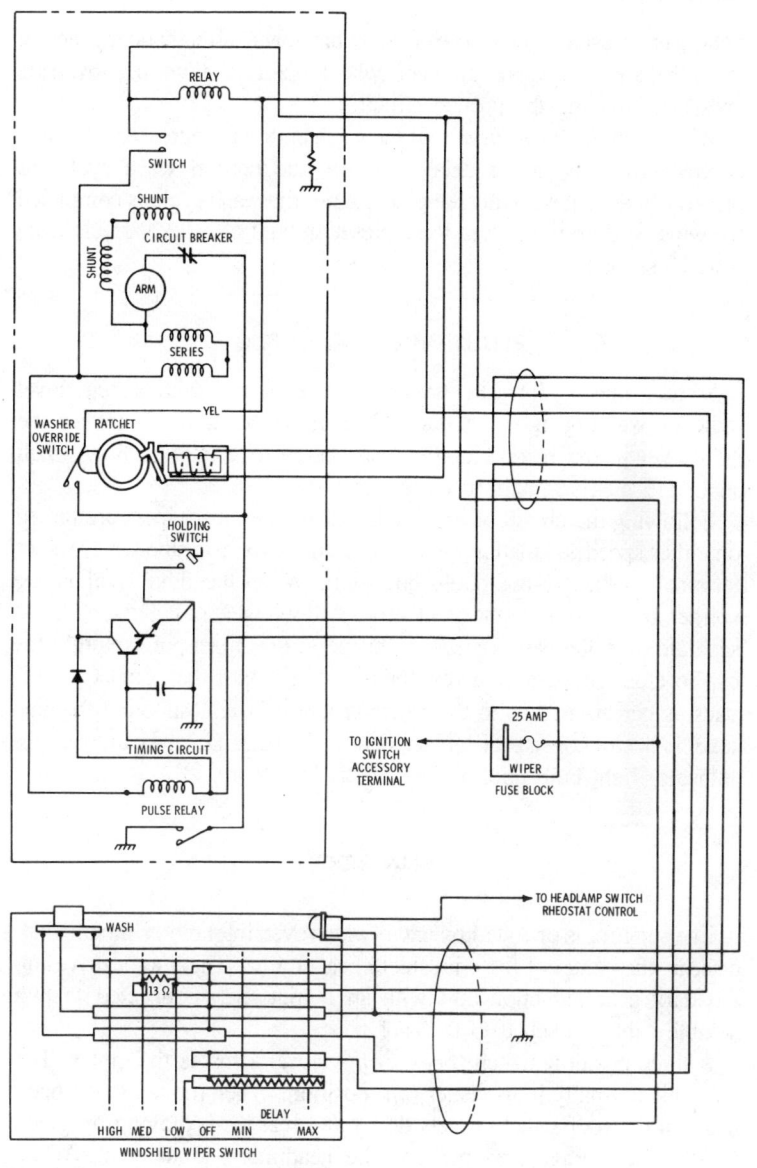

Fig. 3. Typical windshield wiper/washer electrical schematic.

the washer override switch provides the ground circuit. Washer fluid is sprayed on the windshield for five to seven sweeps of the wiper after the button is pressed. Two more sweeps are made after spraying action stops before the washer ratchet wheel opens the washer override contacts, breaking the ground circuit.

Wash With Delay Action — If the wash button is depressed while the control switch is in the delay position, the normal wash cycle, as previously described, will take place. After the wash cycle is completed the wiper system will return to its preset amount of delay variable from 0 to 10 seconds.

FLUID LEVEL INDICATOR

Some windshield washer systems are equipped with a fluid level indicator warning light. The lamp, located on the dash, is lit when the fluid level in the reserve bottle drops below two-thirds full or when about 1½ quarts remain in the bottle.

Following the circuit of Fig. 4, note that when the wipers are turned on either speed, a small amount of current flows from the wiper motor terminal to the washer bottle float unit. When the fluid level in the washer bottle is low, the float drops, allowing a circular magnet to separate from the cap assembly. This permits contact points within the cap to close, bypassing a resistor in parallel with the contact points, causing current to flow to the indicator lamp. Troubleshooting the fluid level indicator consists of replacement of the sensor of the cap, or of the indicator light bulb upon failure of the indicator.

SUN ROOF

The sun roof is operated by a two-way (reversible) motor mounted at, or near, the center of the windshield header area. This motor drives an auxiliary gear reduction unit with an output shaft connected to two flexible cables attached to the roof panel.

A three position switch (*open - off - close*) actuates the motor. The switch is normally in its center (*off*) position. When moved to the open position the roof panel retracts down and rearward, moving on guide rails into a storage area between the headliner and the roof. When moved to the close position, the roof panel moves forward on the guide rails and, as it nears the end of its travel, the rear edge moves upward. This positions the panel flush with the roof, sealing it tightly in the opening.

ACCESSORIES

Adjustments are sometimes critical to insure proper sealing when the panel is closed. For this reason, manufacturer's service procedures must be followed for servicing the sun roof. It may be noted that, in the event of motor or battery failure, the roof panel may be closed manually, by the use of a crank. An electrical schematic of a typical sun roof circuit is given in Fig. 5.

THEFT DETERRENT SYSTEM

Many types of theft deterrent systems, more often called *burgler alarms*, are available; some as new car options and others as "add-on" systems.

One such system, offered as an option by *Cadillac*, has a solid state controller which must be "armed" before it can be "triggered." The controller, accessable only after removing the instrument panel pad assembly, is activated by a manual selector switch located in the glove compartment.

The two positions of the selector switch are labeled *ARM ENABLE* and *ARM PREVENT*. Once the system is armed (arm enable) the selector switch itself becomes a trigger — if moved to the arm prevent position, after it is armed, the alarm is immediately sounded.

The arm prevent position (preset by the driver) is used for certain parking or service situations, such as for valet parking by an attendent. For this controlled situation the system is deactivated.

With the switch in the arm enable position the system is automatically armed in one to one and a half minutes after the ignition switch has been turned off. If, however, a door is held open after the ignition switch is turned off, arming does not occur until after the door is closed. Once armed, the system is disarmed *only* by turning the ignition switch to the accessory or run position. This must be done within twenty seconds after any door is opened — otherwise the alarm will activate.

The alarm is activated by one, or all, of the following: If the manual control switch is moved to the "arm prevent" position; twenty seconds after any door is opened; immediately after the hood, trunk, or glove box is opened; whenever a resistance-type electrical load is turned on; or if the fuse box cover is removed.

Once activated, the horn sounds and the parking, marker, license, and tail lamps flash at a rate of fifty cycles per minute for a period of five minutes. After five minutes the system shuts off and rearms automatically. Further tampering will reactivate the alarm.

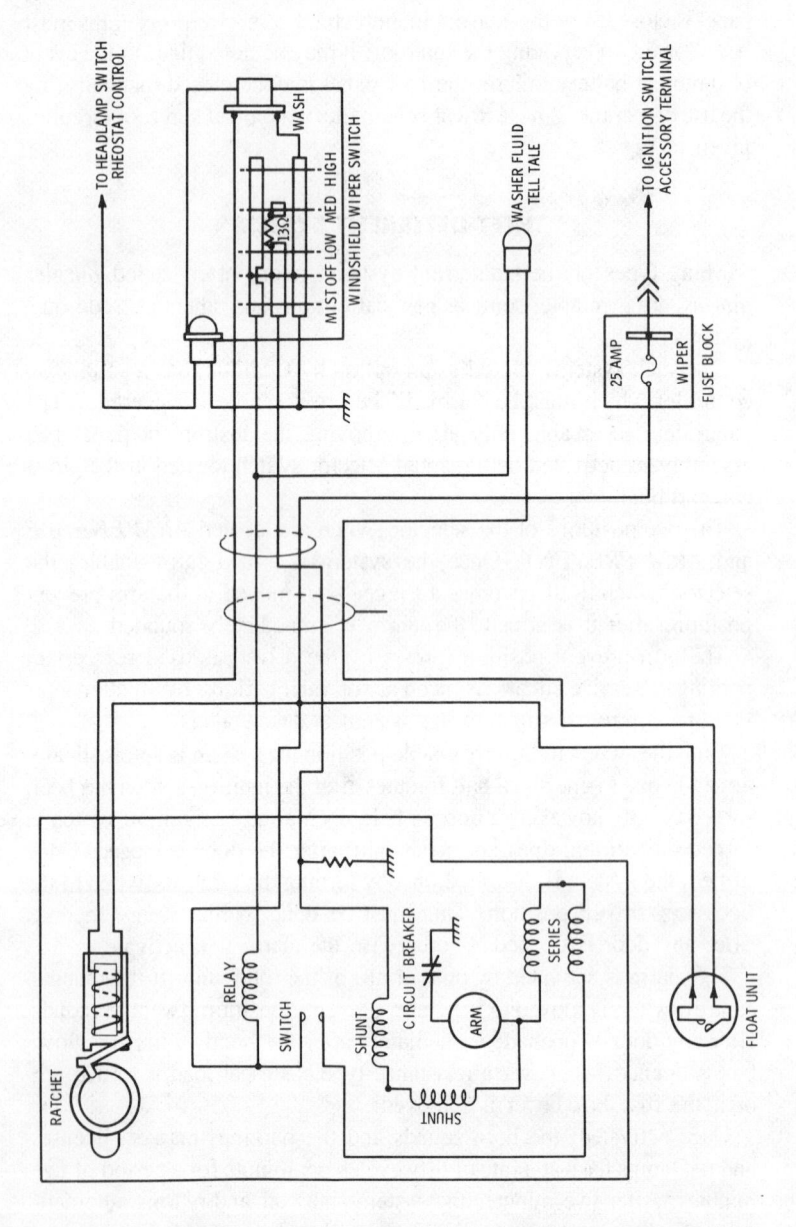

Fig. 4. Typical wiper/washer with fluid indicator schematic.

ACCESSORIES

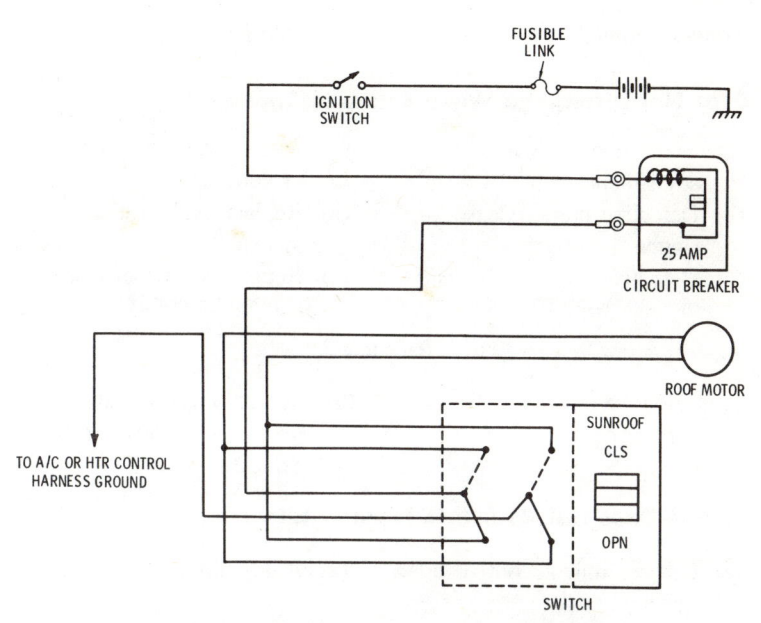

Fig. 5. Typical sun roof electrical schematic.

CRUISE CONTROL TROUBLESHOOTING

Symptoms and Possible Causes

Blowing Fuses

(a) Short or ground in wiring circuit.

Does Not Engage

(a) Blown fuse.
(b) Brake switch out of adjustment.
(c) No current to test point.
(d) Defective engaging switch.
(e) Defective valve body and magnet assembly.
(f) Low-speed switch defective.

Possible Remedies

(a) Check for short or ground. Correct. Replace fuse.

(a) Replace fuse.
(b) Adjust brake switch.
(c) Repair wiring harness.
(d) Replace engaging switch.
(e) Replace valve body and magnet assembly.
(f) Replace low-speed switch.

Automobile Guide

Symptoms and Possible Causes *Possible Remedies*

Does Not Disengage When Brake is Applied

(a) Brake release switch out of adjustment.
(b) Defective brake release switch.
(c) Defective valve body and magnet assembly.

(a) Adjust brake release switch.
(b) Replace brake release switch.
(c) Replace valve body and magnet assembly.

Re-engages When Brake Released

(a) Defective engaging switch.
(b) Improper ground in wiring.

(a) Replace engaging switch.
(b) Repair or replace wiring harness.

Engine Does Not Return to Normal Idle

(a) Control linkage out of adjustment.
(b) Accelerator linkage out of adjustment.
(c) Weak throttle return spring.
(d) Disconnected throttle return spring.

(a) Adjust linkage.
(b) Adjust linkage.
(c) Replace spring.
(d) Connect spring.

Accelerator Pedal Pulsating

(a) Drive cable kinked.
(b) Speedometer cable kinked.

(a) Replace cable.
(b) Replace cable.

Does Not Control at Selected Speed

(a) Incorrect linkage adjustment.
(b) Defective vacuum servo.
(c) Defective vacuum hose.

(a) Adjust linkage.
(b) Replace vacuum servo.
(c) Repair or replace hose.

Controls Speed Three or More mph Above Selected Speed

(a) Centering spring improperly adjusted.

(a) Adjust centering spring.

ACCESSORIES

Symptoms and Possible Causes   *Possible Remedies*

Controls Speed Three or More mph Below Selected Speed

(a) Centering spring improperly adjusted.
(a) Adjust centering spring.

Speed Increases Four mph or More Over a Hill

(a) Vacuum restriction adjusting screw out too far.
(a) Adjust vacuum restriction adjusting screw.

"Hunts" For Correct Speed

(a) Vacuum restriction adjusting screw in too far.
(a) Adjust vacuum restriction adjusting screw.

WIPER TROUBLESHOOTING

Wiper Will Not Operate (Motor Runs)

(a) Defective gear(s).
(b) Crank or output shaft improperly aligned.
(c) Defective latch.
(d) Linkage disconnected.

(a) Replace gear(s).
(b) Align crank and output shaft.
(c) Replace or repair latch.
(d) Connect linkage.

Wiper Will Not Operate (Motor Does Not Run)

(a) Linkage binding.
(b) Linkage bent.
(c) Control switch defective.
(d) Defective motor.
(e) Wiring defect (open or grounded).
(f) Blown fuse or circuit breaker

(a) Correct binding condition as necessary.
(b) Replace or straighten linkage.
(c) Replace switch.
(d) Repair or replace motor.
(e) Repair wiring as required.
(f) Replace fuse or circuit breaker.

No Speed Control (Wiper Operates in One Speed Only)

(a) Defective wiring.
(a) Correct wiring as necessary.

Automobile Guide

Symptoms and Possible Causes *Possible Remedies*

(b) Defective switch.
(c) Defective motor.

(b) Replace switch.
(c) Repair or replace motor.

Blade(s) Will Not "Park" in Proper Position

(a) Arm(s) out of adjustment.
(b) Park switch timing incorrect

(a) Reposition or adjust arm(s).
(b) Adjust park switch as required.

Blades Park in Any Position When Switch Is Turned Off

(a) Defective park switch (open).
(b) Defect in park circuit (open).
(c) Field circuit open.
(d) Defective control switch.

(a) Replace park switch.
(b) Correct as required.
(c) Repair or replace motor.
(d) Replace switch.

Blades Will Not Park When Switch Is Turned Off

(a) Defective park switch (closed).
(b) Defective gear(s).
(c) Defective cam.
(d) Defective armature brake switch.
(e) Defective control switch.

(a) Replace park switch.
(b) Replace gear(s).
(c) Replace cam.
(d) Replace switch.
(e) Replace switch.

Blade(s) "Slap" Against Mouldings

(a) Arm(s) out of adjustment.
(b) Motor crank loose.
(c) Linkage parts loose.

(a) Adjust arm(s).
(b) Tighten or replace crank.
(c) Tighten or replace parts as necessary.

Blade(s) Chatter

(a) Arm(s) twisted or bent.
(b) Bent or damaged blades.
(c) Worn out blades.

(a) Straighten or replace arm(s).
(b) Replace blades.
(c) Replace blades.

ACCESSORIES

Symptoms and Possible Causes *Possible Remedies*

(d) Foreign substances on windshield (such as wax).
(d) Clean windshield.

Excessive Noise

(a) Loose motor.
(b) Motor out of alignment.
(c) Loose or worn linkage.
(d) Defective arm(s).
(e) Defective blade(s).
(f) Foreign substance, such as wax, on windshield.

(a) Tighten motor.
(b) Align and tighten motor.
(c) Tighten or replace linkage as required.
(d) Replace arms (as a pair).
(e) Replace blades (as a pair).
(f) Clean windshield.

WASHER TROUBLESHOOTING

Water Spray But No Wiper Action

(a) Defective switch.
(b) Defective wiring.
(c) Defective wiper motor.
(d) Defective gear(s) or linkage.
(e) Linkage disconnected.

(a) Replace switch.
(b) Repair or replace wiring.
(c) Repair or replace motor.
(d) Repair or replace components as required.
(e) Connect linkage.

Wiper Action But No Water Spray

(a) Defective switch.
(b) Defective wiring.
(c) Defective spray motor or device.
(d) Clogged hose(s).
(e) Disconnected hose(s).
(f) Clogged spray nozzle(s).

(a) Replace switch.
(b) Repair or replace wiring.
(c) Replace motor or device.
(d) Replace hose(s).
(e) Reconnect hose(s).
(f) Clean nozzle(s).

No Water Spray and No Wiper Action

(a) Defective switch.
(b) Defective wiring.
(c) Blown fuse or circuit breaker.

(a) Replace switch.
(b) Repair or replace wiring.
(c) Replace fuse or circuit breaker.

Automobile Guide

Symptoms and Possible Causes

(d) Linkage bent or binding.

(e) Defective motor.

Possible Remedies

(d) Correct linkage as necessary.

(e) Repair or replace motor.

CHAPTER 29

Automobile Air Conditioning

The automobile air conditioner is basically no different from any other type of air conditioning system. The major components, such as the compressor, condenser, and evaporator, are utilized in primarily the same manner as the common room air conditioner. Certain variations and differences are unique to automobile air conditioning systems, such as the power source, method and type of controls, and component design. A typical automobile air conditioner installation is shown in Fig. 1. Power is supplied to the compressor directly from the crankshaft of the engine by means of a V-belt assembly and a series of pulleys, as shown in Fig. 2.

BASIC PRINCIPLES OF AIR CONDITIONING

First, you must understand what is meant by the word "cold." Actually, there is no such thing as "cold." An object is called colder than another object simply because it contains less "heat." Cold, then, is the absence of heat — or at least until you would remove all heat, which would be around $-460°F$.

It is important to understand that car air conditioning systems are not dealing with "cold" — but with less "heat." When you remove the heat it makes the air seem colder. We should now consider the term "heat." There are two kinds of heat that we are concerned with;

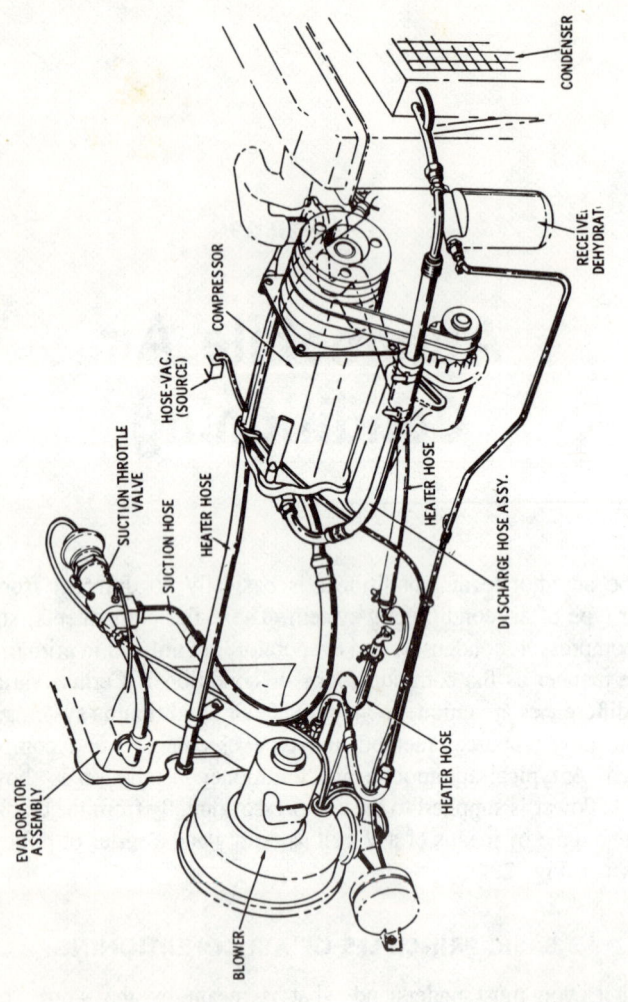

Automobile Guide

Fig. 1. Typical automobile air conditioning system.

sensible heat and *latent* heat. Sensible heat is the heat that you are able to feel and measure with a thermometer. Latent heat (also called hidden heat), is heat that cannot be felt or measured with a thermometer — but we know it is present and must be accounted for. Latent heat can be compared to moisture in the air. When moisture is removed from the air, the sensing temperature does not change.

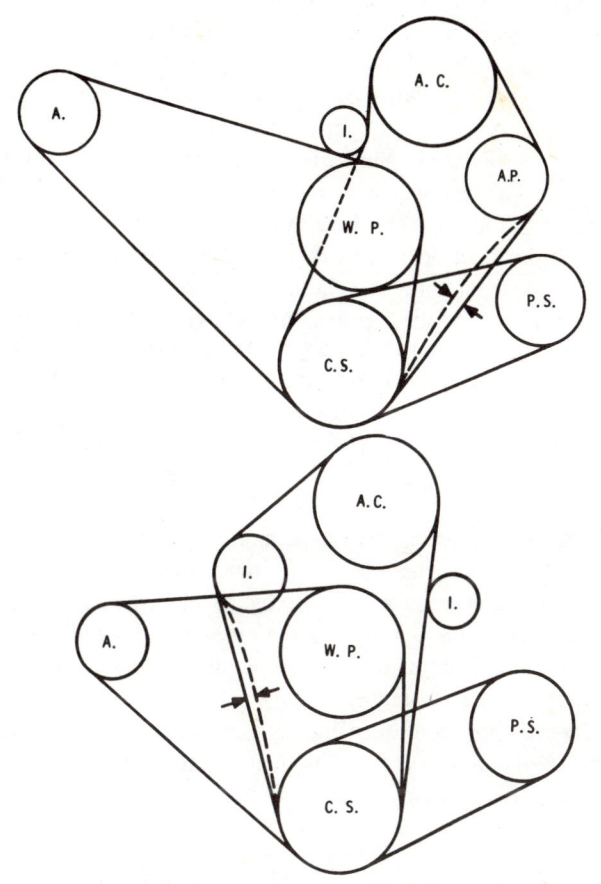

CS = CRANKSHAFT; A = ALTERNATOR; WP = WATER PUMP; PS = POWER STEERING; AC = AIR COMPRESSOR; I = IDLER PULLEYS; AP = AIR PUMP

Fig. 2. Typical belt arrangements in modern automobile engines.

It must be remembered that the car air conditioning system is concerned with both kinds of heat — sensible and latent. Sensible heat and latent heat cannot be destroyed. They can, however, be used for comfort by shifting them from one place to another, or from one object to another.

Heat will shift automatically by itself from one object with a lot of heat content to another object with less heat content. But heat will not shift by itself from an object with less heat to an object that has more heat. Car air conditioning is concerned with this shifting of heat. Heat is to be taken from the inside of the passenger compartment of the car and transferred to the outside of the car.

Two *temperature control* methods are used by automotive air conditioning manufacturers. These are the magnetic (or electric) clutch, and the refrigerant flow control. Normally, the *magnetic clutch* utilizes a stationary electromagnet which is attached to the compressor. The brushes and collector rings can be eliminated with this arrangement, since the electromagnet does not rotate. When a high temperature is present in the passenger compartment of the car, a thermostat (which is set by the driver to a specified temperature) closes the electrical circuit that connects the battery power supply to the stationary magnetic field. This field exists around the electromagnet that is mounted on the shaft of the compressor. A continuously rotating clutch plate then engages the compressor drive shaft and causes the compressor to operate at a higher rate of speed. This clutch plate is mechanically attached to the compressor flywheel which is driven by the V-belt assembly. When the interior of the car reaches the low-temperature setting of the thermostat, the thermostat will open the electrical circuit; the current will cease flowing, and the clutch plate will disengage the flywheel from the compressor. The flywheel will continue to rotate freely until the interior compartment temperature again rises above the thermostat setting. A typical magnetic clutch assembly is shown in Fig. 3.

The *refrigerant flow* control maintains a constant rate of refrigerant flow in the refrigeration system. This equalizing effect is extremely necessary, since the compressor does not operate at a constant rate of speed. The control is located at the suction, or low side of the refrigeration system; its spring-loaded bellows is responsive to the pressure changes that take place in the system. With a decrease in pressure, which accompanies a proportional decrease in interior temperature, the valve closes and thereby restricts the refrigerant flow. This restriction affects the operation of the system by limiting or completely halting the cooling effect, as the case may be. The refrigerant flow control is also responsive to the flow rate of the refrigerant. The valve is closed by an increase in flow rate; this increase causes the refrigerant pressure surrounding the valve stem to decrease and thereby affect the control valve, independent of the low-side pressure.

Sealed systems are highly improbable for use on an automobile, because all systems are, at present, powered by the engine crankshaft, which is an external source. The typical compressor used in the

Automobile Air Conditioning

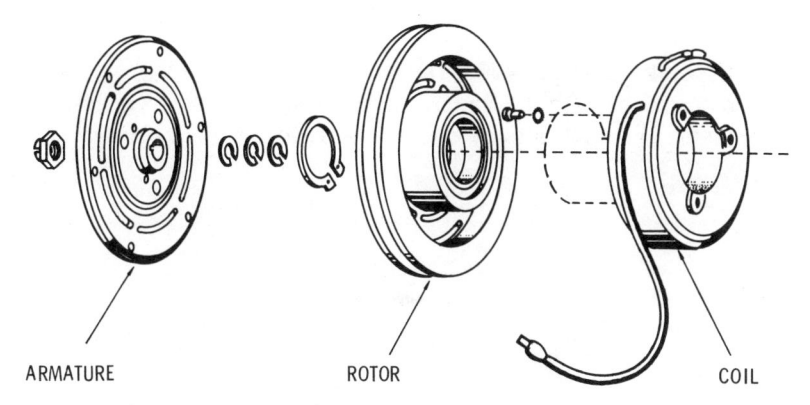

Fig. 3. Exploded view of a typical automotive compressor clutch coil and clutch assembly.

ARMATURE ROTOR COIL

automobile refrigeration system has a large refrigerating capacity as compared to the average room air conditioner (15,000 to 20,000 Btu per hour as opposed to 6000 to 10,000 Btu per hour). This large cooling capacity is due primarily to the large bore and stroke design of the automotive refrigerating compressor, and it is a necessity for automobiles because of the temperature range and poor insulation of the car interior.

The refrigerant most commonly used in the automobile air conditioning system is Refrigerant-12, better known as R-12. It should be noted that this refrigerant is often referred to as *Freon* or *Freon-12*. This term is akin to calling all refrigerators *Frigidaire*. *Freon* and *Freon-12* are registered trade marks of *E. I. du Pont de Nemours and Company*, just as *Frigidaire* is a property of *General Motors Corporation*. Though R-12 is relatively safe when properly handled, extreme caution should be exercised when working on, or in the vicinity, of the system. A poisonous gas, phosgene, is produced whenever R-12 comes into contact with an open flame. For this reason, the system should be completely discharged when any repairs or replacements are to be made on the unit — particularly if the use of heat is involved.

To review these basic principles of air conditioning, it is important to remember that you are dealing not with "cold" but with the shifting of heat from one place to another. Refrigerant is used to shift this heat. Heat transfer from the air inside the passenger's compartment to the air outside the car is accomplished by use of a refrigerant.

AIR CONDITIONING SYSTEM OPERATION

Cool refrigerant gas is drawn into the compressor from the evaporator and pumped from the compressor to the condenser under high pressure (Fig. 4). This high-pressure gas will also have a high temperature as a

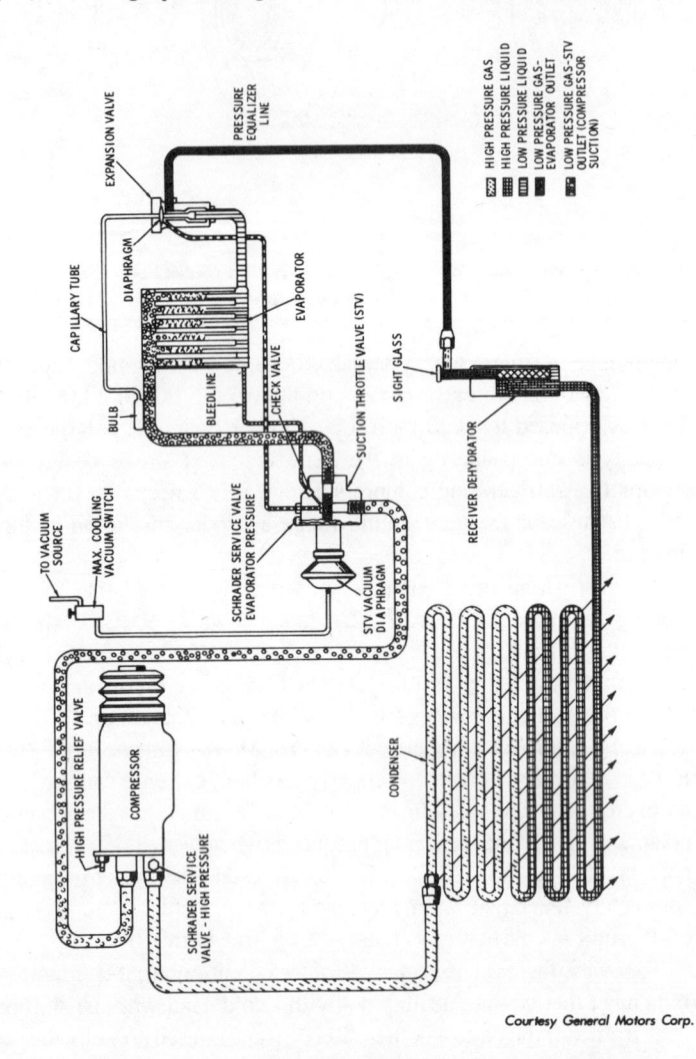

Courtesy General Motors Corp.

Fig. 4. Refrigerant circuit arrangement in a typical automobile air conditioning system.

result of being subjected to compression. As this gas passes through the condenser, the high-pressure, high-temperature gas rejects its heat to the outside air as the air passes over the surfaces of the condenser. The cooling of the gas causes it to condense into a liquid refrigerant. The liquid refrigerant, still under high-pressure, passes from the bottom of the condenser into the receiver-dehydrator. The receiver acts as a reservoir for the liquid. The liquid refrigerant flows from the receiver-dehydrator to the thermostatic expansion valve. The thermostatic expansion valve meters the high-pressure refrigerant flow into the evaporator. Since the pressure in the evaporator is relatively low, the refrigerant immediately begins to boil. As the refrigerant passes through the evaporator, it continues to boil, drawing heat from the surface of the evaporator core warmed by air passing over the surfaces of the evaporator core.

In addition to the warm air passing over the evaporator rejecting its heat to the cooler surfaces of the evaporator core, any moisture in the air condenses on the cool surface of the core, resulting in cool, dehydrated air passing into the inside of the car. By the time the gas leaves the evaporator, it has completely vaporized and is slightly superheated. Superheat is an increase in temperature of the gaseous refrigerant above the temperature at which the refrigerant vaporized. The pressure in the evaporator is controlled by the suction throttle valve. Refrigerant vapor passing through the evaporator flows through the suction throttle valve and is returned to the compressor where the refrigeration cycle is repeated.

Air Conditioning Cycle

Keep in mind the basic principles of air conditioning previously discussed. Look at Fig. 5 and follow the numbered boxes that explain what happens in each part of the air conditioning system during the complete cycle.

1. The cycle begins at the expansion valve where the refrigerant (R-12) enters as a high-pressure liquid. Immediately after the expansion valve, the refrigerant enters the evaporator as a low pressure liquid. The expansion valve is regulated by a sensing bulb, via a capillary tube, that senses the temperature of the refrigerant leaving the evaporator coil. As the temperature of this refrigerant changes, the expansion valve opens and closes to regulate the amount of refrigerant that enters the evaporator coil.

AUTOMOBILE GUIDE

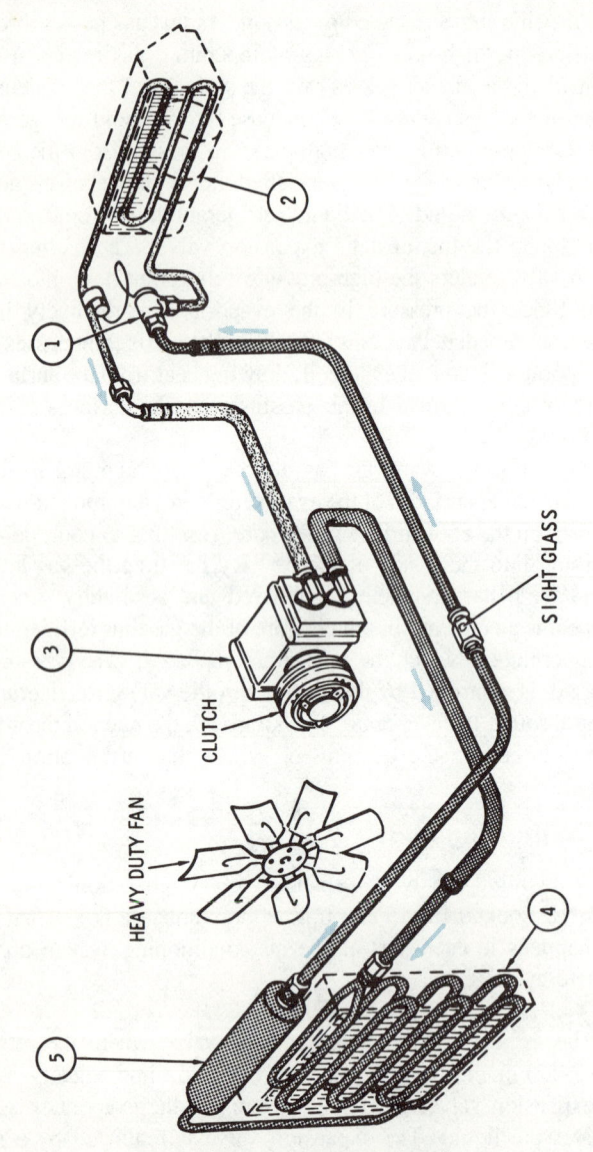

Fig. 5. The air conditioning cycle.

2. The air inside the car is blown over the evaporator fins and coil. The heat in the air goes into these fins and coil and then into the refrigerant inside the coil. The refrigerant inside the evaporator

coil is at a low pressure because it was sprayed into the evaporator through the small orifice at the expansion valve, and because the compressor is sucking it out of the evaporator. As the low pressure refrigerant absorbs the heat from the evaporator coil, it boils, turning into a gas. Since heat was taken out of the air inside the car, its temperature is lower or cooler, and the compartment becomes more comfortable. As the air continues to pass over the evaporator coil, more heat is taken out, and the air continues to get cooler.
3. The refrigerant leaves the evaporator as a low pressure gas with as much heat as it can transport for its pressure-temperature relationship. It goes into the compressor on the low pressure or suction side, is compressed into a high pressure gas and is pumped out the smaller outlet or discharge side of the compressor.
4. The refrigerant enters the condenser at a high pressure and high temperature. As it passes through the condenser coil, the outside air flowing over the coil picks up the heat from the refrigerant. This occurs because the outside air at this point has less heat than the refrigerant in the condenser coil. As this heat leaves the refrigerant, the refrigerant changes from a gas to a liquid, but it remains at a high pressure.
5. The high pressure liquid refrigerant now enters the receiver-drier where it is stored until the expansion valve calls for more. The air conditioning cycle has been completed.

During this air conditioning cycle both the sensible and latent heat have been transferred from the air inside the car to the air outside the car. This was done by changing the refrigerant from a high pressure liquid to a low pressure liquid. Each time the pressure is changed, the refrigerant either picks up or rejects heat, bringing about the heat transfer. The end result is that the air inside the car is cooler and more comfortable. We will briefly cover the component parts in the air conditioning system.

COMPONENT DESCRIPTION

The problems encountered in automobile air conditioning will perhaps be understood by a thorough study of the basic components comprising the system. Figs. 4 and 5 illustrate typical components of an automobile air conditioning unit.

Thermostatic Expansion Valve

The function of the thermostatic expansion valve is to automatically regulate the flow of liquid refrigerant into the evaporator in accordance with the requirements of the evaporator. The valve is located at the inlet to the evaporator core. It consists essentially of a capillary bulb and tube which are connected to an operating diaphragm (sealed within the valve itself) and an equalizer line which connects the valve and the low-pressure suction throttling valve outlet pressure. The thermal bulb is attached to the evaporator outlet pipe. The thermostatic expansion valve is the dividing line in the system between high-pressure liquid refrigerant supplied from the receiver and relatively low-pressure liquid and gaseous refrigerant in the evaporator. The design is such that the temperature of the refrigerant at the evaporator outlet will have 4°F to 7°F of *superheat* before more refrigerant is metered into the evaporator by the expansion valve. *Superheat* is that increase in temperature of the gaseous refrigerant above the temperature at which it vaporizes.

The remote bulb, linked to the expansion valve by a capillary tube, is "charged" with *carbon dioxide* (CO_2) or a heat-sensitive refrigerant, such as R-12. An equalizer passage or external equalizer line is provided to balance pressures on either side of the expansion valve bellows. The remote bulb is attached to the evaporator outlet pipe so it may sense the temperature of the refrigerant leaving the evaporator.

If the temperature differential (td) between the inlet and outlet of the evaporator falls below 4°F to 7°F (depending on system design) the expansion valve will automatically reduce the amount of refrigerant entering the evaporator. If the temperature differential (td) increases, the expansion valve will automatically allow more refrigerant to enter the evaporator. A typical thermostatic expansion valve, externally equalized, is shown in Fig. 6.

The temperature of the air passing over the evaporator core determines the amount of refrigerant that will enter and pass through the evaporator. When the air is very warm, the heat transfer from the air to the refrigerant is great and a greater quantity of refrigerant is required to cool the air and to achieve the proper superheat on the refrigerant gas leaving the evaporator. When the air passing over the evaporator is cool, the heat transfer is small and a smaller amount of refrigerant is required to cool the air and to achieve the proper superheat on the refrigerant gas leaving the evaporator.

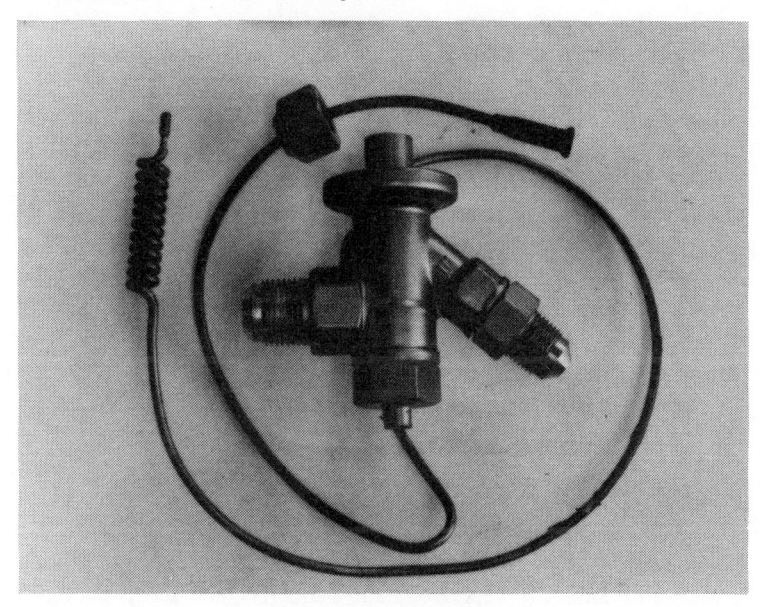

Fig. 6. Expansion valve.

A mechanical adjustment provision, located inside the thermostatic expansion valve, is used to vary the superheat setting of the valve. Adjustment varies the tension of the *superheat spring* which, in turn, alters the point at which the needle valve begins to open or close, thereby regulating refrigerant flow into the evaporator. Since this adjustment feature is inside the valve, *no external adjustment is possible.* All valves are preset at the time of manufacture.

When the air conditioning system has not been operating, all pressures within the thermostatic expansion valve assembly will have equalized at the ambient (surrounding air) temperature, thus the pressure above and below the operating diaphragm and at the inlet and outlet side of the valve will be equal. Pressure under the diaphragm is evaporator pressure. It reaches this area by means of clearance around the operating pins which connect the area under the diaphragm with the evaporator pressure area. While pressures in the expansion valve are almost equal, the addition of the valve adjusting spring pressure behind the needle will hold the needle valve over to close the needle valve orifice.

When the air conditioning system first begins to operate, the compressor will immediately begin to draw refrigerant from the evaporator, lowering the pressure in the evaporator and in the area under the operating diaphragm. As the pressure in this area decreases, the pressure above the diaphragm exerted by the carbon dioxide in the capillary tube will overcome spring pressure and push the diaphragm against the operating pins, which in turn will force the needle off its seat. Refrigerant will then pass through the expansion valve into the evaporator where it will boil at a temperature corresponding to the pressure in the evaporator. This will begin cooling the air passing over the evaporator, and it will also begin to cool the evaporator outlet pipe. The valve adjusting spring is calibrated so that the pressure of the refrigerant in the evaporator outlet pipe and equalizer line to the valve, plus the spring force, will equal the force above the operating diaphragm when the temperature of the refrigerant in the evaporator outlet is 4°F to 7°F above the temperature of the completely vaporized refrigerant in the evaporator.

In other words, the refrigerant should remain in the evaporator long enough to completely vaporize, then warm (become superheated) an additional 4°F to 7°F, depending on design superheat consideration of the system and the valve.

If the temperature differential (td) begins to go below the superheat setting of the volatile gas in the remote bulb, pressure will decrease, exerting less pressure through the capillary tube and the area above the diaphragm. This will allow the valve spring to overcome regulated pressure to move the needle valve toward its seat. This action will, in turn, reduce the amount of refrigerant entering the evaporator through the expansion valve.

Conversely, if the temperature differential (td) begins to go above the superheat setting, the reverse action will take place. Regulated pressure will overcome spring pressure and the needle valve will move away from its seat. This action will increase the amount of refrigerant entering the evaporator.

A sectional view of the thermostatic expansion valve is shown in Fig. 7. Its total purpose in the system is to regulate the flow of refrigerant entering the evaporator as determined by evaporator outlet temperature. Other factors, such as compressor size and choice of refrigerant in the thermal bulb, also affect proper expansion valve operation.

Evaporators

The purpose of the evaporator (Fig. 8) is to cool and dehumidify the air that is flowing over it when the air conditioner is in operation. High-pressure liquid refrigerant flows through the orifice in the thermostatic expansion valve into the low-pressure area of the evaporator. This regulated flow of refrigerant boils immediately. Heat from the core surface is lost to the boiling and vaporizing refrigerant which is cooler than the core, thereby cooling the core. The air passing over the evaporator loses its heat to the cooler surface of the core. As the process of heat loss from the air to the evaporator core surface is taking place, moisture in the air condenses on the outside surface of the evaporator core and is drained off.

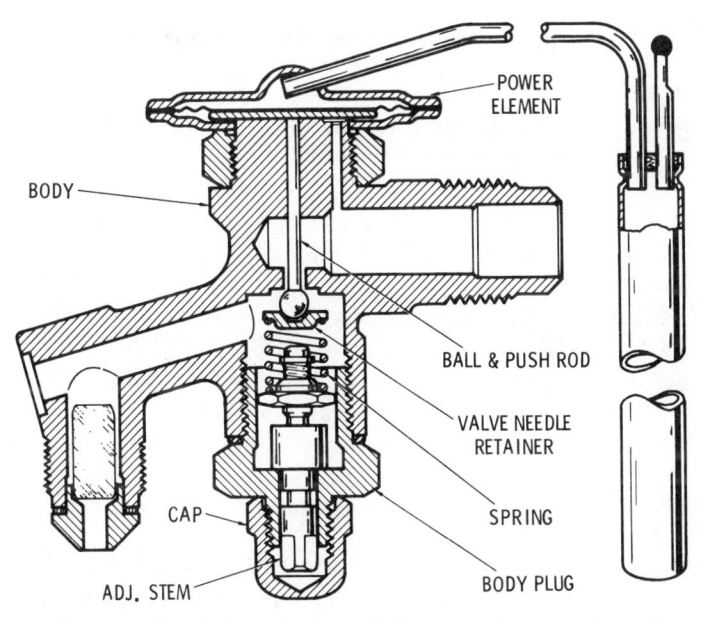

Fig. 7. Sectional view of a typical thermostatic expansion valve.

Since *R-12* will boil at 21.7° below zero F. at atmospheric pressure, and since water freezes at 32°F., it becomes obvious that the temperature in the evaporator must be controlled so that the water collecting on the core surface will not freeze in the fins of the core and block off the air passages. In order to control the temperature, it is necessary to control the amount of refrigerant entering the core, and to control the

Automobile Guide

Fig. 8. Typical automotive "hang-on" evaporator assembly.

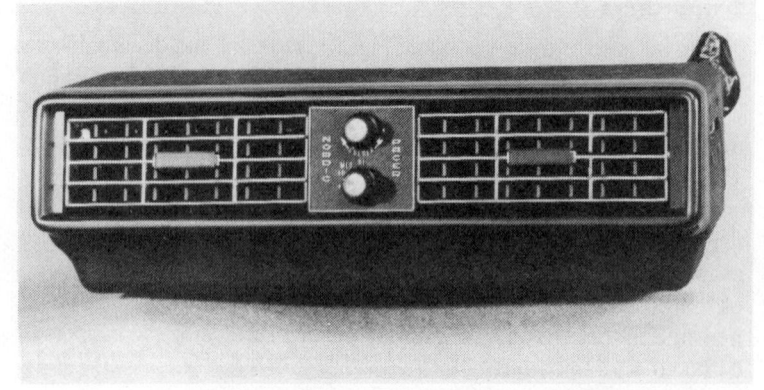

Courtesy The Tamair Company

pressure inside the evaporator. To obtain maximum cooling, the refrigerant must remain in the core long enough to completely vaporize, and then to superheat to a minimum of 4°F. If too much or too little refrigerant is present in the core, then maximum cooling efficiency is lost. A thermostatic expansion valve in conjunction with the suction throttling valve is used to provide this necessary refrigerant volume control.

Basically, there are three problems that may occur, which may result in inefficient cooling. These are as follows:

Coil Leaks — With a minimum of 50 pounds pressure (50 psig) the coil tubes may be checked for leaks with a soap suds solution. The point at which the solution bubbles usually indicated a leak in the system. Leaks are usually repaired in copper tube coils with solder bearing "trace" silver — after the refrigerant has been completely removed.

CAUTION: Using an open flame to solder any component containing even a small amount of refrigerant will create a gas called **phosgene. Phosgene gas is poisonous.** *Before any soldering operation, be certain the system or component is empty.*

Coil Tubes Blocked — If evaporator coil tubes are plugged or blocked, this will restrict the flow of refrigerant. It is recommended that a plugged or blocked coil be replaced with a new one.

Coil Fins Dirty — Dirt or lint on the fins of the evaporator coil will restrict the flow of air through the coil, and will reduce the efficiency of the heat transfer. Clean all dirty fins with a small brush and air pressure, or with water pressure.

Condensers — Air conditioning condensers are similar to the automobile radiator but are designed to withstand much higher pressure. It is normally mounted in front of the car radiator so that it receives a high volume of air. Air passing over the condenser cools the hot high-pressure refrigerant gas causing it to condense into high-pressure liquid refrigerant. Fig. 9 illustrates a typical air conditioning condenser.

Receiver-Driers

The purpose of the receiver-drier assembly is to insure a solid column of liquid refrigerant to the thermostatic expansion valve at all times (provided the system is properly charged). The dehydrator (drier) part of the assembly is to absorb any moisture that might be present in the system after assembly. Also, it traps foreign material which may have entered the system during assembly. A liquid indicator or sight glass is a part of most systems, and is an integral part of the outlet pipe of the receiver-dehydrator. The appearance of bubbles or foam in the sight glass when the ambient temperature is higher than 70° F., indicates air or a shortage of refrigerant in the system. Fig. 10 illustrates the horizontal mounted drier and Fig. 11 illustrates the vertical-mounted drier.

Compressors

In the early days of automobile air conditioning, modified commercial-type compressors were used. Because of the increase in engine speed, the design and development of precision high-speed compressors became necessary. All air conditioning system compressors are presently driven by belt take-off from the engine crankshaft. The compressor speed varies with the speed of the automobile engine, which is considerable. For example, at idling speeds, the compressor turns at a rate of about 400 r/min and develops a refrigerating effect in the area of three-quarters of a ton. In an automobile traveling 55 miles per hour, this same compressor may be turning as high as 3500 r/min and developing capacities in the neighborhood of three to three and one-half tons. This varying capacity has dictated the design of the present automotive control systems.

To obtain a more favorable speed characteristic, a different solution to the problem could be utilized, such as a drive shaft take-off, or an

Automobile Guide

Fig. 9. Typical air conditioning condenser.

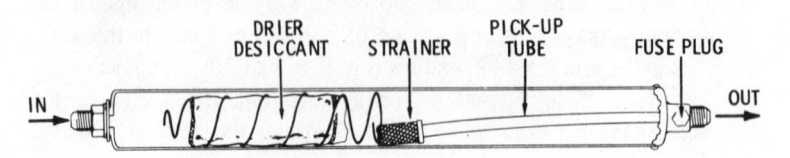

Fig. 10. Receiver-drier—horizontally mounted.

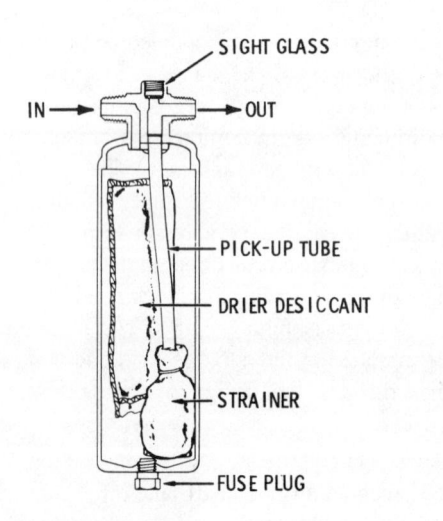

Fig. 11. Vertically mounted receiver-drier.

Automobile Air Conditioning

electric motor drive through an alternator. Although some of these methods of operating the compressor might prove more desirable in forms of operating efficiency, the additional cost of application in addition to space requirement is, without doubt, an important consideration. The compressor has two functions:

1. To pump refrigerant through the system.
2. To raise the pressure of the refrigerant gas received from the cooling coil so that it will condense more readily and give up heat as it passes through the condensing coil.

A typical automotive air conditioning compressor is shown in Fig. 12. This is one of several types of compressor that are popular for "after market" air conditioning installations. Note the exploded view of this compressor in Fig. 13. The reed-type suction and discharge valves are mounted in a valve plate between the cylinder head and main casting of the compressor. A gasket is used on either side of the valve plate to "seal" internal suction and discharge chambers.

The piston and connecting rod assemblies are secured to the crankshaft by use of connecting rod caps — much like those found on the connecting rods of the car's engine. The front end of the crankshaft is usually equipped with a roller or ball bearing while the back end of the shaft may be equipped with a bronze bushing. The shaft seal assembly is found at the front end of the crankshaft.

The oil pump assembly is found at the back end of the crankshaft. Oil is picked up from the compressor "sump" and is pumped to the internal parts. The inner gear fits over a matching "D" flat on the main shaft. The outer driven gear has internal teeth which mesh with the external teeth on the inner drive gear.

A cross-sectional view of a six-cylinder *General Motors* compressor is shown in Fig. 14. This compressor has three sets of double-ended pistons, two heads, and two valve plate assemblies. Internal cross-over passages connect the two heads (suction and discharge sections) together. Instead of the standard gaskets, the GM compressor has teflon-coated head surfaces and "O" ring seals. This compressor is usually found on factory-installed air conditioning systems.

Magnetic Clutch Control

The pulley assembly contains an electrically controlled magnetic clutch, permitting the compressor to operate only when air conditioning

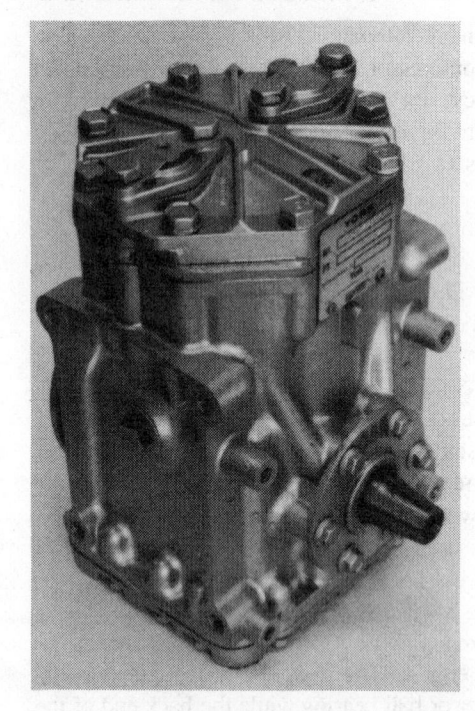

Fig. 12. A typical automobile air conditioning compressor.

is actually desired. When the compressor clutch is not engaged, the compressor shaft does not rotate, although the pulley is being rotated by the belt from the engine. The clutch armature plate, which is a movable member of the drive plate assembly, is attached to the drive hub through driver springs and is riveted to both driver and armature plate. The hub of this assembly is pressed over the compressor shaft and is aligned with a square drive key located in the keyway on the compressor shaft. The pulley assembly consists of three units:

1. Pulley rim.
2. Power element ring.
3. Pulley hub.

A friction material is molded between the hub and rim of the pulley which make up the magnetic clutch assembly. A power-element rim is embedded in the forward face of the molded material which houses the electrical coils and components that make up the electromagnet circuit.

Automobile Air Conditioning

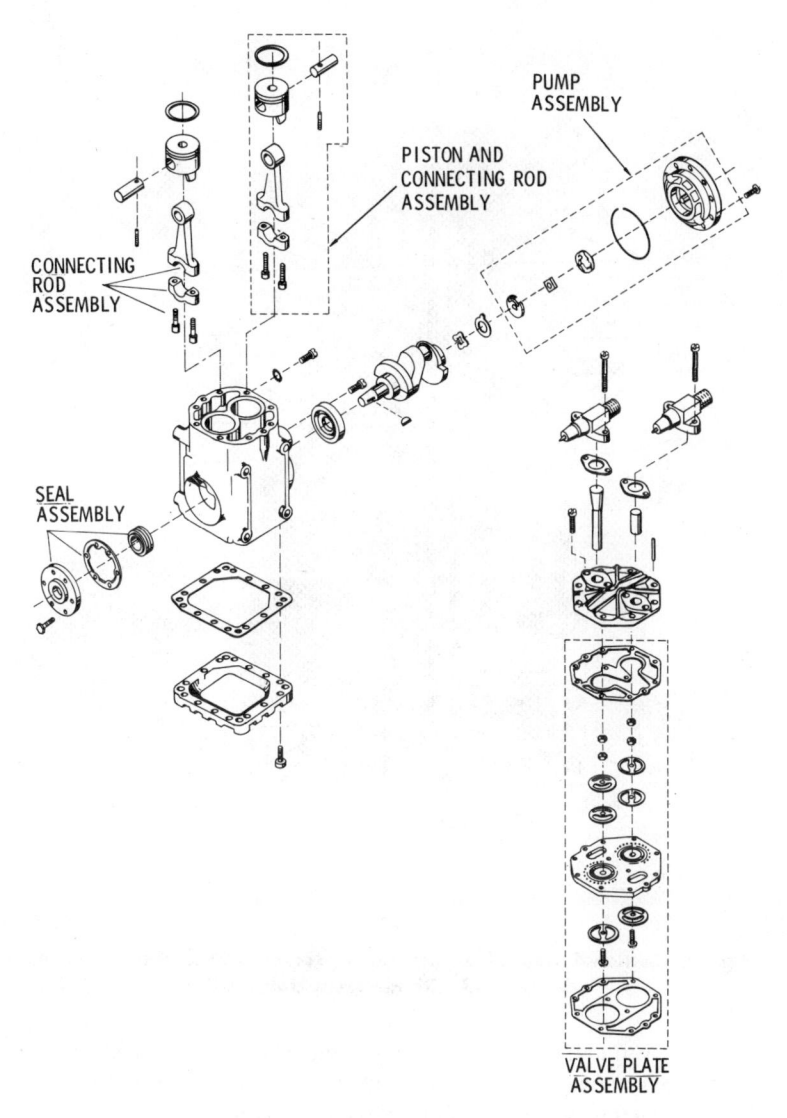

Fig. 13. Exploded view of a typical automotive compressor.

When the air conditioner controls are set for cooling, current flows through the coils, creating a magnetic force which draws the armature

743

AUTOMOBILE GUIDE

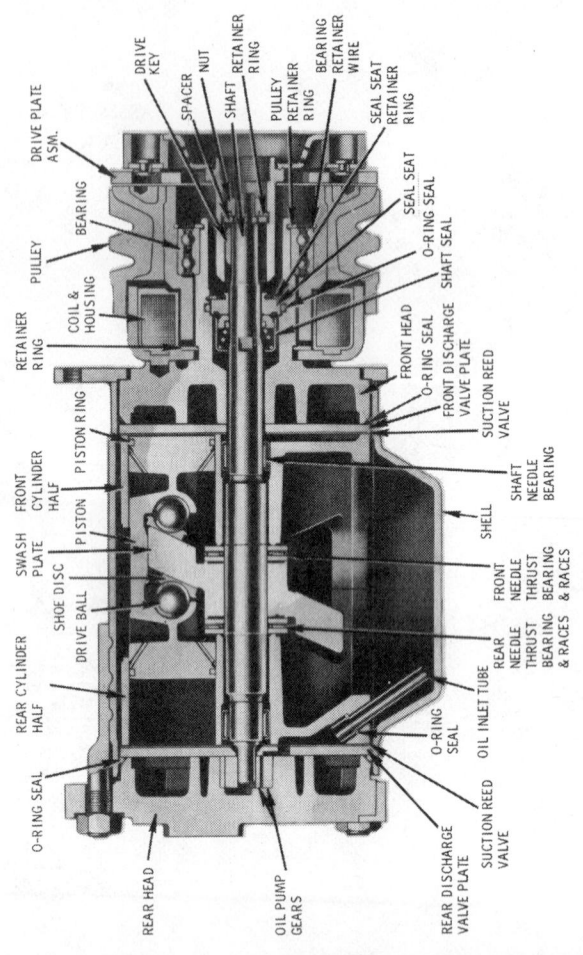

Fig. 14. Sectional view of an air compressor with double-action piston design, and with magnetic clutch coil.

plate forward to make contact with the pulley. This action magnetically locks the armature plate and the pulley together as one unit to start compressor operation. An illustration of a typical magnetic clutch assembly is shown in Fig. 15. Application of a thermostat to the return air in the evaporator provides an off-on cycle. Under extreme conditions, the rapid heat gain of the average automobile interior causes the

Automobile Air Conditioning

clutch to cycle quite often, occasionally several times a minute. Fig. 16 illustrates the various parts used in a typical magnetic clutch assembly.

Compressor-Clutch Trouble Shooting — If compressor or clutch assembly troubles are suspected, first check these units for mechanical or electrical problems, as follows:

Fig. 15. Typical magnetic clutch assembly.

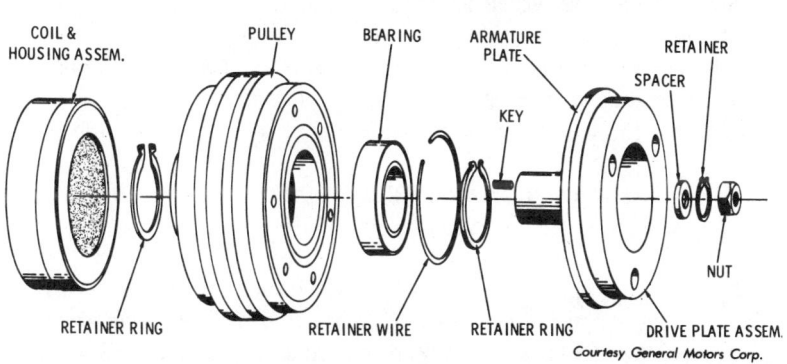

Fig. 16. A view of a magnetic clutch assembly used on automobile air conditioner compressor.

Courtesy General Motors Corp.

1. With the engine running, the blower switch ON, and the thermostatic switch turned to the coldest position, check to see if the compressor crankshaft bolt head is turning. If it is turning, the clutch operation is satisfactory, and the compressor crankshaft is turning.

745

2. If the bolt head is not turning, check for a slipping drive belt. If the belt is satisfactory, check clutch and electrical operation as follows: Disconnect lead wire at the clutch. Connect a jumper wire from the positive terminal of the battery to the disconnected lead wire (leading to the clutch). See if crankshaft bolt head turns. If it does, the clutch is operating and the trouble may be in the thermostatic switch electrical circuit (see Step 3). If the clutch does not operate check the clutch, clutch coil, or brush set (on units so equipped).
3. Before checking thermostatic switch electrical circuit, inspect for blown fuse or faulty lead wire. If satisfactory, proceed as follows: Turn blower switch ON. Then, connect one lead of a test lamp to the end of the thermostatic switch wire and the other lead to ground. If the lamp lights, the electrical circuit to the clutch assembly lead is good. If the lamp does not light, the thermostatic switch or lead wire is faulty.

Blower and Switch

The blower assembly consists of an electric motor and one or two blower wheels. The wheels are mounted on one or both ends of a shaft extending out from the side of the motor case.

The blower wheels will not wear out; however, they could become damaged through carelessness or by accident. If the blower wheels are incorrectly located on the motor shaft, they may contact and rub the case.

The blower switch controls the voltage to the blower motor. If trouble in the switch or motor is suspected, check for cause as follows:

1. Check for blown fuse, faulty lead wire insulation, or broken wire. Check for full voltage at wire leading to switch. Turn on switch and check voltage at output side of switch. If there is a measurable difference in voltage, replace switch. If switch is satisfactory, test motor and check lead wires.
2. Inspect lead wires (from switch to motor) for poor insulation or breaks. For motors that have two or more lead wires, make sure that the ground connection lead from motor to car chassis is good.
3. Test motor by connecting test lead wires from car battery to each of the motor leads. Each lead wire is for different speeds, if equipped with more than two wires. Connect battery to each wire, one at a time, and check motor for operating and for speed

variations. If found to be defective, many small motors cannot be repaired and must be replaced as a unit.

Thermostatic Switch

In many cars with hang-on type air conditioners, the thermostatic switch is used to control the evaporator coil temperature which, in turn, controls the temperature of the air flowing from the evaporator coil. This is accomplished as follows: The thermostatic switch is connected to a temperature sensing tube. The tube is inserted between the evaporator coil fins and held tightly in place by the pressure of the fins. The sensing tube senses the fin temperature, operating the thermostatic switch, which, in turn, starts or stops the flow of current to the clutch. The clutch starts or stops the compressor from pumping refrigerant through the evaporator coil.

If the thermostatic switch troubles are suspected, there may be three possible causes. These are:

1. The sensing tube may be loose in the evaporator coil fins and not sensing the temperature correctly.
2. The contact points may be stuck together and not opening and closing.
3. The sensing tube may have lost its charge.

If the sensing tube or switch is found to be faulty, the thermostatic switch should be replaced as an assembly.

Evaporator Pressure Controls

Evaporator temperature of many factory-installed air conditioning systems is attained by some type of evaporator pressure control device. In *Frigidaire* systems the device, called a *suction throttling valve*, or *positive operated absolute suction throttling valve* is located at the outlet of the evaporator coil. In *Chrysler Airtemp* systems, the device, called a evaporator pressure regulator or evaporator temperature regulator is located inside the compressor — in a cavity under the suction service valve.

The suction throttling valve, illustrated in Fig. 17, consists of a valve body, piston, piston diaphragm, control spring, diaphragm cover, diaphragm cap, and vacuum diaphragm. The suction throttle controls the evaporator pressure and the evaporator outlet temperature. The inside of the piston is hollow and is open to the piston diaphragm

AUTOMOBILE GUIDE

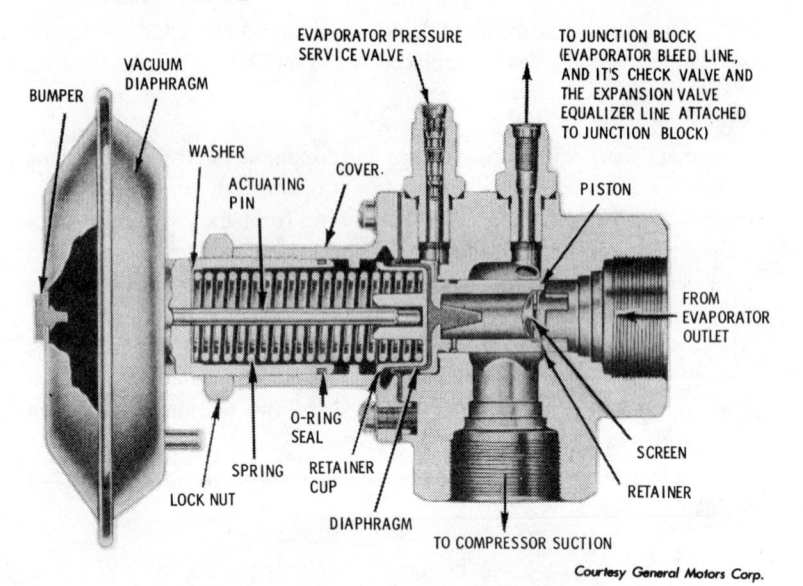

Fig. 17. Typical suction throttle valve.

through small holes in the end of the piston. Located in the lower extremity of the piston is a fine mesh screen held in place by a retainer. The purpose of this screen is to prevent any foreign particles from entering the piston and lodging in the holes drilled in the piston walls.

The piston diaphragm is held in position by the piston on the front side, and by a retainer cup and spring on the rear side. The vacuum diaphragm actuating pin fits in the end of the cup. The body of the vacuum diaphragm threads into the valve cover and determines the amount of spring tension on the cup. The vacuum diaphragm is locked to the cover after it has been set by a lock nut. A vacuum connection on the vacuum diaphragm housing is connected to the vacuum modulator on the instrument panel by a small hose. When vacuum is present on the diaphragm, it is pulled toward the piston and adds spring pressure to the piston diaphragm.

The flow of the low-pressure vapor from the evaporator to the compressor is determined and controlled by the position of the piston in the valve body of the suction throttle valve. The position of the piston in the body is determined by the balance of the forces that are applied to the piston diaphragm. These forces consist of the refrigerant vapor pressure returning from the evaporator on one side and the spring

Automobile Air Conditioning

tension, plus the force of the actuating pin if vacuum is present at the vacuum diaphragm on the other side. Movement of the piston permits vapor to pass by scallops in the piston skirt and then on to the compressor inlet.

During the time that maximum cooling is being produced, the suction throttle valve vacuum diaphragm does not have engine vacuum applied to it. The full flow of low-pressure refrigerant vapor is being returned to the compressor to permit it to exert its full capacity on the evaporator and produce maximum cooling. Under most all operating conditions, the suction throttle-valve inlet and outlet pressures will not be the same, as there will be some throttling to prevent evaporator icing. When the operator desires to raise the temperature within the car, the controls are changed to apply engine vacuum to the vacuum diaphragm. This checks or throttles the flow of the low-pressure vapor returning to the compressor. This results in a higher pressure to be maintained in the evaporator assembly. The suction throttle valve outlet pressure will also increase, but the differential between inlet and outlet will be much greater than when the suction throttle valve is at maximum cooling.

Air Distribution

The air is introduced in the car by various outlets, depending upon the various types and models. The air conditioner distribution system also varies, but is entirely separate from the car-heater distribution system. The air conditioner distribution ducts are usually located forward of the car heater ducts, with one end positioned against the evaporator housing.

Air Conditioner Control System

The operator controls the unit through switches located on the instrument panel or on the evaporator case, depending upon the installation procedure. Follow the manufacturer's instructions for proper operation.

SERVICE AND MAINTENANCE

Since automobile air conditioners do not differ in any important respect from those encountered in home air conditioners, as far as the refrigeration cycle is concerned, such common procedures as evacuating, charging, leak charging, compressor testing, and other standard refrigeration service procedures will be discussed in this chapter.

Testing, adjusting, repairing, and replacement procedures vary for many parts of the system — a different procedure for most every type and style system. For specific procedures manufacturer's specifications should be followed.

Correct Handling of Refrigerant

Safety glasses should be worn to protect the eyes because Refrigerant-12 (R-12) boils, or evaporates, at $-21.7°$ F and may feeeze areas where it contacts. Treat any affected areas where liquid R-12 has been in contact with the skin as frostbite. Flush the affected areas with warm water.

Never heat an R-12 container with a torch, stove, or radiator, to increase the pressure for charging. Warm water, no higher than 125° F., may be used whenever necessary. Never use a torch, weld, solder, or steam clean on or near a system unless the refrigerant has been completely discharged and evacuated. Never inhale large quantities of R-12 vapors, it acts as an anesthetic.

Never discharge the refrigerant from a system where an open flame exists. R-12, when combined with an open flame, produces a very toxic gas called *phosgene*.

Moisture and air in the system is harmful. Use care to prevent moisture-laden air from entering the system. Water is not miscible with R-12 therefore, it will freeze and block the opening in the expansion valve. Chemically, water and R-12 react to form hydrochloric or hydrofluoric acid, which will corrode the metal parts in the system. Water emulsifies lubricating oils forming a sludge which reduces system lubrication.

Immediately seal all lines and components during repairs to prevent the entrance of water. Caps and plugs should be used to close all fitting openings in lines, hoses, and components.

Handling of Lines

It is extremely important that the refrigerant lines be kept dry and clean. Whenever a connection is to be broken, clean all dirt and grease from the connection. Lines removed from the system to be used again should be capped immediately to prevent dirt and moisture from entering the line. The same is true with units in the system, such as the evaporator core, condenser, compressor, and drier.

Automobile Air Conditioning

The lines should be free of kinks that will cause restrictions to the flow of refrigerant. The lines should be carefully stored to avoid crushing or bending.

The proper size wrenches should be used in tightening fittings. Tubing that is left free to vibrate will harden and crystallize the area of the tube at the flare section so that it may become brittle and break. Always use two wrenches when tightening fittings to prevent twisting the soft copper tubing.

Gauge set lines should be kept clean and free of moisture. Always plug when not in use. The compressor lubricant container must not be left open longer than necessary as the special oil is moisture-free and will absorb moisture from the air if left uncapped.

Service Valves

Some compressors are equipped with hand shut-off service valves, though most have "Schrader" type valves. The "Schrader" type is self-opening when a gauge set is installed. This section will cover the proper operation of the hand shut-off type service valve.

The discharge and suction service valves are mounted on the compressor cylinder head. The suction and discharge lines are connected to the compressor at the valves.

The valves have, for all practical purposes, three positions. When the valve stem is turned all the way in, as shown in Fig. 18A, it is said to be "front-seated" and the valve stem closes the line port. The gauge port is open in this position.

With the valve stem turned all the way out, as shown in Fig. 18B, the valve is said to be in the "back-seated" position and the valve stem opens the line port. In this position the gauge port is closed. This is the normal operating position for the compressor service valves. The valve in the midway "cracked" position, as shown in Fig. 18C, opens both the gauge port and the line port. This is the usual service position with the gauges and manifold set installed.

Pressure Gauge Set

The gauge manifold set is used to service the system. A cutaway of the manifold set is shown in Fig. 19. The left guage is a compound gauge calibrated from 0 to about 60 lbs. pressure (0-60 psi), and from 0 to 30 inches vacuum (0-30″). The compound gauge is connected to the suction service valve to check the "low side" pressure, or in some

AUTOMOBILE GUIDE

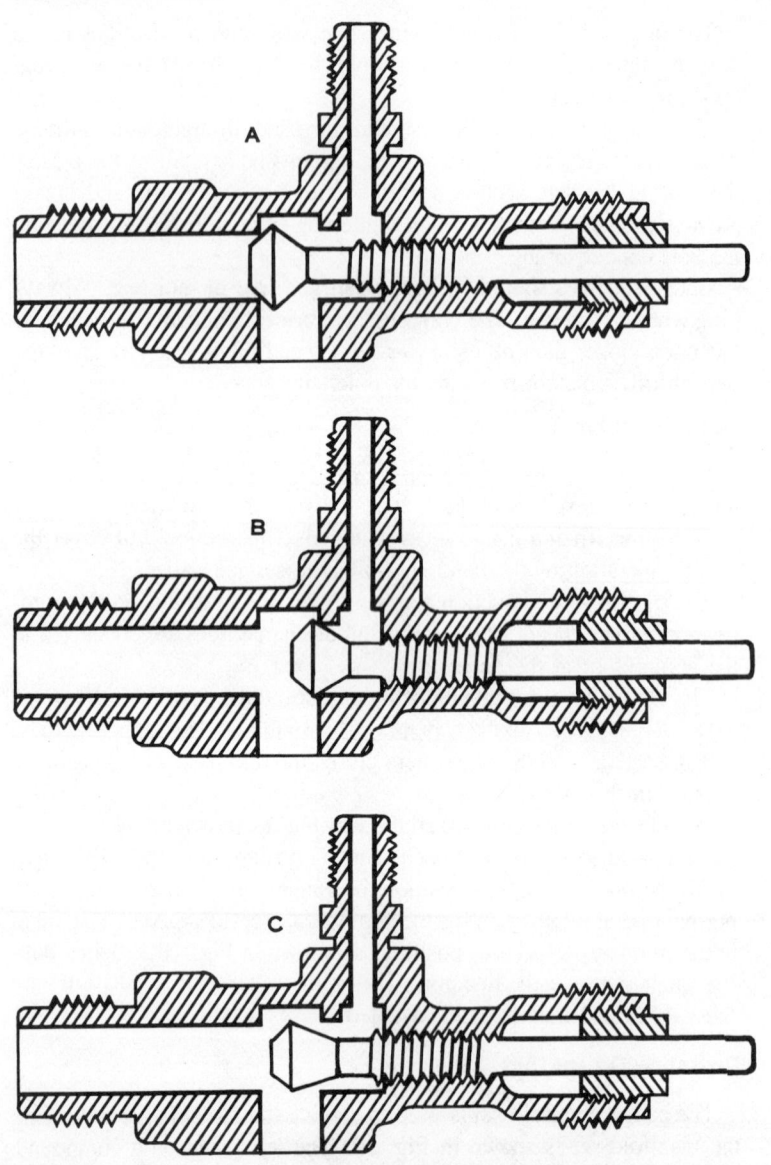

Fig. 18. Service valves; (A) Front-seated; (B) Back-seated; (C) Cracked.

cases, vacuum. The right gauge is the high pressure gauge and is calibrated from 0 to 300 lbs., or more precisely (0-300 psig).

AUTOMOBILE AIR CONDITIONING

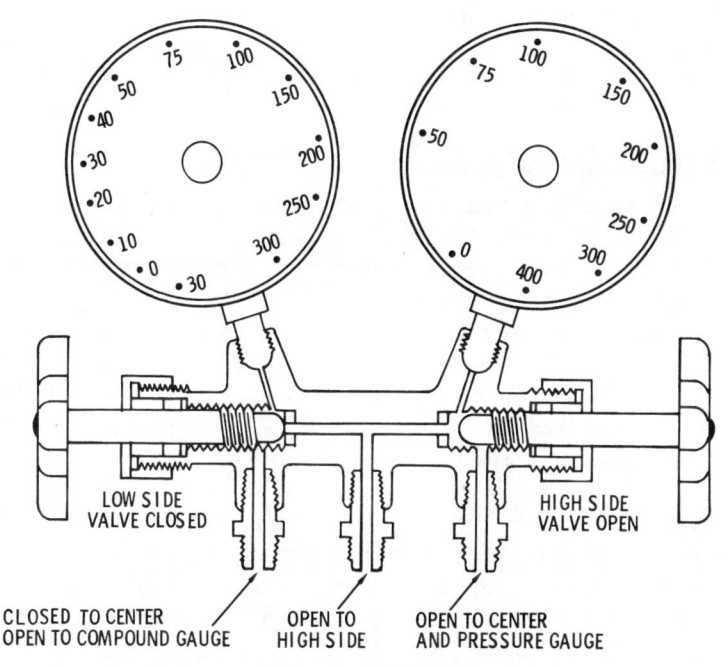

Fig. 19. Cutaway of the manifold set.

Both gauges are calibrated for 0 at sea level atmospheric pressure. Three connections are provided on the manifold. The left connection is used to connect the compound gauge to the suction service valve. The right connection is used to connect the pressure gauge to the discharge service valve. The center connection is used for servicing operations.

Both hand shut-off valves open or close the respective gauge connections to the center service connection or to each other. Pressure will be indicated on the gauges regardless of hand valve position.

Connecting Manifold Gauge Set

Close both hand valves on the gauge set. Connect the compound gauge hose to the suction compressor service valve gauge port. Connect the high pressure gauge hose to the discharge compressor service valve gauge port.

If equipped with hand shut-off service valves, "crack" both compressor service valves. The gauges will now indicate pressures in the

AUTOMOBILE GUIDE

"low" and "high" sides. If equipped with "schrader" type valves, pressures will be indicated as soon as the hoses are connected.

The air conditioner may be operated with the gauge set connected in this manner. The gauges will indicate respective operating pressures.

To Discharge The System

Connect the gauge set to the compressor service valves as indicated. Both manifold hand valves should be closed. "Crack" the high pressure manifold hand valve. The refrigerant will be released through the gauge set center service line.

Release the refrigerant charge slowly. Compressor lubricating oil is mixed with the refrigerant in the system and will be carried out with the gas if discharged too rapidly. Loss of oil should be prevented. The system must be discharged whenever lines or components are to be disconnected or replaced.

Evacuating the System

The system must be evacuated every time it has been opened for a service operation or parts replacement. Evacuation must be performed to remove moisture and air prior to charging the system.

Connect the manifold gauge set to the compressor service valves as shown in Fig. 20. Both hand valves should be in the closed position. "Crack" the suction (compound) hand valve. The system should be free of all refrigerant before beginning evacuating procedures.

Connect the center hose to the vacuum pump and start the pump. Observe vacuum on low-side guage. It should read 28" or less in a few minutes. When this vacuum is attained, close the low pressure hand valve and immediately stop the vacuum pump. The vacuum should remain constant for several minutes. If the vacuum rises it is an indication that there is a leak in the system or in a connection.

Leak Test Procedure

Connect a refrigerant supply to the gauge set center hose with the gauge set connected into the air conditioning system. Loosen the center hose connection at the manifold then "crack" the refrigerant valve. Air in the center line will be purged by the refrigerant gas. Hand tighten the hose connection.

Open the high-side manifold hand valve to admit refrigerant into the system for a partial charge. The gauge set will indicate pressure in both

Automobile Air Conditioning

sides of the system. Close the high-side hand valve when pressure reaches 45-50 psi on the gauges.

External leaks are detected with soap suds or with a *halide torch*. The *halide torch* uses propane fuel and is equipped with a probe. Air is drawn into the tube by the torch, and contacts a heated copper reactor ring in the torch. If refrigerant is present in the sampled air, the normally light blue flame will change to a green color. The color will range from a yellow to green or blue to purple according to the amount of refrigerant present, depending on the severity of the leak.

Halide Torch Operation

Open the halide torch valve slightly and light it. When the copper reactor ring is hot (glows to a cherry red) adjust the flame to about ⅜" above the reactor ring. The smaller flame is more sensitive to refrigerant.

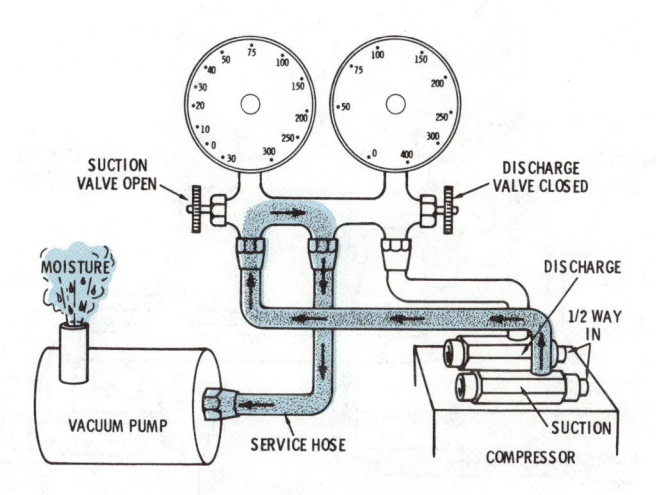

Fig. 20. Evacuating the system.

Hold the open end of the probe close to each joint and connection, passing the end around the joint. Refrigerant is heavier than air, therefore leaks may be more readily detected on the lower side of the areas being checked.

Correct all leaks; discharge, evacuate, and leak test before charging the system. Correct leaks at solder joints using silver solder and silver

Automobile Guide

solder flux. *WARNING: Never solder on the system until all refrigerant has been completely removed.*

CAUTION: Avoid breathing the poisonous fumes and black smoke produced by the torch. Refrigerant in contact with an open flame or heated metal will give off phosgene gas which is highly toxic.

Charging the System

Before charging, the system should be completely evacuated and as free as possible of all moisture and air. With the manifold set hooked into the system, connect the center hose to a refrigerant supply. Invert the refrigerant container so the vapor will push the liquid into the system. Open the high-side manifold hand valve so that refrigerant will be forced into the high side of the system, as shown in Fig. 21.

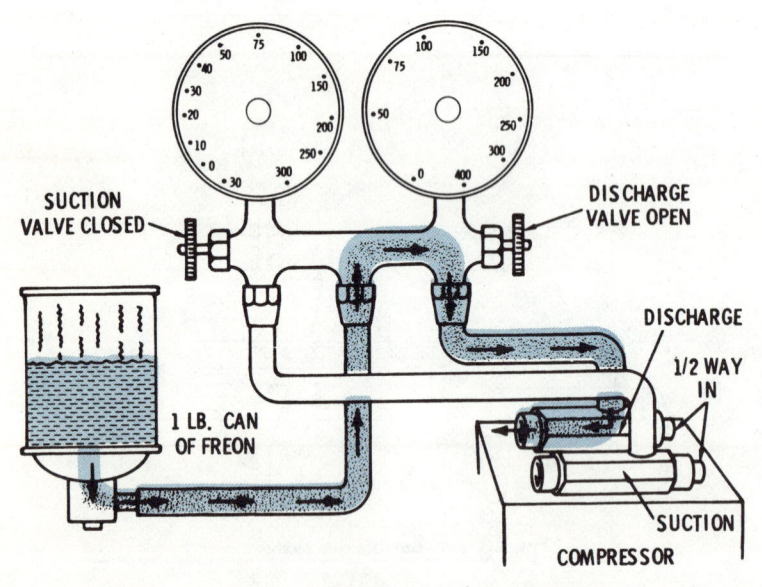

Fig. 21. Charging the system with liquid refrigerant.

WARNING: Never charge liquid refrigerant into a system while the compressor or engine is running.

If using a drum, weigh the drum prior to charging the system and while charging to insure the correct amount of charge. If using

Automobile Air Conditioning

"pound" cans, the correct charge is easier to determine. In the event the system pressure equalizes with the pressure in the can or drum before the correct amount has been installed, it will be necessary to complete the charging through the low side with the refrigerant in a gas form.

To charge in a gas (or vapor) form, turn the refrigerant container upright. It is upright when the dispensing valve is at the top. Close the high-side manifold hand valve and open the low side (compound) hand valve. Start the engine and turn on the air conditioner. Refrigerant will now enter the low side of the system in a gas form due to the action of the compressor.

CAUTION: The refrigerant container must be upright when charging in this manner. If the container is inverted, liquid refrigerant may enter and damage the compressor. Remember: Liquids cannot be compressed.

Charging the air conditioner in a gas form is shown in Fig. 22. When the correct quantity of refrigerant is in the system, close the low-side manifold hand valve and observe the pressures on both sides.

NOTE: At normal temperatures, the high-side pressure should not exceed 250 lbs. per square inch (psi). Operate the air conditioning system for 10 to 15 minutes to normalize and determine if the system will cycle and function properly.

Purging Air From System

The manifold and gauge set is not connected to the system for this procedure. The system should remain idle (off) for several minutes after the compressor has been operating before attempting to purge air. Remove the cap from the gauge port on the discharge (high side) service valve.

"Crack" the discharge service valve to slowly release air from the system. If equipped with "Schrader" type valves the system may be purged of air with a small screwdriver. The screwdriver is used to push the small pin in of the "Schrader" to allow air to escape. Take care not to damage the pin.

Automobile Guide

Compressor Belt

The compressor clutch pulley must be aligned with the engine drive pulley. The drive belt must leave and approach the pulleys in a straight

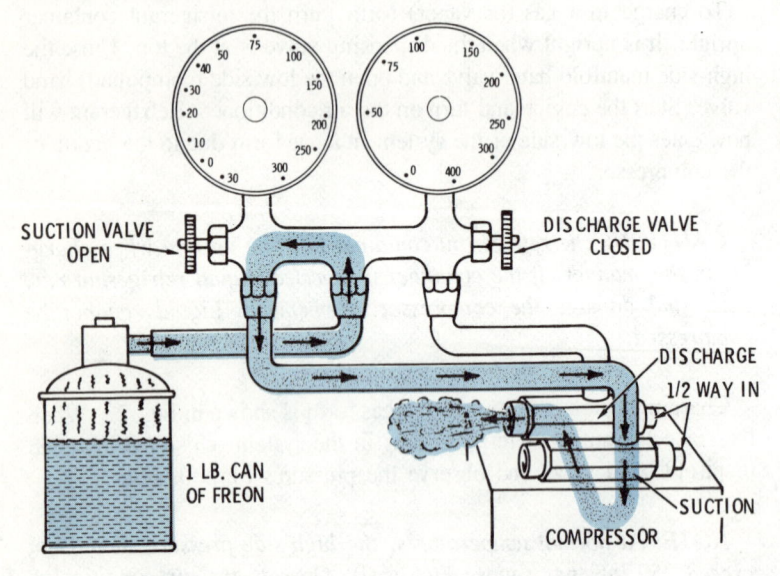

Fig. 22. Charging the system with refrigerant gas.

line. The clutch attaching bolt should be tightened to 18-22 ft.-lbs. of torque. Belt tension is usually tightened by an idler pulley. A belt tension gauge may be used to accurately gauge belt tension. Install the belt tension gauge on the longest belt span and tighten belt to 70-80 lbs. If a belt tension gauge is not available, proper tensioning may be obtained by tightening until there is ⅜" to ½" deflection at the longest span.

Insufficient or No Cooling

In a system incorporating a magnetic clutch and thermostatic switch, the first check is to make certain that the compressor is running. The electrical system should also be checked. The condition and tension of the belt should be checked; in fact, correct tension on the belt is one of the most important service checks to be made. The tremendous load and high speed of these belts mean they must be kept very tight. Deflection of the belt between pulleys should not be over one-quarter of an inch. If a belt is replaced, this deflection should be checked after about one-half hour running period, and tightened again if necessary.

Air Output Not Normal

When it has been determined that the compressor is operating properly, blowers should be checked to make certain they are delivering air. The blower control should be set at high. The temperature control level (if there is one) should be set at maximum cooling. Insufficient discharge of air would indicate an obstruction in the evaporator, or electrical problems with the blower motor.

Air Output Normal

Assuming that actual air delivery at the discharge grill is about normal (around 300 cfm), the next check is the position of the bypass dampers. It is a well-known fact that the condensation of the refrigerant depends upon air passing over the condenser as the automobile travels on the road. To simulate this condition in the shop, a large fan should be placed in front of the car. Head-pressure readings will vary somewhat with the ambient air temperatures. A fast idle (about 1500 r/min) and an ambient temperature of 75°F should result in a normal head pressure of about 140 psig. For every 1°F increase in the ambient temperature, an increase of about 2.5 psig will occur. In a shop situation, without adequate "ram" air, high ambient temperature (110°F or higher) could result in head pressures as high as 300 psig. Extreme head pressures may also indicate one of the following:

1. Overcharge of refrigerant.
2. Engine overheating.
3. Air in the system.
4. Overcharge of oil.
5. Dirt or debris on the condenser.
6. Defective (clogged) drier.

Complete removal of air from the refrigerating system, by means of a vacuum pump, is essential for two reasons:

1. To prevent excessive head pressures when the air volume over the condenser is low.

2. To prevent decomposition of the oil which is accelerated by the normally higher operating temperatures encountered in these systems.

It is not too uncommon to find that an inexperienced person has serviced the air conditioning system and overcharged it, causing a high head pressure.

Checking Suction Pressures

Suction pressures normally run about 16 to 25 psig at 75°F. Any wide variation from these pressures indicates the usual service problems resulting from this condition. Abnormally high suction pressures indicate wide-open expansion valves, a loose feeler bulb, or leaky compressor valves. Valve plates usually can be replaced on these compressors. The normal refrigeration procedures for checking compressor operation are recommended.

Checking Control Systems

Refrigerant control of the air conditioning system will be by one of the following means:

1. Thermostatic expansion valve only.
2. Thermostatic expansion valve with suction pressure control device.
3. Expansion tube with suction accumulator.

Special features of some of these control devices may dictate variations from normal refrigeration service practices. Manufacturer's specifications, found in specific service manuals, should be consulted for specific testing procedures and pressures.

Air Distribution

If an air conditioner distribution system is not functioning properly, first check the vacuum hose connections, the control cable, and vacuum switch adjustments. If the controls and cables operate properly, check for vacuum at valve diaphragms, for proper functioning of the vacuum switches, and for the correct position of the air valves. If the air flow changes or shuts off when the car is accelerating, check for a faulty valve at the intake manifold. If there is no vacuum to the suction throttle valve when the cool switch is on, check for a disconnected vacuum hose at the vacuum modulator.

Defective Compressor

Compressor malfunctioning will appear in one of four ways:

1. Noise.
2. Seizure.
3. Leakage.
4. Low discharge pressures.

Resonant compressor noises are no cause for excessive alarm, but irregular noises or rattles are likely to indicate broken parts. Seizure will be indicated by the failure of the compressor to operate, if the clutch is in good operating condition and there is no break in the electrical system. (A wiring diagram of a typical automobile air conditioner is shown in Fig. 23.) Continued operation of a partially seized compressor will result in damage to the clutch. To check for seizure, de-energize the clutch and attempt to rotate the compressor by using a wrench on the compressor shaft. If the shaft will not turn, the compressor is seized. Leakage of compressor refrigerant may be detected through routine leak detection. Low discharge pressures may also be caused by insufficient refrigerant or a restriction elsewhere in the system. These should be checked out prior to compressor servicing.

Compressor Clutch

If the compressor is inoperative, the electrical lead to the clutch should be checked first. If there is current to the clutch and the compressor is not seized, the clutch coil or the clutch is defective and should be repaired or replaced as necessary.

Condenser

There are two types of possible condenser malfunction. The condenser may leak, resulting in loss of refrigeration and a low system pressure. The condenser may also have a restriction, resulting in excessive compressor discharge pressures and inadequate cooling. If a restriction occurs and some refrigerant passes the restriction, icing or frost may occur on the external surface of the condenser in the area of the restriction. If the air flow through the condenser is restricted or blocked, high discharge pressures will result. It is important that the external fins of the condenser and radiator core are not plugged with bugs, dirt, etc.

Automobile Guide

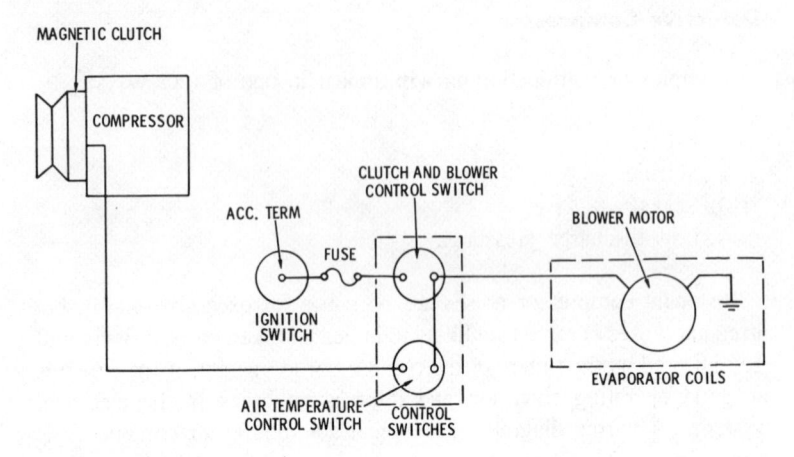

Fig. 23. Schematic wiring diagram of an electrical circuit in a typical automobile air conditioner.

Thermostatic Expansion Valve

If malfunction of the valve is suspected, make sure the power element bulb is in proper position, securely attached, and well insulated from the outside air temperatures. If the thermostatic expansion valve fails, it usually fails in the power element and the valve remains closed. This will be indicated by low high-side or discharge pressures. Also the inlet screen could be plugged. The screen may be cleaned with liquid refrigerant.

Evaporator

Dirt or other foreign matter on the core surface or in the evaporator housing will restrict the air flow. A cracked or broken housing can result in leakage of cold air and can result in insufficient air or warm air delivered to the passenger compartment.

Refrigerant Lines

Restrictions in the refrigerant lines may be indicated as follows:

1. High-pressure liquid line (low head pressure, no cooling).
2. Suction line (low suction pressure, low head pressure, little or no cooling).
3. Discharge line (compressor blow-off).

AUTOMOBILE AIR CONDITIONING

4. Receiver-drier (Leakage of refrigerant indicates a defective unit. This cannot easily be checked, but if the system has been exposed to outside air for a considerable length of time, the unit should be replaced).

Restrictions in the receiver-drier can also cause system malfunction. If the inlet tube is blocked, it is likely to result in high head pressure. If the outlet tube is blocked, head pressure is likely to be low and there will be little or no cooling.

Suction Throttle Valve

If the suction throttle valve is defective, it may cause evaporator pressure to be too high (air outlet temperature too warm) or it could cause the evaporator pressure to be too low (air outlet temperature too low which may cause icing of the evaporator core). If the vacuum diaphragm of the suction throttle valve is defective, there would be no means to change (increase) the air outlet temperature. Refrigerant leakage of the suction throttle valve may be detected through routine leak detection.

Before servicing the suction throttle valve, it should be determined that it is actually the cause of the complaint. If evaporator pressure remains too high when checking and adjusting the suction throttle valve, the low-pressure gauge line should be attached to the valve located on the compressor suction line. If the compressor suction pressure is too high, the compressor or possibly the thermostatic expansion valve may be the cause of the trouble.

Use of Receiver Sight Glass for Diagnosis

A clear sight glass will indicate a properly charged refrigeration system. The occurrence of slow moving gas bubbles, or a broken column of refrigerant for momentary periods during normal operation, should not be considered an indication of refrigerant shortage if the sight glass is generally clear and performance is satisfactory. The tendency of the sight glass to indicate refrigerant shortage when the system is under light load should be considered.

If the sight glass consistently shows foaming or a broken liquid column, it should be observed after partially blocking the air to the condenser. If under this condition the sight glass clears, and the performance is otherwise satisfactory, the charge shall be considered adequate. In all instances where the indications of refrigerant shortage continues, additional refrigerant should be added in ¼ lb. increments until the sight glass is clear. An additional charge of ½ lb. should be added as a reserve. In no case should the system be overcharged.

INSTALLATION PROCEDURE

There are two ways to acquire automobile air conditioning:

1. Factory installations.
2. Universal-type installations.

Factory installed air conditioners are furnished with the car, usually with instructions for its proper maintenance and operation. In such installations there are several types of evaporator assemblies. Many such installations combine the heating system with the cooling system, as shown in Fig. 24, with the evaporator coil and heater core located in the same enclosure. One significant service problem that should be pointed out here is the function of the bypass dampers.

A common complaint of no cooling is corrected by proper adjustment of the bypass dampers. In many installations they are controlled by cables, which operate dampers to furnish outside or recirculated air. These control cables are connected to a control panel in such a way that the combined functions are accomplished or controlled through a single lever. A more recent refinement in damper controls is shown in Fig. 25. Here, vacuum actuators are used with pushbutton control. Installations of this type mean that servicemen must thoroughly acquaint themselves with the basic operating principle governing this type of control. They are similar in many respects to those controls used in pneumatic-controlled air conditioning systems.

The evaporator housings resemble the old-fashioned car heaters that were suspended under the dash. This construction, popular with independent automotive air conditioner manufacturers, simplifies installation. Its operating characteristics are the same as factory-installed units. Fig. 26 illustrates a typical automotive air conditioning system condenser, which is usually located in front of the radiator. Circulation of air over the condenser depends upon either ram air resulting from the forward movement of the car, or from air drawn across the unit by the engine fan.

Automobile Air Conditioning

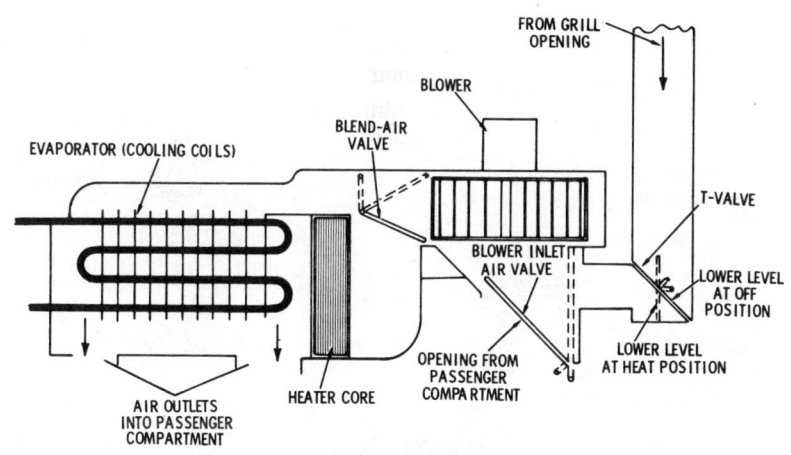

Fig. 24. Schematic diagram which shows the heating and cooling coil arrangements.

It is interesting to note that head pressures vary on the highway when the car travels with or against the wind. When traveling "downwind," head pressure usually runs 10 to 15 lbs. higher than when traveling against the wind. Most road tests, however, have proven that the condenser does not materially affect temperature of the car engine. One major problem encountered is the head pressure increasing substantially when the engine is left idling, such as in slow moving or stalled traffic. Normally, air circulation over the condenser is supplied by the forward movement of the car; at high speeds, the ram effect of this air does an adequate job of cooling the condenser. At more moderate speeds, the fan draws sufficient air over the condenser to keep head pressures normal, but when the car is stalled or is traveling very slowly, air volume is not sufficient to keep head pressures within operating limits. Some systems provide a *fast-idling* control, which increases the engine speed sufficiently to supply air over the condenser.

Location of the condenser in front of the car contributes to accumulation of dirt and debris on the finned surface. Recently developed service tools for effectively cleaning finned surfaces are available. Also shown in Fig. 26 is the system receiver. An innovation is encountered here through the frequent practice of placing a drier core within the receiver, thus resulting in a combination receiver-drier unit. This construction may pose a question to some servicemen. With the drier located within the receiver, how can this component be replaced?

AUTOMOBILE GUIDE

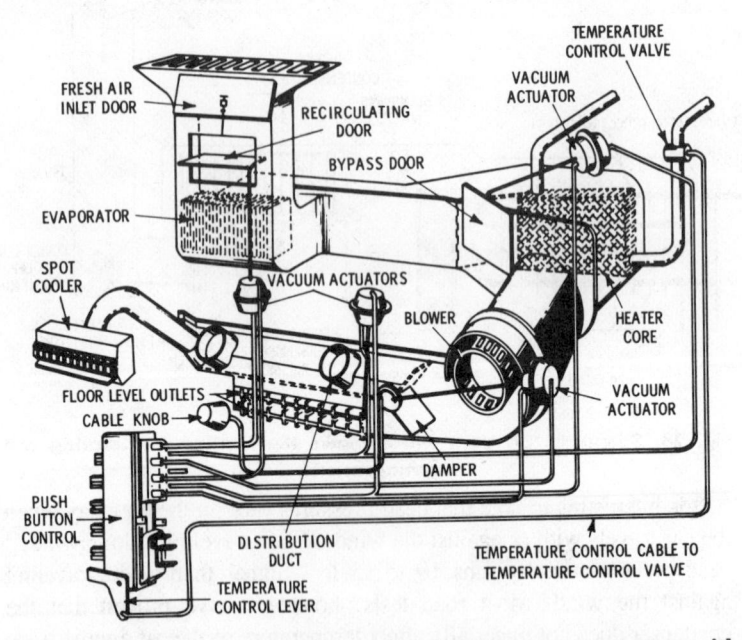

Fig. 25. Typical damper control assembly showing vacuum actuators with pushbutton controls.

Since present automobile air conditioning systems make no provision to "pump down" the unit, there is no need for a liquid line valve. The only valves available are the suction and discharge service valves at the compressor. This simply means that if any service operation is required away from the compressor itself, the refrigerant must be removed from the system. The drier cartridge inside the receiver also usually provides a filter. Many times this is the only filter or screen in the system since the expansion valve is not always equipped with a screen.

TROUBLE CHART

The trouble chart which follows lists the most common operating faults along with possible causes and suggested checks and correction for each. This chart is intended to provide a quick reference to the cause and correction of a specific fault.

AUTOMOBILE AIR CONDITIONING

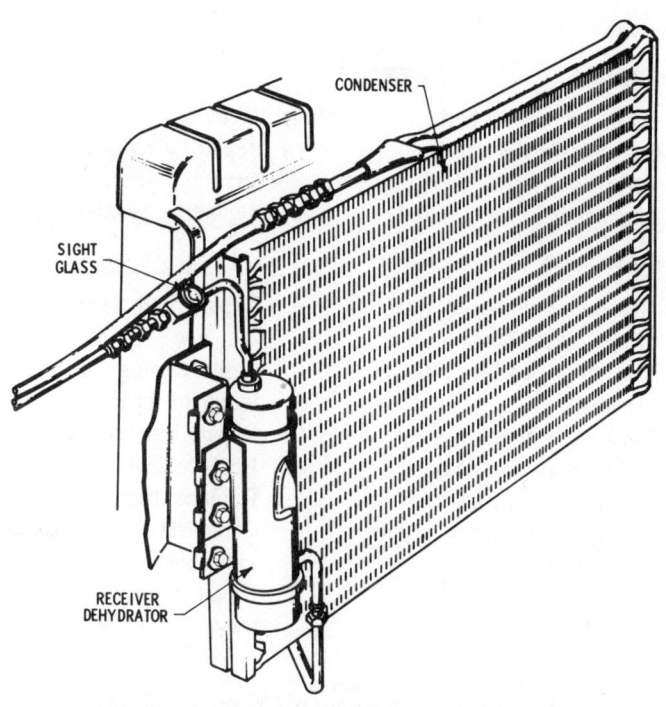

Fig. 26. Condenser and receiver installation in a typical automobile air conditioner system.

AIR CONDITIONING TROUBLES AND REMEDIES

Symptoms and Possible Causes

Electrical

(a) Blown fuse.
(b) Broken or disconnected electrical wire.

(c) Clutch coil defective or disconnected.
(d) Thermostat defective.
(e) Blower motor defective.

Possible Remedies

(a) Replace fuse.
(b) Check all wiring for loose connections. Check wiring for hidden breaks.
(c) Check voltage at clutch. Replace coil if defective.
(d) Replace thermostat.
(e) Replace or repair blower motor.

Automobile Guide

Symptoms and Possible Causes *Possible Remedies*

Mechanical

(a) Loose or broken belt.
(b) Compressor defective.

(c) Expansion valve defective.

(a) Tighten or replace belt.
(b) Repair or replace compressor.
(c) Replace expansion valve.

Refrigeration

(a) Broken or damaged refrigerant line or hose.
(b) Defective fusible plug in system.
(c) Leak in system.
(d) Compressor seal leaking.
(e) Clogged screen in drier.
(f) Clogged screen in expansion valve.
(g) Plugged hose or coil.

(a) Repair or replace refrigerant line.
(b) Replace plug (do not attempt to repair).
(c) Repair leak as necessary.
(d) Replace seal.
(e) Replace drier.
(f) Clean screen in expansion valve and replace drier.
(g) Clean or replace as necessary.

System Produces Insufficient Cooling

Electrical

(a) Blower motor "sluggish."

(b) Clutch slipping.

(c) Clutch cycles too often.

(a) Repair or replace blower motor.
(b) Check voltage at clutch; if correct replace clutch.
(c) Check thermostat for proper operation. Replace thermostat if not correct.

Mechanical

(a) Compressor clutch slipping.
(b) Low volume of air flow.

(a) Check voltage at clutch. If correct, replace clutch.
(b) Check for clogged evaporator coil. Clean evaporator coil.

AUTOMOBILE AIR CONDITIONING

Symptoms and Possible Causes	*Possible Remedies*
(c) Not enough air flow over condenser.	(c) Check for dirt or bugs. Clean if necessary. Install heavy duty fan or reposition condenser.
(d) Temperature control unit defective.	(d) Adjust temperature control unit, or replace as necessary.

Refrigeration

(a) Low refrigeration charge.	(a) Charge system until bubbles disappear from sight glass.
(b) Expansion valve thermal bulb loose.	(b) Clean "contact area" and tighten thermal bulb.
(c) Partially clogged screen in drier.	(c) Replace drier.
(d) Partially clogged screen in expansion valve.	(d) Clean screen in expansion valve and replace drier.
(e) Moisture in system.	(e) Purge system of refrigerant, replace drier and recharge.
(f) Air in system.	(f) Purge system of refrigerant, and recharge.
(g) Excess refrigerant in system.	(g) Purge system until refrigerant capacity correct.
(h) Thermostat defective.	(h) Replace thermostat.

System Cools Intermittently

Electrical

(a) Defective circuit breaker.	(a) Replace circuit breaker.
(b) Defective blower switch or motor.	(b) Repair or replace defective part.
(c) Defective clutch coil or brush set.	(c) Replace defective part.
(d) Loose ground connection to blower motor or clutch coil.	(d) Correct as necessary.

AUTOMOBILE GUIDE

Symptoms and Possible Causes	Possible Remedies
(e) Loose connection in wiring harness, or wiring.	(e) Correct as necessary.

Mechanical

(a) Clutch slipping.	(a) Check voltage at clutch. If correct, replace clutch.

Refrigeration

(a) Moisture in system.	(a) Replace drier.
(b) Expansion valve improperly adjusted.	(b) Readjust or replace expansion valve.
(c) Thermostat improperly adjusted or defective.	(c) Adjust or replace thermostat.
(d) Defective or sticking temperature control valve.	(d) Repair or replace temperature control valve.

Noisy System

Electrical

(a) Defective connection at clutch coil.	(a) Repair as necessary.
(b) Defective clutch coil.	(b) Check voltage at coil; if correct, replace coil.

Mechanical

(a) Loose or worn drive belts.	(a) Tighten or replace belts.
(b) Noisy clutch.	(b) Check voltage at coil; if correct, replace clutch rotor.
(c) Noisy compressor.	(c) Check mounting and clutch for tightness. Tighten as necessary. If tight, repair or replace compressor.
(d) Loose panels in car.	(d) Check and tighten as necessary.
(e) Blower fan rubbing.	(e) Adjust blower fan(s) as necessary.

AUTOMOBILE AIR CONDITIONING

Symptoms and Possible Causes *Possible Remedies*

(f) Wear in blower motor.
(g) Idler bearing defective.

(f) Replace blower motor.
(g) Replace idler bearing and/or pulley.

Refrigeration

(a) Excess charge of refrigerant.
(b) Moisture in system.
(c) Low charge of refrigerant.

(a) Purge refrigerant until correct.
(b) Replace drier.
(c) Add refrigerant until sight glass is clear.

Gauge Pressure Readings

(a) Suction pressure LOW
    Head pressure NORMAL

(a) Defective thermostat.
    Expansion valve screen clogged.
    Restriction between drier and expansion valve.
    Moisture in system.
    Defective expansion valve.

(b) Suction pressure HIGH.
    Head pressure NORMAL

(b) Defective expansion valve.
    Loose thermal bulb on expansion valve.
    Defective thermostat.

(c) Suction pressure HIGH.
    Head pressure LOW

(c) Defective compressor.
    Defective compressor reed valve(s).

(d) Suction pressure HIGH.
    Head pressure HIGH.

(d) Air in system.
    Excessive refrigerant in system.
    Excess oil in system.
    Air flow across condenser blocked or restricted.
    Restriction in drier, condenser, or high pressure lines and hoses.
    Engine overheating.

CHAPTER 30

Tables and Charts

The following conversion tables may be used to conveniently convert english measure into metric measure or metric measure into english measure.

CONVERSION TABLES

All tables give conversion measure from 1 unit to 99 units. The column across the top is for units (1, 2, 3, 4, etc). The column at the left of the table is for tens of units (10, 20, 30, 40, etc).

To find the conversion of feet to meters for, say, 27 feet first locate two-tens of units (20) in the left column, then seven units (7) in the top column. Read to the right at 20 and down at 7. Where the two lines intersect is the conversion.

In the example given the conversion is 34 kilometers to miles. Note the intersecting line from three-tens of units in the left column to four units in the top column. The conversion is 21.127 miles.

km	0	1	2	3	4	5	6	7	8	9
	mil	mil	mil	mil	mil	mil	mil	mil	mil	mil
		0.621	1.243	1.864	2.486	3.107	3.728	4.350	4.971	5.592
10	6.214	6.835	7.457	8.078	8.699	9.321	9.942	10.562	11.185	11.805
20	12.427	13.049	13.670	14.292	14.913	15.534	16.156	16.776	17.399	18.019
30	18.641	19.263	19.884	20.506	21.127	21.748	22.370	22.990	23.613	24.233
40	24.855	25.477	26.098	26.720	27.341	27.962	28.584	29.204	29.827	30.447
50	31.069	31.690	32.311	32.933	33.554	34.175	34.797	35.417	36.040	36.660
60	37.282	37.904	38.525	39.147	39.768	40.389	41.011	41.631	42.254	42.874
70	43.497	44.118	44.739	45.361	45.982	46.603	47.225	47.845	48.468	49.088
80	49.711	50.332	50.953	51.575	52.196	52.817	53.439	54.059	54.682	55.302
90	55.924	56.545	57.166	57.788	58.409	59.030	59.652	60.272	60.895	61.515

Table 1. Kilometers To Miles

km	0	1	2	3	4	5	6	7	8	9
	mil	mil	mil	mil	mil	mil	mil	mil	mil	mil
		0.621	1.243	1.864	2.486	3.107	3.728	4.350	4.971	5.592
10	6.214	6.835	7.457	8.078	8.699	9.321	9.942	10.562	11.185	11.805
20	12.427	13.049	13.670	14.292	14.913	15.534	16.156	16.776	17.399	18.019
30	18.641	19.263	19.884	20.506	21.127	21.748	22.370	22.990	23.613	24.233
40	24.855	25.477	26.098	26.720	27.341	27.962	28.584	29.204	29.827	30.447
50	31.069	31.690	32.311	32.933	33.554	34.175	34.797	35.417	36.040	36.660
60	37.282	37.904	38.525	39.147	39.768	40.389	41.011	41.631	42.254	42.874
70	43.497	44.118	44.739	45.361	45.982	46.603	47.225	47.845	48.468	49.088
80	49.711	50.332	50.953	51.575	52.196	52.817	53.439	54.059	54.682	55.302
90	55.924	56.545	57.166	57.788	58.409	59.030	59.652	60.272	60.895	61.515

Table 2. Miles To Kilometers

mile	0	1	2	3	4	5	6	7	8	9
	km	km	km	km	km	km	km	km	km	km
		1.609	3.219	4.828	6.437	8.047	9.656	11.265	12.875	14.484
10	16.093	17.703	19.312	20.921	22.531	24.140	25.750	27.359	28.968	30.578
20	32.187	33.796	35.406	37.015	38.624	40.234	41.843	43.452	45.062	46.671
30	48.280	49.890	51.499	53.108	54.718	56.327	57.936	59.546	61.155	62.764
40	64.374	65.983	67.593	69.202	70.811	72.421	74.030	75.639	77.249	78.858
50	80.467	82.077	83.686	85.295	86.905	88.514	90.123	91.733	93.342	94.951
60	96.561	98.170	99.779	101.39	103.00	104.61	106.22	107.83	109.44	111.04
70	112.65	114.26	115.87	117.48	119.09	120.70	122.31	123.92	125.53	127.14
80	128.75	130.36	131.97	133.58	135.19	136.79	138.40	140.01	141.62	143.23
90	144.84	146.45	148.06	149.67	151.28	152.89	154.50	156.11	157.72	159.33

Table 3. Meters To Feet

m	0 ft	1 ft	2 ft	3 ft	4 ft	5 ft	6 ft	7 ft	8 ft	9 ft
		3.2808	6.5617	9.8425	13.1234	16.4042	19.6850	22.9659	26.2467	29.5276
10	32.8084	36.0892	39.3701	42.6509	45.9318	49.2126	52.4934	55.7743	59.0551	62.3360
20	65.6168	68.8976	72.1785	75.4593	78.7402	82.0210	85.3018	88.5827	91.8635	95.1444
30	98.4252	101.7060	104.9869	108.2677	111.5486	114.8294	118.1102	121.3911	124.6719	127.9528
40	131.2336	134.5144	137.7953	141.0761	144.3570	147.6378	150.9186	154.1995	157.4803	160.7612
50	164.0420	167.3228	170.6037	173.8845	177.1654	180.4462	183.7270	187.0079	190.2887	193.5696
60	196.8504	200.1312	203.4121	206.6929	209.9738	213.2546	216.5354	219.8163	223.0971	226.3780
70	229.6588	232.9396	236.2205	239.5013	242.7822	246.0630	249.3438	252.6247	255.9055	259.1864
80	262.4672	265.7480	269.0289	272.3097	275.5906	278.8714	282.1522	285.4331	288.7139	291.9948
90	295.2756	298.5564	301.8373	305.1181	308.3990	311.6798	314.9606	318.2415	321.5223	324.8032

Table 4. Feet To Meters

ft	0	1	2	3	4	5	6	7	8	9
	m	m	m	m	m	m	m	m	m	m
		0.305	0.610	0.914	1.219	1.524	1.829	2.134	2.438	2.743
10	3.048	3.353	3.658	3.962	4.267	4.572	4.877	5.182	5.486	5.791
20	6.096	6.401	6.706	7.010	7.315	7.620	7.925	8.230	8.534	8.839
30	9.144	9.449	9.754	10.058	10.363	10.668	10.973	11.278	11.582	11.887
40	12.192	12.497	12.802	13.106	13.411	13.716	14.021	14.326	14.630	14.935
50	15.240	15.545	15.850	16.154	16.459	16.764	17.069	17.374	17.678	17.983
60	18.288	18.593	18.898	19.202	19.507	19.812	20.117	20.422	20.726	21.031
70	21.336	21.641	21.946	22.250	22.555	22.860	23.165	23.470	23.774	24.079
80	24.384	24.689	24.994	25.298	25.603	25.908	26.213	26.518	26.822	27.127
90	27.432	27.737	28.042	28.346	28.651	28.956	29.261	29.566	29.870	30.175

Table 5. Liters To U.S. Gallons

L	0	1	2	3	4	5	6	7	8	9
	gal	gal	gal	gal	gal	gal	gal	gal	gal	gal
		0.2642	0.5283	0.7925	1.0567	1.3209	1.5850	1.8492	2.1134	2.3775
10	2.6417	2.9059	3.1701	3.4342	3.6984	3.9626	4.2267	4.4909	4.7551	5.0192
20	5.2834	5.5476	5.8118	6.0759	6.3401	6.6043	6.8684	7.1326	7.3968	7.6610
30	7.9251	8.1893	8.4535	8.7176	8.9818	9.2460	9.5102	9.7743	10.0385	10.3027
40	10.5668	10.8310	11.0952	11.3594	11.6235	11.8877	12.1519	12.4160	12.6802	12.9444
50	13.2086	13.4727	13.7369	14.0011	14.2652	14.5294	14.7936	15.0577	15.3219	15.5861
60	15.8503	16.1144	16.3786	16.6428	16.9069	17.1711	17.4353	17.6995	17.9636	18.2278
70	18.4920	18.7561	19.0203	19.2845	19.5487	19.8128	20.0770	20.3412	20.6053	20.8695
80	21.1337	21.3979	21.6620	21.9262	22.1904	22.4545	22.7187	22.9829	23.2470	23.5112
90	23.7754	24.0396	24.3037	24.5679	24.8321	25.0962	25.3604	25.6246	25.8888	26.1529

Table 6. U.S. Gallons To Liters

U.S. gal	0	1	2	3	4	5	6	7	8	9
	L	L	L	L	L	L	L	L	L	L
		3.7854	7.5709	11.3563	15.1417	18.9271	22.7126	26.4980	30.2834	34.0638
10	37.8543	41.6397	45.4251	49.2105	52.9960	56.7814	60.5668	64.3523	68.1377	71.9231
20	75.7085	79.4940	83.2794	87.0648	90.8502	94.6357	98.4211	102.2065	105.9920	109.7774
30	113.5528	117.3482	121.1337	124.9191	128.7045	132.4899	136.2754	140.0608	143.8462	147.6316
40	151.4171	155.2025	158.9879	162.7734	166.5588	170.3442	174.1296	177.9151	181.7005	185.4859
50	189.2713	193.0568	196.8422	200.6276	204.4131	208.1985	211.9839	215.7693	219.5548	223.3402
60	227.1256	230.9110	234.6965	238.4819	242.2673	246.0527	249.8382	253.6236	257.4090	261.1945
70	264.9799	268.7653	272.5507	276.3362	280.1216	283.9070	287.6924	291.4779	295.2633	299.0487
80	302.8342	306.6196	310.4050	314.1904	317.9759	321.7613	325.5467	329.3321	333.1176	336.9030
90	340.6884	344.4738	348.2593	352.0447	355.8301	359.6156	363.4010	367.1864	370.9718	374.7573

Table 7. Liters to Imperial Gallons

L	0 gal	1 gal	2 gal	3 gal	4 gal	5 gal	6 gal	7 gal	8 gal	9 gal
		0.2200	0.4400	0.6599	0.8799	1.0999	1.3199	1.5398	1.7598	1.9798
10	2.1998	2.4197	2.6397	2.8597	3.0797	3.2996	3.5196	3.7396	3.9596	4.1795
20	4.3995	4.6195	4.8395	5.0594	5.2794	5.4994	5.7194	5.9394	6.1593	6.3793
30	6.5593	6.8193	7.0392	7.2592	7.4792	7.6992	7.9191	8.1391	8.3591	8.5791
40	8.7990	9.0190	9.2390	9.4590	9.6789	9.8989	10.9189	10.3389	10.5588	10.7788
50	10.9988	11.2188	11.4388	11.6587	11.8787	12.0987	12.3187	12.5386	12.7586	12.9786
60	13.1986	13.4185	13.6385	13.8585	14.0785	14.2984	14.5184	14.7384	14.9584	15.1783
70	15.3983	15.6183	15.8383	16.0582	16.2782	16.4982	16.7182	16.9382	17.1581	17.3781
80	17.5981	17.8181	18.0380	18.2580	18.4780	18.6980	18.9179	19.1379	19.3579	19.5779
90	19.7978	20.0178	20.2378	20.4578	20.6777	20.8977	21.1177	21.3377	21.5576	21.7776

Table 8. Imperial Gallons To Liters

IMP gal	0	1	2	3	4	5	6	7	8	9
	L	L	L	L	L	L	L	L	L	L
		4.5460	9.0919	13.6379	18.1838	22.7298	27.2758	31.8217	36.3677	40.9136
10	45.4596	50.0056	54.5515	59.0975	63.6434	68.1894	72.2354	77.2813	81.8275	86.3732
20	90.9192	95.4652	100.0111	104.5571	109.1030	113.6490	118.1950	122.7409	127.2869	131.8328
30	136.3788	140.9248	145.4707	150.0167	154.5626	159.1086	163.6546	168.0005	172.7465	177.2924
40	181.8384	186.3844	190.9303	195.4763	200.0222	204.5682	209.1142	213.6601	218.2061	222.7520
50	227.2980	231.8440	236.3899	240.9359	245.4818	250.0278	254.5738	259.1197	263.6657	268.2116
60	272.7576	277.3036	281.8495	286.3955	290.9414	295.4874	300.0334	304.5793	309.1253	313.6712
70	318.2172	322.7632	327.3091	331.8551	336.4010	340.9470	345.4930	350.0389	354.5849	359.1308
80	363.6768	368.2223	372.7687	377.3147	381.8606	386.4066	390.9526	395.4985	400.0445	404.5904
90	409.1364	413.6824	418.2283	422.7743	427.3202	431.8662	436.4122	440.9581	445.9041	450.0500

Table 9. Kilograms To Pounds

kg	0 lb	1 lb	2 lb	3 lb	4 lb	5 lb	6 lb	7 lb	8 lb	9 lb
		2.205	4.409	6.614	8.818	11.023	13.228	15.432	17.637	19.842
10	22.046	24.251	26.455	28.660	30.865	33.069	35.274	37.479	39.683	41.888
20	44.092	46.297	48.502	50.706	52.911	55.116	57.320	59.525	61.729	63.934
30	66.139	68.343	70.548	72.752	74.957	77.162	79.366	81.571	83.776	85.980
40	88.185	90.389	92.594	94.799	97.003	99.208	101.41	103.62	105.82	108.03
50	110.23	112.44	114.64	116.84	119.05	121.25	123.46	125.66	127.87	130.07
60	132.28	134.48	136.69	138.89	141.10	143.30	145.51	147.71	149.91	152.12
70	154.32	156.53	158.73	160.94	163.14	165.35	167.55	169.76	171.96	174.17
80	176.37	178.57	180.78	182.98	185.19	187.39	189.60	191.80	194.01	196.21
90	198.42	200.62	202.83	205.03	207.23	209.44	211.64	213.85	216.05	218.26

Table 10. Pounds To Kilograms

lb	0	1	2	3	4	5	6	7	8	9
	kg	kg	kg	kg	kg	kg	kg	kg	kg	kg
		0.454	0.907	1.361	1.814	2.268	2.722	3.175	3.629	4.082
10	4.536	4.990	5.443	5.897	6.350	6.804	7.257	7.711	8.165	8.618
20	9.072	9.525	9.979	10.433	10.886	11.340	11.793	12.247	12.701	13.154
30	13.608	14.061	14.515	14.969	15.422	15.876	16.329	16.783	17.237	17.690
40	18.144	18.597	19.051	19.504	19.958	20.412	20.865	21.319	21.772	22.226
50	22.680	23.133	23.587	24.040	24.494	24.948	25.401	25.855	26.308	26.762
60	27.216	27.669	28.123	28.576	29.030	29.484	29.937	30.391	30.844	31.298
70	31.751	32.205	32.659	33.112	33.566	34.019	34.473	34.927	35.380	35.834
80	36.287	36.741	37.195	37.648	38.102	38.555	39.009	39.463	39.916	40.370
90	40.823	41.277	41.730	42.184	42.638	43.092	43.545	43.998	44.453	44.906

Drill Sizes

Letter Sizes	Drill Diam. Inches	Wire Gage Sizes	Drill Diam. Inches	Wire Gage Sizes	Drill Diam. Inches	Wire Gage Sizes	Drill Diam. Inches
Z	0.413	1	0.2280	28	0.1405	55	0.0520
Y	0.404	2	0.2210	29	0.1360	56	0.0465
X	0.397	3	0.2130	30	0.1285	57	0.0430
W	0.386	4	0.2090	31	0.1200	58	0.0420
V	0.377	5	0.2055	32	0.1160	59	0.0410
U	0.368	6	0.2040	33	0.1130	60	0.0400
T	0.358	7	0.2010	34	0.1110	61	0.0390
S	0.348	8	0.1990	35	0.1100	62	0.0380
R	0.339	9	0.1960	36	0.1065	63	0.0370
Q	0.332	10	0.1935	37	0.1040	64	0.0360
P	0.323	11	0.1910	38	0.1015	65	0.0350
O	0.316	12	0.1890	39	0.0995	66	0.0330
N	0.302	13	0.1850	40	0.0980	67	0.0320
M	0.295	14	0.1820	41	0.0960	68	0.0310
L	0.290	15	0.1800	42	0.0935	69	0.0292
K	0.281	16	0.1770	43	0.0890	70	0.0280
J	0.277	17	0.1730	44	0.0860	71	0.0260
I	0.272	18	0.1695	45	0.0820	72	0.0250
H	0.266	19	0.1660	46	0.0810	73	0.0240
G	0.261	20	0.1610	47	0.0785	74	0.0225
F	0.257	21	0.1590	48	0.0760	75	0.0210
E	0.250	22	0.1570	49	0.0730	76	0.0200
D	0.246	23	0.1540	50	0.0700	77	0.0180
C	0.242	24	0.1520	51	0.0670	78	0.0160
B	0.238	25	0.1495	52	0.0635	79	0.0145
A	0.234	26	0.1470	53	0.0595	80	0.0135
		27	0.1440	54	0.0550		

Gages

GAGE NO.	U.S. STANDARD GAGE* Approx. Thickness—Inches	AMERICAN WIRE or B & S GAGE Thickness—Inches
0000000	0.490	
000000	.460	0.5800
00000	.429	.5165
0000	.398	.4600
000	.368	.4096
00	.337	.3648
0	.306	.3248
1	.2757	.2893
2	.2604	.2576
3	.2451	.2294
4	.2298	.2043
5	.2145	.1819
6	.1991	.1620
7	.1838	.1443
8	.1685	.1285
9	.1532	.1144
10	.1379	.1019
11	.1225	.0907
12	.1072	.0808
13	.0919	.0720
14	.0766	.0641
15	.0689	.0571
16	.0613	.0508
17	.0551	.0453
18	.0490	.0403
19	.0429	.0359
20	.0368	.0320
21	.0337	.0285
22	.0306	.0253
23	.0276	.0226

Gages (con't)

GAGE NO.	U.S. STANDARD GAGE* Approx. Thickness—Inches	AMERICAN or B & S GAGE Thickness—Inches
24	.0245	.0201
25	.0214	.0179
26	.0184	.0159
27	.0169	.0142
28	.0153	.0126
29	.0138	.0113
30	.0123	.0100
31	.0107	.00893
32	.0100	.00795
33	.0092	.00708
34	.0084	.00630
35	.0077	.00561
36	.0069	.00500
37	.0065	.00445
38	.0061	.00397
39	.0057	.00353
40	.0054	.00314
41	.0052	
42	.0050	
43	.0048	
44	.0046	

Decimal and Metric Equivalents

Fractions	Decimal In.	Metric mm.	Fractions	Decimal In.	Metric mm.
1/64	.015625	.39688	33/64	.515625	13.09687
1/32	.03125	.79375	17/32	.53125	13.49375
3/64	.046875	1.19062	35/64	.546875	13.89062
1/16	.0625	1.58750	9/16	.5625	14.28750
5/64	.078125	1.98437	37/64	.578125	14.68437
3/32	.09375	2.38125	19/32	.59375	15.08125
7/64	.109375	2.77812	39/64	.609375	15.47812
1/8	.125	3.1750	5/8	.625	15.87500
9/64	.140625	3.57187	41/64	.640625	16.27187
5/32	.15625	3.96875	21/32	.65625	16.66875
11/64	.171875	4.36562	43/64	.671875	17.06562
3/16	.1875	4.76250	11/16	.6875	17.46250
13/64	.203125	5.15937	45/64	.703125	17.85937
7/32	.21875	5.55625	23/32	.71875	18.25625
15/64	.234375	5.95312	47/64	.734375	18.65312
1/4	.250	6.35000	3/4	.750	19.05000
17/64	.265625	6.74687	49/64	.765625	19.44687
9/32	.28125	7.14375	25/32	.78125	19.84375
19/64	.296875	7.54062	51/64	.796875	20.24062
5/16	.3125	7.93750	13/16	.8125	20.63750
21/64	.328125	8.33437	53/64	.828125	21.03437
11/32	.34375	8.73125	27/32	.84375	21.43125
23/64	.359375	9.12812	55/64	.859375	21.82812
3/8	.375	9.52500	7/8	.875	22.22500
25/64	.390625	9.92187	57/64	.890625	22.62187
13/32	.40625	10.31875	29/32	.90625	23.01875
27/64	.421875	10.71562	59/64	.921875	23.41562
7/16	.4375	11.11250	15/16	.9375	23.81250
29/64	.453125	11.50937	61/64	.953125	24.20937
15/32	.46875	11.90625	31/32	.96875	24.60625
31/64	.484375	12.30312	63/64	.984375	25.00312
1/2	.500	12.70000	1	1.00	25.40000

Index

A

Accelerator pump system, 138
Air cleaners
 filters, 169
 thermostatic control, 169
Air conditioning
 air distribution, 749
 basic principles, 725
 component description,
  blower and switch, 746
  compressors, 739
  evaporator, 737
  evaporator pressure control, 747
  magnetic clutch control, 741
  receiver-drier, 739
  thermostatic expansion valve, 734
  thermostatic switch, 747
 installation procedures, 764
 service and maintenance,
  charging system, 756
  connecting manifold gauge set, 53
  discharging system, 754
  evacuating system, 754
  handling refrigerant, 750
  leak test procedure, 754
  pressure gauge set, 751
  purging air from system, 151
  service valves, 751
 system operation,
  air conditioning cycle, 731
 troubles and remedies, 766
Air suspension
 air,
  compressor, 529
  spring unit, 527
  storage tank, 529
 height control valves, 528
 manual control valve, 530
Alternators
 construction, 385
 diode tests and replacement, 392
 on-the-vehicle-tests, 388
 regulators,
  all-transistorized type, 395
  internal-type,
   indicator lamp check, 404
   static check, 402
  relay-type, 394
Analog oscilloscope, 359
Automatic choke, 152, 158

Automatic transmissions, 647
Automotive accessories
 controlled-cycle wiper and washer system, 713
 fluid level indicator, 716
 speed control devices,
  electrical, 712
  electro-pneumatic, 711
 troubleshooting, 719
 sunroof, 717
 theft deterrent system, 717

B

Ball joints, 514
Battery,
 cell, 24
 charging methods,
  precautions, 36
  quick-charging, 35
  sealed batteries, 35
 maintenance, 29
 ratings, 25
 reserve capacity, 26
 storage, 32
 testing,
  specific gravity, 37
  high-rate discharge, 39
  troubles and remedies, 41
Bendix drive, 371
Boost
 definition, 111
Brake reaction rod, 515
Breaker points, 46
Brakes
 disc, 470
 drum,
  drums, 475
  hydraulic system, 474
  maintenance and adjustment, 476
  master cylinder, 479
  parking brakes, 475
  shoes, 475
 power,
  cleaning, inspection, and overhaul, 502
  general construction, 496
  operating principles, 498
  testing procedure, 501
 troubles and remedies, 506
 warning system, 503

Index

C

Camber, 581
Camshaft
 bearing replacement, 215
 construction features, 210
 hydraulic lifters, 220
 mechanical lifters, 230
 overhead, 212
 purpose, 209
 servicing, 215
Carbon fouling, 84
Carburetor
 adjustments, 147
 automatic choke, 152, 158
 description, 130
 inlet fuel filters, 147
 manual chokes, 151
 operating principles,
  accelerator pump system, 138
  choke system, 139
  float system, 132
  high-speed system, 136
  idle system, 133
  low-speed system, 135
  power system, 137
  throttle,
   linkage, 141
   return check, 141
   types of, 143
  venturi principle, 131
Caster, 583
Center-point steering, 551
Centrifugal-type clutch, 619
Clutches
 centrifugal-type, 619
 diaphragm-type, 620
 hydraulic-type, 622
 servicing,
  inspection, 624
  reassembly, 626
  removal, 623
 troubles and remedies, 641
Choke system, 139
Coil springs, 516
Cold cranking power, 25
Combination fuel pump, 98
Compressors, 739
Condenser, 52
Connecting rods, 207
Continuous fuel injection, 119
Coolant recovery system, 289
Cooling system
 additives, 280
 coolant,
  flow, 280
  recovery system, 289
  types, 279
 fans, 285
 overflow tanks, 289

radiator,
 caps, 288
 types, 282
 thermostats, 286
 troubles and remedies, 291
water,
 jackets, 281
 pumps, 283
Crankcase ventilation, 260
Crankshaft
 bearing,
  clearance, 200
  failure, 197
  main, 195
  replacement, 202
 connecting rods, 207
 oil seals, 205

D

Dashpot, 141
Diagnostic testing, 360
Diaphragm-type clutch, 620
Differential
 conventional, 683
 gear tooth contact, 692
 locking (anti-slip), 685
Direct fuel injection, 119
Distributor
 breaker points,
  contact pressure, 50
  gap setting, 48
  general, 46
  point alignment, 51
 cam, 53
 condenser, 52
 electronic,
  general construction, 59
 general construction, 45
 shaft bearings, 53
 spark advance,
  centrifugal advance, 54
  vacuum advance, 55
 testers, 60
 testing, 64
Drive lines, 668
Drive shaft
 angularity, 674
 general, 668
 service,
  removal, 675
  universal jiont service, 676
 troubles and remedies, 697
Dry-charged batteries, 29

E

Electric fuel pump, 99
Electric power plants, 18
Electronic distributor, 59

789

INDEX

Electronic fuel injection
  air induction system, 123
  electronic control unit, 121
  fuel delivery system, 121
  sensors, 124
  system description, 120
  troubles and remedies, 127
Electronic spark control, 112
Emission control
  air injection reactor system,
    operation, 266
    pump, 267
  exhaust system, 273
Engine fans, 285
Engine lubrication
  crankcase ventilation, 260
  oil,
    additives, 256
    changing, 255
    classification, 255
    filters, 257
    pressure indicators, 259
    pumps, 258
    viscosity, 253
  pressurized systems, 251
  purpose of, 249
  troubles and remedies, 275
Engine tune-up procedures, 296
Evaporators, 737

F

Float system, 132
Four-barrel carburetor, 144
Front syspension
  air suspension,
    air,
      compressor, 529
      spring unit, 527
      storage tank, 529
    height control valves, 528
    manual control valve, 530
  frame,
    alignment, 531
    repair, 534
  standard suspension
    ball joints, 514
    brake reaction rod, 515
    coil springs, 516
    rubber bumpers, 517
    service procedures, 517
    shock absorbers, 515
    stabilizer bars, 516
    torsion bars, 516
  troubles and remedies, 540
Front-wheel
  alignment,
    adjustments,
      caster and camber, 604

      preliminary inspection, 597
      toe-in, 609
    factors,
      camber, 581
      caster, 585
      frame alignment, 591
      height, 585
      kingpin inclination, 585
      toe-in, 591
      turning radius adjustment, 590
    procedures, 591
    summary, 610
    troubles and remedies, 610
  drive,
    axle, 704
    front suspension, 704
    rear suspension, 705
    transmission,
      fluid check, 703
      troubleshooting, 751
    towing, 705
Fuel
  evaporation control system, 108
  gauge, 432
  injection,
    system components, 119
    types of, 118
  line,
    hose leak test, 103
    types of, 107
  pump,
    operating principles,
      combinations, 98
      diaphragm-type, 95
      electric, 99
    servicing, 100
    testing, 100
    troubles and remedies, 125
  tanks, 106

G

Gas fouling, 84
Generators, 383

H

Halide torch, 755
Headlight
  aiming,
    equipment, 419
    using a wall or screen, 423
  general, 410
  switch and circuit breaker, 415
High-rate discharge test, 39
Hydraulic valve lifters
  operating principles, 220
  servicing, 225
  troubles and remedies, 225

INDEX

I

Ignition testing
  distributor
    breaker points, 318
    condenser, 319
    rotor, 315
  engine testers,
    basic scope patterns, 357
    charging test, 344
    cranking test, 341
    cylinder power balance test, 355
    high-cruise test, 355
    idle test, 346
    low-cruise test, 349
    snap acceleration test, 355
  high-tension wires, 320
  ignition,
    coil, 317
    switch, 315
  primary circuit,
    resistance wire, 316
    tests, 321
  secondary circuit tests, 325
  transistor ignition system, 329
Inlet fuel filter, 147
Instrument panel
  charging indicator, 425
  fuel guage, 432
  instrument voltage regulator, 437
  oil pressure, 435
  speedometer, 429
  temperature indicator, 452

K

Kingpin inclination, 585

L

Lead fouling, 86
Lead-sulfuric type battery, 25
Lear Delta engine, 16

M

Magnetic clutch control, 741
Main crankshaft bearings, 195
Manual choke, 151
Master cylinder, 479
Mechanical valve lifters, 230
Metered port injection, 118
Motor oil
  additives, 256
  classification, 255
  filters, 257
  pressure indicators, 259
  pumps, 258
  viscosity, 253

O

Oil fouling, 84
Oil seals, 205
Overflow tanks, 289
Overhead camshaft, 212
Overrunning clutch, 370

P

Phosgene, 750
Piston
  construction, 178
  fitting, 188
  inspection, 181
  replacement, 179
  rings, 189
  troubles and remedies, 193
Pitman and idler arms, 554
Power brakes, 495
Power steering
  integral-type, 566
  linkage-type, 563
  pumps, 572
  troubles and remedies, 577
Pressure guage set, 751

R

Radiators, 282
Rear axle
  assembly, 682
  noise diagnosis, 693
  service,
    removal, 688
    wheel bearing replacement, 689
    troubles and remedies, 699
    wheel balancing precautions, 697
Receiver-driers, 739
Receiver sight glass, 763
Refrigerant-12, 750
Regapping spark plugs, 88
Regulators, 393
Reserve capacity, 26

S

Shock absorbers
  general, 515
  servicing, 539
Sight glass, 763
Single-barrel carburetor, 143
Spark advance, 54
Spark plug
  construction, 80
  reach, 92
  selection, 90
  service procedures, 86
  troubles and remedies, 83

INDEX

Specific gravity test, 37
Speedometer, 429
Stabilizer bar, 515
Starter
  brushes, 369
  circuit tests, 376
  drives,
    Bendix, 371
    overrunning clutch, 370
  general, 368
  remote control switches,
    magnetic, 372
    solenoid starter switch, 375
Steam power plant, 16
Steering system
  control linkage,
    ball studs, 553
    center-point steering, 551
    pitman and idler arms, 554
    servicing, 552
    tie-rod ends, 554
    toe-in, 546
    turning angles, 544
  power steering,
    integral-type, 566
    linkage-type, 563
    pumps, 572
    troubles and remedies, 577
  steering gear,
    recirculating ball worm and nut, 554
    service and adjustment, 558
    worm and roller, 557
  troubles and remedies, 575
Suction throttle valve, 763
Sun 500 distributor tester
  breaker point,
    alignment test, 71
    spring tension test, 69
  cam lobe accuracy test, 70
  centrifugal advance test, 72
  condenser test, 66
  resistance test, 67
  vacuum spark advance test, 73
Supercharger, 110
Suspension springs, 534

T

Tables and charts, 772
Thermostatic expansion valve, 734
Thermostats, 286
Throttle linkage, 141
Throttle return check, 141
Throttle valve, 133
Temperature indicator, 432
Tie-rod ends, 554
Tire
  balancing,
    dynamic, 464
    run-out and eccentricity, 464
    static, 463
  maintenance, 445
  repair,
    demounting and mounting, 456
    tubeless tires, 453
  troubles and remedies, 467
  types, 446
Toe-in, 546, 591
Torque converter,
  pump, 648, 651
  variable-pitch stator, 648
Torsion bars, 516
Transmission
  automatic,
    gearshift controls, 654
    governor, 653
    oil cooler, 657
    operation, 647
    planetary gears and controls,
      forward clutch, 652
      low-band, 652
    reverse clutch, 652
    service, 657
    starting, 657
    towing, 658
    torque converter,
      pump, 648, 651
      variable-pitch stator, 648
    troubles and remedies, 658
  manual,
    five-speed,
      gear ratios, 635
      operation, 634
    four-speed,
      gear ratios, 632,
      operation, 632
    overdrives,
      operation, 635
      servicing, 641
    three-speed,
      gear ratios, 631
      operation, 628
    troubles and remedies, 642
Transistor ignition system, 329
Trouble charts
  air conditioning system, 767
  air suspension, 541
  automatic transmission, 658
  battery, 41
  cams, lifters, and rocker arms, 233
  carburetor, 171
  charging indicator, 442
  conventional turn signal, 425
  cooling system, 291
  clutch system, 641
  cruise control, 719
  drive shaft and universal joint, 697
  electronic fuel injection, 127

INDEX

front suspension, 540
front-wheel drive, 707
fuel guage, 439
fuel pump, 125
lighting system, 427
lubricating system, 275
manual transmissions, 642
oil pressure indicator, 443
overdrive units, 646
piston and rings, 193
power brakes, 510
rear axle, 699
sequential turn signal, 425
spark plugs, 92
speedometer, 437
springs and shocks, 543
standard brakes, 506
starter, generator and alternator, 406
steering system, 575
temperature indicator, 441
tires, 467
turbocharger, 114
valves, 248
washer system, 723
wheel alignment, 610
wiper system, 721
Troubleshooting section, 303
Tune-up procedures, 296
Turbine power plants, 19
Turbocharger
  boost control, 111
  description, 110
  electronic spark control, 112
  theory of operation, 111
  troubleshooting, 113
  waste-gate troubleshooting, 113
Turbocharging, 110
Turning angles, 544

Turning radius adjustment, 590
Turn signals, 414
Two-barrel carburetor, 144

U

Universal joints
  constant-velocity type, 670
  cross-and-yoke type, 669
  mounting,
    pillow blocks, 673
  slip joints, 673

V

Vacuum pump testing, 103
Valve
  assemblies, 236
  guides, 241
  interference fit, 240
  lifters,
    hydraulic, 220
    mechanical, 230
  seats, 237
  springs, 243
  troubles and remedies, 248
Venturi principle, 131

W

Water jackets, 821
Water pumps, 283
Wheel balancing
  dynamic, 464
  methods, 465
  run-out and eccentricity, 464
  static, 463